The Social Divide

The Social Divide

Political Parties and the Future of Activist Government

MARGARET WEIR

Editor

Brookings Institution Press/Washington, D.C.
Russell Sage Foundation/New York, N.Y.

Copyright © 1998 by

THE BROOKINGS INSTITUTION   RUSSELL SAGE FOUNDATION

The Social Divide: Political Parties and the Future of Activist Government
may be ordered from:

Brookings Institution Press
1775 Massachusetts Avenue, N.W.
Washington, D.C. 20036
Tel.: 1-800-275-1447 or (202) 797-6258
Fax: (202) 797-6004

Library of Congress Cataloging-in-Publication data:
The social divide : political parties and the future of
activist government / Margaret Weir, editor
      p.   cm.
   Includes bibliographical references and index.
   ISBN 0-8157-9288-3 (cloth : alk. paper). — ISBN
0-8157-9287-5 (pbk. : alk. paper).
      1. United States—Social policy—1993– .   2. United
States—Politics and government—1993– .   3. Political
parties—United States. I. Weir, Margaret, 1952– .
   HN59.2.S59   1998
   361.6′1′0973—dc21   97-33819
                                                          CIP

9 8 7 6 5 4 3 2 1

The paper used in this publication meets the minimum requirements of the
American National Standard for Information Sciences—Permanence of Paper
for Printed Library Materials, ANSI Z39.48-1984

Typeset in Palatino

Composition by Cynthia Stock
Silver Spring, Maryland

Printed by R. R. Donnelley and Sons, Co.
Harrisonburg, Virginia

Preface

THIS BOOK had its origins in the first months of the Clinton administration, when Eric Wanner, president of the Russell Sage Foundation, invited a group of political scientists to consider how politics might affect social policymaking during the new administration. We began with a question about Clinton's ambitious—and ambiguous— aspirations to be a new kind of Democrat: would this political impulse create a new generation of social policy that could actively respond to the new social and economic challenges at the century's end? Answering this question required us to identify the distinctive features of the contemporary American political system that shape policymaking and to make sense of the strategies that politicians adopt as they thread their way through this maze of political obstacles and opportunities. Meeting six times over the course of four years, we tracked the progress of key pieces of social policy and collectively monitored the often surprising political developments.

The most striking feature of policymaking across issues was its contentious and intensely partisan character. This highly politicized process, combined with the deeply entrenched institutional barriers to change, prevented the emergence of anything as coherent as a new generation of social policy. But neither can the outcome of these years of intense political conflict be characterized as a stalemate. Instead, a patchwork of failures and achievements underscore the way politics has restricted the range of tools that American policymakers use to respond to new social and economic conditions. Among the features of politics the chapters of this book highlight are sharply divided partisan elites, the difficulty of organizing broad majorities to participate effectively, and the dominance of budgetary politics. These factors made it extremely difficult to negotiate trade-offs or to bring expertise and broad public engagement to bear on policymaking. The result has been to restrict what the federal government can do to promote opportunity and security for all Americans; the most immediate consequence has been to increase greatly the insecurity of the poor. At the same time, policymaking during the Clinton administration has done little to build public support for the idea that government has a role to play in helping Americans as they confront new insecurities. In the face of social and economic trends that are increasing inequality and exacerbating insecurity, the current path is more likely to widen rather than bridge the growing social divide.

Over the course of this project I have benefited from the advice and expertise of many colleagues. The greatest debt is to Eric Wanner of the Russell Sage Foundation, who provided generous financial support and challenged us to keep our eyes on the big picture as we sought to make sense of rapidly shifting political events. At the Brookings Institution, Thomas E. Mann, provided critical support and guidance as well as a congenial work setting in his role as director of the Governmental Studies program; as a leading scholar of politics in Washington, he offered astute advice that greatly strengthened the manuscript. Ira Katznelson was instrumental in helping think through the project from the beginning, and, as a participant in our meetings, he prodded us to think more acutely about our political analysis. I also benefited from the comments of several scholars who participated in a stimulating two-day conference that was critical in giving the book its current shape. They included Demetrios Caraley, Martha Derthick, Morris Fiorina, James G. Gimpel, Hugh Heclo, Jennifer L. Hochschild, Ira Katznelson, Thomas E. Mann, Theodore R. Marmor, David Plotke, Theda Skocpol, Phillip Thompson, Carl E. Van Horn, and Joseph White. Hugh Heclo provided written comments that proved invaluable in making the separate contributions more systematic and comprehensive. I, as well as the other authors, am also grateful to the many administration officials and congressional staff who agreed to individual interviews and to several who held off-the-record meetings with the entire group.

I am particularly indebted to my Brookings colleagues, Sarah A. Binder, E. J. Dionne Jr., Christopher H. Foreman, Stephen Hess, Robert A. Katzmann, Pietro S. Nivola, and Allen Schick. Their combined knowledge of American politics is a rare resource, which they generously shared with me. Two Brookings colleagues deserve special thanks. Joseph White read and offered incisive comments on all the chapters. R. Kent Weaver has been a part of thinking through the project from the start, and his willingness to listen to yet another version of the arguments is deeply appreciated. I have also benefited from thoughtful comments on the papers from Jennifer Klein and James P. Pfiffner and from conversations about the project with Marshall Ganz, Kathleen Gille, Philip Klinkner, and Nick Ziegler.

John Guba and Laurel Imig provided resourceful and efficient research assistance. Tara Adams Ragone went above and beyond the call of duty as research verifier. I would also like to thank Matthew J. Atlas for verifying portions of the manuscript. As editor, Nancy D. Davidson did a heroic job in pressing us for concise arguments and in coordinating the final stages of the project. The project was also greatly assisted by the outstanding administrative support at Brookings from Susan A. Stewart, Inge Lockwood, and Kristen Lippert-Martin and at the Russell Sage Foundation from Nancy Casey, Bianca Intalan, Madge Spitaleri, and Rachel Stevens. They handled the logistics of our meetings and the administration of the project with efficiency and grace. Carlotta Ribar provided proofreading services, and Sherry L. Smith prepared the index.

Finally, I would like to thank my coauthors for a stimulating and productive collaboration. The political events of the past five years gave the project many more twists and turns than we could have predicted at the outset. Their willingness to accommodate my many requests for yet another round of revisions is greatly appreciated, as is their enthusiasm throughout the project.

Margaret Weir

Contents

x   Contents

The Social Divide

Chapter 1

Political Parties and Social Policymaking

Margaret Weir

I N 1993, President Clinton made comprehensive health reform the centerpiece of his political agenda, subordinating all other social policy reforms to this objective. With this decision, Clinton staked his domestic agenda on a goal that had eluded Democrats since the New Deal but was especially important to them because it reconfirmed the federal government's central role in guaranteeing economic and social security for all Americans.

Two years later a triumphant Republican Congress proclaimed a revolution animated by a very different vision. At its core was a much smaller federal government, to be achieved by balancing the federal budget and greatly reducing federal regulation. Complemented by initiatives to devolve key programs for the poor to the states and by reforms to encourage individuals to meet their needs through private means, the Republican policy agenda aimed not only to limit the federal government's social role but also to curb its future growth. Although the 104th Congress passed several bills in a flurry of last-minute legislation and the 1997 budget agreement combined with a buoyant economy to push the budget close to surplus, the grand policy ambitions of both parties remained unfulfilled. Indeed, as electoral considerations took precedence, each party moved to the center, choosing short-term survival over long-term transformation.

For helpful comments on earlier versions, I would like to thank Hugh Heclo, Lawrence Jacobs, Ira Katznelson, Thomas Mann, Sidney Milkis, John Mollenkopf, David Plotke, Ted Perlmutter, Theda Skocpol, R. Kent Weaver, Joseph White, and Daniel Wirls. Laurel Imig provided cheerful and efficient research assistance.

This book examines the extraordinary swings in the scope and content of the social policy agenda during the first Clinton administration, asking what they reveal about American politics and the future of social policy. It argues that these struggles must be understood as key elements in strategies designed to consolidate parties' hold over the federal government. Long frustrated by divided government—the apparent Democratic lock on Congress and Republican command of the presidency—each party exceeded its electoral mandate in hopes of enacting major policy reforms aimed to shift politics in their direction for the foreseeable future. The book has three aims: first, to account for the kind of changes in social policy that each party sought and to explain the pattern of legislative success and failure during the "two halves" of the first Clinton administration; second, to examine and account for the policymaking that has occurred despite the failure of most major legislative initiatives; and third, to explore what this episode of federal stalemate and intense conflict means for social policy and for the future of activist government in the United States.

It is not surprising that social policy became the focal point for intense partisan conflict in the 1990s as the end of the cold war diminished the salience of international concerns. By 1990, social programs accounted for 61 percent of the federal budget and showed every sign of growing.[1] Moreover, economic and social change were creating new inequalities even as they rendered key assumptions underlying New Deal social policy obsolete. The "new economy," characterized by job turnover and wage disparity, greatly limited the effectiveness and reach of employment policies crafted around the assumption of steady lifetime employment interrupted only by temporary economic downturns. Likewise, policies predicated on the existence of a male breadwinner were ill equipped to address the myriad issues raised by growing numbers of families headed by women or with two wage earners. Overlaying these broad but diffuse concerns were the more focused and divisive politics surrounding targeted spending programs for the poor and regulatory policies designed to address racial disadvantage. The continuing collapse of many minority urban communities provoked widespread discontent with existing policies and fueled the cultural cleavage that had characterized national politics since the 1960s. This complex and intertwined set of economic and social issues made social policy an excellent reform target from diverse partisan perspectives. Differing interpretations of social and economic issues created possibilities for setting old allies against one another and creating new coalitions to support alternative policies.

President Clinton and his Republican challengers seized on these tensions in social policy to propose new paths that they believed would consolidate electoral victories. Both faced daunting obstacles simply in defining appropriate policy alternatives. As the essays in this volume show, Clinton's claim to be a New Democrat was inherently ambiguous. What Clinton meant by "New Democrat" shifted over time and across issues; and, in any case, policy initiatives that relied on federal spending or regulation were vulnerable to charges that they amounted to little more than discredited "old Democratic" approaches. But the task for Republicans was not so simple, either. The same Americans who distrusted government and supported a balanced budget were strongly attached to the social insurance programs that constituted the core of American social policy. Whole lifestyles and life plans were predicated on their continued existence. Because the stakes were so high, policy struggles were unusually conflictual; each side realized that success would fundamentally reorder politics and policy for decades to come.

This book highlights the connections between politics and policymaking as it examines proposed and actual changes to social programs. It aims to show how American politics has confronted a widening social divide and, in particular, why government has done so little to address the new inequality. The essays reject simple models of agenda setting that explain policy initiatives in terms of party efforts to locate the center of the political spectrum or that view policy as a mirror of public preferences. The essays move beyond explanations that dwell upon the enduring obstacles to policymaking created by the Madisonian system of separated federal institutions. Instead, the book highlights three features of politics and policymaking distinctive to this era to account for the overreaching and limited legislative success that characterized the first Clinton administration: the polarization of political elites, new forms of connecting people to politics and policymaking as political parties have ceased to be mass-based organizations, and the unprecedented role budgetary concerns play in social policymaking.

The failure to enact many major legislative initiatives does not mean that social policy has remained unchanged. Budget decisions, administrative actions, court rulings, and the decisions of states and localities and the private sector have now taken on greater importance in shaping social policy. The second task of this book is to analyze these often less visible or less dramatic changes in policy and to assess how they are altering the definitions of problems, positioning interests differently, and changing ideas about the public role in addressing social problems. Such de facto policymaking is especially salient in the United States. The power of courts to define minority rights and equal protection have made them pivotal actors in American social policy. Likewise, states and localities play important roles in financing and administering key social policies. The federal devolution of some social programs enhances the significance of state decisions, making it important to understand what drives state and local policy choices.

This analysis of politics and policymaking aims to go beyond an autopsy of Clinton's first term. Future possibilities are rooted in the choices (and inactions) of those four years, when contending parties pressed the boundaries of policy in some areas and failed to address other policy domains. Understanding the political and policy institutions they confronted and the strategies they deployed offers a window onto the future of activist government in the United States.

How Do Major Shifts in Policy Occur?

In the aftermath of the 1994 congressional elections, observers across the political spectrum speculated about whether the long-awaited Republican realignment had at last arrived. Only two years earlier, Democratic analysts had seen in the Clinton victory a Republican "crash" and new potential for reviving Democratic political fortunes.[2] It is not surprising that the election of the first Democratic president in twelve years, followed by the first Republican Congress in over forty, should provoke conjecture about the long-term implications of such major shifts. Yet theories of political realignment are of limited help in assessing the lasting significance of these elections. Electoral shifts—even significant ones— must be ratified by accompanying political and policy changes in order to constitute a lasting realignment of political forces. To assess the pattern of policy success and failure during the first Clinton administration, then, requires turning to theories about policymaking and agenda setting.

Democracy, Ideas, and Policy Change

The sharp global swings in the policy agenda and the limited success of many major legislative initiatives during the Clinton administration suggest a peculiar mix of opportunity and constraint in policymaking. Two families of theory offer insight into this pattern, but neither of them captures the distinctive features that characterize social policymaking today.

The first set of theories highlights the role of public preferences: politicians and policymakers give priority to the issues about which the public cares most, and they try to match their proposals to public preferences. Simple spatial theories of politics argue along these lines, positing that parties will try to find the middle of the political spectrum in order to maximize votes.[3] Similarly, many theories of democracy explain what government does in terms of public demand.[4] Once displaced by group theories of politics, this simpler model has become more compelling as many large political organizations have disintegrated and a more fragmented politics has emerged. The widespread availability and use of information about public views discerned through sophisticated polling technologies has added further weight to the view that public opinion determines the policy agenda.

Yet the idea that public preferences set the public agenda is flawed on several counts.[5] As many critiques of the simple spatial model point out, most issues cannot be described by a single dimension in which center, right, and left are clearly defined. Instead, most issues have two or more dimensions, meaning that more than one optimal strategy exists for winning a majority. Since the late 1960s, social policy debates have been organized along two major dimensions: the "social" issue, in which a focus on individual responsibilities and behavior predominates; and the "economic" dimension, in which concerns about economic security are paramount. In the 1980s, a third dimension—concerned with the affordability of public social protections—became increasingly prominent. The existence of different dimensions and the absence of a single clear "center" gives politicians more room to maneuver than simple spatial models suggest. Politicians may seek to frame issues in distinctive ways so that a center is easier to locate, or they may take advantage of complexity to press for some policies and not for others.

Likewise, politicians and policymakers do not simply accept public opinion as they find it; they seek to shape it, either by activating particular preferences or by actually changing preferences.[6] Views about social welfare policy are especially open to this kind of shaping from above. In 1967, in an influential analysis of American public opinion, Lloyd A. Free and Albert H. Cantril characterized Americans as ideological conservatives and operational liberals when it came to government social programs.[7] Subsequent studies have reconfirmed the fundamental ambivalence of many Americans toward social programs, in which the continuing power of ideas about individualism and freedom makes it difficult even for those who support generous social policies to defend them in terms of general principles. Instead their defense of such programs is typically couched in more pragmatic operational terms.[8] This ambivalence provides politicians and policymakers with considerable room to try to convince the public that their policies best match public preferences. The ability of policymakers and politicians to shape public opinion is also enhanced by the complexity of many social policies: because the effects of particular programs or policy tools are often uncertain—as, indeed, are the causes of the problems they seek to remedy—the public may be persuaded about causes and effects in ways that significantly alter preferences and priorities.[9]

The second family of theories offers a more complex approach to agenda setting and policymaking, including independent roles for ideas to affect policy agendas and for political institutions to influence which policies are actually enacted. Frank R. Baumgartner and Bryan D. Jones's work on agenda setting, for example, argues that ideas play a pivotal role in policy stability and instability. Changes in the way issues are defined can dramatically alter policy by activating new groups to take an interest in the policy, upsetting the existing configuration of support, and inviting new institutions to seek jurisdiction over a policy.[10] John Kingdon's theory of agenda setting offers a similarly complex model in which separate streams of problems, policies, and politics converge to produce change.[11] Both theories emphasize the role of policy "subsystems" or distinct policy communities in generating alternatives.

Yet what is striking about conflict over social policies in the first Clinton administration is how frequently it broke out of these smaller communities. Because the guiding ideas of a broad range of social policies had been under attack for over two decades, the battle over ideas was far more politicized and global than the routine style of policymaking that these theories describe.[12] To make sense of these recent policy conflicts, then, it is necessary to examine the larger partisan struggle over ideas and assess its implications for defining social policy issues and changing the nature of the conflict about them.

Every effort to assess how political institutions shape policymaking in the United States has to consider the effects of the system of separated powers and multiple veto points that characterizes the federal government. Explicitly designed to prevent the tyranny of majorities, the Madisonian system of checks and balances has become the target for critics who argue that American political institutions are not capable of addressing the problems that confront the nation on the eve of the twenty-first century. Lawyer and presidential adviser Lloyd N. Cutler, for example, argues that "the separation of powers between the legislative and executive branches, whatever its merits in 1793, has become a structure that almost guarantees stalemate today."[13] The trouble with such explanations is that these same institutions have at times produced major policy innovations, not just during the extraordinary pressures of the Depression or under Lyndon Johnson's unusually large Democratic majorities, but also during other times, such as Richard Nixon's first term, when Congress enacted the framework for environmental laws as well as major expansions of social security. Political scientist David R. Mayhew has shown that periods of divided government—presumably especially inhospitable to policymaking—have produced no decline in the enactment of important policies.[14] And indeed, important initiatives were passed during the first Clinton administration: the North American Free Trade Agreement, deficit reduction, and welfare reform top the list. Yet the record of accomplishment is also marked by policy initiatives that failed because of opposition by one branch of government or by minorities in Congress. Separated institutions are clearly part of the story, but it is necessary to know more about the specific context in which these institutions now operate to understand the pattern of success and failure in policymaking.

Party Politics and Social Policymaking

This analysis of theories of agendas and policymaking suggests three criteria for making sense of the politics of social policy in the 1990s. First, explanations must take into account the overarching combat of ideas that underlies specific social policy debates; second, they must consider how the links between citizens and politicians are organized, acknowledging that influence runs in both directions; third, they must identify the distinctive constraints, operating across a range of policies, that reinforce the tendency to inaction built into American national institutions. We address these criteria by highlighting three features of contemporary politics and policymaking: polarized political elites contending over the basic features of a public philosophy; new forms of connecting people to politics that make it very difficult to assemble stable support for efforts to change policy; and the "fiscalization of social policy" as budget concerns take precedence in policymaking.

POLARIZED POLITICAL ELITES. The sharp ideological polarization of political elites in the 1990s meant that politics was no longer simply a contest to enact or reform individual policies but a more fundamental struggle over public philosophies. Conflict over social policy became the flashpoint for debates about the fundamental principles that should guide the scope and premises of government activity for the next generation. These unusually sharp ideological divisions among political elites were nurtured and amplified by electoral and institutional shifts that made congressional parties especially homogenized and polarized.[15]

Questions about social policy are controversial in part because of the fundamental uneasiness—greatly magnified in recent decades—that Americans have about the federal government and in part because social policy issues evoke deep tensions in American political life about race, gender, and religious values. Several distinct threads run through the current conflict about government and social policy: what should and can the federal government do to ensure social and economic security; what is the federal role in addressing inequality; and how should government address issues that touch on questions of values and morality? Since the 1960s, political divisions have centered on the last two questions. But concerns about economic and social security also moved to the forefront in the 1990s. Polarization grew as Republicans sought to link these concerns into a single argument for a much-reduced federal role and Democrats split over the design and reach of social assistance and whether to defend existing policies.

Contemplating major shifts in social policy creates an uncertain terrain for politicians of both parties because of the fundamental ambivalence of most Americans about government and social policy. Conservatives and liberals each face distinctive dilemmas posed by the mixture of ideological conservatism and pragmatic liberalism that allows a majority of Americans to support a broad range of social programs providing security and at the same time to express belief in individualism and distrust of government. Conservative attacks on social policies couched in ideological terms may generate broad sympathy but little active support. Liberals, on the other hand, must defend social policy in pragmatic terms, which often means showing that the recipients are deserving or that the programs are working. Public judgments about policies will vary depending on how policy is framed. When social policy issues are framed as remedies for economic inequality or are identified with cultural values that do not prize work and family, the disjuncture between underlying values and government programs is less sharp, and conservative critics have the advantage.[16] When, however, the issue is the basic security of deserving people, conservative arguments about individualism or government are much less appealing.

As I show in greater detail below, conservative challenges to social policy from the 1960s on centered on values, and to a lesser extent, on equality. Conservatives sought policy changes that would make beneficiaries conform to the norms of work and family, and they sought to limit benefits. They also attacked affirmative action programs, which began to grow in the 1970s, as fundamentally at odds with American norms of individual effort and fairness. In the 1990s, as the chapters in this volume show, conservative efforts to reduce the federal social role became much more extensive. Critics applied values arguments to a much broader swath of policies, including social security; they rejected the need for compensatory programs to remedy past inequalities; and they criticized popular programs on the pragmatic grounds that they were not working or were unaffordable. These arguments became the basis for a deeper and more comprehensive effort to eliminate many policies, devolve others to the states, and greatly decrease benefits in other areas. Although people with a range of quite different underlying orientations now shared the mantle of conservatism—including libertarians and social conservatives—a common critique of government and social policy helped forge a remarkable unity of purpose among them.[17]

In contrast, defenders of the federal social role were much more defensively positioned and internally divided. Pragmatic justifications of social programs bore the burden of showing that the policies worked or could be made more effective. Moreover, "old" and "New" Democrats differed on how much to emphasize values versus security and on whether to support federal efforts to remedy racial inequalities. These conflicts became evident in diverging views about whether to defend or reform existing policies and in differing assessments about the risks involved in reform efforts. Such internal divisions made it difficult to present a unified response to conservative attacks on government and critiques of existing policies.

Political divisions over social policy are not new in American politics; what distinguished the 1990s was the centrality of these divisions to party strategies and the extent of polarization. Several changes in congressional partisan politics, outlined in John Ferejohn's chapter, reinforced these tendencies. At the constituency level, the ongoing realignment of the South was a key factor in altering the profile of each party.[18] The movement of southern whites into the Republican party after the 1960s made Democrats in the House of Representatives more homogeneous and more liberal than at any time in the past, despite the considerable divisions that remained. At the same time, the replacement of southern Democratic members of Congress with conservative Republicans pulled the Republican party to the right. No longer tempered by intraparty bargaining among Democrats, white southern antagonism to the federal government, organized labor, and social spending found new expression in the Republican party.[19] Organizational changes in politics, discussed below, further magnified partisan polarization. The new prominence of national campaign organizations increased the division between the parties as congressional party leaders—especially among Republicans—aggressively used these organizations to recruit and finance candidates.

NEW FORMS OF CONNECTING PEOPLE TO POLITICS. The decline in political parties as mass-based organizations has had enormous implications for politics and policymaking. By joining distinct networks of interest groups, local political organizations, and national politicians, parties helped to stabilize electoral coalitions and create a measure of continuity between the resources needed to get elected and those needed to govern. In the past two decades this force for coherence in politics and policymaking has been replaced by a more complex configuration that makes the task of governing much more difficult. Three distinct types of linkages now organize politics: a "detached middle" in the electorate, only loosely connected to politics through the advertising efforts of parties and interest groups; highly organized Washington-based interest groups, often with only weak constituent ties; and pockets of grass-roots political organization. Each mode of politics pushes policy in a different direction, confronting politicians and policymakers with conflicting pressures and distinctive obstacles.

To appreciate the difficulties these new forms of political connections pose for governing, it is useful to consider how political parties helped to organize politics and policymaking before the 1970s. In his celebrated critique of American liberalism, Theodore J. Lowi describes a system of interest group liberalism that created a decentralized and fragmented approach to policy in which members of Congress, interest groups, and bureaucracies made policy in areas of concern to them.[20] Nonetheless, because parties were organized from the bottom up—local party organizations formed the backbone of party power—this system did create links among grass-roots politics, interest groups, and congressional policymaking.

These connections were most highly articulated by Democrats, who dominated congressional politics. The Democratic party that emerged from the New Deal was a collection of local party organizations: mass-based patronage organizations in big cities and elite-dominated low-participation networks in the South.[21] Labor unions, which organized a third of the labor force at their height and had a strong mass base and organizational presence at the local level, provided the other element. What was striking about the alliance between organized labor and the Democratic party was that labor took an active role in politics that went beyond representing the narrow interests of its members. In cities across the nation, labor functioned as a coalition builder for the Democratic party.[22] This kind of connection aggregated interests across functional areas at the local level, reducing the role of narrow interests at the national level.

The local organization of party and unions provided the New Deal and its Democratic successors with the means to connect mass and elite politics. But the limits of that organization stamped the character of the coalition. Both local party organizations and unions were regionally concentrated in the Northeast and Midwest. By contrast, there were few effective grass-roots linkages in the racially exclusive and elite-dominated political organization of the South. Moreover, the character of local political organizations, which were often racially discriminatory and particularistic, shaped the nature of the links between grass-roots and elite politics.[23]

The ability of parties to organize politics and to connect politics and policymaking declined as a consequence of several related shifts in parties and elections that occurred during the 1970s: party reforms replaced local party nomination of candidates with primaries in presidential politics, new campaign technologies increased the importance of television and direct mail, and money and consultants replaced precinct captains and campaign volunteers as the key resource in electoral campaigns.[24]

As parties ceased to be mass-based organizations, politics and policymaking began to proceed on three much more separated tracks. The first is an advertising strategy. Designed to appeal to a "detached middle" that no longer has any stable connections to politics, this strategy dominates presidential elections and many congressional elections. As Lawrence R. Jacobs and Robert Y. Shapiro's chapter shows, this strategy is also important in policymaking and governing: presidents make extensive use of public opinion soundings as they develop their policy agendas and seek to win support for their policies. The strategy of "going public"—attempting to build public support to increase pressure on Congress—reflects the presidents' search for new sources of political influence. This advertising strategy is especially associated with the president but is increasingly practiced by interest groups as well.[25]

The second type of politics is a Washington-based interest group politics. In the past twenty years, the number of Washington-based interest groups has soared, but most of these groups approach policy from a narrow perspective and have only loose constituent ties. On the Democratic side, the decline of organized labor and local party organizations broke up the links that had once existed. In the 1970s, labor grew increasingly defensive and inward looking, beginning to function more as a narrow interest group than as an aggregating force for the Democratic party. In contrast, new groups associated with the Democrats adopted a very different organizational strategy: rather than ground their strength in a local base associated with the party, these new organizations became Washington-based staff organizations whose grass-roots links were often limited to mail-in memberships. These groups sought to influence policy through the courts and their ties with Democratic congressional members. The growing decentralization of Congress facilitated this strategy by making it easier for lobbyists with little grass-roots support to gain a hearing from sympathetic subcommittee and committee staffers.[26] The proliferation of Washington-based interest groups occurred across the political spectrum. One of the most significant developments of the early 1970s was the mobilization of business organizations opposed to mounting federal regulations. Likewise, constituency groups associated with particular policies—such as advocacy groups for the aged—grew dramatically in the 1970s, but the impetus for such groups often came from within the government and most remained Washington-focused groups.[27]

The third type of politics consists of organizations with substantial grass-roots organization and mobilization capabilities. Fragments of old party organizations in some cities and states continue to have such capabilities. But the energy in this form of organization in recent years has been on the right, particularly among groups associated with the Christian right.[28] Begun as a direct mail operation, with little grass-roots mobilization, the Christian Coalition and other similar groups have since the late 1980s developed regular ongoing organizations capable of intervening in politics from the grass roots up. These organizations have an advantage that labor unions possessed in their heyday: they tap into preexisting social networks that have important ongoing significance in their members' lives.[29] They have consciously sought to replicate the precinct, county, and state organizations that had once made organized labor such an important presence in national policies. Although these groups constitute a distinct minority in the electorate, their political significance is magnified by the breakdown of established party ties and the atrophy of other organizations with the capacity to mobilize voters at the grass roots.[30]

Reconciling these three modes of politics poses difficult strategic choices for politicians and complicates the task of policymaking because each pulls in a different direction. The advertising model suggests that finding the "median voter" and gearing political appeals and policy toward the center is the optimal strategy. Yet, as Clinton repeatedly discovered, majorities discerned through public opinion polling are difficult to activate and unreliable as a political resource. Washington-based interest group politics is characterized by a narrow self-interested perspective in which there is little incentive to subordinate narrow priorities to some larger political or policy goal. The proliferation of such narrow groups and their skill in blocking aspects of policy they oppose present a formidable barrier to enacting major policy changes. Yet, on occasion, these groups do build coalitions among themselves and when they do, they can be a powerful political force. Finally, the ability to mobilize at the grass roots is a prized political resource in this relatively demobilized electoral world, but because it is animated by volunteers whose zeal for a particular issue drives them into politics, grass-roots or movement-oriented politics tends toward extremism.[31] This may pose costs in broader political support that offset the benefits of support from grass-roots organizations.

But politicians are not powerless. They can attempt to alter these connections between people and politics to their advantage. Patterns of social mobilization are not independent of politics, and politicians can shape the political impact of social groups. Not only does much social mobilization occur in reaction to political decisions, policy changes can spur mobilization, as New Deal labor law did in the 1930s. In addition, politicians can alter channels of political influence to institutionalize advantages for their allies and disarm opponents. Demobilizing the opposition can be as significant as mobilizing allies. A full understanding of political strategies thus requires attention to how politicians attempt to alter—as well as maneuver within—existing patterns of electoral and interest mobilization.

THE END OF THE ERA OF EASY FINANCE. The final feature of politics and policymaking characteristic of this era is what economist Eugene Steuerle has called the end of "the easy financing era."[32] The new era was in part a product of cumulative shifts in spending over time, grass-roots tax revolts, and deliberate political decisions to make federal spending more difficult. Since the 1980s, as Paul Pierson's chapter shows, budgetary concerns have exercised an unprecedented influence on social policymaking, altering the terms of debates, increasing reliance on regulation rather than spending, and propelling new actors into federal policymaking.

The new prominence of budgetary concerns crystallized in the 1980s during the presidency of Ronald Reagan, but many of the elements that created the new fiscal stringency had been building for decades. Steuerle identifies several features of public finance before the 1980s that allowed the federal government to raise revenues and expand social spending without drawing much attention: cuts in defense spending, increases in social security taxes, and the effects of inflation on bond holders and income tax payers.[33] For example, inflation produced "bracket creep" among income tax payers so that even while the federal goverment cut tax rates, it continued to collect increased revenues from taxpayers pushed into a higher tax bracket by inflation.

After the 1980s, these mechanisms disappeared or became more visible and contentious as revenue raisers. Defense cuts from the 1950s on had greatly reduced the defense budget's share of GNP, although the Reagan buildup did create some future budgetary slack. By 1990, the social security tax rate on individuals had risen to over 7 percent, no longer an insignificant chunk of the paycheck. Most important in making visible the costs of financing government was the 1981 tax reform, which indexed individual income tax to inflation, greatly reducing the fiscal slack created by bracket creep.[34] In the future, Congress would have to increase tax rates or broaden the tax base in order to raise more revenue, but neither route—imposing new costs or stripping older benefits—was appealing to members of Congress.[35]

To cope with these budgetary pressures, Congress instituted a variety of new budget procedures that further increased the visibility of winners and losers. The 1990 Budget Enforcement Act required that increased spending on entitlements be offset by decreases in other spending, and it established caps on discretionary spending.[36] These new rules heightened the difference between the fate of discretionary budgetary expenditures and those protected by federal entitlements. The discretionary programs, many of which served the poor and focused on urban problems, were far more vulnerable to cuts and bore the initial brunt of this new fiscal stringency. Yet this new budgetary environment threatened entitlement programs, too. The budgetary mechanisms initially designed to protect entitlements—trust funds—provided a convenient political target for proponents of reducing or eliminating entitlements. As an aging population and rising medical expenditures increased pressure on social security and medicare—the two most expensive entitlements—projected trust fund bankruptcies became a major weapon in very public arguments about the need to reduce or eliminate entitlements. Program opponents thus sought to use budgetary pressures to shape a public debate about entitlements that was quite different from previous reforms that had been bipartisan, expert-negotiated affairs in which the boundaries of the policy were not in question.[37]

By making winners and losers more visible, the new budgetary climate made it extremely difficult to build coalitions to support policies that required new spending. Likewise, policy reform became more difficult as the time-honored practice of "sweetening the pot" to compensate losers was no longer available. Budget stringency reinforced the propensity of interests to take a narrow and short-term perspective as constituencies set against one another assumed a more defensive posture.

As it became more difficult to rely on spending as a policy tool, policymakers increasingly looked to regulation as a means of pushing costs onto state and local governments or onto the private sector. In the 1980s, much of the rise in "unfunded mandates" reflected the Democratic Congress's efforts to preserve and even enhance social protections without paying the bill.[38] Likewise, as Mark Peterson's chapter shows, Clinton's proposal for comprehensive health reform relied extensively on regulation because the president did not want to impose new taxes and could not increase spending without taking it from some other program. As the president discovered, heavy reliance on such regulatory strategies is difficult to sustain because it arouses opposition from those who are regulated, drawing new actors into the political process and changing the possibilities for coalition building.

Persistent budget deficits and new budgetary rules also change policymaking by heightening the importance of some interests and reducing the influence of others. As Pierson's chapter notes, Clinton's entire social policy agenda was limited from the start because of the decision to emphasize deficit reduction. This decision reflected attentiveness not only to public opinion but also to the increased power of the financial markets.[39] New budget rules changed the disposition of social policy matters in Congress, greatly increasing the power of the revenue-raising committees and reducing the power of subject-oriented committees. These new procedures alter the access that different groups have to policymaking, breaking up many of the old iron triangles that had once characterized policymaking. The most dramatic change in procedure is the use of the reconciliation process to bundle together policy changes into a giant bill. These procedures can facilitate policy trade-offs that would be unlikely if the bills were considered separately.[40]

Social Policy as a Target for Reform

By the 1990s, the federal social role became a pivot for partisan competition, as long-standing tensions and new uncertainties surrounded these programs. The social policy framework erected during the New Deal rested on a distinctive set of racial, economic, and social assumptions that continued to affect social policy despite the additions and adaptations that followed the initial "big bang" of policy innovation in the 1930s. As these assumptions broke down, conflicts and questions about social policy arose in three broad areas: the effectiveness and suitability of policies for the poor and disadvantaged, the scope and organization of policy for working families, and the affordability of policies for the elderly.

The Assumptions of New Deal Social Policy

The rash of federal social programs inaugurated during the New Deal constituted a remarkable leap in the federal social role. Among the hurdles policymakers confronted were a federal system in which the national government was the weak partner; a national economy characterized by huge regional and racial divergences in labor force conditions; and a strong and enduring cultural aversion to unearned handouts to the poor. The social polices adopted during the New Deal threaded a path among these obstacles, but accommodations to them, together with assumptions about family and employment patterns, limited the federal role in reducing inequality.

The central tenet of New Deal social and economic policy was that the federal government had the ability and the responsibility to create a healthy economy. In addition, the federal government had a role in providing for individual economic security. Behind the new framework was the view that workers suffered from unforeseen market forces they could not control and that these forces could produce involuntary unemployment: economic need was not necessarily a sign of individual failure.

These were dramatic new ideas about the role of the federal government and about individual need. But the New Deal did not wholly transform American ideas about government's responsibility toward individuals in need. Suspicion of unearned handouts did not evaporate. At the height of the Depression, when 20 percent of the nation was out of work, 60 percent of Americans thought that relief expenditures were too high.[41] And despite Franklin D. Roosevelt's proclamation of an "Economic Bill of Rights" in 1944, the New Deal did not embrace any sweeping notions of social or economic rights based on citizenship.[42] Instead, New Deal social policies conditioned eligibility on past employment, keyed benefits to individual work histories, and allowed for considerable variation in assistance across the states. The Social Security Act, the cornerstone legislation of the New Deal, reflected these criteria. The only fully federal part of the act, social insurance for the aged, provided uniform federal benefits across the states but tied eligibility and benefits to work histories. The second two legs of the act, insurance for the unemployed and aid to poor children and the indigent elderly and blind, accommodated federalism by allowing states to determine benefit levels and requiring them to provide partial funding. Unemployment insurance benefits were tied to work histories and were available only to those temporarily out of work. The architects of social security believed that the need for federal assistance for the poor would diminish over time as more women received survivors' insurance and as more elderly received coverage under the insurance provisions of the act.

By the 1940s, the development of a "shadow welfare state" of job-based private benefits, such as health insurance and pensions—publicly supported by tax expenditures—further amplified the importance of work. Job-based social benefits also introduced new divisions among workers, since some workers received benefits from their jobs and others did not. Underlying the work-based approach to social policy were Keynesian macroeconomic policies, which aimed to ensure that jobs existed for those willing to work. Laws supporting collective bargaining and the establishment of the federal minimum wage would help boost workers' earnings. Federal policy did little for unemployables and other nonworkers without children; it was up to the states to assist these individuals.[43]

Politically, these arrangements had two important consequences. First, the connection between social policy and work provided a justification for public social provision that fit with American cultural norms. By tying benefits to work, recipients could be viewed as deserving and their claim to assistance deemed moral. Second, the connection between social assistance and work history and status meant that social policies would do little to upset existing patterns of inequality or opportunity in the private sector. The federal-state character of unemployment insurance and aid to families with dependent children (AFDC) further ensured that social policies could be tailored to particular places. In this way, social policy preserved the local organization of power on which the New Deal's federal expansion was predicated. But each of these features created future challenges to the policies' adequacy, organization, and political logic as legalized racial inequality became unacceptable; the numbers of families headed by women grew; unemployment fell out of the cyclical rhythms predicted by Keynesians; and the proportion of elderly in the population mounted.

Social Policy, Poverty, and Racial Disadvantage

Once the challenge of the southern civil rights movement got under way in the 1960s, a whole new set of questions about the proper governmental role in addressing racial segregation, inequality, and poverty dominated social policy. The initial federal response to racially identified poverty, embodied in the war on poverty, aimed to provide equal opportunity through targeted spending programs. By the end of the 1960s, as the war on poverty dissolved in controversy, the most tangible consequences of the policy ferment were increased spending on welfare, relatively high levels of public employment for minorities, and federal assistance to the cities. In the 1970s, the spread of affirmative action added another set of policy tools for addressing disadvantage. But this set of policies quickly drew challenges that questioned their effectiveness and fairness.[44] For over two decades, the fault lines in this debate provided the grist for partisan politics. In the 1990s, Republicans were asking how far they could push these divisions, while many Democrats now wondered how they could be escaped.

Political scientists Edward G. Carmines and James A. Stimson have argued that in the 1960s race and social welfare spending first became connected in the public mind in ways that undermined support for social policy. By linking racial conservatism and antigovernmentalism, Republicans were able to create a new political alignment.[45] But the practical impact of this alignment—how encompassing the identification of social policy and race was—was much less far-reaching than Carmines and Stimson's analysis might suggest. Some programs, such as AFDC, quickly became racially identified (although blacks never constituted a majority of recipients), and by the 1990s benefits had declined by one-third. In addition, numerous work requirements sought to impose responsibility on recipients and to limit their stay on the rolls.[46] But during the 1970s and 1980s, the Republican political alignment that linked race and social policy did not launch an all-out effort to dismantle social welfare programs. Nixon emphasized social conservatism and championed middle-class behavioral norms, but he did not highlight antigovernment themes or advocate reductions in social programs. His administration sought to rationalize the delivery of social programs and to disrupt existing Democratic patronage networks by instituting block grants.[47] In many cases this actually meant expanding the federal role, as in the failed effort to reform welfare in the family assistance plan and the successful initiation of supplemental security income, which provides uniform benefits for the elderly poor and disabled. Social spending also rose substantially during the Nixon administration, and in the case of social security benefits, indexing benefits to the rate of inflation guaranteed future increases.

Antigovernment themes rang more loudly throughout the Reagan presidency. Reagan charged that government not only stood in the way of economic prosperity, it also undermined individual efforts to get ahead, taking from hardworking Americans and giving to the undeserving. Reagan offered a sweeping critique of government, but he reserved his most cutting rhetoric for the least popular, racially identified programs, most notably in his famed attacks on public assistance recipients as "welfare queens." Despite his more far-reaching rhetoric, Reagan accomplished only a sliver of his social policy goals. Some programs particularly associated with Democrats and race, such as aid to cities, were cut substantially.[48] New regulations reduced AFDC payments and restricted eligibility, with the burden falling disproportionately on the working poor. But social spending on individuals—even poor individuals—actually increased during the Reagan administration. Likewise, no dramatic reorganization of federal-state responsibility occurred, despite administration proposals for a "swap" in which the federal government would assume full responsibility for medicaid and the states would take over welfare.[49]

In the 1990s, conservatives outside government launched a much more encompassing attack on social policy and the federal government. Critics charged that existing social programs actually hurt the poor by failing to impose behavioral standards on recipients of social assistance. Some reformers argued for tougher behavioral standards; others took a more libertarian approach, favoring deep cuts in or outright abolition of social programs for the poor.[50] Conservatives also challenged affirmative action as a system of unfair preferences, arguing that government policies should be "color-blind." As a series of Supreme Court decisions in the 1980s indicated that the era of expanding affirmative action had ended, the question now was how far it would be rolled back. At the same time, the issue of crime, which had been important to Republican political success since the urban riots of the 1960s, reemerged with new force in the 1980s as the crime rate soared. As the chapters by Ann Chih Lin and Linda Faye Williams show, the link between drugs, crime, and young black men made crime a racial issue and at the same time tempted federal politicians to take up issues of criminal justice, traditionally the preserve of states and localities. Finally, a new set of concerns about the costs of social programs used by immigrants emerged in the 1980s. Although it was regionally concentrated—and especially potent in California—the emergence of immigration as a social policy issue promised to broaden the attack on social spending by posing questions about deservingness in a new context.

New arguments about how to cope with poverty and disadvantage also appeared among liberals who wanted to revitalize the federal role. One, associated with the work of sociologist William Julius Wilson, contended that many of the problems of the minority poor were economic in origin and needed to be addressed with new policies that emphasized employment. It was crucial, Wilson argued, that these should be race-neutral programs, open to a wide range of people. The aim was both to create new paths to integrate poor minorities into the mainstream economy and to eliminate the negative political connotations associated with racially identified programs.[51] Along similar lines were proposals to expand the earned income tax credit, which bolstered the income of the working poor. Other approaches focused more directly on the urban poor. As John Mollenkopf's chapter shows, some urban advocates argued that the growing strength and capabilities of local community organizations now provided a base on which the federal government could build with a variety of new community development initiatives. Others supported mobility strategies that would help poor minorities move to suburban areas, where entry-level jobs were increasingly located. Although these two approaches were often posed as competing strategies—"people versus places"—many urban advocates supported both.

These proposals of conservatives and liberals provided a menu of possibilities for Republicans and Democrats seeking to blend political advantage with policy change in the 1990s. Because many existing policies designed to assist the poor and disadvantaged had grown so politically weak, this broad area of government action was most susceptible to change. The differing assessments of the causes and consequences of poverty had distinct implications for government action. What was new was that each side now claimed its policies provided the path to opportunity for those who had been left behind.

Does Social Policy Help Working Families?

In the 1970s, key economic and social underpinnings of New Deal social policies began to shift in ways that provoked widespread questions about what social policy had to offer working families.

In the domain of jobs and employment, existing policies assumed that private sector jobs would provide sufficient income for families to achieve economic security, that periods of unemployment would be relatively short, and that workers would find their way back into the labor force without special assistance. The underlying vision of society was one in which workers could bargain directly with business to achieve higher wages, better working conditions, and fringe benefits. New Deal labor law had helped make organized labor a countervailing power capable of winning wages and securing benefits that would support a family.

Each of these assumptions began to unravel in the 1970s. Increased international economic competition meant that Keynesian tools could no longer be counted on to create jobs. The collapse of Keynesianism eliminated the cornerstone of the liberal approach to social policy: the belief that with minimal intervention the federal government could create economic growth to ensure widespread economic security. At the same time, union membership dwindled from a high of 33.2 percent of the labor force in 1955 to less than 15 percent in 1995 (and less than 11 percent of workers in the private sector).[52] The declining power of unions since the 1970s meant that labor was no longer powerful enough to serve as a countervailing power to business. By one calculation, the decline in organized labor accounted for one-fifth of the growth of wage differentials among male workers.[53]

In the wake of these changes, average wages stagnated, the notion of a "family wage" disappeared, and two-wage-earner families became the norm. Economic inequality increased after the early 1970s as the wages of less-educated workers dropped sharply. The real wages of male prime-age full-time workers without a high school education dropped from $22,134 a year in 1973 to $19,169 in 1987.[54] Unemployment also took on a new form. Structural unemployment, which lasts longer and often requires the jobless to change occupations if they want work, became more common than short spells of cyclical unemployment. As a consequence, temporary extensions of the basic twenty-six-week unemployment benefit were needed to cover even half of unemployed workers. In the mid-to late 1980s, when such extensions were not in place, only 32 percent of the unemployed were receiving benefits.[55]

The changed economic conditions altered the relationship of individuals to the private market, creating new needs that existing social policies did not address. There were few publicly supported programs offering job placement or retraining to assist unemployed workers in reentering the labor force. Most existing job training programs had poor reputations and focused on the lower end of the labor market.[56] For those who had jobs, policy did little to ease the new conditions of work. There were few public policies to assist two-wage-earner families in combining work and family responsibilities. For the less educated workers whose wages had fallen, food stamps and the earned income tax credit offered only modest help. Although it had been expanded in 1986, the EITC still fell far short of compensating for the wage declines these workers had experienced. The average family credit in 1990 was $549.[57]

These new economic conditions also affected the "shadow welfare state," as Cathie Jo Martin's chapter shows. By 1991, 181.4 million workers and their families received health insurance from employers.[58] But increasingly, private employers declared that they could no longer pay for the rising costs of health insurance. Now subject to intense international competition, many employers claimed that the costs of fringe benefits hampered their ability to compete. For example, automobile manufacturers maintained that such benefits added $1,100 to the cost of an American car, whereas for their competitors the cost was $500-$600.[59] Many employers attempted to make employees bear some of the costs of their health care; others simply stopped providing such benefits. More strikes during the 1980s were waged over employer efforts to shift some of the costs of health care onto their employees. Moreover, pension laws and regulations governing health insurance assumed that workers would remain with a single company for much of their working life. Substantial barriers and penalties limited the portability of pensions and health benefits. As these limits on employer-provided benefits expanded, new insecurities mounted among workers across the income spectrum.[60]

Moreover, many policies designed to cope with changed economic conditions were defensive measures that did not offer benefits to the majority of workers. For example, as organized labor's ability to protect wages and benefits declined, it defended more tenaciously than ever rules designed to ensure the right to organize and to regulate the workplace. Critics charged that many of these rules impeded productivity, putting American industry at a competitive disadvantage.[61] Other policies enacted to protect unemployed workers—such as the Trade Adjustment Assistance Act, which sought to compensate workers who lost their jobs due to international trade—had arcane eligibility criteria and did little to move the limited numbers of workers it did assist back into the labor force.

But it was not only new economic conditions that affected working families; changes occurred in families themselves. Existing policies assumed that women and children would find economic security through their relationship with a working man, and women with children were not expected to work. Policymakers in the 1930s did not envision large numbers of female-headed families or the many new problems confronting two-wage-earner families as they tried to combine work and family. But by the 1970s, social shifts involving gender roles and family forms had transformed the world envisioned by New Deal era policymakers. The rise in the number of female-headed households is the single most cited social change that has raised new questions about social policy. In 1960, 8.2 percent of households with children were headed by women; by 1994 the figure was 22.5 percent.[62] These trends were a product of increased divorce rates and the rising number of mothers who had never been married. And even in two-parent families, new stresses emerged as more women worked outside the home.

The rising number of female-headed households created a host of new issues that social policies based on the male wage earner did not address. The issue of families headed by nonworking mothers on AFDC has dominated the public agenda, but the problems of combining work and family affect a much broader range of people. Women are the main support for the majority of female-headed families: the percentage of female-headed families receiving child support payments from the absent parent was 46 percent of the total eligible in 1991; another 24 percent received partial payment.[63] Child care became a pressing need if such women were to work. Because women, on average, earn considerably less than men, the economic insecurities caused by low-wage work affected these families most severely. Moreover, because most low-wage jobs do not offer health insurance, the selective coverage of the "shadow welfare state" particularly harmed female-headed families. The labor market also posed specific challenges for young single mothers and older divorced women, who often found it difficult to enter or reenter the labor force. Finally, questions about job flexibility, such as maternity leave and time to care for sick family members, took on greater importance for female-headed and two-wage families alike.

The key question for politicians and policymakers was whether there was a plausible public role in assisting working families to manage these new economic and family conditions. Should government directly assist families with new social programs; should it facilitate their search for private solutions; or should it simply get out of their way by lifting regulations and reducing taxes?

Can We Afford Entitlements for the Elderly?

The rising cost of social insurance programs for the elderly in the 1970s and 1980s provoked new questions about their future. Expenditures were difficult to control because these programs were entitlements, available to all who meet eligibility criteria. In 1965, major entitlement programs accounted for 26.9 percent of the budget; by 1990, they had jumped to 45.3 percent.[64] Questions about social insurance programs for the elderly became more pressing in the late 1980s as growing budget deficits fueled arguments that social security pensions and medical care for the elderly had become unaffordable and would have to be radically transformed to accommodate the coming generation of baby boom retirees.

The rising proportion of elderly in the American population was one cause for increased expenditures on pensions and medical care. In 1950 those over 65 accounted for 8.2 percent of the population; in 1990 they were 12.5 percent.[65] In addition, because social security had been in existence for over fifty years by 1990, a much greater proportion of the elderly was eligible for benefits. Policy changes in the early 1970s made social security pensions considerably more generous: Congress increased benefits and—crucially for later efforts to control costs—indexed them to rise with inflation. Total real outlays for old-age and survivors insurance (OASI) grew from $6.6 billion in 1950 to nearly $223 billion in 1990.[66] Medical care for the elderly posed a special set of financial challenges. By the 1990s, the rate of inflation in the medical sector was two to three times greater than the average rise in prices. Longer lives and improved medical technologies brought benefits whose costs were difficult to control, especially given the fee-for-service organization of medicare.

Arguments about the need to reform social insurance programs drew on three kinds of evidence. The first were projections of future needs, extrapolating from current trends. Projections of a declining work force relative to the number of retirees suggested difficulties for future financing, since these programs are funded on a pay-as-you go basis. A second kind of argument questioned the solvency of the trust funds that financed social security and part of medicare. Originally established as a budgeting device to instill confidence in social security (and later medicare), the trust funds enjoyed a dedicated source of revenue from the payroll tax. As expenses grew in the 1970s and 1980s, however, the trust fund financing mechanism began to have the opposite effect.[67] Reports of the impending bankruptcy of the social security and medicare trust funds helped undermine confidence in the future of social insurance and prompted arguments about the need for rapid and dramatic changes in these programs. A final kind of argument about the need to reform social insurance programs for the elderly relied on claims of generational inequities. Partly as a result of social insurance programs, poverty among the elderly declined dramatically: in 1959 the rate of poverty among the elderly was 35.2 percent; in 1990 it was 12.2 percent. By contrast, child poverty increased, reaching 20.6 percent of the population in 1990.[68] Critics of social insurance cited the rise in child poverty and the increase in spending on the elderly as evidence of generational inequities and argued that public funds should be transferred from the elderly to children.

These pressures on social insurance programs provoked an array of reform proposals, ranging from incremental measures to dramatic changes in the structure and coverage of the programs. Incremental measures included raising the age of retirement, temporary cutbacks in cost of living adjustments, and increases in the payroll tax. Supporters of this approach believed that the temporary increase in spending on social security needed to cover the retirement of baby boomers could be accommodated within the existing structure if small changes were made early enough. More dramatic proposals argued for applying a means test to social security, limiting benefits only to the most needy, and allowing employees to invest all or part of their payroll tax rather than the current practice of investing it for them in government bonds. Because of the rising costs of medicare, even proposals that sought to maintain existing coverage envisioned the need for major organizational reforms that would reduce costs.

The political stakes surrounding social insurance were very high. Throughout the 1980s, most politicians had openly advocated only incremental reforms because of the wide support social security and medicare enjoyed. But defenders and challengers of existing policies both knew that this broad political support could begin to unravel if changes to the programs made private alternatives more attractive or substantially reduced benefits.

Vision and Strategy: New Democrats and Antifederalists

Confronted with the distinctive features of political organization and the social policy ferment outlined above, Clinton and the congressional

Republicans fashioned their policy agendas and their strategies for governing. Clinton sought to refurbish the image of Democrats by donning the ambiguous mantle of "New Democrat." While such ambiguity proved useful in winning the election, the president quickly discovered that it did little to help build coalitions for policymaking. The congressional Republicans also adopted a strategy that blurred internal divisions. Their emphasis on the need to shrink the federal government led some observers to compare them with the antifederalists, who opposed a strong federal government during the debates over ratifying the American Constitution.[69] As they were limited in achieving this goal, their underlying divisions also ultimately came to the fore.

New Democrats?

A common interpretation portrays Clinton campaigning as a moderate but governing on the left. Once in office, the story goes, the president fell prey to the usual Democratic constituencies and embraced "big government." This formulation oversimplifies the inherent ambiguity in Clinton's claim to be a New Democrat.[70] Clinton's early rhetoric and policy proposals (and his staffing decisions) can be read in two ways. One is as a centrist approach designed primarily to inoculate Democrats against criticism on issues of values and big government. But a more ambitious and transformative strategy can also be discerned, which embraced activist government but sought to establish new premises for public action and to create new mechanisms to achieve its goals.

This strategy had three components. First, to counter distrust of the federal government, policy would work through market mechanisms or the states, and it would "reinvent" government. Second, to counter racially charged "wedge" issues, such as crime and welfare, policy would set clear expectations for individual responsibility and impose sanctions on bad behavior. It would, however, provide resources to assist people if they lived up to their part of this bargain. The president encapsulated this bargain in the aphorism, "If you work, you shouldn't be poor." Third, to counter arguments that social spending was too expensive, policy would highlight the long-term benefits of "investing" in people so that they could be productive workers and citizens.

This approach to policy can be distinguished from two Democratic alternatives. It most visibly departed from "old Democratic" policy orientations in its forthright embrace of responsibility and expectations for individual behavior as conditions for beneficiaries. But it also envisioned a different relationship between government and the market than traditional New Deal policies. Old Democratic policies had combined a social strategy of strengthening labor with providing compensation (such as unemployment insurance) for market losers. Growing difficulties with these policies, their inability to improve the lot of most workers, and their failure to reconnect workers to the labor market lay behind Clinton's alternative. Clinton adopted an aggressive market-oriented internationalism, evidenced in his support for the North American Free Trade Agreement (NAFTA). And instead of passive compensation, Clinton championed policies that would assist individuals in making the transitions that markets required.

This approach also differed from the centrist New Democratic orientation of the Democratic Leadership Council (DLC). Formed by a group of moderate southerners in the mid-1980s as an alternative to northern liberal Democrats, the DLC embraced themes of individual responsibility and advocated using market mechanisms rather than government wherever possible.[71] But its agenda did not emphasize public investment or the need to increase benefits along with responsibility. The DLC was concerned with repositioning the Democrats on the existing political and policy spectrum, not with changing prevailing conceptions of left and right.

The expansive version of Clinton's strategy aimed to reinvigorate the Democratic coalition by shifting the axes of debate to overcome the recurring divisions over race and values that had blocked major Democratic social policy initiatives since the 1960s and to revamp government programs to address widespread public concern about new economic and social conditions. The economic populist dimension would promote a commonality of interests among the poor and the middle class, while the emphasis on values would remove a crucial wedge issue dividing them.[72] As the chapters in this book show, these aims are evident in many of the policies the administration proposed, including health care reform, welfare reform, crime legislation, urban policy, and job training proposals. This underlying political aim is also evident in the central priority given to health care reform, as a popular security-oriented program that would benefit both the poor and the middle class.

Yet most of the administration's major social policy initiatives failed. The defeat of comprehensive health care reform by the summer of 1994 was the most severe blow. The centerpiece of Clinton's social reform agenda, health care reform became the focal point for administration opponents. Prospects for welfare reform, which the administration had hoped to enact after the health plan, collapsed soon after. Even the administration's policy successes did not lead to political victories, certainly nothing to lay the groundwork for a new generation of social policy. The budget package of 1993—combining deficit reduction with an increased earned income tax credit for the working poor, enterprise zones for cities, and increased taxes on the wealthy—deeply split moderate and liberal Democrats and attracted no Republican support. The crime bill, passed in 1994, was a balancing act that funded more local police and preventive social programs and also imposed tougher sentencing standards. But, as Lin's chapter shows, the bill's passage did not consolidate a new political coalition; instead it left congressional supporters divided and embittered. Other policy victories, such as the passage of the School-to-Work Opportunities Act of 1994, remained small and contained, with little potential for facilitating alternative coalitions in other policy areas.

The Democratic defeat in the 1994 congressional elections marked the end of this ambitious policy strategy. In the second half of his first term, Clinton adopted a much more defensive stance, backing only the politically strongest policies, such as medicare. The ambitious effort to offer an alternative vision and policy strategy for how government could assist individuals had failed, and the president fell back into a more conventionally centrist policy orientation.

What accounts for the policies Clinton proposed and their fate? The chapters in this book draw on the three features of American politics and policymaking outlined above—polarized elites; the disjointed politics of advertising, interests, and social movements; and budgetary constraints—to account for the shape of Clinton's social policy agenda and the fate of his proposals.

Most striking is the emphasis that Clinton's governing strategy placed on the advertising mode of politics. Hoping to push out of the policy box defined by the enervated group-based politics of New Deal liberalism, Clinton sought to fashion a politics and policy founded on new majorities discerned through public opinion polling. This strategy had a certain logic: the existing Democratic base was weak, and there was no burgeoning grass-roots movement on which to build a more mobilized politics. Moreover, the advertising strategy appeared to open new possibilities for activist government. The Clinton campaign had found that in poll after poll the public responded positively to policy proposals that put the political spectrum together differently or that promised the fruits of activist government without the thumbprint of big government.[73] This strategy called for comprehensive policy proposals with many moving parts to balance left and right, bold repudiation of failed approaches from the past, and a distancing from traditional Democratic interest groups.

But the advertising strategy had numerous pitfalls, especially when it interacted with budgetary constraints and polarized congressional politics. To be convincing, the public opinion strategy required Clinton to offer alternatives to the traditional Democratic policy agenda and to cross key Democratic constituencies. As a result, the president could not rely on even the weakened grass-roots support that Democrats did have. In some instances, this strategy carried few penalties, as Williams's discussion of black congressional leaders and the crime bill shows. In other cases, it was more politically damaging, as Peterson's analysis of organized labor and health reform indicates. The rift between organized labor and the president over the signing of NAFTA reduced labor's efforts to support health reform in the critical months after it was first proposed and weakened the administration's hasty efforts to create a grass-roots coalition to work on its behalf.[74] Moreover, budget constraints meant that much of the economic populist side of Clinton's agenda—especially attractive to grass-roots Democratic support—never received serious consideration. As the chapter by John Mollenkopf and my own chapter show, the ambitious plans to finance infrastructure and to invest in America's workers never got off the ground. This made it difficult for the administration to mollify its grass-roots allies or lure them away from programs that the administration hoped to change, such as trade adjustment assistance in the case of employment policy. Similar problems stymied Clinton's early welfare reform. R. Kent Weaver's chapter demonstrates how budgetary limits stalled the administration's welfare reform proposals as it sought to come up with the funds that would please centrist and liberal Democrats by providing work and supportive services to accompany new time limits on AFDC.

The second problem with the advertising strategy was that public opinion majorities did not provide a lever for building congressional coalitions in the context of sharp partisan polarization. Appealing to the center implies a bipartisan congressional strategy, but, as Peterson's analysis of the health reform shows, partisan divisions in Congress hampered such a strategy from the start. The balancing act embodied in Clinton's policies made them attractive in the abstract but multiplied the difficulties in securing congressional majorities to enact them. Any notion that broad public pressure would force Congress to accept Clinton's agenda quickly died. Nowhere was this more evident than in health reform, where the president could not translate polls showing high levels of support for the comprehensive reform into active support. Budget constraints magnified the hurdles involved in coalition building by preventing the president from offering the kind of payoffs that had long characterized Democratic deal making. As a result, ideas, which in theory created overarching new coalitions, were pulled apart into separate initiatives in legislative politics. This was problematic because Clinton's individual policies packaged together numerous components, all of which had to be enacted to achieve the desired goal. For example, as Weaver notes, health reform was needed "to make work pay" and to support the ambitious plan to move welfare recipients into work. Enacting only part of the policy created political and policy outcomes far different from those that had been initially envisioned. Moreover, as Lin's chapter on crime policy suggests, the context of divided partisan politics meant that even when the administration won a policy battle with bipartisan support, it did not build enduring coalitions. Each victory was transient and unconnected to broader political change.

Finally, the advertising strategy exposed the dangers of policymaking by slogan. As Weaver's chapter on welfare reform shows, the rhetoric useful in selling policies can later limit the president's room for maneuver, particularly in the context of sharp partisan polarization. Congressional Republicans used Clinton's much-publicized promise to "end welfare as we know it" to induce him to sign a bill that bore little resemblance to the administration proposal two years earlier.

Gingrich and the Antifederalists

The stunning victory of congressional Republicans in 1994 created new possibilities for revitalizing a conservative vision of social policy that had languished during the Bush presidency. Politically, the Republican strategy was the obverse of Clinton's. Whereas Clinton hoped to neutralize concerns about unpopular and racially loaded social policies, such as welfare, Republicans sought to draw attention to these issues to gain support for a much more comprehensive attack on "the welfare state."[75] Republicans also highlighted the costs of social policy, heightening doubts about affordability.

Congressional Republicans adopted three linked policy strategies that paralleled Clinton's themes of reinventing government, promoting individual responsibility, and enhancing public investment. The first was devolution. By defending the superior ability of the states to tailor social programs to the needs of their residents, congressional Republicans were able to deflect charges of mean-spiritedness or consigning the weak to the harsh discipline of the market. Devolution also helped to mute the internal party conflicts between the social conservatives and the small government advocates by delegating many potentially divisive decisions to the states. Second, the new Republican social policy vision redefined the values issue by identifying government as the culprit in the deterioration of values and behavior. Charles Murray had advanced this argument ten years earlier;[76] congressional Republicans now deployed it to link concern about values to proposals to reduce the government role. Further elaborations of this theme posited that government activity squelched community efforts to cope with social problems: remove government, and private initiatives would flourish.[77] The third element of the Republican vision was a balanced budget, achieved through reduced federal spending and tax cuts. Throughout the 1980s, the growing deficit had come to serve as a powerful symbol of a federal government out of control. Congressional Republicans fortified this argument and linked it to social policy by insisting that families, not government, know best how to spend tax dollars. They also portrayed a balanced budget as the compassionate choice because it was key to a prosperous future for the nation's children.

The central policy initiative of this agenda was a comprehensive plan to reach a balanced budget in seven years. A major reform of the medicare program would produce the bulk of the savings required to reach this goal. In addition, medicaid and AFDC would be converted to block grants to the states and the federal guarantee of assistance withdrawn. These structural changes would reduce the costs of these programs and make future expenditures easier to control. The challenge for the congressional leadership was to keep the balanced budget center stage: this focus would direct public attention to the broad ideological issues involving government and freedom and away from individual programs.

It would also head off distributional conflicts within the ranks of Republicans.

Congressional Republicans had a number of political advantages in seeking to enact this agenda and, for a time, came very close to meshing effectively the advertising, interest group, and grass-roots movement politics in support of their agenda. The polarization that had hurt Clinton worked in favor of Republicans. As Ferejohn's chapter shows, changes in congressional rules provided the potential for a much stronger leadership role, which Speaker Newt Gingrich deployed to its fullest. Moreover, Gingrich had built a strong political network through which many of the freshman and sophomore representatives had been recruited, and whose loyalty he further secured by getting them publicly to sign on to the Contract with America. The simple fact of having been out of power for forty years reinforced these strategic moves. The congressional landscape was free of entrenched committee-based baronies, and, as Minority Leader Richard Gephart put it, "When you've been in the desert 40 years, your instinct is to help Moses."[78]

This unusual unity allowed Republicans to exert considerable control over interest group fragmentation. The promise of reduced federal regulation induced many interest groups to subordinate their more specific concerns to this broad goal. And as Martin's chapter shows, Republicans aggressively used "reverse lobbying" to keep interest groups in line. Republicans also benefited from their energized grass-roots network. Republican strategists had been laying the organizational groundwork for connecting elite and mass politics for over a decade, and many of the grass-roots groups now had a more sophisticated leadership that was willing to forgo immediate victory on its issues in order to ensure Republican ascendancy.[79]

The budget constraints that so hurt Democrats also worked in favor of congressional Republicans. The budget not only provided a pretext for congressional Republican unity; years of budget stringency and mandates also induced Republican governors to press for devolution. The willingness of the Republican governors to trade lower funding for control over programs was a significant departure, and, as Weaver argues, it provided a way out of some of the obstacles that had limited welfare reform in the past. In addition, as Peterson shows, the Republicans seized upon the weakness of the medicare trust fund to argue for major program changes.

Why, despite their unprecedented unity and momentum, did congressional Republicans fail to enact their ambitious agenda? Essentially, Republicans lost the advertising game. The policy agenda that their interlocked networks of politicians and grass-roots activists supported was considerably to the right of the median voter. Congressional Republicans were testing whether their grass-roots base among social conservatives, when fortified by generalized antigovernment sentiment, was strong enough to support an assault on social insurance programs that benefited a wide range of Americans, such as medicare. These efforts revealed the inherent instability in the issue alignment that linked opponents of racial liberalism to opponents of social policy: many whites continued to support key social policies that benefited them and their families. Once the focus moved from balancing the budget or changing social programs implicated in the values debate, there was no broad coalition opposed to social policy. Republicans sought to skirt this problem by framing the public debate with an advertising strategy focused on the budget and big government and then by using their congressional unity to forge ahead despite growing public opposition.[80] But without control of the presidency this strategy was risky. After Clinton's decision to call their bluff provoked three federal government shutdowns, congressional Republicans surrendered.

What Changed?

Some political observers point to the deadlock of the first Clinton administration as evidence that policy change is impossible in a system so dominated by powerful interest groups.[81] Indeed, over time, the growth of a permanent interest group community in Washington has made it extraordinarily difficult for political leaders today to enact bold initiatives comparable to those associated with only a handful of presidents in the past.[82] But the failure of most major legislation in the first Clinton administration did not leave social policy unchanged nor the terrain for future policymaking unaltered.

To make sense of the policy shifts that did occur requires explaining the accommodations that Republicans and Democrats made to one another's agenda. In each case, the pattern of accommodation represented a shift from the transformative efforts of earlier initiatives to a strategy of inoculation. Both parties accepted compromises that aimed to neutralize their greatest vulnerability in the broad arena of advertising politics. Thus Clinton calculated that adopting the Republican welfare reform bill as his own would head off attacks associating him with a style of Democratic liberalism that did not embrace mainstream values. The president's somewhat more ambiguous agreement to balance the budget in seven years demonstrated his will to get government under control. Republicans, on the other hand, sought to ward off charges that they were mean-spirited and placed the interests of private business above those of ordinary Americans. These policy compromises also revealed internal party divisions. On each issue, congressional Democrats had to decide whether to go along with the president or prod him toward their more liberal perspective. Congressional Republicans had to contend with emerging regional and ideological differences as the 1996 elections approached. Clearly, both parties compromised, but the scope of the concessions that the president made took Democrats much further away from the transformative impulse that was once part of their agenda.

Plan of the Book

The chapters that follow show how political conflict shaped the social policy agenda and the patterns of policy success and failure in the first Clinton administration. The first section analyzes the three key features of politics that helped organize these political conflicts: polarization, the divide between elite and mass politics, and the politics of the balanced budget. John Ferejohn examines the causes of increased partisan polarization in Congress, exploring both its electoral roots and institutional changes in Congress that have promoted more cohesive congressional parties. His analysis suggests that the overreaching that characterized both the 103d and the 104th Congresses was not due to misjudgment alone, but rather was the product of cumulative political and institutional shifts that promise to repeat the cycle of overreaching and electoral reaction.

Lawrence R. Jacobs and Robert Y. Shapiro consider the growing role of public opinion in policymaking. Their examination of the public provides a counterpoint to Ferejohn's analysis of Congress: as political elites have become more partisan, the decline of parties in the electorate has left much of the mass public politically unanchored. Politicians use advertising or promotional politics to frame policy issues to their political

36   Margaret Weir

advantage and then seek to mobilize the public to back their objectives. The underlying public ambiguity about social policy—combining philosophical conservatism and operational liberalism—makes this policy area particularly suitable to such competing partisan appeals.

Paul Pierson shows how the overarching factor dominating policy-making in the 1990s—the deficit—became a central political issue and highlights the asymmetrical effects of budgetary politics on Democrats and Republicans. For Democrats, the budget presented a massive obstacle to moving policy in the direction of activist government; for Republicans, the deficit presented an opportunity to argue for the smaller government that they preferred. Although the insistence of congressional Republicans on pursuing both tax cuts and a balanced budget and the popularity of middle-class entitlements derailed the 104th Congress's agenda, President Clinton's acceptance of the balanced budget cast a long shadow over future possibilities for activist government.

The chapters in the second section examine the political struggles over policies designed to appeal to the middle class—the prize for which both parties battled. They also assess the outcomes of these conflicts. In his examination of health care, the key target of reform of both Democrats and Republicans, Mark Peterson shows health care reform was central to each party's agenda. For Democrats, it offered a bold initiative, designed to bring Democratic constituencies together and to establish an ongoing social role for the federal government; for Republicans, reform of existing health programs was essential to reach their goals of a smaller government and a balanced budget. Although both initiatives failed, Peterson shows how, in the wake of defeat, the managed care revolution in the private sector began to reduce costs and to benefit key provider interests such as insurance companies. Some consumer regulation passed, but the issue of universal access to health care was pushed to the side in this market-led reform.

Cathie Jo Martin examines developments in employer-provided benefits, the "shadow welfare state" from which most middle-class working people receive social benefits, such as health insurance and pensions. Because business is so centrally involved in providing social benefits, business leaders are key actors in debates about social reform. Martin examines the role of business in limiting the Family and Medical Leave Act passed in the first weeks of the Clinton administration and in the debates over Clinton's proposed health reform and the Republican efforts to reform medicare. She shows that although many big businesses would either benefit from or be unaffected by a more active government role in these areas, big business was an unreliable ally for Democrats. Its least-common-denominator form of organization blocked any consensus on active government. Small business, by contrast, united around a strong opposition to any government social role and proved a loyal and effective ally for Republicans.

I consider why issues concerning wages and jobs—the source of much broad public anxiety in the first half of the 1990s—failed to occupy a more central part of either party's policy agenda. I argue that the bitter divisions between organized labor and employers and the strength of business and weakness of organized labor meant that neither of the key players in this policy area was interested in the consensual approaches promoted by the Clinton administration. Budget politics meant that less conflictual initiatives, such as greatly increased job training programs, could not even be proposed, much less win approval in Congress. As politicians failed to mobilize public support—with the brief exception of the campaign for the increased minimum wage—the arena of conflict remained narrow. Public disengagement and stalemate around a status quo that favored business remained the order of the day in labor policy.

Ann Chih Lin examines federal crime policy. As widespread fear of crime shot to the top of public concern in 1993, the Clinton administration, anxious to show its distance from liberals who were soft on crime, sought to respond. But crime policy proved to be a policy area that evoked as many intraparty rifts as it did divisions between the parties. Although a federal crime bill eventually passed and Clinton could claim to have neutralized the crime issue for Democrats, success came at great political cost to both parties. Moreover, it remained questionable whether the federal role was more than symbolic. Despite federal action, states and localities continued to dominate policymaking for criminal justice.

The final section of the book examines the effort to reform policies directed at the poor and disadvantaged. The intertwined issues of race, poverty, and cities had provoked public controversy and marked a line of division between Democrats and Republicans since the 1960s. The concentrations of poor people and minorities in cities were exhibit number one in the Republican case against the welfare state. The chapters show that political debates about policies for the poor were heavily influenced by the central partisan conflict around the battle for the middle class. R. Kent Weaver examines the politics of policies designed to assist low-income families, including welfare, the focal point of controversy, and the much less visible earned income tax credit. He shows how Clinton's desire to distance himself publicly from the traditional Democratic support for welfare set the ball rolling toward comprehensive reform, ending the sixty-year guarantee of federal assistance for poor families.

Linda Faye Williams examines the politics surrounding policies designed to address racial disadvantage, including affirmative action. Because minorities were so central to the Democratic coalition and the issue of race so politically volatile, Clinton had to play a delicate balancing game, signaling his openness to minority leaders but publicly emphasizing his independence. The debate over affirmative action in the second half of the administration showed that Republicans also approached racial politics with surprising caution, fearful that a concerted attack on affirmative action could backfire in the months before the 1996 presidential election. Yet the spread of anti–affirmative action movements in the states and continuing unfavorable Supreme Court rulings suggest that affirmative action may be substantially weakened even without a confrontation in national politics.

John Mollenkopf examines the politics of urban policy, showing how any expectations that President Clinton would revive traditional Democratic activism in this area were quickly contradicted. He assesses a range of smaller initiatives proposed by the administration to promote urban development, such as community lending institutions, and the more controversial but minor efforts to promote a metropolitan perspective on urban problems. Mollenkopf shows that, although congressional Republicans did not succeed in overhauling housing policy or eliminating Clinton's programs, other changes in social policy, such as devolution and time limits on welfare and the new restrictions on food stamps, will have a heavy impact on poor urban communities and city budgets.

The book concludes with my assessment of what the experience of these four years suggests for the future of activist government. Even though the transformative agendas of both parties stalled, the battles they engaged in, the policies they enacted, and the responses by states, localities, and private actors will all affect what politicians try to do in the future and how they try to do it. Although the most immediate consequence was a standoff and an unusual timidity on the part of political leaders of both parties, the underlying sharp partisan differences suggest that this was only the opening round in what promises to be a long debate on the future of the federal social role.

Notes

1. This is the proportion of the federal budget devoted to human resources, including education and job training, health, medicare, income security, social security, and veterans' benefits and services. See *Budget of the United States Government, Fiscal Year 1997, Historical Tables,* table 3.1, p. 49.

2. See, for example, the remarks of Senator Phil Gramm and Republican analyst William Kristol in Dan Balz, "After the Republican Sweep; Clinton, GOP Leaders Offer Cooperation," *Washington Post,* November 10, 1994, p. A1; and Stanley B. Greenberg, *Middle Class Dreams: The Politics and Power of the New American Majority* (Times Books, 1995), pp. 3–22.

3. Anthony Downs, *An Economic Theory of Democracy* (Harper and Brothers, 1957).

4. See Joseph A. Schumpeter, *Capitalism, Socialism, and Democracy* (Harper and Brothers, 1942).

5. See the discussion in Kenneth Finegold and Elaine K. Swift, "Major Parties out of Power and How They Respond: A Theory," paper prepared for the 1996 annual meeting of the American Political Science Association; John H. Aldrich, *Why Parties? The Origin and Transformation of Political Parties in America* (University of Chicago Press, 1995), pp. 39–41; and Bryan D. Jones and Billy Hall, "Issue Expansion in the Early Clinton Administration: Health Care and Deficit Reduction," in Jones, ed., *The New American Politics: Reflections on Political Change and the Clinton Administration* (Boulder, Colo.: Westview Press, 1995), pp. 191–211.

6. On the idea of activating preferences in the early Clinton administration, see Jones and Hall, "Issue Expansion in the Early Clinton Administration."

7. Lloyd A. Free and Hadley Cantril, *The Political Beliefs of Americans: A Study of Public Opinion* (Rutgers University Press, 1967).

8. See Stanley Feldman and John Zaller, "The Political Culture of Ambivalence: Ideological Responses to the Welfare State," *American Journal of Political Science,* vol. 36 (February 1992), pp. 268–307; and Jennifer L. Hochschild, *What's Fair? American Beliefs about Distributive Justice* (Harvard University Press, 1981).

9. For an interesting discussion, see Deborah A. Stone, "Causal Stories and the Formation of Policy Agendas," *Political Science Quarterly,* vol. 104 (Summer 1989), pp. 281–300.

10. See Frank R. Baumgartner and Bryan D. Jones, *Agendas and Instability in American Politics* (University of Chicago Press, 1993).

11. John W. Kingdon, *Agendas, Alternatives, and Public Policies* (Little, Brown, 1984).

12. See the discussion of macropolitics in Baumgartner and Jones, *Agendas and Instability in American Politics,* pp. 21–22.

13. Lloyd N. Cutler, "To Form a Government," *Foreign Affairs,* vol. 59 (Fall

1980), p. 127. For other arguments that stress the effects of the separation of powers, see Charles O. Jones, *The Presidency in a Separated System* (Brookings, 1994). For an overview of these arguments, see R. Kent Weaver and Bert A. Rockman, "Assessing the Effects of Institutions," in Weaver and Rockman, eds., *Do Institutions Matter? Government Capabilities in the United States and Abroad* (Brookings, 1993), pp. 1–41.

14. David R. Mayhew, *Divided We Govern: Party Control, Lawmaking, and Investigations, 1946–1990* (Yale University Press, 1991).

15. For an elaboration of this argument, see David W. Rohde, *Parties and Leaders in the Postreform House* (University of Chicago Press, 1991). The argument I develop below, however, stresses the role that partisan leaders play in helping to create the homogeneous preferences of their followers.

16. On the cultural value that Americans attach to work, see, for example, Daniel T. Rodgers, *The Work Ethic in Industrial America, 1850–1920* (University of Chicago Press, 1978).

17. See David Frum, *Dead Right* (Basic Books, 1994); and E. J. Dionne Jr., *Why Americans Hate Politics* (Simon and Schuster, 1991), pp. 147–282.

18. The argument about party realignment in the South and Congress is presented in Rohde, *Parties and Leaders in the Postreform House*, esp. pp. 40–81; for a closer look at the southern realignment (and especially its lengthy nature), see James M. Glaser, *Race, Campaign Politics, and the Realignment in the South* (Yale University Press, 1996); and Gary C. Jacobson, "Reversal of Fortune: The Transformation of U.S. House Elections in the 1990s," paper prepared for the 1997 annual meeting of the Midwest Political Science Association.

19. See Edward G. Carmines and James A. Stimson, *Issue Evolution: Race and the Transformation of American Politics* (Princeton University Press, 1989), for the argument that the Democratic party became identified with social spending and racial liberalism in the 1950s and 1960s, while Republicans linked racial conservatism with conservative positions on social policy. White southern antagonism to social spending was a departure from the period immediately after the New Deal, when southern Democrats tended to support such spending. See Ira Katznelson, Kim Geiger, and Daniel Kryder, "Limiting Liberalism: The Southern Veto in Congress, 1933–1950," *Political Science Quarterly*, vol. 108 (Summer 1993), pp. 283–306.

20. Theodore J. Lowi, *The End of Liberalism: The Second Republic of the United States*, 2d ed. (Norton, 1979).

21. David R. Mayhew, *Placing Parties in American Politics: Organization, Electoral Settings, and Government Activity in the Twentieth Century* (Princeton University Press, 1986).

22. See J. David Greenstone, *Labor in American Politics* (Knopf, 1969).

23. See Mayhew, *Placing Parties in American Politics*.

24. See Nelson W. Polsby, *The Consequences of Party Reform* (Oxford University

Press, 1983); Larry J. Sabato, *The Rise of Political Consultants: New Ways of Winning Elections* (Basic Books, 1981); and Hugh Heclo, "Clinton's Health Reform in Historical Perspective," in Henry J. Aaron, ed., *The Problem That Won't Go Away: Reforming U.S. Health Care Financing* (Brookings, 1996), pp. 15–33.

25. Presidents use the public opinion strategy to "go over the heads of Congress" to appeal directly to the public. See Samuel Kernell, *Going Public: New Strategies of Presidential Leadership*, 3d ed. (Washington: CQ Press, 1997). On interest groups' use of mass advertising techniques, see John T. Tierney, "Organized Interests and the Nation's Capitol," in Mark P. Petracca, ed., *The Politics of Interests: Interest Groups Transformed* (Boulder, Colo.: Westview Press, 1992), pp. 209–11.

26. For a discussion of these strategies in the field of environmental policy, see Marc K. Landy, Marc J. Roberts, and Stephen R. Thomas, *The Environmental Protection Agency: Asking the Wrong Questions* (Oxford University Press, 1990), p. 26.

27. See Jack L. Walker Jr., *Mobilizing Interest Groups in America: Patrons, Professions, and Social Movements* (University of Michigan Press, 1991); and John B. Judis, "The Contract with K Street: Washington Lobbyists vs. American Democracy," *New Republic*, December 4, 1995, pp. 18–25.

28. The National Rifle Association also had a mobilized mass base. For an excellent survey of the mobilization of these groups, see Dan Balz and Ronald Brownstein, *Storming the Gates: Protest Politics and the Republican Revival* (Little, Brown, 1996), pp. 113–245.

29. One Christian activist noted that the "pre-political" nature of the networking made it easy to build political power. See Mark J. Rozell and Clyde Wilcox, "Second Coming: The Strategies of the New Christian Right," *Political Science Quarterly*, vol. 111 (Summer 1996), p. 279.

30. By the 1994 election, the Christian Coalition controlled or exerted strong influence on the Republican party apparatus in a majority of states. See John C. Green, "The Christian Right and the 1994 Elections: An Overview," in Mark J. Rozell and Clyde Wilcox, eds., *God at the Grassroots: The Christian Right in the 1994 Elections* (Lanham, Md.: Rowman and Littlefield, 1995), pp. 1–18.

31. See Jane J. Mansbridge's analysis in *Why We Lost the ERA* (University of Chicago Press, 1986).

32. See C. Eugene Steuerle, "Financing the American State at the Turn of the Century," in W. Elliot Brownlee, ed., *Funding the Modern American State, 1941–1995: The Rise and Fall of the Era of Easy Finance* (Woodrow Wilson Center Press and Cambridge University Press, 1996), pp. 409–44. An insightful analysis of the effects of the deficit on politics is contained in Daniel Wirls, "Busted: Government and Elections in the Era of Deficit Politics," in Benjamin Ginsberg and Alan Stone, eds., *Do Elections Matter?* 3d ed. (Armonk, N.Y.: M.E. Sharpe, 1996), pp. 65–85.

33. Steuerle, "Financing the American State," pp. 420–23.

34. See R. Kent Weaver, *Automatic Government: The Politics of Indexation* (Brookings, 1988), pp. 191–210.

35. The 1986 tax reform did some base broadening. See Timothy J. Conlan, Margaret T. Wrightson, and David R. Beam, *Taxing Choices: The Politics of Tax Reform* (Washington: CQ Press, 1990).

36. Increases in entitlement spending due to changes in economic conditions are not required to be offset; the act applies only to increases that are a result of legislation. See Allen Schick, *The Federal Budget: Politics, Policy, Process* (Brookings, 1995), pp. 39–41.

37. For an account of the 1983 reform of social security, forged by a bipartisan commission, see Paul Light, *Artful Work: The Politics of Social Security Reform* (Random House, 1985).

38. U.S. Advisory Commission on Intergovernmental Relations, *Federal Regulation of State and Local Governments: The Mixed Record of the 1980s* (Washington, July 1993), p. A-126.

39. For the administration's attentiveness to the bond market as they crafted their deficit reduction strategy, see Bob Woodward, *The Agenda: Inside the Clinton White House* (Simon and Schuster, 1994), pp. 69–70.

40. The most famous use of reconciliation was in Reagan's first budget. See the discussion in Schick, *Federal Budget*, pp. 82–86.

41. Leo P. Ribuffo, "Why Is There So Much Conservatism in the United States and Why Do So Few Historians Know Anything about It?" *American Historical Review*, vol. 99 (April 1994), p. 442.

42. On the "Economic Bill of Rights," see Alan Brinkley, *The End of Reform: New Deal Liberalism in Recession and War* (Knopf, 1995), p. 260. On the lack of a tradition of economic rights, see Rogers M. Smith, *Liberalism and American Constitutional Law* (Harvard University Press, 1985), pp. 138–66.

43. See the discussion in Hugh Heclo, "The Political Foundations of Antipoverty Policy," in Sheldon H. Danziger and Daniel H. Weinberg, eds., *Fighting Poverty: What Works and What Doesn't* (Harvard University Press, 1986), pp. 312–40.

44. Michael K. Brown and Steven P. Erie, "Blacks and the Legacy of the Great Society: The Economic and Political Impact of Federal Social Policy," *Public Policy*, vol. 29 (Summer 1981), pp. 299–330; and Jill Quadagno, *The Color of Welfare: How Racism Undermined the War on Poverty* (Oxford University Press, 1994). On the rise in welfare, see Frances Fox Piven and Richard A. Cloward, *Regulating the Poor: The Functions of Public Welfare* (Pantheon, 1971). On affirmative action, see John David Skrentny, *The Ironies of Affirmative Action: Politics, Culture, and Justice in America* (University of Chicago Press, 1996).

45. Carmines and Stimson, *Issue Evolution*.

46. See Martin Gilens, "'Race Coding' and White Opposition to Welfare,"

American Political Science Review, vol. 90 (September 1996), pp. 593–604; and Desmond King, *Actively Seeking Work: The Politics of Unemployment and Welfare Policy in the United States and Great Britain* (University of Chicago Press, 1995).

47. Block grants gave more to county governments and to states, two constituencies more likely to be governed by Republicans than were cities. See John H. Mollenkopf, *The Contested City* (Princeton University Press, 1983), pp. 130–33.

48. See Demetrios Caraley, "Washington Abandons the Cities," *Political Science Quarterly,* vol. 107 (Spring 1992), pp. 1–30.

49. Timothy Conlan, *New Federalism: Intergovernmental Reform from Nixon to Reagan* (Brookings, 1988), pp. 179–98.

50. On tougher standards, see Lawrence M. Mead, *Beyond Entitlement: The Social Obligations of Citizenship* (Free Press, 1986). The libertarian argument is made in Charles Murray, *Losing Ground: American Social Policy, 1950–1980* (Basic Books, 1984).

51. See William Julius Wilson, "Race-Neutral Programs and the Democratic Coalition," *American Prospect,* no. 1 (Spring 1990), pp. 74–81; and Wilson, *When Work Disappears: The World of the New Urban Poor* (Knopf, 1996).

52. Bureau of Labor Statistics, *Employment and Earnings,* vol. 44 (January 1997), pp. 211–13.

53. See Richard B. Freeman, "How Much Has De-Unionization Contributed to the Rise in Male Earnings Inequality?" in Sheldon Danziger and Peter Gottschalk, eds., *Uneven Tides: Rising Inequality in America* (New York: Russell Sage Foundation, 1993), p. 134.

54. McKinley L. Blackburn, David E. Bloom, and Richard B. Freeman, "The Declining Economic Position of Less Skilled American Men," in Gary Burtless, ed., *A Future of Lousy Jobs? The Changing Structure of U.S. Wages* (Brookings, 1990), p. 32.

55. *Overview of Entitlement Programs: 1994 Green Book: Background Material and Data on Programs within the Jurisdiction of the Committee on Ways and Means,* Committee Print, 103 Cong. 2 sess. (Government Printing Office, 1994), p. 266. (Hereafter *1994 Green Book.*)

56. See Margaret Weir, *Politics and Jobs: The Boundaries of Employment Policy in the United States* (Princeton University Press, 1992).

57. *1994 Green Book,* p. 704. The EITC was originally enacted in 1976 to offset increases in the payroll tax.

58. *Statistical Abstract of the United States: 1995,* p. 118, table 169.

59. These figures are cited in Clay Chandler, "Health Reform's Competitiveness Case: Oversold? Most Economists Predict Little Impact on Trade and Investment," *Washington Post,* November 7, 1993, p. H1. The article notes that this number was not universally accepted since it does not take into account the age differences in the auto companies and the quality of care provided.

60. See Daniel J. B. Mitchell, "Employee Benefits in Europe and the United States," in Sanford M. Jacoby, ed., *The Workers of Nations: Industrial Relations in a Global Economy* (Oxford University Press, 1995), pp. 54–75.

61. See, for example, Commission on the Skills of the American Workforce, *America's Choice: High Skills or Low Wages!* (Washington: National Center on Education and the Economy, 1990).

62. *Statistical Abstract of the United States: 1961*, p. 39, table 34; and *1995*, p. 58, table 66.

63. *Statistical Abstract of the United States: 1995*, p. 391, table 616.

64. *Budget of the United States Government, Fiscal Year 1997, Historical Tables*, table 8.3, p. 111.

65. *Statistical Abstract of the United States: 1952*, p. 26, table 20; and *1995*, p. 15, table 14.

66. These data have been adjusted to 1990 dollars. See *1994 Green Book*, p. 5; on indexing of social security, see Weaver, *Automatic Government*, pp. 67–92.

67. See Eric M. Patashnik, "Unfolding Promises: Trust Funds and the Politics of Precommitment," *Political Science Quarterly*, vol. 112 (Fall 1997), pp. 431–52.

68. See *1994 Green Book*, p. 1158.

69. See, for example, George F. Will, "Greenhorns of the Year," *Washington Post*, November 23, 1995, p. A23.

70. E. J. Dionne Jr., *They Only Look Dead: Why Progressives Will Dominate the Next Political Era* (Simon and Schuster, 1996), p. 279.

71. See the DLC manifesto: Will Marshall and Martin Schram, eds., *Mandate for Change* (New York: Berkley Books, 1993).

72. For an elaboration of this strategy, see the arguments of the president's pollster in Greenberg, *Middle Class Dreams*.

73. See ibid.

74. See Theda Skocpol, *Boomerang: Clinton's Health Security Effort and the Turn against Government in U.S. Politics* (Norton, 1996).

75. A staple of Republican Speaker Newt Gingrich's speeches illustrated this strategy: "No civilization can survive for long with twelve-year-olds having babies, fifteen-year-olds killing one another, seventeen-year-olds dying of AIDS, and eighteen-year-olds getting diplomas they can't read. Yet every night on the local news, you and I watch the welfare state undermining our society." Newt Gingrich, *To Renew America* (Harper Collins, 1995), pp. 8–9.

76. See Murray, *Losing Ground*.

77. Gingrich often referred to the work of Marvin Olasky to make this point. See his *The Tragedy of American Compassion* (Washington: Regnery, 1992).

78. Quoted in David S. Broder, "At 6 Months, House GOP Juggernaut Still Cohesive," *Washington Post*, July 17, 1995, p. A1.

79. On the Christian Coalition, for example, see Rozell and Wilcox, "Second Coming," pp. 271–94.

80. See Thomas B. Edsall, "The GOP's Flawed Fable: The Miracle of Michigan Traps the Party's Thinking," *Washington Post*, January 21, 1996, p. C1.

81. See Jonathan Rauch, "The End of Government," *National Journal*, September 7, 1996, pp. 1890–95.

82. Stephen Skowronek, *The Politics Presidents Make: Leadership from John Adams to George Bush* (Belknap Press of Harvard University Press, 1993).

PART ONE

Political Institutions, Legislative Coalitions, and Social Policy

Chapter 2

A Tale of Two Congresses: Social Policy in the Clinton Years

John Ferejohn

STUDENTS of American politics have long been accustomed to viewing Congress as an obstacle course, if not a graveyard, for complicated and controversial legislative proposals. And, in many domains—most recently, campaign finance and health care reform—this image still seems to have much validity. But in other contentious policy arenas, recent Congresses have been surprisingly successful in enacting controversial policy proposals into law. The accomplishments of the 103d and 104th Congresses include, among other things, NAFTA, the renewal of GATT, telecommunications reform, a major crime bill, family leave legislation, minimum wage legislation, the line item veto, and, not least, welfare reform. This is a fairly impressive list of achievements. But the two Congresses also left behind an equally impressive list of failures. Most notable were the collapse of health care reform and the disappearance of welfare reform in the 103d Congress and the failure of the 104th Congress to reform or cut entitlements or to enact significant tax cuts.

There were several striking parallels between the two Congresses. Both began with high expectations about the possibility of transforming gov-

I wish to thank Joshua David Clinton and Tino Cuellar for invaluable research assistance and to express gratitude for perceptive and stimulating comments on earlier versions of this paper to the participants in the Russell Sage project on Clinton's social policy, seminars at Cornell University and Columbia University, and David W. Brady, Morris P. Fiorina, Thomas E. Mann, and Douglas Rivers.

ernmental practices. Clinton's election, ending twelve years of divided government, encouraged Democrats to work toward a redefinition of their party's message, permitting it to appeal to electoral groups—union workers, Catholics, southerners—that had been migrating to the Republicans for twenty years. Similarly, their party's dramatic gains in 1994 encouraged Republicans to believe that America was finally ready to reject New Deal governmental approaches. Both Congresses pursued ambitious legislative agendas that exhibited these transformative expectations. The Democrats of the 103d Congress pushed a social policy agenda centered on using an active, but lean, government to foster health security, support families, widen labor force participation, and develop human skills. The Republicans, when their turn came, pushed for increasing individual autonomy and self-reliance, downsizing government, and deregulating the marketplace. In both Congresses, the partisan ambition and enthusiasm that was so abundantly on display at first collapsed in the second session as the election season approached. And, in both Congresses, it was on the shoals of the individualistic, idiosyncratic, and nonmajoritarian Senate that many initiatives foundered.

But, for all their similarities, the legacies of Clinton's first Congresses were quite different. The collapse of the president's congressional agenda in the 103d Congress produced a crisis of morale among Democrats. While it was clear that Clinton's attempt to define a "New Democrat" approach to government had failed, there was no less urgency that the crisis be resolved. By contrast, when Republican efforts stalled in the Senate or were vetoed by the president, Republicans responded with confrontational tactics at first and compromise later, but did not lose faith that they were moving in the right direction. And, where the 103d Congress failed to create a new and expansive entitlement to health care, the 104th Congress succeeded in enacting welfare legislation that recast both the rhetoric and the reality of the social safety net.[1] Why were the Republicans able to succeed in shifting the ground of social policy where the Democrats had failed?

The Republicans were better able to keep their members together at the various stages of the legislative process than the Democrats of the 103d Congress. The stunning defection of both liberals and conservatives in the initial House vote on Clinton's crime bill in 1994 is only the most obvious example of the ways that Democrats came apart at crucial times in that Congress. The last-minute bargaining between the White House and various congressional Democrats over the 1993 budget was an earlier and perhaps more ominous case. The cacophony of health care proposals that emanated from various wings of the party is yet another.[2] But why were Republicans so much more disciplined than the Democrats?

The usual explanation is to point to recent electoral outcomes—1994 in particular—as effecting a realignment of political forces strong enough to break the gridlocked system of the last quarter century and produce propitious conditions for policy change. A partisan realignment, it is argued, produces an influx of ideologically unified and motivated partisans impatient with decentralized congressional institutions—committees and seniority—ready to back party leaders in disrupting old ways of doing business and creating new ones. By bringing in so many members who were young (the average age of House freshmen in 1994 was less than 45), inexperienced (more than half the House Republican members were first or second termers), and ideologically committed, electoral realignment produced the relative clarity of purpose of the Republicans and, concomitantly, their high degree of party unity.

By contrast, Democrats in the 103d Congress, having habituated themselves to what seemed like permanent majority status, felt secure in the decentralized, committee-based, policy networks that flourished in the modern Congress, especially in an era of divided government. While they were pleased to welcome a Democratic president, they were not disposed to follow his leadership uncritically. This reluctance became more pronounced with the mistakes that the young president made in appointments and policy. His enthusiastic embrace of policy details annoyed committee leaders, who thought they had better ideas on welfare and health policy and, certainly, on whether gays should be permitted to serve in the military. And, as always, matters got worse in the second session as unpredictable foreign crises arose and election season approached, and members of Congress began running away from an unpopular president.

It now seems doubtful that the 1994 elections fundamentally realigned party strength throughout the nation. But even if 1994 did not mark a partisan realignment, at least not outside the South, the Republicans may nonetheless have believed that such a fundamental shift had occurred, and they acted accordingly. If so, this was probably a mistake. If there was no realignment, but merely a sharp and temporary rejection of Democratic policies, newly elected Republican freshmen from marginally Republican districts should not have been eager to adopt sharply defined ideological postures in their first terms. They should have been careful to avoid identifying themselves with national Republican themes that might not play well at home. Such actions would only be an invitation to local electoral retribution. Instead, freshmen from marginally Republican districts should have worked to win the trust of all of their constituents as members have done since time immemorial (at least since the 1960s) by providing constituency services and supporting local projects on a nonpartisan basis.

The pragmatism and relative moderation of the second session of the 104th Congress suggests that many Republicans eventually turned to such tactics, and the electoral setbacks that some Republicans suffered in the 1996 House elections suggest that, for some, this adjustment came too late. If so, the very cohesiveness of the Republicans, especially the House freshmen, which permitted them rapidly to alter congressional institutions and commit themselves to "revolutionary" policy change, came at a high cost. In view of the fact that Republicans neither controlled the presidency nor had a filibuster-proof majority in the Senate, the risks taken seemed great compared with the prospects of immediate policy achievement. Excepting the real changes in welfare policy, many of the dramatic Republican successes in the House did not lead to changes in law and were instead victories of what David R. Mayhew has called "position taking," rather than of substantive policy.[3]

The difference between the House Republicans in 1995 and earlier congressional majorities may not be that they overinterpreted their mandate—every winning party does that—but that they had enough cohesion to enable them to act on this misinterpretation. In contrast, it is not surprising that the Democrats were able to adopt a coordinated legislative agenda in the 103d Congress because they could rely on presidential resources and visibility to commit their congressional party to an ambitious course of legislation. Even if the president was leading them down a blind alley, it would be difficult not to follow him—at least at first. But, lacking these advantages, the Republicans of the 104th Congress had to rely on enthusiasm, energy, and a willingness to sacrifice individual goals for shared purposes, which seems far more unusual. It is remarkable, in this regard, that this unity of purpose and action was sustained for most of the first session, even in the face of repeated warnings of electoral danger.

Both congressional parties have been exhibiting growing levels of party cohesion for two decades, and the effects of increasing party unity have put pressure on many traditional congressional practices. A number of congressional scholars have, for example, seen the decline in the regional and ideological fragmentation of the Democratic party as the source of changes in congressional institutions and procedures since 1970 that have reinforced the strength of parties and party leaders. Similar changes in congressional procedures effected by the Republicans in 1995 may be traced to the same source. The effects of increased party unity have also reached into the constituencies, altering the kinds of expectations that constituents have of Congress and their representative and, possibly, how members see their jobs. Increasingly, citizens are seeing members of Congress in more partisan and ideological terms. These changes, and others associated with the changing landscape of campaign finance, in turn suggest that a different kind of person, more partisan and more ideological, is attracted to run for congressional office. Both parties are more willing and more able to act cohesively on partisan beliefs than they have been in a long time. This capacity exposes the congressional parties to more risk, to repetition of the cycle of overreaching and electoral reaction that took place in 1994 and 1996.

Clinton's First Congress

In 1992, after twelve years of Republican administrations, many Democrats believed that their party needed a serious policy overhaul if it was to compete regularly with the Republicans for national office. President Clinton's recognition of this need was expressed in his embrace of the enigmatic New Democrat label during the campaign. But while the ambiguities of that concept made it useful for bringing together diverse constituencies during the presidential campaign, it did not give much guidance to those charged with crafting Clinton's initial legislative program. Instead Hillary Clinton, Ira Magaziner, Robert Reich, Mary Jo Bane, Robert Rubin, and, of course, Bill Clinton himself, were free to make of it what they would.

Clinton's idea of a New Democrat, whatever else it implied, involved an active federal government role in addressing issues of social policy while reducing the burdens that large government imposed on the economy. This offered the hope of building programs that would attract widespread support among both traditional and newer Democratic constituencies. In the near term, it involved using federal regulation rather than budgetary resources as the principal policy tool. It also required reducing deficits so that it would become feasible to launch new on-budget programs, which ruled out substantial tax reductions in the near term. Health care, support for families, environmental policy, and crime reduction seemed tailor-made issues from this viewpoint. There was plenty of evidence of deep and developing problems in these areas, and many Americans had profound concerns about health, family life, and crime. Moreover, it seemed likely that legislative solutions in these domains would attract middle-class support to the Democrats without dividing their existing constituencies, something that could not be said of welfare reform proposals.

Clinton had not arrived in Washington with a powerful mandate to do anything in particular. He had won only 43 percent of the vote, his party had lost seats in the House in 1992, and he had run behind almost every successful candidate on his ticket. Despite his emphasis on New Democratic themes, his victory was probably due as much to turning the election into a referendum on George Bush's presidency as anything else. These political circumstances made it seem likely that, insofar as the administration pushed a social policy agenda, it would try to steer toward the center of the political spectrum and to actively engage moderates of both parties. At any rate, the Democrats would need to adopt policies that could get sixty votes in the Senate if they were to have a realistic chance of leaving a legislative mark.

It was surprising in this respect that the administration chose to structure decisionmaking in ways that largely cut moderate Republicans and centrist Democrats out of the process. The budget, the economic development plan, the welfare plan, and, most significantly, the health plan were all substantially designed in closed White House settings with little congressional influence apart from the party leaders. Backbenchers and moderates of both parties had little influence or access to these venues and they began, early on, to complain about this. These administrative task forces were told repeatedly to get the policy right and leave the politics to the president. Not surprisingly, in view of who was consulted and who drafted the plans, the early Clinton policy proposals were ambitious, complicated, hard to explain, and *dirigiste* in ways that moderates of both parties found worrying.

Whatever anyone thought being a New Democrat entailed before the election, once the administration was in Washington it became a commitment to deficit reduction through increased taxes, jobs stimulus, a big universalistic health care plan, increased federal involvement in crime prevention, and a general willingness to provide federal support for families. Absent were a welfare reform plan (though there was continued rhetorical endorsement of the idea) and tax reduction, both of which had been promised by the number one New Democrat during the campaign but presumably would come later after the initial legislative push. Whether by intention or inadvertence, the legislative package bore an unmistakable liberal stamp.

The administration's effort to blend left and right in a variety of areas including health policy, gays in the military, and budget policy failed politically. Not only did Clinton forgo any realistic chance of Republican support for his domestic initiatives, he also managed to exacerbate the ideological divisions within his own party and to lose a number of key Democratic supporters as well. While this tactic did not necessarily produce floor defeats in the House, it was a disastrous course in the Senate. By putting welfare reform on a slow track, leading off with substantial tax increases and big government programs (health and crime), and pushing gun control, gay rights, and abortion rights, Clinton made it easy for Republicans to paint his program as a typical "old Democratic" program barely concealed in disingenuous rhetoric. And if things were not bad enough, Clinton seemed to go out of his way to annoy critical members of his party—moderate Democrats from southern and border states—with policy proposals that seemed to underscore their weakness within the party (the energy tax, gun control, and various environmental initiatives of Interior Secretary Bruce Babbit).

By tying his administration so closely to the fate of the controversial health care reform plan, Clinton gave Republicans an immense opportunity for delay and sabotage. Two things were clear about the health care plan. First, Democrats were not united behind several of its key features, so the administration would eventually need Republican support in the Senate in order to get it enacted. Second, the way in which the package was developed left very little room for Republican or moderate Democratic input. The administration's bottom-line insistence on employer mandates and universal coverage until late in the summer of 1994 made the fate of the legislation hostage to events that the White House could not control. While it is not clear which events were more important—the collapse of the crime bill in the House, which fifty-eight Democrats failed to support; the invasion of Haiti and the ensuing congressional brouhaha; the continuing impasse over Bosnia; or Clinton's desperate need for Republican support on GATT—they combined to keep Con-

TABLE 2-1. *Electoral Success of Democratic Incumbents, 1994*

Independent variable	Equation 1	Equation 2	Equation 3
1992 Clinton two-party vote	0.07**	0.09**	0.08**
Strong challenger	−0.84**	−0.90**	−1.1**
South	0.50*	0.56*	. . .
Presidential support	. . .	−0.03**	−0.03**
Constant	−3.01**	−0.98	−0.50
N	225	224	224
Percent correctly predicted	84.9	86.2	84.8

**Significant at the 0.05 level.
*Significant at the 0.10 level.

gress tied up for weeks. And because House Democrats were not willing to vote before the Senate on a health bill containing unpopular features that might then be compromised away, the fate of health care came to rest on securing the sixty senators needed to end a filibuster and this, in turn, meant the need to secure the support of five or more Republicans.[4]

Thus, even leaving aside questions of the president's character and personal morality, the missteps and bad luck on presidential appointments, and the awkward handling of gays in the military, the mismanagement of Clinton's legislative initiatives presented Republican candidates with campaign opportunities that would have been hard to pass up. And, as Republicans learned just how weak was popular support for the administration's initiatives, they began to sense that there was a chance to take over the Senate in November (only Newt Gingrich seemed to think control of the House was in prospect) and lost any interest in reaching legislative compromises. If Senate support for a health care plan was ever possible in the 103d Congress, such a possibility disappeared long before August of an election year.

One can get a sense of some of the implications of these events by examining the results of the 1994 elections. Table 2-1 reports probit analyses of the 1994 election for Democratic incumbents running for reelection, aimed at examining the effects of presidential support on election outcomes after adjusting for other influences. It was to be expected that Democratic incumbents would do well in 1994 where support for Democratic candidates was generally strong (measured by using Clinton's 1992 vote percentage) and where they were lucky enough to face an inexperienced challenger.

TABLE 2-2. *Democratic Electoral Success and Key Roll Call Votes, 1994*

Independent variable	Equation 1	Equation 2
1992 Clinton two-party vote	0.12**	0.11**
Challenger strength	−0.83**	−1.02**
Hyde amendment	−0.06	−0.07
Second crime vote	−0.80**	−1.1**
1993 budget vote	−0.83**	−0.94**
Banning gays in military	0.67*	0.89**
South	0.26	. . .
Brady bill	. . .	0.42
Constant	−3.9**	−3.3**
N	212	211
Percent correctly predicted	86.3	85.3

**Significant at the 0.05 level.
*Significant at the 0.10 level.

As expected, Democratic incumbents ran well where Clinton had enjoyed most support in 1992 and, ceteris paribus, ran somewhat stronger in the South than elsewhere in the nation.[5] It is also no surprise that those incumbents who faced strong challengers, as indicated by whether the challenger had previously held electoral office, were less successful at the polls.[6] Evidently, controlling for these other effects on election outcomes, Democratic incumbents' support for President Clinton's legislative program was costly at the polls.[7] These estimates imply that the probability of reelection would have increased by 15 percent if someone had shifted from the highest to the lowest level of support exhibited by a Democratic incumbent.

The effect of presidential support can be disaggregated by looking at the influence of a small number of critical votes that took place during the 103d Congress. Table 2-2 contains probit analyses of Democratic electoral success as a function of a number of important roll call votes. The results of this table are congruent with those in the previous one in the sense that they show a decomposition of the effects of the presidential support scores into individual roll call votes. In fact, the effect of presidential support disappears once the issue variables are included.[8] Moreover, the region effects remain weak compared with the issue effects. More important, these estimates show how particular aspects of Clinton's legislative program affected Democratic incumbents. As expected from popular media coverage, the 1993 budget vote and the second 1994 crime

TABLE 2-3. *Vote for Democratic Incumbents and Attitudes toward Health and Welfare, 1992 and 1994*

Independent variable	1992	1994
Ideological distance to incumbent	−0.32**	−0.47**
Health care satisfaction	−0.34	−0.52*
Decrease welfare spending	−0.13	−0.39*
Constant	1.52**	2.04**
Percent correctly predicted	74.6	78.3
N	205	378

**Significant at the 0.01 level.
*Significant at the 0.05 level.

vote substantially harmed the electoral prospect of Democratic incumbents. The impact of the vote on gays in the military is a bit weaker but still significant. Each of these votes was politically costly for members from marginally Democratic districts—districts from the South and Midwest that Democrats had to hold on to in order to retain majority status—and a number of incumbents paid a price for casting them. The price paid was made more painful by the fact that in some cases it probably did not, in retrospect, have to be paid at all. Several times during the Congress President Clinton forced House members to make hard votes as a way of increasing his bargaining leverage in the Senate, only to recede from the House position in subsequent negotiations with the Senate.[9]

One cannot, of course, use congressional roll call data to examine the effect of Clinton's legislative choices in the areas of health or welfare policy, arguably the two policy domains most central to his claim to be a New Democrat. These issues never came before the 103d Congress for decision. However, data on the 1994 elections collected by the National Election Study (NES) can provide some insight into voter reactions to these issues during the 1994 campaign period. Table 2-3 contains probit estimates of a simple model of the vote for Democratic incumbents in 1992 and 1994. A vote for the incumbent candidates is assumed to depend on the ideological distance between the voter and the incumbent and issue attitudes toward health and welfare. Attitudes toward welfare are indicated by whether a respondent wished to decrease welfare spending, and health attitudes are indicated by the respondent's satisfaction with his or her current health plan. The respondent's designation as to which party was best able to deal with the health care issue could have been used, with no substantial change in the results.

These estimates suggest that, after taking account of ideological distance, voters in 1994 reacted much more strongly to health and welfare issues during the congressional campaigns of 1994 than they had in 1992, and (more controversially) that the negative impact of this reaction was probably felt by Democratic incumbents. This suggests that the failure of the health proposals and the absence of visible administration proposals on welfare had specific consequences, quite apart from whatever overall rightward shift may have occurred in the electorate. Moreover, even though Clinton's health plan became quite unpopular, it is important to point out that public support for government spending on health care remained very high (63 percent wanted to increase spending, according to the 1994 NES data), suggesting that it was the regulative aspects of the health proposals that dominated public reaction rather than a rejection of a government role.

These analyses support the argument that even if the electoral reaction to Clinton's legislative tactics was primarily short run in nature, it was strongly rooted in specific issues that are fairly central to the more activist elements within the Democratic party. The opportunity that the Republicans had to solidify their 1994 gains and perhaps even to become a majority party was therefore rooted in a public reaction against issues and policies that divided moderate Democrats and liberals. While the public might have been reacting to the missteps and foibles of the early Clinton presidency, or expressing lingering dissatisfaction with the unevenness of the economic recovery, these results suggest that public reaction was connected to what the administration was trying or not trying to do. These popular reactions seem to have been especially sharply expressed against members of the House of Representatives. Indeed, there were fewer Democrats from marginal seats (in the South or in white working-class suburbs) after the 1994 election than before and, no doubt, some of the preelection retirements and postelection party switching reflected pessimism that their district interests could ever be accommodated within the party.[10]

Thus, however attractive the New Democratic ideas may have been in the heady days of early 1993, and whatever early legislative successes the administration enjoyed, it is obvious that the first Clinton program failed completely as a political strategy aimed at successfully repositioning the Democratic party as an electorally viable national party. It is not clear, even in hindsight, exactly why this was so. The extraordinary ineptness of the administration's handling of appointments and of the gays in the military issue, as well as the steady background noise of scandal, surely did not help. Neither did the careless way that Clinton exposed his political supporters on Capitol Hill to electoral retaliation by forcing them to cast difficult votes on bills that he would ultimately not defend. Moreover, congressional Democrats were by no means unified as to the practicality or attractiveness of reshaping the party and were at best reluctant to embrace Clinton's specific policy initiatives. But the deeper problem rests with design of the programs themselves, or better, with the conception of a New Democrat that these programs placed before the public.

Opponents easily characterized the New Democratic consensus as committed to large governmental programs, intrusive regulations, and higher taxes—in a word, like an old Democratic program. It also looked like a program crafted together to placate minorities, public employees, gays, and other Democratic constituencies. Moreover, while Clinton's legislative successes on NAFTA, family leave legislation, the 1993 budget bill, gun control, and, ultimately, the crime bill and GATT cannot be denied, the centerpiece of the program—the health care plan—failed so completely as to color the entire enterprise. When one also takes into account congressional rejection of the economic stimulus package and the costly compromises and close votes on the 1993 budget act, the travails of the crime bill in 1994, and the disappearance of promised welfare reform legislation and the middle-class tax cut, the 103d Congress must be accounted a failure by any plausible political standard. Moreover, these legislative travails made it easy for Republicans to cast the Democratic party as a party of big government, old ideas, and fractious interests.

These results were both surprising and disheartening to those who saw in the election of Bill Clinton the genuine possibility of redefining the Democratic party while maintaining its apparently permanent hold on Congress. While Clinton's New Democratic emphasis on investing in people and health security may yet provide a basis for refashioning the Democratic coalition, it was hard to see much progress on that front by late 1994. Indeed, by the time the dust had settled after the November election debacle, the remaining congressional Democrats were, if anything, even more liberal, more urban, more tied to minorities, and more attached to traditional Democratic programs than they had been at the beginning of the 103d Congress. If Clinton accomplished anything with his efforts to define a New Democratic party, it was to show both how fractured his party is and how committed much of it is to maintaining traditional social programs. However inadvertently, by painting the Democrats as the party tied to big government, Clinton handed the Republicans a golden opportunity to turn the election into a referendum on old Democratic ideas, placed in their most unattractive light. Tempted though they must have been by character and competence issues, Republican leaders grasped at the opportunity to base the campaigns on national themes, and, without either Ronald Reagan or Tip O'Neill to provide the visuals, the electorate provided a remarkably univocal response to Democratic congressional rule.

Clinton's Second Congress

Whether or not Republican gains in 1994 marked fundamental partisan transformation, there seems little doubt that the new majority in the House of Representatives had a great deal of immediate success in seizing control of the political agenda and forcing the president as well as the Senate to negotiate on its terms and to defend long-held assumptions about the responsibilities and powers of the national government. The Republican legislative successes in the 104th Congress, even if many of them were confined to the House of Representatives, are all the more striking in contrast with the collapse of the president's legislative program in the previous Congress.

Following their resounding victory in 1994, House Republicans were determined to shake journalistic notions about the powers of the imperial presidency by showing that policy leadership could emanate from the popular branch. They started by transforming institutions and procedures in the House in a manner that would make that chamber more capable of rapid and centrally directed action than it had been in nearly a century. Within weeks of arriving in Washington, House Republicans had overturned the Democratic "subcommittee bill of rights," restoring to committee chairs control over subcommittee staffs and the selection of subcommittee chairs. Committee proceedings were to be broadcast, proxy votes prohibited, and internal votes published, making it easier for outsiders to monitor internal committee deliberations. Committee chairs were also subjected to term limits, as was the Speaker. At the same time, the Speaker was given an increased role in selecting committee members and chairs. Three committees (albeit ones with substantial Democratic clienteles) were abolished, and committee seniority was violated several times as committee chairs who were thought to be energetic and committed to the Republican agenda were chosen.[11] Perhaps as important, the Republicans chose to make extensive use of party task forces, rather than the committees, as forums for policy development.[12]

The parallels between the Republicans' legislative tactics in 1995 and Clinton's in 1993 are striking in many respects. Whereas the Republicans might be forgiven for thinking that the electorate had given them a clear mandate for policy change, the political circumstances were not propitious. Not only did they not have a filibuster-proof Senate majority, they also lacked the votes in either chamber to override a presidential veto. These numbers meant that even if they could maintain unprecedented levels of party unity, they would need support from moderate Democrats if they were to succeed in enacting new policies. This support would have to come either from policy proposals attractive to moderates or from a public clamoring for policy change. The Republican strategy seemed to count on the latter occurrence. As Clinton had, the Republicans adopted a leadership-driven model of policy formulation, making extensive use of ad hoc task forces to propose legislation and leaving to the committees the more mundane tasks of hearing complaints from the minority party and filling in details. As Clinton had, the Republicans made extensive use of omnibus legislative vehicles associated with the budget process in an attempt to package potentially unattractive components of their proposals. And, as the Democrats had, they made extensive use of restrictive rules to prevent these packages from being picked apart by amendments.

Part of the reason for these choices was, of course, the self-generated urgency of the agenda of the Contract with America. There was simply too little time to permit cumbersome committee processes to develop legislation. Besides, if legislative committees were used, Democrats would have opportunities under the rules to delay, publicize, and embarrass Republicans unnecessarily. The same logic that drove Clinton health policy formation into the White House drove Republican welfare and budget policymaking in the 104th Congress into closed venues.

In many ways the consequences of these choices were similar. As there was little need to compromise during the early stages of policy formation, the resulting initiatives tended to be much more extreme than anything that could be enacted, and moderate Republican concerns were often ignored. Like the Clinton proposals, the Republican agenda was easy to characterize as partisan, ideological, and out of touch with the concerns of average Americans. Even if these initiatives were merely initial bargaining positions, the Republicans were forced to defend these extreme positions fiercely if they were to be credible in negotiations with the president. And, like much of the Clinton agenda, many of the Republican plans ran aground in the Senate. And, of course, unlike the Democrats of the 103d Congress, the Republicans also faced, increasingly, the prospect of the presidential veto.

One result of Republican tactical choices was a heightened degree of partisanship during the first session of the 104th Congress. Another was that party members from marginal districts were pressed to take positions that would make them vulnerable back home. If the president had forced a number of Democrats to "walk the plank" for him in 1993 by making them cast unpopular votes, the Republicans did so on their own, forcing those from marginal districts to take unnecessary positions that could be exploited by potential opponents. Not surprisingly, a number of these Republicans, especially those from traditionally Democratic districts, paid a price for this at the polls.

In any case, throughout most of 1995 President Clinton watched helplessly and irrelevantly, unable to do anything more than minor damage control, as Republican congressional majorities ripped into the fabric of the welfare state. While the president was more willing to use his veto pen to bargain with the Republicans, he had to permit threatened domestic programs to limp along on reduced funding, with continued anxiety for their long-term existence.[13] The Department of Health and Human Services did expand its waiver policy to encourage the states to experiment with welfare under existing law, and Housing and Urban Development attempted to forestall congressional action by proposing to consolidate housing programs, but these actions had little effect on Republican momentum. The president tried, sporadically, to defend programs for children and, with more relish, those with middle-class appeal: medicare, medicaid, social security, and the environment. Marginal groups were left out of the spotlight. Unlike the "legislative president" of the 103d Congress, Clinton became much more an executive and administrative president, discovering the attractions of foreign policy, antiterrorism, school uniforms, and the V-chip and leaving legislative initiative to Congress.

Circumstances changed radically when congressional Republicans forced a prolonged confrontation over the budget late in 1995, producing governmental shutdowns, cutting off government checks, and furloughing civil servants. Even though the president vetoed the appropriations that closed the government, the public clearly blamed confrontational congressional tactics for the stalemate. Opinion shifted sharply against Republicans and their congressional leaders, and they did not begin to recover this lost ground until just before the election. After the shutdowns, Clinton took a more aggressive stance on a number of issues, employing the veto both as a symbolic device and a bargaining tool, and Republican cohesiveness began to decline. When it became clear that House Republicans had become dangerously exposed on middle-class entitlements and environmental programs, and even on welfare reform, the administration pushed its veto strategy harder. As the elections approached, Republicans became anxious to nail down some actual legislative accomplishments. Their leaders became increasingly willing to bargain, permitting the administration to obtain significant concessions on the welfare reform plan and to enact a modest health insurance reform bill. Most surprisingly, congressional Democrats, together with organized labor, mounted a successful campaign to increase the minimum wage, chipping off support from moderate Republicans in both chambers.

Thus, while the Republican-led 104th Congress can validly lay claim to significant achievements—most notably the passage of welfare legislation and the commitment to budget balance in the near term—momentum shifted away from the Republicans sharply in the second session. Whether this shift was due to a tactical miscalculation on the government shutdown or to the unattractiveness of their policy portfolio is impossible to say with any certainty. What is clear is that the 1996 elections were at least a partial repudiation of the House Republicans: eighteen of their incumbents lost while only three Democratic incumbents did. Although the Republicans did pick up an additional pair of Senate seats, these gains were in Alabama and Arkansas and might best be seen as part of the long-term shift of southern states toward the Republicans rather than as an endorsement of the policy direction signaled by the 104th Congress.

While it is still really too soon to see the electoral consequences of specific Republican initiatives, preliminary evidence suggests that a political price was paid in 1996 for support of the Contract with America,

TABLE 2-4. *Predicting Republican Losses in 1996*

Independent variable	Equation 1	Equation 2
Constant	−9.5**	−9.4**
Clinton percent, 1992	0.09**	0.09**
Republican vote, 1994	−2.9**	−2.8**
Contract with America	0.06*	0.06**
Freshman	. . .	0.12
Percent correctly predicted	89.8	89.8
N	215	215

**Significant at the 0.05 level.
*Significant at the 0.10 level.

at least by Republican veteran incumbents. Although the Republicans did manage to hold onto their House majority and to increase their lead in the Senate, table 2-4 shows that support for the Contract with America had consequences for Republican incumbents.

Controlling for the strength of the incumbent's party in the previous election and the overall party balance in the district, support for the Contract with America had a small but negative effect on the survival of Republican incumbents. Support for the contract could not actually have caused many losses—the effect of changing from the highest to the lowest score in the sample raised the probability of winning a seat by only about 3 percent—but it probably tightened many races that would otherwise have been won more easily. It is important, however, to hold some things in mind when interpreting these data. First, there was very little variability in the contract scores among the freshmen: the standard deviation for freshmen was 2.2 versus 9.7 for nonfreshmen, so that made it impossible to get a very precise estimate of the effects of contract support for freshmen. Second, few Republican incumbents lost in 1996, which implies that variability in the dependent variable in the probit analysis is small. To get a more precise picture of the impact of support for the contract on freshmen and nonfreshmen Republican incumbents, it is necessary to examine regression results on the vote margins of Republican incumbents (see table 2-5).

The estimates in table 2-5 suggest that, for the nonfreshmen, the effect of changing one's contract score could be substantial, depending on how big a change in the score would be plausible. For example, a decrease of one standard deviation in the contract score would increase a Republi-

TABLE 2-5. *Vote Margins of Republican Incumbents, 1996*

Independent variable	All Republicans	Nonfreshmen	Freshmen
Constant	144***	143***	100***
Percent Clinton, 1992	−0.77***	−0.75***	−0.68**
Republican vote percent, 1994	0.19***	0.12*	0.57***
Contract with America	−0.60***	−0.54***	−0.43***
R^2	0.37	0.26	0.35
N	215	142	71

*Significant at the 0.10 level.
**Significant at the 0.05 level.
***Significant at the 0.001 level.

can incumbent's vote proportion by almost 6 percent. But the contract scores are so skewed that a change of this magnitude is probably not plausible; I consider instead a change from the seventy-fifth quantile to the twenty-fifth, a drop of about six points, which would increase a nonfreshman's vote margin by about 3 percent. Four nonfreshman Republican incumbents lost by 3 percent or less, so that for these ex-members, contract support might have been quite crucial. For the freshmen, the picture is similar, though (for reasons already discussed) less precise. A six-point decrease in support for the contract (that is, a decrease from the seventy-fifth quantile to the twenty-fifth) would increase their vote share by nearly 3 percent. As six freshmen Republicans lost by a margin this close, this suggests that for them contract support might have been critical.

Unlike the results reported for the 103d Congress, the effects of the Contract with America support scores into specific roll call votes could not be decomposed in any stable or consistent way. It appears that it was support for the contract itself, rather than any specific pattern of votes that stuck in the voters' minds. No particular roll call vote—in either the first or second session of the 104th Congress—made any reliable difference in the electoral fortunes of Republican incumbents: not the vote on minimum wage, not support or opposition to welfare legislation, not floor support for medicare legislation, and not for the budget legislation. Unlike the Democrats in 1994, the Republicans were apparently punished not so much for specific votes as for appearing to be too doctrinaire for their districts.

The comparative picture that emerges of the electoral ecology of the 103d and 104th Congress is this. In both cases, voters responded to what members of the congressional majority did in Washington. Voters appeared to pay attention to and respond to policy choices and roll call voting to a greater extent than in earlier Congresses. The differences between the two Congresses are these: the Democrats suffered much more profoundly for their support of President Clinton's legislative program than the Republicans did for their support of the contract. Blame suffered by the Democrats appears to be connected to particular policies and votes to a greater degree than for Republicans. Both parties are now operating in far more ideologically structured environments than in earlier Congresses, but the terrain seems more difficult for Democrats than Republicans.

Internal Transformations in Congress

The Clinton years have so far been eventful from a congressional standpoint. The turnover of seats has been high by postwar standards, party control has shifted to the Republicans, and the nature of congressional politics seems quite different from that of earlier Congresses. The old image of a stable Democratic majority, operating quietly in seniority-dominated committees and doling out governmental benefits to a heterogeneous electoral coalition, seems increasingly out of date. The congressional agenda now seems to have more thematic coherence, and party leaders rather than committees seem to be running the show. Moreover, the analysis of congressional elections suggests that the electorate is, in the aggregate, responding to the new congressional politics in kind by judging incumbents according to how they voted. In these respects, Clinton's Congresses seem quite dramatically different from earlier ones and perhaps, for that reason, historical aberrations.

There is good reason to think that the "new" congressional politics is not transient and that it is not all that new either. Rather, the main features of the recent Congresses and congressional elections are best understood as continuations of processes of longer duration. These processes can be described at two levels—the institutional and the electoral—and I think that the electoral transformation is the more fundamental. But important transformations have been happening at both levels for a third of a century.

While the rise of acrimonious partisanship and ideological division has dominated recent popular discussion about American politics, a generation of congressional scholars has been reexamining the role of parties in congress, especially in the House of Representatives, over the last two decades. Everyone agrees that Congress has gradually changed from a loosely structured locus of committees and subcommittees operating fairly independently, with party leaders serving largely as "traffic cops," to a more coherent, collegial, partisan, and sometimes even centralized institution, where significant policymaking activity sometimes takes place in the offices of party leaders, in party caucuses, and on the chamber floors. These changes have gone farther and happened faster in the House of Representatives than in the Senate, which was never as decentralized as the House to begin with, but they have been visible in both chambers to varying extents.

While many scholars have remarked on aspects of this transformation over the years,[14] I think it is fair to say that no one fully foresaw the consequences that these changes could have following an electoral shift of the kind that took place in 1994. At this point it does not seem an exaggeration to say that in 1995, after 200 years (and not counting the Reconstruction Congresses) the House of Representatives shows more signs of fulfilling the hopes of (small *d*) democrats and the fears of the Founding Fathers than anyone would have thought possible. How has this transformation come about?

Most of the changes in House procedures since 1970 have had the effect (and the purpose) of enhancing the influence of the majority party in congressional policymaking. As liberals became a majority of the House Democrats in the 1960s, their growing frustration with conservative committee chairs led to a series of reforms aimed at enhancing the power of the party caucus over the committees. The earliest of these changes was to permit the Speaker to control the Rules Committee. Later reforms included reducing the power of committee chairs to select members, leaders, staffs, or jurisdictions of subcommittees; increasing the openness of internal committee proceedings by recording committee roll calls; and establishing a norm of open markup sessions. Perhaps the most significant of these changes was requiring that chairs be selected in caucus by secret ballot, a reform that led to the toppling of several chairmen and, no doubt, to an increase in caucus responsiveness among the others. The results of these innovations were complex, producing an increasing decentralization of decisionmaking as well as an increase in the influence of the majority party.

The procedural changes implemented by the 104th Congress largely continued to pursue similar goals. Like the Democrats in 1970, the Republicans of 1995 were determined to increase the responsiveness of congressional processes to the will of the majority. Because the role of subcommittees was diminished, the internal operations of committees were easier to monitor, and party leaders had more control over the membership and leadership of the committees, legislation was more likely to conform to the wishes of the majority party caucus. Thus, though the Republican caucus did not play a day-to-day decisionmaking role on every issue, instruments were created to ensure that its will was felt in places where the everyday decisions were made. Although the Republicans did reverse some of the earlier Democratic reforms, such as the subcommittee bill of rights, they did so only because these innovations no longer suited their partisan purposes. On the whole the Republican procedural reforms of the 104th Congress, like those of their predecessors, served to increase majority party influence in committees.

Perhaps as important as the changes in committee procedures were the increased powers of the majority party to work its will directly during floor proceedings. The various legislative creatures that had evolved out of the operation of the budget act—principally the reconciliation bill and the continuing resolutions—permitted the construction of omnibus legislative vehicles, at least in part, outside the committee process. The availability of these omnibus instruments, which are generally protected from amendments by special rules (in the House) and negotiated agreements (in the Senate), not only increases the opportunity for policy coordination within Congress but enhances the ability of party majorities to structure the legislative agenda. Perhaps most important in a period of chronically divided government, omnibus vehicles permit majorities to bundle legislative proposals together to gain bargaining leverage with a hostile president. The Democratic Houses of the early 1980s perfected this technique in negotiating budget agreements with the Reagan administration. The Republicans' use of the same tool in late 1995 illustrates both its potential to sharpen issues and its political costs.

As always, things were more complicated in the Senate. The Senate never conferred on its committees the high degree of autonomy that characterized House procedures in the 1950s; thus there was less need to adopt reforms aimed at curbing the powers of chairs. The Senate has chosen more collegial and consensual decisionmaking practices than the House, permitting individual members much greater latitude to influ-

ence individual bills. Unlike the House, the Senate has never been attracted to majoritarian rules for limiting debate and has chosen indi-
vidualist norms in preference to the more collectivist ones found in the
House. Thus, while Senate Republicans in the 104th Congress did change
procedures somewhat by opening up committee processes and subject-
ing chairs to secret ballot within the committee and party caucus, these
changes have had only limited effects in increasing the influence of the
majority party. The only innovations in Senate procedures with this potential are those associated with the budget process, especially the possibility of invoking majoritarian cloture on budget legislation.

Although the detailed pattern of reforms may seem complicated and
distinctions have to be made between the chambers, all of the procedural changes point in the same direction: increasing the influence of
the majority party in congressional decisionmaking. One reason for this
was suggested in a seminal paper by Joseph Cooper and David W. Brady,
whose theme has since been pursued in the developing literature on
congressional parties under the name "conditional party government."[15]
According to this theory, ideologically homogeneous parties are willing
to delegate much more extensive powers to their leaders than heterogeneous ones. The reason for this willingness is that party leaders and followers have similar preferences and the risks of delegation are relatively
low in such circumstances.

Applied to the Congresses of the last quarter century, this argument
implies that Republicans (as the more homogeneous party) would be
more willing than Democrats to delegate extensive powers to their party
leaders. Moreover, as a party becomes more unified—as the Democrats
have in the past two decades—it should be expected to exhibit stronger
party leadership. Conditional party government theory suggests why
both parties have been pushing congressional institutions in the same
direction, why House parties have moved faster than the more heterogeneous Senate parties to centralize decisionmaking procedures, and why
the House Republicans have gone the furthest in this regard.

Members of Congress and the Electorate

Conditional party government theory posits a causal relationship between electoral results, which presumably shape the preferences of members of Congress, and congressional institutions and procedures. And,
no doubt, much of the increase in partisanship is traceable to changes in

the nature of electoral outcomes.[16] The one-man, one-vote decisions of the Supreme Court in the early 1960s and the 1965 Voting Rights Act changed the nature of congressional constituencies in a relatively short period of time. When combined with demographic and other forces, these changes in law forced relatively conservative southern congressional candidates to pay attention to the interests and needs of African Americans, and the effects on the congressional parties were dramatic. Increasingly, the South is represented in Congress by either white conservative Republicans or black liberal Democrats. Racial and social conservatives have largely deserted the congressional Democratic party, which means that the principal source of internal party division has mostly evaporated, producing a much more liberal and homogeneous party than ever before. The replacement of conservative southern Democrats by very conservative Republicans has also transformed the Republican party in two ways: it has made it more homogeneously conservative than it was, and the influx of southerners has increased the party's attachment to social conservatism.

Without denying the importance of electoral change in shaping congressional behavior and institutions, I want to emphasize that there is some evidence that the causal relations are more complicated than this simple picture. Leaving aside the fact that Congress enacted voting rights legislation and the Court imposed constitutional regulations on districting, the congressional passage of campaign finance legislation in the 1970s encouraged the creation of new kinds of national party organizations. In significant ways these new creations have altered the terrain of competition for congressional seats. National parties and committees have come to play a major role in recruiting, training, and financing candidates for Congress in both parties and have probably worked to attract relatively partisan candidates. Gary C. Jacobson and Samuel Kernell have argued that national parties can work, and have done so, to amplify the effect of national forces on local electoral outcomes.[17]

In addition, the growth in the size of Democratic majorities in Congress, just as the reforms were kicking in, produced circumstances in which Democrats, especially in the House, did not really need Republican votes on important legislation. As Steven S. Smith has shown, House Democrats learned to use rules and institutions of the reformed House to cut Republicans out of the action.[18] The result was a growth in combative and belligerent Republican reactions against Democratic control of the congressional agenda.

FIGURE 2-1. *Voters' Perception of Ideological Distance between House Candidates, 1978–94*

Difference in liberal-conservative placements

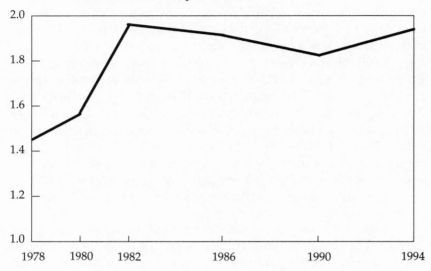

Source: *American National Election Studies, 1948–1994* (University of Michigan, Institute for Social Research, May 1995).

Moreover, changes in congressional behavior directly altered the way that ordinary citizens appraise their representatives in Congress. The growth in congressional partisanship, for example, has not gone unnoticed in the districts. Over the past twenty years, more and more voters have tended to see congressional elections as contests between sharply different parties. Figure 2-1 charts the perceived distance between the candidates (in those districts with two-candidate races) on the NES liberalism-conservativism scale. Generally, voter perceptions of party differences are a little higher during presidential election years than in off years, but these data indicate a growing awareness of party differences and steadily declining differences between off and on years. They also suggest that the big increase in perceived party differences may have occurred more than a decade ago. To a growing extent, voters are coming to see the parties and candidates as relatively extreme rather than centrist. It is only a small exaggeration to say that, as far as many voters

FIGURE 2-2. *Proportion of Respondents Placing Themselves Ideologically between the Parties, 1978–94*

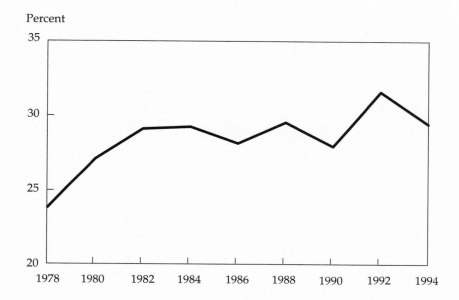

Source: *American National Election Studies.*

are concerned, the choice in a congressional contest is increasingly between two committed partisans.

Figure 2-2 graphs the proportion of respondents placing themselves ideologically in between the two parties. The same picture could have been drawn for intermediate placement between the two candidates, but the estimates would have been based on less information. As was shown in the previous figure, the jump in candidate separation occurred in the early Reagan years.

As members of Congress have become more partisan and their constituents have come to see them in those terms, the traditional relationship between members and their districts has begun to shift. There has been a perceptible drift away from the image of the representative as a neutral service provider for the district—the dominant mode of the relationship between members and constituents from the 1960s to the 1980s—and in the direction of more partisanship and issue responsiveness. This

74   John Ferejohn

FIGURE 2-3. *Reasons for Contacting Members of Congress, 1978–94*

Percent contacting member

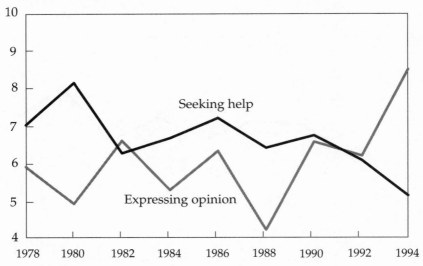

Source: *American National Election Studies.*

movement can be traced in survey evidence from the mid-1970s and in a variety of more indirect sources as well. For example, while there is little evidence of a trend in the proportion of people who report having contacted their member of Congress, more of those contacts involve the expression of opinions and less are seeking help. As can be seen in figure 2-3, since 1980 constituents have been less and less inclined to go to their members to seek help with a government program (the regression relationship is highly significant and negative). Unlike the pattern of figures 2-1 and 2-2, this change is spread out over the whole period and not concentrated in time. By contrast, there has been less of a trend in contacting incumbents to express opinions, with a real jump visible only in 1994.

Figure 2-4 provides further insight into this pattern. A diminishing proportion of constituents think that their member of Congress would be very helpful if they needed assistance (again, a significant negative relationship). Indeed, even though respondents of the other party have always thought the incumbent would be less helpful than those of the same party, the decline in expectations of helpfulness is independent of

FIGURE 2-4. *Expectations of Representative's Helpfulness, 1978–94*

Percent expecting member to be helpful

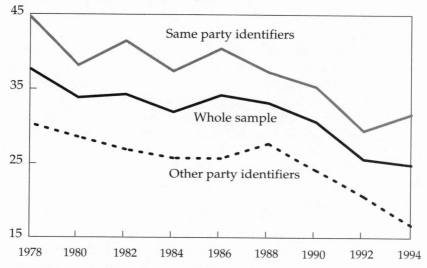

Source: *American National Election Studies.*

whether the respondent identifies with the same party as the incumbent. The rise in the proportion of respondents who think the incumbent would not be helpful if asked is perhaps even more dramatic, increasing by about 50 percent over the period since 1978.

There has also been a gradual decline in recall rates for both incumbents and challengers until 1994, when possibly for quite temporary reasons, there was a surge in these rates (the regressions are negative and significant at the 0.10 level). Citizens are also somewhat less able than previously to recall anything that their member has done for the district. Thus, since 1978 there seems to have been a steady erosion in the image of the incumbent as a neutral servant of the district. While none of these changes is huge, all of them point in the same direction and suggest that the period of the congressional ombudsman may be transient.

Although members do remain closely tied to their districts, the content of this tie seems to be shifting. Individual constituents increasingly expect their representatives to behave as partisans and are increasingly inclined to evaluate them in terms of whether they agree with them. It is becoming more difficult for members to insulate themselves from national tides by providing services to the district, and apparently members are a little less inclined to try to do so. As a consequence, members are coming to see their fates as more bound up with issues and how their parties are doing nationally. Over time these tendencies should produce an increased sorting of members into ideologically congenial districts. The growth of Republican strongholds in the South and the intermountain West and the solidifying Democratic strength in the Rust Belt fit this pattern. Such sorting is consistent with very high rates of reelection; however, such high rates would not be due to advantages of incumbency but rather to the fact that most districts lean ideologically to the party that already represents them.

Although the increasing homogeneity of the parties has been evident for more than a decade, I think it is safe to say that no one forsaw what the consequences might be if a truly homogeneous party took control of Congress. Although the Democrats have become more unified over the past two decades, there are still serious divisions among their constituencies. The divisions have not usually divided congressional Democrats, partly because their leadership has kept divisive issues from coming up for votes. There simply have not been many roll calls on affirmative action policies, busing plans, abortion on demand, and the like over the last twenty years or so. The increased unity of congressional Democrats, while genuine in comparison with the regional fragmentation of the New Deal alliance, was at least partly due to Democratic control of the congressional agenda.

The Republicans, of course, have their own internal cleavages, especially on social issues, and their leaders worked assiduously to keep divisive issues from coming up for votes during the 104th Congress. Until now their underlying base of support has been much less fractured than the Democrats. That is why Republicans were willing to delegate a large amount of authority to Newt Gingrich, Richard Armey, Tom DeLay, and John Kasich during the first session of the 104th Congress, permitting party leaders to craft compromises privately that could be rolled into omnibus legislative proposals.

It is not clear, however, if the image of Republican homogeneity will survive the transition to majority status. That transition entails adding new districts to the Republican coalition, but many of these districts are southern and deeply attracted to the kinds of social issues that could divide the Republican party. The domination of southern leaders within the party, which became more pronounced with Trent Lott's selection as Senate majority leader in 1996, may present members from the North and far West with some difficult problems in the future.

For their part, the Democrats in the House found it difficult to stick together during the first session of the 104th Congress. When, on occasion, they were able to agree to concert their efforts to try to stop the Republican steamroller—as when ex-Democrat Nathan Deal of Georgia offered a compromise welfare plan—the fragility and shallowness of their shared interests was only underscored. Ultimately, Deal and several others from marginally Democratic seats simply saw no room for them and their constituents in the party and resigned, leaving a more homogeneously liberal Democratic party in their wake.

Conclusion: Congress and Social Policy Reconsidered

In one sense, it is easy to see why President Clinton's efforts to reposition the Democratic party failed. This effort was based on the belief that the nation was prepared to accept, and a Democratic Congress prepared to enact, new programs that combined private sector flexibility with governmental activism. Whether or not the public was ready to embrace such a redefinition of the Democratic agenda, congressional Democrats were not able to agree on what that redefinition would be. Clinton's effort at redefining the Democratic agenda was symbolized in the health care plan, which was presented to the public and to Congress as a nonintrusive, nonbureaucratic program that would revolutionize health care without increasing taxes. It is clear in retrospect that neither Democrats nor Republicans could believe this.

The defining setting for Clinton's strategy was in the Senate, and here there were just two choices. If the president could have convinced Senate Democrats to roll major policy proposals—such as the health care plan—into the reconciliation process, he could have relied wholly on Democratic support to enact them. When that failed, Clinton needed to get sixty votes in the Senate to enact any substantial social legislation and, in effect, this meant he would have to depend on centrists like David Boren of Oklahoma and Sam Nunn of Georgia—senators from marginally Democratic constituencies, who were likely to be skeptical of new social programs. And, if these moderates were not included centrally as policymakers and agenda setters, it is not clear why they would wish to cooperate. So, although Clinton did enjoy some partisan victories in the more majoritarian House, and he did succeed in pushing bipartisan legislation such as NAFTA and GATT, it should have been obvious from early on that enacting anything resembling the health care plan, as it was envisioned, was pretty much out of the question.

A viable New Democratic agenda, like the old Democratic agenda, must be based on finding or constructing a set of interests shared by the diverse constituencies of the party. As long as fiscal constraints were not too tight, Democrats were able to do this by developing federally funded programs that distributed government benefits to their segmented constituencies. As things became fiscally tighter during the 1970s, it became increasingly necessary to substitute regulatory policies and unfunded mandates for spending programs. Such policies look and feel coercive to the average American. Regulation, more than distribution of public largesse, demands justification and explanation, and the very diversity of the Democratic coalition made coherent rationales hard to come by. Cumulatively, increased reliance on regulation has been disastrous for Democrats. Such programs often divide Democratic constituencies, putting racial and ethnic minorities in direct conflict with working-class white men. Moreover, regulations increasingly generate opposition from small businesses, states, and local governments. This is what made the old Democratic strategy increasingly vulnerable to libertarian and cultural critiques.

Clinton failed to recognize the intractability of this political problem and to see that the Democrats had effectively become the party of the status quo and that, even if their diverse constituencies could not agree on how to go forward together, they had big stakes in protecting what they were getting from government. Failing to see this, Clinton campaigned as the candidate for change, promising to end welfare as we know it, and to provide health security for all Americans, all while opening up the American marketplace to international competition. These and other, smaller initiatives entailed a mass of new regulatory restrictions on ordinary people and business and, worse, jeopardized support for existing programs. Although it is impossible to know what would have happened if he had moved rapidly on welfare policy, his health and crime programs were easily portrayed as intrusive, big-spending, regulatory programs. The costs of this miscalculation are just beginning to become apparent.

The 1994 elections changed everything in one sense, but in another, more important, sense things remained the same. After the elections it was the Republicans who took responsibility for crafting legislative proposals, and, as argued earlier, the strategic choices they made resembled those made by the Democrats. The Republican had campaigned for revolution rather than mere change. Like the Democrats, the Republicans built a legislative agenda that did not involve moderates of either party, and that agenda predictably ran into trouble in the Senate and with the president. Both Clinton and the Republicans put deficit reduction up front and let that priority guide the policy agenda. For Clinton, concern with deficits meant that the health care plan had to be a regulatory program, not a spending program. For the Republicans, the same concern with deficits led to attempts to trim middle-class entitlements.

Although proposals for change often emanate from elsewhere, the Senate remains the crucial battleground and, once again, it is a question of counting to sixty (or to sixty-seven). The pivotal voter in the Senate is, as before, a moderate (probably someone like John H. Chafee of Rhode Island or Maine's Olympia Snowe). The pickup of two seats in the 1996 election makes the Senate somewhat more tractable for the Republicans, but President Clinton's reelection means that often sixty-seven votes will be needed to enact veto-proof major legislation. This means that several Democratic votes will be required. The freshman Republican senators, several of them having arrived from the more partisan lower house, seem less inclined to seek moderation and compromise than their predecessors. But the arithmetic of power suggests that centrists will remain in a strong position in that chamber.

In the House, the tightening of the party balance probably enhances the bargaining position of Republican moderates. The narrow margin by which Gingrich was able to hold onto his speakership was instructive in this regard. There is no doubt that the Speaker realizes that his leadership depends on the support of moderate Republicans, who see him as a more pliable and pragmatic leader than other Republicans who might take his place. But his position depends as well on his relationship with the large group of second and third termers who, like him, retain visions of building a permanent Republican majority. Even after the electoral scare that the Republicans suffered in 1996, they still have the votes and the cohesion to have a large effect on the national agenda even if they lack the votes to enact substantial new legislation in the Senate or to override presidential vetoes. One would expect therefore that congressional politics in the near term will remain what it has been for four years, a ballet of positioning and posturing, in which each party struggles to define a vision of social policy that can attract the support and enthusiasm of a skeptical electorate.

Notes

1. Indeed, simply reviewing the fate of legislative initiatives of the 104th Congress probably understates its impact on policy by ignoring the fact that various administrative agencies, including the Departments of Health and Human Services and Housing and Urban Development, changed administrative practices significantly in anticipation of possible legislative action.

2. See Theda Skocpol, *Boomerang: Clinton's Health Security Effort and the Turn against Government in U.S. Politics* (Norton, 1996).

3. David R. Mayhew, *Congress: The Electoral Connection* (Yale University Press, 1974), p. 61.

4. A number of Democratic leaders in both the House and Senate wanted to push some health care plan to a vote just to ensure that the Republicans would be on record in opposition. While this course was workable in the House, neither Speaker Tom Foley nor Majority Leader Richard Gephardt had any enthusiasm for it. Haynes Johnson and David S. Broder, *The System: The American Way of Politics at the Breaking Point* (Little, Brown, 1996), pp. 476–510.

5. These results also hold if the Dukakis vote is used as a measure of Democratic party strength or if one uses Clinton's proportion of the three-way vote by including the Perot vote.

6. Strong challengers do not strike randomly. A probit analysis of the 1994 results shows that highly qualified Republican challengers were more likely to appear in districts where Clinton ran poorly in 1992, where the Democratic incumbent exhibited weakness in 1992, and where the incumbent had a high rating by Americans for Democratic Action in the 103d Congress.

7. The results remain stable if the incumbent's previous vote proportion is included on the right-hand side, though the significance of the coefficient on South is reduced. The same analysis in the Senate produces a similar sign pattern—ceteris paribus, support for the president reduced a senator's reelection chances—but the coefficients are insignificant at the 0.05 level. There were too few senators up for election to pursue the questions of this section with any detail or confidence in the results.

8. Gary Jacobson has carried out a somewhat more elaborate analysis of the electoral support for incumbent Democrats in 1994, measured in share of the two-party vote, and has found similar results. He finds that the 1993 budget vote had a major impact on vote shares after taking full account of campaign spending, and in his specification, though not in mine, support for NAFTA hurt

Democratic incumbents. He shows that the incumbent votes were costly both directly, by reducing vote share, and indirectly, by inducing better-funded opposition candidates to run against them. Gary C. Jacobson, "The 1994 House Elections in Perspective," *Political Science Quarterly*, vol. 111 (Summer 1996), pp. 203–23.

9. There was no evidence of a presidential support effect on challenger entry of the sort found in table 2-1, and the effects of particular votes were weak and inconsistent. Indeed, only the 1993 budget vote had any effect, and that effect was negative: ceteris paribus, Democratic incumbents who voted for the budget agreement were actually less likely to have a strong challenge. These results suggest that while Republican challengers, and perhaps the national party committees, may have attempted to challenge liberals in marginal districts, they did not seem to focus on particular issues as much as the electorate did.

10. It is important to note that although moderate Democrats ran poorly in 1994, the marginal effect of policy moderation among Democrats, once account is taken of the strength of the party in the district, was to enhance reelection prospects. It is this apparently divergent pattern that places the Democrats in a difficult political circumstance now and in the future. It is to be expected, after all, that when a party moves from majority to minority status, the seats retained will be those that are fairly safe for the party.

11. For a more complete description and analysis of these changes, see Steven S. Smith and Eric D. Lawrence, "Party Control of Committees in the Republican Congress," in Lawrence C. Dodd and Bruce I. Oppenheimer, eds., *Congress Reconsidered*, 6th ed. (Washington: Congressional Quarterly Press, 1997), pp. 163–92.

12. There were also substantial change in Senate procedures, but, except for making chairs stand for election by secret ballot, none that would alter the Senate's character as an individualistic and slow-moving deliberative chamber. See ibid.; and C. Lawrence Evans and Walter J. Oleszek, "Congressional Tsunami? The Politics of Committee Reform," in Dodd and Oppenheimer, eds., *Congress Reconsidered*, pp. 193–211.

13. Rod Kiewiet and Mathew McCubbins have argued that the president's legislative powers are, in fact, quite uneven in their effects. Armed with proposal and veto powers, presidents can be much more successful in stopping a profligate Congress from busting the budget than in persuading a tightfisted one to spend more than it wishes to. D. Roderick Kiewiet and Mathew D. McCubbins, *The Logic of Delegation: Congressional Parties and the Appropriations Process* (University of Chicago Press, 1991).

14. Among many others, see John H. Aldrich, *Why Parties: The Origin and Transformation of Party Politics in America* (University of Chicago Press, 1995); Stanley Bach and Steven S. Smith, *Managing Uncertainty in the House of Representatives: Adaptation and Innovation in Special Rules* (Brookings, 1988); Steven S. Smith, *Call to Order: Floor Politics in the House and Senate* (Brookings, 1989); Steven

S. Smith, *The American Congress* (Houghton-Mifflin, 1995); Gary W. Cox and Mathew D. McCubbins, *Legislative Leviathan: Party Government in the House* (University of California Press, 1993); Kiewiet and McCubbins, *Logic of Delegation*; Keith T. Poole and Howard Rosenthal, "Patterns of Congressional Voting," *American Journal of Political Science*, vol. 35 (February 1991), pp. 228–78; and David W. Rohde, *Parties and Leaders in the Postreform House* (University of Chicago Press, 1991).

15. Joseph Cooper and David W. Brady, "Institutional Context and Leadership Style: The House from Cannon to Rayburn," *American Political Science Review*, vol. 75 (June 1981), pp. 411–25. The theory was worked out more completely and applied to current circumstances in John H. Aldrich and David W. Rohde, "Theories of Party in the Legislature and the Transition to Republican Rule in the House," paper prepared for the 1995 annual meeting of the American Political Science Association.

16. For differing descriptions of fluctuations in partisanship, see Poole and Rosenthal, "Patterns of Congressional Voting"; and Joseph Cooper and Garry Young, "Partisanship, Bipartisanship, and Crosspartisanship in Congress since the New Deal," in Dodd and Oppenheimer, eds., *Congress Reconsidered*, pp. 246–73. These papers show that the low levels of party unity in the 1950s were unusual in congressional history and that partisan divisions in the 1990s represent a return to more typical political patterns. Poole and Rosenthal show how the "dimensional structure" of roll calls in that period was also unusual.

17. Gary C. Jacobson and Samuel Kernell, *Strategy and Choice in Congressional Elections* (Yale University Press, 1981). For a careful assessment of this theory in the elections in the 1980s and 1990s, see Gary C. Jacobson, *The Politics of Congressional Elections*, 4th ed. (New York: Longman, 1997).

18. Smith, *Call to Order*.

Chapter 3

The Politicization
of Public Opinion:
The Fight for the Pulpit

Lawrence R. Jacobs and Robert Y. Shapiro

HEALTH CARE REFORM was one of Bill Clinton's top priorities during his first term. Following the textbook accounts on how modern presidents promote their agenda, he took to the bully pulpit in September 1993 and January 1994 to champion health reform and start an avalanche of public support that would bury the opponents of reform in Congress and elsewhere in Washington. These were classic—even electrifying—illustrations of a president capitalizing on the unique visibility of his office to go over the heads of Washington elites and command the country's attention. While chief executives must share constitutional authority with other branches of government, they alone—according to the textbook on the public presidency—can exercise the distinctive power to "go public" and thereby "monopolize" national debate and persuade Washington elites to cooperate.[1]

The authors thank the following people for research and other assistance: Shmuel Lock, John Bies, Michael Zis, Greg Shaw, Alan Yang, John Lapinski, Matt Stevens, Charles Riemann, Jennifer Baggette, Greg Haley, Sue Zayac, Elizabeth Brennan, and Eric Osterman. Steven S. Smith, Wendy Rahn, Mark Peterson, Charles Cameron, and members of the Russell Sage Foundation Social Policy Group offered valuable advice. This research was supported by grants from the Russell Sage Foundation and the Robert Wood Johnson Foundation, and was conducted at the University of Minnesota and at the Paul F. Lazarsfeld Center for the Social Sciences, Columbia University. The responsibility for the analysis and interpretations reported here is the authors'.

The textbook account of the public presidency, however, presents an overly one-sided characterization of elite strategies to mobilize support from the mass public and, indirectly, other political actors. In particular, this view falsely equates presidents with public promotion and mistakenly presumes that presidents who "go public" will dominate national debate. Today, many political activists—from members of Congress to interest groups and journalists—are engaged in public promotion. Public promotion now defines elite mobilization strategies: contending leaders visibly compete to influence public opinion. Focusing on the single person with the loudest voice ignores the potentially deafening, sustained chorus of an army of speakers.[2]

The story of health care reform, of course, did not stop with Clinton's two addresses. Both were followed by hard-hitting televised rebuttals that received widespread media coverage. In the days and weeks following the president's speeches, journalists, members of Congress, interest groups, and others weighed in with their own comments. The result was that the president's promotion of universal insurance and other principles was drowned out by what became a familiar incantation of the faults of Clinton's health reform effort: too much big government, an unwieldy and secretive task force, and overly ambitious policy objectives. Clinton's health reform campaign did, of course, focus national attention on the issue for nearly two years, which was a significant feat. But Clinton (like other presidents before him) found that other political activists competed for control over the policy agenda. Clinton's first term was marked by notable issues like gays in the military and balancing the budget, on which competing elites took to the airwaves, successfully pushed their positions into national prominence, and forced Clinton to acknowledge them. In short, Clinton and Republican leaders struggled over social policy by appealing to Americans to support their policies and oppose their competitors'.

The strategy of public promotion has three distinctive characteristics. First, it engages numerous actors, from officeholders to journalists. Policymakers intent on influencing government decisions now make routine public appeals to produce tangible evidence of widespread support for their positions. Second, the journalistic norm of providing "balanced" coverage and the news media's hunger for audience-grabbing stories of conflict ensure that presidents face competition in presenting policies on which elites disagree. The bully pulpit is overflowing with members of Congress and interest groups who fight to get their side represented in the national debate. Journalists zero in on the fight because conflict and controversy are expected to capture and keep audiences. Finally, political activists have increasingly used public opinion research to calibrate their public presentations in order to evoke desired reactions from Americans. Aside from the immediate periods around elections, political struggle today is defined by opponents who carefully track public opinion and then fashion competing messages to capture public support.

Political elites have turned to strategies based on public promotions because of profound changes in American politics. Before 1970 elites relied on political parties, unions, and other organizations that mobilized the mass public in order to build durable coalitions among voters and Washington policymakers. Enduring alliances among a relatively small number of peak interest groups and decentralized subunits within Congress and the executive branch largely governed the everyday distribution of government benefits. However, the unraveling of political parties in the electorate and other political organizations after the 1960s left large groups of both elites and the mass public unmoored; the result was to alter the strategic calculations of elites and to make public opinion, more than organized interests and constituencies, the focal point of today's struggle over social and fiscal policy. Mobilizing public opinion promised to expand scarce political resources and to provide the epoxy to bond together supportive coalitions in a fractured government and a disjointed polity.

Elected officials use public appeals for the quite different purposes of responding to the public's policy evaluations and attempting to direct them. Political conditions and the electoral cycle affect how public appeals are used. Successful politicians shift their public appeals between following the policy preferences of their constituents in order to maximize their electoral chances and attempting to shape public opinion in order to achieve their personal ideological goals and policy preferences. Both strategies combine elements of responding to and directing public opinion.

During periods when they did not directly face election, the policy proposals of the Clinton administration (1993–94) and the Republican-controlled Congress (1995 and early 1996) were largely driven by their respective policy preferences or ideological beliefs. Although Clinton and the Republicans responded to the most prominent problems on the public's agenda, they were less responsive to the public in the actual formulation of social policies. Rather, they aimed at bolstering their political leverage by influencing public opinion to adopt their desired policies—some of which represented extreme positions far from the center of public opinion. Contending leaders responded to public opinion by focusing on problems that ranked high on the public's agenda and using language and arguments that registered favorably in polls and focus groups. But their responsiveness was geared toward sculpting, not implementing, the public's policy preferences: information about public opinion was exploited to craft and target messages that would help manufacture public support. Although *instrumental* responsiveness is a style of political conflict that did not begin with Clinton's inauguration nor with the election of the 104th Congress in 1994, Clinton and the Republicans heightened the focus of the policymaking process on swaying public opinion.

In the wake of the new political conditions produced by the 1994 elections and the approach of the 1996 elections, the Clinton administration and then congressional Republicans moved to the political center in search of compromises that would produce legislation and attract voters not strongly attached to either major political party. The results during the fall of 1996 were heightened *substantive* responsiveness to public opinion and campaigns that claimed credit for legislative success in hiking the minimum wage, increasing education funding, reorganizing the welfare system, and enacting modest health care reforms.

Disorganized Democracy: Political Institutions and the Mass Public

The emphasis of today's policymakers on building direct connections to public opinion reflects a strategic adjustment to the historic development of American institutions and public opinion. At the turn of the century, a decentralized America was reshaped by the emergence of corporations, large trade unions, national political parties, and national governmental capacity. America's search for order in a chaotic world produced large and more centralized organizations.[3] During the 1930s, the Democratic party and labor unions established a powerful organizational presence in American politics, aggregating public preferences and creating institutional linkages that facilitated governing. By contrast, during the last third of the twentieth century, political organizations and the electorate have developed in the nearly opposite direction—toward disorganization.

American political parties and labor unions have weakened over the past fifty years. Despite some signs of resurgence, today's political parties fall short of their previous position in American politics: the electorate's attachment to political parties has eroded, and the parties' organizational capacity for directing electoral campaigns and linking the lawmaking branches has deteriorated. The breakdown of parties led to the increased importance of independents and weak partisans as swing voters and paved the way for candidate-dominated electoral campaigns based on individual candidates' personal following and organizations. Moreover, the decline in membership of labor unions from over 30 percent to 17 percent of the work force eroded an important source of organizational and financial resources, and it has weakened a critical cue or guide for Americans in evaluating electoral candidates and government policies.

The diminution of political organizations undermined the governing capacity of Congress and the presidency, not in an absolute sense but in relation to the rising responsibilities and expectations placed upon them. Most presidents share the same objectives: win reelection for themselves or their party, satisfy widespread expectations of prosperity at home and peace abroad, and secure a venerable place in history. America's constitutional system, however, frustrates presidents' attempts to achieve these objectives: the chief executive's political resources are constrained by the dispersion of constitutional authority and the divergence of political interests between presidents, who are elected to represent national interests, and members of Congress, who are selected in subnational elections to represent more localistic interests. These enduring limitations on presidential resources have been intensified during the postwar period by the unraveling of political parties, the increase in international pressures, and the growing scrutiny and visibility of the mass media, especially television.

Members of Congress, who are no less intent on winning reelection and directing government policy, face many of the same constitutional constraints. In addition, the weakness of political parties, combined with the institutional and electoral incentives for initiatives by individual members, has typically frustrated collective congressional efforts to direct national policymaking during the postwar period.

The shifting of power within Congress to individuals remains a defining characteristic of the institution despite Newt Gingrich's success in strengthening his institutional position to direct the House. Clearly, the Speaker increased the size and authority of his office as he pushed through a series of changes that circumscribed the committee system.[4] But it is equally clear that the Speaker remained significantly constrained by individual members. Members demanded and received things from Gingrich in the 104th Congress that would have been unlikely in an earlier age when individualism was not prevalent. The Speaker himself conceded that he was leading a "collegial" and not a hierarchical institution that could be directed from the top.[5] The point, then, is that the collective behavior of congressional Republicans as they voted for a series of highly contentious bills did not indicate that members had given up their individuality. Rather, it suggests that members viewed their electoral and policy interests as coinciding; they saw their votes as being in their personal interest.[6]

The fragmentation of political institutions and organizations has both reflected and contributed to the splintering of voting patterns and public policy preferences. In particular, the fading of unions and parties has undermined cognitive mechanisms for sorting through complex and vast information regarding policies and candidates and fostered ambivalence, instability, and the proliferation of divergent groupings of voters.

American politicians can no longer rely on appeals to large blocs of voters defined strictly by regional or socioeconomic cleavages. Today's mass public is characterized by multiple, cross-cutting cleavages; a decisive working-class vote, if it ever existed, has been replaced by a set of increasingly complex and diverse social groupings.[7] National elections (especially presidential contests) are now determined by independents and weak partisans who defect from their regular political party and are not persistently drawn to either major party. The result is that neither party has a winning base among American voters.

Three pronounced characteristics of the American electorate have developed since the 1950s: a decrease in the percentage of self-identified (especially "strong") Democrats; an increase in the proportion of Republican-leaning independents; and a rise in the number of genuine independents who lean toward neither party. Self-identified Democrats still exceed Republicans; about 35 percent identify themselves as Democrats and about 30 percent as Republicans.[8]

But the strong Democratic New Deal coalition and short-lived Great Society coalition are now gone. National Election Study surveys and exit poll data show that the Democratic party can no longer build a durable electoral majority based on substantial support by Catholic and Jewish voters as well as voters from the South, labor unions, and urban areas. White voters have defected from the Democrats in the South, and the party's support among Catholics and, less so, Jewish voters has also dipped.

Slippage among Democrats has been partly offset by increasing support since the 1960s among black and women voters. Democrats have also maintained support among urban and union voters, but these voters constitute a much smaller proportion of the electorate than in the past. (In addition to the nearly 50 percent drop in union membership, suburban voters outnumber central-city voters by about two to one.) Moreover, the 1996 presidential election suggests that some Catholic voters (especially Latinos) may remain reliable Democratic supporters.[9]

The Democratic losses have helped to boost support for the Republicans in the South and among religious conservatives. But the Democrats' misfortune has certainly not produced a Republican majority in the electorate as a whole. Instead it has produced a rise since the 1950s of self-identified independent voters, who now constitute about a third of the electorate. Loyal supporters of the Democratic or Republican parties represent isolated pockets of party loyalty. The number of independent voters explains the appeal that Colin Powell had (and may later have) as a candidate and that Ross Perot has had as a candidate and party founder. Independent voters now represent a national base, as evidenced by Ross Perot, who in 1992 received approximately the same percentage of the vote (19 percent) in every state. (In the 1996 election, his support dropped by more than half.) Powell and Perot's Reform party were significant new developments, but previous presidential candidates were also able to capitalize on the large pool of voters unhappy with the major parties: John B. Anderson attracted almost 6 million in 1980, and even the little-advertised campaign of Eugene J. McCarthy in 1976 drew more than 750,000 supporters.[10]

A good part of the nonaligned electorate is ideologically moderate. Overall, a plurality of voters identify themselves as moderate. For example, *New York Times*/CBS surveys in the 1990s showed about 20 percent self-identified liberals, an average of over 40 percent moderates, and 30–35 percent conservatives.[11]

The disjointed quality of the American polity is further complicated by significant disloyalty among partisans. According to exit polls, as many as 26 percent of Democrats have defected to Republican candidates in their presidential vote in elections since 1976, and as many as 13 percent of Republicans have voted Democratic. (These are very likely underestimates because vote choice may have influenced reported party identification.) In the 1992 elections, with Perot's third-party candidacy, 27 percent of Republicans and 23 percent of Democrats defected. (The 1996 figures were 19 percent and 15 percent, respectively.) Another sign of electoral splintering is that split-ticket voting has at least doubled since 1952. About 20 percent of voters, if not more, choose different parties when selecting congressional and presidential candidates.[12]

The declining partisan cohesiveness of social groupings has meant that candidates (especially in presidential contests) cannot rely on stable blocs of voters. Bill Clinton acknowledged the reality of America's splintered polity when he embraced the New Democrats' commitment to cease relying on blocs of voters allied with unions and other longtime party allies. Republicans have also been in a tenuous position, with many members of Congress elected by narrow margins in 1994 and 1996. The campaigns of both George Bush and Robert Dole starkly demonstrated that Republican candidates face the unenviable task of simultaneously appealing to conservative activists, party moderates, and disaffected Perot supporters. Candidates from both political parties are left with the onerous and uncertain task of appealing across economic and social groupings in order to stitch together a winning coalition from an atomized polity.

The fragmentation evident in voting patterns is also evident in the multiple and competing considerations that characterize the public's policy preferences. The combination of genuine public ambivalence toward government social policy and the changing contours of elite debate and media coverage produced significant variations in the problems that received public attention during Clinton's first term. For instance, Gallup polls indicated that the proportion of Americans who identified general economic problems as the most important problems facing the country swung from 27 percent in July 1995 to 36 percent in January 1996.[13] Specific economic and social problems on the public's agenda also experienced volatility. The evolution of crime, health care, the budget deficit, and other issues up and down the agenda closely followed elite debate and media coverage. For example, Gallup polls indicate that up to 31 percent identified health care reform as a major problem and persistently ranked it as the one or two top issues facing the country during the height of Clinton's campaign for reform; it sank to its low of

7 percent after the Republicans assumed control of Congress and focused on other issues. The federal budget deficit was surpassed by other general economic concerns and unemployment during Clinton's first two years but became the top issue by January 1996 during the Republican balanced budget campaign. Welfare reform was a prominent campaign issue in 1992, slipped from public attention during Clinton's first two years in office, and then regained its salience after the Republican victory in 1994. The public's agenda has varied as elites and the media have shifted their attention.[14]

Americans' attitudes toward social policies are historically rooted in genuine ambivalence regarding individual self-reliance, collective social responsibility, and limited government. Americans' devotion to the ideals of individual self-reliance and minimal government have been consistently found in both studies of early national values and analysis of contemporary public opinion surveys.[15] CBS News/*New York Times* polls during the 104th Congress confirm that about two-thirds of Americans believe that government does too many things that are better left to business and individuals. About the same proportion in a February 1996 survey by the same group favored a smaller government providing fewer services.[16]

In addition, the public's sense that Washington policymakers listen to them and can be trusted has declined since the late 1980s. The trend of declining trust first began in earnest during the 1970s because of a number of developments: growing pessimism about an economy that was producing sustained structural change and dislocation; rising crime rates; social upheavals; and the crises of Vietnam and Watergate. The result was to undermine Americans' confidence in the government's ability to solve problems and their sense of efficacy—the feeling that their political activities influence government actions.[17] After improving from the all-time lows reached in 1980, the level of trust and affection for Washington began to decline significantly after the mid-1980s to levels that were now near or at all-time lows. The current dissatisfaction was driven by greater attention to domestic politics because of the cold war's end, and by successive recessions and the failure of aggregate economic gains to be passed along to many working individuals.

Americans' philosophical support of individualism and limited government in the abstract mixes, however, with competing values and attitudes. Americans recognize the government's social responsibility to protect the country as a whole and to help individuals, whether the aged on medicare and social security, the poor who need medical and financial assistance, or college students in need of educational loans. Survey data suggest stable patterns of support for assisting the country's disadvantaged and elderly populations.[18] Moreover, the February 1996 CBS/ *New York Times* survey reported that 55 percent support the federal government doing more to regulate the environmental and safety practices of business (23 percent felt the government was doing enough; 17 percent favored it doing less); two-thirds supported the government guaranteeing a job for everyone who wanted to work. A 1995 survey by Princeton Survey Research Associates reported that 78 percent agree that the "government should play an active role in improving health care, housing, and education for middle-income families."[19]

The public is genuinely ambivalent toward many social policies, including desegregation, welfare, and regulation.[20] Stanley Feldman and John Zaller's study of Americans' attitudes toward social policy found considerable uneasiness with significant government involvement in redistributing resources.[21] Even those most supportive of government involvement remained uncertain about social policies and were unwilling to offer egalitarian justifications for them.

Public opinion toward health care illustrates Americans' ambivalence toward social policy. Americans perceive a strong personal and family stake in the current health care system, with polls persistently revealing a high and stable level of personal satisfaction. Americans' personal satisfaction with their own health care coexists, however, with anxiety about the price of that care and about the status and future of the health care system. In addition to concerns about their personal circumstances, Americans worry about overall national conditions regarding health care, with strong support for extending health insurance to the uninsured, guaranteeing health care for all Americans, and overhauling the current system. The bottom line is that Americans are haunted by multiple and competing considerations: the public is predisposed to hang onto the status quo because of satisfaction with their own situation and uneasiness that increased government intervention could undermine quality, and yet Americans nonetheless favor government funding and regulatory oversight in health care.

Americans' ambivalence toward social policy is further complicated by major demographic and historically rooted cleavages in the electorate. The public's preferences toward economic and social policy differ based on geographic location (southerners and midwesterners tend to be more conservative than northeasterners), race (blacks are among the most liberal on economic and civil rights issues), and gender (men have tended to be somewhat more conservative than women, though this varies by specific issues of concern, age cohort, and women's economic and social experiences and circumstances).[22]

Americans' ambivalence regarding policy issues and electoral candidates is sustained and perhaps aggravated by the public's quite understandable reliance on information conveyed by the media. Journalists, however, do not simply report reality; their selection of sources and stories introduces interpretations that highlight differences among elites. The professional norm of objectivity requires presenting the "other side," and the economic pressures on the media encourage journalists to portray conflict, which is expected to draw audiences.[23] The result is that media coverage of salient social policy debates is likely to be geared toward presenting opposing points of view that reinforce Americans' ambivalence.[24]

The War of the Airwaves

The process for making government policy has been profoundly affected by the development of fractured institutions and a disjointed electorate. Up through the 1960s, the medium for influencing the policymaking process involved overt political behavior: strikes and social movements in unusual times and grass-roots efforts to mobilize supporters in more normal periods. By the 1990s, however, the medium of political activism had become public promotion, and the aim of policymakers has been to make routine appeals that evoke public support for individual politicians or specific policies. In an environment of institutional and political disorganization, winning public opinion is strategically attractive because it augments scarce political resources and offers the means to build supportive coalitions.

Presidents as well as congressional leaders and interest groups all recognize the strategic advantage of acquiring public support and building the institutional capacity to make public appeals routinely and effectively. Public promotions by competing sets of elites ensure that presidents—or another coherent group of political activists—rarely, if ever, control the terms on which policies are understood by Americans.

Clinton and Republican leaders pursued what can be described as a "framing" strategy. Research in political psychology suggests that changes in public opinion involve more than simply one set of political activists quickly persuading Americans to change their minds. Rather, changes in the public's evaluations of policy proposals can result from manipulating the salience of other already existing or related attitudes. Visible statements by political activists and the media's selective coverage of them can highlight or activate within individuals one set of existing attitudes. Because of the increased prominence of these attitudes, they are given greater priority and weight.[25] For political gladiators, the political battle, then, is over which set of already existing attitudes is foremost in an individual's mind.

Political conditions and the electoral cycle affected whether President Clinton and Republican leaders used their public appeals to respond to the public's policy evaluations or to lead them. As we describe further below, Clinton in 1993–94 and the Republicans in 1995 and early 1996 exercised opinion leadership by pursuing a strategy of instrumental responsiveness: they responded to what the public considered pressing problems but were largely not driven by public opinion during the formulation of social policy. The designing of specific policy proposals was driven by the increasing ideological and partisan polarization among politicians. Clinton and the Republicans sought to draw on existing attitudes that were supportive of their proposals in order to promote the new policies, while their respective opponents seized on genuine oppositional values: in 1994 the Republicans appealed to individualism and dread of government, and in 1996 the Democrats drew on both self-interest and collective social responsibility. The strategy of elites was to "frame" or activate competing strains in Americans' policy preferences that best comported with their personal or ideological position. Public opinion was carefully tracked in order to "test market" presentations and pinpoint the phrases and arguments that would resonate with some component of Americans' ambivalent social policy attitudes and summon public support.[26]

Under the pressure of approaching elections, however, Clinton and then the Republicans adjusted their strategy and became more responsive to the public's substantive policy preferences. Clinton after the 1994 election and Republicans in mid-1996 selectively staked out positions to solidify their respective bases of loyal partisan support, but they devoted most of their energy to capturing the independent or swing voters who would determine presidential and congressional elections. The fight for these critical voters pushed both Clinton and the Republicans toward appealing to the midpoint of public opinion. Informed in part by extensive public opinion research that pinpointed voter preferences, Clinton and the Republicans moderated their positions to correspond substantially with centrist opinion on particular issues and in general.

Bill Clinton's Appeals for Public Support

At the turn of the century, direct presidential appeals for public support were considered inappropriate violations of elite norms and dangerously demagogic.[27] The dissatisfaction of successive postwar presidents with their enduring political weakness in the face of rising responsibilities has prompted chief executives since John F. Kennedy to augment their scarce political resources by rallying public support. Presidents calculate that strong approval ratings or strong support for their policy proposals enhance their leverage when bargaining with members of Congress, administrators in the executive branch, and intransigent sectional interests.

The commitment by presidents (and other political activists) to establishing a direct connection with the public has relied heavily on new technology, from television to the latest methods of public opinion research. It is certainly plausible that the development of modern public relations technology has itself led to increasing efforts at opinion leadership. Technology, in our view, is a necessary but not sufficient condition. Timing is especially instructive: the technology for opinion leadership has been around since Kennedy's presidency and certainly since Nixon's, but it was neither visibly wielded by presidents nor widely used by other political activists. The key factor was that institutional and political developments created new incentive structures, which increased the political demand for and use of the new technology.

The political attraction to public opinion research is evident in the institutional development of the White House. Since Kennedy's election, the White House has developed a public opinion apparatus to assemble opinion data and conduct expanded public relations activities. Centralized in the White House and evolving as an extension of presidential election campaigns, this apparatus provides a regular and enduring organizational capacity to carefully track and lead public sentiment. Richard Nixon, Jimmy Carter, Ronald Reagan, and George

Bush each maintained the apparatus and spent millions from their political parties and campaign funds to gauge the pulse of public opinion. Indeed, Bush placed his pollster (Robert Teeter) in charge of his reelection campaign.

Beginning with his 1992 presidential campaign, Bill Clinton set a new standard in terms of a president's visible reliance on public appeals for support. Previous postwar presidents have cautiously downplayed—in public—the presence and use of information about public opinion in the White House. Kennedy stored his private polls in the Justice Department under the watchful eye of his brother in order to distance himself from an image as a slick politician eager to appeal for public support. Nixon kept many of his polls in a vault and publicly denied that he used them, even as he decisively expanded Johnson's already significant operation for analyzing public opinion. Carter advertised his defiance of public opinion as a sign of his responsible "trustee" style of leading, though he too commissioned and used private surveys.[28]

What stood out about the behavior of President Clinton during his first term was the intensity and openness with which he courted public opinion. In a style that was more open and concerted than that of his predecessors, Clinton readily acknowledged his use of public opinion polling and unabashedly used his communication skills to regularly solicit citizens' support for himself and his policies. During Clinton's first term, journalists were fed stories about the president reviewing and altering the questionnaires that his pollster used. Other politicians reported conversations in which the president signaled his genuine interest in one of their policy proposals by promising to test the ideas in the White House's next survey.[29]

Clinton's interest in and use of polls was extensive. Interviews with advisers and officials in the administration suggest that the White House received a steady flow of survey data based both on private polls and compilations of published material. Stanley Greenberg, Clinton's pollster in 1993–94, reported that the president even regularly received regression analyses to assist him in understanding the polling results.[30] In addition, the White House received regular reports based on focus groups. During the White House's budget battles with Republicans in late 1995 and 1996, opinion surveys were at times conducted and analyzed by Richard Morris, Mark Penn, and Douglas Schoen nearly every night; during the campaign they were conducted continuously to produce rolling estimates of shifting political fortunes.[31]

It is indicative of the centrality of pollsters in the modern White House that Clinton reacted to the Republicans' triumph in the 1994 elections by replacing his pollster. He started his term in 1993 by carrying over his campaign pollster, Greenberg. Following the 1994 elections, Clinton brought in political consultant Richard Morris and the team of Penn and Schoen to help reposition him toward the center of public opinion. Morris had navigated Clinton back from defeat as Arkansas governor in 1980 by counseling him to respond to centrist opinion. In 1994, Clinton again turned to Morris to analyze public opinion in a way that was unconstrained by Democratic party affiliation or ideological orientations. A senior administration official explained after Morris's resignation in August 1996 that "his polls are his bible. . . . He did not have a core. His judgments were all based on the latest poll—and what wins based on the latest poll."[32]

The White House's public opinion information contributed to policymaking, but its influence was more varied and complicated than suggested by conventional assumptions of "pandering" politicians who obsequiously follow the public. Clinton used the institutional capacity for managing public opinion for two specific but interrelated purposes: to respond to the public's policy preferences and to influence Americans' attitudes by managing press relations and making direct appeals publicly through speeches and other events. During 1993–94, the White House tilted toward leading public opinion; in the second half of Clinton's first term, he emphasized greater responsiveness (as later discussed in connection with the Republican Congress). In both periods, White House strategies combined elements of both responsiveness and direction of public opinion.

In 1993–94, the public's agenda of pressing problems, found in poll results, had a moderate impact on the president's agenda. The president's early attention to the major campaign issue of health reform corresponded with one of the public's greatest concerns, and the surge of anxiety about crime rocketed that issue to the top of his agenda in 1994 even though it was not a top campaign priority. Moreover, the president avoided labor, urban and racial issues, which were not major public concerns. The early administration did, however, focus on issues that were not the most prominent on the public's agenda (gays in the military, gun control, and, to lesser extent, deficit reduction), and it relatively neglected other issues like welfare reform, which had been a prominent concern during the 1992 campaign.

Although the administration generally addressed the public's concerns, public opinion's impact on the formulation of policy was decidedly mixed. On the one hand, the president followed the broad contours of public preferences on some issues, adopting the popular principle of universal insurance coverage and generous benefits in health reform, a get-tough approach on crime and gun control, and a work-based approach on welfare reform that continued to provide supports for women and children.

On the other hand, public opinion did not generally drive the formulation of specific social policies. Some policies contradicted public preferences. Clinton's proposal to allow gays in the military was inconsistent with the public's deep-seated attitudes toward homosexuality,[33] and his sweeping health reform proposal openly defied sustained public fears regarding excessive government interference and erosion of quality and choice of care. More generally, White House documents and interviews with administration officials reveal that the administration's public opinion information had no direct impact on policy decisions. Both extensive interviews and examination of confidential White House records indicate that Greenberg, the president's primary pollster during 1993 and 1994, was locked out of the process of formulating health care policy.[34]

Public opinion information was most consistently used during 1993–94 to direct public opinion by fashioning an appealing presentation of decided policy. Interviews with administration officials and White House records indicate that the primary purpose of tracking public opinion was not to pander but to educate, lead, or otherwise influence public attitudes toward the president and his policies. Mandy Grunwald, a media consultant who has advised Clinton, likened polls to tools, which Clinton wielded to get the message out on his desired policy: "He uses polls to help make an argument in a way that people understand."[35]

Battles over Clinton's social policy during his first two years in office involved both administration initiatives to respond to and direct public opinion and Republican counterattacks that exploited the public's ambivalence. For instance, on health care reform, Clinton tried to sell his proposal by appealing to all sides of the public's ambivalence. On the one hand, he downplayed the significant expansion of government involvement from financing to the provision of care. He orchestrated presentations to reassure those satisfied with their own care and wary of government solutions by heralding his plan's commitment both to preserving patients' freedom of choice and quality of care and to relying on competition among private health plans. On the other hand, the president appealed to Americans' sense of collective social responsibility and future insecurity by promising long-term security for all.

The Republicans' counterattack on health reform, which was also guided by polls, paid deference to the public's anxieties by acknowledging that access needed to be expanded but appealed to the public's distrust of government and its satisfaction with the current system. The president's plan, Senator Robert Dole warned, meant "more government, more bureaucracy," and—according to Senator Phil Gramm—"tearing down the greatest health care system in the history of the world."[36] Television advertisements such as the Harry and Louise series were skillfully targeted by polls to activate public concerns about excessive government interference and disruption of existing arrangements.[37]

The Republican strategy of drawing on genuine public ambivalence contributed to noticeable conservative shifts in public opinion on health care and other social welfare issues beginning in 1994; the result was to reverse liberal shifts in attitudes toward social policies that had occurred during the 1980s and early 1990s.

The general conservative shift in public opinion that followed the Republican counterattack was evident in the area of health care. Support for the Clinton plan plummeted 15 percentage points from September 1993 to the summer of 1994 (from 59 percent to 44 percent). The Republican attacks were associated with a significant jump during this period in the proportion of people who felt that the president's plan was not fair to them and created "too much government involvement." Those worrying that Clinton's plan relied excessively on the government increased from 40 percent in October 1993 to 47 percent in March 1994.[38] In an election-night survey in November 1994, the Henry J. Kaiser Foundation found that a substantial majority (especially among those who voted Republican) concluded that the Democrats' proposed reform introduced too much "government bureaucracy" and would reduce the quality of their own care.[39]

The Congressional Pulpit

Members of past Congresses did not identify national opinion leadership as their primary responsibility.[40] Even recent congressional leaders like Speaker Thomas S. Foley or Minority Leader Robert H. Michel avoided routine and conspicuous appeals to the public; they certainly lacked the personal skill, temperament, and capacity to conduct effective public relations efforts.

Perhaps the most striking feature of the Republican congressional leadership after their election in 1994 was their unprecedented effort to track and manage public opinion. House Speaker Newt Gingrich and Senate Majority Leader Bob Dole made direct appeals to Americans in a way that had previously been reserved for presidents. Not only did congressional leaders sound more like presidents on their bully pulpits, but their calculations were also presidential in nature.[41]

Faced with enduring institutional obstacles to achieving an ambitious agenda, the Republican leaders anticipated that rallying public support for themselves and their policies would increase their leverage with their rank and file as well as with the president. As one congressional aide explained to us in an interview, demonstrating public support was politically important in "being able to sell [a policy] in Congress."

To establish and maintain a relationship with public opinion, congressional Republicans used their party to build an institutional apparatus that rivals the White House's organization in providing two critical services: tracking public opinion by commissioning polls and focus groups, and attempting to influence Americans' attitudes by crafting the party's presentations and managing its relations with the media.

In 1995 and 1996, we interviewed a sample of fifty-two senior legislative staff of members of Congress. The interviews provided an opportunity to track patterns and trends in the perceptions and behavior of members of Congress toward public opinion. In particular, we were interested in studying the actual use of public opinion as well as its impact on the strategic calculations of members.[42]

According to the congressional staff we interviewed, members apparently have perceived that Congress as a whole has become more sensitive to public opinion even while they as individuals have not. Among staff of members who have served ten years or more, 68 percent (seventeen of twenty-five) reported that their member's sensitivity to tracking public opinion is less or unchanged. But 68 percent also believed that other members of Congress have become more sensitive to public opinion.

The disjuncture between the perception of collective institutional patterns and the behavior of the individual rank-and-file members may be explained by the prominent role assumed by recent congressional *lead-*

ers in managing public opinion. Staff reported to us that their members conduct very little polling; the surveys that they conducted were largely limited to district or state election campaigns. Instead, individual members rely on traditional contacts with their constituents: face-to-face meetings, mail, and phone calls. When given the opportunity to identify all the ways they monitor public opinion, five of fifty-two staffers (10 percent) reported private polls being conducted (all in the 1996 election year), fifty mentioned that their offices monitored public opinion by relying on letters or phone calls, and twenty-two pointed to personal encounters.

The incentives for congressional leaders to carefully track survey data and focus groups have been greater than for rank-and-file members. Leaders pursue collective goals such as a strong party reputation and majority party status.[43] In particular, Newt Gingrich, who used public opinion information to chart his rise from political obscurity to House Speaker, set up arrangements for receiving a regular flow of surveys and focus group reports, especially from Frank Luntz.

Public opinion information assembled by Republican congressional leaders had a varied and muted impact on their social policy proposals, especially in the period before the fall of 1996. At the height of the Republican ascendancy in January 1995, a CBS poll identified fourteen items that respondents ranked as the most important national problems. Only two of the issues listed in the "Contract with America" corresponded with the public's agenda: crime and the deficit. Americans did not rank the great bulk of the congressional Republicans' initial agenda— from tax cuts and increased defense spending to capping punitive damages in liability and malpractice cases—as among the country's major problems.

Public opinion's impact on the formulation of policy was also decidedly mixed before the fall of 1996. On the one hand, many of the Republicans' broad positions paralleled the general contours of public opinion. A Gallup/CNN/*USA Today* poll in late November 1994 (November 28–29) revealed supermajorities of more than 70 percent favoring tougher anticrime legislation, a constitutional amendment to balance the budget, cutting taxes, limiting welfare payments, establishing a presidential line item veto, and passing term limits. Moreover, Republicans did respond to public opinion by not proposing some reforms of programs that enjoyed strong public support, such as social security.

On the other hand, the formulation of specific proposals to achieve these broad objectives in 1994 did not reflect the public's preferences. The public backed welfare reform but not the punitive approach to children and the poor that the House proposed.[44] Although Americans have shifted a bit away from backing environmental protection at all costs, Republican policies for relaxing regulations were inconsistent with public opinion that remained highly supportive of such protection and regulation. House Majority Whip Tom DeLay was far from the midpoint of public opinion when he compared the Environmental Protection Agency to the Gestapo and insisted, "I can't think of one [regulation I would keep]."[45] Moreover, Republicans proposed increasing defense spending while the public's support for defense spending remained at a near all-time low. Polling data also indicated that the Republicans' proposals ran counter to the public's preferences toward medicare and medicaid, health and safety regulation, school lunches, student loans, Americorps volunteers, and education and training.[46] In addition, the 104th Congress (like its predecessors) failed to act on political reforms like term limits and lobbying regulations, despite their popularity. In short, many of the Republicans' particular policies during much of the 104th Congress contradicted public preferences.[47]

At least three factors help to account for the Republicans' relatively low responsiveness to public opinion before the fall of 1996. First, the Republicans' opinion information may have been faulty because they distrusted representative scientific opinion surveys and overvalued focus groups. Our interviewees persistently asserted that polls were easily manipulated and therefore could be neither trusted nor regularly used to monitor public opinion and make policy. Sixty-two percent (thirty-two of fifty-two) of those we interviewed reported that their offices commissioned no surveys and, not surprisingly, nearly three-quarters (thirty-eight of fifty-two) indicated that no one in their office had special responsibility for analyzing them. (No significant differences existed among Democrats and Republicans.) As one Republican staffer insisted, "We discount any polling—it all depends on how questions are asked, who is asked. Who designs [a poll] can make it say what they want. We trust direct contact with constituents instead."

In place of polls, political activists and, especially, Republicans have turned to focus groups, which are unstructured conversations among a dozen or so "ordinary" Americans. Although the findings from focus groups are not (by design) representative of the views of the entire country, they have nonetheless been treated as such by political activists. One of the most notorious examples of the misuse of focus groups was the campaign of Frank Luntz to promote the Contract with America. While focus group research drove Luntz's design of the contract, he publicly heralded its ten main proposals to reporters as enjoying the support of at least 60 percent of Americans in his polls. Under pressure from reporters who pointed to discrepancies between published polls and the contract's planks, Luntz conceded in November 1995 that he never rigorously measured the contract's popularity in the first place.[48]

A second factor contributing to the Republicans' relatively low responsiveness to the public's substantive preferences was the widespread conviction among members that public opinion was an inappropriate consideration in formulating policy. When we pushed our staff respondents on the usefulness of public opinion information in policymaking, a common response was that public opinion was not directly considered. For instance, when staffers were asked whether existing opinion today or anticipated future opinion influenced decisions, eighteen of twenty-four spontaneously volunteered that public opinion was of no use. Nine of twenty-five responded to a separate question about how public opinion weighed in the member's decisions about specific policies like health care or welfare reform by again spontaneously challenging the question's premise and insisting that their member's decisions were not guided by public opinion.

The third and perhaps decisive explanation for Republicans' low responsiveness was that members' policy positions were guided by their personal beliefs and judgments. (The personal predilections of many Republicans were backed up by like-minded interest groups such as the Christian Coalition, the National Rifle Association, and the National Association of Small Businesses.)

In our interviews, staffers regularly emphasized their members' determination to "do what's best" according their personal values. As one Republican respondent explained: "On policy, beliefs are more important than public opinion." Another explained that the member "just does what he feels he needs to do. Public opinion is not at all useful in day-to-day policymaking." Forty-six of fifty-two acknowledged that public opinion information was used to lobby their offices but argued that it had no influence on the member; their member "stuck" to his or her beliefs and distrusted the results because the "numbers are so easy to manipulate" to serve the interests of the lobbyist, whether it was an interest group, another member, or the White House. The bottom line is that if Republican leaders pushed for compromise legislation that responded to public opinion they would face a rank and file that was guided by personal and ideological orientations and was suspicious of public opinion.

It is certainly possible that our interviews may have simply invited the expected answers to politically loaded questions on whether members "pandered." Our interviews with individual congressional offices are, however, consistent with a large body of quantitative research on the relationship between individual members of Congress and constituency preferences in the members' districts. The findings of these studies indicate that public opinion has a measurable but modest and highly contingent impact on members' voting decisions and electoral prospects.[49] Part of the explanation for the muted impact of constituents is that their policy preferences have but a small influence on congressional elections; voters give substantial weight to personal characteristics and party in their voting decisions and know little about (and often do not act on) members' policy positions or records.[50] Evidence, then, that constituency opinion is not a decisive influence on individual members corroborates the persistent and unequivocal downplaying of public opinion by the staff we interviewed.

Polling for the Message

Congressional behavior presents a puzzle: the rank and file and, especially, the leadership regularly monitored public opinion, but this information did not normally appear to affect their substantive policy decisions. The explanation for the apparent disregarding of public opinion amidst studious monitoring is that members used their public opinion apparatus to direct Americans' attitudes by crafting the party's presentations and managing its relations with the media. In other words, members and, especially, leaders devised their proposals—based on public opinion research—in order to build public support or at the very least prevent opposition from building.

Congressional Republicans shared the long-standing objective of successive presidents to rally public opinion to their side. Gingrich significantly enhanced his party's institutional capacity by assembling a "vast communications army," which was supported by the Republican National Committee (RNC), the House Republican Conference, and corporate pressure groups. To communicate the House Republicans' messages, Gingrich established CommStrat, which was staffed by congressional and party press secretaries and coordinated through the Speaker's office. CommStrat met daily to design their "message for the day" as well as the RNC's fax for the day and the talking points that would guide Republican press secretaries in their discussions with reporters.[51] The purpose of the communications operation, according to its director in the House (Ernest J. Istook Jr. of Oklahoma), was "to make sure radio-talk-show hosts, political pundits, editorial writers all receive the *same* information, *contemporaneously*, with the same parts *accented*."[52]

Like successive presidents, Congressional Republicans concluded that they had to "*punch through* the establishment media" to reach the public with their message.[53] Haley Barbour, chairman of the RNC, worked closely with Gingrich to flood reporters with the House Republicans' presentations; his motto at the RNC was "Repeat it until you vomit." Stealing another page from the White House, Gingrich and his supporters monitored the stories filed by journalists and lobbied them to adopt their preferred interpretations. During the medicare debate, for instance, Barbour and John R. Kasich of Ohio, the chair of the House Budget Committee, vigorously pressed journalists to present their plan as slowing the program's rate of growth rather than as a cut in it.[54]

Congressional leaders seized upon information about public opinion as a valuable resource for identifying the language and arguments that presented Republican proposals in an appealing manner and defined Democratic positions in negative terms. One Republican staffer likened public opinion information to "intelligence gathering in war"; others repeatedly emphasized that it was a "tool to shape our message," "educate the citizens," and "learn what messages we need to get across." As one Republican staffer commented, opinion information is "not the source of decisions on policy but rather is helpful in showing the kinds of things [a member] is not communicating . . . and therefore the need to try to educate further."

Our interviews produced a persistent theme that polls were "useful in terms of framing what you were going to do anyway." Thirty-one of fifty-two congressional staff indicated that public opinion information had been used to frame already decided policy decisions. More of those we interviewed indicated that public opinion information was useful for leading or educating Americans than for responding to them (47 percent versus 35 percent). Republicans tended to see this information as more important for leading than responding (47 percent versus 30 percent), while Democrats were nearly evenly split. In addition, 67 percent of the staffers—drawn equally from both parties—viewed public opinion as an opportunity that enhanced their political resources and ability to lead rather than as a constraint. Only two respondents identified it as a pure constraint. (Eight identified public opinion as neither a constraint nor an opportunity; seven classified it as both.)

Republican leaders in particular have treated words as weapons, adapting the techniques of test marketing that were common in campaigns, commercial marketing, and White House operations to the business of crafting their policy presentations.[55] According to Gingrich, political success went to those who "test [words], deliver them and repeat them in ways that devastate the opposition or provide the best protection against enemy attack."[56]

Gingrich and his supporters recognized that public opinion information served a number of purposes. In addition to pinpointing presentations that were most likely to sway the public, it was also useful for lobbying reporters and reassuring his own rank and file. During the debate over changing the school lunch program, the House leadership commissioned Richard Wirthlin, who polled for Republican presidents. Wirthlin's report that Republicans could "redefine compassion" by using "power phrases" like "hope" in describing their initiatives was widely circulated within the House in order to solidify wavering members.[57]

The political significance of polls was underscored by Gingrich's outburst against the *New York Times* in October 1995 for devoting its lead column—on the morning of a critical House vote—to its poll that found public opposition to Republican proposals. Gingrich accused the *Times* of using "deliberately rigged questions that are totally phony," and called it "a disgraceful example of disinformation."[58]

Dueling for Public Support

Debate over social policy for much of the 104th Congress was characterized by competing strategies to appeal for public support. Republicans visibly promoted their proposals to win public backing while Democrats counterattacked by exploiting genuine public ambivalence. For Democrats and, specifically, Clinton, defeating the Republicans' plans provided an opportunity for political rehabilitation in time for the upcoming 1996 elections. Clinton's objective was clear: deter primary challengers from within the Democratic party and build broad support for the general election. The president's strategy was to highlight both his responsiveness to public opinion and the distance of "extreme" Republicans and entrenched liberal Democrats from the midpoint of public opinion. The combination of facing an upcoming reelection fight amidst a disorganized electorate and aggressive Republican majorities in Congress reinforced Clinton's New Democratic inclination toward centrist opinion. Clinton's strategic shift prompted him to give increased prominence to problems that Americans identified as important, such as welfare reform and social issues, and to adjust his actual policy stances—including his adoption of a largely Republican welfare bill and the balanced budget goal—to correspond to centrist opinion.[59]

The two biggest battles over social policy involved Republican proposals in 1995 and early 1996 on health care reform and the budget. Holding down projected medicare spending was essential for achieving the Republicans' plans to cut taxes and the government budget. Gingrich and his advisers did appreciate from their public opinion research that Americans opposed balancing the budget by restricting medicare spending; they knew they would need a carefully crafted presentation to win over Americans' support.

Their strategy was to devise a presentation that straddled the divide in Americans' health care attitudes between individualism and social responsibility. RNC Chairman Haley Barbour took charge in unifying the themes in the Republicans' communications. By proposing vouchers and medical savings accounts, they aimed to tap into the public's commitment to individual responsibility and distrust of government. To pay homage to Americans' sense of collective responsibility, Republicans emphasized that their proposal for dramatic changes in medicare was essential to saving the program from financial insolvency. Luntz's research steered Republicans away from talking about their actual fiscal objectives and toward emphasizing that their proposals would "preserve, protect and improve" the program.[60] Indeed, independent surveys confirmed that the Republicans' argument enjoyed public support: 54 percent reported in a September–October 1995 Harris survey that they favored cutting future medicare costs to save the program from bankruptcy.[61]

The Republicans' opponents—not unlike the Republicans themselves two years earlier—capitalized on Americans' ambivalence. The counterattack by Democrats and, specifically, Clinton were directed at highlighting the Republicans' distance from centrist opinion. Initially, Clinton was reportedly reluctant to challenge Republicans on medicare because of fear that he would appear as defending "special interests."[62] But, after reassuring polling results, Clinton joined with congressional Democrats in launching a well-scripted and coordinated campaign against the Republicans' medicare reforms that warned of draconian cost hikes and disruption in the care received by current medicare beneficiaries. In addition to rousing seniors, the Democrats directly appealed to the general public's concern for social responsibility. As Clinton warned in a ceremony to commemorate the thirtieth anniversary of the medicare program, the Republicans' plan would create a situation in which "a 75-year-old man . . . goes broke trying to supplement his health care plan because his voucher doesn't go far enough, [and] a 70-year-old heart patient . . . needs home care but cannot afford $1,400 annual copayments."[63]

The opponents of health reform in 1995 (like those in 1993 and 1994) successfully emphasized Americans' ambivalence. Two polls (a CNN/ *Time* poll in May 1995 and a CNN poll in January 1996) showed lopsided majorities of about 65 percent preferred a budget-balancing plan that involved smaller reductions in the growth of medicare and forgoing a larger tax cut. A number of additional surveys in the fall of 1995 and early months of 1996 confirmed that large majorities opposed reducing the growth of medicare expenditures in order to balance the budget or to deliver tax cuts.[64]

Moreover, a September 1995 *Los Angeles Times* poll revealed that 51 percent opposed medical savings accounts (38 percent supported them, with 11 percent offering no opinion).[65] A July–August 1995 NBC News/ *Wall Street Journal* survey reported that 55 percent opposed reforming medicare by introducing vouchers (whereas 32 percent supported this and 13 percent were not sure).[66] The Republicans' reform proposal simply lost credibility with the public; 57 percent of a *Los Angeles Times* survey sided with the Democrats in questioning the Republican claims that their plan was simply intended to save medicare.[67] Between October 1995 and mid-January 1996, when President Clinton's defense of medicare intensified, the public's approval of the president's handling of medicare jumped from 47 percent to 58 percent, while confidence in the Democratic party's handling of medicare jumped from 33 percent in June 1995 to 50 percent in January 1996.[68]

The battle over the budget followed a similar script. Luntz's advice to the House Republican Conference was to communicate the "moral force for balancing the budget" by "turning the issue of 'fairness' against the Democrats" and focusing "the general rhetorical attack on the 'Washington bureaucracy.'"[69] The Republican strategy for winning public support for restructuring fiscal policy was once again to straddle Americans' value conflict: balancing the budget would deliver collective benefits that lifted the less fortunate and fulfilled Americans' longing for less government and more freedom for individual initiative. The assumption was that steadfast pursuit of the Republican strategy—even if it meant closing the government—would win public support and then force Clinton to cave in.

On the budget, as well as on medicare, the Republicans overreached what Americans, Clinton, or moderate members of Congress were willing to accept. Their strategic blunders were the cumulative result of the ideological commitments of House Republicans, an exaggerated Republican confidence in the potential for moving public opinion, and a one-sided focus on the aspects of Americans' value conflict that valued individualism and distrusted government.

Clinton's counterattack was carefully gauged to capitalize on the Republicans' vulnerability by using their positions to reposition himself toward the center of public opinion and to depict the Republicans as occupying the extreme margin. With the aid of Morris's public opinion research, Clinton pursued a triangulation strategy that responded to public opinion by distancing himself from long-time Democratic party allies who opposed a balanced budget as well as from Republicans who took an "extreme" approach to achieving one.[70] Morris's research prodded Clinton to use his own balanced budget proposal to turn the debate into a referendum on how to accomplish this goal that larger majorities had long supported. The president changed his budget proposal from one in early 1995 that envisioned successive annual deficits of $200 billion to a proposal a few months later that embraced the Republican call for a balanced budget over seven years. As Clinton himself explained, his shift offered "people for the first time . . . a clear sense of what the choices were between the Congressional Republican vision . . . and my vision."[71]

Clinton's counterattack—joined by congressional Democrats—of emphasizing the "extreme" individual and collective costs of the Republicans' proposals effectively activated the public's sense of self-interest and social responsibility. While Americans supported the objective of a balanced budget as much as ever, they did not prefer the Republicans'

policies for achieving it. Survey data showed that instead of deficit reduction, majorities preferred to forgo tax reduction and to avoid cuts in
programs such as college loans, medicare and medicaid, and school
lunches. In short, the Republicans' failure to win public support stemmed
from both the Democrats' success and Republicans' unresponsiveness
to public opinion from the outset of the 104th Congress.

During the government shutdowns in December 1995, Gingrich spot-
ted the impending political train wreck and the damage to his party's
national reputation that the shutdown caused. But he needed several
frantic weeks at the end of December 1995 and early January 1996 to
temper the ideological convictions of his rank and file—especially the
sophomore and freshman House members—and to win the support of
his own leadership team, which had unanimously voted in late December against reopening the government. Gingrich garnered only a bare
majority for an interim spending bill (fifteen Republicans voted against
him, including twelve freshman members).[72]

The Republicans' failure to win public support for their fiscal policies
produced political dividends for the Democrats and hurt the GOP's national reputation. A February 1996 CBS/New York Times poll showed that
a majority blamed the Republicans in Congress more than Clinton for
the budget impasse.[73] The public perceived Clinton as more flexible than
the Republicans in searching for a compromise that would resolve the
standoff: two separate questions in a January 1996 CBS/New York Times
survey indicated that 62 percent concluded that Clinton was "really trying" to find a solution, while only 42 percent felt the same about the
Republicans. Moreover, between July 1995 and February 1996, when the
battles over the budget and medicare intensified, the public's approval
of Clinton's performance rose nine percentage points (from 43 percent
to 52 percent) while approval of Congress dropped nine percentage points
(from 31 percent to 22 percent.)[74] New York Times polls indicated that
registered voters began to reconsider Clinton's orientation, with more
Americans seeing him as moderate in mid-1996 than in mid-1993. A
Gallup analysis in February 1996 found that medicare, the budget, and
the economy primarily accounted for Clinton's lead over Robert Dole.[75]

Faced with electoral punishment, Republicans rethought their political strategy of opinion leadership in the weeks before the presidential
conventions, and by the fall of 1996 they were ready to compromise in
earnest and move toward centrist public opinion. Senator John McCain
of Arizona summarized the consensus among many Republicans—in-

cluding the ideologically driven House—that they had pushed "too far, too fast." The motto in the fall of 1996 was "Get things done, retain the majority and then be able to do more. If we don't compromise, we risk losing everything."[76]

The Republicans' tactical retreat in late 1996 produced a stream of compromise legislation in which Republicans abandoned earlier proposals to cut or eliminate established programs and signed off on policies identified with Democrats. The surge produced new money for education (including the largest increase in maximum Pell grant awards in twenty years), wider access to health insurance, a higher minimum wage, reauthorization of the Safe Drinking Water Act, and a rewriting of federal pesticide laws. In addition, Republicans abandoned their campaign for a major tax cut—the "crown jewel" of the Contract with America—and a constitutional amendment to balance the budget. In one policy after another, Republicans conceded—as Gingrich did on the environment—that they had "mishandled" the issue and had to reverse course.[77]

In short, competing political leaders pursued a dynamic strategy toward public opinion. Both Clinton and the Republicans in the 104th Congress began their terms by attempting to frame policy proposals in order to direct or lead public opinion. In particular, they drew on genuine public ambivalence in a contested effort to craft and target their messages in order to obtain support for their proposals. Republicans repeatedly returned to the public's long-established adherence to the abstract principles of individualism and minimal government. Democrats countered by focusing on Americans' sense of social responsibility and on their tendency to be "operational liberals" when it came to specific government efforts to help citizens.[78] The approach of the 1996 elections, however, prompted Republicans and Democrats to shift toward a median voter strategy that emphasized passing compromise legislation that responded to centrist public opinion, even at the cost of tempering ideological convictions.

The Ineffectiveness and Dire Consequences of Elite Mobilization Strategies

Clinton and Republican leaders pursued a strategy of mobilizing public opinion that was at once enticing and yet perilous. The opportunity to augment scarce political resources was almost irresistibly seductive. In an era of disorganized democracy, mobilizing public opinion seemed to promise a degree of influence that neither political parties nor other mass organizations such as unions could marshal.

The False Allure of Promotional Politics

The strategy of mobilizing public support, however, backfired on Clinton in 1993–94 and the Republicans in 1995–96. By counting on their ability to win public opinion, Clinton and the Republicans were lured into championing social policies that overreached what Americans or Washington moderates were willing to accept. Opposing leaders effectively capitalized on their rivals' inflated confidence and political miscalculation: as we suggested earlier, the Republican attack during Clinton's first two years in office contributed to a conservative shift in public opinion, while the Democratic onslaught during the 104th Congress prompted a moderating shift back in a liberal direction. The opposition's success prompted retreat and a frenzied search for compromise as electoral pressures mounted.

The promotional strategy failed to mobilize public opinion as elites expected because their strategy rested on two tacit but untenable assumptions: that their message could dominate, and that the public was available to be won. If elites are to direct public opinion, then the public needs to receive clear or nearly uniform information regarding which direction to head in. The institutional structure of the policymaking process, however, nearly guarantees that Americans will typically receive conflicting messages. Individual political activists have significant discretion; launching oppositional messages is attractive to individual political entrepreneurs because it offers them an opportunity to garner attention and influence. Moreover, journalists actively seek out political activists that represent the "other side" because of both the professional norm of objectivity and the economic pressures on the media to portray conflict in order to attract audiences.[79] The result is that the media report opposing messages from mainstream leaders. In short, competing political leaders use public presentations to underscore policy differences, and journalists seize on the ensuing conflict.

Second, the reliance of elites on mobilizing public opinion falsely presumes that Americans, in effect, passively receive and accept information. As we suggested earlier, Americans do not begin policy debates as blank slates; instead, they already hold fairly stable and complex core values and attitudes that are not susceptible to dramatic change, especially within a short period. The implication is that one-sided and well-orchestrated propaganda campaigns are susceptible to effective counterattacks that emphasize competing considerations. Indeed, oppositional leaders were quite effective from 1993 to 1996 in prompting Americans to weigh conflicting values and attitudes and oppose the proposals offered by rival political factions.

Moreover, social science research suggests that ordinary individuals engage in interpretation much like politicians and journalists. They select, reject, or ignore new information; they redefine terms, infer meaning, draw parallels, and make connections. Far from behaving passively, individuals are active agents in constructing their own interpretations based on information from the mass media as well as from personal experience and conversation.[80]

In short, promotional strategies failed because they rested on a set of faulty assumptions. The targeted presentations of one side were countered and offset by journalists who amplified the conflicting messages offered by rival elites; Americans followed the acrimony and wrestled with their own multiple and competing considerations to reach their conclusions.

The success of oppositional leaders in changing public opinion can be evaluated using two distinct approaches. First, the impact of elites on public opinion can be studied at the aggregate level after the fact. Indeed, as we have already suggested, aggregate public opinion responded to the counterattacks that were launched by oppositional leaders: the Republican attacks in 1993–94 were followed by a conservative shift in public opinion, while the Democratic onslaught in 1995–96 prompted a moderating shift back in a liberal direction.

A second approach, which we pursued in December 1994 after the congressional elections, was to use an experimental design to study the possible impact on public opinion of a change in the framing of public debate.[81] We used a "split ballot" in a national telephone survey of just over 800 adults between late December 1994 and mid-January 1995. One half of the sample was first asked about their general confidence in the national government's ability to carry out its programs; these respondents were then asked about their confidence in the federal government in the specific policy areas of national defense, medical care, social security, the environment, and welfare. In contrast, the other half of the sample was asked first about confidence in specific government programs and then about the government more generally. This second format would tell us to what extent respondents evaluated government more positively if they were first reminded in even a subtle way about specific policies for which the national government was responsible.

We found that respondents who were first asked about specific policies were, indeed, somewhat more confident in government overall (by eight percentage points) than the respondents to the first ballot. The most striking finding, however, involved an important set of subgroup differences: politically knowledgeable and self-identified Republicans were the most affected by being reminded of specific government policies. They were more than twenty percentage points more confident than their counterparts in the first ballot.[82] Those who listened to talk radio (often considered a mainstay of the Gingrich following) were among the most strikingly affected by first being reminded about government policies.

These results show how the different Democratic and Republican strategies for shaping public opinion can have significant effects. When the Democratic strategy in 1995–96 succeeded in focusing on specific programs and government accomplishments in accepting social responsibility, attentive voters became more likely to evaluate government more favorably. Conversely, when Republicans in 1993–94 diverted discussion away from actual policies and government operations and toward overall government performance in the abstract, Americans reached a less favorable evaluation of government because they paid less attention to what specific government programs actually did.

Any single strategy of mobilizing public opinion is vulnerable, then, to counterattacks by opposing leaders who seek to exploit Americans' ambivalence toward social policy. The increasing ideological and partisan divisions among politicians—especially within Congress—fueled elite efforts to sharpen already existing divisions among Americans. Both Clinton's policy initiatives in 1993–94 and the Republicans' proposals after the 1994 elections were cases when opponents successfully activated public doubts and mobilized against new policy initiatives.

The Consequences of Promotional Strategies

The attempt by elites to mobilize public opinion has accentuated public ambivalence toward public policy instead of fostering deliberation that helps the public develop informed, consistent, and stable preferences. The presumption underlying the elite strategy of opinion mobilization is that the public's innate intelligence and wisdom are not high; Americans are essentially contradictory, misinformed, and soft or susceptible to wild fluctuations.[83] The implication is that elites' muted responsiveness is both responsible and even necessary for the public good.[84]

The public's views, however, are institutionally conditioned; they are not an autonomous and completely external force that pounds on the doors of government. Rather, public opinion echoes the context in which Americans reach judgments; the public's preferences are influenced by politics. A growing body of research supports the view that the public responds in an identifiable and understandable manner to events, political mobilization strategies, and information transmitted by elites.[85] The public is not a sequestered jury that reaches judgment in a vacuum detached from ongoing policy debates.

Consider, for instance, an apparently obvious case of contradictory public preferences during the Clinton presidency: Americans both supported a balanced budget and opposed cuts in specific programs. Interpreting this as evidence of public confusion ignores the fact that the public does support approaches to deficit reduction that avoid social program cuts; polls suggest that the public favors reducing defense spending, forgoing tax reduction, limiting net benefits received by the rich (including even medicare and social security), and raising taxes on the rich and on tobacco and alcohol. The problem is that the public's preferred approach was ruled out by elites.

Public opinion during Clinton's first term was interpreted as irrational because it was perceived both as misinformed (for example, Americans believed that their taxes went up even though most tax hikes fell on the most affluent) and too volatile (support for Clinton's health reform bill reversed within half a year). It is certainly true that the public's perceptions have not always been accurate, and they may also have changed more in recent years than during previous periods: we have reported elsewhere a twofold increase in the number of cases of opinion changes on certain social policies since 1984.[86]

The source of the public's misperceptions is certainly not a mystery. On the tax issue, journalists assiduously covered the Republicans' broad attacks on Clinton's first budget in early 1993 for raising the taxes on a broad segment of Americans. (Clinton did not help matters: when he conceded in a widely reported comment that he probably increased taxes too much, Americans all across the country nodded their heads.) The public's limited knowledge that the tax increase fell on the affluent was an understandable conclusion from the information environment.

The dynamics of public opinion are also a product of the institutional and informational context. First, it should be stressed that although there has been general stability in public preferences toward a range of policies from spending on education and medical care to maintaining social security and fighting crime, many of the instances of change in public opinion have involved evaluations of particular proposals that elites have been actively and visibly debating. The public's evaluations of proposals may change because oppositional elites are quite skilled in framing their presentations to garner media coverage and to fuel the ambivalence and apprehension that Americans already harbor. On health reform, Republican leaders used information on public opinion to counter Clinton's emphasis on security by highlighting and thereby activating opposing considerations in the public's mind, such as the undesirable consequences of government intervention. Even as the Clinton health plan failed, Americans continued to support universal access to health insurance and to perceive a need for health reform.

A major consequence, then, of the current process of political debate and policymaking is to make it harder than in the past for the public to form accurate perceptions and consistent and stable preferences. Indeed, the current process has created a cycle of vocal conflict that has constrained the efforts of both Democrats and Republicans to build support for their respective governing philosophies. Because Americans are genuinely ambivalent about social policies, politicians have every incentive to accentuate and arouse the side of the public's value conflict that best comports with their position. The media have only been too eager to carry the gore of a fierce political fight. These activities serve to maintain Americans' ambivalence and to frustrate Americans' expectations of government effectiveness. By opting for an opinion mobilization strategy that adapts to institutional disorganization and electoral splintering, political elites have promoted divisiveness, short-term change, and even confusion among Americans.

The Politicization of Public Opinion

Presidents and members of Congress face a paradox. They face enormous incentives to appeal for public support. Checks on their formal constitutional authority and their informal extraconstitutional resources make public mobilization attractive as a potentially powerful means to augment their scarce political resources. The "right" communications strategy seemingly offers the means for swaying public opinion and winning it all. But once political leaders go to the airwaves, they find their political opponents successfully competing for media coverage and for the public's attention. Opinion leadership is a political snare.

The strategy of opinion mobilization breeds a go-for-broke confidence that invites overreaching. First Clinton and then congressional Republicans pursued comprehensive reforms in an environment characterized by political constraints. Echoing Gingrich's own confession, Clinton conceded that he "overestimated" his political resources.[87]

It is, of course, conceivable that the disappointments that Clinton and the Republicans experienced could prompt political leaders to avoid opinion mobilization; after all, it could deliver neither Clinton's health plan nor the Republicans' Contract with America.

In reality, however, the political pain inflicted on Clinton and the Republicans is unlikely to reduce future reliance on opinion leadership strategies. First, neither is likely to view the opinion mobilization strategy as a complete failure. It did, after all, work quite effectively as a strategy in opposition; Republicans drowned out Clinton on health reform, and the administration defined the policy debate in 1995 and 1996. Moreover, both Clinton and the Republicans blamed their defeats on the tactics they used to implement the mobilization strategy, not on the strategy per se. Clinton ultimately attributed the defeat of his health plan to "the enormous amount of organizational effort and funding" that opponents committed.[88] In terms nearly identical to those used by Clinton, Republicans blamed their losses— as did one of the congressional staff we interviewed—on "the amount of organized resistance . . . [and] vast amounts of money . . . thrown out to stop us." Gingrich blamed the Republicans' troubles on the Democrats' ability to circulate messages that "lied about what we were doing about Medicare," and House Judiciary Committee Chairman Henry J. Hyde of Illinois pointed to being "late in communicating."[89]

Democrats and Republicans attributed their various defeats to the same problem: tactical errors in the timing and use of resources for communicating and winning public opinion. What persists is the presumption that public support for policy proposals can be won and that opinion leadership offers the most feasible basis for mobilizing a supportive coalition of elites.

The current political calculus, however, is nearly backward: only significant elite agreement can mobilize public opinion; autonomous public opinion cannot be reasonably expected to unify a divided set of elites. Competing efforts to lead public opinion will only reinforce or deepen public ambivalence and elite conflict. The opinion leadership strategy that was used during Clinton's first term encouraged just the developments it hoped to escape: fractious and ideologically divided elites.

Notes

1. Samuel Kernell, *Going Public: New Strategies of Presidential Leadership*, 2d ed. (CQ Press, 1993); Jeffrey K. Tulis, *The Rhetorical Presidency* (Princeton University Press, 1987); and Bruce Miroff, "Monopolizing the Public Space: The President as a Problem for Democratic Politics," in Thomas E. Cronin, ed., *Rethinking the Presidency* (Little, Brown, 1982), pp. 218–32.

2. Competition among elites to promote themselves and their policies may explain the persistent finding that even strong public approval of presidents has little measurable impact on the White House's success in converting negative or wavering floor votes in the House and Senate. George C. Edwards III, *At the Margins: Presidential Leadership of Congress* (Yale University Press, 1989); Mark A. Peterson, *Legislating Together: The White House and Capitol Hill from Eisenhower to Reagan* (Harvard University Press, 1990); and Jon R. Bond and Richard Fleisher, *The President in the Legislative Arena* (University of Chicago Press, 1990); but compare Terry Sullivan, "The Bank Account Presidency: A New Measure and Evidence on the Temporal Path of Presidential Influence," *American Journal of Political Science*, vol. 35 (August 1991), pp. 686–723; and Benjamin I. Page and Robert Y. Shapiro, "Presidents as Opinion Leaders: Some New Evidence," *Policy Studies Journal*, vol.12 (June 1984), pp. 649–61.

3. Robert H. Wiebe, *The Search for Order: 1877–1920* (New York: Hill and Wang, 1967); Richard Hofstadter, *The Age of Reform: From Bryan to F.D.R.* (Vintage Books, 1955); and Stephen Skowronek, *Building a New American State: The Expansion of National Administrative Capacities, 1877–1920* (Cambridge University Press, 1982).

4. Gingrich's reorganization reduced the number of committees and committee staff, defunded the caucuses, which represented independent power centers for influencing the committees, downgraded seniority's role in the selection of committee chairs, limited chairs to six-year terms, and strengthened the Republican Conference's influence over committees (allowing subcommittee chairs to be removed if they fail to follow the conference's agenda). Power flowed from the committee system to the Speaker's Advisory Group.

5. Connie Bruck, "The Politics of Perception," *New Yorker*, October 9, 1995, pp. 50–76.

6. We thank Steven S. Smith for sharing this observation with us.

7. On recent changes in the social structural and ideological basis of the U.S. party system, see Jeffrey Levine, Edward G. Carmines, and Robert Huckfeldt, "The Rise of Ideology in the Post–New Deal Party System, 1972–1992," *American Politics Quarterly*, vol. 25 (January 1997), pp. 19–34; and Edward G. Carmines and Geoffrey C. Layman, "Issue Evolution in Postwar American Politics: Old Certainties and Fresh Tensions," in Byron E. Shafer, ed., *Present Discontents: American Politics in the Very Late Twentieth Century* (Chatham, N.J.: Chatham House, 1997), pp. 89–134.

8. Norman R. Luttbeg and Michael M. Gant, *American Electoral Behavior 1952–1992*, 2d ed. (Itasca, Ill.: F.E. Peacock, 1995).

9. Marjorie Connelly, "Portrait of the Electorate," *New York Times*, November 10, 1996, p. 28.

10. Richard M. Scammon and Alice V. McGillivray, eds., *America Votes: A Handbook of Contemporary American Election Statistics*, vol. 14 (Washington: Congressional Quarterly Press, 1981), pp. 16, 18.

11. Roper database, Storrs, Conn.

12. Luttbeg and Gant, *American Electoral Behavior 1952–1992*, p. 41; and Connelly, "Portrait of the Electorate."

13. The Gallup Organization and other pollsters regularly ask Americans, "What do you think is the most important problem facing this country today?" The "most important problem" question is a common source of information on the public's policy agenda.

14. Shanto Iyengar and Donald R. Kinder, *News That Matters* (University of Chicago Press, 1987).

15. Louis Hartz, *The Liberal Tradition in America: An Interpretation of American Political Thought since the Revolution* (Harcourt Brace Jovanovich, 1955); and Herbert McClosky and John Zaller, *The American Ethos: Public Attitudes toward Capitalism and Democracy, A Twentieth Century Fund Report* (Harvard University Press, 1984).

16. CBS News/*New York Times* poll, February 22–24, 1996.

17. Trust and efficacy are highly associated. Steven J. Rosenstone and John Mark Hansen, *Mobilization, Participation, and Democracy in America* (Macmillan, 1993). For instance, John Brehm and Wendy Rahn used pooled data from the General Social Surveys from 1972–94 to examine the relative influence of economic resources, psychological involvement with community, cognitive ability, and other factors. The cross-sectional analysis revealed that perceived government responsiveness was strongly related to confidence in government (though they do not precisely estimate the reciprocal relationship between the two). John Brehm and Wendy Rahn, "Individual-Level Evidence for the Causes and Consequences of Social Capital," *American Journal of Political Science*, vol. 41 (July 1997), pp. 999–1023.

18. Fay Lomax Cook and Edith J. Barrett, *Support for the American Welfare State:*

The Views of Congress and the Public (Columbia University Press, 1992); and Benjamin I. Page and Robert Y. Shapiro, *The Rational Public: Fifty Years of Trends in Americans' Policy Preferences* (University of Chicago Press, 1992).

19. Princeton Survey Research Associates poll, October 25–30, 1995, for the Times Mirror Center for the People and the Press.

20. Page and Shapiro, *Rational Public*; and John R. Zaller, *The Nature and Origins of Mass Opinion* (Cambridge University Press, 1992).

21. Stanley Feldman and John Zaller, "The Political Culture of Ambivalence: Ideological Responses to the Welfare State," *American Journal of Political Science*, vol. 36 (February 1992), pp. 268–307.

22. Page and Shapiro, *Rational Public*, pp. 285–320.

23. Thomas E. Patterson, *Out of Order* (Vintage Books, 1994).

24. Zaller, *Nature and Origins of Mass Opinion*.

25. Jon A. Krosnick and Donald R. Kinder, "Altering the Foundations of Support for the President through Priming," *American Political Science Review*, vol. 84 (June 1990), pp. 497–512; Zaller, *Nature and Origins of Mass Opinion*; Iyengar and Kinder, *News That Matters*; Shanto Iyengar, *Is Anyone Responsible? How Television Frames Political Issues* (University of Chicago Press, 1991); and Lawrence R. Jacobs and Robert Y. Shapiro, "Issues, Candidate Image, and Priming: The Use of Private Polls in Kennedy's 1960 Presidential Campaign," *American Political Science Review*, vol. 88 (September 1994), pp. 527–40.

26. Polling's growing popularity is evident in a more than fourfold increase in the number of polls conducted during presidential campaigns between 1960 and 1988 and the shifting of polling from campaigns to governing. We discuss the increased use of polls later. See Ronald D. Elving, "Proliferation of Opinion Data Sparks Debate over Use," *Congressional Quarterly Weekly Report*, August 19, 1989, pp. 2187–92; and Lawrence R. Jacobs and Robert Y. Shapiro, "The Rise of Presidential Polling: The Nixon White House in Historical Perspective," *Public Opinion Quarterly*, vol. 59 (Summer 1995), pp. 163–95.

27. Tulis, *Rhetorical Presidency*; but compare Gerald Gamm and Renee Smith, "Presidents, Parties, and the Public: Evolving Patterns of Interaction," paper prepared for 1995 annual meeting of the Midwest Political Science Association; Mel Laracey, "Popular Rhetoric in George Washington's Time: Proscription or Prescription?" paper prepared for 1994 annual meeting of the Midwest Political Science Association; Laracey, "The Presidential Newspaper 1836–1860: The Rest of the Story," paper prepared for 1995 annual meeting of the American Political Science Association; and Laracey, "Presidents and Public Communication in the Late 19th Century," paper prepared for 1996 annual meeting of the Midwest Political Science Association.

28. Jacobs and Shapiro, "Rise of Presidential Polling"; Lawrence R. Jacobs, "The Recoil Effect: Public Opinion and Policymaking in the U.S. and Britain," *Comparative Politics*, vol. 24 (January 1992), pp. 199–217; Lawrence R. Jacobs,

"Institutions and Culture: Health Policy and Public Opinion in the U.S. and Britain," *World Politics*, vol. 44 (January 1992), pp. 179–209; Jacobs and Shapiro, "Issues, Candidate Image, and Priming"; Diane Heith, "Staffing the White House Public Opinion Apparatus 1969–1988," paper prepared for 1996 annual meeting of the American Political Science Association; and Charles O. Jones, *The Trusteeship Presidency: Jimmy Carter and the United States Congress* (Louisiana State University, 1988).

29. Michael K. Frisby, "Clinton Seeks Strategic Edge with Opinion Polls," *Wall Street Journal*, June 24, 1996, p. A16.

30. Lawrence Jacobs, interview with Stanley Greenberg, presidential pollster, 1994.

31. Frisby, "Clinton Seeks Strategic Edge with Opinion Polls"; and Francis X. Clines, "The President's Strategist Puts His Faith in Timing and Telephone Calls," *New York Times*, August 9, 1996, p. A12.

32. Dan Balz, "Dick Morris's Fall From Grace," *Washington Post National Weekly Edition*, September 16–22, 1996, p. 11.

33. Alan Yang, "The Polls—Trends: Attitudes toward Homosexuality," *Public Opinion Quarterly*, vol. 61 (Fall 1997), pp. 477–507.

34. Our evidence of the muted impact of public opinion on health policy formulation is echoed by Theda Skocpol in her recent book, *Boomerang: Clinton's Health Security Effort and the Turn against Government in U.S. Politics* (Norton, 1996), pp. 113–20.

35. Frisby, "Clinton Seeks Strategic Edge with Opinion Polls."

36. "Congress Defeats Clinton's Crime Bill," *ABC World News Tonight*, August 11, 1994, transcription 4159.

37. Joseph N. Cappella and Kathleen Hall Jamieson, "Public Cynicism and News Coverage in Campaigns and Policy Debates: Three Field Experiments," paper prepared for 1994 annual meeting of the American Political Science Association; Darrell M. West, Diane Heith, and Chris Goodwin, "Harry and Louise Go to Washington: Political Advertising and Health Care Reform," *Journal of Health Politics, Policy and Law*, vol. 21 (Spring 1996), pp. 35–68; and Elizabeth Kolbert, "Special Interests' Special Weapon: A Seeming Grass-Roots Drive Is Quite Often Something Else," *New York Times*, March 26, 1995, p. A20.

38. Lawrence Jacobs and Robert Shapiro, "Public Opinion Trends toward Health Care," University of Minnesota and Columbia University, October 1994.

39. Henry J. Kaiser Family Foundation poll, November 15, 1994, "National Election Night Survey."

40. See Susan Herbst, *Numbered Voices: How Opinion Polling Has Shaped American Politics* (University of Chicago Press, 1993).

41. Forrest Maltzman and Lee Sigelman, "The Politics of Talk: Unconstrained Floor Time in the U.S. House of Representatives," *Journal of Politics*, vol. 58 (August 1996), pp. 819–30.

42. The interviews were conducted on a confidential basis and were based on a preset questionnaire in order to facilitate comparisons across the interviews. Twenty-one of the interviews were completed during the summer and early fall of 1995; thirty-one were conducted in 1996, mostly in June and July. To reflect the partisan balance in Congress and the larger size of the House of Representatives, we oversampled both Republicans and House members. Of our fifty-two interviews, forty-one were with House staff (eleven with Senate staff) and thirty with Republicans (twenty-two with Democrats). (The number of interviews reported is at times less than fifty-two because time constraints prevented some staff from finishing the interview.) The response rate was approximately 40 percent. The nonresponse occurred because some staff could not give a detailed and time-consuming interview.

43. Lawrence Jacobs and others, "Congressional Perceptions of Public Opinion and Health Reform," *Political Science Quarterly* (forthcoming); and R. Douglas Arnold, *The Logic of Congressional Action* (Yale University Press, 1990).

44. R. Kent Weaver, Robert Y. Shapiro, and Lawrence R. Jacobs, "The Polls—Trends: Welfare," *Public Opinion Quarterly*, vol. 59 (Winter 1995), pp. 606–27.

45. Dan Morgan, "A Revolution Derailed," *Washington Post National Weekly Edition*, October 28–November 3, 1996, p. 21.

46. Thomas W. Smith, "How Much Government? Public Support for Public Spending, 1973–1994," *Public Perspective*, vol. 6 (April–May 1995), pp. 4–6.

47. Benjamin I. Page, "Who Gets What from Government," paper prepared for the 1995 Richard S. and Nancy K. Hartigan Lecture on Politics and Government, Loyola University, Chicago.

48. Andrew Ferguson, "The Focus-Group Fraud," *Weekly Standard*, October 14, 1996, pp. 18–23; and Frank Greve, "GOP's 'Contract' Poll Not Adding Up," *Knight-Tribune News Service*, November 10, 1995.

49. Warren E. Miller and Donald E. Stokes, "Constituency Influence in Congress," *American Political Science Review*, vol. 57 (March 1963), pp. 45–56; Aage R. Clausen, *How Congressmen Decide: A Policy Focus* (St. Martin's, 1973); Robert S. Erikson, "Constituency Opinion and Congressional Behavior: A Reexamination of the Miller-Stokes Data," *American Journal of Political Science*, vol. 22 (August 1978), pp. 511–35; and Barbara Sinclair, *Congressional Realignment 1925–1978* (University of Texas Press, 1982).

50. Bruce Cain, John Ferejohn, and Morris Fiorina, *The Personal Vote: Constituency Service and Electoral Independence* (Harvard University Press, 1987); and Robert A. Bernstein, *Elections, Representation, and Congressional Voting Behavior: The Myth of Constituency Control* (Prentice-Hall, 1989).

51. Michael Weisskopf and David Maraniss, "Republican Leaders Win Battle by Defining Terms of Combat: Medicare Pitch Became 'Preserve and Protect,'" *Washington Post*, October 29, 1995, pp. A1, A26.

52. Bruck, "Politics of Perception," p. 70.

53. Ibid., p. 62.

54. Weisskopf and Maraniss, "Republican Leaders Win Battle by Defining Terms of Combat."

55. Michael Kelly, "Clinton's Escape Clause," *New Yorker*, October 24, 1994, pp. 42–53; and Michael Weisskopf, "Playing on the Public Pique: Consultant Taps Voter Anger to Help GOP," *Washington Post*, October 27, 1994, pp. A1, A26.

56. Weisskopf and Maraniss, "Republican Leaders Win Battle by Defining Terms of Combat."

57. Ibid.

58. Ian Fisher, "Gingrich Attacks Times-CBS Poll, Claiming Bias against G.O.P.," *New York Times*, October 27, 1995, p. D21.

59. Richard Stengel and Eric Pooley, "Masters of the Message: Inside the High-Tech Machine That Set Clinton and Dole Polls Apart," *Time*, November 18, 1996, pp. 76–96.

60. Bruck, "Politics of Perception"; and Haynes Johnson and David S. Broder, *The System: The American Way of Politics at the Breaking Point* (Little, Brown, 1996), pp. 577–78.

61. Louis Harris and Associates poll, September 28–October 1, 1995.

62. Frisby, "Clinton Seeks Strategic Edge with Opinion Polls."

63. John F. Harris and Eric Pianin, "Parties Swap Fire in Fight on Medicare: Details of Plans Remain Hidden," *Washington Post*, July 26, 1995, p. A4.

64. Roper Center for Public Opinion Research.

65. *Los Angeles Times* poll, September 16–18, 1995.

66. NBC News/*Wall Street Journal* poll, July 29–August 1, 1995.

67. *Los Angeles Times* poll, September 16–18, 1995.

68. Louis Harris and Associates polls, September 28–October 1, 1995, and January 18–22, 1996; and NBC News/*Wall Street Journal* poll, June 2–6, 1995.

69. Frank Luntz, "Attention! All Sales Reps for the Contract with America!" *New York Times*, February 5, 1995, p. E7.

70. Stengel and Pooley, "Masters of the Message." Evaluating Morris's influence on Clinton in an even-handed manner has eluded many political commentators. Although Morris was persuasive on some issues such as the budget, Clinton rejected his advice on others, such as affirmative action (Morris recommended elimination), school prayer (he advocated a constitutional amendment), and a budget deal with the Republicans in the period of government shutdowns. Balz, "Dick Morris's Fall from Grace"; and Alison Mitchell, "Clinton Campaign Finds Harmony after Exit by Morris," *New York Times*, October 15, 1996, p. C19.

71. Alison Mitchell, "Despite His Reversals, Clinton Stays Centered," *New York Times*, July 28, 1996, pp. A1, A10–12.

72. Indicative of the ideological split within the House Republican caucus, twenty-five to forty-five Republicans were preparing to support Democratic

proposals to reopen the government in early January 1996. Michael Weisskopf and David Maraniss, "Behind the Stage: Common Problems," *Washington Post National Weekly Edition*, February 5–11, 1996; and Jason DeParle, "Rant/Listen, Exploit/Learn, Scare/Help, Manipulate/Lead," *New York Times Magazine*, January 28, 1996, p. 34.

73. Fifty percent blamed Republicans, 31 percent attributed the standoff to Clinton, 14 percent blamed them both equally, and 5 percent offered "don't know" or no answer. CBS News/*New York Times* poll, February 22–24, 1996.

74. CBS News/*New York Times* polls, January 18–20, 1996, and February 22–24, 1996.

75. David W. Moore, "Most Important Issues in Presidential Campaign: Medicare, Budget Deficit, and the Economy," *Gallup Poll News Service*, February 9, 1996, pp. 1-3.

76. Quoted in Helen Dewar and Eric Pianin, "A Switch in Time That May Have Saved the GOP," *Washington Post National Weekly Edition*, October 7–13, 1996, pp. 9–10; and Helen Dewar and Eric Pianin, "Choosing Pragmatism over Partisanship," *Washington Post National Weekly Edition*, August 12–18, 1996, p. 12.

77. Morgan, "A Revolution Derailed."

78. See Lloyd A. Free and Hadley Cantril, *The Political Beliefs of Americans: A Study of Public Opinion* (Rutgers University Press, 1967).

79. Patterson, *Out of Order*.

80. W. Russell Neuman, Marion R. Just, and Ann N. Crigler, *Common Knowledge: News and the Construction of Political Meaning* (University of Chicago Press, 1992); and William A. Gamson, *Talking Politics* (Cambridge University Press, 1992).

81. Shmuel T. Lock, Robert Y. Shapiro, and Lawrence R. Jacobs, "Political Discontent: Reminding the Public What the Federal Government Does—An Experiment," revised version of paper prepared for 1996 annual meeting of the Midwest Political Science Association.

82. Political knowledge was determined by correct answers to factual questions about politics. Zaller, *Nature and Origins of Mass Opinion*; and Michael X. Delli Carpini and Scott Keeter, *What Americans Know about Politics and Why It Matters* (Yale University Press, 1996). We could not pinpoint the influence of any one particular policy on knowledgeable Republicans.

83. Julie Kosterlitz, "Dangerous Diagnosis," *National Journal*, January 16, 1993, pp. 127–30.

84. Giovanni Sartori, *The Theory of Democracy Revisited* (Chatham, N.J.: Chatham House, 1987).

85. Page and Shapiro, *Rational Public*; and Zaller, *Nature and Origins of Mass Opinion*.

86. Lawrence R. Jacobs and Robert Y. Shapiro, "Debunking the Pandering Politician Myth," *Public Perspective*, vol. 8 (April–May 1997), pp. 3–5. We cannot rule out the possibility that increased opinion change was due to more polling

over time. But decisions to do additional polling and to focus on specific issues are partly affected by the anticipation of finding opinion shifts.

87. Mitchell, "Despite His Reversals, Clinton Stays Centered."

88. "Clinton Is Seeking Some Limited Goals," *New York Times*, July 30, 1996, p. B8.

89. Dewar and Pianin, "Choosing Pragmatism over Partisanship"; Adam Clymer, "The President and Congress: A Partnership of Self-Interest," *New York Times*, October 2, 1996, pp. A1, C23; and Mitchell, "Despite His Reversals, Clinton Stays Centered."

Chapter 4

The Deficit and the Politics of Domestic Reform

Paul Pierson

IN the spring of 1981, Reagan administration strategists David Stockman and Richard Darman sat in the back of a room on Capitol Hill as swing voters in the House frantically added "ornaments" to the "Christmas tree" of tax cuts that was to become the Economic Recovery and Tax Act (ERTA). "I hope they're enjoying this," Stockman whispered. "They've just put themselves out of business for the rest of the decade."[1] Although he captured the significance of the moment, Stockman was wrong in three respects. The deficit was to stay at the center of American politics for almost two decades; the decision did not put Congress out of business, but it fundamentally changed the way that business is done; and this change was less a result of the specific decisions taken in 1981 than a consequence of long-term, gradual shifts in the structures of American taxing and spending.

The Reagan tax cuts are generally seen as the beginning of a new period of conservative governance in which the push for smaller government and lower taxes was to become the rule. Yet in crucial respects, ERTA represented the end of an era rather than the beginning; it was the last time federal politicians were in a position to legislate massive benefits without engaging in agonizing struggles over how to cover the costs. As Eugene Steuerle has put it, the late 1970s and early 1980s signaled

I am grateful to Martha Derthick, R. Kent Weaver, and Joseph White for very thoughtful comments on earlier versions. The Russell Sage Foundation has provided generous financial and administrative support for this project. Robert Shapiro kindly shared polling data, and Ben Garcia provided valuable research assistance.

the end of the "easy financing era" and the arrival of the "fiscal strait-jacket era."[2] This new context did not mean the end of policy change, but it profoundly affected the kinds of policies that could be advanced, the strategies that were employed, and the political process that shaped eventual outcomes. The main road to new policy now led through the budget, and that road was a rough one. Politicians aspiring to produce "change" must first confront the deficit. Domestic politics in the United States had been *fiscalized*.

The emergence of the budget deficit fundamentally altered the politics of national policymaking. It shifted attention away from the merits and limitations of individual programs to broader, more abstract arguments about the appropriate scope of government; it altered the nature of legislative politics as massive budget bills became the major instrument for generating policy change; it gave preexisting policy commitments a formidable political advantage over any new policy initiatives; and it helped generate an atmosphere of austerity conducive to what R. Kent Weaver has called the "politics of blame avoidance" rather than the traditional politics of credit claiming.[3]

All of these changes were evident in the recent efforts of the Clinton administration and congressional Republicans to pursue major reforms through budget strategies. Although the broader aspirations of these two coalitions were obviously quite different, the parallels between the two initiatives are striking. Indeed, these parallels suggest the extent to which the deficit came to define and confine American politics. Both coalitions were drawn to deficit reduction in part because it seemed the only plausible vehicle for their considerable legislative ambitions. Action on the budget represented a fast track in a system prone to stalemate. Both Clinton and congressional Republicans also saw deficit reduction as a way to reframe policy debates and garner public support for changes that would otherwise be untenable—to claim credit for attacking the deficit rather than attract blame for imposing austerity. Each sought not only a redistribution of the costs and benefits of governance but a more lasting transformation of the possibilities for activist government. In short, each coalition hoped that a serious assault on the deficit would serve to consolidate recent electoral gains and help to fashion an enduring political majority.

The most important parallel of all is that in both cases the immediate political results of their efforts were overwhelmingly negative. Although the Clinton administration eventually achieved some of the legislative goals contained in its original budget proposals, this victory came at a very high price. Action taken on the budget foreclosed the possibility of progress toward several of the administration's most prized policy ambitions, and the deficit reduction initiative contributed directly to the electoral debacle of 1994. Congressional Republicans invested even more heavily in a budgetary strategy, rolling almost all of their major legislative initiatives into an enormously ambitious budget package. The collapse of negotiations with the Clinton administration in January 1996 meant the collapse of the Republican policy agenda for the 104th Congress. Again, the political costs were extremely high. The failed budget gambit brought the Republican revolution to an abrupt halt and resurrected Clinton from his extremely weak electoral position at the end of 1994. Thus the final parallel: both reform coalitions discovered what others who had taken the lead on deficit reduction had learned before—that while the public applauds the rhetoric of deficit reduction, it often deplores the practice.

This essay explores these twin political catastrophes.[4] It considers why the budget became the main instrument of reform for each coalition, why particular strategies were chosen, and how to explain the political results. I argue that the broadly parallel outcomes were, in fact, more similar than they needed to be. Although the budget created severe problems and activated deep internal cleavages in each coalition, it constituted a far more favorable terrain for Republican reformers. The budget deficit was a massive obstacle between the Clinton administration and its main aspirations. For the Gingrich coalition, the deficit offered a direct pathway—albeit a hazardous one—to political and programmatic success. Like the Clinton administration on health care, however, congressional Republicans fell victim to hubris. With very considerable policy achievements within reach, Republicans exaggerated the scope of their mandate, underestimated Clinton, and consequently overreached. On the budget, the Clinton administration was dealt a bad hand, while the Republicans' stronger hand was badly played.

If this interpretation is correct, it has fundamental implications for an understanding of the contemporary political environment. The events of the past five years in budget politics reveal the importance of key political actors' strategic choices as well as the significance of long-term processes and institutional constraints. Yet the claim that Clinton had a bad hand while the Republican hand was badly played suggests a basic asymmetry in the prospects for those seeking to expand or curb the policy capacities of government. Although not especially conducive to radical retrenchment, the budget deficit functioned as a very effective lid on the public sector. Trends in taxes, spending, and the deficit—both as facts and as the subjects of an evolving public discussion—created formidable constraints on the possibilities for new public initiatives. Even if the Balanced Budget Act of 1997 signals the emergence of a new budgetary climate, the era of deficits will leave a lasting legacy. The lid on new spending initiatives is unlikely to be lifted anytime soon.

The Evolution of the Deficit as a Political Issue

Discussion of the Clinton and Gingrich budget strategies must be placed in a broader historical and political context.[5] First, a review of taxing and spending trends since 1981 is necessary because the trends, and previous responses to them, helped to shape the possible range of budgetary strategies in the 1990s. More important, the facts about taxes, spending, and the deficit suggest the limitations of the simplest and most common hypothesis concerning agenda development, namely, that major assaults on the deficit have taken place because budgetary imbalances were massive and hence reform was unavoidable. Explaining the widespread attention focused on the deficit is usually taken to be a nonpuzzle. Casting doubt on the claim that the need for dramatic action has been self-evident is a necessary first step to developing a more politically mediated interpretation of the evolving political agenda.

There is a simple but critical point to be made about broad trends in taxes, spending, and the deficit over the past two decades: this is a story of increasing policy rigidity. There was no sharp break in political behavior as elected officials indulged themselves by ladling out tax cuts, new social programs, or fancier and more plentiful military hardware. Instead, the federal government has lost some of the flexibility it needs to make modest budgetary adjustments. Partly through the relentless logic of compound interest, imbalances have then been perpetuated in the form of continuing deficits.

The data presented in figure 4-1 indicate that the deficit did not result from massive tax cuts. The Reagan tax cuts, often identified as the primary culprit in the deficit story, rolled taxes back only moderately from historically high levels.[6] This is not to suggest that there were no important changes in tax policy in the early 1980s. Most important, the index-

FIGURE 4-1. *Taxes, Spending, and Deficits, Fiscal Years 1970–97*[a]

Percent of GDP

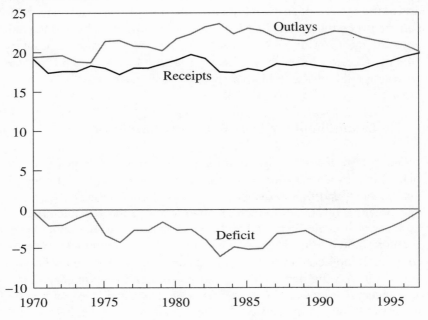

Source: Congressional Budget Office, *The Economic and Budget Outlook: Fiscal Years 1998–2007* (January 1997), app. F, table F-5; and Congressional Budget Office, *Monthly Budget Review* (October 3, 1997).

a. Data for 1997 are estimates.

ation of tax brackets introduced in 1981 made it far more difficult to raise revenues without voters noticing. After 1981, elected officials seeking higher taxes would face the politically precarious task of voting openly for new revenues.[7] One might argue that without bracket indexation taxes would have increased sufficiently in the early 1980s to prevent the deficit from rising. Yet while taxes might have moved somewhat higher, and the distribution of taxation would have been different, this counterfactual is difficult to sustain. Indeed, the stability of American tax revenues over time is striking. Since 1962 federal receipts have never fallen below 17 percent of GDP and have never risen as high as 20 percent. The historic high of 1981, reflecting the impact of high inflation on the pace of bracket creep, had already fueled deep disenchantment and probably made some adjustment inevitable. It seems unlikely that politicians could have pushed that level up to 22 or 23 percent at a time of stagnating household incomes.[8]

Steuerle has persuasively argued that the decision to end bracket creep in 1981 was only part of a broader series of transitions that altered the character of federal finances.[9] The late 1970s also marked the virtual exhaustion of the "peace dividend," through which declining relative allocations for defense had created fiscal slack for domestic programs. A long period of cheap borrowing, in which debt incurred at times of low interest rates was paid off in inflated dollars, was also coming to an end. Aversion to higher payroll taxes—a traditional source of low-visibility finance for social security and medicare—was growing.

Although the federal government has faced new and serious pressures on the revenue side, it is crucial to recognize that federal receipts as a percentage of GDP have fluctuated within a narrow band since 1980. Payroll taxes have risen further, and some tax expenditures have been cut to offset losses of revenue elsewhere. What ended was the era of *easy* finance. In recent years, increasing federal receipts has required more visible allocations of pain than was true in the past. Not surprisingly, politicians have become more skittish about the actions required to do so.

If the deficit cannot be blamed on Reagan tax cuts, it also cannot be attributed to the tendencies of spendthrift politicians to vote for big increases in benefits or new federal programs in the past fifteen years. For those inclined to blame government spending, one common claim is that Reagan's defense buildup was key. Yet sizable as it was, the Reagan defense buildup was short-lived (see figure 4-2). By 1990 defense spending as a percentage of GDP was no higher than it was in 1980, and it has dropped considerably since then. Whether or not the rising defense expenditures of the early and mid-1980s made sense, it is hard to sustain a claim that they have much to do with the long-term budgetary situation.

As figure 4-2 indicates, the most important sources of growing public expenditure are the mandatory spending or "entitlement" programs, enacted much earlier, and the rise in interest payments (itself a delayed result of the deficits of the early 1980s). New government activities, or recent legislation funding old activities more generously, have not played a significant role.

Rising spending in mandatory programs, except for modest expansions of medicaid, largely reflects the interaction of preexisting statu-

FIGURE 4-2. *Changes in Major Spending Categories, Fiscal Years 1970–96*

Percent of GDP

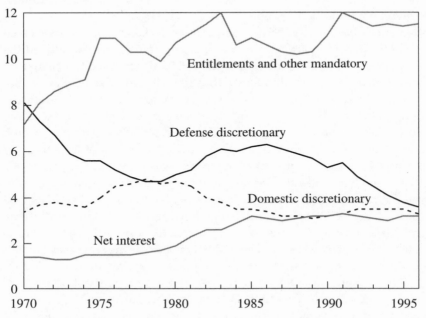

Source: CBO, *Economic and Budget Outlook,* tables F-9, F-11.

tory requirements with societal changes (including shifts in demographics
and the distribution of income and, especially, rampant health care inflation). Thus, where there has been higher spending, it has been driven
by the unfolding implications of decisions taken much earlier.[10] Indeed,
policy changes introduced in social security and medicare over the past
fifteen years have almost always been in the direction of retrenchment
rather than expansion. The heavy hand of the past looms large, both in
the form of legal rules requiring the provision of benefits to those meeting specified criteria, and in the form of interest payments that reflect
the lagged effects of previous policy decisions.

Figure 4-3 provides more detail on spending trends and makes clear
that the overwhelming source of expenditure strain has been the increase
in health care outlays. Federal expenditures for medicare and medicaid
rose from 1.7 percent of GDP in 1980 to 3.7 percent in 1995. As Mark

FIGURE 4-3. *Outlays for Entitlements and Other Mandatory Spending, Fiscal Years 1970–96*

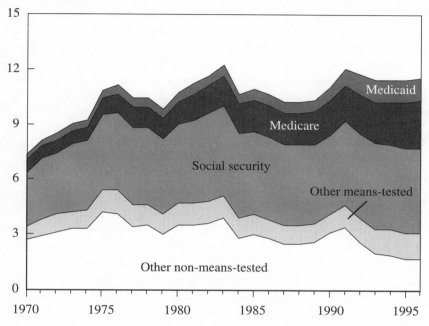

Percent of GDP

Source: CBO, *Economic and Budget Outlook*, table F-13.

Peterson's chapter demonstrates, these increases have mostly reflected rising costs in the health care sector as a whole.

Higher spending also came from rising interest costs and smaller increases in some other entitlement programs. These rising outlays, however, were more than offset by relative declines—including, in many cases, real cuts in spending—in other programs. As a percentage of GDP, federal outlays were lower when Clinton took office in 1993 than they had been in 1981. In particular, the "discretionary" elements of the budget have faced a sharp squeeze. Defense and domestic discretionary spending have fallen by roughly equal amounts, although the path of defense spending has been more volatile. Combined spending on the two sets of programs was 10.1 percent of GDP in 1981 but only 7.6 percent in 1995.

It is worth emphasizing that what stands out, especially in comparative perspective, is the remarkable spending constraint in the United States. In virtually every advanced industrial democracy, demographic pressures, the maturation of public programs, and economic difficulties have led to considerable growth in the size of the public sector. Whether the time frame is the past thirty-five years or the past decade, the relative capacity of the American political system to contain expenditure growth is striking.[11]

Thus, as a share of the economy, both taxes and outlays have been essentially flat since 1981. Broad rhetoric about out-of-control spending is really applicable only to health care, and there it has been evident in both the public and private sector. Beginning with a deficit of 2.8 percent of GDP in Carter's last year and leaving aside the first few years of Reagan's first term, what emerged in the 1980s were relatively small gaps between taxes and spending. These gaps were in turn perpetuated and accentuated by growing interest payments, which now constitute a substantial share of federal spending.

The deficit is a product of long-term pressures on spending and equally long-term changes that have made life more difficult on the revenue side. The gaps have not been huge. The possibilities for adjustments have diminished, however, as the budget has become more rigid. With the end of easy finance, possibilities for automatic or low-visibility revenue enhancement have vanished. Efforts to move taxes modestly upward have become perilous. Adjustments on the outlay side have also become more difficult. Between 1963 and 1993, discretionary outlays fell from 70.4 percent of the budget to 37.2 percent. As mandatory spending has crowded out discretionary spending, outlays are determined more and more by broad social trends and prior policy commitments and less and less by year-to-year adjustments of policymakers.[12]

The end result of these trends—a disjuncture between receipts and outlays, combined with increasing rigidity—must be carefully examined. One of the striking features of public discussion of the deficit, including much elite and even scholarly discourse, is the widespread use of inappropriate benchmarks, including very misleading discussions of trends in nominal dollars over extended periods of time. These statistics gave rise to an image, firmly embraced by the public, of an inexorably rising federal deficit. At a minimum, deficit numbers need to be adjusted for inflation, but the best simple indicator of the nation's ability to handle borrowing requirements is to consider the deficit as a percentage of GDP.

By this benchmark, deficits peaked in Reagan's first term and declined considerably thereafter (see figure 4-1).

There have been, however, important fluctuations. In particular, the deficit took an upward turn at the end of the Bush administration, primarily because of recession, rising health care costs, and the savings and loan bailout. This rise in the deficit helped set the stage for the Perot phenomenon and Clinton's determination to focus on deficit reduction. Real trends fueled the sense of urgency in 1992 and 1993. It is hard to say the same of the past few years. By 1995 the deficit as a percentage of GDP was lower than it had been when Reagan took office and considerably lower than the deficits in most other OECD countries. Yet after the 1994 election, Republicans described the deficit as a national crisis, and polls showed the public saw it as the nation's most important problem. Clearly, something besides raw numbers was driving the political agenda.

One needs, therefore, an account of agenda setting that explains why the deficit has occupied such a prominent place in policy debates. This analysis must operate at two levels, because the evolution of the issue involved a complex interplay between elites and mass publics. The perspective of the mass public is hardest to grasp, not least for politicians seeking to satisfy a seemingly fickle electorate. If pollsters ask about a balanced budget, respondents have always been overwhelmingly favorable, although this result is nothing new. Public enthusiasm is much more muted, however, if voters are asked to explicitly consider particular tradeoffs that might be required to eliminate the deficit. Doubts about the extent to which voters care about the deficit may also be found in surveys asking respondents to identify the "most important issues" facing the country. These numbers fluctuate wildly in ways that have little connection to movements in the deficit itself. Instead, the issue seems to rise sharply in importance when public figures decide to make the issue prominent, as they did in 1990, 1993, and 1995. Whether or not the deficit becomes a focus of popular attention—which tends to be limited to only a few issues at a time—is crucial, and here the evidence suggests that elite opinion and partisan competition are often critical.[13]

Less concretely, however, the deficit has become for many an important symbol in the last few years of the larger failings of the American political system.[14] The prominence and seeming clarity of an unbalanced budget has lent itself to effective public rhetoric. Amidst the vast confusion of politics and policy, the idea of budget balance offers a powerful focal point for a public operating with very limited information.[15] As the rise of Ross Perot signaled, the deficit has become a powerful frame for advancing a larger critique of domestic policy and a lightning rod for public anger about government. All politicians faced growing pressure to take the appropriate public stance.

This popular sentiment has evolved in a complex interaction with elite-level opinion in the media, academia, and government. A strong and growing consensus among economists holds that deficits represent a serious problem. The precise explanation for *why* deficits are so troubling has changed: in the late 1970s and early 1980s deficits were seen as an inevitable source of inflation; now they are seen as a cause of diminished savings and investment.[16] The elite media have accepted these analyses with enthusiasm. Again, balancing a budget offers a clear and dramatic goal that lends itself to effective portrayal within the constraining structures of commercial news.

This conventional wisdom in academia and the media spilled over into political circles as well. Especially in Congress, repeated struggles over budget packages fostered the view among moderate Democrats and Republicans that controlling the deficit should be a priority. This broadening political consensus deserves close examination.

The attitude of Republicans is not hard to understand. Republicans stand to benefit if the deficit serves as the central frame for policy reform, since it draws attention from reductions in popular programs to the overarching imperative to "clean house." As Gingrich put it in an interview with the *New York Times*, "It changes the whole game. . . . You cannot sustain the old welfare state inside a balanced budget."[17]

Given these political realities, it is the growing enthusiasm of Democratic politicians for deficit reduction that requires explanation. Here, of course, one needs to recognize that there were important internal divisions. Deficit reduction was more popular among moderate to conservative Democrats. Over time, however, this stance became more prominent in the party. In the Senate, Democrats such as David Boren, John Breaux, and Bob Kerrey became advocates of an ambitious agenda of deficit reduction. A similar group emerged in the House around figures like Charles Stenholm and Tim Penny.

A number of factors were involved here. First, the consensus among economic analysts and the media undoubtedly made resistance to deficit reduction more difficult. Beyond its intrinsic power to persuade, the elite media helped to define what behavior qualified as "statesmanlike." Refusing to take a tough rhetorical stance on the deficit could lead to accusations of "pandering," with the implication that a political figure lacked *gravitas*. Second, the declining role of traditional constituencies and trends in campaign finance altered the balance of political interests within the Democratic party, encouraging a more aggressive stance on the deficit. Finally, as rhetoric on the deficit began to resonate with the public, the Democrats faced growing pressure to respond to effective Republican challenges that they represented the old politics of tax and spend. Standing tough on the deficit was a way to signal that one was a new kind of Democrat, especially as the deficit came to symbolize government failure. The Perot campaign, with its effective appeal to some traditionally Democratic constituencies, further heightened the pressure.

One factor that has not received sufficient attention in accounting for the evolving position of Democratic politicians is the impact of American political institutions. The existence of divided government throughout the 1980s made a commitment to deficit reduction especially attractive for moderate Democrats. Split control over political authority opened tremendous opportunities for "cheap talk." Democrats could embrace deficit reduction rhetorically in the confidence that divided government made serious initiatives unlikely.[18] The political system offered plenty of opportunity to shift blame and obscure accountability for failures to take the tough steps that a real attack on deficits would require.

This institutional configuration facilitated a sequence of strategic steps that, over time, recast the terms of debate. Given the short time horizons typical in electoral politics, the cheap talk solution made considerable sense. Indeed, since the deficit represented one of President Reagan's few political weak spots, it was a difficult target for Democrats to resist. Over time, however, this rhetorical stance helped transform deficit reduction into an issue that allowed only one public position. In turn, this transformation left Democrats in an awkward position when the 1992 elections gave them control of both branches.

Thus by early 1993 the deficit was to cast a long shadow over the incoming Clinton administration. The numbers themselves justified concern. The sense of urgency, however, was heightened by a public dialogue that had sharpened over the course of a decade. The deficit had become a powerful symbol of what was wrong in American government, an easy target for those eager to show that they favored reform, and an issue on which many politicians felt they were committed to taking some significant action.

Reform Coalitions and the Development of Budget Strategies

As Margaret Weir notes in her introduction to this volume, both the Clinton administration in 1993 and the Republican congressional coalition in 1995 had worked out, over an extended period of time, relatively clear and cohesive plans for generating policy initiatives that would facilitate long-term political success. For each coalition, budget strategies emerged as critical components of these broader ambitions. By budget strategies I mean a reform coalition's (at least semicoherent) plans for using budgets and alterations of the budgeting process to advance a wider political agenda. Budget strategies involve two interconnected projects: a redistributive project to transfer resources toward a governing coalition, and a structural project designed to alter governmental capacities in ways that lock in the coalition's agenda and facilitate further transfers in the future.[19]

Budgets are the main vehicles for distributing the costs and benefits of governance. Of course, the budget is not simply a zero-sum, redistributive tool. Reform coalitions generally hope that their efforts will promote economic growth and will therefore have a substantial "positive-sum" component. Yet all reform coalitions seek to redistribute the burdens and benefits of government activity. Establishing a sustainable political position requires that benefits be extended to those who will be incorporated into the governing majority, and that wherever possible the costs of government be displaced onto the excluded minority. Two groups, in particular, are the most important recipients of new resources: organized actors that a coalition draws on for crucial political resources (such as unions in the case of Democrats, small business interests for Republicans), and the median or floating voters needed to put the electoral coalition over the top.

Sustaining political power also requires a structural project. The ability to pursue policy initiatives depends in part on governmental capacities.[20] These capacities, in turn, reflect the rules that govern political processes (such as the vulnerability of new initiatives to vetoes) and the extent of administrative and fiscal resources. Because a particular reform coalition knows that it will not always be in control, a crucial task for those committed to lasting reform is to advance a structural project that changes the rules and allocates governmental resources in ways that alter the range of possible policy action.[21] Of course, such changes need not occur through the budgetary process (term limits and campaign finance reform would be good examples). As the budget has grown in importance, however, it has become an increasingly popular mechanism of structural reform. This is true both because the budget is itself the core element of government policymaking and because budgetary legislation is easier to move through the veto-ridden institutions of the federal government. Budgets must be passed, and they are exempt from the sixty-vote cloture rule that creates such an obstacle to policy change in the Senate.

Both the Clinton administration and congressional Republicans advanced budget strategies that included significant redistributive and structural projects. The contrast between the two efforts is revealing. In each case, the "negative-sum" arithmetic of deficit reduction generated severe tensions within the reform coalition. Yet deficit reduction presented a greater problem for the Clinton administration than it did for the Republicans. This is partly because of the relationship between program cutbacks and redistribution. Although Republican constituencies benefit in many ways from government spending, they rely on it less heavily than Democratic constituencies do. Cuts in spending are much more easily incorporated into a Republican budget strategy than a Democratic one. Equally important, the Clinton administration wished to reduce spending to create the fiscal and political space for *new* programs. Thus Democrats had to pursue unpopular policies in the hope that this would somehow create a starting point for their real ambitions. For Democrats, success on the budget could only be a prelude. If these actions generated no political capital, they would represent a total failure. By contrast, Republicans wished to cut programs because they sought smaller programs and lower taxes. Each step, politically painful as it might be, was itself a significant move in the right direction. Even if successful budget actions ultimately proved unpopular, Republicans would at least have furthered their programmatic agenda.

The Clinton Administration: Activist Government in the Shadow of the Deficit

Very early on, the Clinton administration chose to latch much of its domestic agenda to the single vehicle of a massive deficit reduction initiative. This effort, presented as a necessary effort to put the government's house in order, was arguably the crucial decision of Clinton's first two years. Framing the issue as one of deficit reduction forced the administration to downplay the campaign's theme of "investment" policies designed to reallocate resources toward domestic programs targeted on the working and middle classes. At the same time, the administration's posture increased the leverage of conservative Democrats in Congress by legitimating their main concern. Already empowered by their status as swing voters, the deficit focus placed conservatives within the party in a position to dictate key terms of the budget agreement. Finally, decisions taken on the budget—and the unexpectedly lengthy and difficult struggle to final passage—were to have ripple effects, mostly unfavorable, on the administration's other domestic initiatives.

The Decision to Pursue Deficit Reduction

Why did the administration bet so much political capital on a plan to hike taxes, cut spending, and reduce the deficit by almost $500 billion over five years? The puzzle stems not only from the wisdom of hindsight but from a major shift in the administration's orientation. Although the campaign had focused on "investment"—a priority reiterated in Clinton's economic summit following the election—the administration's initial economic program revealed a new emphasis on budgetary stringency.

A number of conjunctural factors have been offered as possible explanations for this switch. The appointment of prominent deficit hawks among the president's leading economic advisors certainly encouraged this shift. So did the worsening of deficit projections in the months preceding Clinton's inauguration, when Clinton aides vigorously criticized OMB Director Richard Darman for his "Christmas present" of bad budgetary news. Yet various published accounts cast doubt on these explanations. Top figures in the campaign had known at least since the summer that the deficit numbers were far worse than was publicly acknowledged and that Clinton's promises on the deficit, taxes, and spending could not possibly add up. While it is true that Clinton's economic team was heavily populated with deficit hawks, these appointments themselves presumably reflected Clinton's own priorities. The case that Clinton was "captured" is further weakened by the fact that Clinton chose the most aggressive of five options his advisors assembled for addressing the deficit.[22] Given the profound consequences of this choice, clarifying its origins is critical to understanding the evolution of the administration's domestic agenda.

Four factors were crucial: a sense that the deficit's size constituted an immediate economic problem, as signaled by nervous financial markets; a desire to reach out to Perot voters and establish Clinton's "New Democrat" credentials; the recognition that conservative Democrats favoring deficit reduction held the balance of power in Congress; and the belief that deficit reduction created an opportunity to put the administration's legislative priorities on a fast track. In combination, these arguments added up to a persuasive case for moving quickly and aggressively on the deficit.

Of critical significance was the administration's sense that movement on deficit reduction was economically necessary.[23] Deficit projections worsened throughout 1992. By December the Bush administration forecasts of a 1993 deficit topping $300 billion set off alarm bells.[24] Here the role of financial markets, and the bond market in particular, was of central importance. When Clinton entered office, the historically large gap between short- and long-term interest rates was viewed as a sign of market skepticism about government handling of the deficit. The administration's deficit hawks, in particular, saw high long-term interest rates as a major brake on the economy and a credible deficit plan as a necessity for bringing them down. Lower interest rates would in turn allow homeowners to refinance their mortgages and increase consumer spending, fueling the economy. This argument took hold. Over time, an interest rate strategy virtually supplanted the administration's earlier investment strategy for economic growth. Success of this interest rate strategy hinged on serious deficit reduction.[25]

More directly political goals also drove the decision to put the deficit at the center of the administration's efforts. Foremost among these was the continuing concern to position Clinton as a New Democrat who could appeal to disillusioned voters. From the outset, the Clinton administration knew that its political fate lay in the hands of Perot voters. In the 1992 election, Clinton won only 43 percent of the vote. Assuming a two-way race in 1996, Clinton would need roughly half the Perot vote to win. In fact, Perot voters were as likely to lean toward Clinton as toward Bush, suggesting that the Democrats could have won a two-person race in 1992. But Clinton had been the outsider, the voice of "change" in 1992, and he would be an insider in 1996. Given the hostility of Perot voters to Washington politics and "business as usual," Clinton needed to strengthen his appeal to this crucial group.

As Clinton pollster Stanley Greenberg has argued, the administration believed that winning this group over to an activist domestic agenda was a formidable but not impossible challenge.[26] Indeed, the emergence of the Perot vote could be seen as only the latest stage in the electoral shift that had motivated much of the Clinton campaign's strategic thinking from the outset: the disaffection of formerly Democratic constituencies among white working-class males. The key to winning over this group, it was argued, was to demonstrate a commitment to political reform and to new policies that would make government work better. According to Greenberg, Perot voters' concern with the deficit was not based on a strong commitment to austerity. Instead, the deficit held symbolic significance as an indicator that government was incompetent and out of control. Attacking this symbol, in the minds of many in the administration, would be a clear way to signal Clinton's New Democrat credentials. If successful, the effort would prime skeptical Perot voters for a "new" activism, embodied in the administration's plans for investments and health care reform.

The dynamics inside the Beltway pointed in the same direction. Clinton's modest electoral victory and nonexistent coattails left him heavily dependent on moderate-to-conservative Democrats in Congress who had less than total enthusiasm for ambitious new federal initiatives. Clinton's dependence on conservative Democrats reflected the small size of the Democrats' congressional majorities and the position of Republicans, who had little interest in a deficit package built around significant revenue increases.

That the vast majority of Republicans would refuse to go along with the administration's budget initiative was evident from the start. The events of 1990, when even a Republican president seeking a considerably smaller set of tax increases could not carry the majority of his own party in the House, were a watershed.[27] The 1992 election results—which many conservatives attributed to Bush's flip-flop on taxes—had confirmed the commitment of most Republicans to a strong antitax stand. In a calculation that proved to be well justified, they saw little to be gained in helping the Democrats spread the blame for tax increases. When Republican Gerald Solomon of New York introduced an alternative budget resolution containing tax increases, it received only twenty votes, and the Republican conference reaffirmed its opposition to any new taxes.

The Democrats' budget bills were to receive not a single Republican vote, in committee or on the floor of either chamber, throughout the process. Thus the Clinton administration found itself trying to achieve something never accomplished in postwar history: the passage of major legislation without any support from the opposition party. Democrats therefore needed almost every vote within their own caucus. The margin was especially thin in the crucial Senate Finance Committee, where the Democrats held only an 11–9 majority.

It is here that the contrast between Clinton and the reform presidents he hoped to emulate is most evident. Lyndon Johnson and Franklin D. Roosevelt could point to Democratic landslides and worked with large majorities in both chambers. In 1992 members of the House and Senate in increasingly marginal Democratic seats were less than awed by Clinton's showing but quite impressed by the scope and substance of the Perot phenomenon. Partly for this reason, at the beginning of 1993 deficit reduction was considered much more important within Congress than among the mass public.[28]

A final factor pushing Clinton toward an ambitious deficit plan was the administration's belief that it presented the most promising vehicle for a substantial legislative agenda. Here, Clinton clearly sought to emulate the Reagan administration's example of 1981. Creating a large budget package offered three advantages. First, rules governing the budget streamlined the actions of Congress and diminished the blocking power of minorities. Given that Clinton's working majority was at best a slim one, a procedure governed by simple majorities was a considerable advantage. Second, budget packages offered maximum flexibility, creating space for bargaining within the coalition and facilitating efforts to accommodate legislative priorities that would have stood no chance of passage on their own. Finally, presenting such a major package could reframe the legislative issue for congressional Democrats as one of supporting or opposing the first Democratic president in twelve years. Since the fragmentation of the party meant that aspects of the administration's agenda were sure to be troubling for various factions, the administration could maximize the costs of a vote against it by raising the stakes of political failure. As I will discuss below, Republicans were to be drawn to a budget strategy in 1995 for many of the same reasons.

Thus, far from being a case of an administration hijacked by a few hawkish advisors, the decision to move forward on the deficit appears to have been overdetermined. The forecasts of future deficits were indeed daunting, and they prompted understandable anxieties that restless financial markets would trigger immediate economic problems. Yet political imperatives greatly amplified these economic concerns. The message of the Perot campaign, the posture of moderate Democrats in Congress, and the need for Clinton to husband his modest political capital all pointed in the same direction.

Creating the Budget Package

Many of these same factors played a critical role in shaping the administration's budget package. The task facing the administration was formidable: it sought to generate sufficient "fiscal slack" to both substantially reduce the deficit *and* permit significant new spending for its own legislative priorities. Three linked decisions were central: how big the deficit package should be, how much new revenue to seek, and how much the administration should attempt to reallocate spending within the federal budget.

As already noted, Clinton chose the most ambitious deficit target offered by his advisors. Decisionmaking seems to have centered on determining a credible figure for a variety of audiences. Federal Reserve Chair Alan Greenspan warned that financial markets expected something near $500 billion. Rumblings in Congress also suggested the need for an ambitious effort. Finally, the administration wanted to send a strong signal that Clinton was striking out in a new direction. The administration estimated the total deficit reduction in its package at about $500 billion over five years, although the Congressional Budget Office soon suggested that the total was more like $430 billion.

The most politically delicate issue at the outset was a decision about how much revenue to seek and how that revenue was to be produced. The Clinton administration recognized that it could not cut the deficit sharply and introduce new or expanded programs without new revenues. Yet taxes were clearly a dangerous issue for the Democrats. Given the Republican experience of 1990 and Bush's fate in 1992, it was a near certainty that Republicans would refuse to go along with a proposal containing sizable new taxes. Democrats alone would be held accountable for the resulting package.

The administration eventually settled on a formula that it hoped would provide the best combination of revenue increases with minimal political fallout. The main decision was to concentrate tax increases on the well-off by raising the top income tax rate, limiting deductions for high-income households, increasing taxes on social security benefits for the relatively well-to-do, and removing the income cap on the medicare payroll tax. These changes accounted for roughly three-fourths of the tax increases in the administration's original plan. The administration thus sought to partially reverse the declining progressivity of the tax system that had occurred during the 1980s. Indeed, it exploited an opportunity to largely shelter the middle class from burdens associated with the push to generate new revenue.

The one exception to this distributional outcome was the administration's proposal for a Btu tax. This new energy tax, weighted to provide incentives to burn cleaner fuels, was projected to generate $73 billion over the five-year period, about one-fifth of the total planned tax increase. In addition, the Btu tax offered significant possibilities for structural reform. For those seeking to loosen the federal government's fiscal straitjacket, the tax had attractive features: its connection to environmental and energy conservation issues gave it a potentially persuasive rationale, while the fact that it was indirect was likely to make it less unpopular. Opening up a source for future revenue expansion would be a major achievement in an era when traditional sources of revenue growth had diminished potential. Of course, as the administration was to find, this implication also made the proposal controversial.

While the determination of tax and deficit numbers dictated the overall scope for spending, a final set of decisions focused on the allocation of spending within that total. The administration needed to decide how much it would push for new investment spending and where the savings would be generated elsewhere in the budget to make these targets viable. Here the administration's initial inclinations were reasonably ambitious but hardly radical. The plan called for major cuts in defense and an extension of tough overall caps on discretionary spending. The discretionary caps would tightly squeeze those programs not receiving favored treatment within the administration's investment priorities.

The largest source of potential funds within the existing budget was entitlement spending, especially for social security, medicare, and medicaid. Social security was widely regarded as untouchable. Many in Congress saw the rapidly growing health care programs as a target for major savings, but the administration needed to preserve these options to help finance its plans for health care reform. Ultimately, the administration's plan did draw on entitlement programs for savings: taxes on the social security benefits of more affluent retirees were to generate $29 billion, and roughly $50 billion would come from medicare and medicaid. Yet these changes represented very modest adjustments in the government's most expensive domestic programs. Combined with smaller cuts elsewhere and reductions in interest payments resulting from the smaller anticipated deficits, however, these changes in entitlements meant that spending cuts would roughly match the tax increases in contributing to a lower deficit while leaving significant funds for the administration's domestic agenda.

As is detailed elsewhere in this volume, the administration's proposed investment initiatives marked a significant shift from the spending priorities of the Reagan and Bush administrations. Over the four years of 1994–97, the administration asked for $160 billion in additional spending for infrastructure, education, health care, and tax incentives for the private sector.[29] While it is clear that the administration stretched the definition of "investment" to cover its spending priorities, the budget did call for a reorientation toward programs geared to the promotion of human and physical capital.

Nonetheless, with few exceptions the proposals were restrained, even at the outset. In many cases, the administration sought only to partially offset reductions in real spending levels made during the 1980s. While packaging the new spending initiatives in a large budget bill gave the administration a better opportunity to shape priorities, the need to reach the deficit targets meant that the scope for activism was limited. Overall, the administration's package contained only a modest redistributive project. As was to become clear after 1994, it is far easier for the Republicans to design a redistributive project around deficit reduction than it is for the Democrats. In the administration's plan, redistribution was built around the increases in taxes on the wealthy and the new investments (especially the earned income tax credit), but the economic magnitude of these efforts was relatively small.

Given this characterization of the administration's initial proposals, one should ask whether there was any realistic alternative. Since budget constraints presented the chief limit on possibilities for a more activist agenda, it is worth considering options that might have produced greater fiscal slack. Two such options existed but were not attempted: an attack on tax expenditures and the introduction of a capital budget.[30] Brief discussion of these roads not taken can help to clarify both the administration's political calculations and the character of contemporary budgetary constraints.

The federal government operates a vast, largely hidden array of policies that subsidize private activities through the tax code.[31] Most economists agree that these subsidies are analytically equivalent to budgetary outlays. The only difference is that the government, rather than writing a check to a particular group, simply indicates to the favored party that it can write a smaller check to the government. These tax expenditures have a number of features that would seem to make them prime targets for a Democratic administration: they are expensive, and therefore cutbacks would have considerably eased the administration's budget problems; they have grown with very little scrutiny and almost no sense of whether they serve any important public purpose; and they provide a large majority of their benefits to those well above the median income level, so the costs of reform would have fallen most heavily on Republican constituencies.[32]

The idea of a capital budget has remained at the fringes of policy discussion for the past decade.[33] The argument in favor of such an accounting approach is that the government (like private firms and most state governments) should distinguish between consumption and investment expenditures, and that it is appropriate to borrow for the latter in anticipation of future economic returns. Introducing a capital budget would have highlighted one of the administration's main arguments for government activism: the need to invest in the physical and human capital required to compete in the rapidly changing global economy. At the same time, introducing a capital budget would have reframed the deficit issue, calling into question the apocalyptic scenarios associated with government borrowing.[34] Loosening this constraint might have created the opening for Clinton proposals that would cost money in the short run.

At first glance, both these options look like potential winners: each would have greatly eased the government's fiscal constraints while transferring resources toward Clinton's key constituencies. The reasons for their rejection clearly indicate that the Clinton administration was deeply concerned from the outset about public resistance to taxes and big government. There is no evidence that a capital budget was seriously considered.[35] The antideficit mood in Congress was such that it would have been widely derided as a gimmick. There was simply no political appetite in Washington for creating the kind of fiscal slack that such a plan might have generated. Furthermore, Clinton's economic advisors would certainly have argued that the approach would not be credible on Wall Street.

The tax expenditure strategy received somewhat more attention but never became a serious option. When the implications of the deficit reduction plan for the administration's investment agenda became apparent, Labor Secretary Robert Reich made an attempt to put tax expenditures on the table. The White House reacted with alarm: any effort to curb these subsidies would be interpreted as a "tax hike on the middle class" and provide a dangerous opening for the Republicans. Reich's initiative was effectively silenced. Only after the 1994 election did the administration begin to discuss tax expenditures (again at Reich's urging), and then the discussion was limited to "corporate welfare." Mentioning the huge tax expenditures for private pensions, health care, and mortgage interest that overwhelmingly benefit the well-to-do remains taboo.

These nonepisodes highlight the administration's narrow room to maneuver in budgetary policy. In particular, the growth of well-hidden, untouchable, and massive subsidies for the upper middle class is now a crucial constraining feature of American social policy. While social security and medicare become increasingly vulnerable to the charge that they are poorly targeted and inefficient, criticisms of the programs most deserving of such challenges remain beyond the pale. Budget analysts have long wanted to tackle this issue (note the initial Treasury plans for tax reform in both the late 1970s and mid-1980s), but the political barriers appear insurmountable. Although these programs clearly constitute a variant of public spending, Republicans (and a wide range of organized interests that benefit from these subsidies) are quick to jump on any proposed reform as a "tax increase." Because the Clinton administration had no viable response to these charges, the most sensible route to a serious reorientation of public commitments was closed off. The complexity of the tax code, the difficulty of explaining the concept of tax expenditures, and the salience of the word *tax* in contemporary American politics has made it impossible to convince middle-income Americans to support the policy reforms that might have allowed a more activist agenda.[36]

Passing the Budget Act

Events following Clinton's announcement of his budget plan suggest that the president had not underestimated the possibilities for activism. The deficit reduction package's journey through Congress was a high-wire act from start to finish. Close to a humiliating defeat on several occasions, the administration ultimately prevailed by a single vote in each chamber. Although the administration had correctly calculated that the reconciliation process would give it significant advantages, Clinton was forced to trim back his aspirations. The ultimate package roughly followed the outlines of the administration's initial effort. Where it had changed, however, the moves were relentlessly in the direction of making it "tougher" and scaling back new initiatives. Deficit reduction goals were raised, spending cuts were increased, and new revenues were scaled back. Moreover, the process further tarnished the appeal of federal activism; indeed, it served to reinforce the enthusiasm of those seeking even further attacks on public expenditure.

The fight over the budget was a fierce six-month battle, ultimately resolved only when Senator Bob Kerrey of Nebraska—one of Clinton's main rivals in 1992—dramatically announced, after months of criticism of the president, that he would not cast the vote to bring the administration down. Kerrey's decision opened the way for Vice President Gore's tie-breaking vote on final passage.[37] All the adjustments in the intervening period had underscored the weakness of Clinton's position and the constraints on policy activism. With congressional Republicans showing no interest in pursuing a deficit reduction package along lines anything like those which the administration envisioned, holding on to Democratic votes was crucial. Early on, these swing voters indicated their strong preference for greater deficit reduction, engineered through deeper spending cuts rather than increased tax hikes. Legislative success required holding these deficit hawks on board.

When the CBO initially scored the administration's plan as $60 billion short of its deficit target, the House responded by passing a budget resolution calling for $63 billion in further spending cuts, engineered by an additional tightening of the caps on discretionary spending.[38] The demise of the administration's stimulus package in the Senate in April created further trouble. Although Senate Republicans would not have the filibuster as a weapon in the budget fight, they had shown the potential for portraying the administration and its allies as business-as-usual, tax-and-spend Democrats.

As Congress moved from the general expressions of support contained in the budget resolutions to the specific decisions required to turn those aspirations into law, further difficulties arose. Most important was opposition to the Btu tax. This proposal was a chief target of Republicans, who saw the one major tax increase not focused on the well-to-do as a shrewd place to make their stand. Ultimately, however, it was conservative Democrats, especially from oil- and gas-producing states, who killed the proposal. A modified Btu tax, increasingly weakened by exemptions, survived the House, but only after the administration promised further modifications in the Senate. Led by Oklahoma Democrat David Boren, who held the swing vote on the critical Finance Committee, the Senate happily obliged. The Btu tax was dropped in committee, eliminating what might have been one of the more lasting implications of the administration's budget initiative. The lost revenues were plugged by a 4.3 cent increase in the gasoline tax and further steps on the spending side: scaled-down investments and deeper cuts in medicare and medicaid.

Thus, by the time the legislation finally passed, the limited spending initiatives of the administration's proposal had been further curtailed. The administration had made some difficult choices and could justly claim a major step toward lower deficits. On the spending side, there were some notable changes, including a major expansion of the earned income tax credit (EITC). It is no accident that the main vehicle for redistribution was a subsidy for low-wage workers, which was more acceptable than other forms of social spending to moderate and conservative Democrats as well as to business.[39] Although priorities in the discretionary budget were reoriented and a number of programs gained, the overall lid established on spending was extremely tight.[40]

As a redistributive project, the 1993 budget legislation must be judged a modest success at best. Indeed, the agreement bore more than a passing resemblance to the 1990 budget accord between congressional Democrats and a Republican president.[41] The two packages were similar in size, although after adjusting for inflation the 1990 agreement was somewhat larger. Each agreement hiked the gas tax about a nickel and raised the top rate of income tax; each got its expenditure savings largely from defense cuts, slower growth in medicare, and tightened "caps" on domestic discretionary spending; and each offered an expanded earned income tax credit to make the package more progressive. The biggest difference was on the ratio of taxes to spending. The 1993 package relied much more heavily on taxes.

The debacle over Clinton's stimulus package, the curtailment of provisions to increase investment, and the demise of the innovative (and unpopular) Btu tax all signaled the failure of the administration's budget strategy to move the congressional center of gravity significantly to the left. This defeat is suggested not only by the erosion of Clinton's redistributive project but by the collapse of the administration's structural project.

The administration had hoped that a strong deficit package would restore the possibilities for activism in two respects. New revenues, and a new revenue base, would make it easier to escape the fiscal straitjacket that limited the possibilities for innovative public policy. Equally important, tough action on the budget would restore the Democrats' credibility and expand popular support for public action. The revenue package largely failed to meet the first goal, at least for the long term. While moderately raising receipts, it did so by targeting the well-to-do in a way that was unlikely to be repeated. The failure of the Btu tax, and the bitter fight over a trivial increase in the gasoline tax, signaled the difficulty of introducing any tax increase on the middle class. Thus the revenue initiatives left little on which to build. In the words of one senior budget aide, "Tactically it was terrible. . . . We won the battle but lost the war."[42]

Nor did the administration's initiative restore public confidence in activist government or succeed in taking the deficit issue off the table. Indeed, within Congress the administration's actions seemed only to fuel the appetite for spending cuts. By the fall of 1993, House deficit hawks were already back looking for more. Despite intense administration opposition, a tough bipartisan deficit reduction bill sponsored by Democrat Tim Penny of Minnesota and Republican John Kasich of Ohio lost by only four votes in the House. Penny-Kasich would have had devastating consequences for Clinton's agenda, blocking most of the planned "investments" and initiating further medicare cuts the administration desperately needed to finance health care reform.[43]

This near debacle reflected a broader breakdown of the administration's strategy. The structural project within Clinton's deficit initiative sought to lay the electoral foundation for renewed government activism. Clinton, whatever his protestations, clearly held a strong belief in the need for extensive new government activities to combat domestic problems. Health care—one-seventh of GDP—is the obvious and massive example, but as a number of chapters in this volume indicate, the administration had considerable ambitions in other areas. The main political obstacle to its aspirations was public skepticism about new policy initiatives and resistance to higher taxes. The deficit plan, it was hoped, would "clear the decks" by showing that Clinton was not afraid to go after government waste and that money would be spent sensibly. Perot voters were to be convinced that an activist administration was on their side.

This plan failed totally, as Perot voters split two-to-one in favor of Republicans in the 1994 congressional elections. The Clinton budget was quite unpopular. Polling results suggest that this was in part a problem of marketing. The public remained largely unaware of the redistributive elements of the plan (the rise in rates on the wealthy; the expansion of the EITC to "make work pay"); most people believed (wrongly) that their own taxes were scheduled to go up significantly; and few people even knew that the plan had reduced the deficit. Thus Clinton failed to inoculate himself against the charge that he was an old-style tax-and-spend Democrat and to lay the ground for a new round of activism. Indeed, by shifting the debate from the campaign's emphasis on new investment to the need to "clean house" and rein in an overextended government, the budget fight of 1993 may well have made voters even more skeptical of new initiatives.

There is good reason to doubt, however, that the administration's failures simply reflect a bad sales job. One of the clear lessons of the past fifteen years—both here and abroad—is that the most popular form of deficit reduction is the kind that never gets implemented.[44] Voters also repudiated the Senate Republican initiative of 1985 and Bush's effort of 1990. Deficit reduction requires visible pain in return for diffuse and uncertain benefits. The "negativity bias" of voters means that they have a strong tendency to focus on the unpleasant things politicians do. Clinton's initiative marked the third successive time that the champions of deficit reduction had been punished at the polls.[45]

For an administration with such high aspirations, it is hard to imagine a more dismal result than the political outcome of Clinton's two-year experiment with deficit reduction. The administration's budget strategy only modestly advanced its redistributive project, and the structural project completely failed—indeed, it had helped set the stage for radical Republican efforts to push in the other direction. Yet this account is not meant to highlight the tactical failings of the administration. Rather, it suggests that Clinton probably had no good options. The 1992 election results, combined with a sizable deficit and a set of mass and elite expectations of swift action, left a president eager for activism in an impossible bind. Deficit reduction turned out to be a losing strategy for a Democratic administration, but it is far from clear that there was a realistic alternative.

Budget Policy and the Gingrich Revolution

Following the 1994 election, controlling the deficit quickly became the rallying cry for those within the Republican coalition who felt the time was finally ripe for a sustained assault on the welfare state. As the data on long-term expenditures suggest, the deficit had served as an effective brake on new social spending during the Reagan, Bush, and Clinton administrations. Yet it had failed to prompt the dismantling of social programs anticipated by some conservatives and feared by many liberals. Some programs were eroded, others (such as the EITC) expanded, but most faced relatively incremental changes.[46] In the wake of their stunning victory, congressional Republicans mobilized to try again.

The Role of the Budget in Republican Strategy

Although the new Republican agenda was far more sweeping than Clinton's, a budget strategy was once again the centerpiece. As with Clinton's budget strategy, the Republican budget initiatives contained both a redistributive and a structural component. Each of them, however, made Clinton's ambitions look modest. The redistributive element—an unusually aggressive effort to alter who gets what from government—was apparent in both the tax and spending proposals. As is discussed in detail elsewhere in this volume, expenditure cuts were to fall very heavily on traditional Democratic constituencies, especially the poor and cities.[47] The reductions in planned expenditure on low-income programs were to be much larger than anything the Reagan administration had proposed.

Cutbacks in programs for the middle class were comparatively modest, although given the magnitude of the total reductions desired and the current distribution of federal spending, they were inevitably quite large. Social security was put off the table at the outset, but the huge and rapidly growing medicare program was not. Indeed, medicare cuts represented by far the largest single target for reductions. As the budget debate proceeded, voters were to learn that even cutbacks in programs ostensibly targeted at the poor (such as medicaid) might have far-reaching consequences for nonpoor families.

The Contract with America, as well as the budget resolution approved by the House in May 1995, also contained radically redistributive tax cuts. Rather than concentrating on lower rates, the budget proposals were full of tax expenditures—activist government in conservative clothing. Many of these benefits were offered to businesses and were scheduled to start small but expand just beyond the budgetary horizon. The contract also called, however, for a significant expansion of the "hidden welfare state." Sharp cuts in on-budget spending were to be accompanied by new subsidies for "American Dream" savings accounts, adoption, long-term care insurance, elderly dependent care, and the costs of child rearing. The well-to-do elderly were to get more favorable treatment of their earnings, and the "marriage penalty" was to be reduced.

Since these subsidies had to be paid for by other people's taxes, borrowing, or cuts in spending, economists would say that these proposals were financially indistinguishable from the "tax and spend" initiatives that Republicans castigated. Politically, however, there are crucial differences. Tax expenditures generally subsidize private sector activity rather than building up the public sector. Unless specifically means-tested (like the EITC), they are extremely regressive and therefore highly favorable to important Republican constituencies.[48] Equally important, these new benefits for particular groups could be presented as "tax cuts" that simply give people back their money rather than as instances of government largesse. Furthermore, past experience with tax expenditures suggests that while Republicans would get credit for introducing these benefits, voters were unlikely to attribute their good fortune to government for long. Thus Republicans could reap the political gains of new social spending without encouraging public tolerance for government action. In combination with the Republicans' proposals for deep cuts in on-budget spending, this tax subsidy package promised a sweeping redistribution of the costs and benefits of government.

The Republicans' structural project easily matched this bold redistributive agenda. Republicans sought nothing less than a radical reduction in the political capacities of the federal government. This effort extended far beyond budgetary policy, involving an equally vigorous attack on the regulatory state. Yet the budget was seen as crucial. The Republicans advanced two major institutional reforms, the line item veto and a balanced budget amendment. Each proposal would change the rules in ways that strengthened the hands of those seeking retrenchment. Few analysts, however, expected that the line item veto would have much effect, and even the impact of a balanced budget amendment was open to serious question. Despite these uncertainties, each would signal the depth of Republican commitment to smaller government.

Of course, the budget cuts themselves were an essential part of the structural project. Lower spending meant smaller government in the short run, contributing directly to the main Republican agenda. Moreover, by creating an intensely Darwinian budgetary climate, Republicans could also pit the constituencies for government spending against each other. With large parts of the budget—defense, interest payments, and social security—off limits, competition among other groups promised to make the Democrats' job of coalition building more difficult. Finally, because government programs often provided an important resource base for groups favoring the Democrats, spending reductions would further weaken these constituencies, possibly clearing the way for further cutbacks in the future.

The tax cuts were also a crucial component of structural reform. Indeed, by 1994 many leading Republicans saw tax levels, not the budget, as the decisive issue in American politics. In the long run, they argued, it was tax rates that determined the size of government. This legacy of Reagan had become increasingly prominent in the Republican party following the traumatic rebellion over Bush's 1990 budget initiative.[49] The revolt, which had signaled the ascendance of the Gingrich wing of the party, established the priority of tax reductions as a litmus test for true believers. Rather than achieving fiscal stabilization, the goal was to establish a dynamic in which tax cuts forced spending cuts, allowing further tax cuts, and so on. The 1995 Republican budget plan met this structural goal not only by including large tax cuts, but by designing the cuts in such a way that they would grow just beyond the time horizon of the budget scorecards.[50]

Profound structural reforms also were contained in the policy revisions within the Republican budget. The most prominent and important were proposals related to devolution. As I will discuss in greater detail below, block grants were intended not just to meet spending targets for 2002 but to shift the balance of political power between spending advocates and their opponents and exploit the "competitive deregulation" potential of federalism. The devolutionary reforms of medicaid, aid to families with dependent children (AFDC), and other federal programs were not simply gambits for short-term spending reductions but radical initiatives to alter the relationship among policymaking institutions and curtail the long-term policy capacities of the federal government.

Finally, the budget process also became the favored vehicle for policy initiatives that would produce structural reforms but faced certain filibusters or vetoes if considered alone. Republicans sought to attach to major pieces of budget legislation proposals such as the Istook amendment (an aggressive effort to "defund the left" by restricting the political activities of those receiving federal money) and various curbs on regulatory authority. Thus changes in budgeting rules, spending cuts, lower taxes, devolution, and scattered institutional reforms were all part of a systematic assault on the long-term possibilities for activist government.

Advantages and Problems for the Republicans

In pursuing this ambitious budget strategy, Republican reformers had several advantages over their Democratic predecessors. As mentioned at the outset, while Democrats pursued deficit reduction as a prelude to their principal agenda, the Republican proposals *embodied* Republican goals. The Republicans' budget strategy had far greater potential for advancing structural reform and redistributing resources toward their key constituencies. While the proposals required a great deal of pain, the bulk of it would be felt by those outside the Republican coalition. Their tax cut proposals would also provide tangible benefits for important supporters.

Deficit reduction also played to Republican rhetorical strengths. Unlike the Democrats, Republicans had no need to engage in torturous reasoning about "reinventing" government or cutting bad and inefficient programs to make room for more effective ones. Rather, they could hammer away at simple, familiar, and Republican-friendly themes: government had gotten too big, programs were out of control, Americans had to take back their lives from Washington bureaucrats. Persuading voters to support smaller government was a task that Republicans could embrace with conviction.

In politics, the sequence of strategic action is often crucial. Republicans benefited in several respects from going second. Ironically, it was Clinton's previous actions on the deficit, fiercely opposed by Republicans, that gave the Gingrich coalition its biggest boost. With Clinton having brought the deficit part of the way down, Republicans could plausibly set their sights on the one deficit reduction goal that might truly capture the public's imagination: a balanced budget.[51] Gingrich, in particular, was convinced that the possibility of reaching zero was a tremendous opportunity and argued vigorously against those (including John Kasich) who advocated a more modest target. A great believer in the role of symbols (especially numerical ones), the Speaker saw a unique opportunity to frame deficit reduction in the heroic terms that would make it an achievable goal.[52]

The enthusiasm that Democrats, and Clinton in particular, had shown for deficit reduction two years earlier also made it difficult for them to criticize the Republicans' zeal for a balanced budget. By 1995 a fierce commitment (at least rhetorically) to deficit reduction had become a bipartisan consensus. The political cover this situation presented was potentially invaluable. Given the possibilities for blame generation associated with deficit reduction, this apparent disarming of the political opposition represented a rare advantage. There is considerable evidence that the absence of such political cover from the opposing party has created major obstacles to retrenchment initiatives, both in the United States and abroad.[53]

The lessons drawn from the 1994 election further bolstered Republican resolve. The Democrats' debacle at the polls helped to keep Republicans' feet to the fire: deficit reduction might anger people, but failing to bring about "real change" would create even bigger electoral problems. The message from the states reinforced this interpretation. Republican leaders made much of John Engler's experience. The Michigan governor had plummeted in the polls following the introduction of tough budget cuts, only to recover and win reelection by a landslide. In explaining its strategy to the congressional rank and file, the Republican leadership recited the same message over and over: making the hard choices now would pay off in the end, as voters rewarded a party that kept its promises. Engler became the toast of Republican Washington, often brought in to rally wavering congressional troops when the going was rough.

Republicans had learned not only from the 1994 elections but from more than a decade of experience with deficit politics. Although there were inevitable tactical blunders (such as the school lunch issue and the early talk of orphanages), the Republican initiative was generally well orchestrated. The immediate exemption of social security, the stress on medicare's financial problems and the need to "save" it, the backloading of the most severe cutbacks, the simultaneous assault on a broad range of issues to disorganize, divide, and demoralize opponents, and the reliance on block grants and the empowering of states were all responses to previous failed attempts at budget cutting.

The most important tactical initiative was to control the way that the central issues were framed. Given the complexity of modern policy-making and the weak information base of most voters, the focus of public attention was crucial. Tremendous advantages could be gained through concentrating debate on the most favorable dimensions of political action.[54] Drawing on the opportunities created by the Perot campaign, Clinton's 1993 deficit reduction plan, and a prevalent perspective in the elite media, the Republicans made a continual effort to direct the spotlight on the goal of a balanced budget. As Gingrich observed, "Balancing the budget [is] the only fight which allows you to focus the country's attention on reshaping the entire federal government."[55] House Majority Leader Dick Armey was even more blunt: "Balancing the budget in my mind is the attention-getting device that enables me to reduce the size of government. Because the national concern over the deficit is larger than life. . . . So I take what I can get and focus it on the job I want. If you're anxious about the deficit, then let me use your anxiety to cut the size of government."[56]

This attempt to focus attention was one of the main purposes of the initiatives to obtain a line item veto and balanced budget amendment. The powerful image of protecting children, which Democrats had long enlisted in support of social spending, was appropriated to underline the moral imperative of a reduced national debt. The Republicans continuously emphasized the crusade to clean up the deficit mess rather than their plans to cut specific programs. Their hope was that by shifting discussion to the target of a balanced budget, they could transform the politics of program cutting from an exercise in blame avoidance into an opportunity for credit claiming.

A final important advantage for Republican strategists was the state-level electoral sweep that accompanied the change of power in Congress. Indeed, the prominence of devolution was the most striking change between the Contract with America developed in the summer of 1994 and the Republicans' actual legislative proposals.[57] Devolution presented important opportunities to avoid blame for unpopular cutbacks. Reform could be framed as a matter of getting government "closer to the people" and out of the hands of Washington bureaucrats rather than as an ugly business of undercutting support for the needy. Yet devolution would clearly promote retrenchment. The block grants themselves contained very considerable cuts in real spending, but this would be only the beginning. Especially for programs targeted at the poor, devolution would predictably create pressure at the state level to rein in spending.[58] Before

1994, such an initiative would have met fierce opposition from state-level officials, as was ultimately the case for Reagan's much milder New Federalism proposals of 1982.[59] With conservative Republicans now prominent at the state level, however, the political climate had changed. As a result, Republicans could hope to hand a large share of the deficit reduction effort over to the states through a potentially popular program of block grants.

Despite these considerable advantages, the Republican budget strategy remained a risky undertaking. Two major problems loomed. The first was the intrinsic political danger associated with serious deficit reduction. In the past, mild public sympathy for cutbacks had evaporated quickly as details of the proposed program reductions became more widely known. Three previous attempts to cut the deficit—in 1985, 1990, and 1993—had generated fierce political backlashes. And by 1994, most of the easy targets in the federal budget were long gone. The preceding decade had been a period of budgetary Darwinism, in which programs without politically convincing rationales or strong clienteles had fallen by the wayside. With defense spending, interest on the debt, and social security off limits, finding more than $200 billion in annual cuts was a formidable challenge. Democratic constituencies would be the first targets, of course, but voters the Republicans needed would be affected as well. The initial poll results—often a high-water mark for major policy initiatives—were not encouraging for Republicans: 60 percent opposition to the House budget resolution, 56 percent opposition to the Senate plan.[60]

The second problem was that while the Republican electoral victory was remarkable, it was still of limited scope. Despite having achieved historic breakthroughs in Congress, the Republicans had only a 53 percent majority in each chamber. Even a demoralized Democratic minority would be well placed to exploit the instruments of obstruction that characterize American institutions, especially in the Senate. More important, Republicans still faced a Democratic president. Clinton had been weakened considerably; his public insistence on his continued "relevance" in April 1995 was widely taken to suggest just the opposite. Yet he retained significant political resources: the veto and the presidency's inherent potential for rallying public opinion. The latter could be crucial where the Republicans' chosen course did not command broad popular support. The veto weapon was particularly important for the critical issue of entitlement reform. Congress had leverage in pursuing discretionary spending cuts, since future spending required new legislation. In the case of entitlements, by contrast, spending would continue unless a new agreement was reached.

The Unreconciled Tension between Republican Unity and Public Appeal

The thin congressional majorities were also worrisome because Republicans had to cope with substantial internal cleavages. As had been true for the Democrats in 1993, there were deep disagreements within the Republican coalition over the redistributive elements of their plan. An important source of division concerned existing government spending. Many Republican constituencies relied heavily on federal largesse, and their demands created major problems in crafting such radical reforms. Among the most important groups were defense interests, the farm lobby, and the recipients of what came to be called "corporate welfare." Moderates, especially in the Northeast, worried about the political ramifications of major cuts in social programs.

The sharpest internal divide, however, was over taxes. Many House Republicans saw tax cuts as the most important part of the package, but moderates worried about the distributional implications while fiscal conservatives saw large cuts as irresponsible. Before the tax cuts reached the House floor, 102 Republicans—almost half the Republican caucus—wrote to Gingrich asking that the income ceiling for the child tax credit be reduced from $200,000 to $95,000. On average, Senate Republicans were more concerned about deficit reduction and blanched at the magnitude of spending cuts required to yield both a balanced budget and substantial tax cuts. Like the House, however, the Senate contained sharp divisions on the issue, with a growing faction that placed tax cuts front and center. This cleavage was certain to produce serious conflicts during the legislative process, and the Clinton administration could be expected to exploit such divisions.

Given the modest size of their majorities, Republican strategists faced two potential dangers in advancing their budget agenda. Failure to accommodate important interests within the party could undermine the internal cohesion that was crucial to Republican success. Yet accommodation to particular interests might produce a package that was politically unpopular. In broad terms, the Republicans appear to have decided that internal unity was more important: the most powerful interests within the coalition escaped relatively unscathed from the budget proposals. Indeed, many were generously rewarded by the tax provisions. The Republican strategy was to present a united front and take their chances that the public's eagerness for reform would lead it to tolerate a package heavily skewed toward core Republican constituencies.

One factor pushing Republican strategists to the right was their determination to avoid the kind of centrist, bipartisan outcome that had brought the party to grief in 1990. Given Clinton's desire for "triangulation," the existence of significant support for deficit reduction among congressional Democrats, and the considerable distance between moderate Republicans and the more committed supporters of radical reform, the possibility of such a centrist outcome was always present. The decision of the House leadership to stand up to moderates' calls for a more targeted child tax credit signaled early on that steps toward the center would be resisted. Fearful that such a move would split the party, the leadership held moderates on board with the traditional plea for party cohesion: to vote against the leadership would sink the party's agenda, with calamitous electoral consequences. Gingrich placed the vote on tax cuts, which he had termed the "crown jewel" of the contract, at the end of the first one hundred days, and correctly calculated that it would be politically impractical for moderates to defect. As Gingrich explained the task facing potential rebels: "You're now going to go to these guys and say, on final passage, why don't you kill the piece de resistance of the entire contract so you can go home . . . and have every Republican in your district ask you if you've lost your mind."[61] Although moderates had little success in watering down their party's more conservative initiatives, Republican solidarity remained impressive (except on environmental issues) throughout 1995.

For the most part, and for similar reasons, Republicans also rejected efforts to reach out to moderate and conservative Democrats. A significant faction of Democrats, the "Blue Dog" coalition, advanced a serious balanced budget proposal. Republican efforts to work with this group might have considerably weakened Clinton's position, undermining his strategy of triangulation. As Kent Weaver shows in his chapter, this was to be the case on welfare reform. On the budget, however, there was a large distance between the Republican proposal and the position of the Blue Dogs. This was especially true on taxes, where the Blue Dog proposal called for no cuts at all. The central status of tax cuts within the Republican agenda effectively precluded movement toward a bipartisan coalition.[62]

Of course, the Clinton administration was bound to seize the political opening that this strategic choice created. To the extent that the Republican leadership possessed a plan for dealing with this, it was based on the belief that the president was in a weak position and would back down if pushed. Although Clinton retained the veto power, House Republicans thought that the bargaining context gave them the upper hand. Clinton was in a strong position on entitlements, but failure to reach agreement on discretionary spending would have radical consequences: the "train wreck" of a government shutdown. Republicans signaled early on that they would use this weapon if necessary to force the administration to accept a balanced budget.

The upshot of this high-stakes bargaining game was a dramatic confrontation between the branches.[63] What House Budget Committee Chair John Kasich described as a remake of "High Noon" culminated in a string of high-level negotiations and two partial government shutdowns (one lasting a record twenty-one days). After negotiations collapsed in mid-January, Republicans were forced to retreat. Although they eventually succeeded in passing a tough reconciliation bill in late April 1996, forcing substantial cuts in domestic discretionary spending, the bill was only a modest first step toward the ambitious seven-year targets for discretionary programs. Even worse, the failure to reach agreement meant that structural reform would have to await the outcome of the 1996 election. The opportunity to lock in substantial changes in federal tax and spending policies had slipped away.

Disappointing as these policy outcomes were for Republicans, the political ramifications were at least as bad. The fight over the budget was the principal catalyst for Clinton's remarkable political comeback. As Republican poll numbers dropped, Clinton's approval rating reached the highest sustained level of his presidency. By the outset of the 1996 presidential campaign, Clinton had simultaneously consolidated his base and positioned himself to appeal to moderate swing voters. This striking reversal of fortunes suggested that the Republican revolution might well have been stopped rather than merely postponed.

The fierce conflict over the budget involved many twists and turns, and it is possible to give substantial weight to tactical choices and the impact of key personalities.[64] Certainly the Clinton administration's strategy was executed relatively well, while the Republican leadership made important blunders—most prominently Gingrich's well-publicized remarks that seemed to link the Republican decision to shut down the government to a perceived snub on Air Force One. Yet two deeper, linked factors run through the negotiations and help to account for the serious Republican setback.

The first factor was the dynamic of public opinion in response to a serious attempt to impose austerity. One can ask why Republicans miscalculated so badly, since the response of public opinion to serious budget cuts has been remarkably consistent both in the United States and abroad. Support for broad goals like budgetary balance gives way rather quickly once policymakers are forced to reveal concrete proposals for major reductions in planned expenditure. As publicity about the Republican budget increased, support dropped. Some of this had to do with specific missteps—for instance, a badly mishandled initiative on school lunches—and the effective campaign of Clinton and congressional Democrats, but the basic trend in public opinion conformed entirely to previous experience.

Republicans seriously misread this crucial political variable. While recognizing that public support for cutbacks was likely to be soft, the congressional leadership counted on the appeal of a balanced budget to keep the bottom from dropping out. Crucially, Republican strategists also believed their position would gradually improve as they received credit for making tough choices: "promises made, promises kept" was a central Republican slogan. This view understated the strength of public attachment to public programs. More important, it overlooked the *relational* character of public opinion on the budget and the way divided government transformed that relational quality into political trouble. Each downward step in approval for the Republicans translated into greater support for Clinton, which in turn increased the president's latitude to take a tougher public stance.

The relational quality of public attitudes on the budget revealed the flaw in the Engler analogy, which had been a key to Republican strategy. Republicans expected their poll ratings to drop but then to recover as they received credit for moving the budget toward balance. In a context of divided government, however, their legislative proposals increased the president's popularity, allowing him to move more aggressively to block Republican policy ambitions. The Republicans found themselves in the same position the Clinton administration had been in only a year before. Unable to deliver, Republicans bore the brunt of blame for unpopular decisions without achieving the legislative record necessary to claim credit for producing change.[65]

Despite internal divisions and some wavering, the White House seems to have grasped the potential of its position early on. Whether the Clinton administration had learned from bitter experience or simply benefited from the new opportunity to defend popular programs, it did an impressive job of taking its case to the electorate. The administration and its congressional allies employed a two-step strategy of first vigorously challenging the Republican plans and then slowly introducing Clinton's outline of a more moderate alternative. A series of gradual, partial concessions on the Republican demand for a true balanced budget suggested the president's willingness to compromise and contrasted with the Republicans' continuing threats of an imminent confrontation. At the same time, the administration effectively sought to refocus attention on Clinton's priorities—the overwhelmingly popular government responsibilities of medicare, education, and the environment—suggesting that a commitment to these goals represented the real point of disagreement.

As Mark Peterson's chapter shows, congressional Democrats and the administration achieved their greatest public relations success with medicare. Once the Republicans decided to pursue large tax cuts and take social security off the table, they were inevitably led to pursue major changes in medicare. It was not difficult for Democrats to determine that the program's prominence and significance for the middle class made it the ideal target for a public relations offensive. Republican efforts to convince the public that they sought only to save a medicare system verging on insolvency largely failed. The House leadership had some difficulty explaining why $270 billion in savings were required from a program facing a trust fund shortfall of roughly $100 billion. The proximity of the $270 billion figure to the $240 billion in Republican tax cuts made it easy for Democrats to argue that the cuts were being made to finance "tax breaks for the rich," a message they drove home relentlessly. Congressional Republicans had made great gains among the elderly in the 1994 election, but this crucial voting group moved away from the party in droves over the course of the budget fight. By the late spring of 1996, Clinton's lead over Dole among the elderly was over twenty points, the highest margin of any age group.

The medicare story was the most dramatic, but the same struggle was repeated on a smaller scale over other programs. Clinton positioned him-

self as the advocate of a "sensible" balanced budget that would eliminate the deficit while preserving his priorities. His stance allowed him
to walk a fine line, signaling both conviction in protecting programs (that
conveniently happened to be popular) and receptivity to a bipartisan
solution. The success of this strategy also strengthened his resolve and
his bargaining position.

The Republican misreading of public opinion proved costly. When the
final confrontation arrived in the two government shutdowns, the Republicans found themselves badly exposed. By almost two-to-one margins, the public blamed Republicans for the impasse and expressed
overwhelming hostility to their tactics. Not only had Clinton not capitu-
lated, but he had used the confrontation to restore his badly tarnished
image. Meanwhile, Republicans had expended a large share of their sizable and painfully constructed stock of political capital and had virtually no policy achievements to show for it.

That the battle of the budget ended without major policy changes in
1996 has much to do with the other important feature of the struggle: the
unwillingness, or inability, of the Republican leadership to accept a partial victory. Exactly what the Republicans could have obtained is impossible to determine. Yet by January 1996 the Clinton administration had
acceded to the Republican demand of a seven-year plan for a balanced
budget, scored by the Congressional Budget Office. The administration's
plan clearly involved some "creative" budgeting—cuts in outlays were
backloaded, and a tax cut was conveniently (and implausibly) scheduled to expire two years before the 2002 deadline for a zero deficit—but
it would nonetheless require major policy changes. Despite the fact that
all previous deficit reduction packages had involved tax increases, and
despite the unprecedented ambition of the deficit targets discussed in
1995, even the administration's plans called for *lower* taxes. Against the
backdrop of anything other than the Republicans' own proposals, this
stance represented a fundamental shift in policy, implying deep cuts in
public spending. Nor was it presented as the administration's bottom
line. Presumably, the Republicans could have pushed the president at
least somewhat further in their direction.

Table 4-1 indicates the rough outlines of the offers on the negotiating
table when bargaining broke down. These numbers should be treated
with some caution, but they indicate that the differences in spending
reductions between the two sides had actually closed considerably. More
fundamentally, they suggest the distance that had been traveled since

TABLE 4-1. *The Evolution of Budget Proposals, 1995–97*
Billions of dollars

| | Republicans | | Democrats | | Budget |
| | December 1995[a] | January 1996[a] | December 1995[a] | January 1996[a] | and tax acts |
Budget category					of 1997[b]
Medicare	201	154–68	97	102	112
Medicaid	116	85	37	52	7
Welfare	60	60	38	38	c
Discretionary	384	349	259	295	89[c]
Net tax cut[d]	−223	−117	−70	−17	−81

Sources: Ann Devroy and Eric Pianin, "Pessimism Grows on Budget Deal: Neither Side Sees Solution to Impasse," *Washington Post*, January 11, 1996, p. A1; and Congressional Budget Office, *The Economic and Budget Outlook: An Update* (September 1997), tables 10, 11.

a. Seven-year savings, 1996–2002.

b. Five-year savings, 1998–2002.

c. Excludes significant savings produced between January 1996 and the enactment of 1997 budget and tax acts.

d. Minus signs indicate increase in budget deficit.

October 1994. Neither plan on the table in January 1996 bore a remote resemblance to the rather similar deficit reduction initiatives of 1990 and 1993. Deficit reduction goals were more ambitious; tax increases had been replaced with tax cuts; program reductions were much larger than had been true previously and far more heavily skewed toward those of greatest importance to low-income groups. In short, Republicans had fundamentally refashioned the terms of debate.

In two respects, however, Clinton and the congressional Republicans remained far apart. The first dispute, which is suggested by the figures in table 4-1, concerned taxes. Support among Democrats for tax cuts had always been very limited, and the inclusion of tax cuts in Clinton's first budget plan of 1995 was widely criticized. As negotiations proceeded, and the Clinton administration was driven to accept tougher and tougher targets for deficit reductions, its position on taxes actually moved away from the Republicans. In order to protect Clinton's spending priorities, the tax cuts were scaled back and various tax subsidies ("corporate welfare") were reduced to offset the revenue loss.

As I have suggested, for key Republicans this aspect of the administration's position was simply unacceptable. For many of the first- and second-term members, and for elements of the leadership such as House Majority Leader Dick Armey, taxes were not just one part of the package but the centerpiece. To reach a balanced budget without sizable tax cuts would not represent the fundamental change they sought.

Not surprisingly, the second fundamental disagreement was on structural reform: the elements of the Republican budget proposal designed to induce a long-term shift in the political balance of power. The relatively small distance between Clinton and the Republicans on spending masked a chasm on structural changes in medicare, medicaid, and AFDC. Again, Republicans were reluctant to give up the opportunity to fundamentally restructure these programs. Reforms that would have produced irreversible changes in the basic governance of the American welfare state, which had seemed within reach a few months before, were hard to jettison.

Both items at the center of the dispute—taxes and structural reform— reveal clearly that for many Republicans deficit reduction had always been a means to an end. The broader objective of radically reduced policymaking capacity at the federal level required not just a balanced budget but continuing downward pressure on spending through lower taxes and the establishment of a more decentralized policymaking structure. For the more radical members of the Republican coalition, achieving a balanced budget without accomplishing these objectives would be a hollow victory.

By January 1996, however, these bold aspirations were clearly beyond reach. Even if he had wanted to, Clinton could not have moved much further toward the Republicans without losing the majority of an already skeptical caucus of congressional Democrats. In any event, given his rising approval ratings, the president saw little need for such a shift. The question at hand was whether Republicans would settle for reductions in spending that would have been unimaginable eighteen months earlier. In the heady atmosphere created by their new political strength, they would not.

As John Gilmour has recently argued, "strategic disagreement" occurs when a participant in negotiations chooses to reject agreement on terms that it appears to prefer to the status quo.[66] Gilmour suggests three principal reasons why strategic disagreement may occur: one side may believe it can do better at a later date, it may not wish to blur distinctions between the two sides in the public eye, or it may fear that the most zealous members of its own coalition will be outraged by an attempt at compromise. Of these three factors, the third seems to have been most central to the calculations of the Republican leadership. It is not clear whether Gingrich and Dole ever seriously contemplated an attempt to fashion a compromise, but the painful experience of 1990 must have made such an option unappealing. The positions many House Republicans had adopted by that point would have made it difficult for them to accept any proposal that could have commanded significant support among Democrats, so any agreement would likely have split the party. The Republican leadership preferred to walk away rather than risk this outcome. Instead of moving toward compromise, negotiations broke down and attention shifted to the presidential campaign. Republicans had gotten their train wreck; it was to take them a long time to find their way out of the debris.

The Strange Death of the Budget Deficit

Little more than a year after the dramatic collapse of negotiations, a freshly reelected President Clinton and the Republican leadership assembled to announce final agreement on a plan to balance the budget by 2002. The plan sailed rapidly and relatively uncontroversially through Congress, and Clinton was able to sign the twin bills, the Balanced Budget Act and Taxpayer Relief Act, in August 1997. How, after the bitter struggle of only a year before, did such a seemingly easy resolution emerge?

A critical factor in generating agreement was the improved budgetary situation itself. By early 1997, a variety of factors had substantially reduced the magnitude of reforms needed to generate budgetary balance. A relatively robust economy lowered outlays in some programs while enhancing tax revenues. Slower than expected growth in some spending areas, especially medicaid and medicare, also lowered projected deficits. Finally, cutbacks the Republicans had achieved in discretionary programs during 1995 and 1996 were producing significant savings. All in all, the package required far less painful choices than had been true only a year before. Again, a critical background condition was the already quite dramatic decline in the budget deficit that had occurred by the end of 1994.

Yet the lower financial hurdles were not enough to assure agreement. The relaxation of pressure to lower the deficit could just as easily have intensified demands for larger tax cuts or smaller spending cuts. Indeed, as deficit projections became ever more rosy over the course of the year, negotiators worried that the increasing latitude for new initiatives would jeopardize their search for compromise. The administration at times went to considerable lengths to hide indications that the deficit situation was improving.[67] A conviction on both sides that agreement was imperative remained crucial.

The rapid and relatively nonacrimonious achievement of consensus reflected the reluctance of each side to revisit the harsh conflicts of 1995. Republicans had received telling signals during 1996 about the dangers of confrontation and the possible rewards of bipartisanship. The Clinton administration badly wanted a balanced budget as a way of signaling a clear, tangible policy achievement, doubted that it could be sure of success in a second round of brinkmanship, and worried that a drawn-out conflict would jeopardize the possibilities for progress on other fronts.

The congressional leadership and the White House thus agreed fairly quickly on a basic formula of lowering their sights and meeting halfway. With more modest aspirations on overall savings, radical reform proposals would be jettisoned, and the two sides would basically split the difference in compromising among their remaining priorities. Each side would be given a few victories to take back to its constituents. For Clinton, the agreement allowed modest initiatives on health care and immigrant aid along with education tax credits for the middle class. For the Republicans, there were tight caps on discretionary spending and a variety of tax cuts, including lower capital gains and estate taxes and an expansion of individual retirement accounts.

Two fundamental features of the budget agreement stand out. First, the composition of the package was considerably to the right of all previous budget agreements signed since 1981 (that is, those of 1982, 1984, 1990, and 1993). Unlike earlier programs to reduce the deficit, this one included net tax reductions rather than increases. These tax reductions were not only heavily weighted toward the well-to-do but were designed to increase considerably in size over time. Indeed, while both the modest spending initiatives and the tax benefits for middle-income families (the education and child credits) declined in real terms over time (because they were not indexed), benefits for the affluent were carefully designed to start small (often producing net revenue increases in the first few years) but grow rapidly in later years. Funding for five of the six significant social program initiatives either terminates or declines after the first few years. Total spending on these initiatives is lower in the second five years (fiscal years 2003–2007) than in the first five years (1998–2002) of the budget plan. By contrast, the revenue loss from high-income tax cuts is over four times as great in the second five-year period as it is in the first period.[68] The front-loading of benefits for the middle class combined with the back-loading of benefits for the affluent provides a striking example of how policymakers manipulate the visibility of their activities in tailoring legislation.

In addition, despite the fact that the poor had taken by far the hardest hits from budget cuts in 1995 and 1996, little effort was made to mitigate the impact of austerity on these groups in the 1997 agreement.[69] Unlike 1990 and 1993, when the expansion of the earned income tax credit was a major part of deficit reduction packages, the Clinton administration's initiatives to add "balance" to the legislation seemed based on a median-voter strategy, clearly targeting the middle class. Thus both in its treatment of taxes (revenue cuts replacing revenue increases) and in its distribution of burdens and benefits, the 1997 agreement revealed the growing weight of Republican priorities in fiscal politics.

Yet one must also recognize the second fundamental characteristic of the 1997 agreement. Republican victories, while evident, were all modest elements of what remained an essentially incrementalist package.[70] Whatever the composition of the package might be, the package itself was simply not large enough to make much of a direct impact on the fiscal and policy posture of the federal government. The Congressional Budget Office recently estimated that the net tax reduction in the year 2007 as a result of the package would be $35 billion—about 1.4 percent of total federal revenues projected for that year ($2.45 trillion), or less than 0.3 percent of GDP.[71] The cap on discretionary spending is quite tight, but much of the pain is back-loaded until the last few years of the budget agreement and thus must be regarded as highly uncertain. In any event, this provision essentially continues the policy stance on discretionary spending of recent years.

Thus the final act of nearly twenty years of deficit sturm und drang ended on an oddly quiet note. The 1997 agreement made no bold departures. Rather, a bipartisan majority essentially pocketed the results of economic good fortune and the painful budget choices of 1990, 1993, and 1994–95, declared victory, and went home. Nothing symbolized this more clearly than the awkward news in the early fall of 1997 that the current budget was essentially in balance already, and that the greatly hyped new legislation would actually increase the deficit slightly in the short term.

Conclusion: After the Era of Deficit Politics?

For almost two decades, the deficit has been a crucial feature structuring political struggles over domestic reform. This centrality partly reflected actual trends in taxing and spending, especially the gradual loss of flexibility on both the revenue and expenditure sides. Yet the prominence of the deficit has also been a political construct. The evolution of both elite and mass opinion interacted with the incentives of politicians to turn a significant issue into something more like a moral crusade. For ambitious reformers, the budget's potential for escaping gridlock proved irresistible. Thus it is no accident that both of the major reform initiatives of the 1990s placed deficit reduction at their core.

This defining feature of recent American politics was not neutral. It fundamentally favored those who opposed an activist federal government. In the aftermath of Clinton's stunning political revival, itself in large part a result of the Republican effort to attack the deficit, this conclusion may be surprising. But Clinton's victory was made possible only by a dramatic retreat from his original aspirations. Although the deficit created opportunities and constraints for both coalitions, it was the constraints that were more evident for the Clinton administration. The administration's attempt at political jujitsu—seeking to turn a heavy burden into an advantage—was perhaps unavoidable but nonetheless disastrous. Activist government in the shadow of the deficit was a political impossibility.

The negative-sum nature of deficit reduction presented a profound challenge for Republican reformers as well, and they botched their first attempt to address the issue. Yet continuing public preoccupation with the deficit over almost twenty years reinforced a sense of an unwieldy government, and it provided a powerful weapon for attacking programs that have proven impervious to direct assault. Difficult as the process of confronting the deficit might be, Republicans possessed one considerable advantage over the long run. They, at least, were heading in the direction that they truly wished to travel. Thus, although Republicans failed to dismantle the core features of federal spending, they have engineered a considerable shift in the public debate and have placed an effective lid on public expenditure at a time when the maturation of entitlement programs might have seemed to imply inexorable expansion.

Recent history suggests that budget projections should be treated with great caution, but it now looks as though the country is entering a period when concern over the deficit will recede. If so, there will be new possibilities for quite different political struggles over taxes and spending. The deficit has been a factor for so long that it is hard to imagine what new dynamics will emerge. Within both parties, there will be those pushing for continued fiscal conservatism, with one eye on the debt and the other on the looming pressures associated with population aging. Yet others will certainly attempt to exploit this newfound fiscal flexibility for spending initiatives or more aggressive tax cuts. This essay suggests that those advocating tax cuts are likely to be in a stronger position. For twenty years, concern over the deficit helped sustain a near-constant refrain about the need to curb government activism and bring Washington under control. We are not simply returning to the predeficit era of American politics. Rather, we are entering a postdeficit era profoundly shaped by this long period of austerity.

Notes

1. David A. Stockman, *The Triumph of Politics* (Harper and Row, 1986), p. 262.

2. C. Eugene Steuerle, "Financing the American State at the Turn of the Century," in W. Elliot Brownlee, ed., *Funding the Modern American State, 1941-1995: The Rise and Fall of the Era of Easy Finance* (Woodrow Wilson Center Press and Cambridge University Press, 1996), pp. 409–44.

3. R. Kent Weaver, "The Politics of Blame Avoidance," *Journal of Public Policy*, vol. 6 (October–December 1986), pp. 371–98.

4. To make the discussion manageable, I focus only on the direct clashes over the budget and deficit reduction. As discussed in other chapters, the deficit has also had profound effects on policy disputes in every sector of government.

5. The best treatment of budget politics in the 1980s is Joseph White and Aaron Wildavsky, *The Deficit and the Public Interest* (University of California Press and Russell Sage Foundation, 1989).

6. C. Eugene Steuerle, *The Tax Decade: How Taxes Came to Dominate the Public Agenda* (Washington: Urban Institute Press, 1992).

7. For a discussion of the political implications of bracket indexation, see Paul Pierson, *Dismantling the Welfare State? Reagan, Thatcher, and the Politics of Retrenchment* (Cambridge University Press, 1994), pp. 153–55.

8. In this context, it is worth commenting on Daniel Patrick Moynihan's famous claim that Reagan's tax cuts represented a "Trojan horse," consciously introduced to sabotage the welfare state. Republicans quickly discovered that the deficit was a powerful weapon for enforcing expenditure constraint. However, the crucial decision to index tax brackets was actually proposed by Senate Republicans, was not expected to pass, and was initially opposed by the Reagan White House. For a detailed account, see R. Kent Weaver, *Automatic Government: The Politics of Indexation* (Brookings, 1988), chap. 9.

9. Steuerle, "Financing the American State."

10. Richard Rose, "Inheritance before Choice in Public Policy," *Journal of Theoretical Politics*, vol. 2 (July 1990), pp. 263–91; Paul Pierson, "The Politics of Pensions," in Keith G. Banting and Robin Boadway, eds., *The Reform of Retirement Policy* (Kingston: Queen's University, School of Public Policy Studies, 1996), pp. 273–93; and Joseph Cordes, "How Yesterday's Decisions Affect Today's Budget and Fiscal Options," in C. Eugene Steuerle and Masahiro Kawai, eds., *The New World Fiscal Order* (Washington: Urban Institute Press, 1996), pp. 95–116.

11. Among the European members of the OECD, total government outlays rose from 31.3 percent of GDP in 1960 to 47.6 percent in 1989, while in the United States they rose from 27 percent to 36.1 percent. Most of the spending rise in the United States was at the state and local level. Federal outlays in the United States were 18.3 percent of GDP in 1960 and 22.1 percent in 1989. OECD, *Historical Statistics, 1960-1990* (Paris: OECD, 1992), p. 68; and *Budget of the United States Government, Fiscal Year 1996, Historical Tables*, table 1.3.

12. See the comments of Norman Ornstein in "Symposium: President Clinton's Budget and Fiscal Policy: An Evaluation Two Budgets Later," *Public Budgeting and Finance*, vol. 14 (Fall 1994), pp. 7–10.

13. Bryan D. Jones, *Reconceiving Decision-Making in Democratic Politics: Attention, Choice, and Public Policy* (University of Chicago Press, 1994).

14. Stanley B. Greenberg, *Middle Class Dreams: The Politics and Power of the New American Majority* (Times Books, 1995).

15. See John A. Ferejohn and James Kuklinski, eds., *Information and Democratic Processes* (University of Illinois Press, 1990).

16. For evidence of these shifting rationales along with useful critiques, see White and Wildavsky, *Deficit and the Public Interest;* and James D. Savage, "Deficits and the Economy: The Case of the Clinton Administration and Interest Rates," *Public Budgeting and Finance*, vol. 14 (Spring 1994), pp. 96–112.

17. Quoted in Jason DeParle, "Rant/Listen, Exploit/Learn, Scare/Help, Manipulate/Lead," *New York Times Magazine*, January 28, 1996, p. 39.

18. It is difficult to distinguish between the pragmatic and the principled adoption of the "hawkish" stance on the deficit. One significant piece of evidence for the "cheap talk" hypothesis was the elaborate dance over a balanced budget amendment in the spring of 1995. Faced with the possibility that the amend-

ment might actually pass, a number of Democrats began a desperate search for a way out of their earlier verbal commitments to an amendment. Several had some success in redefining their position as an effort to protect social security, and others were taken off the hook when the Democrats successfully reached the magic number of thirty-four needed to block the proposal. All the Democrats were helped by the decision of Senator Mark Hatfield, Republican of Oregon, to oppose the amendment, since the outcry among his Republican colleagues drew attention away from the sharp divide between Republicans and Democrats on the issue. For a detailed discussion of this episode, see Elizabeth Drew, *Showdown: The Struggle between the Gingrich Congress and the Clinton White House* (Simon and Schuster, 1996), pp. 152–66, 189. This dynamic was repeated in the spring of 1997, when Republicans again predicted that they had enough support, only to fall one vote short in the Senate.

19. On systemic retrenchment—strategies to alter the political environment to facilitate long-term cutbacks in social programs—see Pierson, *Dismantling the Welfare State?* chap. 1.

20. On the concept of governmental capacities, see, for example, Peter Katzenstein, ed., *Between Power and Plenty* (University of Wisconsin Press, 1978); and Theda Skocpol, "Bringing the State Back In," in Peter B. Evans, Dietrich Rueschemeyer, and Theda Skocpol, eds., *Bringing the State Back In* (Cambridge University Press, 1985), pp. 3–37.

21. Terry M. Moe, "The Politics of Structural Choice," in Oliver E. Williamson, ed., *Organization Theory: From Chester Barnard to the Present and Beyond* (Oxford University Press, 1990), pp. 116–53.

22. Bob Woodward, *The Agenda: Inside the Clinton White House* (Simon and Schuster, 1994).

23. For discussions see Savage, "Deficits and the Economy"; and Paul Starobin, "Time to Get Real," *National Journal*, December 19, 1992, pp. 2878–82. Despite a tendency to reduce everything to a struggle between the "investment team" and the "deficit team," Woodward's *The Agenda* also contains useful information about the impact of financial markets on administration discussions.

24. One irony is that these estimates turned out to be way off the mark. With a recovery under way since the summer of 1992 and gathering steam, the deficit in 1993 would ultimately turn out to be $255 billion.

25. This argument presents an important case of what Charles Lindblom has called the "imprisoning" effects of markets in democratic polities. Business and financial interests exert influence not only through overt lobbying but through the market signals that induce politicians to gravitate toward particular policies. Charles E. Lindblom, *Politics and Markets* (Basic Books, 1977).

26. Greenberg, *Middle Class Dreams*.

27. On the 1990 accord and its electoral implications for Republicans, see Gary C. Jacobson, "Deficit-Cutting Politics and Congressional Elections," *Political*

Science Quarterly, vol. 108 (Fall 1993), pp. 375–402. For an excellent discussion of the growing strength of antitax sentiments in the Republican congressional delegation, see Dan Balz and Ronald Brownstein, *Storming the Gates: Protest Politics and the Republican Revival* (Little, Brown, 1996), pp. 126–58.

28. Bryan D. Jones and Billy Hall, "Issue Expansion in the Early Clinton Administration: Health Care and Deficit Reduction," in Bryan D. Jones, ed., *The New American Politics: Reflections on Political Change and the Clinton Administration* (Boulder: Westview Press, 1995), p. 197.

29. Viveca Novak, "Spending Spree?" *National Journal*, February 27, 1993, p. 510.

30. I have already discussed the reasons why a third option—an aggressive effort to scale back entitlements—was not seriously considered.

31. Christopher Howard, *The Hidden Welfare State: Tax Expenditures and Social Policy* (Princeton University Press, 1997).

32. In 1993, the revenue loss from tax expenditures totaled $49.4 billion for corporate retirement pensions, $46.9 billion for corporate health insurance, and $78.2 billion from the mortgage interest deduction and other tax breaks for homeownership. *Budget of the United States Government, Analytical Perspectives, Fiscal Year 1995*, table 6.2. Tax expenditures tend to be regressive because high-income households are generally able to spend more on the activities that are subsidized, and the value of the deduction is greatly affected by one's tax bracket. Households earning more than $30,000 a year received 97.7 percent of the value of the mortgage interest deduction, with 59.1 percent going to households earning at least $75,000. Joint Committee on Taxation, *Estimates of Federal Tax Expenditures for Fiscal Years 1994-1998* (Government Printing Office, 1993).

33. See Robert Eisner, *How Real Is the Federal Deficit?* (Free Press, 1986).

34. A capital budget would have made the deficit look far less imposing. In fiscal year 1995, the federal government spent $20 billion on direct nondefense capital projects, $38 billion on grants to states and localities for such projects, $69 billion on research and development (including defense), and $47.2 billion on educational grants. Louis Jacobson, "A Capital Idea, or a Fiscal Sand Trap?" *National Journal*, April 1, 1995, pp. 816–17.

35. Though interview comments by Letitia Chambers, chief budget adviser to the transition team, and John Dill, counsel to the transition's budget group, point vaguely to ambitions along those lines. See Viveca Novak, "Previewing Bill Clinton's First Budget," *National Journal*, January 9, 1993, pp. 83–86. Labor Secretary Robert Reich tried to persuade Clinton to propose a capital budget in March 1995 in response to the balanced budget initiative of congressional Republicans, but the president rejected the idea. Drew, *Showdown*, p. 223.

36. On the difficulties of explaining complex policy arguments to inattentive publics, see R. Douglas Arnold, *The Logic of Congressional Action* (Yale University Press, 1990).

37. For a summary of the many twists and turns, see *1993 Congressional Quarterly Almanac*, pp. 82–139.

38. It is unclear that the administration, and Clinton in particular, fully understood how severely these caps would eventually curtail his investment agenda. By one report, gradual recognition eventually produced an outburst from the president: "How could we not have spent more time on it? Why wasn't there a whole strategy on it? This is a Republican budget. We're Eisenhower Republicans!" Sidney Blumenthal, "The Education of a President," *New Yorker*, January 24, 1994, p. 37.

39. See Paul Pierson, "The Creeping Nationalization of Income Transfers in the United States, 1935–1994," in Stephan Leibfried and Paul Pierson, eds., *European Social Policy: Between Fragmentation and Integration* (Brookings, 1995), pp. 301–28. The EITC increase was scaled back from the administration's proposal of $28.3 billion over five years to $18.3 billion in the Senate to help plug the hole left when the Btu tax was dropped. Pressure from the Congressional Black Caucus led to the restoration of some funds in conference: the final total was $20.8 billion.

40. The severe impact of the caps would be evident by the time of the administration's second budget and would get worse over time. See Paul Leonard and Robert Greenstein, *Life under the Spending Caps: The Clinton Fiscal Year 1995 Budget* (Washington: Center on Budget and Policy Priorities, 1995); and Lance T. Leloup and Patrick T. Taylor, "The Policy Constraints of Deficit Reduction: President Clinton's 1995 Budget," *Public Budgeting and Finance*, vol. 14 (Summer 1994), pp. 3–25.

41. George Hager, "1993 Deal: Remembrance of Things Past," *Congressional Quarterly Weekly Report*, August 7, 1993, pp. 2130–31; and David R. Mayhew, "The Return to Unified Party Control under Clinton: How Much of a Difference in Lawmaking?" in Jones, ed., *New American Politics*, pp. 111–21.

42. Hager, "1993 Deal," p. 2131.

43. *1993 Congressional Quarterly Almanac*, pp. 140–45.

44. Paul Pierson, "The New Politics of the Welfare State," *World Politics*, vol. 48 (January 1996), pp. 143–79.

45. For evidence of the budget vote's contribution to the poor showing of Democrats in 1994, see John Ferejohn's chapter in this volume.

46. Pierson, *Dismantling the Welfare State?*

47. Some Republicans made an issue of the vocabulary for describing policy change, arguing that increases in nominal expenditures should not be described as cuts. The case for describing declines in real spending (that is, after correcting for inflation) as "cuts" seems fairly straightforward. Reductions from planned expenditures (which reflect growth in demand as well as sector-specific cost increases) raise more difficult issues of interpretation. Of course, Republicans have been happy to describe reductions in planned *tax* levels as "cuts," even

when legislative changes would still imply rises in nominal or even real levels of revenue. In this essay, "cuts" or "cutbacks" refer to reductions in planned expenditures.

48. High-income households are generally able to spend more on the activities that are subsidized, and the value of the deduction is greatly affected by one's tax bracket: high-income families are subsidized 33 cents for every dollar spent, while working class families receive a subsidy of only 15 cents. The poor, who pay no income taxes, receive no benefits from such programs.

49. Balz and Brownstein, *Storming the Gates*, pp. 130–50.

50. In February the Congressional Joint Tax Committee estimated that while the five-year cost of the House Republican tax proposals was a little over $200 billion, the ten-year cost would exceed $700 billion. Eric Pianin, "Budget-Balancing Considerations Weaken Hill Push for Tax Cuts," *Washington Post*, February 8, 1995, p. A4. For a discussion of some of these provisions, see Philip Harvey, Theodore R. Marmor, and Jerry L. Mashaw, "Gingrich's Time Bomb: The Consequences of the Contract," *The American Prospect*, no. 21 (Spring 1995), pp. 44–52.

51. Herbert Stein, "Board of Contributors: What Happened?" *Wall Street Journal*, May 31, 1995, p. A16.

52. Drew, *Showdown*, p. 85.

53. Pierson, "New Politics of the Welfare State."

54. See especially Jones, *Reconceiving Decision-Making*; and John W. Kingdon, *Agendas, Alternatives, and Public Policies* (HarperCollins, 1984).

55. Drew, *Showdown*, p. 85.

56. Balz and Brownstein, *Storming the Gates*, p. 154.

57. For an excellent discussion see R. Kent Weaver, "Deficits and Devolution in the 104th Congress," *Publius*, vol. 26 (Summer 1996), pp. 45–85.

58. Paul E. Peterson, *The Price of Federalism* (Brookings, 1995).

59. Timothy Conlan, *New Federalism: Intergovernmental Reform from Nixon to Reagan* (Brookings, 1988).

60. *Washington Post*–ABC News Survey, May 10–14, 1995, in Richard Morin, "Poll Finds Disapproval of GOP's Budget Plans," *Washington Post*, May 16, 1995, p. A1.

61. Eric Pianin, "Domenici to Attack Deficit and Ignore GOP Tax Cut," *Washington Post*, March 29, 1995, p. A4. On this incident see also Drew, *Showdown*, pp. 172–83.

62. The only occasion on which such a coalition became salient was during the first government shutdown. Indications that many moderate Democrats were drifting toward agreement with Republicans on plans to reopen the government appear to have played a role in pushing Clinton toward a stopgap agreement.

63. For useful accounts see Drew, *Showdown*; Balz and Brownstein, *Storming the Gates*; and David Maraniss and Michael Weisskopf, *"Tell Newt to Shut Up!"* (Simon and Schuster, 1996).

178 Paul Pierson

64. For analyses along these lines see especially Drew, *Showdown*; and Maraniss and Weisskopf, *"Tell Newt to Shut Up!"*

65. Gingrich acknowledged as much: "We made a mistake. . . . We expected that there would be a slump in our poll numbers, but we didn't calculate that a surge in Clinton's numbers would cause him to dig in even more." See Gingrich quoted in Drew, *Showdown*, p. 360.

66. John B. Gilmour, *Strategic Disagreement: Stalemate in American Politics* (University of Pittsburgh Press, 1995).

67. At the beginning of 1997, the Office of Management and Budget was projecting a budget deficit for the fiscal year of just under $100 billion. The fiscal year 1997 deficit would ultimately be just $23 billion, 0.3 percent of GDP—the lowest figure since 1970. Congressional Budget Office, *Monthly Budget Review: Fiscal Year 1997* (October 3, 1997), p. 3.

68. Robert Greenstein, "Looking at the Details of the New Budget Legislation" (Washington: Center on Budget and Policy Priorities, August 12, 1997).

69. Entitlement programs for the poor constitute only 23 percent of entitlement spending but accounted for 93 percent of entitlement cuts (which totaled $65.6 billion for 1996–2002) introduced in the 104th Congress. Real appropriations for low-income discretionary programs fell by 10 percent from fiscal year 1995 to fiscal 1997, compared with a 5 percent drop for other domestic discretionary programs. Robert Greenstein, Richard Kogan, and Marion Nichols, "Bearing Most of the Burden: How Deficit Reduction during the 104th Congress Concentrated on Programs for the Poor" (Washington: Center on Budget and Policy Priorities, December 3, 1996).

70. Incrementalism became even more the order of the day when the Congressional Budget Office provided much more optimistic budget projections late in the negotiating process. With an extra $250 billion over five years to work with, negotiators backed away from the more painful subjects of discussions, such as more significant medicare reforms and possible adjustments to the consumer price index. They added more funds for Clinton's social initiatives and for tax cuts and eased up a bit on proposed cutbacks in discretionary spending.

71. Congressional Budget Office, *The Economic and Budget Outlook: An Update* (September 1997), tables 2, 10.

PART TWO

The Battle for the Middle Class

Chapter 5

The Politics of Health Care Policy: Overreaching in An Age of Polarization

Mark A. Peterson

FOR proponents of national health care reform, September 22, 1993, was a date to remember. After months of delay, President Bill Clinton was finally presenting to a joint session of Congress and the American public the kickoff of his comprehensive plan to reorganize the U.S. health care system to guarantee every American affordable universal health insurance coverage that can "never be taken away." Hillary Rodham Clinton, who formally orchestrated the formulation of the president's plan, called it "the Social Security Act of this generation, the reform that would establish the identity of the Democratic Party and be the defining legislation for generations to come."[1]

Little more than a year later, however, an entirely different persona, possessing an even more expansive view of history and the future, addressed the House of Representatives and the nation with a strikingly contrasting message. On January 3, 1995, the self-proclaimed Republican revolutionary Newt Gingrich presided as the new Speaker over the opening day of the first Republican House in two generations. Health care reform had gone down in flames the previous September, a defeat

I owe special thanks to the Robert Wood Johnson Foundation for an Investigator Award in Health Policy Research, which in addition to the Russell Sage Foundation supported the overall research project; Adam Gearing, Michael Aleprete, and especially Ranjan Chaudhuri for their research assistance; Ira Magaziner and Rima Cohen for sharing their files; all those who granted interviews; and R. Kent Weaver, Theodore Marmor, and Joseph White for suggestions that transformed this chapter.

that Republicans, under Gingrich's leadership, engineered and then leveraged in the 1994 midterm elections to help propel themselves into majorities in both chambers of Congress.

Driven by their goals of balancing the federal budget and reducing taxes, prerequisites to fulfilling the core objective of sharply curtailing the scope of government, Gingrich and his compatriots set their sights on something equally as daring as Clinton's proposed Health Security Act. Instead of offering a new, vast entitlement, they sought to shrink, privatize, and in some respects dismantle existing federal health care commitments. Hundreds of billions of dollars would be cut from projected federal expenditures for medicare and medicaid. Both programs would also be fundamentally restructured. Bill Clinton, politically emasculated, hardly seemed much of an obstacle. Yet within a year the Republican effort to reverse federal health care policy dramatically died just as assuredly and loudly as did Clinton's proposed health reforms. Clinton rode a backlash that he helped stimulate against Republican "extremism" to a second term in the White House.

Each party's health care agenda generated stiff and ultimately effective opposition, with profound implications for politics beyond the health policy domain. How is it that both parties perceived their opportunities for success so at odds with the realities? Why was neither party able to wrestle any kind of legislative victory on issues so prominent on its agenda and so tied to its political fortunes? What are the consequences of these respective policy failures for the course of the health care system? In the absence of explicit federal action, where is health policy being determined, and to what effect?

Both the Clinton administration and the congressional Republicans gambled that they could achieve major legislative successes that would in turn yield enormous political returns, literally shifting the electoral landscape. Although their predecessors had in the past been unable to enact comparable policy agendas, the political and institutional setting now offered new opportunities for legislative mastery. Health care thus emerged as a defining issue separating the increasingly polarized Republican and Democratic parties. The leadership of each party recognized and responded to the enormous political stakes involved. The unusual intensity of the interparty competition reflected significant changes in the political arena. Neither party waged its health care battle with only conventional lobbying in the legislative domain, where compromise is instrumental. Instead, each mounted a decidedly public campaign to woo the "detached middle"—people worried about economic and social dislocations but skeptical of government and politicians. Each party saw its proposed changes in the health care system as an opportunity to win the detached middle's allegiance, to mobilize the party's own loyal base, and to deal a strong blow to its opponents. But each party made serious miscalculations, and in the end neither could overcome resistance to major change in public policy. In response, the private sector launched an unprecedented revolution in the health care marketplace that would, directly and indirectly, make Republicans the claimants to a broader victory.

The Opportunities for Major Health Policy Change

The health policy domain of President Clinton's first term bore little resemblance to the setting that ensnared health care issues under previous presidents. To begin, the nature and dimension of the problems confronting the health care system had been transformed. Since the end of the Great Depression, insurance coverage had steadily expanded through a combination of more employers offering health benefits and new publicly financed programs for the elderly and poor. Starting in the mid-1980s, however, the ranks of the uninsured—mostly workers or their dependents—began to rise in number and as a proportion of the population. More significantly, the costs to employers, individuals, and state and federal governments of financing medical services appeared to escalate out of control. Health care expenditures emerged as a major concern in the 1970s, but by the early 1990s many business leaders, citizen group advocates, and policymakers had concluded that nothing short of government intervention would stem the tide. Medical inflation was 12 percent or higher each year, typically twice the overall consumer price index. Between 1970 and 1989, employer spending on wages and salaries, controlling for inflation, went up just 1 percent, but for health benefits, it rose 163 percent. In the fiscal year before the 1992 presidential election, federal expenditures for medicare climbed 13.4 percent and for medicaid, nearly 30 percent. State spending on medicaid rose 20.8 percent in real terms from 1990 to 1992 and climbed past 15 percent of state budgets. Despite the rise in public spending, more after-tax income of the elderly went to pay for medical care than before the start of the medicare program. Overall, by the end of the 1980s, the nation was committing nearly 12 percent of its gross domestic product to health care services, far more, and increasingly so, than any other advanced industrial state, all of which had systems that provided universal coverage. Employers, the middle-class electorate, and policymakers could no longer view health care reform as simply a matter of access for the uninsured: it necessarily became the business of everyone, from proponents of government expansion to advocates of public sector retrenchment.[2]

The institutional terrain in which the politics of federal health policy would play out had also changed significantly. The previous alliance of medical, business, and insurance interests that had always prevented the federal government from enacting comprehensive reform was split in every conceivable way.[3] For example, the membership of the American Medical Association (AMA) declined from an estimated 90 percent of physicians in private practice and over two-thirds of all physicians as recently as the 1960s to 41 percent in the 1990s. Scores of specialty organizations with an invigorated Washington presence, including the American College of Surgeons and American Academy of Family Physicians, challenged the AMA's position on health care reform and its role as medicine's voice. The AMA itself became more receptive to some versions of reform. By 1993 members of the Health Insurance Association of America (HIAA), the core trade association for the commercial insurance industry, issued only a third of the nation's private health insurance policies. Small carriers that could not do well under any reform regime had moved to the new Council for Affordable Health Care, and the largest carriers, which became heavily committed to managed care, departed to form the Alliance for Managed Competition. Changes in insurance practices, such as the movement toward experience rating individual employer groups and cherry picking employers with healthy workers, produced strains between the commercial insurers and the nonprofit plans represented by the Blue Cross–Blue Shield Association. Large employers felt they were paying for the health care of small business employees, while small employers challenged corporate willingness to support government intervention in the marketplace. The service sector was at odds with old-line manufacturers, and employers with union work forces, especially those with many early retirees, countered nonunion firms. In addition, although organized labor had declined significantly as a force in the workplace and as a coalition leader in the political arena, on the health care issue it was now joined by an array of increasingly politically sophisticated consumer, aging, disability, and religious groups.[4]

As shown in the chapter by John Ferejohn, Congress and its members had also changed in ways bearing great significance for health care policymaking. As a result of the institutional reforms begun in the early 1970s, the House of Representatives was no longer an institution dominated by the highly autonomous committees under the considerable influence of powerful baronial chairmen that blocked major health policy change in the past. On the one hand, along with the Senate, it had become far more fragmented, with individual members wielding greater influence as policy entrepreneurs. On the other hand, new rules and the invigoration of the party caucuses granted party leaders previously unavailable opportunities to manage legislation and encourage party-based coalitions. By the 1990s, committees of health jurisdiction had become neither the certain deathtraps of ambitious health care proposals nor reliable building blocks of successful coalitions. Both advocates and adversaries of major policy change had to develop alternative strategies for advancing their interests, each likely to begin with a partisan base.[5]

Bill Clinton's Strategy for Health Care Reform

On the closing day of the 103d Congress's first session, President Bill Clinton's Health Security Act was finally introduced after many delays and well after the "first one hundred days" deadline he announced upon taking office. The 1,342-page bill that the president presented—touted as "managed competition under a budget"—would affect every corner of the health care system.

A mandate on employers to offer and pay most of the costs of their employees' private health insurance, along with the retention of medicare as a public insurance program, would ensure coverage for most Americans. Subsidies for the unemployed and the poor, replacing medicaid, would fill the remaining gaps in coverage. All individuals, except medicare beneficiaries and employees of the largest businesses (which could establish their own alliances), would purchase their health insurance through "health alliances," nonprofit entities established by the states to oversee competing private insurance plans and provide plan information to consumers. All insurance plans would have to offer a standard package of comprehensive benefits, eventually including long-term care coverage and more extensive mental health protection. Seniors would also get pharmaceutical coverage, which, like most aspects of long-term care, was not currently provided by medicare. The Health Security Act would establish a web of government regulations designed to ensure the quality of insurance coverage, prevent risk selection, promote a more efficient allocation of physician specialties, and influence myriad other details of health system operation. Competition among plans within the mandatory health alliances and large corporate alliances would, the administration anticipated, effectively restrain costs while promoting quality. But to protect against cost escalations even in this newly defined world of competition, the government would impose insurance premium caps to keep overall health expenditures within specified spending targets. Private insurance and employer "shared responsibility" would be mixed with some public financing and government regulation to meet the standard of universal, affordable health care provided without interruption.[6]

By any measure this was a bold and sweeping initiative, probably more ambitious than anything proposed by any previous president. It was also initially popular. When Clinton first announced the plan in September, a *Washington Post*/ABC News poll at the time showed 67 percent of the public favored it, while only 20 percent were opposed.[7] Yet, a year later, the president's plan and all the alternatives to it, however modest, were dead. Congress recessed without ever having taken a floor vote in either house on any health care reform initiative.

Some analysts argue that this outcome was inevitable. According to Sven Steinmo and Jon Watts, the Madisonian decentralization of governing institutions in the United States, further fragmented by a series of late twentieth century party and congressional reforms, overwhelmingly biases the system against major policy change. Clinton's plan was doomed regardless of what he did or what the plan contained. But some of the very dynamics that appeared to further fragment influence and authority in American politics served to break up antireform coalitions that had effectively vetoed comprehensive plans in the past.[8]

Other observers posit that, in fact, it was health care reform that was well-nigh inevitable, and that the Clintons, by their bumbling, failed to deliver. As *Newsweek* put it, "the Clintons . . . squandered a historic opportunity."[9] This assessment ignores the broader institutional issues appropriately raised by Steinmo and Watts. It also fails to account for the particular challenge Clinton confronted resulting from the 1992 election. He was a plurality president who led the Democratic congressional candidate in only four House districts. His party lost seats in both the

House and Senate, producing one of the leanest postwar congressional majorities for a Democratic president. Any reform initiative would necessarily include regulatory provisions that imposed concentrated costs on well-organized stakeholders.[10] Several unanticipated intervening events—such as the fight to ratify NAFTA; the Whitewater investigations; crises in Russia, Haiti, and Bosnia; and, yes, administration blunders and personality clashes—aggravated the political situation.

In fact, health care reform was neither doomed nor foreordained. First, Clinton knew what he was up against. It was an audacious gamble for someone with a predilection for living "on the edge."[11] Perhaps, as Allen Schick intones, "a weak president should not make strong demands," but this one did, with reason.[12] Given the contributions of the rapidly growing medicare and medicaid programs to future federal deficits,[13] without health care reform there was little hope of redirecting federal financing toward the kinds of social investments Clinton desired or re-establishing the public credibility of federal action. Both were prerequisites for establishing a record that would generate greater popular support for himself and his party in the next election.[14]

Second, there was opportunity as well as risk. Long before Governor Bill Clinton plunged into the presidential lottery, health care reform had a momentum of its own, for reasons both practical and political. More people were uninsured, and everyone was struggling with unrelenting rising costs. The stunning come-from-behind special election victory in Pennsylvania of Democrat Harris Wofford to the U.S. Senate in 1991, with his explicit campaign focus on health care reform, firmly settled the issue on the agenda in minds of interest group leaders and elected officials.[15] Only 6 percent of the public nationally thought that the health care system was working "pretty well" and needed "only minor changes." Ninety-two percent favored either "fundamental changes" or "completely rebuilding" the health care system, a forty-year high. When he entered office, the public "favored Clinton and the Democrats over the Republicans . . . on improving health care" by 55 points.[16]

In addition, a significant proportion of the interest group community had the potential to be organized in support of a Democratic president's plans for reforming the health care system. Fully 85 percent of groups interested in the health care reform debate perceived "an important difference between the two major political parties" on this issue, and nearly 90 percent participated in at least one formal or ad hoc coalition to influence reform policymaking. Taken together, potential "Democratic tar-

get" groups—those who were interested in the issue of federal involvement in health and human services, favored government action to ensure universal insurance coverage, perceived an important distinction
between the parties, and participated in coalitions—represented about
half of the relevant interest organizations. And they possessed considerable resources of political relevance. Over 80 percent reported large or
medium-sized staffs (closely associated with the size of a group's revenues), and three-quarters had members in every or nearly every state.[17]

Reform would, as a result, be debated in "the most favorable conditions in this century."[18] Still, the substantial interests of stakeholders, the
complexity of the health care system, and the fragmentation of American political institutions meant that enacting legislation was going to
require all of the pieces fitting into place.

To exploit this opportunity, Clinton developed the strategy of using
the substantive design of his health security proposal and a public campaign on its behalf to capture the detached middle, excite its interest,
and compel enough bipartisan support in Congress to enact a bill. The
plan would have to attract multiple majority coalitions in a number of
congressional venues. To forestall a filibuster and points of order on projected additions to the deficit, it would also require a sixty-vote coalition
in the Senate either for reform itself or at least in opposition to stalemate.
When it came to final passage, the administration would thus need moderate and conservative Democrats and some moderate Republicans.[19]
The "center" in Congress would have to hold. Clinton's fatal miscalculation was to believe that this could be accomplished by innovative policy
design. Instead of dissipating the opposition and weaving together a
disparate coalition in support, as he intended, the very design of his
health initiative—and the manner in which it was drafted—revitalized
his opponents, especially conservative Republicans lying in wait; fueled
their rhetoric to instill fear in the public; and inhibited the mobilization
of organized allies.

Clinton's Legislative Strategies

There were three potential legislative strategies for bringing the congressional moderates along. First there was the conventional process
approach: working from the start with both Democrats and Republicans
to identify a viable reform alternative. Major social policy change in the

United States typically occurs only when legislation attracts substantial support from both parties. Nearly two-thirds of important laws from 1949 to 1994 had bipartisan majorities in the House. As the administration took office, the bipartisan strategy had at least surface appeal. The president had been elected as a self-proclaimed New Democrat, seeking solutions between the past divisions of American politics. Several Republican moderates, especially in the Senate, had a record of working earnestly in the health care reform vineyards and claimed that they were prepared to work with the administration.[20]

A bipartisan strategy at the policy formulation stage, however, was complicated by the contemporary congressional terrain. For the first time in history, Democratic leaders and committee and subcommittee chairs in both houses almost unanimously supported enactment of comprehensive health care reform. In the House, single-payer supporters represented the largest single bloc of members. They were unlikely to look favorably upon *starting* the debate from a position of compromise on first principles. Recent experience had also already tested the proposition that the key to unlocking health care reform was a bipartisan process. Neither the U.S. Bipartisan Commission on Comprehensive Health Care (Pepper commission) nor, soon after, a bipartisan group formed by Republican and Democratic senators from the Finance Committee and Labor and Human Resources Committee had been able to achieve a bipartisan consensus and move legislation.[21] Finally, bipartisan outcomes do not require bipartisan engagement early in the policy formulation process. Quite often the process is "copartisan," with "parallel" development of initiatives by the two parties, setting the stage for bargaining from these established positions, as happened with the social security crisis in the early 1980s.[22] Indeed, in 1993 Senate Republicans resisted starting discussions with Democrats about working out a deal until they had introduced their own bill.[23]

The second potential way to claim the middle ground involved identifying a specific legislative initiative that appealed to moderates in both parties. There were two possible variations to this median legislator approach. One was an incrementalist strategy, which would take the minimalist common denominator among most plans, such as forbidding the use of preexisting condition exclusions, and avoid the contentious issues of coverage expansion, cost control, and financing. The other median approach fell under the rubric of major reform: "pure managed competition," as identified by the Jackson Hole Group. Summed up by its main intellectual progenitor, Stanford economist Alain C. Enthoven, "Managed competition was meant to be a moderate, centrist approach, using market forces, minimal government controls, certainly no price controls."[24] Median legislator approaches, however, would have created enormous substantive and political problems for the administration. Evaluations of "moderate" proposals showed their potential to harm the middle class and their incapacity to stem the federal deficit tide.[25] Even more encompassing initiatives would run into trouble. The Managed Competition Act of 1993, a "pure" managed competition plan promoted by conservative House Democrat Jim Cooper of Tennessee that garnered substantial bipartisan support, fared poorly when scored by the Congressional Budget Office.[26]

To gain the support of moderates for a program that had the large political payoff he desired, Clinton chose a third approach that would blend together in one comprehensive plan features promoted by advocates to the left and to the right of center:

> Bringing everyone into an insurance pool would please the Left; letting private insurers and providers compete for business in that pool would please the Right. Letting market forces discipline inflation would please the Right; having a ceiling on overall spending, as a backup, would reassure the Left.[27]

The detached middle among the public wanted health security but worried about government. This plan solved the dilemma, Clinton thought, because it would ensure comprehensive benefits, but without overt taxation, without "government" insurance, and with private institutions, even for millions of Americans currently enrolled in the public medicaid program.

This "liberal synthesis," as Jacob Hacker labels it, emerged from an evolving intellectual milieu in the community of health policy specialists.[28] In the summer of 1992 Ira Magaziner, the long-time Clinton friend, campaign associate, and future engine of the president's health care task force, had begun a series of conversations with Paul Starr, a Princeton sociology professor who was then circulating a draft of his book manuscript, *The Logic of Health Care Reform*. It outlined the integration of liberal objectives for health care reform with the market-oriented approach of managed competition developed by Enthoven and the Jackson Hole Group. This represented the culmination of a number of efforts by designers of modified single-payer plans to introduce private insurance and some competition into a system overhaul grounded on government action.[29] These ideas provided the means to make the shift from conventional Democratic proposals for health care reform that worried moderates—such as the government-financed single-payer model or the pay-and-play alternative that would require employers to provide insurance or pay into a large public insurance program—and still lay claim to the Democratic heritage and single-payer coalition.

Once in office, the Clinton administration sought a coordinated strategy for drafting a formal presidential proposal and mobilizing support that would sustain the program's claim as centrist despite its unprecedented substantive scope and reassure the public and congressional moderates. It depended on transforming health care reform from a legislative, "inside Congress" issue to a major public campaign with all of the elements of electoral attention to rhetoric and mobilization.

Reflecting the bridge design of the health care plan, the theme of inclusiveness, and the depoliticized public rhetoric, the strategy for mobilizing interest group support had three essential components.[30] First, unions, aging groups, nursing associations, and a variety of consumer groups, liberal provider associations, religious associations, and organizations representing women, children, and minorities—mostly single-payer supporters committed to reform and universal coverage—were to be the administration's natural allies. They brought valuable resources to coalition building. Senior citizen associations had "the grassroots ability to be a counterweight to the small business groups" almost certain to be opponents of the president's plan. Consumer groups "have more credibility [with the public] than any other group on the health issue."[31] Second, potential allies outside the liberal base were to be enticed by features of the plan. The strategy was designed to "win significant enough business support, from both large and small businesses, to reassure conservative Democrats and moderate Republicans, and to overcome the almost certain opposition of . . . conservative business groups."[32] Third, recognizing the tensions within the previous antireform alliance, the administration would "keep the health industry divided, sector from sector and within sectors. . . . We need to both keep the different major sectors— doctors, hospitals, insurers, pharmaceuticals—shooting at each other, and we need to make sure some players in each sector are with us." Concluding that "we have to have *all* of these groups to win," interest-group liaison official Mike Lux observed that "the trick in passing health care reform has always been in part to figure out a package that can draw some business and provider support, while exciting the people who should be our base."[33]

This inclusive policy-package-as-political-strategy approach had to square several circles at once: engaging activist government without laboring under the charge of big government; financing universal coverage, even in the short run, without being singed by the dreaded "tax" word; stimulating enthusiasm and grass-roots activism in the Democratic party's base and organized groups long committed to universal health care while simultaneously attracting enough support from skeptics of reform in both parties to neutralize the influence of antagonists; and advertising the virtues of flexibility in deliberations while benefiting Clinton's own reelection by showing the middle class early tangible returns from the rapid implementation of reform.

Central to finding the right technical fix were the estimates of the program's cost and the revenues to be generated to pay for it. The success of the plan (or any plan) in Congress depended on the scoring of the bill by the Congressional Budget Office. Under the "pay-as-you-go" ("paygo") rules adopted by Congress in the 1990 Budget Enforcement Act, the administration needed the CBO's cautious analysts to confirm that the Health Security Act could get to universal coverage with its proposed financing structure and without exacerbating the federal deficit (a stipulation that pure managed competition, without some sort of budget caps, could not meet).[34] This had long been the major source of contention both among Clinton's advisers and with outside experts.

Using managed competition under a budget as a "third-way" bridge across the historical schisms in the health care reform debate was not implausible.[35] Moderates in both parties felt much more comfortable with this generic formulation than others that emerged from the Democrats' liberal wing or leadership. Even more conservative Republicans accepted that Clinton moved the debate toward a "common language" with which serious discussions could go forward.

No such convergence occurred, however. Clinton and his advisers had misjudged the position of too many Republicans on health care reform, the effects of increasing polarization on Capitol Hill, and the potency of the new antireform alliance of organized interests that worked in spirited conjunction with the large conservative Republican contingent in Congress.

An Effective Opposition

Republicans had been vulnerable on the issue when the 103d Congress opened. Many in the White House calculated that the GOP could not outright block and defeat reform, that members of Congress of either party could not face their constituents in the fall of 1994 without having taken some kind of favorable action. Prominent Republicans, such as Senate Minority Leader Robert Dole, did waffle on reform early in the debate. But by mid-1994, with the exception of moderates like Senator John Chafee, Republican of Rhode Island, who worked until the end to achieve a workable compromise, Republicans were dead set against passing reform.

Motivating the emerging Republican opposition was the reasonable belief among conservative activists that Clinton's proposed health care reform was not just a matter of policy but in fact a menace to their political future. They understood what the Clinton gamble was all about. Bipartisanship, even copartisanship, would be self-defeating for the GOP. House Minority Whip Newt Gingrich concluded very early on that it was essential to stall and defeat Clinton on all fronts, especially health care.[36] William Kristol, founder of the Project for a Republican Future (PRF), unleashed a series of memos (widely faxed throughout Washington), essays, and interviews arguing that Republicans should adopt a course of unrelenting opposition to the Clinton health care plan. Kristol wanted to "puncture the sense of inevitability" that surrounded health care reform even at the end of 1993 and early in 1994. This approach itself was a major gamble. For the Gingrich-Kristol faction to prevail, the GOP had to unify behind hostility to health care reform. Clinton's gamble required that only a limited number of Republican moderates side with reform. "Our most important problem, from the political side," recounted GOP pollster Bill McInturff, "was not letting those people defect and pass a health care plan."[37] The Republican opposition required an effective rhetoric to keep the "detached middle" from attaching to Clinton, influential allies among organized interests to deliver the message, and the time necessary to orchestrate the counteroffensive.

Clinton's strategy, ironically, granted his adversaries precisely what they needed. The administration's central miscalculation was attempting to formulate in precise legislative language a comprehensive policy initiative that compelled private institutions to provide universal coverage and cost control without relying on existing public agencies or explicit public funding, and to do so in accord with CBO scoring. The sheer complexity of the Health Security Act enervated allies and invigorated adversaries. Grass-roots mobilization by the administration's base groups was stalled because they were "having to devote enormous amounts of resources to educate their *activists*, let alone their members. . . . Until they get ahead of the curve on this process, grassroots pressures on our side will be relatively sparse."[38] Probably more important, the detail and complexity ceded to opponents the rhetorical edge. The Clinton plan could be characterized not as a simple extension of the predominantly employer-based insurance system but rather as big government, socialized medicine, a bureaucratic nightmare, a taking away of one's cherished choice of doctors, and any number of other indictments, without providing the means for an easy and concise response. As lamented by AARP's John Rother, "If you're explaining it, people's eyes glaze over. If you're attacking it, you need only that one rhetorical salvo."[39]

A conference room at the Citizens for a Sound Economy became the "nerve center" of the "No Name Coalition," the behind-the-scenes network of organizations unifying in opposition to reform. This coalition was determined to bury the Health Security Act under the oft-repeated label "government-run health care." It worked closely with Gingrich and other Republicans to develop and maintain a cohesive strategy of opposition.[40]

The National Federation of Independent Business (NFIB) led the charge against the Health Security Act. The most conservative of small business trade associations, it was implacably opposed to the employer mandate and regulatory provisions of the plan. With 600,000 members scattered across every state and congressional district, and with millions of dollars committed to its two-stage campaign of grass-roots mobilization and heavy inside lobbying against the president's proposal, the NFIB alone was a formidable source of opposition. Other groups with similar capabilities joined together against Clinton, including the National Restaurant Association, the Independent Insurance Agents of America, and the Christian Coalition and its allies. Large-scale hostile media campaigns were launched, in particular by the Pharmaceutical Manufacturers Association and the Health Insurance Association of America. The HIAA, most noted for its "Harry and Louise" television advertisements, invested $50 million in its media strategy and its overall lobbying effort. Although its ads aired in only a few selected markets, they were intended to spawn the impression of public doubt in districts of members of Congress who mattered the most. Press coverage of Harry and Louise gave them even more scope. HIAA activities "produced more than four hundred fifty thousand contacts with Congress—phone calls, visits, or letters—almost a thousand to *every* member of the House and Senate."[41]

The No Name Coalition strove to create the impression that "a spontaneous ground swell of [public] opposition was forming."[42] Bombarded with the message that Clinton proposed a government takeover of medical care that even threatened doctors and patients with jail terms if they violated the rules, the public grew increasingly worried about the ramifications of reform. Focus groups conducted by Republican pollsters revealed that people desired reform and supported Clinton's efforts but also highlighted their concern that government did not have the competence to do it right. Since the vast majority of the public had little comprehension of the core concepts upon which the administration's plan rested, their fears were easily aroused. Instead of stoking popular appeal by linking his plan to medicare and social security, symbols that most people understood and believed in, Clinton focused on managed competition and health alliances, foreign terms to most people. Much of the public, the detached middle largely unassociated with the kinds of organizations that could have countered these themes, was captured by the opposition's rhetoric.[43]

This rhetorical transformation of the health reform issue and an effective mobilization against reform could not be accomplished overnight. It did not have to be. While a number of external events intervened to postpone the drafting and announcement of the president's Health Security Act, the choice of managed competition under a budget as the framework, with multiple ancillary minutiae, took time to develop into workable provisions. People in the White House knew that "delay will embolden our opponents, and give them even more time to build their infrastructure and attack our general plan." "Delay proved fatal," indeed.[44] It mitigated the possibly divisive Republican dilemma about whether or not to stand in the way of health care reform in the face of initial popular support for it. Growing obstructionism by congressional Republicans—unanimously rejecting Clinton's 1993 budget act, defeating the president's economic stimulus package, exploiting the Senate filibuster as an instrument of partisan opposition—resulted in neither public gains for Clinton nor public damage to Republicans by the time attention turned to health care reform. Instead, Clinton's job approval never consistently rose much higher than his 43 percent of the popular vote in the 1992 election, while the GOP proceeded to win one congressional special election after another.

When the health debate lapsed into late 1994, Democrats in the House—already burned by the budget experience in 1993, when they voted to retain contentious provisions later dropped in the Senate—would not start floor debate on health care until they saw what provisions could attract the sixty Senate votes necessary to overcome a filibuster. At the same time, Gingrich and his colleagues were increasingly convinced that the Republicans would take back the House in the upcoming elections. Presidential electoral politics also intruded, as the competition for the Republican nomination between Senators Phil Gramm and Bob Dole pulled the Republican center of gravity further to the right on health care. In the House, serious participation by Republicans in efforts to reach a "moderate" compromise effectively ended. A frustrated President Clinton "complained . . . that Republicans moved 'further away' from a compromise on health care each time he reached out to them."[45]

Recognizing that momentum for reform was stalling, business and provider groups that had earlier shown support shifted ground. Expectations that reform would pass, with the belief that it was better to be on the train than run over by it, transformed into the realization that it might well be derailed altogether. The pivotal point in the debate came in the spring of 1994, when John Dingell, the powerhouse chairman of the House Energy and Commerce Committee and long-time advocate of health care reform, could not overcome the opposition of key moderate Democrats to muster the majority needed to report a bill. The groups took notice.[46] As Republicans in Congress enjoyed increased assurance about their own unity, they worked with the No Name Coalition and put pressure, both direct and indirect, on other traditional allies within the interest group community who were wavering on reform. "Lobbied by the lobbyists" and "read . . . the riot act" by Republican conservative activists in Congress, the U.S. Chamber of Commerce backed away from its earlier endorsement of employer mandates. The American Medical Association, facing a similar onslaught, reversed its previous support for employer-based universal coverage.[47]

The credibility and cover that the Clinton administration had hoped to generate for potential supporters in the middle evaporated, while a new antireform alliance of social conservatives, deficit hawks, business representatives, and talk radio hosts produced a powerful "lineup of the stars you just don't get in politics very often."[48] The coalition that was supposed to congeal in support of the president's approach—with all of the potential resources of organized labor, consumer groups, and senior advocacy organizations—never matched the unity, intensity, or resources of its opponents.

President Clinton's third-way strategy to enact health care reform and invigorate Democratic majorities in the future represented the triumph of hope over experience. Intended to merge many constituencies by bridging interests across the policy center, the Health Security Act ended up devoid of any real constituency, even the administration's presumed "base" groups. Liberal organizations participated actively at some levels but ultimately held back because their ardor for the plan, their trust in the administration, and their endorsements had never been secured.[49] Of the potential "Democratic target" groups described earlier, which the administration had to have on board, only 25 percent formally endorsed the president's plan, 23 percent supported it but withheld endorsement, and 49 percent supported some features but opposed others.[50] Instead of enticing moderates from both parties in Congress, Clinton's strategy helped feed the intensifying partisanship in Congress that led both parties away from bipartisanship—or copartisanship—on the issue without, oddly, ever exciting his own party's constituent base.

Republican Health Care: Vanguard without a Revolution

Just as enactment of national health care reform would have risked relegating Republicans to prolonged minority status, its defeat was a critical stepping-stone to the first GOP congressional majorities in two generations. Throughout 1994, Republicans engineered a "referendum" campaign against the president—"morphing" all Democratic congressional candidates into the image of Bill Clinton—and rode a wave of electoral discontent to capture the House and Senate. The Health Security Act, concluded Clinton's own pollster, was "the single item that most directly linked Clinton with big government" and became the centerpiece of the offensive.[51]

The congressional elections handed Republicans their own moment to execute an extraordinary but intriguing gamble, with the potential to reshape the landscape of American politics along conservative Republican contours. They sought not only to arrest the routine expansion of the

New Deal and Great Society social commitments but to actually "repeal the New Deal" altogether through sharply reduced taxes, intense deregulation, and programmatic devolution to states, localities, and the private sector.[52] If the Republicans could disrupt the federal social programs on which the detached middle had become most dependent, including the huge public health insurance programs, the Democrats would lose their claim on the middle-class electorate. Like Clinton before them, however, the Republican congressional leadership miscalculated how far favorable circumstances (by historical comparison), clever strategies, and public communication could take them, especially to overcome the one major obstacle in their way: the president's veto pen. It was now the turn of the congressional Democrats and the administration to recognize the imperative for their own future of defeating the Republican retrenchment and to exploit charges of extremism to prevent the public's acceptance of the conservative agenda.

Restructuring Medicare and Medicaid

The Republican gamble depended on two essential short-term achievements embedded in the Contract with America: massive tax cuts (defunding social programs) and a constitutional amendment to balance the budget (preventing the later rebuilding of the welfare state). Although the amendment fell short of the two-thirds needed, a balanced budget by 2002 became the mantra of the Republican agenda. The math was simple. Lowering taxes by $245 billion and increasing defense expenditures within the context of a balanced budget required enormous cuts of $450 billion in domestic programs. Political expediency kept social security, the largest program, off the table. Medicare and medicaid were the next most expensive programs and likely to grow substantially because of swelling beneficiary populations, advancing technology, and general medical inflation. They thus became natural targets.

Republicans proposed fundamental retrenchment and restructuring of these central embodiments of existing federal health care policy. Projected expenditures for the medicare program, which is entirely financed and administered (through private fiscal intermediaries) by the federal government, were to be reduced $270 billion over seven years. A budgetary cap would also have been imposed for the first time. House and Senate Republicans initially pursued somewhat different policy approaches but ultimately agreed to a package that included unprecedented provisions to implement the cost savings.[53] Some methods did have precedents in earlier Congresses. Those would have required affluent beneficiaries to pay somewhat higher premiums for Part B physician coverage, cut reimbursement rates to health care providers, and decreased subsidies to hospitals for medical education and serving disproportionately poor populations.

Most controversial were the provisions to transform the overall character of the program in respects that had not been considered before. The federal individual entitlement would remain, but it would be capped by moving many beneficiaries into a defined-contribution rather than defined-benefit program. There would be incentives for them to leave the existing public fee-for-service program, which offered the same standard benefits to everyone, and to accept vouchers of set value to choose their coverage from among a range of private insurance options, emphasizing managed care plans. Any difference between the voucher and the coverage selected would be paid out of pocket. In addition, medical savings accounts (MSAs) could be established with the vouchers. Funds that accumulated in the MSAs would pay for routine health care expenses. Money not expended could be saved toward expenses in future years. To protect against the costs of severe illnesses, part of the voucher would be used to purchase very high-deductible insurance.[54]

Conservatives argued that the voucher and MSA provisions would save money by enhancing competition and making people more cost conscious in their health care decisionmaking. MSAs, however, risked taking dollars that previously paid for delivering medical services and transferring them to the accounts of healthy beneficiaries with few if any medical expenses. The Congressional Budget Office cautiously scored the MSAs as costing—not saving—the medicare program $4.5 billion over seven years.[55]

Because medicaid is a state-administered program combining federal and state funding, and caters to a different clientele mix, the Republican approach to spending reductions there was even more dramatic. Although over 70 percent of medicaid spending covers services for the elderly and disabled, much of it for long-term care, about two-thirds of medicaid beneficiaries are women and children who typically obtain coverage as recipients of welfare benefits. Medicaid is thus often most identified with the poor people on welfare, a politically weak and relatively unpopular constituency.[56] Republican reforms would have replaced the explicit individual entitlement to medicaid coverage, as well as other federal health programs for the poor, with "medigrant" block grants to states using a needs-based formula. Under block grants, Washington would budget a set amount of federal funding each year and leave it to the states to determine how and in what form to provide health care coverage to the eligible population. States could supplement federal contributions but would not be required to do so. The vast majority of states would undoubtedly proceed with even greater intensity in their existing efforts, under waivers granted by the Clinton administration, to lower costs by incorporating voluntary or compulsory private managed care plans but without the federal standards.[57]

These types of initiatives helped to unify the slender Republican majorities in Congress. Deficit hawks, like Senator Pete Domenici and Representative John Kasich, the chairs of the Senate and House Budget Committees, wanted to end long years of federal deficit spending. Others saw an opportunity to strike at the heart of the welfare state, and its public base, by privatizing medicare and devolving medicaid, the most popular of welfare programs, to the states.[58] Despite pronounced variations in need, medicare beneficiaries were in a common pool that promoted a constituency with a common interest. Giving them choices in the private insurance market, and especially the opportunity to withdraw the funds into medical savings accounts, threatened to fragment that constituency and create competing and incompatible interests. Killing—astutely—existing middle-class entitlements was the basis for ensuring Republican majorities for years to come. Here was a payoff that was hard to ignore.

The risks of this enterprise were also difficult to ignore. These proposals were every bit as politically hazardous as Clinton's Health Security Act. Although medicare had been cut before, the size of the proposed cuts was unprecedented. Every member was keenly aware of what happened when Congress in the past dealt with medicare in a major way. Most recently, within a year of its heralded enactment, the Medicare Catastrophic Coverage Act was repealed as Congress bowed to the antagonisms of many elderly who were convinced—wrongly—that the program was going to cost them more and provide them less.[59]

A major problem for the congressional Republicans was the gap between their budget strategy, particularly as it applied to medicare, and public opinion. The medicare program was enormously popular with beneficiaries and one of the bulwarks of middle-class entitlements. The

Republican proposals threatened to hit at the heart of the middle-class electorate: both the seniors themselves and the children relieved of the burden of paying for their parents' health care. The public did not recognize anything broken in the medicare program that needed to be fixed. Republican polling results indicated rather starkly that they had to avoid talking about programmatic cuts, especially in the context of funding the tax cuts.[60] In addition, unlike Clinton, Republicans asserted their health policy agenda devoid of an identifiable popular mandate on the issue and without having made health care policy of any sort a defining attribute of their campaign agenda. Nothing was said in the Contract with America about restructuring medicare or medicaid or the major reductions in the growth of spending for these programs that would occupy so much of the later debate.

Congressional Republicans enjoyed a nearly unprecedented opportunity for surmounting these obstacles and risks, however. Democrats, shocked by their losses, were profoundly demoralized. The pall cast over the Clinton White House was so pronounced that the president had to insist publicly that he was still a player.[61] Even though the Republican majorities in the House and Senate were narrower than the Democratic majorities with which the administration unsuccessfully tried to forge health care reform (about twenty seats smaller in the House and three in the Senate), they started out with important coalitional advantages.

Clinton in the 103d Congress needed votes from a Democratic majority whose composition he had done little to effect. It remained ideologically divided over issues central to comprehensive health care reform: mandates, taxes, and regulation. On the issues resting at the heart of medicare and medicaid restructuring—privatization, deficit reduction, and reduced taxes—the new House Republican majority could hardly have achieved greater solidarity. And, as Paul Pierson's chapter argues, the emerging bipartisan consensus about the value of balancing the budget gave further advantage to the Republican health care agenda. The return of the Senate to Republican hands after almost ten years and the first Republican House since the mid-1950s further reinforced a spirit of cooperation among members of the Senate Republican conference.[62]

Republicans in the 104th Congress also learned a couple of important lessons from the Clinton experience. The first was to avoid policy approaches, designed to capture moderates, that would confuse or weaken the resolve of their base coalition. Given the political objectives of the Republican agenda and their consequences for the opposition, there was little to be gained by initiating or talking about a bipartisan process. Neither Democrats in Congress nor administration officials were invited to participate in the development of these programmatic initiatives.[63] Due to the coherence of the Republican majorities in both chambers, building majorities did not require explicit reaching out to moderate or even conservative Democrats.

The second lesson was to execute effectively the very stratagem that they had accused Clinton of trying with health care reform: ramming through a plan at the end of a legislative session with little advance notice of its contents. No details were released until a few weeks before the House vote. A single hearing was scheduled without the actual legislative language being made available. Those wishing to defeat the Republican initiative had little time for mobilization and none of the public specifics with which to launch an early rhetorical attack.[64]

Republican Strategies

Based on these political opportunities and lessons, the Republicans devised a four-part strategy for enacting their proposed changes in medicare and medicaid. First, as John Ferejohn reports in his chapter, House Republican leaders recognized and took advantage of institutional resources that facilitated forging majority coalitions under an aggressive leadership. The committees of jurisdiction—Ways and Means and Commerce—played almost no formal role in formulating the plan to restructure medicare. It was drafted by eight Republican members of Congress whom Gingrich specially chose as the "Speaker's design group," locking Democrats out of the conventional bill-writing process. With far more open rules, including the threat of filibusters, the Senate could not operate in the same terms. Still, early in 1995, "task forces made up of people not on the committees were established on various subjects, to act as an outside force on key issues." Trent Lott, the Senate Majority Whip, and fellow conservatives wanted to "control these committees and their chairmen."[65] The controversial initiatives could thus be written quickly, quietly, and with maximum leverage on Republican members to go along.

This legislative strategy was assisted by budgetary rules that were not available to Bill Clinton for health care reform. Because the medicare and medicaid changes were embedded in the overall budget plan and had deficit-reducing elements, they could be included in the reconciliation bill if and when necessary. That would facilitate orchestrating up-or-down votes on broad packages of both popular (tax cuts) and politically difficult provisions. Only simple majority votes in both houses would be required, since reconciliation bills are protected from filibusters and holds in the Senate. Gingrich had institutionally stripped away many of the problems previously created by a fragmented legislature. Reconciliation ensured the further centralization of the legislative process, giving full advantage to a unified majority party directed by a forceful leadership.

To bolster the legislative regime, the second component of the Republicans' strategy entailed mobilizing support from its powerful allies in the interest group community and silencing potential critics. The first task was fairly straightforward. The campaign to defeat health care reform had invigorated the alliance of conservative Republicans now in command of Congress with the business association and movement activists that had joined forces in the No Name Coalition. Now the alliance was out in the open, "an unambiguous collaboration of political and commercial interests" with "the roles of legislator and lobbyist blurred."[66]

The antigovernment network met as the "Thursday Group" each week, chaired by Representative John Boehner of Ohio and Senator Paul Coverdell of Georgia, to coordinate lobbying and grass-roots support for each element of the Contract with America and other Republican initiatives. Within this framework the Coalition to Save Medicare was established. An alliance of the Healthcare Leadership Council, pharmaceutical companies, the insurance industry, hospitals, and conservative senior groups, it was the organizational wing of the legislative campaign to restructure federal health policy.[67]

But for an issue as volatile as medicare reform, Republican leaders also had to neutralize the likely opposition. The two potentially strongest threats to the medicare (and medicaid) spending reductions—the American Association of Retired Persons (AARP) and medical providers—were treated to specific tactics to mute or limit any opposition. Republicans started by attacking the AARP, questioning its tax status.[68] In the course of writing the medicare proposal, however, Gingrich dealt directly but quietly with the AARP leadership. These discussions moderated some of the initial features of the plan, including provisions that would have made staying in the standard medicare program less attractive. Only after the AARP could not win any significant scaling back of the $270 billion spending reductions did it launch a public, national campaign against the Republican efforts, but this came much later and with more restraint than would otherwise have been anticipated.[69]

Provider and insurance organizations were shown both the carrot and the stick. Gingrich offered to engage the groups directly but with the proviso of "no public dissent" and acceptance of the overall $450 billion reductions in federal medical expenditures. Before getting the message, the American Hospital Association announced its usual public position that cuts of the magnitude being discussed would "devastate medicare." Soon it found itself shut out of meetings and roundly assailed by members of Congress.[70] The AMA, a more natural Republican ally but representing the physicians who could take a big hit in reimbursements, negotiated explicitly with the Speaker. In the process it won enough concessions—including provisions that would facilitate the development of physician-run health plans without the usual financial reserve requirements and promote medical savings accounts without any limits on physician billing—to announce its endorsement of the Republican reforms.[71] A subdued AARP, chastened AHA, and a supportive AMA went a long way toward enfeebling organized opposition to enactment of the health care proposals.

The most dangerous aspect of the Republican agenda was the possible ignition of a public outcry against the proposed policy changes, especially in medicare. As the third leg of their strategy, Republican leaders engineered both a general and specific plan for diffusing public objections to the restructuring of medicare and medicaid.

To begin, following the Reagan budget-cutting strategy of 1981, the controversial reductions in projected spending would be subsumed within the context of the overall economic plan, complete with popular proposals to cut taxes and reduce government intrusiveness. Gingrich and his compatriots sought to make this scheme work within their overall attack on Washington. They knew that there had been "a collapse of faith in government and the political system itself," and that the percentage of citizens who thought the federal government would do "what is right most of the time" was at a historic low.[72] They could present their proposed changes in medicare and medicaid as the means for contracting the reach of Washington and rebuilding faith in a political system newly dedicated to individual aspiration and achievement within the free enterprise system. In addition, not only would they claim to preserve appropriate social commitments, they were reengineering programs like medicaid that were currently "abusing the poor" by "creating a culture of poverty." For medicare, polls and focus groups accentuated the desirability of avoiding terms like "changing medicare," "caps," "cut," or "freeze." They were not cutting the program, but simply "slowing the rate of growth" as a result of improvements that would provide more choices to beneficiaries.[73]

As they were searching for the most effective language, the medicare board of trustees issued its annual report, which warned that the Hospital Insurance Trust Fund, which finances Part A of the program, would be depleted by the year 2002 unless programmatic changes were made. Although the annual reports had issued similar alerts nine times since 1970, to little fanfare, the timing on this occasion, in the words of RNC chair Haley Barbour, was "manna from heaven." Now Republicans would present themselves as "saving medicare from bankruptcy," which Clinton and the Democrats were otherwise letting fall into ruin. After much poll testing and wordsmith refinement, the message settled on a Gingrichian trilogy that mimicked the presidential oath of office: the GOP plans would "preserve, protect, and strengthen" medicare.[74] This line would be sold to the detached middle using the full scope of modern political communications technology.

The final component of the strategy for winning the gamble—dealing with President Clinton—was quite simple. In the face of Republican unity, the mobilization of allied groups and the silencing of the organized opposition, and a public campaign to save medicare and return government to the people, Clinton would not have any choice. He would have to go along. Gingrich and his colleagues "dismissed Clinton as a weak, irrelevant President who would cave under their pressure. They could bend and break him; he would be compelled to accept their budget demands." Gingrich thus wagered that the last potential hurdle for the Republican health care revolution—the constitutional provision of presidential veto authority—would become moot. Clinton would sign the budget on Republican terms.[75]

Compared with the humiliation that President Clinton experienced with health care reform, the Republicans appeared to be on the road to a stunning success. On November 17, 1995, the House and Senate approved the budget reconciliation bill that included the GOP plans for revamping medicare and medicaid, reducing their spending over the next seven years by $270 billion and $163 billion, respectively, and restructuring the programs almost precisely as Republicans had proposed. The legislative part of the strategy had worked. These were stark party-line votes,

237–189 in the House (five Democrats joining the GOP, one Republican defecting) and 52–47 in the Senate (with no Democratic votes and one Republican defection).[76] Unity within their party ranks, the effective use of institutional instruments of legislative leadership (reconciliation and Speaker's powers), and enough political mobilization to maintain the confidence of Republican members in the political viability of their agenda yielded a first-order success.

For a while, President Clinton looked like he might actually fulfill the Republican strategy for him. He vacillated in support of his own 1993 budget and then contributed to legitimizing the Republican rhetorical campaign by initially adapting to their terms of debate. In response to the Republican agenda, congressional Democrats had immediately launched into opposition, attacking the plans for medicare and challenging the very presumption of balancing the budget in seven years. They sensed that they were making political headway, despite the secrecy associated with the development of the programmatic details. But Clinton decided that he "had the responsibility of being in the discussion," and, in his words, "the ticket to admission to American politics is a balanced budget."[77] Once Clinton joined this debate, including proposed reductions in medicare spending, the Democrats on the Hill felt betrayed.

Clinton Resists

In the end, however, the Republicans' triumph was brief. Their leadership had miscalculated their position just as badly as Clinton had done with health care reform, overestimating their ability to surmount an obviously crucial institutional facet of policymaking: the presidential veto. The president had found his voice in budgetary and federal health care politics. As one senior Democrat suggested, Bill Clinton had finally realized that he was a Democrat, and medicare was a cornerstone of Democratic government. It represented the core legacy of the party. Medicaid was another fundamental party commitment. Clinton was not going to "allow himself to be seen by Democrats as selling out his principles, as Bush had been seen by Republicans, when he abandoned his famous 'read my lips' pledge to not raise taxes."[78] The reconciliation process may facilitate legislative politics, but it also grants an opposing president additional leverage. Everything in the package lives or dies as the *overall* politics dictate. Although the huge changes in medicare and medicaid seemed as though they might ride the train of reconciliation into the statute books, they—along with cuts in education and other social investment programs considered vital to Clinton—actually motivated a presidential veto of the budget reconciliation bill on December 6, 1995. "Today I am vetoing the biggest Medicare and Medicaid cuts in history, deep cuts in education, a rollback in environmental protection and a tax increase on working families. . . . With this veto, the extreme Republican effort to balance the budget through wrongheaded cuts and misplaced priorities is over."[79]

Clinton's veto of the reconciliation bill forced Republicans into the situation they had so carefully schemed to avoid: having the details of their proposals out in public, with plenty of time for the opposition to gear up its campaign. Delay would now prove fatal to *their* health care plans. Large-scale budget negotiations, rhetorical contretemps, partial government shutdowns unprecedented in scope and frequency, and ongoing efforts to close the impasse persisted from December 1995 on into the presidential and congressional elections of 1996, without resolution. With the same integration of legislative and communications strategies perfected by the Republicans, the Democratic opposition used this period to pound relentlessly against the medicare initiative, claiming that massive cuts in the program were intended to finance the tax cuts directed mostly at the affluent. Clinton had initially given the Republicans protective cover on medicare, but medicare in turn granted him political protection for blocking the entire Republican budget. He even used the pen with which Lyndon Johnson signed medicare and medicaid into law to do it.[80]

The results were devastating for the Republican revolutionaries. Public opinion surveys showed that the GOP rapidly lost ground with senior citizens. From January 1995 to March 1996, the percentage of people who approved of the way Congress was doing its job dropped from 42 percent to 30 percent. By November 1995 the public opposed cuts in the rate of spending for medicare by 75 percent to 21 percent, and for medicaid, by 66 percent to 30 percent. In December, by almost two to one the public expressed more confidence in the Democrats than Republicans in dealing with medicare and protecting the middle class (44 to 24 percent and 43 to 24 percent, respectively). The 180-degree shift in public opinion was remarkable. Retrospectively, two-thirds of the public now blamed Congress alone for failing to pass health care reform, while only 15 percent thought Clinton was responsible. A month before the 1996 presidential election, according to the Harris poll, 54 percent of the public reported that they would have been "better off" had Clinton's Health Security Act been enacted (37 percent said worse off)—more favorable figures than right after Clinton had announced the plan in 1993. More than two-thirds wanted him to propose "major health care reforms" if reelected.[81]

With the Health Security Act, many observers felt that Clinton had overreached, trying to move health care reform well beyond his electoral mandate and the capacity of the political coalitions he could form. Whatever lessons Republicans learned from the Clinton experience, this was not one of them. They read far more into their electoral victory than the facts could sustain and pressed ahead with a plan that was in many ways even more politically ambitious and risky than the president's. Just as Clinton never fully appreciated the problem of thwarting a filibuster minority in the Senate, they failed to give appropriate weight to the president as a necessary participant in the legislative arena. They perceived him to be so shell-shocked by the 1994 election, and so lacking in firm principles, that he would simply cave. He proved otherwise.

Social Policy as Private Enterprise

The political failures of both the Clinton and congressional Republican agendas for major health care policy change did not leave in their wake a stagnant health care system. Indeed, during President Clinton's first term, the nation witnessed an extraordinary transformation of the health care sector, promulgated largely by market-driven private-sector institutions acting individually on their own initiative. The public so skeptical about both Clinton's and the Republicans' health policy initiatives ended up with a lot more to worry about than what elected officials had introduced. The market wrung certain inefficiencies out of the system, but in the process out-of-pocket costs rose, choice of insurance and providers became more limited, the ranks of the uninsured grew, and fewer resources were available to finance charitable care. In the end, despite losing in the legislative arena, because of the prominence and emphasis of the transformations in the health sector, Republicans could actually claim indirect victory. The market, not government, is now thoroughly the basis of health system organization.

There is nothing unprecedented about private sector activities in the

United States generating significant health policy consequences. Witness the development of employer-based private health insurance and its rapid spread in the 1940s and 1950s. Nonetheless, in their reach and scope these recent changes may have greater impact and have occurred more quickly than any generated by federal health policy in the past. Previously long-standing institutional arrangements and traditional assumptions about the relationships among payers, patients, and providers were fundamentally recast. Some of the changes, such as the rapid rise of managed care, are consistent with elements of both Clinton's initiative and Republican proposals for medicaid and medicare, but they are taking shape undirected by federal strictures.

The most obvious evidence of change in the health care system is a remarkable slowing down of the previous medical care expenditure spiral, by any measure, even in the absence of federal regulation. In 1996, the fully available data for 1994 showed that overall annual health care spending growth had moderated to 6.4 percent, 5.4 percent for per capita costs, and that only 13.7 percent of GDP was committed to medical services. Employers, many of whom had been advocates of reform because of rising costs, saw increases in their stated health care expenditures nearly disappear. Even the public sector was witnessing ameliorated cost pressures.[82] President Clinton announced that the overall health care inflation rate had dropped to 2 percent for the first half of 1996 and could finish the year below consumer prices in general.[83]

Much of this "good" news in the health care sector is somewhat illusory, however. As the economy moved steadily out of the recession of the early 1990s, GDP expanded more rapidly, improving measures of health care expenditures as a proportion of national income without necessarily reflecting real health care savings. The overall rate of inflation also remained low and declined from previous periods. So while the surge in medical care prices abated, until 1996, according to Consumers Union, "medical care inflation continue[d] to exceed general inflation by 61 percent—precisely the same differential that has prevailed since 1980."[84] In addition, at least some of the "savings" experienced by businesses amounts to a form of cost shifting. Fewer large employers were extending coverage to retirees (down to 66 percent in 1995 from 71 percent in 1993), and employees were having to pay more for their coverage.[85] There is also the possibility that providers and insurers temporarily held down costs in the hopes of reducing the appeal of government intervention, a pattern reminiscent of the late 1970s.[86] The dramatic turn-around in health care cost patterns, therefore, has to be viewed in context and cautiously, along with its political implications for federal policy in the years ahead.

That caution, however, should not blind one to the structural revolution that is most certainly taking place in the health care sector. It is a kind of social policy as private enterprise, which most observers agree has contributed to the restraint on health spending, if only momentarily. Without the benefit of tax changes, subsidies, or standardized benefits packages, and the health alliances to oversee plan performance and competition envisioned by the Clinton health plan, managed care arrangements of various kinds have nonetheless taken hold with unprecedented speed.

When Clinton was elected in 1992, enrollment in the various versions of managed care was below 40 million and costs were climbing at double-digit rates. Most individuals covered by firms with 200 or more employees—53 percent—still had indemnity insurance, with 47 percent in managed care. Only about 10 percent of Blue Cross–Blue Shield enrollment around the country involved managed care. In the early to mid-1980s, about 3 percent of medicare and medicaid beneficiaries participated in managed care plans, rising near 10 percent as the health care reform debate began to unfold in full force.[87]

A few years later, the numbers are strikingly different. In 1995 nearly 70 million individuals were enrolled in various HMO product lines (with estimates of about 130 million being projected for 2002), and an additional 91 million participated in more loosely structured "preferred provider organizations" (PPOs). Seventy-three percent of employees participating in employer-sponsored coverage were in managed care plans, and 35 percent of all state government employees. More than half of Blue Cross–Blue Shield enrollees were now in managed care.[88]

Publicly financed programs were restructuring, too. Forty states and the District of Columbia had received waivers from the Health Care Financing Administration to launch managed care programs for their medicaid beneficiaries; thirteen states had received approval to compel participation. As a result, in 1995 about a third of all beneficiaries were enrolled in private managed care plans, including approximately one-half of all mothers and children in the program. Medicare risk contracting with private managed care plans had not yet reached this pace, accounting for under 10 percent of enrollees concentrated in ten states. By the end of 1996, however, 78 percent of managed care plans surveyed by the American Association of Health Plans intended to have medicare risk contracts, up from less than a quarter at the beginning of 1995.[89] Managed care, in all of its many permutations, is becoming the American way of health care financing and delivery.

The reorganization of private and public health insurance toward managed care has brought with it restructuring of the providers of care. The American Medical Association had challenged the concept of prepaid group practice from its inception. That opposition had weakened over the years, but as reform reemerged on the agenda in the late 1980s, most physicians spent the bulk of their time practicing fee-for-service medicine. Fifty-seven percent of physicians in 1986 were not involved with managed care at all; in 1995 more than eight in ten had at least one managed care contract, nearly doubling in one decade, and a third of physicians participated in group practices. Managed care has also contributed to lower physician incomes and to a rapid and dramatic reversal in the practice intentions of medical students, with most identifying primary care—the heart of managed care—as their career path instead of other specializations.[90]

Established patterns in the operation of hospitals were even more disrupted. Managed care discounting both reduced the overall financial viability of many hospitals, especially public institutions, and threatened to alter the flow of funds that major academic health centers and other facilities relied on to help finance medical training and clinical research. It has also created incentives for rapid consolidation of the hospital industry, part of the 623 health care sector mergers and acquisitions that occurred in 1995 alone.[91]

The final major transition in the health care sector, consistent with the market as opposed to government serving as the engine of change, has been a general process of corporatization. Where not-for-profit institutions, most of them state or local, once dominated the scene, for-profit enterprises, typically regional or national in scope, have now gained the upper hand. Nonprofit HMOs still had a majority of HMO enrollees in 1991, but for-profit ones took a substantial lead by 1994, reporting hundreds of millions of dollars in profits. Even traditionally nonprofit Blue Cross and Blue Shield plans began to participate in the corporatization of health care by becoming outright for-profit entities, selling out to for-profit hospital networks, or creating separate for-profit managed care lines. As a result, 84 percent of HMO enrollment in 1994 was already in corporate HMO chains.[92]

Where have these non-policy-derived changes left the health care system? Managed care and competition among such plans may bear some similarities to the Clinton vision of 1993–94, but the future of cost restraint, the impact on insurance coverage, and the implications for access to treatment, choice over providers, and the quality of care are not what the president intended from reform. The very things the public had been led to fear from Clinton were in fact being generated in the marketplace by the private interests that organized in opposition to reform. Not "Big Government," but "private power was poised to take over people's health care and therefore their lives."[93] The benefits of cost reduction are real, for example, but perhaps only temporary, without any overt mechanisms to contain any future eruptions in health spending. Once the large-scale transition to managed care is nearly complete and consolidations have run their course, the "easy savings" will disappear.

Corporate managed care plans may have incentives to sell a quality product for those who can purchase insurance, but there are none for expanding coverage to those without it, especially those with a history of medical conditions. Employers have also cut back on coverage as another way to restrain what they view as their own health care expenditures. Various indicators have shown either a continuing climb in the number and proportion of people without insurance or, at best, no diminution, despite a resurgent economy. According to the U.S. Bureau of the Census, the number of uninsured rose from 34.7 million in 1990 to 38.6 million in 1992, 39.7 million in 1994, and 40.3 million in 1995, about a 16 percent increase. In addition, 14.2 percent of children under 18 years old lacked insurance—the highest percentage since 1987 and despite the expansion in children's coverage under medicaid in the 1980s.[94]

Although the uninsured previously often received less and lower quality care than those with health care coverage, they conventionally had been given access to medical services through "safety-net" institutions: hospitals, clinics, and various health practitioners that provided discounted or uncompensated care financed by surpluses generated from the fees charged private patients, medicare, and medicaid. Managed care plans, however, because of their emphasis on trimming the costs of those they cover and their effectiveness at negotiating capitated payments or discounted reimbursement rates, sliced deeply into the funding stream for uncompensated care. The formation of vast networks also often excludes consideration of the poor in general. Publicly owned facilities bore the greatest brunt of the market changes.[95]

Managed care had a potentially more positive effect for some medic-aid beneficiaries. Where they have been shifted into managed care, either voluntarily or by force, many recipients had sustained access for the first time to primary care physicians and specialists in settings outside either emergency rooms or crowded clinics. But even here the story about access is mixed. Other medicaid beneficiaries have found themselves victimized by corrupt marketing practices, signed up for HMOs located far from where they live, or joined managed care plans that failed to meet their needs.[96] With very high turnover rates in medicaid eligibility, and thus health care enrollments, managed care plans have less incentive to serve client demands.

Even the vast bulk of middle-class individuals enjoying the benefits of "good" health insurance coverage through their employers began to experience the deficiencies as well as benefits of the managed care revolution. Where Clinton proposed to offer them the choice of no fewer than three insurance plans through a health alliance, with at least one of them offering traditional fee-for-service coverage, in the current market individuals have few choices of plans and most decisions are still made by employers. Only a little more than half of employers that provide health benefits offer a choice of more than one plan; 52 percent of mid-sized firms grant no choice.[97]

Once in a managed care plan, enrollees have not always been happy with the results. As the managed care revolution unfolded, the media began reporting numerous stories of dissatisfaction and even outrage, especially as the gatekeeping function of managed care denied some individuals coverage for various treatments or more lengthy hospital stays. In a 1995 national survey of managed care executives, slightly more than half agreed that "there is a significant backlash coming in response to managed care's emphasis on cost." More than two-thirds of the executives from not-for-profit plans expressed that view.[98]

In this environment of social policy as private enterprise, and the backlash that started to form, state-level policymakers began to act. Following implementation of Hawaii's employer mandate in 1974, a number of states, such as Massachusetts, Oregon, Minnesota, Washington, Florida, and Vermont, had either enacted their own reform plans or appeared to be on the verge of doing so. When the federal initiatives were thwarted in 1994, some observers anticipated that the states would assume leadership of the reform issue. That did not happen. Not only were states stymied by the federal Employee Retirement Income Security Act

(ERISA), which placed about half of the health insurance market beyond their regulatory authority, but the conservative political wave that swept Congress in 1994 also washed across myriad states. Even in states that had enacted reform measures, the newly Republican legislatures rescinded those efforts.[99]

States across the country, however, did launch policy responses to the market transformation of health care. By 1996, almost all were at some stage of planning or implementing incorporation of managed care in their medicaid programs in order to reduce costs, and, in some instances, such as Tennessee's TennCare program, to make some strides toward expanding insurance coverage with the presumed savings. When public spending was involved, the states joined the private sector bandwagon.[100] At the same time, however, the backlash that was mounting among the middle class against the perceived nefarious effects of managed care led most state legislatures to consider a variety of bills to regulate the managed care industry. Several hundred bills have been introduced, ranging from mandates that managed care plans accept "any willing provider," which twenty-four states have enacted, to minimum periods of covered maternity length of stay in hospitals, under consideration in thirty-four states and passed by eleven. By summer of 1997, twenty-seven states had enacted statutes prohibiting HMOs from restricting the information provided by physicians to their patients. Eighteen states had also adopted patient protection acts, many modeled on an omnibus package of proposals originally advocated by the AMA.[101]

Neither Congress nor the White House could resist the temptation to join the bandwagon. At the close of the 104th Congress, Clinton signed legislation that would require insurers to pay for forty-eight-hour maternity hospital stays and mandate parity in lifetime limits for coverage of mental health and physical illness.[102]

The Lure of Redemption: Everyone Needs a Win

With the medical care system changing under its own dynamic, the political election cycle reignited the interest of federal elected officials in some kind of government action. Although election years typically aggravate divisive partisanship—certainly apparent in the gridlock that pervaded Capitol Hill in the spring of 1996—they often close with a torrent of enacted legislation that benefits candidates from both parties wishing to demonstrate accomplishments back home.[103] Having each suffered defeat on their major health care initiatives, in 1996 Clinton and the Republican congressional majorities were looking for a legislative win, an impulse that brought modest health care reform back to the legislative agenda. The question remained, however: what kind of mutually agreeable deal could be struck in the wake of such intense political warfare, heightened partisanship, fierce group mobilization and countermobilization, and public anger and confusion? Keeping the issue a matter of more conventional legislative process rather than public rhetoric eventually mitigated these divisions.

President Clinton was the first to resolve the strategic dilemma. In his 1996 State of the Union address, he said he was "eager to associate himself with" a bipartisan proposal introduced by Senator Nancy Landon Kassebaum, the Republican chair of the Senate Labor and Human Resources Committee, and Democratic Senator Ted Kennedy, the previous chair and now ranking member.[104] This stripped-down "consensus" bill would lessen the fear of losing health insurance protection, among people who already had it, due to changes in employment status. It would inhibit insurers from denying coverage for preexisting conditions and provide a bridge between the group and individual insurance markets.[105] These were issues upon which liberals and conservatives, Democrats and Republicans, could readily agree. By all accounts, the public wanted this protection. It was also the one element of health care reform on which the potential Democratic and Republican target groups could agree (such insurance market reforms were formally supported by 77 percent and 68 percent of these organizations respectively, with virtually no official opposition).[106] The incrementalist threat rejected by Clinton two years before became potential fuel for his political redemption.

Conservative Republicans were not as easily tempted. They decided to block the Kassebaum-Kennedy bill, which would impose unprecedented federal regulation of the health insurance market without market-oriented provisions more to their liking. As the opposition geared up, it looked like 1994 repeated, albeit on a smaller scale. Even this most incremental of legislation could not be insulated from the intense and divisive partisan politics that characterize the contemporary Congress and dominated the debate over comprehensive health policy change.

The fate of the legislation hinged on the ideological battle over medical savings accounts, a core item on the conservative social policy agenda championed by Bill Archer, Republican of Texas and chair of the House

Ways and Means Committee. The renewed MSA debate reinforced the partisan divisions about social policy. MSAs—in this case allowing individuals and families to make tax-deductible contributions to an account from which they would cover routine health care expenses, save what they do not use in a given year, and obtain high-deductible insurance coverage for catastrophic expenses—represented a form of social policy as both private *and* personal enterprise. Healthy individuals in particular, especially those with the financial resources to make MSA contributions, would have the incentive to withdraw from conventional insurance risk pools, taking their money with them, and self-insure all but exceptional medical needs. Insurers with catastrophic product lines would also have market incentives to cherry pick the healthy. Liberals and most Democrats argued that the scheme was a direct challenge to the idea of even private insurance and the spreading of risk along with its burdens. In the words of one consumer advocate, MSAs "funnel money away from doctors' bills and into accounts that will help healthy people accumulate wealth." Those without MSAs would face rising costs.[107]

Unlike the duels over comprehensive reform and the transformation of medicare and medicaid, however, this dispute rarely engaged precincts outside Washington. This was not a struggle between high-pitched media campaigns to capture the detached middle of the electorate and full-tilt efforts at grass-roots mobilization. Although the HIAA objected to the bill, Harry and Louise did not return to America's homes. The public was not highly engaged. Only 43 percent responding to a midsummer 1996 poll had even heard of the overall bill, and just 30 percent knew about the MSA provisions. When MSAs were explained in the poll, only 28 percent expressed support for them.[108] In addition, since the whole packet of proposals in the bill generated only modest costs, easily compensated, budgetary politics played no role.

The president's promotion of a narrow, pragmatic initiative this time made it more politically difficult for conservative Republicans to kill the initiative. Clinton's likely opponent in the upcoming presidential race, Senate Majority Leader Robert Dole, brought the bill to the floor. After defeating an MSA provision (supported by Dole), the Senate passed the legislation 100 to 0. Ultimately, with the 104th Congress nearly at an end and the fall campaigns on the horizon, Kennedy and Archer were finally able to negotiate a compromise that permitted passage of the Health Insurance Portability and Accountability Act. It authorized a far more confined MSA experiment than conservatives were previously willing to consider. Up to 750,000 individuals or families could make tax-deductible contributions to MSAs during a designated four-year period, with specific limits set on the size of deductibles and out-of-pocket obligations for the associated catastrophic insurance. Only people self-employed or working for firms with fifty or fewer employees would be eligible. Congress would then assess the results. For the MSA program to continue after the four-year experiment, Congress would have to take explicit action. With this issue settled, the conference report passed unanimously in the Senate and with only two dissenting votes in the House.[109]

Once the law was in hand, debate returned to symbolic politics. Democrats and Republicans declared partisan victories precisely in the terms developed during the health care reform debate and fine-tuned for the 1996 election campaigns. Democrats claimed the law and Clinton's promotion of it "shows their devotion to the security of working families." Robert Dole, formally the Republican nominee for president, declared that the statute "includes many of the important health insurance reforms I've promoted for years and should end once and for all the Clinton prescription of big-government health care."[110]

Clinton got his Rose Garden signing ceremony and Republicans got their claim that they enacted the kind of health care reform they always supported, and not "government-run health care." But as enacted, stripped of earlier provisions, the law does little more than extend federal ratification of provisions that the vast majority of states had already implemented.[111] For 20 million to 25 million people moving between jobs, the act could provide some real protection, although early evidence indicates that some insurers are actively undermining its provisions.[112] The legislation also does virtually nothing for the 40 million Americans without health insurance. It may also do relatively little for those with preexisting conditions, who could still face waiting periods and steep premiums. In general, the law makes insurance more available but not necessarily more affordable.[113] Perhaps most important, the Health Insurance Portability and Accountability Act does not impose any limits on how high insurers can set premiums.[114] States could intervene, but the federal law itself permits individual insurance premiums to rise beyond the reach of many of those technically eligible for the coverage. Finally, the MSA experiment may, in the end, be unassessable. Because the participants are distributed throughout the country, and the vast majority of people use few medical services in most years, it will be extremely difficult to judge the potential adverse effects of MSAs on insurance markets, especially over such a short period of time. Congress might authorize a permanent MSA program without being aware of what disruptions it could bring to the health system.[115]

Conclusion

President Clinton's first term presented the public with a partisan duel over social policy the likes of which it has rarely seen. Major health care initiatives were the primary ammunition in that confrontation. First Clinton and then the subsequent congressional Republican majorities hoped to use federal health policy to alter the long-term political landscape. Of course, neither the president nor the congressional Republicans succeeded in enacting their respective visions of health care policy changes and thus could not achieve the political transformations to which they aspired. The Kassebaum-Kennedy portability act passed at the end of the 104th Congress neither seriously expanded the role of the state nor did much to advance the privatization of the federal health care programs. (Although the statute permitted 375,000 MSAs by April 30, 1997, only 10,000 accounts had been established.)[116]

The battle over federal health policy during Clinton's first term would thus seem to be a political wash. Following the 1996 elections, so influenced at all levels by the health policy debates, neither party gained the boost it had been trying to engineer. Instead, the nation stood dramatically divided between the two political parties. It was not a symmetry likely to breed more than episodic moderation, however. At the same time, Congress and the nation have grown increasingly polarized.[117] With the departure of many moderates from Congress by retirement and defeat, the ideological divisions are likely to grow more stark.

This is the setting in which the immediate future of federal health policy, especially the enormous challenge of putting medicare on a secure footing in anticipation of the aging of the baby boom, would have to be addressed. In his initial major address after the 1996 election, President Clinton, in familiar New Democratic terms, sought to cast himself as a unifying leader within these divisions. After having waged a presidential campaign based on divining the middle path, he announced that "I stand ready to forge a coalition of the center, a broad consensus for creative and consistent and unflinching action" that includes "a balanced budget that restructures Medicare and Medicaid while protecting both from deep cuts and expanding coverage for children." Republican congressional leaders also expressed willingness to pursue more cooperation and less confrontation, facilitated by new budget estimates for medicare, medicaid, and other programs that narrowed the gap between their and the administration's proposals for reaching a balanced budget.[118] The result was major bipartisan legislation enacted in 1997, signed by the president, that would bring the budget into balance by 2002. It included the most sweeping changes in medicare since its inception, including significant remnants of the Republican agenda, such as more aggressive expansion of privated managed care options for beneficiaries and an MSA experiment. The budget deal also launched a new federal block grant to the states to provide coverage for uninsured children, allowing for either expansion of medicaid or use of private insurers.[119]

Despite the surprising if temporary emergence of bipartisanship, Republicans and their interest group allies probably came away from the intense struggles and then deal making of the mid-1990s with the greatest overall claim to success. The GOP may have lost its bid to recapture the presidency and suffered some losses in the House in 1996, but it has transformed the agenda, altered the terms of debate, and helped unleash a private sector transformation of the health domain that is entirely consistent with its long-term political project of balancing the federal budget, reducing federal spending, and promoting the activist market in place of the activist state. Market-oriented approaches to health care—now even embedded in medicare, the Democratic bastion of social policy—have distinct winners who reap the rewards of the redistribution of resources they generate.[120] It is the Republican base—business, insurers, some health care providers, pharmaceuticals, movement conservatives, all of the members of the erstwhile No Name Coalition—that has profited from this transformation. It remains to be seen, however, whether the electorate wants or will tolerate the rise of corporate managed care, hospital downsizing, reduced employer-provided benefits, and a rising tide of uninsured with more limited access to care, or whether these trends will return statist policy alternatives to the agenda.

Notes

1. Interviews with participants; "Clinton Urges Congress To Seize 'Magic Moment' of Reform," *Congressional Quarterly Weekly Report*, September 25, 1993,

p. 2583; and Haynes Johnson and David S. Broder, *The System: The American Way of Politics at the Breaking Point* (Little, Brown, 1996), p. 511.

2. Jill D. Foley, "Uninsured in the United States: The Nonelderly Population without Health Insurance: Analysis of the March 1990 Current Population Survey" (Washington: Employee Benefit Research Institute, April 1991), pp. 7–8; Robert Pear, "34.7 Million Lack Health Insurance, Studies Say; Number Is Highest Since '65," *New York Times*, December 19, 1991, p. B17; "The State of America's Health Care System and Health Care Crisis: A Reference Guide," DPC Special Report, Senate Democratic Policy Committee, SR-40-Health, August 16, 1994, p. 31; J. Ian Morrison, Ellen M. Morrison, and Jennifer N. Edwards, "Large Employers and Employee Benefits: Priorities for the 1990s," in Robert J. Blendon and Jennifer N. Edwards, eds., *System in Crisis: The Case for Health Care Reform* (New York: Faulkner and Gray, 1991), p. 104; Congressional Budget Office, *Rising Health Care Costs: Causes, Implications, and Strategies* (April 1991), pp. 3, 46; Julie Rovner, "Governors Ask Congress for Relief from Burdensome Medicaid Mandates," *Congressional Quarterly Weekly Report*, February 16, 1991, p. 416; James W. Fossett and James H. Wyckoff, "Has Medicaid Growth Crowded Out State Educational Spending?" *Journal of Health Politics, Policy and Law*, vol. 21 (Fall 1996), p. 420; Spencer Rich, "Despite Medicare, Elderly Health Costs Up, Study Says," *Washington Post*, February 26, 1992, p. A3; Laurene A. Graig, *Health of Nations: An International Perspective on U.S. Health Care Reform* (Washington: Wyatt Company), pp. 25–27; and Paul Starr, "The Middle Class and National Health Reform," *American Prospect*, no. 6 (Summer 1991), pp. 7–12.

3. Mark A. Peterson, "Interest Groups as Allies and Antagonists: Their Role in the Politics of Health Care Reform," paper prepared for the 1995 annual meeting of the Association for Health Services Research and Foundation for Health Services Research.

4. Mark A. Peterson, "Political Influence in the 1990s: From Iron Triangles to Policy Networks," *Journal of Health Politics, Policy and Law*, vol. 18 (Summer 1993), pp. 395–438; Barnaby J. Feder, "Medical Group Battles to be Heard over Others on Health-Care Changes," *New York Times*, June 11, 1993, p. A22; Elton Rayak, *Professional Power and American Medicine: The Economics of the American Medical Association* (Cleveland: World Publishing, 1967), pp. 2, 12; Julie Rovner, "Congress and Health Care Reform, 1993-94," in Thomas E. Mann and Norman J. Ornstein, eds., *Intensive Care: How Congress Shapes Health Policy* (AEI and Brookings, 1995), p. 198; Cathie Jo Martin, chap. 6 in this volume; and Peterson, "Interest Groups as Allies and Antagonists."

5. Mark A. Peterson, "From Vested Oligarchy to Informed Entrepreneurship: New Opportunities for Health Care Reform in Congress," paper prepared for the 1994 annual meeting of the Midwest Political Science Association; C. Lawrence Evans, "Committees and Health Jurisdictions in Congress," in Mann and Ornstein, eds., *Intensive Care*, pp. 33-34; and Frank R. Baumgartner and Jeffrey C. Talbert,

"From Setting a National Agenda on Health Care to Making Decisions in Congress," *Journal of Health Politics, Policy and Law*, vol. 20 (Summer 1995), p. 442.

6. White House Domestic Policy Council, *The President's Health Security Plan: The Clinton Blueprint* (Times Books, 1993).

7. Darrell M. West, Diane Heith, and Chris Goodwin, "Harry and Louise Go to Washington: Political Advertising and Health Care Reform," *Journal of Health Politics, Policy and Law*, vol. 21 (Spring 1996), p. 50.

8. Sven Steinmo and Jon Watts, "It's the Institutions, Stupid! Why Comprehensive National Health Insurance Always Fails in America," *Journal of Health Politics, Policy and Law*, vol. 20 (Summer 1995), pp. 329–72; and Mark A. Peterson, "Institutional Change and the Health Politics of the 1990s," *American Behavioral Scientist*, vol. 36 (July 1993), pp. 782–801.

9. Steven Waldman and Bob Cohn, "Health Care Reform: The Lost Chance," *Newsweek*, September 19, 1994, p. 29.

10. Mark A. Peterson, *Legislating Together: The White House and Capitol Hill from Eisenhower to Reagan* (Harvard University Press, 1990), p. 179; see Lawrence R. Jacobs, "Politics of America's Supply State: Health Reform and Technology," *Health Affairs*, vol. 14 (Summer 1995), pp. 143–57; and Hugh Heclo, "The Clinton Health Plan: Historical Perspective," *Health Affairs*, vol. 14 (Spring 1995), p. 93.

11. Elizabeth Drew, *On the Edge: The Clinton Presidency* (Simon and Schuster, 1994).

12. Allen Schick, "How a Bill Did Not Become a Law," in Mann and Ornstein, eds., *Intensive Care*, p. 266.

13. See Henry J. Aaron, "End of an Era: The New Debate over Health Care Financing," *Brookings Review*, vol. 14 (Winter 1996), p. 35.

14. Heclo, "The Clinton Health Plan," p. 94.

15. For the best treatment of the Wofford effects, see Jacob S. Hacker, *The Road to Nowhere: The Genesis of President Clinton's Plan for Health Security* (Princeton University Press, 1997), chap. 1.

16. Harris Poll results from 1991 reported in Lawrence R. Jacobs and Robert Y. Shapiro, "Don't Blame the Public for Failed Health Care Reform," *Journal of Health Politics, Policy and Law*, vol. 20 (Summer 1995), p. 416; and Thomas Byrne Edsall, "The Protean President," *Atlantic Monthly* (May 1996), p. 43.

17. Data derived from 120 responses to a mail survey of a diverse, purposively selected sample of interest groups likely to be interested in the issue of health care reform and representing providers, various types of businesses, the insurance industry, "disease" associations, religious organizations, citizen advocacy groups, unions, and state and local government officials, among others.

18. Johnson and Broder, *The System*, p. 604. Every person I interviewed at both ends of Pennsylvania Avenue and from both parties agreed that there was a "window of opportunity" to enact a version of significant health care reform in the 103d Congress.

222   Mark A. Peterson

19. David W. Brady and Kara M. Buckley, "Health Care Reform in the 103d Congress: A Predictable Failure," *Journal of Health Politics, Policy and Law,* vol. 20 (Summer 1995), pp. 447–54.

20. Interviews with participants; Schick, "How a Bill Did Not Become a Law," p. 250; Charles O. Jones, "The Clinton Administration in the Separated System: A Presidency at Risk?" *Extensions: A Journal of the Carl Albert Congressional Research and Studies Center* (Spring 1996), p. 5; and Charles O. Jones, *The Presidency in a Separated System* (Brookings, 1994).

21. Mark A. Peterson, "Momentum toward Health Care Reform in the U.S. Senate," *Journal of Health Politics, Policy and Law,* vol. 17 (Fall 1992), pp. 553–73.

22. Jones, *Presidency in a Separated System,* pp. 20–21; and Paul Light, *Still Artful Work: The Continuing Politics of Social Security Reform,* 2d ed. (McGraw Hill, 1995).

23. Interviews with participants.

24. Michael Wines and Robert Pear, "President Finds Benefits in Defeat on Health Care," *New York Times,* July 30, 1996, p. A8.

25. One 1994 study, for example, estimated that already insured families with incomes between $20,000 and $75,000 would pay more for insurance under plans that made incremental changes in the insurance market without guaranteeing universal coverage. "Study Concludes That Incremental Reforms Would Force Middle Income Families to Pay More for Their Health Care," Press Release, Senator Rockefeller's Office. n.d.

26. Congressional Budget Office, "An Analysis of the Managed Competition Act," April 1994, pp. xi-xii.

27. Johnson and Broder, *The System,* p. 86.

28. See Hacker, *Road to Nowhere,* for detailed examination of the development of the ideas behind the Clinton Health Security Act.

29. Hacker, *Road to Nowhere;* Theda Skocpol, *Boomerang: Clinton's Health Security Effort and the Turn against Government in U.S. Politics* (Norton, 1996), chap. 1; Paul Starr, *The Logic of Health Care Reform* (Knoxville, Tenn.: Whittle Direct Books, 1992), p. xv; Johnson and Broder, *The System;* and interviews with participants.

30. Lisa Disch, "Publicity-Stunt Participation and Sound Bite Polemics: The Health Care Debate 1993-94," *Journal of Health Politics, Policy and Law,* vol. 21 (Spring 1996), pp. 3–33; Memorandum for Ira Magaziner, from Mike Lux, "Memo We Discussed This Morning," March 31, 1993, p. 1; and Memorandum for Hillary Rodham Clinton, from Mike Lux, "The Politics of Remaining Major Health Care Decisions," May 18, 1993.

31. Memorandum for Hillary Rodham Clinton, from Mike Lux, "Interest Group Strategy on Health Care," April 19, 1993; and Memorandum to Celia Fisher, from Mike Lux, "The Grassroots Campaign for Health Care Reform," March 22, 1993, p. 3.

32. Memorandum for Ira Magaziner, from Mike Lux, March 31, 1993, p. 1.

33. Memorandum for Hillary Rodham Clinton, from Mike Lux, "Organizational Strategy on Health Care," March 9, 1993, pp. 2–3; Memorandum to Ira Magaziner, from Mike Lux, "Memo We Discussed This Morning," March 13, 1993, p. 2; Memorandum for Hillary Rodham Clinton, from Mike Lux, April 19, 1993; and Memorandum for Hillary Rodham Clinton, from Mike Lux, "Positioning Ourselves on Health Care," May 3, 1993.

34. Joseph White, "Budgeting and Health Policymaking," in Mann and Ornstein, eds., *Intensive Care*, pp. 54–55. See pp. 70–74 for a discussion of how the paygo rules adversely affected the 1990s health care reform debate by empowering critics and sponsors of marginal bills.

35. Interviews with participants in both parties.

36. Dan Balz and Ronald Brownstein, *Storming the Gates: Protest Politics and the Republican Revival* (Little, Brown, 1996), p. 251; and Johnson and Broder, *The System*, pp. xi, 11–12.

37. Johnson and Broder, *The System*, p. 428.

38. Memorandum for the President, from Mike Lux, December 15, 1993.

39. Johnson and Broder, *The System*, p. 154.

40. Johnson and Broder, *The System*, pp. 52–53, 195, 223–24, 373, 466, 499, 630.

41. Balz and Brownstein, *Storming the Gates*, pp. 181, 320–24; Haynes Johnson and David S. Broder, "Health Reform vs. Harry and Louise," *Pittsburgh Post-Gazette*, April 22, 1996, p. A-6; West, Heith, and Goodwin, "Harry and Louise Go to Washington," pp. 48–49; Johnson and Broder, *The System*, pp. 197, 213; and Skocpol, *Boomerang*, chap. 5.

42. Johnson and Broder, *The System*, pp. 197, 220.

43. Skocpol, *Boomerang*, pp. 122–23; and Mollyann Brodie and Robert J. Blendon, "The Public's Contribution to Congressional Gridlock on Health Care Reform," *Journal of Health Politics, Policy and Law*, vol. 20 (Summer 1995), pp. 403–10.

44. Memorandum for Ira Magaziner, from Mike Lux, "The Case Against Delay," July 20, 1993; Balz and Bernstein, *Storming the Gates*, p. 100; and Adam Clymer, Robert Pear, and Robin Toner, "For Health Care, Time Was a Killer," *New York Times*, August 29, 1994, pp. A1, A8.

45. Interviews with participants; Adam Clymer, "House Is Letting Senate Go First on Health Care," *New York Times*, August 5, 1994, pp. A1, A8; David Maraniss and Michael Weisskopf, *"Tell Newt to Shut Up!"* (Touchstone, 1996), pp. 122–23; Jeffrey Talbert, "Congressional Partisanship and the Failure of Moderate Health Care Reform," *Journal of Health Politics, Policy and Law*, vol. 20 (Winter 1995), pp. 1033–50; Johnson and Broder, *The System*, p. 498; and Robin Toner, "Partisan Jockeying on Health Care Becomes Intense," *New York Times*, July 28, 1994, p. A20.

46. Interview with participant.

47. Schick, "How a Bill Did Not Become a Law," pp. 241–43; Cathie Jo Martin, "Stuck in Neutral: Big Business and the Politics of National Health Reform,"

Journal of Health Politics, Policy and Law, vol. 20 (Summer 1995), pp. 434–35; Johnson and Broder, *The System*, p. 323; and Robert Pear, "Health Care Tug-of-War Puts A.M.A. under Strain," *New York Times*, August 5, 1994, p. A18.

48. Republican health adviser Deborah Steelman, quoted in Johnson and Broder, *The System*, pp. 197, 499.

49. Memorandum for the President, from Mike Lux, December 15, 1993, pp. 1, 3; Memorandum for Distribution, from Mike Lux, "Mobilizing the Base," February 21, 1994; and Memorandum for Harold Ickes and Greg Lawler, from Mike Lux, "Update on Constituency Action Plan," January 31, 1994.

50. Results from the mail survey of interest groups.

51. Balz and Brownstein, *Storming the Gates*, pp. 25, 36, 45.

52. Elizabeth Drew, *Showdown: The Struggle between the Gingrich Congress and the Clinton White House* (Simon and Schuster, 1996), p. 81.

53. Colette Fraley, "Medicare Conferees Face Some Major Differences," *Congressional Quarterly Weekly Report*, November 4, 1995, pp. 3379–80.

54. Alissa J. Rubin, "Medicare: Throwing Down the Gauntlet," *Congressional Quarterly Weekly Report*, May 13, 1995, p. 1304; Colette Fraley, "Using Vouchers for Medicare May Help GOP Cut Costs," *Congressional Quarterly Weekly Report*, July 22, 1995, pp. 2189–90; and Colette Fraley, "Conference Agreement Entails Sweeping Medicare Changes," *Congressional Quarterly Weekly Report*, November 18, 1995, pp. 3536–37.

55. Linda Bilheimer, "The High-Deductible/MSA Option under Medicare: Exploring the Implications of the Balanced Budget Act of 1995," CBO Memorandum, March 1996, p. 28.

56. Julie Rovner, "Cost of Medicaid Puts States in Tightening Budget Vise," *Congressional Quarterly Weekly Report*, May 18, 1991, p. 1277–81; and Karl Kronebusch, "Medicaid and the Politics of Groups: Recipients, Providers, and Policymaking," *Journal of Health Politics, Policy and Law*, vol. 22 (June 1997), pp. 839–78. This medicaid eligibility will continue for the same population even under the welfare reform law enacted by Congress and signed by President Clinton in 1996.

57. Colette Fraley, "Key Medicaid Provisions," *Congressional Quarterly Weekly Report*, November 18, 1995, p. 3540; and R. Kent Weaver, "Deficits and Devolution in the 104th Congress," *Publius*, vol. 26 (Summer 1996), pp. 45–85.

58. Jason DeParle, "Rant/Listen, Exploit/Learn, Scare/Help, Manipulate/Lead," *New York Times Sunday Magazine*, January 28, 1996, p. 39.

59. Maraniss and Weisskopf, *"Tell Newt to Shut Up!"* p. 37; Stephen Gettinger, "Beware Past History of Medicare Cuts," *Congressional Quarterly Weekly Report*, September 23, 1995, p. 2950; and Peter B. Rutledge, "Prescription for Repeal?" senior honors thesis, Department of Government, Harvard University, 1992.

60. Maraniss and Weisskopf, *"Tell Newt To Shut Up!"* p. 132; and Connie Bruck, "The Politics of Perception," *New Yorker*, October 9, 1995, p. 76.

61. "Presidential News Conference: Clinton Lays Down Challenge on Welfare Reform Bill," *Congressional Quarterly Weekly Report*, April 22, 1995, p. 1140.

62. Interviews with participants.

63. Interviews with Republican and Democratic congressional and executive branch officials.

64. Interviews with participants; Bruck, "Politics of Perception," p. 76; and Johnson and Broder, *The System*, p. 580.

65. Drew, *Showdown*, p. 79.

66. Johnson and Broder, *The System*, pp. 567–69; Maraniss and Weisskopf, *"Tell Newt to Shut Up!"* pp. 11–17, 111–17; and Balz and Brownstein, *Storming the Gates*, pp. 15, 184.

67. Maraniss and Weisskopf, *"Tell Newt to Shut Up!"* p. 139.

68. Senator Alan Simpson visited the AARP board and stated directly, "I want you to know that the intensity of my investigation of AARP will vary directly with the intensity of your efforts to fight the Medicare changes." Johnson and Broder, *The System*, pp. 588–89; and Colette Fraley, "Simpson Zeroes In on AARP and Its Tax Exemption," *Congressional Quarterly Weekly Report*, June 17, 1995, p. 1749.

69. Marilyn Werber Serafini, "Newtral Actions," *National Journal*, November 25, 1995, p. 2918; and Drew, *Showdown*, p. 316.

70. DeParle, "Rant/Listen," p. 56; and Johnson and Broder, *The System*, p. 588.

71. Stuart Schear, "The Ultimate Self-Referral," *American Prospect*, no. 25 (March–April 1996), p. 71.

72. Balz and Brownstein, *Storming the Gates*, pp. 12–13.

73. Interviews; Bruck, "Politics of Perception," p. 76; and Drew, *Showdown*, p. 204.

74. Johnson and Broder, *The System*, p. 576; Maraniss and Weisskopf, *"Tell Newt to Shut Up!"* pp. 128, 129–35.

75. Johnson and Broder, *The System*, pp. 580, 595; Maraniss and Weisskopf, *"Tell Newt to Shut Up!"* p. 151; and interviews with participants.

76. Alissa J. Rubin, "Congress Readies Budget Bill for President's Veto," *Congressional Quarterly Weekly Report*, November 18, 1995, p. 3512; and Colette Fraley, "GOP Score on Medicare, But Foes Aren't Done," and "Scaled-Back Medicaid Savings Plan Emerges from Conference," *Congressional Quarterly Weekly Report*, November 18, 1995, pp. 3535, 3539.

77. Drew, *Showdown*, p. 234.

78. Ibid., p. 308.

79. George Hager, "Harsh Rhetoric on Budget Spells a Dismal Outlook," *Congressional Quarterly Weekly Report*, December 9, 1995, p. 3721.

80. Ibid.

81. Handout by Peter Hart, based on NBC/*Wall Street Journal* poll, January 1996; Handout, Democratic Congressional Campaign Committee, based on ABC/

Washington Post poll data and unpublished NBC/*Wall Street Journal* poll, December 1995; *USA Today*/CNN-Gallup Poll, November 10, 1995, reported in George Gallup Jr., *The Gallup Poll: Public Opinion 1995* (Wilmington, Del.: Scholarly Resource Inc., 1996), p. 272; Wines and Pear, "President Finds Benefits in Defeat on Health Care"; "Surveys and Polls—Harris: More than Two-Thirds Support More Health Reforms," *Healthline*, October 9, 1996 (from the Internet); David W. Moore, "Polling on Health Care and Medicare: Continuity in Public Opinion," *Public Perspective*, vol. 6 (October–November 1995), p. 14.

82. The mid-session budget report for fiscal year 1996, for instance, revealed that medicaid expenditures were up just 2.5 percent, not the approximately 20 percent a year of the early 1990s, even with increased enrollments. Bruce Vladeck, "Seminar on the Future of Medicaid in the Commonwealth of Pennsylvania," University of Pittsburgh, Institute of Politics and Health Policy Institute, July 26, 1996 (author's notes).

83. Paul B. Ginsburg and Jeremy D. Pickreign, "Tracking Health Care Costs," *Health Affairs*, vol. 15 (Fall 1996), pp. 140–49; Katharine R. Levit, Helen C. Lazenby, and Lekha Sivarajan, "Health Care Spending in 1994: Slowest in Decades," *Health Affairs*, vol. 15 (Summer 1996), pp. 130–44; "A Look at Employers' Costs of Providing Health Benefits," *Medical Benefits*, vol. 13, August 30, 1996, p. 1; Vladeck, "Seminar on the Future of Medicaid in the Commonwealth of Pennsylvania"; and "Remarks by the President to the Community of the Pittsburgh Area," Robert Morris College, September 25, 1996.

84. "Health Care Check-Up: Consumers at Risk," *Medical Benefits*, vol. 13 (June 15, 1996), p. 8.

85. About three-quarters of employees in 1995, compared with one-half in 1983, directly paid part of their health insurance premiums, an expenditure that on average doubled from $45 a month for a family to $107. Fewer workers were participating in employer-offered plans, in part reflecting a decline in employer sponsorship of health benefits. Information on employers comes from "National Survey of Employer-Sponsored Health Plans 1995," *Medical Benefits*, vol. 13 (February 29, 1996), p. 2; and "A Look at Employers' Costs of Providing Health Benefits," *Medical Benefits*, vol. 13 (August 30, 1996), p. 2.

86. Levit and others, "Health Care Spending in 1994," pp. 133–34.

87. "HMO Industry Report," *Medical Benefits*, vol. 13 (April 30, 1996), p. 1; Robert Kazel, "Blues Growth Tied to Managed Care: Plans Reorganize to Compete," *Medical Benefits*, vol. 13 (June 30, 1996), p. 7; "Medicare HMOs' Rapid Enrollment Growth Concentrated in Selected States," *Medical Benefits*, vol. 13 (April 15, 1996), p. 10; and *Medicaid Facts* (Washington: Kaiser Commission on the Future of Medicaid, May 1996), p. 1.

88. "Managed Care Thrives as HMO Enrollment Soars," *Medical Benefits*, vol. 13 (October 15, 1996), p. 10; "HMO Industry Report"; "1995 AAHP HMO & PPO Trends Report," *Medical Benefits*, vol. 13 (July 30, 1996), p. 1; "1995 Survey

of State Employee Health Benefit Plans," *Medical Benefits*, vol. 13 (January 15, 1996), p. 5; Gail A. Jensen and others, "The New Dominance of Managed Care: Insurance Trends in the 1990s," *Health Affairs*, vol. 16 (January–February 1997), p. 126; and "Blues' Managed Care Enrollment Surpasses Fee-for-Service," *Medical Benefits*, vol. 13 (September 15, 1996), p. 6.

89. "1995 AAHP HMO & PPO Trends Report." See also Jonathan B. Oberlander, "Managed Care and Medicare Reform," *Journal of Health Politics, Policy and Law*, vol. 22 (April 1997), pp. 595–631.

90. Rosemary Stevens, *American Medicine and the Public Interest* (Yale University Press, 1971); Paul Starr, *The Social Transformation of American Medicine* (Basic Books, 1982); and Carol J. Simon and Patricia H. Born, "Physician Earnings in a Changing Managed Care Environment," *Health Affairs*, vol. 15 (Fall 1996), pp. 124–33.

91. Kenneth E. Thorpe, "The Health System in Transition: Care, Cost, and Coverage," *Journal of Health Politics, Policy and Law*, vol. 22 (April 1997), pp. 339–61; Robert E. Mechanic and Allen Dobson, "The Impact of Managed Care on Clinical Research: A Preliminary Investigation," *Health Affairs*, vol. 15 (Fall 1996), pp. 72–89; and Deborah Haas-Wilson and Martin Gaynor, "Antitrust Policy and the Transformation of Health Care Markets," paper prepared for 1996 annual meeting of the Robert Wood Johnson Investigator Awards in Health Policy Research Program.

92. "Mega Managed Care Deal Redefines Market," *Medical Benefits*, vol. 13 (April 30, 1996), p. 5; Marc Levinson, "Health Care: Profit Motive," *Newsweek*, April 22, 1996, p. 56; and "HMO-PPO Digest, 1995," *Medical Benefits*, vol. 13 (March 15, 1996), p. 2.

93. Johnson and Broder, *The System*, p. 534; and Robin Toner, "Health Cares: Harry and Louise Were Right, Sort of," *New York Times*, November 24, 1996, sec. 4, pp. 1, 3.

94. Bureau of the Census, U.S. Department of Commerce, *Statistical Abstract of the United States 1996*, 116th ed., p. 120, table 173; "Sources of Health Insurance and Characteristics of the Uninsured," *Medical Benefits*, vol. 13 (November 30, 1996), p. 4; Wines and Pear, "President Finds Benefits in Defeat on Health Care," p. A8; "More in U.S. Lose Health Coverage," *Pittsburgh Post-Gazette*, September 11, 1996, p. A9; and "Health Insurance for Children: Private Insurance Coverage Continues to Deteriorate," *Medical Benefits*, vol. 13 (August 15, 1996), p. 7.

95. Thorpe, "Health System in Transition."

96. Joseph Berger, "In Westchester County, Welfare Meets Managed Care," *New York Times*, September 9, 1996, p. A1; and Marsha Gold, "Markets and Public Programs: Insights from Oregon and Tennessee," *Journal of Health Politics, Policy and Law*, vol. 22 (April 1997), pp. 633–66.

97. "Health Benefits in 1996," *Medical Benefits*, vol. 13 (November 15, 1996), p. 2.

98. "1995 Managed Care Executives National Survey," *Medical Benefits*, vol. 13 (February 15, 1996), p. 8.

99. Pamela Paul-Shaheen, "The States and Health Care Reform: The Road Traveled and the Lessons Learned from Seven That Took the Lead," *Journal of Health Politics, Policy and Law*, forthcoming; and Mary Ann Chirba-Martin and Troyen A. Brennan, "The Critical Role of ERISA in State Health Reform," *Health Affairs*, vol. 13 (Spring II 1994), pp. 142–56.

100. Gold, "Markets and Public Programs"; and Colleen M. Grogan, "The Medicaid Managed Care Policy Consensus for Welfare Recipients: A Reflection of Traditional Welfare Concerns," *Journal of Health Politics, Policy and Law*, vol. 22 (June 1997), pp. 815–58.

101. "State Managed Care Legislative Activity," *Medical Benefits*, vol. 13 (April 30, 1996), p. 4; Jill A. Marsteller and others, "The Resurgence of Selective Contracting Restrictions," *Journal of Health Politics, Policy and Law*, vol. 22 (October 1997), pp. 1133–99; and Robert Pear, "Laws Won't Let H.M.O.'s Tell Doctors What to Say," *New York Times*, September 17, 1996, p. A9.

102. Robert Pear, "Conferees Agree on More Coverage for Health Care," *New York Times*, September 20, 1996, p. A11; and "Statement by the President," signing of H.R. 3666, Departments of Veterans Affairs and Housing and Urban Development, and Independent Agencies Appropriations Act, FY 1997, The White House, Washington, D.C., September 26, 1996.

103. Peterson, *Legislating Together*, pp. 123–24.

104. Todd S. Purdum, "Clinton Signs Bill to Give Portability in Insurance," *New York Times*, August 22, 1996, p. A14.

105. The bill was intended to help provide portability of insurance as workers changed jobs or became unemployed. The bill, however, does not fulfill conventional notions of portability. Workers do not carry their existing insurance coverage with its range of benefits from one job to another. The actual coverage they would receive might have quite different benefits and costs.

106. Based on responses to the mail survey of interest groups.

107. Robert Pear, "Deal in Congress Gives Health Bill a New Momentum," *New York Times*, July 26, 1996, A7. One study estimated that if only 25 percent of healthy individuals chose MSAs over traditional insurance, the cost of a comprehensive health insurance policy for those who retained it would jump 63 percent. Marilyn Moon, Len M. Nichols, and Susan Wall, "Tax-Preferred Medical Savings Accounts and Catastrophic Health Insurance Plans: A Numerical Analysis of Winners and Losers," Working Paper 06571-002 (Washington: Urban Institute, April 1996).

108. Adam Clymer, "Public Lacks Strong Opinions on Health Bill, Survey Shows," *New York Times*, July 31, 1996, p. A11.

109. The law included a number of other provisions, such as increasing health insurance deductibility for the self-employed, giving long-term care insurance premiums the same tax status as health insurance premiums, and tax protection of accelerated death benefits. Steve Langdon and Alissa J. Rubin, "Health Insur-

ance Bill Fight Ends with Deal on Savings Accounts," *Congressional Quarterly Weekly Report*, August 3, 1996, pp. 2198–99.

110. Robert A. Rosenblatt, "Health Reform Bill Is Signed," *Pittsburgh Post-Gazette*, August 22, 1996, p. A20.

111. Thomas R. Oliver and Robert M. Fiedler, "State Government and Health Insurance Market Reform," in Howard M. Leichter, ed., *Health Policy in America: Innovations from the States*, 2d ed. (Armonk, N.Y.: M. E. Sharpe, 1997), chap. 3.

112. Robert Pear, "Health Insurers Skirting New Law, Officials Report," *New York Times*, October 5, 1997, p. 1.

113. To acquire individual insurance, one must have previously been in a group insurance plan, left that coverage without having any other group options, and expired COBRA coverage first. Most individuals cannot afford the costs of COBRA insurance. Of the 14.5 percent of employees eligible for COBRA coverage, fewer than one in five elect it. "Portability of Health Insurance: COBRA Expansions and Small Group Market Reform," *Healthcare Trends Report*, vol. 10 (February 1996), p. 7.

114. Todd S. Purdum, "Clinton Signs Bill to Give Portability in Insurance," *New York Times*, August 22, 1996, p. A14.

115. "Finally, A Health Bill," *New York Times*, July 27, 1996, p. 22.

116. "Unintended Consequences," *Medical Benefits*, vol. 14 (September 30, 1997), p. 6.

117. Average voting scores for 1995 assembled by the liberal Americans for Democratic Action (ADA) show almost complete separation of the parties in Congress, and more so than just two years before. "ADA's 1995 Voting Record Shows Dramatic Polarization in Congress: More Than Twice as Many House Members Score Zero," *ADA Today: A Newsletter of Liberal Activists*, vol. 51 (March 1996), p. 1.

118. Todd S. Purdum, "Clinton Promises to Create a 'Coalition of the Center,'" *New York Times*, December 12, 1996, p. A16; Francis X. Clines, "Gingrich Sees Improved Relations between Congress and Clinton," *New York Times*, December 4, 1996, p. A18; and Richard W. Stevenson, "Deficit Estimates of the Two Sides Are Edging Closer," *New York Times*, December 2, 1996, pp. A1, A11.

119. Mary Agnes Carey, "Critics: Law Could Be Unhealthful for Elderly—and for Medicare," *Congressional Quarterly Weekly Report*, September 13, 1997, pp. 2146–49; and Robert Pear, "$24 Billion Would Be Set Aside for Medical Care for Children," *New York Times*, July 30, 1997, p. A13.

120. Robert G. Evans, "Going for the Gold: The Redistributive Agenda behind Market-Based Health Care Reform," *Journal of Health Politics, Policy and Law*, vol. 22 (April 1997), pp. 427–66.

Chapter 6

Inviting Business to the Party: The Corporate Response to Social Policy

Cathie Jo Martin

DURING President Bill Clinton's first term, both Democrats and Republicans attempted to make profound changes in the nation's system of social provision. Clinton sought to require employers to grant their workers family leave and proposed a fundamental overhaul of the health financing system; the Republicans proposed to cut medicare radically and to erode guarantees of health coverage for elderly people. A greatly pared-down Family and Medical Leave Act passed, but both health bills failed.

Big business interests were at least initially considered to be important players in these legislative campaigns. First, because many social benefits in the United States are dispensed through private companies, public policy changes have profound implications for corporations. This blend of public and private provision means that pressures on one sector inevitably affect the other; for example, questions about the adequacy of company medical plans (coverage, portability, and costs) prompted discussion about public health reform.

Second, the new politics of the budget deficit left both parties needing business support and offering corporate managers very different rationales for signing onto the parties' political programs. For the Democrats, the deficit made expanded or new public programs politically impossible; instead, the party decided to use the employer-based system of social benefits to achieve its new social goals. Thus, in a sharp break with New Deal social prescriptions, the Clinton administration sought not to create new spending programs, but rather to impose new regulations on the private sector.

The Democrats tried to attract corporate backers by framing their initiatives as part of a larger project to reorganize social policy. Clinton argued that markets failed to provide American industry the resources necessary to capture world market share: government should assist industry with economic and social investment policies to maximize America's competitive advantage. Because employers were already paying a large share of social benefits, the Democrats hoped that mandates would seem like a logical extension of the status quo. Corporate payers had good reasons for wanting nonpayers to assume their fair share: many companies with benefits were in fact paying for workers without coverage either through hospital-imposed surcharges for the uninsured or through family benefits.

For the Republicans, their goals of balancing the budget and reducing government were the rationale for asking business to back social spending cuts. The GOP assumed that exploding nonwage labor costs and pressures of international competition would make corporate payers and nonpayers wary of new social burdens. Rationalizing costs might be appealing, but mandating new benefits could be frightening, especially to labor-intensive, low-wage companies. Thus the Republicans offered managers a move in the opposite direction from the Democrats: less social provision, lower taxes, and substantial reductions in public programs such as medicare to inject market rationality into the public system (and incidentally to create new profit opportunities for the health care industry.)

Third, business managers were key as agents of change. For the Democrats, company providers were necessary to implementing the new social initiatives. Clinton planned to use markets as a way of achieving social ends; as private providers of social benefits, big business managers were critical to this market restructuring.

The parties also saw employers as sources of political power and sought to include them in legislative coalitions. The Democrats had limited success mobilizing corporate support. Although much big business opinion was favorable toward the Clinton health plan in the prelegislative period, the initial interest later evaporated. The Republicans fared better with their allies, organizing an impressive business show of force to support their balanced budget and antiregulatory agenda. But they, too, ultimately fell short of their goals.

This essay considers the possibilities for bringing business managers into policy coalitions, exploring the failure of the Clinton administration to secure much corporate support for its social initiatives and the greater

Republican success in rallying business allies. Business support for spending reduction is not inherently surprising. But the GOP success diverges from conventional wisdom. Although the Republican party has historically been portrayed as a handmaiden to leaders of industry, small business was the backbone of support for the Republicans' social policies. Many big business managers were quite wary about the Republican social agenda; for example, they stood to lose much from the medicare reform through increased cost shifting onto private payers.

I argue that it has become increasingly difficult for Democrats to bring corporate allies into social reform coalitions because of the institutional organization of U.S. big business and the difficulties that Democrats face in simultaneously winning support from key interest groups and mobilizing public opinion. First, institutional features of American business have always made it difficult to mobilize corporate leaders in support of long-term policy change, and recent changes within business have exacerbated this problem. Corporate receptiveness to social policy legislation depends on how business is organized. Although American business managers are very good at acting on their own narrow, short-term self-interests, they are not organized in ways that support broad collective goals. Without a unitary peak employer association, corporate managers lack a forum to make difficult zero-sum decisions and to commit collectively to a course of action.

Second, business involvement in social policy legislation depends on policy entrepreneurs' strategies vis-à-vis business, but the Democratic party today has a much more difficult time incorporating sympathetic corporate elites into its policy coalitions. In matters of both message and strategy, the party finds it hard to reconcile the equity concerns of the "have-nots" with the human investment interests of corporate sponsors. Populist appeals designed to excite the first serve only to alienate the second.

In comparison, Republicans have been much more successful at building business coalitions. Small business allies are much better organized, and the GOP has a less diverse coalition and a less activist agenda than the Democratic party.

Employment-Based Social Benefits under Pressure

Business and social policy have little in common at first glance, and one might wonder why politicians would reach out to corporate America for support in this area. But for years large employers have been a major source of social benefits, filling in the vacuum left by the very limited government welfare state. Employers began offering employee benefits in the late nineteenth century to curb labor unrest. Initially hostile to company plans, unions viewed benefits as weapons to halt the advance of collective bargaining and to trap workers in onerous jobs. But the creation of the National War Labor Board (NWLB) during World War II precipitated a dramatic expansion of the employee benefit system. Anxious to prevent inflation, the NWLB limited wage increases but did not regulate benefits, so workers negotiated benefit increases as a way to expand their total compensation package. The excise profits tax also pushed the growth of benefits, because firms could pay for benefits with pretax dollars. Shortly after the war the labor movement expanded its earlier campaign for greater government social provision to include private sector benefits.[1]

Today, while other countries have public health insurance, training programs, child allowances, and pensions, the United States has a patchwork system of benefits in which private employers play a key role. This "shadow welfare state" is heavily subsidized by the federal government because business expenditures for health insurance and pensions are tax deductible. Tax expenditures for these purposes amounted to $64.4 billion for employer health plans and $55.4 billion for employer pensions in 1996.[2] Business is at the heart of the health care system: almost two-thirds of the nonelderly population is covered through employers.[3] Business health care spending climbed from 2.2 percent of salaries and wages in 1965 to 8.3 percent by 1989.[4] Even the biggest government benefit program, social security, has enormous help from the private sector in funding retirement income: in 1993 social security old-age benefits (combined with disability insurance) paid individuals $297.9 billion, and private employer pensions paid out $192.6 billion.[5] Many employers also provided supplemental unemployment, disability, and life insurance.

Significant as it is, the coverage of the system of employer-provided benefits is quite uneven. Less-educated and lower-paid workers are much less likely to receive benefits from their employers. For example, in 1992, only 28.4 percent of family heads who had not completed high school received health benefits from their employers, compared with 81 percent among those who had completed college.[6]

Recent economic and political changes have eroded the social provision of many firms. International trade has pushed firms to price competitively and often to reduce total compensation costs. Companies worry about providing benefits when nonpaying firms shift social costs onto paying ones. For example, many large companies provide health benefits to the spouses of their workers when these spouses cannot obtain coverage through their own employers.

A tighter competitive climate has prompted firms to scale back services and to shift social risk to their workers. In 1982, 84 percent of employees were enrolled in defined-benefit plans, which pay benefits based on workers' years of service and salary history. By 1994 only 56 percent were in such plans; the remainder were in defined-contribution plans, in which benefits are based solely on the accumulated contributions of workers and firms.[7] Employer-provided health benefits also declined, and workers had to make up the difference. In large and medium firms, employers fully financed health insurance for 56 percent of their employees in 1988; only five years later that number had dropped to 37 percent. The extent of family coverage in health insurance also declined. In 1988, 36 percent of employees participated in health insurance plans in which the employer fully paid for benefits for the worker's family; by 1993 only 21 percent of employers picked up the tab for an entire family.[8] Moreover, the number of temporary workers—least likely to receive benefits from their employers—has grown in recent years.[9] Thus, just when workers are needing an expanded safety net, the private welfare state has less to offer. *Business Week* remarked:

> The relationship [between company and worker] isn't what it was. The new compact between company and worker dismisses paternalism and embraces self-reliance. Bid farewell to unconditional lifetime employment, even at the bluest of blue-chip companies that once implicitly turned on such an ethic.[10]

Economic competition may be forcing companies to reevaluate their programs of social provision, but social changes are creating new needs. By 1987 working mothers represented 65 percent of the labor force. Female executives have urged their companies to accommodate these dramatic gender changes in the composition of the work force with a variety of family-oriented policies such as parental leaves and help with child care.[11]

Globalization is challenging all countries to alter their systems of social provision, as the national regulatory structures suited for the 1950s and 1960s seem inappropriate to the new rules of global economic battle. But despite consensus about the problem—the need to remain competitive in a changed economic world—there is much dissension in business over the best course of action. Managers disagree about the impact of labor market institutions and social supports on market efficiency and company profits. Some are drawn to a laissez-faire approach that considers social provision detrimental to these goals; others, to a high-performance work force approach that considers social investment a necessary component.

The laissez-faire approach would cut social spending in both the private and public realm in order to reduce labor costs and free up investment capital. In this view, social policies, especially those that impose regulations on employers, limit companies' ability to hire and fire in downturns; therefore, firms avoid hiring extra workers and the system actually augments unemployment. The minimum wage allows workers to stay unskilled, so that firms would be less willing to hire them. Social security taxes swell the cost of labor, as do fringe benefits. Health insurance limits worker mobility and thereby harms efficiency. Social programs can enlarge the tax burden and budget deficits.[12] Thus social policies detract from economic growth in this zero-sum world.

The high-performance workplace approach recommends rationalizing, targeting, and often expanding social investment spending by governments or firms in order to develop the competent, productive work force necessary to knowledge-intensive, high-tech production. This approach links the well-being of workers to a strong bottom line for the firm. Social investments are part of the solution, because the new era of flexible manufacturing entails greater investment in the work force. Flexibility is necessary to postindustrial manufacturing, when products and production processes are changing quickly, consumer tastes cry out for variety (operationalized as limited production runs), and computer technologies favor the jack-of-all-trades over the assembly-line automaton.

Managers in some companies have been attracted to government social investment policies for several reasons. Companies that already provide social benefits would like government to force their competitors also to offer benefits; for instance, much of the corporate debate about national health reform fixed on ending cost shifting. Some big corporate spenders (often with firm commitments to their unions) would like the government to bail them out by assuming some of the costs of social provision. Again, some automobile and steel companies sought national health reform to evade their commitments to unionized workers who retired early. Finally, some firms believe that a coherent government policy could rationalize the current system of social delivery and encourage greater provision of a collective benefit. But even those business managers who advocate social investment do not want broad new government programs of the New Deal vintage; rather, they look for solutions that work through existing private markets and do not interfere with their own private programs.

Constructing Preferences and Choosing Sides

How do companies choose between these competing visions about limiting or expanding social investment in workers? To some extent the battle lines separate firms that already provide benefits from those that do not and, consequently, large from small firms. Large and small employers have substantially different interests in social investment: small firms tend to be less involved in international markets and have less incentive to ensure that worker skill levels meet European standards. Large corporate providers want to end cost shifting; because small firms tend to offer fewer benefits and are the source of cost shifting, they have no interest in a level playing field. Typically labor-intensive enterprises, small companies are likely to oppose social investment policies that place any additional labor costs on firms.

The data reflect big businesses' greater involvement in social provision. In a 1986 study, all sampled firms with over 500 employees offered health benefits, while only 55 percent of small companies had programs; 79 percent of the big companies had pension plans, compared with 16 percent of the smaller firms.[13] In a 1994 study, small firms with under 100 workers spent 84 cents per hour worked (5.7 percent) on health benefits, while large companies with over 500 workers spent $1.84 (7.9 percent). Eight percent of the small companies in one study provided paternity leave in 1992; 53 percent of large and medium companies provided it in 1993.[14] The American Management Association found that companies with fewer than 50 employees were much more likely to fear operational stability would be harmed by the Family and Medical Leave Act (55 percent) than larger companies (28 percent).[15] Distinctions also separate manufacturing and service sectors. In 1994 the retail trade sector spent $2.03 an hour on all benefits for its employees, or 22 percent of total compensation. Manufacturing firms spent $7.03 an hour on all benefits, or 34 percent of total compensation.[16]

But this distinction between large and small does not tell the whole story. Obviously small high-technology companies have very different social investment needs from grocers; large insurers' interests in health system restructuring are quite unlike those of large auto producers. At least some companies' interests are difficult to pigeonhole. Firms, like people, have conflicting goals. Managers cannot be sure that their actions will achieve the intended outcomes; widespread concern about a problem does not translate into agreement about its cause and effect.[17] In situations where interests are complex and uncertain, business managers' grasp of complicated social issues will depend in part on whether they have the institutional resources to learn about technical policy problems and are organized to take action based on this learning.

American Business Organization and Collective Social Goods

The essential question, of course, is whether the laissez-faire approach or that favoring social investment in workers will carry the day. The marginal contribution of business mobilization to social investment initiatives is likely to reinforce those espousing the laissez-faire approach for three reasons: the nature of the tasks facing the two groups, the organizational clout of each, and the business mobilization capacities of each side's primary party allies.

The Nature of the Task

First, the business supporters of laissez-faire are likely to have more impact on social investment policy (or the lack thereof) because they have a simpler task. It is generally easier to attack than to support in the U.S. political system because proactive positions require collective action.[18] Firms have difficulty bearing social costs on their own; rather they need organizational cover that will commit all to a social course and will increase their trust that they will not be punished for their collective behavior.[19] In addition, payroll issues are directly linked to the bottom line for labor-intensive small employers, but they are typically of somewhat less importance to capital-intensive large firms, which often save their political capital for more relevant battles.

Organizational Superiority

A second reason the forces behind laissez-faire are likely to win is that the small business groups at the heart of the coalition are much better organized. Large employers who favor expanded public social provision have no distinctive voice (apart from the Business Roundtable, which seldom expresses anything more than general principles), and the groups responsible for representing big companies' political views almost never reflect the full extent of positive business attitudes toward social initiatives.

Scholars tend to assume that weak business organization enables greater welfare state development.[20] Yet business managers' political capacity to support collective social goals depends on their cognitive ability to perceive the link between social investment and economic growth and their organizational discipline to focus on broad, mutual concerns over narrrow self-interest. Therefore a higher degree of business organization may actually increase corporate support for social investment initiatives. Organization of business in the United States is likely to discourage corporate support for expanded social initiatives.[21] American business is politically quite fragmented, and the explosion of narrow interest groups since the 1960s has prevented business managers from articulating a broad, collective vision of their own long-term interests.[22] The development of in-house political expertise within the firm has exacerbated the proliferation of voices. Although government affairs offices provide companies with greater knowledge of public policy, they paradoxically accelerate the fragmentation of the business perspective by creating the means for identifying a separate firm interest.

A least-common-denominator politics within the big umbrella associations (the most likely sources of centralized thinking and planning among business leaders) also limits collective thinking. American business managers have a more difficult time finding common ground than their counterparts elsewhere, which reflects a weakness in the organizations that represent employers in the political realm. Unlike business managers in many advanced industrialized countries, U.S. business-people have no single peak association to aggregate their interests at a class level.[23] Rather, the Chamber of Commerce and the National Association of Manufacturers compete to represent the entire business community, and the Business Roundtable claims to represent big business. In addition, industrial sectors have trade associations that operate as independent agents, further fragmenting the business voice.

Competition among groups claiming to represent business compels these various entities to function as sales organizations—competing to win new members—rather than as democratic decisionmaking bodies. Unable to make difficult choices, employer organizations tend to defer to vocal minorities and to neglect the sentiments of the more silent majority. Constant catering to minority objections means that associations resort to a least-common-denominator politics, expressing only broad, inoffensive but empty principles and seldom providing leadership. Since change always offends somebody, these groups find it easier to voice short-term objections than to endorse broader, long-term change. Thus, despite its impressive reputation for political power, big business is so politically fragmented that its representative associations usually engage in only the most limited of political activities. As one business respondent put it, "I can't tell you how many times I've sat in a room where all but one person supported a position; and if that one person objected, we didn't do it."

These constraints typically do not affect action toward the narrowly targeted self-interests of companies; when a few large firms or sectors have very direct economic interests, managers often dominate the policy process.[24] But where a wide spectrum of companies shares broad collective goals, employers are hard pressed to find common ground. Without being certain that other companies will go along, it is hard for even the most farsighted to take long-term positions because they might be punished for their behavior. If they train workers, they run the risk of these workers being raided by other companies. If they offer health benefits, they can be undersold by companies not offering these benefits.

The profile of small business groups offers a sharp contrast to the behavior of umbrella organizations and reinforces the importance of organization. First, media and public appeals have come to dominate modern political life, making the ability to exercise spin control and to shape public perception of an issue extremely important to political outcomes. Small businesses evoke the same kind of nostalgic reminiscences as farmers; this mom-and-pop-store profile allows the little guys to win very favorable approval ratings from outside publics. For example, in 1982,

71 percent of journalists found small firm proprietors credible, but only 50 percent believed CEOs of big corporations.[25]

Even more important in this going-public world, small business groups such as the National Federation of Independent Business (NFIB) and the National Restaurant Association have a connected mass base that they can call upon in every congressional district to demonstrate a public show of organizational force.[26] The very weakness of small employers in the old days when Washington was a closed community—their numbers, diversity, and lack of prestige—is a source of strength today. The well-heeled corporate lobbyist who wielded such power behind closed doors lacks the television charisma of hundreds of restauranteurs storming Congress. Innovations in computer technologies have augmented the advantage of small business groups: grass-roots computer mailings first made popular by public interest groups are perfectly suited to their large and varied membership.

Second, the most prominent of these groups have developed organizational decision rules to augment the natural advantages of a broad-based, numerous membership. The NFIB avoids the least-common-denominator politics of larger umbrella groups by grounding its policy positions in regular membership polls. This practice both gives the organization's positions legitimacy and enables it to reach zero-sum decisions that adversely affect a minority subset of members. *Roll Call* has called the NFIB "the most powerful advocacy group in Washington."[27]

Of course, even the most inclusive of small business groups has an easier time of it: they enjoy a more homogeneous membership than umbrella organizations that include both large and small employers. Indeed, the Chamber of Commerce has suffered from a sort of schizophrenia as it has flip-flopped between its big and small business constituents over the years. After a period of relative inaction, the chamber grew dramatically in the late 1970s and early 1980s, moved to the ideological right, and developed a grass-roots operation called Citizen's Choice, which organized mass telephone calls to legislators before key congressional actions. The chamber's budget for research and political action increased threefold between 1974 and 1980. This period marked a close relationship with the small employer members of the chamber (about 59 percent have fewer than ten workers), whom the organization viewed as an enormous source of power in lobbying Congress.[28] The move to the right alienated the chamber's big business members, and in the late 1980s the organization shifted dramatically toward its international, high-technology, big business wing. Then in 1993 it swung back to the right again.

But small business enjoys less ideological homogeneity than one might think; indeed, opinion polls show a polarization among small employers. Some want no government interventions in areas such as health and family policies; others want even more government involvement than that desired by large employers, believing that small firms cannot hope to offer social investment support on their own. Thus the NFIB found a quarter of its members favored a government single-payer plan in health reform.[29]

Finally, small business groups have overcome the least-common-denominator politics syndrome with single-issue coalitions. Large employers sometimes join these coalitions; for instance, Pepsico was an important actor in the Health Equity Action League's efforts to defeat the Clinton health plan. But groups such as the NFIB, the National Association of Wholesaler-Distributors, the National Restaurant Association, and the National Retail Association are typically at the core of these coalitions and are the leaders in organizational efforts. Indeed, the small business lobby has explicitly tried to establish itself as an independent voting bloc. In the words of NFIB grass-roots organizer R. Marc Nuttle, "Christians did not realize how big they were. Pat Robertson put a face on them and I intend to do that for small business."[30] The NFIB recently passed on to its members David Broder's rhetorical question, "Is there a small business voting bloc?" The association's response was predictable: "Your personal involvement can help make the answer 'Yes.'"[31]

Coalitions evolve when employers are dissatisfied with the umbrella associations' least-common-denominator politics and believe that a new forum dedicated to a single issue can make tougher decisions.[32] Typically organized to influence a specific bill, some outlast their precipitating legislative initiatives. They may be organized by business groups or by public sector policy entrepreneurs within the administration or in Congress. According to Dirk Van Dongen, the groups organized by political figures tend to have a greater sense of direction.

There is a big distinction between a coalition that has an elected official and one that doesn't. The Reagan administration was very adept at providing leadership from the top down. They had a goal and mobilized folks that shared that goal and provided leadership. That type of leadership gave a sense of direction and position that you don't have without that type of leadership. . . . It gives a clarity in the exercise that is not there as much in the absence of that [political leadership].[33]

Not all coalitions achieve discipline, but the most successful have developed decision rules to keep participants committed to general objectives. In exchange for specific benefits, members must pledge to support the entire legislative package and not to make side deals with the other side. The Republican Contract's Thursday Group presents a good example of this decision rule. The leadership asked group members to take a "blood oath" to back the Contract with America in its entirety in exchange for action on their concerns. One participant explained, "We have no independent goals; all goals come from the leadership. We will do whatever the leadership feels we should do."[34]

Mobilization Capacity

Finally, the business supporters of laissez-faire have been strengthened by the Republicans' relatively easier task of mobilization. In the age of deficits, Democratic goals for expansion of social programs are politically harder to achieve than Republican cutbacks. Fiscal constraint has made it harder for the Democratic party to harmonize the needs of both haves and have-nots. Constituency-building dilemmas pose challenges for strategy: a populist mass politics has very different policy implications from business mobilization. Divisions among constituents have been exacerbated by the seeming inability of the Democrats to find a strong ideological message that could unify diverse factions. Despite Clinton's efforts to create a new public philosophy, "tax and spend" Democrats have been unable to reinvent themselves as investors in human resources in part because they need to address the very real concerns of society's disadvantaged.

The Republican program of contracting government spending in a period of deficit restraint—combined with ideological unity, less constituency conflict, and greater organizational strength—has made it easier to mobilize business allies. But the Republicans also face political problems in their attack on programs that have enormous legitimacy and public support. The Republicans are also likely to face distributional conflicts between business and radical right constituents. Thus the GOP leadership must persuade supporters among business managers to buy into the broad project of contraction even when this project attacks specific interests.

The following discussion of initiatives during the two halves of the first Clinton administration reveals how the policy legacies of the private welfare state involved employers in public policy reforms and how the different organizational strengths of big and small business affected political outcomes.

The Family and Medical Leave Act

The Family and Medical Leave Act, signed into law in 1993 after seven years of legislative failure, revealed the strength of small businesses, which opposed the measure, and the relative quiescence of big businesses, many of which already provided such benefits. First proposed in 1985, the measure granted unpaid leave to workers after the birth or adoption of a child or for serious family medical problems. The bill failed in 1985 and was successfully filibustered in the Senate in 1988. Congress passed the bill twice in 1990 and 1991, only to have it vetoed by President George Bush. The overwhelming popularity of the measure ensured its passage once Clinton was elected. According to pollster Ethel Klein, by 1989, 93 percent of Americans believed that individuals should have a right to take a leave to care for a newborn or sick parent without the threat of losing their jobs.[35] Nonetheless, the delay in enactment is rather astounding, given the high level of public support and the ubiquitous presence of leaves in the industrialized world; small business groups may take full credit for the procrastination and for the limited reach of the bill the president ultimately signed.

Business Positions

Many large companies are sympathetic to work-family issues, especially because of the perceived links between productivity and family policies. New mothers in firms with flexible leave policies and health care express greater satisfaction, have lower levels of absenteeism, take less time off during pregnancy, and are more likely to return to their jobs.[36] As Carol Sladek of Hewitt Associates put it, "Companies that are perceived as being family-friendly realize that it's good for that company's bottom line."[37] Turnover is enormously expensive for a company. The Families and Work Institute calculated that it costs 75 to 150 percent of an employee's salary to replace a worker but only 32 percent to grant him or her a leave. Merck estimated that a six-month parental leave policy actually saved $12,000 per employee by eliminating turnover costs. In a Fortune 1000 sample, 55 percent feared potential future labor shortages.[38]

One might think that family and medical leave would be an easy policy for large employers to endorse, since it ratified the status quo for many big firms. Yet big business experts in work-family issues had practically no involvement with the national legislative debate, largely because of their lack of political organization. Work-family experts have a more tenuous position within the firm than managers in other social investment areas because they are often brought in from the outside and placed in new divisions rather than incorporated into the traditional human resources departments, which have close relations with government affairs. Because these experts are predominantly women, their issue connotes feminist overtones. Finally, this relatively new issue has no corporate organizational sponsor to organize business followers, to spread the word in the larger business community, and to push the issue in the public arena.[39]

Where large employers largely ignored the issue, small business trade associations made opposing family leave a cause célèbre for seven years. Conservative critics sought to frame the policy as a new entitlement.[40] Participants like Michael Roush at the NFIB worried that the family leave act set a precedent for mandates and promised to be a first step in a slippery slope toward an expanded welfare state. Opponents also feared that the requirement for unpaid leaves would become the ubiquitous camel's nose under the tent leading to paid leaves.[41] Small business predicted dire economic effects on companies; small firms especially would be hit with high costs for hiring and training replacement workers.[42] Chamber of Commerce lobbyist Virginia B. Lamp argued that the leave motivated employers to discriminate against women in hiring decisions. Parental leave would also replace other goodies in the employee benefits "pie" and reduce the flexibility to negotiate alternative compensation packages.[43]

Business Mobilization

When first introduced in 1985, as the Parental and Disability Leave Act, the measure covered all businesses, provided up to eighteen weeks of unpaid leave for mothers and fathers of newborn or adopted children, and granted up to twenty-six weeks of leave for workers with disabilities and sick children. Over the next eight years, the initial core of feminist and liberal Democratic supporters expanded their congressional coalition by increasing the reasons leave could be granted, by exempting small businesses, and by reducing the weeks of guaranteed leave. The interest coalition they built included such pro-family groups as the Catholic Conference, as well as more traditionally liberal groups such as organized labor and the American Association of Retired Persons, which signed on when provisions for eldercare were added to the bill. Throughout consideration of the bill, small business proved the principal and most staunch opponent of the Family and Medical Leave Act.[44]

The U.S. Chamber of Commerce initially led the small business attack on family leave policy, but in 1987 some fifty-eight companies and groups contributed $175 each to form a new coalition, the Concerned Alliance of Responsible Employers (CARE).[45] The coalition met on a weekly basis, often in close coordination with the Reagan administration, to discuss new information, tally congressional positions, and distribute assignments.[46]

Both the chamber coalition and CARE fought to defeat family leave with the usual arsenal of coalition strategies: spin control, Mailgrams, and media events. Presented with formidable public enthusiasm for family leaves, the small employers tried to cast the issue in a less attractive light. CARE conducted its own public opinion poll showing that even while many Americans supported family leaves, they remained ambivalent about mandating this benefit. Small business picked up Phyllis Schlafly's (Eagle Forum) refrain that family leave was a "yuppie" issue.[47]

Small business opponents did a series of massive direct mail campaigns urging members to contact legislators each time the bill seemed to progress. In the fall of 1987 CARE's major offensive made the bill lose legislative sponsors. CARE's Mary Tavenner quipped, "We've been all over those guys like a cheap suit." In August 1988 the chamber urged members to "blitz" legislators with Mailgrams and phone calls.[48] By October the Senate had killed the family leave bill, with very few moderate Republicans defecting from their party's majority. Senator Christopher Dodd, Democrat of Connecticut, blamed business lobbying for the defeat, angrily adding that "groups that support parental leave or child care don't have any political action committee money."[49]

The Bush administration offered less political leadership than its predecessor to the antileave contingent. Candidate Bush worried that opponent Michael Dukakis would seize control of the family issue, so he promised to diverge from Reaganomics with a kinder, gentler approach to public policy. At a meeting of Illinois Republican women he even seemed to lean toward supporting mandated leave by stating, "We need to assure that women don't have to worry about getting their jobs back after having a child or caring for a child during a serious illness. That is what I mean when I talk about a gentler nation."[50] This campaign strategy prompted Linda Dorian of the National Federation of Business and Professional Women's Clubs to comment, "We think the Bush campaign is showing some very good signs. There is room for some productive dialogue on this."[51] Once in office, however, the small business antileave coalition was able to secure promises of a presidential veto from John Sununu, White House chief of staff.[52]

Where were big business managers while this struggle against family leave was unfolding? The Women's Legal Defense Fund, which had played a critical role in creating and fighting for the bill, tried hard to bring corporate leaders who supported private sector leave policies into their reform coalition, but was largely unsuccessful. The organization sent letters to the CEOs who headed a *Working Women*'s list of best companies. The response to this exercise was, "We agree with you but we can't alienate our colleagues."[53]

There were a few exceptions to this negative showing. The National Federation of Business and Professional Women's Clubs was a strong proponent of the legislation.[54] Early on, the National Association of Women Business Owners (NAWBO) testified in favor of the family leave concept, but was unable to back the final policy because the group consisted primarily of small firms that considered the length of the leaves beyond their capacity. Selected members of the Conference Board (which had done considerable work on firm family leave policy) also showed interest in the policy, but the organization did not offer formal support.[55] Toward the end of the policy battle, the Women's Legal Defense Fund organized a small group called the Business Leaders for the FMLA, and Business for Social Responsibility endorsed the policy as well. Lawrence Perlman, chief executive officer of Control Data, wrote an influential op-ed piece on the bill.[56]

Although the bill initially had a low public profile, by the 1992 election it had become far more visible, making its high levels of public support more politically salient. Family leave was a natural issue for the unusually large number of women candidates running in what the media dubbed "the Year of the Woman." Candidate Clinton's support for the measure provided a sharp contrast with Bush's two vetoes. With business as the leading opponent, there was danger of a public debate that pitted business against families.[57]

In the endgame the big umbrella associations moved into a position of neutrality. After Clinton's election and with the arrival of a new vice-president at the Chamber of Commerce, Bill Archey, the chamber decided to abstain from the campaign against the Family and Medical Leave Act. The chamber's chair for labor relations explained that the bill was less threatening than other labor initiatives: "We did not support it, but we decided that because over 70 percent of our members give [leave] and because there is a Democrat in the White House who will sign it, we could not develop a veto strategy. We also had to realize that as bad as family leave is, it is not going to kill American industry."[58] The strategy greatly angered the chamber's critics to the right. Grover G. Norquist, president of Americans for Tax Reform, colorfully denounced the chamber's decision to sit out the battle:

> When you don't fight and stake out a position against it, you let the other side have a victory at no cost. It doesn't work for high school girls and it doesn't work for trade associations: You don't get respect by giving in a few times every once in a while. That doesn't make you reasonable; it makes you easy to have, and it makes you had. It doesn't get you invited to the prom. The problem with pragmatism is that it doesn't work.[59]

Family leave was ultimately signed into law, but only with immense effort, significant public support, and the arrival of a Democratic president. Even so, it had been significantly pared down. Businesses with fewer than fifty employees residing within seventy-five miles of the firm were exempt from the provisions of the act. The leave had been cut to twelve weeks; to be eligible, employees had to have worked at least 1,250 hours for their employers. Democrats in Congress voted overwhelmingly in favor of the bill, but Republicans divided, with a significant majority (77 percent in the House and 61 percent in the Senate) voting to oppose the law. By the end, even its opponents recognized that their opposition was somewhat overdrawn: at one point a chamber lobbyist remarked, "This is almost an issue whose time has come and gone."[60]

Clinton's National Health Reform

In 1993 President Clinton proposed the Health Security Act, a major overhaul of the medical financing system and key policy initiative of the president's first term. The bill sought to establish a universal right to health care by mandating employer benefits and to contain costs with a market-oriented system called managed competition. The health reform saga vividly confirms the patterns of corporate engagement evidenced by the Family Leave Act. Initially considered promising allies by the administration, large employers ultimately abandoned the reform effort while Republicans and their small business compatriots carried the day.

Business Positions

As major providers of health benefits, large employers were sure to be affected by national health reform, and the Clinton plan seemed tailor-made to appeal to these likely corporate allies. Health reform had special appeal for large companies currently providing benefits (and often paying for spouses working for firms with fewer benefits) because it would impose costs on those companies' competitors. The Clinton bill was packaged as a way to protect the employer-based system and to work through the market to achieve social ends; thus managed competition was a very small step from the status quo.[61] The employer mandates were not an especially big leap for large employers; many already provided health benefits. Large insurers were initially open to managed competition because they hoped to administer the new Clinton system.[62]

Large companies as a monolithic mass did not rush to endorse national health reform, because various factions had different concerns; during the proposal development stage, however, most big business managers seemed accepting of both systemic reform and employer mandates. The aging industrials (Chrysler and Bethlehem Steel) had given generous benefits to their early retirees, whereas companies such as AT&T, Arco, and IBM had made fewer commitments to their workers. Some large labor-intensive firms such as Pepsico and Mariott opposed systemic health reform, because they provided limited health benefits and wanted to keep the status quo. Insurers and providers wanted a bill that preserved their profits and professional control. In my study of ran-

domly sampled Fortune 200 companies, over half of the business respondents (54 percent) supported mandates and another 19 percent had
mixed opinions on the subject.[63] A survey of CEOs at big companies in
1990 found 90 percent convinced that a major system overhaul was necessary, and one-half favored employer mandates then or in the future. A
Harris poll found two-thirds of a corporate sample at least somewhat
accepting of a mandated standard benefits plan.[64]

Membership polling within the major umbrella associations supported
the findings of academic business surveys. In a 1992 study, 55 percent of
National Association of Manufacturers members favored a "play-or-pay"
approach (complete with employer mandates) as part of overall system
reform.[65] A June 1994 Washington Business Group on Health survey of
large firms showed 72 percent supporting a requirement for all companies to offer insurance, 59 percent wanting firms to pay a portion, and 71
percent objecting to an arrangement that allowed small business to escape the mandate.[66]

Small business managers also had reason to want changes in health
policy, but most business groups opposed comprehensive reform on both
ideological and material grounds. In 1991, 57 percent of the National
Small Business United members surveyed ranked the costs and availability of health insurance as the number one problem facing business.[67]
But many small employers who did not offer coverage and feared creating a new entitlement opposed mandates.[68] The NFIB wanted both to
kill mandates and to improve access to health insurance, but destruction
of the employer mandate became the group's all-consuming goal.[69]

Business Mobilization

If health reform enjoyed widespread acceptance among big business,
why did its proponents ultimately fail to do more to pass such legislation? An easy answer was that business feared the economic consequences of the bill. Large firms worried about losing purchasing power
to the health alliances and getting pushed into the public pool. They
considered the minimum benefits package excessive, were skeptical about
the funding arrangements, found the plan complicated, and worried that
states would have flexibility to experiment with financing mechanisms.[70]

The economic explanation partly explains the failure of big business
to fight for health reform, but much remains puzzling. The administra-

tion assured corporate allies that many of their demands were alternatives acceptable to the president, as laid out in the "endgame scenario" written in the summer of 1993. The initial proposal was much closer to large employers' preferences than the final outcome because legislators granted huge subsidies to small business. Therefore, why did big business not protect its turf better?

While business groups helped to make health reform a political issue, they were crippled by divisions within the ranks and unable to develop support for a specific legislative proposal. The administration initially considered the NAM and the Chamber of Commerce to be important allies, but both ultimately backed away from the Clinton plan, although the chamber went so far as to testify in favor of Clinton after he adopted their small business discount schedule. NAM president Jerry Jasinowski agreed to take the plan to the board if the administration would fix five issues troubling to large employers and, referring to a September 1993 press release, wrote, "I avoided any mention of mandates in order to imply that they may be a cost that business has to pay to get comprehensive reform; and to signal that mandates are not likely to be a top priority concern to manufacturers."[71] But although the administration calculated that a majority of the NAM board was sympathetic to health reform, health care providers and leaders of the fast food industry in the board's minority managed to prevent the NAM from endorsing the proposal.[72] NAM staff remember going into a board meeting in February 1994 having "good things to say about the Clinton bill and having the board do a 180 degree turn."[73] The Business Roundtable did not get as far as the NAM or the chamber because its health care task force was controlled by insurers from the beginning. When the group considered a universal access bill, General Mills and the insurers campaigned to dissuade CEOs from this option.[74]

The inability of large employers to express political support for the proposal made vote-seeking politicians unwilling to take firms' concerns seriously. Legislators instead granted concessions to try to buy off the better-organized small business groups. A study showed that under a partial mandate large employers would cover 14.7 million more individuals than they would under a full mandate; in other words, this extra coverage would be cost shifted from the small employers allowed to escape the mandate.[75] A bill that initially attracted big business by reducing cost shifting was offering to shift more costs than ever onto large firms.

Party strategies also worked against large employer support for health reform: the president designed the bill to appeal to business but failed to bring managers into the reform coalition. Employers felt that the administration refused to take business concerns seriously and confused campaigning and governing by rewarding loyalists and excluding others. In fact, the Office of Public Liaison restricted access to prior enemies in order to protect the privileges of its allies and warned against "wasting a huge amount of staff time 'receiving input' that would not accomplish very much toward actually building the coalition that will help us pass health care reform."[76] As one trade association representative put it, "Outreach to them means access to those who have been with them from the beginning and shutting out everyone else."[77]

The administration contended that it vigorously courted business managers in the early days of reform, but acknowledged that its business mobilization was later compromised by competing priorities. First, the administration was caught in a bind between rallying the mass public with a populist attack on insurers and drug companies and working behind the scenes with its business supporters.[78] Its attack on drug companies elicited emotional, ideological responses that undercut the private sector policy experts' ability to portray the issue in technocratic terms and to sell the plan to their firms.[79] The need to rally mass support also prompted a shift in focus from cost containment to access, but corporate supporters responded best to the administration's plan when the problem was framed as curbing costs. The president's pollster, Stanley Greenberg, argued for the access appeal:

> The dominant goal should be health care security: that people will have health insurance and that they will never lose it, never. . . . Health care security has much more power than the cost argument, and it is much more believable: people think we can deliver on security; they are not sure we can deliver on cost control. There is also an emotion in security (lacking in cost) that empowers our rationale for bold changes.[80]

Second, the administration was torn between conflicting demands from its congressional allies, over whom it had little control in an era of declining party discipline and decentralized legislative decisionmaking. The administration believed that a detailed presidential proposal could unify the diverse factions in Congress, but legislators felt that the executive deal making was premature and in the fall of 1993 forced the Clintons "to shut down the process" of offering concessions.[81] This damaged the administration's credibility with business allies when, suddenly after promises to the contrary, the Clintons refused to adapt to corporate concerns. The administration quietly reassured groups that their demands were consistent with its own "endgame scenarios."[82] But this strategy failed to assuage the fears of the groups' mass memberships, who could judge the Clinton plan only by its public manifestation. Thus NAM president Jerry Jasinowski told Ira Magaziner, "I have a problem with some of my members. They're afraid that you're rope-a-doping me." Others explained to Magaziner:

> [Corporate opponents] say that you're going to roll us and that you won't be flexible. If you made some of the changes that you yourselves admit, even if you don't change employer mandates or benefits, it gives us something to work with.[83]

Third, the growing intrusion of the media limited coalitions with both congressional and corporate allies.[84] Early talk of "detailed briefings to the health care press perhaps two or three times every week" was abandoned when Clinton's media advisors feared that this would distract decisionmakers, shift attention away from the budget, and make controlling the message difficult.[85]

The Republican countermobilization against health reform was more successful. Republicans identified health care as Clinton's Achilles' heel, and most Washington observers ultimately concluded that conservative Republicans were determined to block any bill with a Democratic label, even centrist efforts.[86] Thus Republican strategist William Kristol advised, "Those stray Republicans who delude themselves by believing that there is still a 'mainstream' middle solution are merely pawns in a Democratic game. . . . Our enemy is no longer Clinton, it is Congress."[87]

The Republicans pressured big business to reject reform, directing employers toward incremental alternatives, framing the health debate in larger terms, and capitalizing on the Republican party's historical relations with individual companies. The message to business was that health reform was "a new entitlement" and "a whole package," and that firms should not sell out their broader interests in less government spending and regulation for individual benefits. One aide remembered the admonishment from her member of Congress:

> "If you want our help in killing the Clinton plan, don't do separate deals on other things." Again and again we were trying to lay out the big picture

for them. "Maybe you can accept the deal right now, but think about what can be done to you in 10 years."[88]

The Republicans also threatened to retaliate in other policy areas if companies joined the Democrats on health reform, forcing them to choose between health and issues more directly tied to core production activities. Shortly before the Business Roundtable vote, House Minority Whip Newt Gingrich told two dozen CEOs that "their interests were best promoted by being principled rather than going for short-term deals." When Ameritech, a long-time supporter of health reform, planned to sponsor a presentation by President Clinton, Republican members of the House Energy and Commerce Committee told the company that if it supported the president, it would be punished in other regulatory areas under the committee's jurisdiction. Caterpillar and several telecommunications companies received similar threats. CEOs were told, "If you are going to come back and ask for help in future areas, you should know that it's not in your interests" to support mandates.[89]

Congressional Republicans take much of the credit for the dramatic policy reversal by the Chamber of Commerce. Chamber vice-president Bill Archey worked with his group's Health and Employee Benefits Committee to endorse a package of employer mandates, managed competition, and standardized benefits. This position greatly angered the House Republican Conservative Opportunity Society, which demanded a meeting with chamber president Richard Lesher and Archey and "read them the riot act." Representative Jim Bunning, Republican of Kentucky, gave a speech against big government, big labor, and big business (causing one participant to wonder if Bunning knew that the organization included big Fortune companies.) Representative John Boehner, Republican of Ohio and chairman of the group, sent letters on congressional letterhead to constituents who were members of the chamber saying that they should cancel their membership. The NFIB initiated a membership drive against the chamber. Few members resigned, but the chamber reversed its position on reform.[90]

The Republicans worked closely with small business groups to fight health reform. On the House side, Billy Pitts (an aide for Minority Leader Bob Michel) ran Monday morning meetings of congressional aides on the key committees and business representatives.[91] Pitts would identify the issue of the week, and the group would "brainstorm on strategies, line up key amendments to focus on, and make sure that everyone was pulling in one direction." A big topic of conversation was "when to pull the plug on reform so that it didn't look like the Republicans had pulled the plug."[92] The small business lobby intervened at critical junctures, such as its campaign to prevent the Energy and Commerce Committee from producing a bill. The NFIB sent action alerts to all of its members in the ten districts with swing legislators, urging that legislators oppose the chairman of the committee, John Dingell, Democrat of Michigan. These private sector allies were also very helpful to the Republican leadership in disciplining members of its own party, as when the NFIB did a preemptive strike against Fred Upton, Republican of Michigan. Republican Senators Paul Coverdell of Georgia and Bob Packwood of Oregon led a similar group to keep moderate senators in line, relentlessly arguing to business participants that no bill was better than anything legislated under the Democratic leadership. Lobbyists generally agreed that the Republicans came to this conclusion before most of the business community did so.[93]

By the end, some business representatives opposed to the Clinton plan actually felt the conservative Republicans had gone too far in blocking any bill. One lobbyist explained, "Now we are getting hit from the right and the left. . . . The Republicans want to kill the thing without leaving fingerprints. But we still want health reform." Despite the continued interests of some businesses in enacting health reform, business had played an active role in removing reform from the national agenda.

The Republican Medicare and Medicaid Proposals

The intrabusiness dynamics of Clinton's first two years became even more pronounced after the Republican landslide in 1994. In the second half of Clinton's first term, the new Republican congressional majority mounted a strong effort to reduce medicare and medicaid spending. Because they had avoided cutting these popular programs in their Contract with America, Republicans could not claim an electoral mandate for these efforts. But by the spring of 1995, congressional leaders realized that they could not meet their ambitious deficit and tax reduction targets without cutting these two expensive programs. The Republicans proposed to cut $270 billion over seven years from the medicare budget and $90 billion from medicaid.[94] The GOP turned to the vigorous small business trade associations to help in this ambitious and politically risky endeavor.

Business Positions

Because cutbacks in the public health financing system often result in increased cost shifting to private corporate payers, medicare reform could have enormous implications for the system of private sector social provision. But the GOP hoped to overcome corporate skepticism about the cuts and especially to appeal to those parts of the business community that did not offer health benefits by placing these policy changes in the context of its larger laissez-faire program of regulatory transformation, tax reduction, and budget balancing.

The Republicans also wooed business and health care provider interests with very specific concessions to interested parties but insisted that private sector allies reject side deals with the Democrats. For example, the Republicans wooed the American Medical Association with promises that medicare fees would not be reduced for seven years and with regulatory changes allowing physicians to refer patients to facilities with which they are financially involved.[95]

Small business liked the Republican plan because it worried incessantly about rising payroll taxes. The Chamber of Commerce publication, *Nation's Business,* suggested that the medicare trust fund was considering raising payroll taxes from 2.9 percent to 4.23 percent to pay for medicare hospital insurance. To make medicare solvent for seventy-five years, the payroll tax would be increased to 6.42 percent and 3.2 million jobs would be lost in the process.[96] Efforts to satisfy different interests were not entirely congruous; for example, the Health Insurance Association of America objected to the provision allowing physicians to form managed care arrangements more easily.[97]

Large employers were highly skeptical of the medicare project but had little input into the process. Worried when the Clinton administration proposed cutting medicare to pay for expanded access, big firms were likewise concerned that the Republicans wanted medicare reductions to balance the budget (and pay for the tax cut.) Some large employers feared that the Republican plan did not have sufficient incentives to move beneficiaries into more cost-efficient plans from fee-for-service arrangements. But the largest concern of big business was that the medicare cuts would result in greater cost shifting by hospitals to private payers. One study concluded that the Republicans' plan would shift at least $66 billion onto the privately insured, adding 2.3 percent to the costs for employers, employees, and self-insured individuals.[98]

Business managers also worried that the Republicans' proposal to turn medicaid into a block grant would result in greater cost shifting to private employers, as *Business and Health* warned:

> To the extent that states have been able to control Medicaid spending, they have done so by sharply limiting payments to providers. . . . And guess who makes up the difference? Employers and private insurers. . . . The business community has a strong vested interest in seeing that the Medicaid program gets overhauled carefully. One way or another, it ends up paying the bills.[99]

But as in the battles over the Clinton plan, the voice of large employers was difficult to hear. Big business was silenced in part by its desire for deficit reduction and regulatory relief. A Business Roundtable offshoot, Coalition for Change, planned to spend $10 million in advertising to support nonpartisan deficit reduction.[100] Some business managers also grew less concerned about their own health costs. In 1994 health costs actually declined for the first time in a decade, making some believe that firm-level interventions were working, although costs began to climb again in 1995.[101] In addition, as a lobbyist put it, "Business got a little embarrassed by its association with Clinton." A business representative confirmed this:

> Old manufacturing industries were quick to jump on a Clinton bandwagon. But it divided the business community and embarrassed those like the automobile industry that were too close to the Clinton process. The Arco CEO (Cook) got a nasty piece written about him in the Wall Street Journal. Other CEOs were made to feel like they had knifed business in the back.

The Republicans also met specific concerns of large employers, for example, by backing away from a program for keeping employees in private health plans even after they had retired. The roundtable argued that the government had an obligation to cover medicare recipients and should not shift responsibility to business.[102] Large employers also disliked a Senate proposal to increase the age of medicare eligibility from 65 to 67. The Corporate Health Care Coalition, which represented twenty-five big companies, attacked this aspect of the Republican plan because it would shift significant costs to corporations that provided retiree health benefits. The proposal to raise the eligibility age was quickly dropped under strong Democratic pressure. Ultimately, the Corporate Health Care Coalition supported the plan because it would move the elderly into managed care arrangements. Many from the big business community were also persuaded that the medicare cuts were necessary to the budget-balancing goal that they so strongly desired.[103]

Business Mobilization

To bring the various interests together, the Republican leadership formed a group called the Coalition to Save Medicare, composed of ninety-nine associations from the insurers, providers, small business, seniors, and right-wing citizen activist sectors. The coalition was co-chaired by Pamela Bailey of the Healthcare Leadership Council and Jake Hansen of the Seniors Coalition.[104] The Healthcare Leadership Council, which consisted of players from for-profit hospitals, insurance companies, and drug companies, had been a leader in the campaign against the Clinton bill. Thus the coalition continued a tradition begun by the Republicans during the 1980s of unifying business interests and sympathetic consumer groups in the same coalition.[105] Learning from the Clinton failure to secure commitments, the Republicans met secretly through September 1995 to make deals with various interest groups and demanded ironclad promises of support in return; they unveiled their proposal only when they were ready to legislate.

The Coalition to Save Medicare helped the leadership in innumerable ways. First, members generated seemingly endless cash. Democratic allies trying to defeat the GOP medicare bill had much less money to spend than the Republican supporters that had fought the Clinton health reform plan earlier. For example, the HIAA spent $15 million on advertising attacking Clinton in 1994, while the American Hospital Association spent only $350,000 and the AFL-CIO spent $1 million criticizing Republicans in the first part of 1995.[106]

Second, interest groups helped the Republicans to define the medicare problem in the early stages with a media blitz to convince the public that medicare was going bankrupt. The coalition persuaded Republican senators to give radio commentaries on the bill.[107] Participants hired political consultants to produce ads and polls to spread the word. Allies of the party claimed that this campaign was wildly successful. The Citizens for a Sound Economy's initial focus groups showed a public largely convinced that there was no problem with the medicare system, yet follow-up focus groups a few months later showed a public largely accepting of the Republican line.[108] Public opinion, of course, later shifted away from the Republican plan.

Third, business allies offered public support for the bill. Shortly before the August recess, the coalition held a "mobilization event," offering legislators stirring testimonials to take back to the districts. The coalition also held a series of forums for congressional staffers, entitled "Medicare University," to discuss issues related to the so-called medicare crisis. Thus aides were treated to sessions on "Tax Dilemma without Medicare Reform," "How Choices Can Strengthen Medicare," and "Waste, Fraud and Abuse." The coalition did the occasional grass-roots show of force, as when thirty seniors arrived at Congress with 100,000 "message-grams."[109]

Fourth, coalition members worked to protect Republicans from marginal districts. The Democratic Congressional Campaign Committee targeted fifty narrowly elected House Republicans in the 1996 election who were vulnerable on medicare. The GOP organized its corporate and right-wing allies to show "grass-roots" support for these legislators.[110]

At first the GOP strategy seemed to pay off. A month after its introduction, the Medicare Preservation Act had been passed by both houses. But medicare and medicaid reform was subsequently killed by Clinton's veto and his sudden willingness to stand up to his political enemies. Ironically, many of the Republicans' ambitions were realized in 1997 because Democratic cooperation was secured by trade-offs on other issues in the budget reconciliation process. Chastened by the frustrations of the budget battle during the 104th Congress, the two parties became less combative during the 105th Congress.

Conclusion

The experience of the Family and Medical Leave Act and health reform in the two halves of Clinton's first term suggests important implications, both for the future of political coalitions in social policymaking and for the continuing provision of private sector benefits.

First, the experience casts doubt on the ability of any administration to muster much large employer support for future social initiatives.[111] Although many managers from large companies were sympathetic to the connection between social investment and economic growth, this did little to produce social legislation. The pattern of business political influence during these legislative experiences exposed a fundamental weakness of big business organization and the relative strength of small business associations. Large employers were unable to organize themselves to support or, after the first few months, even to affect the Clinton health plan and were largely absent from the family leave debate. Big business worried that medicare reform would increase its health costs but did little to protect its interests and ultimately was saved only by Clinton's veto.

Small business, on the other hand, has shown itself to be a natural and powerful coalition partner for the Republican retrenchment agenda. With a mobilizable mass base distributed in every congressional district, a deep distrust of new taxes or federal mandates, and a propensity to take intransigent stands, small business rivals the Christian right in its affinity for the Republican agenda. But small business does have its limitations: it has been more successful in blocking (the Clinton health plan) or delaying and cutting back opponents' agendas (the Family and Medical Leave Act) than in developing and passing a social policy agenda of its own.

This episode also has implications for the provision of private sector benefits. In the aftermath of public policy's failure to rationalize the health system and to reduce cost shifting, large paternalistic companies continue to be under pressure to cut benefits. Many have resisted eliminating employee plans by moving full force into managed care arrangements, thus, ironically, completing what Clinton promised with his system of health alliances. A Foster Higgins survey found that by 1995 managed care networks had come to cover 71 percent of workers who received health benefits through their jobs.[112] But important questions about the quality of managed care remain. Companies are also shifting costs onto their employees; indeed 78 percent of a 1995 *Business and Health* survey found firms (often regretfully) anticipating this course of action.[113] Some large firms, such as General Motors, have sought to reduce their obligations to provide health care to retirees.[114]

There is some optimism that the growth in company health costs is dropping off. Towers Perrin consultants found health costs for employees (in their sample firms) increasing only 6 percent in 1994 and 2 percent in 1995, as opposed to 14 percent in 1991. But some employers fear that without a national policy framework health costs will continue to rise, especially if they were artificially restrained during the health reform political cycle in an effort by providers to demonstrate that national legislation was not necessary to curb increases. Towers Perrin found health costs for employers up 4 percent in 1996, a modest growth rate but still above the 1995 figures.[115] Some analysts believe that the declining growth rate in health care costs simply reflects a movement out of fee-for-service plans; when this process is completed, health costs will continue to rise.[116] Business managers also fear that the initial savings from moving into managed care will not be sustained over time.[117] One also wonders what the current wave of mergers and acquisitions within managed care will do to prices.[118]

The pared-down Family and Medical Leave Act has had the anticipated consequences: it has done little to change the status quo, because it reified what many large companies were already doing and exempted many small employers. Nearly 40 percent of all employees were not covered by the act because workers in businesses with fewer than fifty employees were excluded. A majority of the work sites covered by the act already provided some form of leave, although two-thirds of them made some changes in their leave policies to conform with the provisions of the act. A survey conducted after the first two years of implementation found that for the vast majority of employers, providing family leave under the new law had not increased costs or had increased them by only a small amount. Working mothers' behavior changed very little: 78.6 percent took leaves before enactment, and 78.4 percent took leaves after. Only 6 percent of firms reduced health insurance benefits to offset costs of family leave.[119]

As large firms reduce the social benefits they provide to the middle class and as the public sector, crippled by budget constraints and polarized partisan politics, fails to address the growing gaps in coverage and the new concerns of a changing work force, these intertwined social and economic issues are likely to resurface on the public agenda. Because the public and private welfare states are so closely connected and because small business is so strongly organized, politicians of all stripes will have to contend with business interests as they attempt to remake social policy.

Notes

1. Beth Stevens, *Complementing the Welfare State: The Development of Private Pension, Health Insurance and Other Employee Benefits in the United States* (Geneva: International Labor Organization, 1986), pp. 13–19.

2. *Budget of the United States Government, Analytical Perspectives, Fiscal Year 1998*, p. 74.

3. Marilyn J. Field and Harold T. Shapiro, "Summary," in Field and Shapiro, eds., *Employment and Health Benefits: A Connection at Risk* (Washington: National Academy Press, 1993), p. 1.

4. Katherine R. Levit and others, "National Health Care Spending, 1989," *Health Affairs*, vol. 10 (Spring 1991), pp. 117, 127–29.

5. Carolyn Pemberton and Deborah Holmes, eds., *EBRI Databook on Employee Benefits* (Washington: Employee Benefit Research Institute, 1995), p. 14.

6. These figures include both direct and indirect coverage. Employee Benefit Research Institute, "Sources of Health Insurance and Characteristics of the Uninsured," EBRI Issue Brief 133 (January 1993), p. 23.

7. Only 22 percent of employees in small private establishments were in defined-benefit plans. Pemberton and Holmes, eds., *EBRI Databook on Employee Benefits*, p. 14. See also Michael J. Mandel, "Business Rolls the Dice," *Business Week*, October 17, 1994, p. 89.

8. Pemberton and Holmes, eds,. *EBRI Databook on Employee Benefits*, p. 42.

9. Sharon R. Cohany, "Workers in Alternative Employment Arrangements," *Monthly Labor Review*, vol. 119 (October 1996), pp. 31–45.

10. "The New World of Work," *Business Week*, October 17, 1994, p. 76.

11. Julie Kosterlitz, "Family Cries," *National Journal*, April 16, 1988, p. 994; and Marlene Piturro and Sarah S. Mahoney, "Managing Diversity," *EF: Executive Female*, vol. 14 (May 1991), p. 45.

12. See, for example, Organization for Economic Cooperation and Development, *Flexibility in the Labor Market* (Paris: OECD, 1986), pp. 91, 111.

13. Charles Brown, James Hamilton, and James Medoff, *Employers Large and Small* (Harvard University Press, 1990), pp. 43–44.

14. Pemberton and Holmes, eds., *EBRI Databook on Employee Benefits*, pp. 33, 42.

15. "AMA Survey Reveals Perceptions of FMLA," *HR Focus*, vol. 70 (October 1993), p. 11.

16. Pemberton and Holmes, eds., *EBRI Databook on Employee Benefits*, pp. 29–30.

17. Grahame Thompson, "The Firm as a 'Dispersed' Social Agency," *Economy and Society*, vol. 11 (August 1982), p. 233; and Neil Fligstein and Kenneth Dauber, "Structural Change in Corporate Organization," *Annual Review of Sociology*, vol. 15 (1989), p. 83.

18. Mancur Olson, *The Logic of Collective Action* (Harvard University Press, 1971).

19. Robert D. Putnam, *Making Democracy Work: Civic Traditions in Modern Italy* (Princeton University Press, 1993).

20. See Walter Korpi, "Social Policy and Distributional Conflict in the Capitalist Democracies: A Preliminary Comparative Framework," *West European Politics*, vol. 3 (October 1980), pp. 296–315; Francis G. Castles, *The Social Democratic*

Image of Society (London: Routledge and Kegan Paul, 1978); and John O. Stephens, *The Transition from Capitalism to Socialism* (London: Macmillan, 1979).

21. A more narrow organization of business is more likely to lead to means-tested, targeted programs with a smaller scope and clear winners and losers.

22. Kay Lehman Schlozman and John T. Tierney, *Organized Interests and American Democracy* (Harper and Row, 1986), pp. 75–77.

23. Graham K. Wilson, *Business and Politics* (Chatham, N.J.: Chatham House, 1985).

24. James Q. Wilson, *The Politics of Regulation* (Basic Books, 1980).

25. Brown, Hamilton, and Medoff, *Employers Large and Small*, p. 73.

26. See Cathie Jo Martin, *Shifting the Burden* (University of Chicago Press, 1991); and Margaret Weir, chapter 7 in this volume.

27. "NFIB Named 'Most Powerful,'" *Capitol Coverage* (Washington: National Federation of Independent Business, December 1995).

28. Richard Kirkland Jr., "Fat Days for the Chamber of Commerce," *Fortune*, September 21, 1981, pp. 144–58; and Carol Matlack, "Mobilizing a Multitude," *National Journal*, October 17, 1987, p. 2592.

29. Interview with NFIB staffer.

30. Cindy Skrzycki, "Dome Alone II: How Small Business Won Congress' Heart," *Washington Post*, January 6, 1995, p. B1.

31. "Building Bloc?" *Capitol Coverage* (Washington: National Federation of Independent Business, December 1995).

32. William Lanouette, "Chamber's Ponderous Decision Making Leaves It Sitting on the Sidelines," *National Journal*, July 24, 1982, p. 1298.

33. Interview with Dirk Van Dongen, National Association of Wholesaler Distributors, Summer 1994.

34. Interview with industry representative, September 14, 1995.

35. David Anderson, "Survey: Government, Business Should Take on Family Issues," United Press International (June 20, 1989).

36. James T. Bond, "The Impact of Childbearing on Employment," in Dana E. Friedman, Ellen Galinsky, and Veronica Plowden, eds., *Parental Leave and Productivity* (New York: Families and Work Institute, 1992), chap. 1.

37. Fran Hawthorne, "Why Family Leave Shouldn't Scare Employers," *Institutional Investor* (March 1993), p. 31.

38. Ellen Galinsky and Dana E. Friedman, "Introduction," p. iii; J. Douglas Phillips and Barbara Reisman, "Turnover and Return on Investment Models for Family Leave," and Rebecca Marra and Judith Lerner, "The True Cost of Parental Leave," in Friedman, Galinsky, and Plowden, eds., *Parental Leave and Productivity*, chaps. 4, 5; Margaret E. Meiers, "Down with the Wait-and-See Approach," *Management Review*, vol. 78 (January 1989), p. 16; and Ellen Galinsky and Dana E. Friedman, *Education before School: Investing in Quality Child Care* (New York: Scholastic, 1993), p. 17.

39. For a broader discussion of these issues, see Cathie Jo Martin, *Stuck in Neutral*, forthcoming.

40. "Business' Battle over Parental Leave," *Nation's Business*, vol. 74 (August 1986), p. 12.

41. Michael A. Verespej, "Clinton's First Legislative Child," *Industry Week*, March 1, 1993, p. 57; and William Miller, "Employee Benefits: Congress' Mood to Mandate," *Industry Week*, January 12, 1987, p. 48.

42. The Chamber of Commerce originally estimated that employers would spend an extra $16.2 billion a year on labor costs should leave be mandated and then revised this figure to $2.6 billion. The General Accounting Office figured the leave mandate's cost at $147 million. Statement of William J. Gainer, U.S. General Accounting Office, "Statements on Parental Leave Act (S. 249) before Senate Labor Subcommittee on Children, Families, Drugs and Alcoholism," *BNA Daily Labor Report*, April 24, 1987, p. D1. The $16.2 billion figure prompted David Blackenhorn of the Institute for American Values to tell a House committee, "the Chamber uses a statistic like a drunk uses a lamppost, more for support than illumination." Fern Schumer Chapman, "Taking Time Out to Have a Baby," *Washington Post*, September 22, 1987, p. Z12. See also Eliza Newlin, "Driving Force behind Family Leave," *National Journal*, September 14, 1991, p. 2227.

43. Mike Adlin, "Virginia B. Lamp: A Chamber Lobbyist Battles a 'Precedent,'" *National Journal*, August 30, 1986, p. 2080; and testimony by Carol L. Ball, U.S. Chamber of Commerce, "Selected Statements on the Family and Medical Leave Act Delivered Feb. 2, 1989, to the Senate Labor Subcommittee on Children, Family, and Alcoholism," *BNA Daily Labor Report*, February 3, 1989, p. E1.

44. For an account of the bill's movement through Congress, see Ronald D. Elving, *Conflict and Compromise: How Congress Makes the Law* (Simon and Schuster, 1995).

45. Others in the antileave coalition began to resent the chamber's high visibility and felt that it was stealing the spotlight.

46. Interview with Mary Tavenner, formerly with National Association of Wholesaler Distributors, July 1996.

47. "American Public Prefers Flexibility to Federal Mandates according to the Society for Human Resource Management," *PR Newswire*, February 28, 1991; and "Sen. Cochran Will Lead Opposition to Mandated Parental Leave," *PR Newswire*, July 25, 1988.

48. Carol Matlack, "Mobilizing a Multitude," *National Journal*, October 17, 1987), p. 2592; and Pamela Brogan and Judy Sarasohn, "Parent's Leave May Hinge on Dukakis," *Legal Times*, August 29, 1988, p. 8.

49. Joyce Barrett, "Democrats Claim 'Pro-Family' Political Victory,' *American Metal Market*, October 12, 1988, p. 7.

50. Margaret Wolf Freivogel, "Supporters of Bill on Family Leave Try to Head Off Veto," *St. Louis Post-Dispatch*, June 16, 1990, p. 1B.

264   Cathie Jo Martin

51. Associated Press, "Women's Groups Begin Push for Parental Leave Measure," *New York Times,* September 8, 1988, p. 22.

52. Interview with CARE participant, July 1996.

53. Interview with Donna Lenhoff of WLDF, March 31, 1995.

54. Jennifer Dorsey, "Plans for Parental, Medical Leave Divide Congress, Boardrooms; House Small Business Committee," *Travel Weekly,* August 20, 1987, p. 9.

55. Interviews with participants, February, September 1995.

56. The WLDF group included people like Arnold Hyatt, Elliot Lehman, and Lawrence Perlman. Interview with Lenhoff, March 31, 1995.

57. See Elving, *Conflict and Compromise,* pp. 190, 244.

58. Interview with chamber staff, May 1995.

59. Kirk Victor, "Deal Us In," *National Journal,* April 3, 1993, p. 808.

60. Karl Vick, "The Principle behind the Family Leave Bill," *St. Petersburg Times,* May 9, 1990, p. 7A.

61. For details see chapter 5 by Mark Peterson in this volume.

62. They were the primary providers of managed care networks for firms. Interview with industry representative, September 1992.

63. Cathie Jo Martin, "Nature or Nurture? Sources of Firm Preference for National Health Reform," *American Political Science Review,* vol. 89 (December 1995), pp. 898–913.

64. Joel C. Cantor and others, "Business Leaders' Views on American Health Care," *Health Affairs,* vol. 10 (Spring 1991), pp. 98–105; and "Leaders Look at Health Care," *Business and Health,* vol. 9 (February 1991), pp. 8–9.

65. Play or pay was the Democratic predecessor to the Clinton plan, which called for employers to either provide benefits or pay a dedicated health tax. Foster Higgins/NAM, "Employer Cost-Shifting Expenditures" (November 1992). A majority still supported mandates in 1993, according to an unpublished survey provided by the Clinton administration.

66. NAM survey described in interview with Ira Magaziner, September 1995; and "Washington Business Group on Health," paper provided by the administration, n.d..

67. National Small Business United, "Small Business Outlook and Attitudes," 1991, pp. 4–5.

68. Jerry Geisel, "Employers, Unions in Coalition Endorse Play-or-Pay Mandate," *Business Insurance,* November 18, 1991, p. 73.

69. Interview with Mark Isakowitz at NFIB, November 15, 1994. The small business community was not entirely unified. The early alliance between small insurers and small business came under considerable stress when the Health Insurance Association of America (HIAA) endorsed employer mandates. As a sort of preemptive warning, the NFIB "sent a strong signal to HIAA that if they supported mandates, we'd support premium caps." To prevent a fissure, NFIB

chief lobbyist John Motley and HIAA president Bill Gradison met in early 1994. An uneasy truce ensued, which ended when HIAA tried to do a secret deal with House Ways and Means Committee chair Dan Rostenkowski. The NFIB tentatively decided that if Ways and Means supported a mandate, the association would urge the Republicans to vote for premium caps.

70. Richard I. Smith, "Getting Business Support for Health Care Reform," *Washington Post*, June 13, 1994, p. A18. ERISA preemption allowing self-insured firms to avoid state regulations was the major issue for large employers and the only one that unified the business community.

71. Memo, to Ira Magaziner from Bob Patricelli, "Follow-up to March 8, 1993 Meeting," March 18, 1993; and memo, to Magaziner from Jerry Jasinowski, "Administration Health Care Plan," September 15, 1993.

72. Interview with Ira Magaziner, September 1995.

73. Interviews with NAM staff.

74. Letter to [name blacked out] from H. Atwater Jr., chair and CEO, General Mills, December 2, 1993, obtained from White House sources.

75. Association of Private Pension and Welfare Plans, "Unintended Consequences of Excluding Small Firms from an Employer Mandate," Washington, May 1994.

76. Interview with administration official; and Memo, to Mrs. Clinton from Alexis Herman and Mike Lux, "Office of Public Liaison Plan for Health Care Reform Campaign," February 5, 1993.

77. Interview with industry representative, Spring 1994.

78. Bob Woodward, *The Agenda* (Simon and Schuster, 1994), pp. 110, 147.

79. Interviews with industry respondents.

80. Memo, to Ira Magaziner from Stan Greenberg, "The Health Care Joint Session Speech," p. 2, obtained from White House sources.

81. Interviews with Ira Magaziner, July, September 1995.

82. "Passing Health Reform: Policy and Congressional Summary," December 17, 1993, first draft August 1993, pp. 10–14, obtained from the White House.

83. Interview with Magaziner, September 1995.

84. Tom Hamburger, Ted Marmor, and Jon Meacham, "What the Death of Health Reform Teaches Us about the Press," *Washington Monthly* (November 1994), pp. 35–41.

85. Memo, to George Stephanopoulos and Bob Boorstin, from Magaziner, "Health Care Press Strategy," February 4, 1993. The concern about leaks greatly diminished the administration's sharing of ideas and strategy with congressional allies. Interview with Magaziner, September 1995.

86. Republican pollster Bill McInturff told Gingrich that health reform's defeat could lead to a Republican House. Robin Toner, "Pollsters See a Silent Storm That Swept Away Democrats," *New York Times*, November 16, 1994, p. A14. See, for example, Julie Kosterlitz, "Brinksmanship," *National Journal*, July 9, 1994, p. 1648.

87. Memo, to Republican Leaders, from William Kristol, "Health Care: Why Congress Is Now More Dangerous than Clinton" (Washington: Project for the Republican Future, July 26, 1994).

88. Interview with congressional staff in leadership role, September 1994.

89. Ibid.

90. Interview with chamber staff, July 22, 1994.

91. Business groups represented by NFIB, Healthcare Leadership Council, National Restaurant Association, National Retailers Association, and HIAA, among others.

92. Interview with participating lobbyist, September 1994.

93. Interviews with participating lobbyists, September 1994.

94. Robin Toner and Robert Pear, "Medicare, Turning 30, Won't Be What It Was," *New York Times,* July 23, 1995, pp. A1, 24.

95. Robert Pear, "Doctors' Group Says G.O.P. Agreed to Deal on Medicare," *New York Times,* October 12, 1995, p. A1.

96. David Warner, "A Medicare Tax Hike's Impact on Business," *Nation's Business* (October 1995), p. 8.

97. Adam Clymer, "Health Lobby Starts Taking Aim at G.O.P. Plan," *New York Times,* October 10, 1995, pp. A1, 18.

98. Interviews with industry participants, 1995, 1996; and Milt Freudenheim, "Business May Pay More for Health as Congress Cuts," *New York Times,* November 4, 1995, p. 1.

99. Steven Findlay, "Block Grants for Sale," *Business and Health,* vol. 13 (August 1995), p. 55.

100. Peter H. Stone, "From the K Street Corridor," *National Journal,* August 12, 1995, p. 2063.

101. Milt Freudenheim, "Survey Finds Health Costs Rose in '95," *New York Times,* January 30, 1996, pp. D1, 21.

102. Sharon McIlrath, "GOP Health Plan Blitz," *American Medical News,* October 9, 1995, p. 1.

103. Robert Pear, "Retirees' Group Attacks G.O.P. Health Plan," *New York Times,* October 6, 1995, p. A22; and David Segal, "Will GOP Medicare Cuts Backfire on Business?" *Washington Post,* November 5, 1995, p. H1.

104. William Miller, "Battle Looms," *Industry Week,* September 4, 1995, p. 82.

105. Martin, *Shifting the Burden.*

106. Marilyn Werber Serafini, "Turning Up the Heat," *National Journal,* August 12, 1995, p. 2053.

107. Peter H. Stone, "Rallying the Troops," *National Journal,* September 2, 1995, p. 2152.

108. Interview, September 14, 1995.

109. Mary Jane Fisher, "Both Parties Turning Medicare into Huge Political Football," *National Underwriter,* August 14, 1995, p. 8; Fisher, "Coalition Hold-

ing 'Medicare University' Briefings," *National Underwriter,* September 4, 1995, p. 36; and Fisher, "Medicare Reform Is Turning Congress into a Circus," *National Underwriter,* October 9, 1995, p. 10.

110. Serafini, "Turning Up the Heat," p. 2052.

111. Employment and training initiatives had a very different politics. See Martin, *Stuck in Neutral.*

112. Freudenheim, "Survey Finds Health Costs Rose in '95."

113. Wayne J. Guglielmo, "Business Has a Mixed Message for Doctors," *Medical Economics,* January 15, 1996, p. 180. This was up from 48 percent in 1991. Norma Harris, "Managed Care Right Course, Employers Say," *Business and Health,* vol. 10 (July 1992), p. 32.

114. General Motors sought to reduce its obligations to workers who took early retirement benefit packages between 1974 and 1988. Its effort was rejected by a federal appeals court. See Nichole M. Christian, "GM Ordered to Pay Health Benefits to Early Retirees," *Wall Street Journal,* August 15, 1996, p. B7.

115. Towers Perrin, "1996 Health Care Cost Survey" (New York: Towers Perrin Employee Benefit Information Center, March 1996).

116. J .P. Donlon and Barbara Benson, "The New Anatomy of Health Care," *Chief Executive,* no. 110 (January 1996), p. 52.

117. This concern was echoed in a majority of the companies I surveyed that had some experience with managed care plans.

118. Karen Davis, Karen Scott Collins, and Cynthia Morris, "Managed Care: Promise and Concerns," *Health Affairs,* vol. 13 (Fall 1994), pp. 178–85.

119. U.S. Department of Labor, "Employers Find the Family and Medical Leave Act Is Good Business" (Washington: Federal Document Clearing House, May 1996); James T. Bond and others, *Beyond the Parental Leave Debate* (Watertown, N.Y.: Families and Work Institute, 1991), pp. ii–viii; and Jaemin Kim, "Workplace: Leave Law Drops Employers into the Family Circle," *Chicago Enterprise,* vol. 7 (May 1993), p. 10.

Chapter 7

Wages and Jobs:
What Is the Public Role?

Margaret Weir

O N THE EVE of the 1994 congressional elections, Secretary of Labor Robert Reich put his finger on a central political and economic issue facing both Republicans and Democrats. "Our national challenge," he declared, "is to affirm that the American dream of broadly shared middle-class prosperity still endures, that if you work hard you can get ahead, and that our children can lead even better lives than ours."[1] Reich's remarks reflected widespread public doubts about the continued viability of the American dream of economic opportunity, individual mobility, and rising standards of living. Public unease about finding security in the new economy mounted during the recession of the early 1990s and lingered even as the economy began to recover. Despite considerable concern, however, federal employment policies dealing with labor relations, workplace regulation, and job training changed very little during the first Clinton administration. This chapter asks why employment policies were so marginal when the issues of economic security they address loomed so large in the lives of ordinary Americans.

I argue that the institutional and social terrain on which both Clinton and the Republicans operated was ill suited to facilitate the policy changes that each sought, although the starting point was far more favorable to Republicans. Anxious to avoid taking sides between business and labor, Clinton adopted a top-down consensual strategy, attempting to find common ground between them on a range of reforms. But administration

I am grateful for helpful comments from Stephen Amberg, Ann Lin, David Plotke, Carl Van Horn, and Joseph White. John Guba and Laurel Imig provided expert research assistance.

initiatives foundered on the sharp antagonism and unequal power between business and labor and on the traditionally weak role of government—apart from regulation—in this arena. The administration had little power to compel business and labor to compromise, nor did it rouse broader public interest in its agenda. Republicans, by contrast, embraced a much more explicit social strategy, hoping both to please business constituencies and to win public support by linking a strongly probusiness agenda in labor policy with tax cuts. But when their tax cuts failed after being pitted against the competing goals of balancing the budget and preserving medicare, Republicans found that the probusiness agenda commanded much less popular support. Not only did Republicans have to pull back from their most sweeping initiatives, they also lost on key issues such as increasing the minimum wage. Despite their limited success, Republicans maintained the advantage in the face of Clinton's failure to alter the fundamental facts in labor policy: a business community far more powerful than labor, weak public institutions, and public antipathy to excessive corporate power tempered by doubts about the desirability of expanding the public role.

Old Policy in the New Economy

Between 1970 and 1990, a number of discrete economic and social changes combined to create a new economic world. Although economists dispute the weight of different factors in causing the new conditions, chief among the engines of change are technological innovations, increased international economic competition, and the decline of unions.[2] The central features of the new economy—wage stagnation, growing economic inequality, employment instability, and low productivity growth—upset longstanding assumptions held by both families and firms. These shifts also provoked doubts about existing labor and employment policies, which had been crafted for quite different economic circumstances.

For growing segments of the American work force, the new economy meant reduced prospects for economic advancement. After 1973, average real wages rose very slowly and the wages of men with less education fell precipitously. The real wages of white male prime-age full-time workers without a high school education dropped from $22,134 a year in 1973 to $19,169 in 1987.[3] During the 1980s, the premium paid to college-educated workers increased, paving the way for growing inequality. Brookings economist Gary Burtless estimates that average real earnings for men in the bottom quintile of the income distribution declined by 15 percent between 1969 and 1993 and those in the second lowest quintile declined by 9 percent. For men in the top quintile, earnings increased by 17 percent. Social trends exacerbated these inequalities: rates of marriage among men in the bottom quintiles declined markedly and by 1993 were far smaller than those of men in the top quintile. The entry of more high-earning women into the labor force between 1969 and 1993 further increased inequalities among families because these women were far more likely to marry high-earning men.[4]

Changes in employment and job stability also introduced new economic insecurities for workers. Recessions continued to drive unemployment rates up periodically, but average rates did not change much: the unemployment rate in the 1970s was 6.2 percent, and in the 1990s it has been 6.3 percent.[5] However, new problems related to job security now complicated unemployment. Over the past twenty years, the rate of job loss has increased, especially among younger and less educated workers. Moreover, unemployment is now more likely to be structural than cyclical. Because workers who lose their jobs are less likely to be called back, finding a new job more often means changing employers or occupations. The consequences of this displacement are most severe for less educated workers, who are less likely to become reemployed after a job loss than more highly educated workers.[6] There are also rising numbers of part-time, temporary, and contingent workers, the majority of whom are women and minorities, who tend to have lower wages and higher turnover than regular workers. Contingent workers, moreover, typically do not enjoy employer-provided benefits such as health care and pensions and often are ineligible for public benefits such as unemployment insurance.[7]

These changes in the American economy undermined key assumptions behind existing employment policies—many of which traced their origins to the New Deal—and created new problems that these policies were ill equipped to handle. From the 1940s until the 1970s, national economic policymaking was dominated by the Keynesian idea that federal spending and tax cuts could stimulate the economy and reduce unemployment. Policymakers assumed that the key problem for workers was the rate of unemployment, a product of cyclical downturns that could be remedied by economic stimulus.[8] Unemployment insurance would provide temporary assistance to those out of work during recessions. Unions, whose right to organize was protected by federal law, would ensure decent working conditions and wages through the collective bargaining process. The minimum wage would provide a floor under the income of the poorest workers. During the 1960s, a variety of short-term job training programs, oriented toward "disadvantaged workers" at the bottom of the labor market, was added to the policy mix. And in the 1970s, an array of federal regulations, including antidiscrimination and occupational health and safety hazards measures, provided additional protections for workers.

Over the next two decades, this edifice appeared increasingly unable to promote the twin objectives of economic security and prosperity. A more open international economy meant that individual nations were less able to fine-tune their economies: Keynesian stimulus was less effective in this new environment. Unemployment insurance offered only temporary respite for the growing number of workers who would not be rehired by their former employers. The ability of workers to secure good working conditions and wages through collective bargaining declined throughout the 1970s and 1980s as unions lost power to a much more assertive business community, intent on creating a flexible labor force able to compete internationally. Job training programs, focused on the bottom of the labor market, had little to offer most workers affected by economic change or employers facing international competition. Employers, moreover, charged that the growing number of regulations made it more difficult for them to compete and that unions, even though weakened, imposed rigidities that reduced productivity.

Initially, federal policymakers responded to the economic shifts with increased protection for workers through public jobs and temporary income support. In 1973 Congress enacted the Comprehensive Employment and Training Act (CETA), job training legislation that quickly turned into a public service jobs program as unemployment rates soared in the mid-1970s. At its height, during the Carter administration, CETA spent $10.2 billion and provided 739,000 public service jobs, employing 12 percent of unemployed workers.[9] Congress also temporarily extended unemployment benefits, so that many claimants could receive benefits for up to sixty-five weeks, more than doubling the basic twenty-six-week benefit. In addition, Congress loosened eligibility requirements for benefits authorized under the Trade Expansion Act of 1962, which assisted workers who had been displaced by import concessions granted in trade negotiations. Although no benefits had been authorized in the 1960s, in the 1970s the number of beneficiaries soared. Trade adjustment assistance (TAA) expenditures ballooned from $150.3 million in 1976 to $1.6 billion in 1980.[10]

By the 1980s, this patchwork approach came under fire from conservatives offering a different diagnosis of the economy. Rather than increase demand to boost employment, the "supply-side" approach endorsed by the Reagan administration relied on reducing taxes and regulation. Such burdens on business, conservatives argued, depressed economic growth and limited job creation. This new perspective marked a fundamental shift: now the key to economic prosperity was business freedom, not government spending or well-timed tax reductions.

In this view, most existing employment policies were counterproductive. Expanded eligibility for unemployment benefits and extended benefits simply encouraged people to remain unemployed; instead, conservatives argued, eligibility for unemployment insurance should be tightened to reduce unemployment. Numerous changes to the system in the 1980s did indeed tighten eligibility. These changes, along with demographic shifts, the increased portion of the work force covered by the unemployment insurance system, and the decline in unionization, substantially reduced the percentage of workers receiving unemployment benefits. The nadir was reached in 1984, when only 28.5 percent of the unemployed received unemployment insurance and trade assistance spending had been cut back by 97 percent.[11]

Congress also reduced and overhauled existing jobs programs. Criticized as wasteful and ineffective, CETA became a prime target after Reagan's election and was the only program totally eliminated in 1981. A bipartisan congressional agreement produced the Job Training Partnership Act (JTPA), which, with significantly reduced funding, provided block grants to the states for job training only, not job creation. JTPA placed much more control in the hands of governors and local business groups, organized into Private Industry Councils. This new structure aimed to connect publicly sponsored job training programs to the private sector but retained the remedial focus of its predecessors.[12]

Finally, under Reagan, the federal government threw its weight behind employers in labor-management conflicts. The administration sanctioned the use of permanent replacements for striking workers, and an unsympathetic National Labor Relations Board (NLRB) made union organizing more difficult. The administration also fought to limit employment regulations. Although Congress rejected proposals for a subminimum "training wage" for youth, efforts to increase the minimum wage to keep pace with inflation failed throughout the 1980s. A significant increase in 1990 still left the real value of the wage well below what it had been in 1980. Enactment of new federal employment regulations also slowed substantially in the first part of the 1980s. But by the latter half of the 1980s, Congress had enacted a variety of new employment regulations, including the Americans with Disabilities Act, which passed with bipartisan support in 1990 and imposed a significant new burden on employers.[13]

Thus, by the time Clinton took office, industrial relations policy was an area of intense conflict, in which business held the upper hand. Workers won protection less through collective bargaining and more by regulation. Income support programs designed to cushion unemployment had been weakened, but government had few active policies to assist workers in adjusting to economic change or to reduce growing economic inequalities. Labor market policies remained either passive or remedial.

Business-Labor Conflict, Partisan Polarization, and Labor Policy

The new economic conditions pitted business and labor against one another more starkly than they had been since the 1930s. As business became more organized and assertive in the 1970s, its desire to limit—and even eliminate unions—became more pronounced. Faced with a hostile environment and declining membership, unions grew inward-looking and defensive. These developments exacerbated partisan polarization. Organized labor had long been a key Democratic ally, and, although big business cooperated with Democrats, it had stronger ties to Republicans. The political mobilization of business in the 1970s and 1980s and the growing political significance of small business, discussed in Cathie Martin's chapter, reinforced the business-Republican connection. These divisions shaped the politics of employment policy since business and labor had sharply different views about how government should respond to economic change.

By the 1970s, the strong ties between organized labor and Democrats had begun to fray. Labor's capacities to mobilize voters became less significant after the 1960s as locally based party organizations declined in strength and money replaced people as the currency of politics. At the same time, the spread of primaries deprived labor of its dominant role in candidate selection. Declining union membership further reduced labor's importance to Democrats. By 1995 the combination of job loss in the heavily unionized manufacturing sector and concerted anti-union campaigns by employers had diminished labor's strength to less than 15 percent of the labor force (and only 10.4 percent of the private sector).[14]

Despite all these drawbacks, organized labor still had political resources important for Democrats. Although union households were not as reflexively Democratic as they had once been, they continued to vote for Democrats at higher rates than the electorate as a whole, giving majorities to Democratic presidential candidates in every election since the New Deal, except in 1972.[15] Moreover, especially in the cities of the Northeast and Midwest, labor's mobilizing activities were still important for voter turnout. And even in a money-dominated electoral system, organized labor was a valuable resource for many Democratic candidates: despite their decline, unions still possessed formidable fundraising capacities.

These conflicting pulls are evident in the relationship between the congressional Democrats and organized labor. In the 1970s, the rise of more independent-minded moderate suburban Democrats cut into labor's traditional strength among northern Democrats, making their support for labor issues more tenuous.[16] Labor's influence in Congress weakened further after Reagan's election. But in the second half of the 1980s, Democratic Speaker Jim Wright forged closer ties between unions and the congressional leadership. Despite the complaints of many moderate and conservative Democrats who resented having to vote on labor-related issues, the leadership persisted, believing that labor's Washington-based lobbying capabilities were essential to revitalizing a broader Democratic agenda.[17] Yet, reflecting the new political environment, this version of the labor-Democratic alliance concentrated on inside-the-beltway politics, not grass-roots mobilization.

In contrast to labor, business became more organized and politically active in the 1970s and 1980s. Business leaders created new organizations, such as the Business Roundtable, which brought together the heads of major corporations; they also revived older groups, such as the Chamber of Commerce. The original purpose of the roundtable was to stem the power of unions; although it quickly took on a much broader agenda, this sharp antagonism to unions remained a central theme.[18] Also fueling business mobilization was opposition to economic and regulatory policies identified with Democrats. Such antagonism to Democrats was new: many businesses had established good working relationships with Democratic administrations in the 1960s.[19] By the 1980s, the antigovernment tenor of business sentiment intensified as small business organizations, such as the National Federation of Independent Business (NFIB), became important players.

Although these groups were not formally aligned with the Republican party, over the 1970s and 1980s their activities within the party simultaneously bound it closer to them and pushed it further to the right. The same changes in party organization and elections that had made labor less important to Democrats enhanced the value of business, particularly its fundraising abilities, to Republicans. Moreover, these business organizations had local bases that made them potent congressional lobbyists.

Reflecting these developments, partisan polarization around key aspects of labor and employment policy intensified after the 1970s. The outcomes largely favored business, most often big businesses.[20] Proposals to alter labor laws to strengthen unions and make organizing easier, including common situs picketing legislation and labor law reform in the 1970s, were most divisive along party lines, although in each case some Republicans and southern Democrats defected from the position of their party's majority. On both issues, mobilized business played a key role in pushing Republicans to defeat the legislation; indeed, the common situs legislation failed only when President Gerald Ford, under business pressure, withdrew his earlier support and vetoed the measure.[21] Likewise, reductions in assistance to the unemployed through taxes on unemployment insurance and restrictions on TAA were highly polarized along party lines, especially in the House. New partisan divisions began to appear in the long-consensual area of trade policy.[22] Other legislation was more consensual. Minimum wage legislation often split Republicans and drew bipartisan support. Social regulation that imposed new costs on business, including the Americans with Disability Act and the Family and Medical Leave Act (FMLA), passed Congress with overwhelming bipartisan support, although President George Bush vetoed the FMLA. Most consensual was job training legislation, as indicated by the overwhelming bipartisan support for JTPA in 1982.

Thus as Clinton took office some clear patterns of partisan polarization and consensus were in place. Moreover, labor and business each had an agenda it hoped the new president would support. For labor, the list was long and hopes were high that the first Democratic president in twelve years would back labor priorities. These included labor law reform to make organizing easier, a ban on the use of permanent replacements for striking workers, defeat of the proposed NAFTA or addition of substantial protections, an increase in the minimum wage, preservation of TAA, and strengthened social regulation, including family leave and occupational health and safety laws. Business took the opposite position on most of these issues. Business leaders preferred the status quo in labor law, although they wanted to relax section 8(2)(a) of the National Labor Relations Act, which outlawed company-sponsored work committees. A recent NLRB ruling had cast doubt on the legality of new management techniques that relied on nonunion labor-management committees to solicit worker input.[23] Business also opposed labor on other issues. including NAFTA, social regulation, and the minimum wage. Job training was the one area in which there was little business-labor conflict. Some sectors of business strongly supported existing programs, but such public job training programs were not central priorities of either business or labor.

Consensual Strategies and Polarized Politics

The Clinton administration sought to reduce the polarization in employment policy in several different ways. In contrast to previous Democratic presidents, Clinton established some distance between his priorities and those of organized labor. His policy initiatives sought to temper the divisions between business and labor and link employment policy to national goals of economic prosperity by winning support for such consensual ideas as the high-performance workplace (changing the supply of jobs) and a more skilled work force (changing the supply of labor). Both initiatives could also temper polarization by making employment policies relevant to a much broader range of workers, thus broadening their constituency.

But the administration had few resources to make such a consensual strategy work. This was in part a result of the president's own choices: his priority on cutting deficits and enacting comprehensive health reform left little funding for employment policy. But there were other problems: the weakness of labor and the strength of business made each resistant to compromise, and Clinton did not command sanctions or incentives that would budge either. Most of the administration's new initiatives did not have ready-made constituencies nor could they be easily implemented through existing institutions. Building broader support for a new approach to employment policy meant not only overcoming or bypassing the entrenched polarization of labor and business but also making a convincing case that the federal government could effectively assist workers in the new economy. Little in the legacy of previous labor and employment policies paved the way for the new approach.

Keeping Labor at Arm's Length

Organized labor posed a political dilemma for the new president. On the one hand, the administration was anxious to establish its independence from labor: labor's inward-looking stance, its continued decline, and the new organization of politics all suggested that a conspicuous alliance with labor would not produce the broader appeal that the president needed. But it made little sense for Clinton to antagonize labor unnecessarily, since unions continued to provide a key organized resource base for Democratic candidates. For its part, labor hoped that Clinton would embrace its backlog of initiatives. Once he took office, however, unions and their congressional allies were reminded that "a Democrat from Arkansas is not the same as a Democrat from Michigan."[24]

Initial appointments to the Department of Labor signaled the administration's determination to expand beyond the department's traditional constituency of organized labor. Robert Reich, appointed as secretary, was well known as an innovative and liberal thinker on economic policy issues, but he did not enter office with ties to organized labor. Labor was initially pleased with the appointment because of Reich's close ties to the president and his status as a key player in the administration's economic team. This promised the department more access to the centers of power than it had enjoyed in many years. But Reich did not immediately identify his objectives with those of organized labor. In a statement that reverberated throughout the labor movement, Reich declared at a 1993 administration-sponsored conference on the workplace that "the jury is still out on whether the traditional union is necessary for the new workplace."[25] Over time, however, Reich grew closer to organized labor and became one of its strongest proponents within the administration. Other appointments balanced labor-aligned old Demo-crats and self-identified New Democrats, some of whom had antagonistic relationships with organized labor. These tensions set the stage for difficult relationships with key congressional committees, where labor-aligned "old Democrats" looked with suspicion on the proposals of some Clinton appointees.

The most bitter policy rift occurred in the fight over NAFTA. Since the 1970s, organized labor, heavily concentrated in manufacturing industries battered by international competition, had grown increasingly protectionist. Democrats, once staunch internationalists, now divided over trade as members of Congress who were aligned with labor began to oppose trade liberalization. NAFTA was a classic confrontation between congressional Democrats tied to labor, often representing older urban areas, and Democrats from suburban districts where labor was weaker.[26] Clinton had announced his support for NAFTA during the campaign, and, although he negotiated side agreements on labor and environmental concerns, labor rejected them as too weak and refused to support the legislation. NAFTA passed in 1993 with support from a coalition of Republicans and a minority of Democrats.

The president backed away from labor's priorities on other issues as well. As a candidate, Clinton had pledged to support the minimum wage; once in office he failed to support it. Secretary Reich put the minimum wage on the agenda in mid-1993 with a memo to the president proposing a twenty-five-cent increase and floating the idea of indexing the minimum wage. Even this modest increase—a significant scaleback from the one-dollar increase that administration officials had discussed earlier in the year—unleashed a roar of protest from business groups and especially from small business. Within weeks, the White House induced Reich to withdraw the proposal. Acutely aware that they needed business support to pass their health care and trade proposals, administration officials were anxious to avoid further antagonizing business. The provision for mandates in the health proposal had already alienated much of the small business community, and other segments of business were upset by tax increases in the budget passed that summer.[27]

Even more important to labor was legislation to ban the use of permanent replacements for striking workers. Although Clinton had supported the measure in his campaign, he put it on the back burner once in office. This issue was so central to labor that its congressional allies introduced their own bill. When they were unable to pass the legislation, organized labor and many congressional Democrats blamed the administration for refusing to invest the political capital needed to pass the bill.[28]

The administration did tilt the scales in labor's favor in less visible administrative venues, most notably in the National Labor Relations Board, which is responsible for overseeing collective bargaining. Before the 1980s, the board represented a careful balance of labor and business allies, but during the Reagan years it had become markedly probusiness. Delays and unfavorable rulings had made it more difficult for unions to challenge unfair labor practices. Clinton's appointment to head the board was much more favorable to labor and quickly drew the ire of business leaders.[29]

Clinton's public distance from labor signaled his intention to be a different kind of Democrat and his desire to avoid policies that would entangle him in confrontations with business. As Cathie Martin's chapter notes, the administration very much sought to maintain business support. Nor did the administration pay a high price for its distance from labor. Labor's active support for health reform diminished in the aftermath of NAFTA, but ultimately labor had nowhere else to go.

The Failed Public Investment Strategy

Throughout the presidential campaign, Clinton stressed the need "to invest in America's future" and proposed a federal investment program of $20 billion a year for four years to "rebuild America."[30] The investment theme conveyed the campaign's populist economic message; politically, it offered traditional Democratic constituencies—especially labor and mayors—the spending they desired but, using the language of investment, it linked spending to new arguments about national productivity and competitiveness. This attempt to recast spending as investment was a resounding failure.

Neither the intellectual nor the political groundwork had been laid for the investment strategy. Once the administration embraced deficit reduction as its primary economic policy, there was very little left over for investment. The major program promised in the campaign became a $16.26 billion "stimulus package," which the administration described variously as a "down payment for investment" and as an emergency short-term economic stimulus needed for a stagnant economy.[31] Many of the specific spending proposals in the package could not realistically be defended as investment. For example, it included $4 billion (nearly a quarter of the total) for a temporary extension of emergency unemployment compensation.[32] Other elements, including $1 billion for summer youth employment, could be (and were) defended as investment in the nation's human resources, but the relatively poor record of such programs made them an easy target for opponents. Similarly, the $2.5 billion for community development block grants could be justified as investment in physical capital, but, as grants doled out for small projects designed by local governments, they could also be labeled "pork" by the administration's enemies.

These choices reflected the administration's desire to appease key constituencies but left the package open to Republican charges that Democrats were engaged in the same old "tax and spend" approach. Temporary jobs programs and spending for local projects have always been vulnerable to charges of "pork." Senate Republicans, betting there would be few repercussions if they voted against pork, unified to block the bill, agreeing only to approve the extended unemployment benefits.[33]

The failure of the stimulus package marked a political turning point because it demonstrated that the president could be defeated, even with a Democratic majority in Congress. But it is unlikely that, even had it passed, the stimulus package would have appreciably strengthened arguments for public investment. The rationale for the measure and the programs it supported did not make a strong enough case to challenge the antideficit message that politicians and mainstream economists had promoted for the past decade.

Public Policy for the High-Performance Workplace

Attracting much more attention among experts were new ideas about reorganizing the workplace and training the American work force. In the late 1980s, an emerging issue network of liberal policy experts and centrist organizations tied to big business issued a flood of policy reports and recommendations about the need for "high-performance workplaces" founded on consensual relationships between labor and management, worker participation, and skilled labor for high-quality production.[34] Politically, this approach emphasized consensus; it promised to resolve labor-management conflict around conceptions of mutual interest and to reduce inequality in a process that would be beneficial to all. The administration launched two types of initiatives in this area. The first was a Commission on the Future of Worker-Management Relations (chaired by veteran labor mediator and former secretary of labor John T. Dunlop), which was to build a consensus on labor law reform, in essence striking a grand bargain between business and labor from above. Second was the creation of a new Office of the American Workplace in the Department of Labor, charged with disseminating the new ideas about the high-performance workplace, a more bottom-up strategy of building grass-roots support for workplace innovation. The difficulties of each revealed just how few political and institutional tools the federal government had for affecting workplace practices.

Aware that there was little point in proposing legislation in the divisive area of labor law, the administration instead appointed the Dunlop commission, charged with producing recommendations about new methods or institutions to enhance workplace productivity through cooperation. The commission was also asked to recommend changes in law or collective bargaining to support such practices. This was no small charge. Although both business organizations and unions expressed generalized support for the high-performance workplace, labor law was the most polarized and politicized arena of labor-business conflict. Business and labor held diametrically opposed views about needed reforms. Labor wanted legal changes that would make organizing and union recognition easier, creating what it viewed as a more level playing field to reverse labor's decline. Business, by contrast, had little interest in any labor law reform other than a relaxation of the restrictions on nonunion forms of representation and reduction of other employment regulations.[35] Business leaders particularly wanted changes in labor law that would explicitly sanction quality circles and other new management practices that relied on worker participation.

The hope was that the commission could broker a grand bargain between business and labor in which business would agree to changes in the law that would facilitate union organizing and labor would consent to changes that permitted employer-initiated work groups. The potential for breaking the logjam rested on finding segments in labor and business receptive to the trade-off. Within the AFL-CIO, the idea of worker participation committees had won some acceptance among a younger cohort that did not believe such groups necessarily posed a threat to labor. In the business community, employers who played by the rules with regard to union organizing might be induced to discipline others who engaged in unfair labor practices.[36]

Both business and labor praised the commission's initial fact-finding report. Labor approved its finding that the labor force was becoming bifurcated into high- and low-wage sectors and that unions had a role to play in arresting this trend. Business applauded its acknowledgment that worker-management committees were important for enhanced productivity.[37] Yet, the potential deal—with unions getting changes in labor law to support organizing and business gaining more freedom to form worker-management committees—was never struck. The weakness of labor and the strength of business made each side fundamentally uninterested in changes that required moving from their current position.

Winning these changes in labor law required either far more trust between labor and management than currently existed or a credible threat that even less desirable changes would occur unless each side agreed to compromise. But the Clinton administration had few tools for creating trust or for enforcing any grand bargain through threats. Both business and labor knew that the administration could not push pro-union labor law reform through Congress even if it sought to do so. Although Secretary Reich supported the commission, there was little backing within the rest of the Department of Labor, where long-standing ties to organized labor bred skepticism about the idea of remaking the social compact. Internal discord delayed the commission's recommendations until December 1994, and the final recommendations displeased both business and labor. Former United Auto Workers' president and commission member Douglas Fraser dissented from the recommendations because they opened the door to nonunion employee-participation committees.[38] But the wording did not go far enough for business, which also disapproved of the changes recommended to support union organizing. By the time the commission reported, the election of the Republican Congress had made its recommendations moot.

The more grass-roots initiative overseen by the new Office of the American Workplace fared little better. The office was charged with promoting innovations in workplace organization to replace conflict with cooperation and thereby create the conditions for a high-performance workplace. As a newly created office with little funding, it spent most of its two years of existence seeking to define its role. It had limited avenues to pursue its mission. A handful of Washington-based organizational forums, including the Council for Competitiveness and the National Planning Association, had developed a robust dialogue about the high-performance workplace. But there was no public organizational framework for diffusing these ideas and no funds to create one. The

most the new office could do was support research and add a supportive public voice.

The failed grand bargain and the limited activities of the Office of the
American Workplace suggested that the United States did not have the
social institutions for launching a national economic strategy organized
around the idea of the high-performance workplace. While individual
firms and unions reached agreements around new workplace practices,
whether the federal government could do much to encourage such practices remained unclear. The failure of these initiatives left the Clinton
administration with no strategy to affect the supply of jobs.

Reinventing Government to Create a Skilled Work Force

Creating a skilled labor force was the second leg of the high-performance strategy. During the 1980s, diverse arguments about the benefits
of a more skilled work force emerged from a range of public and privately sponsored studies and commissions, gelling into what one scholar
called "a new consensus" on skills and training.[39] Advocates of training
promised benefits, not just for workers, but for the entire economy. In
the dramatic language of a 1990 report by the Commission on the Skills
of the American Workforce, the United States faced the choice between
"high skills or low wages."[40]

Advocates of a high-skill work force criticized American training programs as short term, fragmented, poorly administered, too focused on
the lower end of the labor market, and poorly linked to the private sector. Most evaluations of federal training programs judged them modestly effective at best.[41] Moreover, private employers offered training to
their college-educated workers, not to the majority of noncollege workers. Compounding these problems in adult training was a weak system
of vocational education and the absence of standards to allow employers to judge the skills of noncollege workers. Both made the transition
from school to work very difficult for noncollege youth.

Supporters of the high-skill approach were well placed in the Clinton
administration. Hillary Clinton had served on the William T. Grant
Foundation's Commission on Work, Family and Citizenship, which urged
new policies to enhance the education and training of noncollege youth.
Ira Magaziner, the architect of the president's health plan, had chaired
the Commission on the Skills of the American Workforce. Secretary Reich

was well known as a strong proponent of investing in workers' skills. Key interests also supported training. Business organizations had joined in the chorus of voices arguing for more training, and, although it was not high on organized labor's priorities, unions generally supported training. In Congress, training programs had a history of bipartisan consensus.

Despite this considerable support, the administration made very little headway in creating a new system for job training. Business objections killed the 1.5 percent payroll training tax that Clinton had endorsed during the campaign. The decision to finance health reform with employer mandates made administration officials reluctant to impose a mandate for training.[42] Divisions within the Labor Department blocked the efforts of Assistant Secretary for Employment and Training Doug Ross—a self-identified New Democrat—to convert existing job training programs into a system of vouchers.[43] The administration's major legislative initiative, the Reemployment Act, never made it out of committee in Congress. The legislative successes—the School-to-Work Opportunities Act and the National Skills Standards Board—were very inexpensive programs that emphasized state and private voluntary action.

Despite the apparently widespread interest in training, business and labor objected to key features of the administration's proposals, and no broader engagement in the issue emerged to widen the arena of conflict and make change possible. Part of the problem was funding: job training programs required discretionary expenditures subject to the stringent rules imposed by the 1990 budget act. New initiatives had to be funded by taking from existing programs. But the problem was deeper. Public training programs were not high on the list of business priorities, and organized labor had little interest at all in this area. In fact, few workers, organized or not, took much interest in public training programs because only a tiny proportion of the labor force had any experience with them. Broad public engagement could not be rallied in a policy arena of such low salience.

The administration's proposed Reemployment Act represented a first step toward a key goal: to redirect resources away from the passive income support system toward programs that actively inserted unemployed workers back into the labor market. By one estimate, the resources spent on such passive assistance account for 95 percent of all federal spending on the unemployed.[44] The bill consolidated six existing programs that provided assistance to dislocated workers and would cost $13 billion over five years.[45] It also remedied the arbitrary pattern of coverage that existed in such programs as TAA; under the Reemployment Act any workers permanently laid off and unemployed for at least six months could get retraining and placement advice in a training program. They would also receive income support during training, financed through the unemployment system. The program's universal character was essential to the new vision. Secretary Reich emphasized this objective in his congressional testimony on the bill: "It will counteract past tendencies to create wholly different services and access channels for different sets of workers—often segregating the disadvantaged into separate service delivery systems—and encourage moves toward mainstream programs serving all citizens."[46] The act also provided incentives for the states to set up "one-stop career centers."

Business objections quickly limited the scope of training under the act. The bill initially offered income support to workers in long-term training, using funds from the extended unemployment benefits program. Under existing programs, most dislocated workers could not receive enough income assistance to support them in longer-term training programs. The new guarantee for assistance would be paid for by the permanent extension of an existing 0.2 percent surcharge on the unemployment payroll tax. When business vigorously opposed using the tax for training and congressional Republicans expressed concern that the act might be the opening wedge toward a new training entitlement, the administration dropped the guarantee for long-term assistance. Once their concerns about creating a new entitlement were addressed, major business organizations supported the bill and worked closely with the administration in designing it.

Organized labor, however, blocked the bill. Labor vigorously objected to folding trade adjustment assistance into the Reemployment Act. Unions regarded such assistance as an entitlement for workers displaced by trade and did not want conditions of job search attached to it. Union members were the chief beneficiaries of TAA because unions played a key role in ensuring that their laid-off members applied and qualified for TAA benefits. For manufacturing unions hard hit with downsizing, preserving these funds was a top priority.[47]

Labor also had concerns about the administrative structure of the proposed legislation. In the early deliberations over the act, considerable friction developed within the department and with union leaders about the role of the Employment Service. In existence since 1933, the Employment Service had a poor record as a job placement agency, and employers primarily used it as a source of low-wage workers. Since the 1960s, its poor performance had been a source of frustration for advocates of a national training system. Assistant Secretary Doug Ross strongly advocated bypassing the Employment Service altogether by providing job training vouchers directly to workers.[48] Labor staunchly opposed reforms that would jeopardize the Employment Service because the service's work force was unionized. Bypassing it placed 20,000 union jobs in jeopardy.[49] Faced with intense union opposition, the administration dropped vouchers and proposed comprehensive career centers that could be run by different entities, including the Employment Service.

Despite this concession, labor continued to oppose the measure. The key House committees responsible for considering the legislation were dominated by labor-aligned Democrats who bottled the bill up in committee. The climate in which Congress considered the bill did not help its chances. There was little new money to sweeten the pot; the task was one of "rearranging existing money."[50] Added to this was the severe rift between "old" and "new" Democrats in this policy area. Finally, labor's mistrust of the administration was at an all-time high in the aftermath of NAFTA, the very period when the Reemployment Act was being devised. But advocates of the bill also blamed the weakness of its proponents.[51] Business groups supported the act but were not willing to expend much energy to see it passed. No broader public support emerged.

The two successful legislative initiatives, the 1994 School-to-Work Opportunities Act and the National Skills Standards Board, both were modest measures that provided incentives for private actors and state and local governments to begin to build new systems of training. Initially authorized at $300 million for the first year, the School-to-Work Opportunities Act provided seed money, granting the states substantial freedom to design a range of programs that linked schooling and job training.[52] The federal job was to award competitive grants based on national criteria. After five years the program would be phased out, with the expectation that the systems it helped to create would continue with the support of other federal funding. The National Skills Standards Board—part of the Goals 2000 educational standards legislation—provided funds for states to establish voluntary educational standards. Such voluntary national skill standards would be building blocks of a national system of training in which employers could easily judge the job preparation of their noncollege work force.

In both cases, many of the controversial issues had already been aired

in earlier bills introduced during the Bush administration. Potential conflicts around the role of the federal government and concern about protecting existing labor and business prerogatives were headed off by
concessions to the concerned interests. But in each case, the limited cost
of the act, the emphasis on local and voluntary action, and the lack of
threat to existing programs made bipartisan agreement possible.[53]

The limited achievements in employment and training legislation
underscored the shallowness of the bipartisan and interest group consensus on training. Business blocked any major new government role,
and labor resisted reforms to existing programs. But the administration
did modestly increase spending on existing programs. Appropriations
for employment and training rose by 14 percent in 1994 and were slated
to increase by 9 percent as the Republican Congress took power.[54]

Federal Tools for Reducing Economic Inequality and Insecurity

The barriers to action in labor and employment policy prompted the
administration to look to other venues to address inequality and job insecurity. Most of the administration's initiatives on inequality centered
on tax and social policy. The proposals for universal health care coverage and an expansion of the earned income tax credit (EITC) would be
important steps toward improving bad jobs and removing disincentives
to work. With the failure of the health plan, the expansion of the EITC
stood as the most far-reaching achievement in reducing income inequality.

Other tools to address economic inequality, such as direct job creation,
were simply off the agenda. Labor Department officials worked with
the drafters of the crime bill to include a program of wage subsidies for
youth, in hopes of creating an opening wedge toward a universal guarantee of jobs that paid $6 to $7 an hour as an attractive alternative to
crime. The program was dropped in the final negotiations over the bill.[55]
Likewise, the agenda of the Women's Bureau, which shifted from a focus on "glass ceiling" issues in the Bush administration to the problems
of contingent workers, remained largely sidelined. Improving the position of contingent workers through legal changes collided with the Labor Department's commitment to promote more workplace flexibility.
Efforts to address the problems of the heavily female part-time and temporary work force centered on a voluntary campaign to recognize employers who were "good corporate citizens."[56]

To address job insecurity, the president increasingly looked to higher education, rather than job training. Education was a more promising tool for a variety of reasons. Education had the universal characteristics that job training, with its remedial orientation, lacked; the middle class already cared deeply about higher education. Existing programs assisted the middle class with loan guarantees on which students had become more dependent as education costs rose. Yet higher education was not exclusively a middle-class concern; federal assistance to poorer students was available through Pell grants. Expanding access to higher education also faced fewer institutional problems. Private and public universities and community colleges offered a range of educational opportunities. Moreover, Clinton had already launched several popular initiatives in the area of higher education financing, including direct student loans that bypassed the banking system, thus reducing the cost of lending. He had also initiated income-contingent loans in conjunction with his national service program. The plan called on the federal government to create a fund from which all Americans could borrow to finance college expenses. The loans could be paid back either through public service or "as a small percentage of [recipients'] income over time." Although this remained a small program, it was a dramatic departure that could underwrite public service activity and expanded access to higher education.[57]

Immediately after the 1994 election, Clinton sought to build on this support for education by proposing a "Middle Class Bill of Rights." The bill of rights took a page from the Republicans' book by featuring tax cuts geared to the middle class, but it retained the administration's emphasis on building a highly skilled work force by including a $10,000 annual federal tax deduction for college tuition or other post–high school training expenses. The proposal was an unabashed ploy to win middle-class support, showing scant attention to the poor, who would derive little or no benefit from the tax deduction.

The Republican Stalemate

Upon taking over Congress in 1994, Republicans had a two-track strategy to address public concerns about economic security and inequality. The centerpiece of their policy for working Americans was tax reduction. Reflecting their close alliance with business, congressional Republicans supported changes in labor law to permit nonunion employee committees, opposed increases in the minimum wage, and backed sharp reductions in workplace regulation. None of these initiatives succeeded. Republicans failed to attract broad public support for tax cuts, their efforts to enact workplace reforms and overhaul regulation failed, and they ended up presiding over an increase in the minimum wage. Their efforts to reform job training programs ended in stalemate. The record was not one of total failure, however. Republicans reduced funding for jobs programs, curbed some workplace regulation, and won substantial tax concessions for small business in return for the minimum wage increase.

The Republicans' inability to enact a distinctive agenda in labor and employment policy is striking, given the political weakness of labor, the close ties of Republicans to business, and broad public antipathy to government and taxes. Explaining the stalemate requires understanding how the election of the new Congress altered the political landscape, activating new interests and changing the positions of those already active. After 1994, Clinton moved closer to unions, embracing labor as a key ally and endorsing policies he had once only tepidly supported. The activation of governors and right-wing groups around job training policies introduced new complications and divisions among Republicans that ultimately made it impossible for them to agree on a reform strategy. Finally, the aggressive promarket rhetoric of the Republican leadership and the impending election allowed congressional Democrats and organized labor to broaden the scope of attention around the minimum wage in 1996. By activating popular support for an increase, they were able to divide Republicans. But the administration limited its alliance with labor, shying away from sharp rhetoric that evoked class warfare.

Living Standards, Tax Cuts, and Entitlements

The promise to reduce taxes was the central Republican initiative designed to address the economic concerns of working people. The argument that federal taxes were responsible for declining standards of living resonated widely in public opinion and was reinforced by widespread antigovernment sentiment.[58] Republicans sought to rally this opinion behind their proposals for federal tax cuts totaling $240 billion. To their surprise, public support never consolidated behind the cuts, and they were eventually abandoned.

As Paul Pierson's chapter notes, the constrained budget climate meant that tax cuts were for the first time pitted against middle-class entitlements, most notably medicare. Throughout the 1960s and 1970s, public spending actually increased while taxes were cut. In the 1980s, Reagan's tax cuts were accompanied by spending reductions, but these reductions occurred in discretionary programs, not in the core programs of middle-class entitlements, where spending actually rose. The trade-off between tax cuts and social insurance was especially transparent in 1995 because proposed tax cuts would cost the federal treasury $240 billion, very close to the $270 billion congressional Republicans proposed to take out of medicare. When presented with the choice of tax cuts or preserving existing benefits provided by social insurance programs, the public backed away from tax cuts. Stripped of arguments about burdensome federal taxes, congressional Republicans had little to offer a public concerned about job security and wages. Their remaining initiatives in the area of labor and employment policy primarily addressed business concerns and never attracted broad interest.

Labor Policies

In policies regulating workplaces, congressional Republicans pressed for a range of business priorities. Congress passed a bill lifting the restrictions on nonunion worker-management committees, with near unanimous support from Republicans in both houses. Congressional Republicans also sought to curb the power of the NLRB by imposing deep spending cuts and proposed a major overhaul of the Occupational Safety and Health Administration (OSHA) that would dramatically limit its regulatory powers.

The president played a key role in defeating or limiting each of these initiatives. Although a proportion of congressional Democrats had long been aligned with labor, Clinton's moves reflected a change in strategy. Clinton's veto killed the bill to permit nonunion employee-involvement committees. Likewise, the president's promise to veto curbs on OSHA's powers, together with a threatened Democratic filibuster, blocked Republican efforts.[59] And while the president could not prevent cuts in the 1996 NLRB budget, the following year the agency actually received a small increase as Democrats and Republicans raised spending on education and training. Nor could congressional Republicans prevent Clinton's NLRB head, William Gould, from issuing rulings that favored labor; in 1995 the NLRB issued a record 104 injunctions, many of which ordered immediate reinstatement for discharged workers.[60]

Clinton's new support for organized labor went beyond defending against Republican initiatives; he also energetically supported measures he had avoided during his first two years in office. For example, in May 1995 Clinton signed an executive order—ultimately struck down in federal court—denying federal contracts to companies that used permanent replacements for striking workers. By moving Clinton closer to organized labor, the election of the Republican Congress had altered the political calculations surrounding labor policies; simple majorities were not enough to enact the probusiness agenda.

The Stand-off over Job Training

The implications of the Republican congressional victory for job training policies were not immediately clear. Reflecting on federal job training programs in December 1994, the policy director of the House Republican Conference, Edward W. Gillespie, suggested the Contract with America's proposal to allow tax-free withdrawals from individual retirement accounts would be sufficient for individuals to finance their own training. But existing job training programs enjoyed strong bipartisan support: JTPA had been the handiwork of Republican Senator Dan Quayle.[61] Moreover, the JTPA was business-friendly, granting local business leaders a central role in shaping the program on the ground through Private Industry Councils. With outright elimination of programs off the agenda, conflict centered on whether job training funds should be fully devoted to the states or whether existing programs should be replaced with individual vouchers issued by the federal government. Crosscutting this conflict were differences over whether job training programs should serve dislocated workers or provide training for welfare recipients. Each of these issues, but especially the first, divided the parties internally so that the sharp partisan divisions evident on many other issues were less prominent on job training.

Immediately after the 1994 elections, Clinton proposed to abolish sixty existing employment and training programs, replacing them with "skill grants" worth $2,000 to $3,000 available to individuals who needed retraining. A national data bank would collect information on training programs so that trainees could make informed choices about which programs to select.[62] The new proposal reflected the impact of the Republican victory inside the Department of Labor. As the status quo looked increasingly difficult to defend, advocates for vouchers, stymied in the first two years of the administration, saw an opening to press their case. The resources for job training might be salvaged, they argued, if they were repackaged in a way more attractive to Republicans.

Working with moderate Republicans on the Education and Economic Opportunities Committee, the administration built support for consolidating existing job training programs into four block grants to the states.[63] The grants did not give governors much discretion. States were required to set up the features of school-to-work and job training systems favored by the administration, including "one-stop centers" and local work force development boards. The adult training grant required the creation of "career grants" or vouchers. Administration advocates argued that vouchers were compatible with Republican themes of individual empowerment. They also appealed to suspicions of state bureaucracy: was bureaucracy in Sacramento any better than bureaucracy in Washington?[64] Through this work, they built a bipartisan coalition for the voucher proposal in the House.

A minority of House Democrats remained opposed, believing that the job training information system would not be sufficient to steer participants into good training programs. Fraud and mismanagement by proprietary schools had been a routine feature of the training system sponsored by JTPA, as had simple incompetence: many participants were trained for jobs that did not exist.[65] Many Democrats were also unhappy with the proposal because it cut current spending by 15–20 percent. In the end, however, a majority of House Democrats joined all but three Republicans in favor of the measure.

Governors, who preferred block grants they could control, proved the biggest obstacle. Republican governors wanted job training funds to play a role in their devolution strategy. Most federal job training money was already allocated as block grants, but regulations governed how and where the funds could be spent. Federal regulations, for example, established walls between the job opportunities and basic skills (JOBS) program for training welfare recipients on the one hand and job training programs for dislocated workers and disadvantaged workers covered by JTPA on the other. Governors wanted to retain funding but remove the regulations so that they could deploy the funds wherever they saw fit. Although they held up the bill for several months attempting to gain more control over the funds, the House bill as passed still imposed significant limits on governors' discretion.[66]

Governors were more successful in the Senate, where the new chair of the Senate Labor and Human Resources Committee, Nancy Kassebaum, Republican of Kansas, strongly advocated program consolidation and block grants controlled by the governors. Senate Democrats, including former Labor committee chair Edward Kennedy, had also backed program consolidation. As passed, the Senate bill practically eliminated federal oversight over job training by replacing it with a National Workforce Development Board. The Senate debate also directly confronted the question of whether job training funds could be used for welfare reform. Hoping to force Democrats to support welfare reform, Kassebaum made a brief attempt to include the work force training bill in the welfare reform legislation in September 1995. But she and her allies backed down in the face of sharp Democratic denunciations that Republicans had, in the words of Senator Barbara A. Mikulski, Democrat of Maryland, "decided to rob job training for middle-class, dislocated workers to fund programs for the poor." Even so, the walls between welfare reform and job training were not strong in the final Senate bill.[67]

Although job training proposals passed each house with overwhelming bipartisan majorities, a bill never emerged from conference committee. Republicans could not bridge their differences over how much control to give governors. As their broader budget project failed, they found it harder to reach consensus on less central issues, such as job training.[68] Moreover, as the bill languished, opponents on the far right, opposed to any federal job training role—for adults, but particularly for school-to-work programs—launched a campaign to defeat the legislation that cut into Republican support in the House.[69] The 104th Congress adjourned without taking action. Congressional inaction was in many respects a victory for the administration: it had successfully warded off undesirable system changes and had limited cuts to training programs.

Throughout the 104th Congress, Clinton made education and training the sticking point in his budget negotiations with congressional Republicans. In his rhetoric, the president grouped job training and education together, aiming to regain the political offensive by winning over the middle class. Clinton cast his first veto on a 1995 measure to rescind $16.4 billion in education and training funds, although he later signed a bill that was only symbolically different. Congressional Republicans cut employment and training funds by some 27 percent in 1995.[70]

Again, in the conflict over the 1996 budget, Clinton singled out the cuts in education and training as unacceptable. He held out successfully for Congress to restore $2.7 billion in education and training programs in the protracted drama over the 1996 budget, which ultimately registered a small increase in employment and training expenditures.[71] As the 1996 election approached, congressional Republicans fell into a bidding war with Democrats that actually increased spending on employment and training programs by 14 percent and on Pell grants by over 20 percent. Still, by 1997, spending in both categories had dropped by 6 percent from their highs in 1994.[72]

The Politics of the Minimum Wage

When congressional Republicans launched their revolution in January of 1995, few would have predicted that President Clinton would sign an increase in the minimum wage during the closing months of the 104th Congress. The congressional vote to increase the minimum wage from $4.25 to $5.15 an hour reflected the strong public support for the measure: in April 1996, 84 percent of the public supported an increase. But by itself, public support is not sufficient to explain why Congress increased the minimum wage in 1996.[73] On the Democratic side, the closer alliance between the president, congressional Democrats, and a newly activated AFL-CIO on the issue was essential to making public opinion salient. On the Republican side, a weakened congressional leadership with few legislative accomplishments and an impending election allowed underlying fissures to surface.

As part of his closer alliance to organized labor, President Clinton resuscitated the proposal to raise the minimum wage in his 1995 State of the Union address, proposing a ninety-cent increase over two years. Senate Majority Leader Bob Dole initially expressed some interest in trading Republican support for an increased minimum wage with Democratic support for a capital gains cut, but no agreement was reached. In 1996, however, presidential politics began to heat up, and Republican presidential candidate Pat Buchanan's campaign showed the unexpected vitality of economic insecurity as a political issue. Congressional Democrats seized upon this climate to reintroduce legislation increasing the minimum hourly wage, this time by one dollar. The effort to raise the minimum wage did not remain confined to the halls of Congress, however.

Under new leadership, the AFL-CIO launched a public campaign to win support for the measure. A spate of television advertisements targeted moderate Republicans from districts with a high percentage of union members.[74]

The split over the minimum wage was the first breach in Republican unity, the first sign that the congressional leadership was losing its unusual power as the 1996 election approached. Underlying differences that the leadership had suppressed in favor of a common project now took center stage. Many Republicans supporting the increase were from the Northeast, where wages, the cost of living, and union membership are higher than in the rest of the country.[75] Unable to kill the measure by attaching a variety of unpopular conditions, the Republican leadership eventually used it as a vehicle to enact a range of corporate tax breaks. Working with their allies in the NFIB and other business organizations, congressional Republicans—joined in some instances by Democrats— turned the minimum wage bill into a measure in which tax cuts for business were at least as significant as the impact on wages.[76]

Class Warfare?

The emergence of economic security as an issue early in the 1996 presidential campaign and the renewed activism of organized labor suggested new prospects for a class-oriented politics. Attacks on big business and corporate greed were a staple of the rhetoric that had catapulted Pat Buchanan into the public spotlight. The AFL-CIO picked up similar themes in its public campaign around the idea that "America needs a raise." Both stressed the effects of corporate greed and business's irresponsibility toward working people as the causes of the economic insecurity that now troubled American workers. As the 1996 election approached, Clinton briefly flirted with these themes but ultimately chose not to embrace the "class warfare" strategy. Allowing Secretary Reich to inject themes of corporate irresponsibility into the public debate, the president embraced a much-diluted argument favoring corporate good citizenship without allying himself too closely to organized labor or antagonizing business.

For Democrats, labor's decision to take a more aggressive political posture than it had in decades presented new resources for a class-based politics. Ruing labor's fall from "political powerhouse to a political patsy,"

new AFL-CIO president John Sweeney vowed to launch an unprecedented grass-roots effort in the 1996 election.[77] The organization soon
approved a special assessment on members to finance a $25 million cam-
paign fund for the 1996 elections. Moreover, the new labor leadership
embraced a rhetoric that went beyond the narrow concerns of organized
labor and converged with Clinton's attention to the middle class. The
AFL-CIO's new political director, Steve Rosenthal, responded to Republican criticism by asserting that unions' political activities were not about
parties but about "beginning to rebuild the base of working families who
will stand up for basic middle-class American values."[78]

The Department of Labor also began to sound a class-oriented rhetoric and establish a forthright alliance with organized labor. The shift toward organized labor was evident in Reich's willingness to identify
labor's concerns as essentially the same as those of all workers, unionized or not. It was also apparent in Reich's attack on "corporate welfare," his campaign to highlight growing economic inequality, and his
crusade for "corporate responsibility." These initiatives placed the Department of Labor in a "class warfare mode," in the words of one department official.[79]

With his talent for framing an issue, Reich directed public attention to
the emergence of an "anxious class" concerned about economic
downsizing. His campaign for corporate responsibility pressed the idea
that corporations had responsibilities to their employees as well as to
their stockholders and that downsizing and lowering wages were not
the answers to concerns about productivity.[80] Reich worked with congressional Democrats to craft legislation that would establish a special
class of corporation, the A-Corps, that would be taxed at a lower rate.
Approved firms would have a number of characteristics, including 2
percent of payroll devoted to employee training, a limit on highest-paid
employees' earnings to no more than fifty times that of the lowest paid,
profit-sharing plans open to half the work force, and health and pension
plans. Congressional Democrats—many long aligned with organized
labor—also unveiled proposals to strengthen labor laws protecting workers and communities from corporate downsizing.[81]

The resurgence of these economic themes revived the debate between
economic populism and middle-class values that had vied within the
Clinton camp since the 1992 campaign. The failure of the 1993 stimulus
bill and the decision to emphasize deficit reduction had wiped economic
populism off Clinton's agenda, but public concerns about corporate

downsizing now raised the possibility of relaunching these themes as political issues. Supporters of this path argued that such economic concerns had historically been the most potent themes for Democrats, providing a bright line to distinguish Democrats from Republicans. A series of public opinion studies commissioned by the AFL-CIO in the spring of 1996 offered some support for this strategy. Half of those surveyed believed that they were falling behind economically, and a majority believed that "corporate greed" was responsible for the nation's economic problems.[82]

Others in the Clinton camp rejected this route as too divisive, preferring instead to build the campaign around preserving middle-class entitlements, such as medicare. They pointed to ambiguities in public opinion to support their arguments for this more conservative route. The same survey that found public disapproval of corporate greed also showed that more Americans were more worried about moral and social problems than economic problems. And although Americans blamed corporate greed most for economic woes, their second culprit was a government that took too much in taxes. Finally, the survey indicated that Americans were "not necessarily in a 'corporation bashing' mood." Only 30 percent of those surveyed expressed negative feelings toward corporations—the same as toward labor unions.[83]

Within the administration there was little support outside the Department of Labor for policy initiatives to enforce corporate responsibility. The National Economic Council and Treasury Secretary Robert Rubin were particularly incensed at Reich's moves into areas that were within their purview.[84] The overall tenor of economic policy set in 1993 was much more conservative than a new class-oriented politics would require. The "Eisenhower Republicanism" that Clinton had rued—but embraced—in deliberations over his first budget was premised on winning support from Wall Street, not on arousing the ire of business.[85]

Ultimately, Clinton rejected Reich's initiatives and the stronger class rhetoric they implied. Instead the president embraced a much more consensual approach. Convening a day-long meeting of business and labor to discuss corporate citizenship, Clinton implored workers and managers to "join together in a great journey as Americans" to create better workplace practices. Rather than support regulation or the certification process proposed by Reich, the president backed tax breaks for corporations that provided education for their workers and the establishment of an award for corporate citizenship.[86]

Clinton thus restricted his move toward organized labor. The more conservative economic path the administration had already charted, the continued weakness of organized labor despite its new activism, and the ambiguities of public opinion relevant to the "class warfare" strategy all supported arguments against reviving economic populism as an essential element of a new Democratic majority. Moreover, the organization of politics—premised around raising money rather than mobilizing people—meant that an electoral strategy of winning over swing voters in the middle class was much safer than one that sought to reengage disaffected working-class voters around a new set of issues. Antagonizing business, an important source of campaign funds, would not help such an electoral strategy.

The Future of Employment Policy

Although labor policies remained caught in the stand-off between labor and business, two major directions for reforming job training policies emerged from Democratic and Republican initiatives. The first is a federal human capital strategy that would provide training vouchers for workers and, if fully developed, would lead to a new federal entitlement to "lifelong learning." A second path would devolve responsibility for job training to the states, allowing governors considerable leeway in designing programs. Each route—especially if taken without accompanying reform of workplace practices—would encounter distinctive political and institutional obstacles that could leave significant gaps in public efforts to address economic insecurity and inequality. However, possibilities for the future rest not only on public initiatives, but perhaps more important, on the dispositions of private actors in business and labor and in the now mostly disengaged public.

The Federal Human Capital Strategy

Clinton's embrace of vouchers and tax cuts for higher education after the 1994 election charted a new direction for federal employment and training policy. Instead of pursuing elusive system reforms, the federal government would simply provide individuals with the means to secure their own training. One of the obvious political benefits of this approach is that it allows the government to assist workers but to avoid the tag of "big government." Because it relies on tax credits or checks rather than government institutions, this route makes it easier to adopt a more universal approach to training, without separate remedial tracks for the less well off. And although it removes the federal government from institution building, the community college system across the country provides the institutional base on which to build such a strategy. In recent years, community colleges have played an integral role in providing vocationally oriented training and, more recently, customized training programs desired by employers.[87] Moreover, vouchers provide a way of extending job training to a wider range of recipients, potentially building broad new support for federal job training efforts.

One of the major drawbacks of this approach as a way to remedy economic insecurity and inequality are doubts about whether training has the benefits its supporters claim.[88] As was pointed out during the 1995 debate over job training, vouchers and tax credits would do little to remedy fraud and incompetence in proprietary training schools, and it is questionable whether providing information about schools would sufficiently address this problem. There is also the question of whether the mere presence of more highly trained workers will increase the supply of "good jobs." How, for example, does this strategy alter the practice of relying on contingent and part-time workers? Such concerns remain significant; the human capital strategy alters the supply of workers without directly affecting the demand for highly skilled workers. Moving employers from a low-wage to a high-skill, high-wage strategy may require both organizing employers at the regional level and building cooperation that allows them to see the benefits of highly trained workers and to influence the type of training that workers receive. The creation of such employer consortia is especially important for small businesses, which have less often utilized public training programs.[89] Other analysts argue that it is necessary to cut off employers' options to take the low-wage strategy by imposing regulations, such as a greatly increased minimum wage.[90]

Finally, significant obstacles remain to expanding this system—or any other—to create a new entitlement to training. Business opposition to direct a small part of the unemployment tax surcharge toward training during the debate over the reemployment bill indicates the obstacles that efforts to find new sources of dedicated revenue will encounter. Similarly, labor's opposition to using trade assistance adjustment funds for training purposes provides only a preview of the resistance that efforts to turn passive into active assistance will encounter. The Clinton administration did institute some reforms in unemployment insurance that move it toward a more active system, notably requiring states to profile claimants in order to identify those unlikely to be reemployed at their old jobs and move them to new employment or training. But more direct efforts to limit unemployment insurance in favor of training will encounter stiff resistance from organized labor.[91]

Devolution and State Initiative

A second path for employment and training policy relies on the states. States already play an important role in job training. JTPA provides block grants to the states, and many states have also undertaken a variety of training programs with their own funds.[92] With or without formal devolution, states will continue to shape public efforts at job training. The advantage of state action is that states are more able to engage in the kind of system building that is simply too difficult to orchestrate from Washington. Some Clinton administration initiatives recognized this: thus, the school-to-work initiative provided incentives for states to build new connections between employers and schools, with the federal role limited to reviewing applications from the states.

But purely state-directed job training systems have several potential pitfalls. One problem was suggested during the Senate debate over job training in 1995: job training programs could become little more than an adjunct of welfare reform. As states confront new pressures to employ former welfare recipients in the wake of the 1996 welfare bill, job training funds could be used as a flexible resource to support this effort. While providing training for welfare recipients is an important objective, it could give public job training an even more remedial cast, thereby undermining the objectives of building a more universal system designed to assist all workers and improve the overall health of the economy. A second danger in a purely state-run system is that job training would become an adjunct of state economic development objectives. As the federal government has reduced its social and economic role in the past twenty years, states have taken a much more active role in promoting economic development. An increasing number of states have used promises of customized job training to bring important employers to the states. The problem with this approach is that it can allow employers to play states off against one another so that the states end up providing training that the firms would have provided anyway and there is no net new benefit: job training becomes primarily a subsidy to business. State training programs linked to economic development are also likely to underserve disadvantaged workers, as indeed most current state programs of this sort do.[93]

Regardless of federal action, it is likely that states will continue to develop job training programs. Given the incentives that governors have to use these programs for purely economic development objectives, pressure from other groups, including labor and minorities, will be needed to push these programs further to build state systems that promote competitiveness and benefit workers as well as employers.

Whose Concern?

As important as public initiatives are, future possibilities for labor and training policies will be shaped both by the positions of employers and unions on proposed policies and by firm-level agreements about training and workplace practices. The level of public attention and engagement around these issues will also affect policy, as will community-based efforts to create new job development strategies. Many of the institutional failures that have limited labor and training policies stem from inadequate organization among business and labor. Because institution building involves the organization of social interests, not simply what government does, the activities of private groups and the support within them for new forms of workplace organization and training are key in determining future possibilities.

Although labor and business have been sharply polarized around labor law reform, some firms and their workers have built new forms of cooperation in the workplace. By one estimate, approximately 25 percent of American firms engage in "high-performance workplace" practices.[94] Among the most successful examples are unionized firms that have struck deals with labor over workplace changes designed to benefit both management and labor. Expanding this model faces opposition from both business and labor. Employer control of workplace organization is a deeply embedded feature of American industrial organization that many employers are loath to alter. Moreover, many American employers have succeeded in international markets with low-wage, flexible work strategies in which skilled workers and worker participation play little part. It will be difficult to move some employers away from that model in the absence of regulatory measures—such as a much higher minimum wage—that make that option less viable.

An essential element of labor practices and policymaking over the past quarter century has been the growing organization and aggressiveness of business and the weakness of labor. Organized labor's current efforts to rebuild through new organizing drives and active engagement in politics may open new possibilities for labor policy. But if these changes are to be linked to new workplace practices, labor will have to become more interested in expanded training and less suspicious of new workplace practices. Although individual unions have reached innovative agreements with firms, organized labor as a whole has granted little more than lip service to these ideas.[95] A more forward-looking posture on the part of labor is critical if new workplace practices are to expand and achieve their promise of mutual gains for employers and workers.

A persistent problem for labor and training policy has been its low public salience, which allows the polarized perspectives of business and labor to dominate policymaking. The narrow scope of this policy arena reflects public ambivalence about whether the government can play a constructive role in ensuring job security. Surveys taken in 1996 found a majority of American concerned about downsizing but revealed doubts about what government could and should do. For example, when asked who should bear primary responsibility for ensuring job security, 36 percent of respondents said individual workers, 30 percent said employers, and only 18 percent identified government.[96] When asked whether Congress *could* do something about layoffs and job loss, 64 percent responded positively, but when asked whether the government *should* do something about layoffs, only 47 percent answered yes.[97]

Although broad-based pressure to expand the public role in addressing economic security and inequality is likely to remain elusive in the near future, community-level engagement around these issues has grown and is creating new models for job training and development. Confronted by job loss and growing inequality, some community organizations have taken the lead in developing programs that move beyond training to job development by establishing connections with employers and winning guarantees of good jobs at the end of training. The Industrial Areas Foundation's Project Quest in San Antonio provides an example of the new approach to training that engages community organizations and employers.[98] These initiatives are as yet small scale, but they are important because they broaden the scope of engagement and build new connections between community groups and employers and, in some cases, with organized labor as well. They also provide models for redesigning public efforts. The Bush and Clinton administrations, for example, both used the highly successful California employment and training program as a model for connecting job training to employers.[99]

In addition to these job development efforts, community organizations have become active in "living wage" campaigns in over thirty cities. Community groups have aligned with organized labor to win agreements that city contractors be required to substantially increase their minimum pay to $7.70 an hour, the amount a full-time worker would need to support a family of four—a figure well above the minimum wage. Although the effort has been successful only in Milwaukee and Baltimore—and only on a limited basis—it provides a new model of coalition building and political mobilization around the issue of low wages.[100]

Because government action in the area of labor and employment policy has been so troubled, the perspectives of private actors are especially important. The actions of labor, business, and community organizations and public views are important in their own right, but they also feed back into policymaking as models for possible future innovation and markers of the likely limits of public action.

Conclusion

The failure of Clinton and the congressional Republicans to put their distinctive stamps on employment policy reflected the substantial political barriers that blocked efforts to depart from existing policies. In both cases the key barriers were the polarization of business and labor around workplace policies, budget constraints that made compromise difficult, and public disinterest that kept the arena of conflict narrow. Clinton's proposals for consensus building around labor and job training programs had no ready-made constituencies, and the president lacked the resources—either inducements or sanctions—to create new interest or compromises. Where broad public pressure could be mobilized, as in the minimum wage struggle, change was possible. But because Clinton's political and policy strategy was fundamentally consensual, he chose not to rally support for more conflictual measures that also had public appeal, such as corporate responsibility. The Republican effort was more straightforward politically; the public had long backed tax cuts, and business strongly supported reductions in workplace regulation. But the politics of budget constraints and entitlements stripped Republicans of their most powerful argument and most popular initiative regarding living standards. They were left with a probusiness agenda that the Democratic minority—now joined by the president—could limit.

Yet the impasse left Republicans and their business allies with the upper hand in employment policy. Democrats and their supporters face formidable challenges if they are to reestablish the connections between general economic strength and workers' well-being that Keynesian economic policy once did. The tasks they confront require political mobilization as well as institutional creation. New regional institutions that link workers and employers, alliances between labor and community organizations to raise wages, firm-level experiments in workplace innovation, and a revived and broadened labor movement are all essential elements for expanding the policy arena and altering the political calculus that has greatly circumscribed the scope for reform. As these goals suggest, future action must go beyond compromises negotiated from above and the purely consensual approach preferred by the Clinton administration.

Notes

1. Robert Reich, "This Administration 'Snubs' No One," *Washington Post*, November 4, 1994, p. 25.

2. For an analysis of these factors in comparative perspective, see Richard B. Freeman and Lawrence F. Katz, "Rising Wage Inequality: The United States vs. Other Advanced Countries," in Richard B. Freeman, ed., *Working under Different Rules* (New York: Russell Sage Foundation, 1994), chap. 2.

3. McKinley Blackburn, David E. Bloom, and Richard B. Freeman, "The Declining Economic Position of Less Skilled American Men," in Gary Burtless, ed., *A Future of Lousy Jobs?* (Brookings, 1990), p. 32.

4. Gary Burtless, "Worsening American Income Inequality: Is World Trade to Blame?" *Brookings Review*, vol. 14 (Spring 1996), p. 28.

5. *Economic Report of the President, February 1997*, p. 346, table B-40. Lester Thurow estimates, however, that the real rate of unemployment was 14 percent in early 1996. See Thurow, "The Crusade That's Killing Prosperity," *American Prospect*, no. 25 (March–April 1996), pp. 54–59.

6. See Henry Farber, "The Changing Face of Job Loss in the United States, 1981–1995," *Brookings Papers on Economic Activity, Microeconomics: 1997* (forthcoming).

7. U.S. Department of Labor and U.S. Department of Commerce, Commission on the Future of Worker-Management Relations, *Fact Finding Report* (May 1994), p. 21.

8. That stimulus took the form of automatic stabilizers in the 1940s and 1950s. Not until the 1960s did the federal government engage in active stimulus in the form of tax cuts. See Herbert Stein, *The Fiscal Revolution in America* (University of Chicago Press, 1969). On the narrow definition of the problem, see Margaret Weir, *Politics and Jobs* (Princeton University Press, 1992), chaps. 2–3.

9. See Donald C. Baumer and Carl E. Van Horn, *The Politics of Unemployment* (Washington: Congressional Quarterly Press, 1985), pp. 19, 110.

10. C. Michael Aho and Thomas O. Bayard, "Costs and Benefits of Trade Adjustment Assistance," in Robert E. Baldwin and Anne O. Krueger, eds., *The Structure and Evolution of Recent U.S. Trade Policy* (University of Chicago Press, 1984), p. 184.

11. Daniel P. McMurrer and Amy B. Chasanov, "Trends in Unemployment Insurance Benefits," *Monthly Labor Review* (September 1995), p. 34; on TAA benefits, see *Overview of Entitlement Programs: Background Material and Data on Programs within the Jurisdiction of the Committee on Ways and Means*, Committee Print, 104 Cong. 2 sess. (Government Printing Office, 1996), p. 374.

12. On the critiques of CETA and the creation of JTPA, see Baumer and Van Horn, *Politics of Unemployment*, chaps. 3–6. On the creation of JTPA, also see Richard F. Fenno, *The Making of a Senator: Dan Quayle* (Washington: Congressional Quarterly Press, 1989).

13. On the move to increased regulation and use of employment law, see Commission on the Future of Worker-Management Relations, *Fact Finding Report*, chap. 4.

14. Bureau of Labor Statistics, *Employment and Earnings*, vol. 44 (January 1997), pp. 211–13.

15. See Harold W. Stanley and Richard G. Niemi, *Vital Statistics on American Politics*, 4th ed. (Washington: Congressional Quarterly Press, 1994), table 3-10.

16. See James W. Singer, "Labor and Congress: New Isn't Necessarily Better," *National Journal*, March 4, 1978, pp. 351–53.

17. See Taylor E. Dark, "Organized Labor and the Congressional Democrats: Reconsidering the 1980s," *Political Science Quarterly*, vol. 111 (Spring 1996), pp. 83–104.

18. Thomas Byrne Edsall, *The New Politics of Inequality* (Norton, 1984), p. 121.

19. Cathie J. Martin, *Shifting the Burden: The Struggle over Growth and Corporate Taxation* (University of Chicago Press, 1991), chaps. 1–4.

20. Edsall, *New Politics of Inequality*, pp. 125–26.

21. James W. Singer, "Life Isn't as Grand for Labor When the Grand Old Party's in Power," *National Journal*, May 22, 1976, pp. 698–703.

22. See the discussion in I. M. Destler, *American Trade Politics*, 3d ed. (Washington and New York: Institute for International Economics and Twentieth Century Fund, 1995), chap. 7.

23. See Thomas A. Kochan and Paul Osterman, *The Mutual Gains Enterprise* (Harvard Business School Press, 1994), pp. 201–02; and James R. Rundle, "The Debate over the Ban on Employer-Dominated Labor Organizations: What Is the Evidence?" in Sheldon Friedman and others, eds., *Restoring the Promise of American Labor Law* (Ithaca, N.Y.: ILR Press, 1994), chap. 11.

24. Interview, congressional staff, March 20, 1996.

25. Louis Uchitelle, "Union Leaders Fight for a Place in the President's Workplace of the Future," *New York Times*, August 8, 1993, p. 32.

26. See Thomas B. Edsall, "NAFTA Debate Reopens Wounds in the Body of the Democratic Party," *Washington Post*, October 24, 1993, p. A4.

27. Steven Greenhouse, "Labor Official Retreats on Higher Minimum Wage," *New York Times*, October 30, 1993, p. 9; and Greenhouse, "Labor Secretary to Urge Clinton to Propose Minimum Wage Rise," *New York Times*, October 13, 1993, p. 18.

28. Interview, congressional staff, March 20, 1996.

29. Kirk Victor, "Ready, Aim, Fire," *National Journal*, September 10, 1994, pp. 2079–82; on the declining usefulness of collective bargaining, see Paul Weiler, *Governing the Workplace: The Future of Labor and Employment Laws* (Harvard University Press, 1990).

30. Bill Clinton and Al Gore, *Putting People First* (Times Books, 1992), p. 9.

31. See the discussion in Jon Healey, "Spending Increases Come First in Rush to Pass Package," *Congressional Quarterly Weekly Report*, February 20, 1993, pp. 365–69.

32. For a list of the initial proposals, see Executive Office of the President, Office of Management and Budget, *A Vision of Change for America* (February 17, 1993).

33. Jon Healey, "Democrats Look to Salvage Part of Stimulus Plan," *Congressional Quarterly Weekly Report*, April 24, 1993, pp. 1001–04.

34. The best overview of these arguments is presented in Kochan and Osterman, *Mutual Gains Enterprise*. Among the key reports were Commission on the Skills of the American Workforce, *America's Choice: High Skills or Low Wages!* (Washington: National Center on Education and the Economy, 1990); and William T. Grant Foundation Commission on Work, Family and Citizenship, *The Forgotten Half* (Washington, 1988). Among the business reports were the National Alliance of Business, *Shaping Tomorrow's Workforce* (Washington, 1988); and the Research and Policy Committee of the Committee for Economic Development, *Work and Change: Labor Market Adjustment Policies in a Competitive World* (New York and Washington: Committee for Economic Development, 1987).

35. See the essays in Friedman and others, eds., *Restoring the Promise of Ameri-*

can Labor Law; and Kirk Victor, "Labor's New Deal," *National Journal*, April 24, 1993, pp. 978–82.

36. Interview, Department of Labor official, June 17, 1996.

37. See Commission on the Future of Worker-Management Relations, *Fact-Finding Report*; Kirk Victor, "Try, Try Again," *National Journal*, July 9, 1994, pp. 1623–26; and "Economy: Study Commends Worker Participation, But Says Labor Laws May Be Limiting," *Wall Street Journal*, June 3, 1994, p. A2.

38. U.S. Department of Labor and U.S. Department of Commerce, Commission on the Future of Worker-Management Relations, *Report and Recommendations* (December 1994).

39. See James J. Heckman, "Is Job Training Oversold?" *The Public Interest*, no. 115 (Spring 1994), pp. 91–115.

40. Commission on the Skills of the American Workforce, *America's Choice*.

41. See, for example, the evaluations in Robert J. LaLonde, "The Promise of Public Sector-Sponsored Training Programs," *Journal of Economic Perspectives*, vol. 9 (Spring 1995), pp. 149–68.

42. Beverly Geber, "Because It's Good for You," *Training*, vol. 30 (April 1993), pp. 17–25; and interview, Department of Labor official, September 15, 1995. A central recommendation of the Commission on the Skills of the American Workforce was a training tax of 1 percent of payroll, to increase over time. See *America's Choice*, p. 82.

43. See his chapter in the Progressive Policy Institute's agenda for Clinton: Doug Ross, "Enterprise Economics on the Front Lines: Empowering Firms and Workers to Win," in Will Marshall and Martin Schram, eds., *Mandate for Change* (Berkley Books, 1993), chap. 3.

44. Carl E. Van Horn, "Federal Programs Try to Cushion the Blow," in Twentieth Century Fund Task Force on Retraining America's Workforce, *No One Left Behind* (New York: Twentieth Century Fund Press, 1996), p. 131.

45. The six programs were economic dislocation and worker adjustment assistance; trade adjustment assistance; NAFTA transitional adjustment assistance; the defense conversion adjustment program; the clean air employment transition assistance program; and the defense diversification program.

46. See Reich's testimony before the House Committee on Education and Labor, March 16, 1994.

47. Interview with Department of Labor official, September 15, 1995.

48. See Weir, *Politics and Jobs*, pp. 80–83; Marc Bendick Jr., "Matching Workers and Job Opportunities; What Role for the Federal-State Employment Service?" in D. Lee Bawden and Felicity Skidmore, eds., *Rethinking Employment Policy* (Washington: Urban Institute Press, 1989), chap. 4; and Ross, "Enterprise Economics on the Front Lines."

49. Interviews with Department of Labor official and congressional staff, March 16, 1996; April 3, 1996; March 20, 1996.

50. Interview with congressional staff, March 20, 1996.

308   Margaret Weir

51. Interviews with Department of Labor official and National Economic Council staff, March 16, 1996; June 17, 1996; April 13, 1996.

52. Rochelle L. Stanfield, "A Test, Maybe, for the Reinventors," *National Journal*, September 1, 1993, pp. 2197–98; and "Clinton Signs School-to-Work Bill," *1994 Congressional Quarterly Almanac*, pp. 400-01.

53. Rochelle L. Stanfield, "Hire Learning," *National Journal*, May 1, 1993, p. 1043.

54. "Labor-HHS Bill Requires Trade-offs," *1994 Congressional Quarterly Almanac*, p. 520; and "Huge Bill Funds Labor, HHS, Education Department," *1993 Congressional Quarterly Almanac*, p. 633.

55. Interview with Department of Labor official, June 17, 1996.

56. Interview with Department of Labor official, June 5, 1996.

57. See Steven Waldman, *The Bill* (Viking, 1995).

58. Ruy A. Teixeira and Joel Rogers, "Volatile Voters: Declining Living Standards and Non-College Educated Whites," Working Paper 116 (Washington: Economic Policy Institute, August 8, 1996).

59. See Kirk Victor, "Up the Creek?" *National Journal*, April 8, 1995, pp. 859–63; Frank Swoboda, "GOP Bills on OSHA Face Veto by Clinton," *Washington Post*, February, 20, 1996, p. C1; David Masci, "Panel OKs OSHA Changes, But Bill Has Uphill Fight," *Congressional Quarterly Weekly Report*, March 9, 1996, p. 625; and Jonathan Weisman, "Panel OKs Measure to Ease Worker Safety Regulations," *Congressional Quarterly Weekly Report*, April 20, 1996, p. 1052.

60. Steven Greenhouse, "Labor Board Chief Takes Assertive Stance," *New York Times*, June 2, 1996, p. 32. However, political pressure could be the cause for the reduced number of injunctions in 1997. See Aaron Bernstein, "How Business Is Winning Its War with the NLRB," *Business Week*, October 27, 1997, p. 59.

61. Rochelle L. Stanfield, "Rutsville," *National Journal*, December 3, 1994, pp. 2837–39; and Fenno, *Making of a Senator*.

62. See Ann Devroy, "Clinton Proposes 'Middle Class Bill of Rights,'" *Washington Post*, December 16, 1994, p. A1.

63. The areas were youth and education, adult training, rehabilitation, and adult education. Advocates for the disabled later succeeded in having rehabilitation grants removed from the mix. The final House bill created three block grants: the youth development and career preparation consolidation grant, the adult employment and training consolidation grant, and the adult education and family literacy consolidation grant. See Robert Marshall Wells, "Job Training Bills Compared," *Congressional Quarterly Weekly Report*, November 4, 1995, p. 3396, for a detailed description of the House and Senate bills.

64. Interview with Department of Labor official, March 16, 1996.

65. On the skills grants, see Robert Marshall Wells, "Job Training Programs Could Get Pink Slip," *Congressional Quarterly Weekly Report*, January 28, 1995, pp. 284–87; and Asra Q. Nomani, "Politics and Policy: Many U.S. Programs

Face Radical Changes, but Critics Question the Payoff in Efficiency," *Wall Street Journal*, December 19, 1994, p. A16. Even though they would benefit, proprietary schools were not strongly involved in the debate. Lobbyists for community colleges were heavily involved in arguing for the legislation.

66. Some representatives resented appropriating funds for governors. In the markup of the Careers Act, committee chair Bill Goodling, Republican of Pennsylvania, remarked that if governors wanted to decide how to spend money, they should raise it themselves. Interview with Department of Labor official, March 16, 1996.

67. Judith Havemann, "A New Welfare Bill Complication," *Washington Post*, August 24, 1995, p. A17; and Rochelle L. Stanfield, "Training Wheels," *National Journal*, December 16, 1995, pp. 3085–89.

68. This was despite the fact that House Majority Leader Dick Armey had placed the legislation on his "must pass" list. See Dick Armey, "A Republican Agenda to Reverse the Clinton Crunch," Heritage Foundation, February 27, 1996.

69. Adam Clymer, "A Job-Training Bill Is Being Attacked by Conservatives," *New York Times*, March 31, 1996, p. A1; and interview with congressional staff, April 3, 1996.

70. Dan Morgan and Ann Devroy, "Clinton to Veto $16 Billion Rescissions Package," *Washington Post*, May 17, 1995, p. A1; "Labor-HHS Bill Requires Tradeoffs"; and "Labor-HHS Bill in Limbo at Year's End," *1995 Congressional Quarterly Almanac*, p. 11-56. See the discussion of the 1995 rescissions bill in "$16.3 Billion Cut from 1995 Spending," *1995 Congressional Quarterly Almanac*, pp. 11-96–11-105.

71. Jerry Gray, "Senate Republicans Add Money for Education and Job Programs," *New York Times*, March 13, 1996, p. A1; and Eric Pianin, "House-Senate Budget Agreement Is Said to Be Near," *Washington Post*, March 29, 1996, p. A6.

72. Jeffrey Katz, "Education Programs Get Big Boost in Spending," *Congressional Quarterly Weekly Report*, October 5, 1996, p. 2870.

73. "The Minimum Wage: A Portrait," *New York Times*, April 19, 1996, p. A26. For an argument about the importance of public opinion and the preferences of legislators regarding the minimum wage, see David W. Rohde, "Parties, Institutional Control, and Political Incentives: A Perspective on Governing in the Clinton Presidency," paper prepared for colloquium on "The Clinton Years in Perspective," Université de Montreal, October 6-8, 1996.

74. See Helen Dewar and David S. Broder, "Democrats' Cents of Unity," *Washington Post*, April 25, 1996, p. A1.

75. Ibid.; and Jackie Koszczuk and Jonathan Weisman, "GOP Bending on Raise in Minimum Wage," *Congressional Quarterly Weekly Report*, April 20, 1996, pp. 1047–48.

76. See Eric Pianin, "How Business Found Benefits in Wage Bill," *Washington Post*, February 11, 1997, p. A1.

77. See Tim Curran, "Labor's Political Rebirth?" *Roll Call*, November 6, 1995, pp. 1, 24; and Peter T. Kilborn, "Delegates of Labor Gather, Battered but Now Buoyant," *New York Times*, October 22, 1995, p. 1.

78. Thomas B. Edsall, "GOP Plans Counteroffensive on Labor," *Washington Post*, March 22, 1996, p. A16.

79. Victor, "Up the Creek?"; and interview with Department of Labor official, September 15, 1995.

80. See, for example, Robert B. Reich, "How to Avoid These Layoffs?" *New York Times*, January 4, 1996, p. A21.

81. Clay Chandler, "Sensing Advantage as GOP Debate Shifts, Democrats Unveil Plan on Jobs, Growth," *Washington Post*, February 29, 1996, p. A24; and Adam Clymer, "Help Companies That Treat Workers Well, Kennedy Says," *New York Times*, February 9, 1996, p. A27.

82. The Mellman Group and Peter D. Hart Research Associates, "AFL-CIO: Summary of Key Findings" (Washington, May 1996).

83. Ibid.; and memo to AFL-CIO Executive Council from Peter D. Hart Research Associates and the Mellman Group (Washington, May 6, 1996), pp. 12–13. The survey found strong public sympathy for small business.

84. Clay Chandler, "Reich's 'Responsibility' Issue Irritates Colleagues," *Washington Post*, March 8, 1996, p. F1.

85. See Bob Woodward, *The Agenda: Inside the Clinton White House* (Simon and Schuster, 1994).

86. Clay Chandler, "Clinton Unveils Initiatives for Businesses," *Washington Post*, May 17, 1996, p. F3.

87. Paul Osterman and Rosemary Batt, "Employer-Centered Training for International Competitiveness: Lessons from State Programs," *Journal of Policy Analysis and Management*, vol. 12 (Summer 1993), pp. 456–77.

88. Heckman, "Is Job Training Oversold?"

89. Osterman and Batt, "Employer-Centered Training," pp. 468–69. On small business, see Laurie J. Bassi, *Smart Workers, Smart Work* (Washington: Southport Institute for Policy Analysis, 1992).

90. See, for example, Eileen Appelbaum and Rosemary Batt, *The New American Workplace* (Ithaca, N.Y.: ILR Press, 1994), pp. 168–69.

91. See Jane McDonald-Pines and Jack Sheinkman, "Dissent," in Twentieth Century Task Force, *No One Left Behind*, pp. 53–54.

92. See Carl E. Van Horn, "Economic Change and the American Worker," in Twentieth Century Fund Task Force, *No One Left Behind*, chap. 5; Evelyn Ganzglass, ed., *Excellence at Work* (Kalamazoo, Mich.: W.E. Upjohn Institute, 1992); and Osterman and Batt, "Employer-Centered Training."

93. Osterman and Batt, "Employer-Centered Training."

94. See Commission on the Future of Worker-Relations, *Fact Finding Report*; Appelbaum and Batt, *New American Workplace*; Paul Osterman, "How Common

Is Workplace Transformation and Who Adopts It?" *Industrial and Labor Relations Review,* vol. 47 (January 1994), pp. 173–88; and David I. Levine, *Reinventing the Workplace: How Business and Employees Can Both Win* (Brookings, 1995).

95. See AFL-CIO Committee on the Evolution of Work, *A Labor Perspective on the New American Workplace: A Call for Partnership* (Washington: AFL-CIO, February 1994).

96. *Time*/CNN/Yankelovich Partners Poll, May 8–10, 1996. There were large gender and race differences in these responses: 42 percent of men said that individuals should bear primary responsibility for job security, compared with 30 percent of women; 36 percent of women believed employers should be responsible for job security; and blacks and Hispanics were markedly more likely to identify government as primarily responsible for job security.

97. This *New York Times* poll was taken December 3–6, 1995. See Elizabeth Kolbert and Adam Clymer, "The Politics of Layoffs: In Search of a Message," *New York Times,* March 8, 1996, p. A23.

98. See Bennett Harrison and Marcus Weiss, "Networking across Boundaries: CDCs and CBOs in Regionally Engaged Workforce Development Alliances" (Boston: Economic Development Assistance Consortium, July 7, 1996), pp. 100–12. W. Norton Grubb notes, however, that job training by community-based organizations may be more subject to political goals or interference that can greatly reduce their effectiveness. See W. Norton Grubb, *Learning to Work* (New York: Russell Sage Foundation, 1996), pp. 101–02.

99. Many of these replication efforts have encountered problems; see Harrison and Weiss, "Networking across Boundaries," pp. 93–100.

100. See Louis Uchitelle, "Some Cities Flexing Fiscal Muscle to Make Employers Raise Wages," *New York Times,* April 9, 1996, p. 1.

Chapter 8

The Troubled Success
of Crime Policy

Ann Chih Lin

CRIME was the stealth issue of the Clinton administration. In January 1993, as President Clinton was inaugurated, a Gallup survey found that only 9 percent of Americans felt crime to be one of the country's most important problems. That was much lower than the 35 percent who named the economy, the 22 percent who named unemployment, or the 18 percent who mentioned health care. But merely a year later, crime topped the list. Of those polled in January 1994, 37 percent considered crime the most important problem facing the country, a figure that rose to 49 percent after the president's "three strikes and you're out" State of the Union address.[1] And despite the passage of a massive crime bill in August 1994 and encouraging reports of reductions in crime in the next two years, public concern remained unabated. In 1996, both Clinton and his Republican opponent, Bob Dole, made crime a central element in their campaigns: Clinton touted his distribution of federal funding for police, while Dole attacked the administration's record on drugs.

The clear prominence of crime as a public concern and a national issue is matched by its substantive legacy. The legislative record is impressive: a $30.2 billion crime package signed into law in August 1996; an antiterrorism package including restrictions on death row appeals, a provision for which Republicans had been fighting since the Reagan administration; and a raft of smaller bills, most prominent a sexual-offender community notification bill, commonly known as Megan's law. These measures represent the ascendancy, in both parties, of the belief that the rights of individuals can be restricted, even substantially curtailed, to satisfy perceptions of the common good. They also firmly establish the federal government as a player in an arena which is, for most intents and purposes, a state and local concern.

On the surface, these bipartisan legislative successes would seem to challenge the trends this book describes in other policy areas: an unusually conflict-ridden policy process, the fragmentation of the political environment, and the increasing devolution, both formal and informal, of social policy initiatives to the states. A closer examination, however, shows that these forces were present even when they did not prevent legislative success. Polarized elites jockeying for power within the parties, unstable interest group coalitions with fluid relationships, and state-centered policy reform describe the politics of crime policy in this era. The result was a split between the rhetoric and the substance of crime policy.

On the rhetorical level, President Clinton was able to challenge the Republican party's symbolic ownership of crime policy. His successful redefinition of "tough crime policy" as gun control and police funding and his willingness to challenge traditional Democratic elites over their support for civil liberties established crime as a credible issue for Democrats. But while the partisan battle at the national level was joined over the definition of "tough on crime," actual crime policy at the local level was largely unaffected. Except in some areas, where local grass-roots movements rather than national rhetoric were the motivating force, localities did not become tougher; in many cases, localities had been pursuing tough policies for decades. Instead, localities struggled with the federal government over the right to maintain autonomous policies, to define for themselves what a tough policy would be. By accepting federal largesse, however, they opened the door to federal influence and intergovernmental competition in the future. Crime policy thus illustrates the possibilities and the limits of the national government as a force for social policy change at the end of the twentieth century: it is a government that affects but cannot determine the content of change.

From Polarized Parties to Polarized Elites

By the beginning of the 1990s, crime, a perennial American concern, was a growing American preoccupation. Gallup polls show that from 1989 to 1992, 84–89 percent of Americans believed that there was more crime, each year, than there had been a year earlier. From 1985 to 1993, the percentage of people who said that they themselves were a victim of crime in the last year jumped from 5 to 11 percent.[2] And all this occurred despite survey results from the National Criminal Victimization Survey, widely accepted as the most accurate national measure of crime rates, that showed crime rates to be level, though fluctuating.

The divergence suggests that the fear of crime is at least partially self-inflicted: a 1996 Pew Research Center study finds, for instance, that 84 percent of the population reports following news stories about crime "very closely" or "somewhat closely," far outpacing the 59 percent who report the same thing about "political figures and events in Washington," the 57 percent who follow entertainment, or the 54 percent who follow sports.[3] But it is also true that the effect of crime is not well measured by its annual rate of incidence. When a person hears one year that two neighbors' homes were robbed and in the next year that a different neighbor was mugged, she does not rejoice that the crime rate has decreased by 50 percent. Instead, her perception is that there is "more crime" (three incidents rather than two), and it is that perception that drives political mobilization.

This explanation helps to make sense of the fact that concern about crime has stayed high even as annual rates have stayed constant or gone down. It makes even more sense when the absolute amount of crime is considered; one is more likely to be the *victim* of a violent crime than to be injured in a motor vehicle accident, although one is only half as likely to be *injured* in a violent crime as one is to be injured in an auto accident. Moreover, while crimes among adults stayed constant in the 1980s, violent crime experienced by people aged 12 to 24 increased.[4] Juvenile violence has a particular hold on public beliefs; it outrages popular perceptions of childhood innocence and of children as the icons of the future. President Reagan's "war on drugs" exacerbated the image of children run amok: news coverage of drug dealers and drug trafficking focused on gangs of youths who defended their business with guns and murdered both associates and strangers in the pursuit of drug profits. And popular media sustain it: juvenile violence is increasingly visible as a staple of television, movies, and popular music.

In this environment, Democrats were increasingly tagged as not taking crime seriously enough. By 1988, 40 percent of those surveyed thought that Republicans were better able to handle crime, while only 24 percent thought that about the Democrats.[5] This perception was anchored in the historical commitments of both parties. From the 1960s to the 1990s, national Democrats and Republicans had largely predictable views on crime. In the turmoil of their party's re-creation in the 1960s, Democrats had taken stands on crime that paralleled their stands on other social issues. Thus crime was identified as a symptom of job-lessness, urban decay, poor education, and the lack of hope. Well aware that civil rights activists were routinely accused of criminal actions as a form of intimidation, Democrats were also quick to point out that diatribes against crime were often ill-concealed diatribes against African Americans. Extending the analogy to other groups—protesters, prisoners, the poor—Democrats developed strong commitments to the rights of the accused. These commitments were evident in policy positions, such as summer jobs for youth, the identification of bias crimes, or support for freedom of speech and freedom from unlawful search and seizure. They were also evident in campaign rhetoric: when George Bush's 1988 presidential campaign superimposed the picture of a black criminal atop a shadowy picture of a prison with streams of men exiting, Democrats were quick to attack Bush's campaign as race baiting and Bush as a racist.

As that incident suggests, Republicans had also developed a firm set of positions on crime. In his 1964 campaign, Barry Goldwater tied the theme of "law and order" to a backdrop of civil rights protests. The theme resonated with those who saw protests, civil rights demands, or both as a disruption of social order. By the 1970s, when antiwar protests were commonplace and the prospect of urban riots had become all too real, the crime issue became a constant in Republican presidential campaigns. This culminated in President Reagan's federal war on drugs: a package of legislation that included greatly increased sentencing for drug offenses, an expanded list of federal drug crimes, money for drug interdiction, and civil asset forfeiture provisions that financially rewarded police departments for the investigation and capture of drug dealers. This emphasis on law and order linked together several important themes: traditional notions of punishment for criminals and respect for duly constituted authority, and thus support for harsh sentencing and civilian law enforcement. Republicans also forged strong ties with police groups and attacked the courts for interference with police discretion and state administration.

But while Republicans clearly enjoyed an advantage in the perceptions of a crime-fearing public, their traditional commitments were also beginning to cause problems. Although neither the percentage of gun owners (roughly 50 percent) nor the margin of public support for stricter gun laws (about two-thirds) changed in this period, both gun owners and gun control advocates became more vocal.[6] The 1986 McClure-

Volkmer Act, which repealed past laws to allow for the legal interstate sale of guns and make it easier for gun merchants to operate, underlined the reputation of the National Rifle Association (NRA) as an unbeatable lobby. But handgun control advocates were also mobilized by McClure-Volkmer; and police groups, who formerly had been firm supporters of both the NRA and the Republican party, began to break ranks in order to speak out for more gun control, arguing that their lives were threatened by the spread of guns and gun use in crime. The ensuing debate put guns and crime in the national spotlight; and it suggested the opportunity for partisan repositioning on crime.

Both parties seized the opportunity, moving away from some traditional stands and redefining others. But as the party leadership moved in one direction, influential elites in both parties saw their cherished policy positions threatened. Groups who felt threatened by their changing position in the post–New Deal era, such as blacks in the Democratic party, tried to make changes in legislation so as to combat their marginalization; groups who saw their influence rising, such as anti-government conservatives, hoped to consolidate their gains. This resulted in a crime debate as bitter within the parties as between them. The legislative story of crime is thus not just a chronicle of painful coalition assembly in a fragmented system; it is also a snapshot of parties trying to re-form.

Consensus without Agreement, 1992–94

Shifts in public opinion and the public debate on crime in the 1980s were accompanied by general shifts in the political makeup of the country. The development of a swing "Reagan Democrat" vote led politicians of both parties to create middle-class appeals. Redistricting accomplished under the Voting Rights Act of 1965 concentrated both African American voting strength and white voters, especially in the South. The decline in the growth rate of family income, frequent recessions, and the visibility of plant closings and downsizing all helped to create anxiety and frustration. The popularization of the growth of an "underclass" in American cities gave politicians a symbol of racial fear and social disorder.

Public anxiety about crime could be linked to all of these factors. Concern about law and order and support for the police were issues that resonated with the middle class. As a symptom of social disorder, crime was a proxy for generalized anxiety about a society where "things fall apart." And racial overtones were clearly present within the crime debate; in one Gallup survey, while a third of whites believed that racial prejudice motivated law-and-order politicians, over half of blacks did.[7]

President Clinton's crime strategy was designed, in large part, to capitalize on these conditions. As the introduction to this volume describes, Clinton hoped to move away from the Democratic party's identification with the poor and minority groups and toward a middle-class appeal that would also include traditional constituencies like African Americans. He needed, therefore, to create a message that would speak to public anxiety about crime and middle-class anxiety about social disorder without intensifying racial cleavages. His crime strategy attempted to do so in four ways. First, by advocating funding for the police, Clinton hoped to deemphasize Democratic identification with social spending and social programs. Second, by supporting the death penalty and tougher federal sentences, he hoped to send a message that "responsibility," rather than "rights," would typify his administration's approach to government programs. Third, by emphasizing community policing and deemphasizing indictments of racial bias, he hoped to move away from the identification of Democrats with racial and ethnic minorities and toward a vision of an inclusive, color-blind society. And finally, by emphasizing federal-state partnerships in crime fighting, he hoped to move away from the identification of Democrats with the federal government and toward his own experience as a governor who knew both the possibilities and limits of federal involvement.

But while the candidate Clinton realized that crime could have these advantages for him, President Clinton had other preoccupations, especially at first. One of President Clinton's most-repeated lines, on the campaign trail and in the White House, was his promise to "put 100,000 new police officers on your streets." But that line was preceded not by a statement about crime control but by one about cutting the size of government: "[Bush] won't streamline the federal government and change the way it works; cut 100,000 bureaucrats and put 100,000 new police officers on your streets of American cities, but I will."[8] Health care and welfare reform, too, had occupied much more prominent places in the campaign; and above all else, the statement "it's the economy, stupid," was candidate Clinton's rallying call.

As a result, for many in the new White House, economic policy, such as the stimulus package or deficit reduction, came before social policy, such as crime. Those interested in crime policy remember going "hat in hand" to find money in the economic stimulus package for the first police grants and having to make their case to advisors who, they said derisively, wanted the president to be the "chief accountant." Even after Senate legislation was introduced in August 1993, the administration took only a limited role in rallying support for it. Democratic staffers in Congress remember that, apart from a few advocates, "the administration was criticized here when the legislation was going through the Senate, because it just wasn't visible—there was a lot of angst, a lot of anger, about that."[9]

By the fall of 1993, however, those who believed that values issues like crime should take priority were helped by a series of events: high-profile mayoral elections in New York and Los Angeles and a governor's race in New Jersey, all of which focused on crime; the murder of Polly Klass, a young girl in California, by a released felon; a "three-strikes" referendum in Washington State, providing for lifetime imprisonment upon conviction for a third felony, which passed overwhelmingly; and the gunning down of a carful of commuters on the Long Island Rail Road. The reaction to these events demonstrated that not only was crime a popular concern, but voters were willing to base their votes on it. The Senate's crime bill was placed on a fast track. Since it was similar to legislation that had been passed in 1992 but vetoed by President Bush, the bill started with a base of support; to enhance it, the sponsors combined Republican provisions for prison funding with Community Oriented Policing Services (COPS), the White House provision for police funding for localities. Problematic and partisan issues, like habeas corpus reform to limit death penalty appeals, were deliberately put aside. Provisions that had bipartisan histories, such as new death penalty offenses and the Violence Against Women Act, were included. The final bill passed the Senate on November 19, 1993, by 95 to 4.[10]

The White House read this triumph as confirmation that its middle-class, middle-of-the-road policies had struck a chord with the American people. Crime, said Bruce Reed, the deputy assistant to the president for domestic policy,

is the classic example of an issue where there's an enormous center in the country. . . . There's this great center without a party, and without much interest in party, and on this particular issue, most Americans were for trying anything. They weren't just for trying tough punishment, though they were for that. They were also for more police, they were also for the kind of crime prevention that was in the bill, and in the surveys that we saw, our approach was overwhelmingly popular. And of course, the assault weapons ban was overwhelmingly popular. . . . It is really hard to imagine who would be against the kinds of measures that were in our bill.[11]

That last phrase—"It is hard to imagine who would be against the kinds of measures that were in our bill"—neatly encapsulates the advertising strategy distinctive to Clinton's politics. As the chapter by Lawrence Jacobs and Robert Shapiro in this volume describes, Clinton's policymaking was dominated by the belief that proposals that were "overwhelmingly popular" could, in and of themselves, create a coalition for reform. But jumping on, or even creating, a groundswell of support is not the same as creating a legislative coalition. Faith in the permanence of their public support led the administration first to dismiss and then later to underestimate the opposition to their bill in Congress.

The first mistake the administration made was to interpret the overwhelming Senate vote as evidence of the bill's popularity. In fact, the Senate vote was clearly easier because the House had yet to act. While several smaller bills on crime had been introduced in the House, none had been voted on in November 1993. Thus senators were free to vote for the politically popular crime bill without worrying that its controversial provisions, such as the assault weapons ban or the new death penalties, might thereby become law. By the time a bill got through the House, they expected that such provisions would be deleted. Their confidence was well placed. Members like Jack Brooks, Democrat of Texas, a staunch supporter of the National Rifle Association, opponent of gun control, and chair of the House Judiciary Committee, refused to include the assault weapons ban in the House bill. Among his supporters were many senior Democrats, including the Speaker of the House, Tom Foley, and committee chairmen like John Dingell, Democrat of Michigan. At the same time, the Congressional Black Caucus (CBC) insisted that any new death penalties be accompanied by the Racial Justice Act. This provision would allow statistical evidence on the racially discriminatory use of the death penalty to be considered in the sentencing of individuals convicted of death penalty crimes; it was widely opposed in the Senate.

In these two issues, Clinton confronted two groups of Democrats—the veteran congressional leadership and the party's liberal wing—who, though allies, were competing with him for the ability to shape the party's agenda on social policy. As the first major piece of social legislation to come close to enactment, crime policy became the symbol of the conflict. Clinton had publicly committed to an assault weapons ban and had gained political capital by signing the Brady bill, which established a waiting period for handgun purchases, the year before. But support for the NRA was a long-standing commitment for leaders like Foley, Brooks, and Dingell. Clinton needed them, not only to pass the crime bill, but for the rest of his legislative agenda: Foley and Dingell, for instance, were two of the most important players on pending health care legislation.

If he flouted the old Democratic leadership by supporting the assault weapons ban, Clinton was flouting a newly powerful ally by looking to drop the Racial Justice Act. The Congressional Black Caucus was a coalition with influential senior members, such as John Conyers, Democrat of Michigan, and Kweisi Mfume, Democrat of Maryland, and the 1992 elections had given it its largest voting bloc in history. Its strong support for Clinton's stimulus package in the House was the most important of the many favors it had done for Clinton. As Linda Williams points out in her chapter, the Racial Justice Act was a passionate issue for the CBC: blacks are disproportionately sent to death row, and one study of death penalty cases since 1976 found that federal courts found reversible constitutional error in 40 percent of the cases, even after multiple layers of state court review.[12] In addition, the CBC could rightfully see the act as a symbol of Clinton's support for them, especially because Clinton's willingness to identify the Democratic party with predominantly white middle-class voters and to deemphasize issues of discrimination was a source of worry for many African Americans.

These battles plagued the House legislation all through the early months of 1994. Clinton had hailed the Senate bill in his 1994 State of the Union address; thus the pressure was on the House to settle its differences and produce a bill to send to conference.

The House version of the crime bill finally passed on April 21, 1994. As a concession to the CBC and the Democratic leadership, it included the Racial Justice Act and excluded the assault weapons ban. But Clinton's supporters won an important concession from each: the right to bring the controversial provisions up in separate votes before the bill went to conference with the Senate version. And in a victory that stunned all concerned—the White House, Democrats, Republicans, and both the NRA and its chief opponent, Handgun Control Inc.—the assault weapons ban passed the House as a separate provision on May 5, only a week after the House omnibus crime bill had passed. Then, on June 16, the House voted against its own racial justice language. The assault weapons ban victory meant that it could not be left out of a conference bill; the Racial Justice Act's defeat meant that it would. Congressional and administration staff still debate about which event was more to blame, but the result brooks no disagreement: the crime bill did not go to conference with the Senate until well into the summer.

Given that amount of time, the NRA, in conjunction with Republican allies, was able to mobilize a counterattack. Wisely gambling that it would not be able to keep the assault weapons ban out of the conference bill, the NRA decided to attack the entire bill. Using publicity campaigns targeted in two directions—the congressional districts of the Democrats who voted for the ban and conservative talk radio shows, which were fast becoming the common network of the Republican grass roots—the NRA released "anecdotal bite-sized information" like a hail of bullets, "designed to get people mad."[13] They derided the community policing grants as a fraud, claiming that no more than 20,000 police would be funded.[14] They also attacked prevention programs, many of which had been added to reward supporters from both parties, as pork barrel politics.[15]

The NRA campaign, party-line opposition from the Republicans, and defections from the CBC and Democratic NRA supporters all helped to produce an August defeat on the rule for consideration of the conference report. The bill seemed dead—and coming on top of the realization that health care reform would go nowhere before the midterm election, the White House was faced with the possibility of losing every major social policy initiative of its first two years. It responded with a whirlwind of public lobbying and private compromise. Rejecting a private proposal by the Democratic leadership in Congress to remove the assault weapons ban, the administration instead went back to a strategy of individual benefits, this time courting Republicans with spending cuts. Moderate Republican supporters of gun control responded; in the end, thirty-eight Republicans and some Democratic returnees allowed the administration to pass its bill.

President Clinton's crime bill succeeded in changing the center of gravity in the crime debate. Republicans acknowledged his success: "You used to be able to say, easy on crime, tough on crime, but the President does get credit for changing that. Republicans can't make this a black and white issue anymore," said Paul McNulty, a key Republican congressional staffer.[16] Yet the victory was mixed at best. A bill that intended to transfer an extraordinary $8.8 billion to local police departments was attacked as inadequate. A bill that was intended to demonstrate partisan unity, and perhaps even bipartisan cooperation, had instead revealed deep intraparty divisions on gun control and race in sentencing. A bill that was intended to show that Democrats were ready to challenge Republicans for the "law-and-order" mantle had succeeded, but only after attempts to paint it as a bill full of failed Great Society programs had succeeded as well.

Most bitterly of all, the failure of both welfare and health care legislation to move through Congress had left the administration and congressional Democrats little to point to but the victory on crime. With no other legislation to attack, Republicans were able to focus on the inadequacies of the crime bill as a symbol of the inadequacies of Democrats. Thus they not only attacked the crime bill as pork barrel politics in disguise but argued that deceptions like the crime bill were common in the Clinton administration. The bill was fodder for an attack on Clinton's honesty and competence, as Republicans asked whether people weren't "tired of broken promises, tired of being misled, tired of 'spin' from a White House that seems to govern on the principle that you can fool all of the people some of the time"?[17] They also combined those attacks on the president's character with a more general appeal to those who simply distrusted the federal government. Different groups of voters—those who disliked Clinton personally, those who were angry about social programs for the poor and wanted lower taxes for themselves, those who feared centralized government on principle, those who felt that the federal lawmakers had become too entrenched—found that the theme of distrust both expressed what they felt and gave them a target for their anxiety. Thus, to counter Clinton's attempt to build a winning coalition with public opinion, Republicans were able to capitalize on all the reasons why, in the post–New Deal era, people were suspicious about government. The crime bill became a symbol of the larger Republican attack upon social welfare provision.

The strategy was, of course, successful. In the Republican sweep of Congress that followed, 69 percent of gun owners, nearly two-thirds of regular talk radio listeners, and almost 60 percent of small business owners and employees voted Republican; gun owners alone provided one-third of all the votes Republican candidates received.[18] These numbers convinced the Republican leadership that crime could still play an important mobilizing role for them. Provisions on crime were included in the Contract with America, and they were among the first set of promises to be considered when the new majority opened its legislative session in 1995. But crime proved to be as problematic for the Republicans as it was for the Democrats. For one, while parts of his legislation could be repealed, Clinton's legislation seemed to capture most of the crime-fighting ideas on the agenda. For another, the Republican sweep brought in a group of freshmen members whose antigovernment zeal sometimes extended to their own party's leadership. Fueled by principles and righteousness, these members would show scant patience for compromise.

Family Feuding, 1994–96

When the new Republican Congress opened for business in January, the "Taking Back Our Streets Act" was H. R. 3. It included two Republican standbys: habeas corpus reform, which limited death sentence appeals, and "good faith" exemptions to the exclusionary rule, which allowed evidence obtained in violation of a warrant to be admitted into court under certain conditions. Three other issues—victim restitution, criminal alien incarceration funding, and prison construction money— were selected for their popularity and received bipartisan support.[19]

But the most important provision in the contract's crime proposal was a direct slap at Clinton's bill. Instead of direct grants to police departments for new officers, Republicans offered a block grant provision that rolled drug courts, the individual prevention programs, and Clinton's showcase COPS, or community policing grants, into one block grant for localities. It then cut the funding for these programs by almost $4 billion. This was almost the entire amount that prevention programs, excluding provisions of the Violence against Women Act, had received in the 1994 legislation. It passed the House on a party-line vote.

Politically, the drafting of this provision was extremely clever. The legislation drove a wedge between police departments, which would now have to compete for their funding; prevention programs, which the police had previously supported; and mayors, both Democratic and Republican, who would have much more money to control. Clinton's most supportive constituencies could thus be pitted against each other. Even better, the legislation could be sold as an attack on pork barrel programs and as a victory for local control, both themes of the Republican revolution. Win or lose, therefore, the provision threatened Clinton's base and reinforced Republican themes.

Had the Senate been able to move on the crime bill in early 1995, Clinton would have been faced with the prospect of vetoing crime legislation even tougher and more flexible than his own. But the Republican leadership in the Senate was preoccupied, first with the balanced budget amendment and later with welfare. Unfortunately for them, this decision to wait doomed the crime bill. The April 1995 bombing of the Alfred Murrah Federal Building in Oklahoma City diverted attention from the crime bill. In the end its provisions were folded into the appropriations bill for the Justice Department and died in the budget showdown at the end of 1995. All the momentum for new legislation against street crime disappeared.

Crime itself, however, did not disappear as an issue. Its new venue was antiterrorism legislation. The arrest of two right-wing antigovernment militants for the Oklahoma City bombing brought the threat of domestic terrorism to public attention. The threat was reinforced by the start of a trial of a group of Muslim extremists for conspiring to bomb several New York City landmarks. Politicians vied to show that they could put aside partisan quarrels and respond to a national tragedy. Within a month a bipartisan bill had been introduced. To make its passage possible, President Clinton again disappointed traditional Democrats by supporting habeas corpus reform to limit death row appeals. In return, the bill enhanced federal wiretapping authority, allowed the military to assist civilian law enforcement with some terrorism cases, and required the tagging of several types of explosives—all provisions that Clinton had asked for. Two of the most bipartisan contract provisions, victim restitution and the streamlined deportation of criminal aliens, were also included. The result was a classic piece of bipartisan compromise, and the Senate, with support from President Clinton, passed its legislation in July 1995.

But the simple bipartisan calculation came out differently in the House. The antigovernment Republicans, who had been the centerpiece of the Republican sweep, revolted. A small but vocal group, led by Republicans Bob Barr of Georgia, John Boehner of Ohio, the GOP conference chair, and Thomas Ewing of Illinois, chair of the Conservative Opportunity Society, complained that the bill sacrificed limits on federal power for quick political gain. "Now is not the time to be encouraging big government and intrusion into private lives under the guise of preventing terrorism," Ewing wrote.[20] Although the bill passed the Judiciary Committee in June 1995, floor leaders were forced to yank it from the December schedule; vote counts showed it would be defeated. As the memories of Oklahoma City began to recede, so did the possibility for passage.

The factionalism that had plagued Democratic attempts to pass a crime bill had come back to haunt Republicans. On the one side were puzzled party leaders: expanding the powers of law enforcement, after all, had been a Republican policy from the 1960s days of denouncing rioters. Even a conservative guru like Ronald Reagan had expanded the powers of law enforcement greatly through his war on drugs. None of these leaders thought these expansions of government authority violated their antigovernment philosophy; for these leaders, distrust of government was a synonym for an establishment preference for lower taxes and fewer federal social programs. But as the Republican base began to grow, the theme of distrust attracted conservatives of other stripes. These new party members believed that the federal government's restrictions on school prayer stifled their freedoms, that federal gun laws restricted their liberties, that environmental regulations limited their ownership rights, and that affirmative action curtailed their opportunities. For these conservatives, the enemy without was less frightening than the enemy within. Representative Tom Coburn, Republican of Oklahoma, gave perhaps the best description when he asked his fellow members not to let the fear of terrorists deter them from voting against the antiterrorism bill. "There is a greater fear in this country, and that is fear of our own government."[21]

But the Republican approach to dealing with its factions was the opposite of the president's. Clinton had made a calculation that he could disappoint traditional liberals, the CBC, and NRA Democrats; the resulting fracas gave him a bill but a much diminished victory. The Republican leadership, by contrast, first attempted to placate and then gave in to its right flank, betting that the mobilized base these members represented was too important to disdain. Congress sponsored hearings on two key incidents of alleged federal law enforcement abuse: the Waco raid and two shootings at the Weaver cabin in Ruby Ridge, Idaho, in August 1992. The terrorism bill passed during the week of the one-year anniversary of the Oklahoma City bombing, but without the provisions to expand wiretapping, place taggants in explosives, or allow the military to aid civilian law enforcement. The title of the bill that Clinton finally signed reflected its changed purpose: the Comprehensive Anti-Terrorism Act of 1995 was changed to the Effective Death Penalty and Public Safety Act of 1996.[22] Even when a jetliner mysteriously exploded the week before the Olympics began in Atlanta and momentum for stricter terrorism laws returned, conservatives were successful in keeping such provisions out.

These conservative victories, however, lacked the public resonance that successful crime legislation might have had. The major revelation of the Waco hearings was that the leader of the Branch Davidians, David Koresh, had had sexual relations with the young daughter of one of his followers. The Ruby Ridge hearings, in which the director of the FBI admitted culpability, were overshadowed by the congressional drama over medicare reform and budget reconciliation. Thus conservatives fearful of the federal government had their fears replayed through the hearings, but they garnered few converts and little approbation. Nor did fighting the extension of federal antiterrorism powers bring conservatives the gratitude of ordinary citizens. Although 70 percent voiced concern that civil liberties would be restricted by antiterrorism laws, 64 percent favored expanding FBI powers to trace suspects and 74 percent favored expanding the FBI's ability to infiltrate suspect groups.[23] Coburn's "fear of our government" was clearly not widely shared.

Thus, for the antigovernment conservatives in the Republican party, even victories on crime policy only mocked their inability to take long-run control of the party's agenda. By July 1996, the Republican nominee for president, Bob Dole, had moved himself away from their crime policies. In a tacit concession to the 71 percent of Americans who said they approved of the assault weapons ban, Dole shrugged off an earlier promise to the NRA to work for the ban's repeal.[24]

Merely a year and a half after the Republicans' historic victory, therefore, centrist politics had stopped the Republican revolution. But as the introduction to this volume suggests, characterizing the politics of this period as a search for the country's center is too simplistic a story. Certainly the leaders of various party factions hoped that their policies would be popular with a majority of the public. But they were primarily interested in capitalizing on their party's temporary ascendancy to assert their importance within the party and gain control over the party's agenda. In other words, liberal Democrats and antigovernment conservatives did not simply misread the public's mood. Instead, each of these factions claimed that the party had won its victories—in 1992 for the Democrats, in 1994 for the Republicans—because of their efforts, and thus they deserved a share of the policy spoils in return. Their insistence on deference was particularly urgent because crime legislation seemed a natural vehicle for various party factions to introduce policy themes—antidiscrimination, lessened federal involvement—that could apply to other social problems as well.

In this way, the antigovernment conservatives' loss was reminiscent of the Congressional Black Caucus's. Each faction saw, in either the unified Democratic government of 1992 or the Republican sweep of 1994, a chance for one-party dominance in which its philosophy could play a defining role. But they misread the elections: the party's victories in each case heralded not party dominance but instead the weakness of parties that could not maintain stable electoral coalitions. Thus factions within the party were not rewarded for their role in creating the party's victory; instead, they were abandoned as party leaders kept searching for the right electoral formula, the right key to public support.

The pattern suggests that even another decisive win, by either party, would only restart the process. At the end of 1997, neither party has a common philosophy to bind it together; instead, each has a variety of factions determined to use victory as a chance to impose its own version of its mandate. As long as neither party is strong enough to ensure both consistent policy and consistent follow-through, party factions cannot hope to gain their ends by cooperating with others and waiting for their turn. Instead, they will find it more useful to try to dominate the other party factions in the hopes that their ideas can then get the priority they deserve.

Old Groups and New Strategies

Party factions are not the only groups that must be brought into a coalition for parties to achieve legislative success. Party coalitions also need mass-based interest groups. But quarreling between party factions makes stable alliances between interest groups and parties more difficult. In a system where parties are strong enough to promise rewards, interest groups can establish stable relationships with one party, as labor did with the Democrats in the mid-twentieth century, and have a say on issues ranging across the policy agenda. Conversely, interest groups can also count on ties to members in both parties, as the NRA did through the 1980s, to protect its interests in a particular domain. In return, the party can count on the group's loyalty, mobilization effort, and resources, all of which strengthen the party further. When parties are rife with factions, however, mass-based organizations cannot count on stable rewards from party alliances. Thus they have an incentive to wander just as parties need them the most to serve as a dependable, mobilized source of support.

This dynamic has several implications for politics. For interest groups, it means that loyalty to a party is not particularly wise; in the search for new alliances, a party can easily ignore allies with no other place to go. For parties, it means that low-cost ways of maintaining grass-roots support, such as depending on interest groups to mobilize supporters, need to be replaced by the active retention of existing support and the acquisition of new allies. Under this arrangement, groups willing to threaten defection are the ones who can influence policy. By contrast, groups who identify too closely with one party, so that they cannot realistically leave, lose influence.

The National Rifle Association

The NRA's lobbying efforts on Capitol Hill are legendary. Until 1993, it was able to beat back every gun control effort ever mounted in Congress.[25] When it lost on the Brady bill and the assault weapons ban in 1993 and 1994, it responded with such fierce mobilization that Clinton blamed it for the Democrats' 1994 defeat.[26] Yet Bob Dole, running twenty points behind in the presidential race in the summer of 1996, had the courage to go back on a promise to the NRA to repeal the assault weapons ban, even hinting that he would not mind losing the NRA's endorsement. By contrast, Dole's opponent for the presidency, Bill Clinton, picked up the endorsement of three police unions in the fall, including one from the Fraternal Order of Police, which had never endorsed a Democratic president. And to add insult to injury, the speech announcing the endorsement was made on the same day that Dole announced his own major anticrime initiative.

For watchers of crime policy, the juxtaposition was ironic in the extreme. The NRA, with a highly mobilized membership of 3.5 million, once counted the major police organizations among its closest allies.[27]

Many police officers are avid shooters, who own and enjoy guns off the job as well as on. The NRA's instructors provide advanced training to police instructors, and they certify instructors who then go on to train police and to testify to ballistics evidence in court. Up until the mid-1980s, police and the NRA presented a unified front on legislation as well, testifying in favor of the right to bear arms.

But in 1985, major police groups and the NRA split over the Firearm Owner's Protection Act of 1986, more popularly known as McClure-Volkmer. McClure-Volkmer lifted many restrictions on handgun sales and also permitted the sale of "cop-killer" bullets that could penetrate body armor. The issue, an intensely emotional one for police, created a rift between the police and the NRA that later deepened over issues like national waiting periods and semiautomatic weapons bans. Their split gave gun control a high profile on the legislative agenda and encouraged both groups to step up their lobbying activity and burnish their images as crime experts.

At the first, the NRA was the acknowledged master. The NRA not only funds campaigns—distributing almost $230,000 in 1995 to House freshmen alone—but actively recruits and trains candidates who support its positions.[28] In the 1994 campaign, the organization put together a multimedia package for the candidates it supported, giving suggestions for launching an effective anticrime campaign and tips for responding to attacks. The videotape in the package closes with a shot of Tanya Metaska, the executive director of the NRA's Institute for Legislative Action and the organization's second-in-command. Standing in front of the Capitol building, she tells the prospective candidate, "The choice is yours. The NRA, along with our anti-crime coalition, will stand shoulder-to-shoulder with candidates who have the courage to tackle the hard issues of criminal justice. But we'll go head to head with any politician who thinks that attacking gun owners is a good alternative to fighting crime. Support reforms to rebuild our failed criminal justice system, and the politics of crime will work for you, as a candidate, and as an elected leader of your community."[29]

The emphasis on crime fighting as an alternative to gun control was no accident. Active lobbying for anticrime policies is clearly one way for the NRA to rebut the criticism that it is interested in protecting gun rights regardless of the cost in rising crime. Explains Elizabeth Swasey, senior policy counsel for the NRA's Crimestrike division, "Gun-carrying, law-abiding citizens like us here are blamed for crime when it's the failure of our criminal justice system that's at fault . . . . Americans support gun control as a solution for crime only because they're not offered anything else; . . . once they're given a list of possible solutions, they want other ones. It's our job to tell Americans what other solutions to crime are out there."[30]

Formed in 1993, Crimestrike is specifically devoted to promoting crime policies such as truth-in-sentencing, an expansion of prison capacity, the death penalty, victims' rights, and, unsurprisingly, the expansion of rights to use and carry weapons for self-defense. The 1994 crime bill saw it move into high gear. In addition to coordinating the media and talk radio campaign described above, the division organized a conference of conservative researchers and practitioners to attack the provisions in the crime bill and commissioned polling by Frank Luntz, a well-known Republican pollster. Each of these projects gave the NRA more backing for its claim that it was not merely an advocacy group fighting for gun rights but a "full-service organization working for laws fighting crime."[31] Crimestrike, in short, allows the NRA to claim the status of an expert group.

The combination of lobbying savvy, "expert" credentials, and a mobilized membership should have made the NRA an even more effective force in Washington. But just as all these elements came together in the 1994 elections, the NRA chose to use its clout in a way that, though effective in the short term, was self-defeating in the long run. The NRA's clout on Capitol Hill has always been enhanced by the fact that powerful Democrats, as well as Republicans, counted themselves among its beneficiaries and friends. But in the 1994 elections, the NRA primarily targeted Democrats who voted for the crime bill. The Republicans who made final passage of the bill possible all survived.

This suggests that the NRA made the perfectly reasonable calculation that working toward a Republican majority, and thus a leadership sympathetic to its aims, would be a better bet than simply targeting all of those who voted against its interests. But its efforts to defeat even powerful Democrats like Jack Brooks and Tom Foley, who defected on the 1994 crime bill, left Congress with Democrats who never had any fondness for the NRA. They were quick to attack the NRA when, after the Oklahoma City bombing, a fundraising letter excoriating federal law enforcement agents as "jackbooted thugs" was made public. When one NRA staff member was found to have posed as a congressional staffer in order to get information from a witness at the 1994 hearings on the Waco siege, and another was found to be sitting at the Republican staff table during the hearings, Democrats were again quick to charge the organization with improper influence.

In response, the Republican leadership of the House, who had originally scheduled a vote to repeal the assault weapons ban for the day before the NRA's 1995 national convention, backed away from the organization. When the repeal of the assault weapons ban finally did come up in the House in March 1996, Representative Peter Torkildsen, Republican of Massachusetts, spoke for many Republicans when he worried that it would "make the Republican Party look like it's appealing to a narrow interest."[32] The NRA did not lose influence in Congress; its lobbying was certainly influential in restricting the scope of antiterrorism legislation, and it mobilized its membership for the 1996 congressional races. But the legislative record of the 104th Congress was surprisingly meager, especially for a leadership clearly indebted to the NRA for its help just two years before.

The example is less one of duplicity than one of predictable electoral calculation. The NRA's open support for Republican candidates in the 1994 election would have made sense, given parties that were strong enough to reward its friends. But the precarious foothold of the Republican majority meant that when votes could be gained by abandoning the NRA, politicians like Dole calculated that the NRA had nowhere else to go. Nor is it only the political influence of the NRA that suffers when it becomes associated with one party in particular; the ability of the organization to promote itself as an expert on crime issues is diminished as well. This does not mean that the NRA's influence is permanently on the decline; its membership and its money guarantee it a place in future crime debates. But it does suggest that a more entrepreneurial stance toward politics, where its influence and support are issue-based and thus less easy for the parties to count on, will better protect its long-run interests.

Police Organizations

The balance the NRA is looking for is one that police groups have also struggled to achieve. Since McClure-Volkmer, in which the NRA's lobbying tactics ambushed the less-organized police groups, the International Association of Chiefs of Police (IACP) and the major unions, research foundations, and chiefs' groups that coordinate as the Law Enforcement Steering Committee (LESC) have worked to become more politically savvy.[33] In 1987, they made an unprecedented endorsement of Robert Bork as nominee to the Supreme Court, launching a nationwide lobbying campaign in his favor at the same time.[34] Bush won the support of major police unions when running against Michael Dukakis, even though his opposition to the Brady bill earned their criticism.[35] Attracted by Clinton's promises to support community policing and gun control, the National Association of Police Organizations (NAPO) and the International Brotherhood of Police Officers (IBPO) endorsed him in the 1992 election, while the Fraternal Order of Police (FOP) supported Bush.[36]

The willingness of police groups to work with candidates of both parties made it possible for Clinton to bid for their support. He did so, holding substantive meetings with the IACP and LESC and supporting the assault weapons ban, even against the counsel of prominent members of Congress and his own aides. On their advice, he expanded his "Police Corps" proposal, first developed as a part of his national service initiative, to allow for the general hiring of street officers. In return, while not everything in the crime bill won the approval of police chiefs or police unions, all the major police groups came out in uniform to support the administration's bill at every major event. Both Clinton's aides and representatives of the LESC agree that the police organizations' strong support for community policing grants in the COPS program caused Clinton to challenge the 104th Congress, openly making one of his first veto threats on behalf of the program.

The affiliation between police groups and the Clinton presidency raises the possibility that police groups will suffer the same fate as the NRA, becoming dispensable because they have nowhere else to go. Indeed, in the first year of the 104th Congress, mainstream police groups complained privately that their support for Clinton had cost them access to the Republican leadership. Both unions and chiefs' groups are vulnerable to the charge that they are "Washington organizations," out of touch with the cop on the beat; to emphasize this distance, Dole invited a paralyzed police officer, Steven McDonald, to speak at the Republican convention.[37] To counter a partisan affiliation, police groups need, over time, to show the willingness to move away from Democrats, just as they moved away from Republicans in 1992. Just as important, they need to develop an independent public image, appearing in public and releasing statements and reports that stem from their own issue commitments, not one party's electoral or legislative needs.

But police groups do have an advantage that the NRA does not have. For while police officers' votes are certainly important, the symbolic value of a police endorsement or of police testimony is even more crucial. Through phone banks, faxes, and mailings, the NRA can generate political pressure on legislators. Police organizations can do this on occasion as well, but they can also stand in uniform with a candidate and show, by their presence, that "you're being endorsed by somebody tough on law and order, but also by someone with blue-collar middle-class values."[38] Police are also trusted to be experts on crime, a role for which they vigorously claim their fitness. As Daniel Rosenblatt, executive director of the IACP, puts it, "Discussions about legislation are public safety work; it's not politics. We deal with the substance; we never deal with the personalities. Chiefs in this country now see themselves as experts— it's their responsibility . . . to help make good policy."[39] Because the sources of police influence do not come solely, or even primarily, from the electoral base it provides, the label of partisanship is easier to shake. With a few exceptions, candidates cannot take "anti–law enforcement" positions; attacking police for being partisan cannot turn into an attack on police itself.

African Americans

Another way of thinking about this dynamic is to look at the difficulties African American leaders have encountered in their attempts to influence crime legislation. African Americans are overwhelmingly Democratic, and the leadership of African American political organizations is almost completely so. On crime, this alliance is magnified because of the Republican party's explicit use, in the late 1960s, of "law-and-order" policies as a veiled attack upon civil rights protest and unrest. The fact that African Americans are arrested, convicted, imprisoned, and given the death penalty in disproportionately high numbers also means that calls for tougher sentencing as an anticrime policy threaten the African American community in ways that white communities have little sense of. Although blacks are just as likely to be concerned about crime as whites are,[40] both their history and the history of the Republican party mean that Republicans and African Americans write each other off as possible allies.

But the fact that African Americans are solidly ensconced in the Democratic party means that the party does not have any urgency about supporting their interests. On the day when Clinton had announced the crime bill, back in the summer of 1993, Representative Conyers had promised that "without the Congressional Black Caucus signing off on this legislation, it is not going anywhere. Period."[41] A year later, the conference bill the CBC faced lacked the Racial Justice Act, the CBC's top priority. A similar approach characterized Clinton's actions on habeas corpus reform, which members of the CBC had vigorously opposed on the House floor. Habeus corpus reform was meant to limit the amount of time in which a prison inmate could appeal his death row conviction in the federal courts. Supporters argued that death sentences were meaningless because they were postponed for years through the appeals process; opponents argued that given the difficulty of finding lawyers to take cases for indigent inmates, reform would make an already biased system even worse. But Clinton had signaled his willingness to deal with habeas reform in 1993, as the Senate bill was being drafted. And by the time it was moved into the antiterrorism bill, taking a stand against terrorists seemed more important to him than the opposition of the CBC.

The split in the CBC over support for the 1994 crime bill reflects the problematic position in which it found itself. The Clinton administration primarily worked on the CBC by appealing to black mayors to make the case that the cities needed the money in the bill for protection and prevention. In July 1994, for instance, African American mayors were asked to, and did, sign a letter to the CBC, asking that its members not allow their anger at the exclusion of the Racial Justice Act to interfere with their support for the bill. "We cannot afford," the mayors wrote, "to lose the opportunities this bill provides to the people of our cities."[42] After the Republican takeover of Congress, Clinton managed to preserve COPS funding by drawing on money already appropriated to the Justice Department. But COPS was a police priority first, an African American priority second. By contrast, the prevention programs for which the mayors also urged support were, like so many other programs, victims of the ongoing appropriations and budget battles in Congress.

Crime, of course, is not the only or even the major issue on the African American agenda, and on some of the other issues important to African Americans, such as affirmative action, Clinton has been much more supportive. But the failure of the CBC to have more influence on the crime debate speaks to the failure of their primarily partisan strategy. In an era when the stable New Deal coalition has broken down, African Americans can no longer expect that their loyalty to the Democratic party will ensure attention to their interests. Instead, African American groups might heed the lesson of the NRA and revive their mobilization efforts of the 1960s, so that they can pressure politicians with appeals to their reelection as well as their sense of justice. This kind of political power would also give African American groups a credible threat to bargain with both parties for support, especially if their agenda allowed for active coalition building with other groups supportive of the same goals.

The Need for Partisan Independence

An example of how this might happen, even on a small scale, can be seen in a sidenote to the major provisions of the 1994 legislation. After years of discussion and a long battle to win the backing of both Senator Orrin Hatch, Republican of Utah, and Senator Joseph Biden, Democrat of Delaware, a coalition of national and grass-roots women's groups won passage of the Violence against Women Act in 1993. It was attached to the crime bill and became law in 1994. The act allowed women to sue their attackers, under some conditions, for violating their civil rights, and required universities to make rape statistics public. It also provided funding for battered women's shelters, rape prevention, child abuse prosecution, and a national domestic violence hotline. In 1995, when the House Appropriations Committee tried to omit two-thirds of the funding for the domestic violence programs authorized under the law, the groups and representatives who had worked for it swung into action. Hatch and Biden wrote a letter to the chair of the House Appropriations Committee, Bob Livingston, Republican of Louisiana, asking him to reconsider. The offices of senators who supported the bill "got hundreds of calls in the next few days asking what was happening, what could they do about it," said one Senate staffer. "The community on rape and domestic violence is well-organized and it comes out. That's really important at the grassroots."[43] Eventually, Congress preserved the funding.

This victory affected a comparatively small item in the federal budget, but its dynamics are significant. Like African American groups, women's groups have been closely and almost solely affiliated with the Democratic party since the mid-1970s.[44] In this case, women built upon the support offered by a traditional ally, Joseph Biden, the Democratic chair of the Senate Judiciary Committee. But they also mobilized a grass-roots base, built coalitions with universities interested in finding funding for sexual assault prevention centers, and cast the issue in such a way as to make it possible for a Republican as conservative as Orrin Hatch to be a visible supporter. One Senate staffer suggested that national women's groups, though very helpful, were more successful because they did not take the lead. "The interesting thing is that it's totally from the grass roots up. When we started this, we didn't get much interest from the national women's organizations; but once the bill got in and they heard about it from women in the country, they've been very supportive."[45] The strategy they chose was not to discard their Democratic support but to expand outward rather than become dependent upon it.

Cathie Jo Martin's chapter for this volume shows how big business groupings that challenged the Republican agenda during this period found themselves shut out of important policymaking roles; by contrast, business groups that were willing to coordinate with the Republican leadership were guaranteed a seat at the table. Using "reverse lobbying" to keep interest groups in line was absolutely crucial for the Republicans in defeating Clinton's health care bill. But in the long run, it is not clear whether that outcome was also best for the businesses that went along. For the NRA, police groups, African Americans, and women, who faced the same choice, the loyalty that parties seek was not their best option. Instead, the parties' need to rebuild support from one issue to another, and thus their inability to promise consistent rewards for loyalty, means that the most successful groups functioned more as entrepreneurs who maintained the freedom to sell their support to the highest bidder. It may be that some future period of realignment will lock one or more of these groups into, or out of, a stable governing coalition. But until then, interest groups will be more likely to be successful when they hold off on binding partnerships.

Bargaining and Balancing in a Federal System

The structure of interest group influence is not the only thing that has changed with the slow demise of the political and social conditions that made the New Deal possible. The relationship of states and localities to the federal government has changed as well. If the decades after the New Deal can be seen as the period of slow decline of states' rights as the federal government expanded both its resources and its policy reach, the shrinking resources the federal government faces now make devolution, with its trade-off of cost savings for power, a natural alternative. In fact, one of the ironies of the prominence of crime policy as a national issue in this period is exactly this: while the federal government spoke more loudly and vociferously, its actual influence upon state and local policy was modest.

But modest influence is not the same as no influence, and in its own way, the structure of federal influence is interesting precisely because it cannot make use of overwhelming, centralized force. Instead, as with interest groups, the federal government is bargaining: using a small amount of federal money to leverage a larger amount of federal influence, depending on professional networks rather than federal mandates to affect law enforcement priorities. Meanwhile, states and localities, despite all their claims of independence, bargain too: they need federal money and federal guidelines to address their internal problems and resolve multijurisdictional conflicts.

Though ideological advocates of devolution might not agree, therefore, shifting power and money to the states does not remove the federal government from policy influence. Instead, it rechannels that influence, reducing it in some areas but not in most. From the competition to enlist localities as allies, to the use of policy tools such as incentive grants, crime policy offers a particularly good place to explore these bargaining relationships. In social policy areas where the federal government has long had a role, bargaining over power is harder to distinguish from simple coordination. But in the arena of crime policy, the federal government has *never* had a major role in law enforcement. This makes it easier to see when the federal government is trying to enlist localities as allies vis-à-vis the states. It makes it more apparent when strings are attached to a new grant of resources. And it also makes it clearer when the states themselves are trying to convince the federal government to do something that it has heretofore avoided.

Theories of devolution often suggest that it is possible for the federal government to be involved in some policy areas while the states take charge of others. This idea lay behind President Ronald Reagan's attempt, in his first term, to take medicaid for the national government but return welfare programs to the states; it is also prominent in the work of scholars like Paul Peterson, who suggests that the national government should take charge of redistribution while states deal with developmental programs.[46] But while these ideas have an administrative elegance to them, they ignore the realities of political interdependence within a federal system. National, state, and local leaders need each other for policy purposes but also for political support. When national leaders have the chance, they will design programs that help them cement that support and that help them maintain a level of influence in policy.

Community policing and prison construction, the centerpieces of Clinton's crime policy, are a case in point. The 1994 crime bill provided $8.8 billion over six years directly to police departments in local communities for hiring through the COPS program, $3.9 billion for prison construction in all states, and an additional $3.9 billion for states that established "truth-in-sentencing policies." Each of the vast sums involved had a strong individual justification: localities badly needed police officers but did not have the tax base to fund them; prisons were overcrowded in every state; and the federal government could not well encourage states to pass "tough on crime" legislation without realizing that it would lead to even more overcrowding. But the political justifications were equally strong. The COPS program, an unprecedented direct federal grant of money to police departments, bypassed the states' political structures entirely and made localities dependent on a new federal subsidy. By contrast, incentive grants for truth-in-sentencing involved an appeal to a position popular with citizens, as well as a financial spur for states to adopt a policy over which the federal government has no jurisdiction.

The Republican bill, like its Democratic predecessor, was not at all shy in demanding that states be accountable to the federal government. Republican legislation passed by the House in early 1995 would have provided more flexibility to cities but less to states. The $10 billion the House provided for police and prevention grants could be allocated in any way that the cities saw fit; the 1994 legislation had provided more money for police and prevention but specified the amounts that were to be spent in each area. Similarly, prison grants were allocated $2.8 billion more, but only states that increased prison time for violent offenders were eligible for any money at all. While eager to give block grants in some areas, therefore, the party took actions that indicated that some things were too important to leave completely to the states.

Of these two areas, police and prisons, the COPS grants were by far the most obvious attempt to use federal funds to shape partisan coalitions. Before the 1994 legislation, federal assistance for local law enforcement was delivered to the states under the Byrne memorial grant program. States then distributed the money, which led to predictable abuses: governors used the grants to build their political machines, assist friends, or punish enemies, and federal funds sometimes went straight into state coffers without appreciable "trickling" to localities.[47] Cities, naturally, chafed under this "pass-through" system. Through the new police and prevention grants, however, the 1994 legislation gave cities their own claim upon federal funds. Police departments were empowered to apply directly to the federal government for police hires without sending their requests through the state. The 1995 Republican bills went one better, even bumping the policing money from police departments to cities. States understood that this meant they lost power vis-à-vis their localities. Although they did not lose control of the Byrne memorial grants, they were cut out of the new funds being distributed.

The political calculations in which this involved states and cities were tricky. States largely decided not to lobby against direct funding for cities, in order to put their energies into getting prison construction money and in the realization that a fight could be counterproductive for all. But they fretted about the possibility that the grants would create "a connection between the federal government and the localities which is corrosive. Interest groups who get disappointed at the state level know they can go to the feds. . . . It's simpler to persuade one federal government, rather than fifty state governments, to do something a group wants."[48] Exchanges of letters between the National Conference of State Legislatures and the U.S. Conference of Mayors saw the states warning cities, somewhat patronizingly, that federal money might not be a boon a few years down the line.[49]

Meanwhile, cities found themselves entangled in partisan politics at the national level. Police groups and cities had cooperated in advocating for the 1994 legislation; in December 1993, police chiefs and mayors issued a "National Action Plan to Combat Crime" and coordinated their lobbying campaigns. After the Republican congressional victories in 1994, they found their loyalties, to President Clinton and to each other, strained. For the mayors, "all politics aside, the Republican bill is much better for cities. . . . The politics of this are very difficult—the administration is taking a no-compromise position. On the other hand, if this [the Republican bill] is going to happen, we want to be involved. We're hoping we can work with the administration to make that [compromise] happen."[50]

But police groups, as described earlier, were more publicly committed to the administration. They were also the clearest losers under the Republican plan; COPS money, which went directly to police departments as part of the 1994 legislation, was redirected to cities in the Republican House bill. Their interests, therefore, did not let them deal with the Republican Congress as easily as did the cities. And by driving this wedge between the two, the Republican leadership would have effectively muted one of the strongest coalitions in favor of the 1994 legislation. Gridlock over the budget process saved it; new Republican legislation no longer looked inevitable, and the virtues of standing tough against a Republican onslaught acquired some political payoff. Nevertheless, the escape was a narrow one; though police groups might have benefited, in the long run, from seeming less partisan, there would have been few political advantages from being forced to compromise.

By contrast, on truth-in-sentencing prison grants, the parties converged in asserting federal influence against the states. National politicians often try to boost their "tough on crime" images by calling for longer and stricter sentences. The result is that parole for federal crimes was abolished in 1986; federal prisoners are now required to serve at least 85 percent of their sentences. But federal prisoners represent only 8 percent of all prisoners in the United States, and of that number, the percentage of inmates who have committed a violent federal crime is even smaller. To be taken more seriously, therefore, national politicians have to try to influence state policy—a difficult task, as dealing with crime is almost always, and indisputably, a state power.

Incentive grants were the solution. Unlike formula grants, incentive grants are not distributed equally across states; instead, they are distributed to states that meet particular federal standards. The truth-in-sentencing grants in both the 1994 and 1995 bills thus rewarded states that decided to adopt truth-in-sentencing laws that equaled the federal government's 85 percent standard. Whatever the substantive merits of such a provision, it created a serious fiscal dilemma for states. It was quite possible that enacting stiffer sentencing requirements in states with already grossly overcrowded prison systems would cost states *more* than the federal government would provide in incentive and formula grants combined. Thus this program, which seemed to offer assistance to states on the surface, actually concealed an unfunded mandate—an odd contradiction, given the Clinton administration's stated desire to reduce state mandates. And the irony was only further magnified when the Republican House, which had included in its "Contract with America" a call for the prohibition of unfunded mandates, conditioned *all* of its expanded prison funding on tougher prison sentences in the states.

Both the Democratic and Republican authors of the bills understood the inconsistency, even if they did not accept the implied criticism as fair. Bruce Reed argued that "keeping citizens safe is the first responsibility of government. . . . We have to put state and local governments in a position to do that, and that's why we don't just step back from the battlefield and say it's none of our business."[51] For Paul McNulty, the majority counsel of the House Subcommittee on Crime, the Republican approach was equally defensible. "The only states [that call the sentencing conditions attached to prison construction money a mandate] are states that can't get it done at all, and so they're frustrated, and want to call this a mandate. Here's the bottom line. We've got limited money for prison construction, and so what should be the basis for getting that money? . . . Our legislation says that we should reward states that are trying to do this, that have undertaken this burden; it's a burden worth undertaking."[52]

In response, governors and state legislators argued that such provisions clearly violated the spirit of the call to give power back to the states. When the need was as great as it was for prison construction money, they argued, states had little choice but to go along. While welcoming the new money, moreover, organizations such as the National Governors' Association, U.S. Conference of Mayors, National Conference of State Legislatures, and National League of Cities were unanimous in saying that the issue with crime was not "more"—as in more prison space—but "better"—better ways to utilize what they had. Available prison space could be better used if management and alternative sentencing options were funded; prison construction money, a representative of one of these organizations suggested, was "for jobs, for building, not for crime."[53]

These groups suggested that block grants, which Republicans had been so quick to support in other areas, should be extended to prison construction as well. While recognizing the ways block grants had been misused, they largely dismissed those criticisms as politically motivated. As Jon Felde of the National Conference of State Legislatures commented, "The Republicans came in, talking about turning power back to the states, but now we're getting mandates from different philosophical positions. . . . For these people, federalism is just an argument you use for achieving a different end. It's not a systematic way of looking at government."[54] The financial difference, especially under the Republican bill, was vast:

a 1995 Bureau of Justice Report suggested that had incentive grants been available in 1994, only one state—Delaware—would have been eligible. Maine, Kansas, the District of Columbia, Arizona, Oregon, and Washington would have been close; their prisoners served between 75 and 80 percent of their sentences. In the average state, however, the average prisoner convicted of a violent crime served only 48 percent of his sentence. In other words, the average state would have to nearly double the amount of time a prisoner spent in prison to qualify for funding under the Republican bill.[55]

Incentive funding is far from new. Funding for schools under the Elementary and Secondary Education Act was conditioned on district compliance with desegregation plans. Funding for highways is conditioned on state acceptance of the 55 miles per hour speed limit and the 21-year-old drinking age.[56] Such restrictions on states' rights, in the service of national principles and national standards, have long been seen as an effective and powerful tool. Under *South Dakota* v. *Dole*, the Supreme Court has upheld the constitutionality of conditional or incentive funding. Yet the widespread use of such conditions challenges the claim that, under devolution, the federal government returns power to the states to allow them to enact the policies best suited to their needs. And notably, the story of truth-in-sentencing grants seems to show that even political parties that hold devolution dear can use incentive grants without a qualm.

But the involvement of the federal government in crime policy need not produce only new intergovernmental battlegrounds. At its best, intergovernmental alliances can also occur. The Clinton Justice Department was marked by the number of high-ranking appointees who either had experience working with local prosecutors and law enforcement or who had actually served in state and local positions: Janet Reno, attorney general and former state's attorney for Dade County, Florida; Tom Constantine, head of the Drug Enforcement Administration and former superintendent of the New York state police; Louis Freeh, head of the FBI, who in his previous experience at the FBI had worked closely with local and state district attorneys on Mafia prosecutions; Lee Brown, drug czar, a former police chief from Houston and New York. These and other officials developed programs that proactively brought federal assistance to strapped state investigators, coordinated interjurisdictional criminal investigations and information sharing, and resolved conflicts over dual prosecutions and overlapping state and federal laws. Daniel Rosenblatt, head of the IACP, gave an example.

Tom Constantine had 30 years of experience in the New York State Police, where he established mobile teams of state police who could travel around to assist local police. They did their job and moved on to the next emergency. Now he's brought that concept into the DEA. He's set up 18 teams, who can go to all parts of the country, to investigate suspected trafficking, cases of murder that are drug-related, and other drug-related crimes. He can do that because he's aware that this is the help that local DEA agents need, but also that the local police can use. So the old view that the federal government doesn't know anything about local conditions is wrong.[57]

The ability of local, state, and federal law enforcement to cooperate, not only to resolve jurisdictional conflicts but actually to create mutually beneficial partnerships, speaks to a characteristic of federalism that is often overlooked by those who draw strict divisions between state and federal powers. As Paul Peterson, Barry Rabe, and Kenneth Wong point out in their 1986 study, *When Federalism Works*, under conditions of forced cooperation and over time, shared federal-state programs cultivate a network of professionals who develop knowledge of each level's competence, formally and informally rewrite regulations in order to facilitate cooperation, acquire a shared expertise that allows for improved solutions to problems, and mobilize to defend both their programs and their claim to autonomy and expertise. Peterson, Rabe, and Wong see the development of these professional networks as a key characteristic of successful federalism.[58] The creation of law enforcement networks in the Clinton administration, a development led primarily by practitioners rather than by political staff, suggests the importance of their argument.

This kind of cooperation was further enhanced by a commitment within the Department of Justice to cooperative efforts with local communities. The Office of Justice Programs funded several community-based initiatives, from "Weed and Seed" programs started in the Bush administration, to "Project PACT" and "SafeFutures," both of which focused on youth violence. Each of these involved cooperation across federal, state, and local law enforcement, as well as similar cooperative efforts among different levels of social service providers, schools, and community groups. The enterprise zone–enterprise community program, housed primarily in the Department of Housing and Urban Development (HUD), also included a crime-fighting component. Perhaps most interesting, Justice and HUD participated in a group sponsored by foundations and corporations, the "National Funding Collaborative on Violence Prevention." By pooling federal money with nonprofit and private funds, this collaborative sought both to coordinate funding for communities to work on violence prevention efforts and to draw national attention to successful strategies.[59]

All of these efforts are in their infancy; whether they can contribute to greater community safety and involvement in the designated areas has yet to be determined. But it is interesting how little attention they have received, from either politicians or the press, when compared with promises to increase sentences and chase down criminals. They do not fit into the rhetorical framework of the politics of crime policy, which places law enforcement in direct opposition to "social programs" and "prevention." Instead, they present the sight of police working in tandem with community groups, in efforts that look suspiciously like neighborhood services. The challenge to the terms of the crime debate is quiet, but it is significant nonetheless. The seeds of at least one strand of future crime policy are embedded in it. Whether they grow, however, depends on the political climate as much as on their own potential.

The Future of National Crime Policy

All through the 1996 presidential campaign, President Clinton reminded voters that the nation's crime rate had declined each year of his term. In their first debate, however, his Republican opponent, Bob Dole, challenged that statement. "Crime has gone down, but it's because of mayors like Rudy Giuliani, where one-third of the drop happened in one city, New York City."[60] Indeed, New York City, with less than 3 percent of the American population, accounted for 33 percent of the total national decline in crime between 1993 and 1995. By way of comparison, nine of the country's twenty-five largest cities had higher crime rates in 1995 than in 1993.[61]

Both the debate, and the statistic, say something important about the national role in fighting crime. The federal government is an important shaper of crime rhetoric: it can highlight crime-fighting techniques, popularizing some and discrediting others; it can raise national awareness and leverage local spending with even a limited commitment of national funds. But the substance and ultimately the results of crime policy originate from states and localities. President Clinton can promise to put 100,000 police on the streets, but for most communities, this has worked out to one or two new officers. National politicians can publicize "three strikes and you're out" laws, but, in the end, prosecutors and judges will file different types of charges or overlook previous convictions in order to restrict the law's reach.[62]

State and local politicians, of course, face the same public pressures for tougher crime policy that national politicians do. It was Alabama, not the federal government, that tried to reinstitute chain gangs; it is California whose "three strikes and you're out" law is the most punitive in the country.[63] Budgetary pressures can also work to curtail state activity, of course: warehousing in overcrowded prisons, or the move to pass off some corrections responsibilities to private prisons, can be seen as movement away from an activist policy approach. But one important difference is that budgetary pressures, which limit the federal government's involvement in state and local crime policies, also work at the state and local level to encourage innovation in crime fighting. States that rushed to lengthen sentences in the 1980s and 1990s are now experimenting with a range of alternative sentencing programs, from drug courts to boot camps.[64] Law enforcement officials are beginning to state publicly that police funding, gun control, antidrug efforts, and restructuring the justice system are only "relatively short-term responses to violent crime. . . . If we are to stem the tide of violence, however, we must address the root causes of crime and violence in a comprehensive and seamless manner."[65]

By contrast, the federal government's activity in crime policy is beginning to face challenges in the courts. Attempts by the national government to participate in crime policymaking at the local level have, in fact, played roles in two important cases defining the limits of national power: United States v. Lopez (1995), a case about the Drug-Free Schools Act, and Printz v. United States (1997), a case challenging the enforcement of the 1993 Brady bill. In United States v. Lopez, the 5–4 majority decided that a federal law prohibiting the possession of a firearm in a school zone was a trespass upon state authority. The decision restricted the scope of Congress's power to legislate under the commerce clause, which gives Congress the power to regulate interstate commerce.[66] Printz v. United States could be an additional hobble on the federal government's ability to require state cooperation. Now that the Court has prohibited the federal government from requiring local police and sheriffs to do a background check on gun purchasers, there is no telling how many other federal mandates, enforced at the local level by state and local authorities, might also fall.

Taken together, these cases suggest that federal crime policy, despite its increasing political prominence, may prove to be primarily sound and fury. If the Supreme Court prevents the federal government from making popular laws against crime where federal jurisdiction is doubtful and prohibits it from enlisting state and local law enforcement to carry out federal provisions against crime, the federal government would have few crime-fighting options left. Indeed, two of the crime-fighting measures crafted in the last days of the 104th Congress—Megan's law, a measure requiring community notification when sex offenders are released and take up residence in a neighborhood, and a law to prohibit anyone convicted of a misdemeanor domestic violence charge from buying a gun—are at least questionable under *Lopez* and *Printz*. In an era of budgetary restrictions, laws such as these are popular: they allow for bipartisan cooperation and require no federal money. Without the ability to pass such laws, the federal government's crime-fighting options would be limited to taking symbolic action against crime in areas of direct federal jurisdiction—Indian reservations, the city of Washington, D.C., military bases—or encouraging states to fall into line with its rhetoric through the use of incentive grants or task forces.

Another way of thinking about the limited role of the federal government in crime fighting is to examine how the federal government allocates its spending on criminal justice. As figure 8-1 shows, in real terms the federal investment in crime activity has more than doubled in the past twenty years. Assistance to states and localities for criminal justice spending has risen 82 percent in that time, certainly not an insignificant figure. But as table 8-1 shows, far larger increases in this period are found in other categories of federal spending: 158 percent in border enforcement, 252 percent in civil and criminal prosecutions, 203 percent in the federal judiciary, and 327 percent in federal correctional activities. These figures reflect the cost of the war on drugs, but, by and large, they do not represent spending on the type of violent street crime that politicians in this period condemned. Nor does this spending reflect a reorientation of priorities toward assisting states and localities to deal with violent crime. Criminal justice assistance to states and localities in 1997 occupies only 13 percent of the federal criminal justice budget, a slight decrease from the 17 percent it represented in 1978.

In a world where states and localities are the primary source of anticrime policies, then, what role is left for the federal government? Two possible directions come to mind. An open debate about the protection

FIGURE 8-1. *Total Federal Criminal Justice Budget Authority, 1978–97*[a]

Millions of 1994 dollars

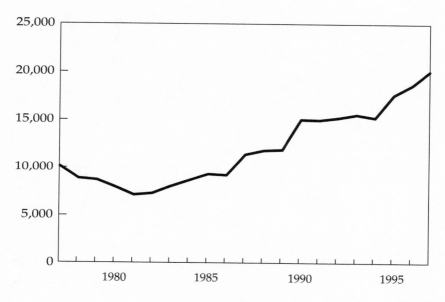

Source: *Sourcebook of Criminal Justice Statistics,* annual volumes, 1979–94.
a. Estimates from the 1994 volume are included for 1995–97.

of civil liberties could force a national reexamination of both crime fighting and incarceration alternatives. Given the importance of the federal judiciary in such controversies, this kind of debate would of necessity involve the federal government and the national parties in shaping a context for crime policy. This may seem almost inconceivable, given developments in this period. But the issue of how to fight crime while protecting civil liberties is one that promises to become more contentious as enhanced law enforcement powers create their own backlash. While the Supreme Court's unanimous decision in 1996 to uphold the antiterrorism bill's restrictions on habeas corpus appeals (*Felker* v. *Turpin*) underlines this era's willingness to restrict civil liberties, signs of a swing on the political pendulum are already appearing. The odd juxtaposition of the American Civil Liberties Union and the NRA, uniting their efforts to

TABLE 8-1. *Average Annual Budget Authority, by Presidential Term, 1978–97*

Millions of 1994 dollars unless otherwise indicated

Budget category	Carter (1978–80)	Reagan 1st term (1981–84)	Per-centage change	Reagan 2nd term (1985–88)	Per-centage change	Bush (1989–92)	Per-centage change	Clinton 1st term (1993–97)[a]	Per-centage change	1978	1997	Percentage change, 1978–97[a]
Federal law enforcement activities												
Criminal investigations	1,580	1,730	9	2,219	28	2,831	28	3,472	23	1,687	3,929	133
Alcohol, tobacco, and firearms investigation	277	227	-18	242	6	319	32	394	23	293	417	42
Border enforcement activities	1,514	1,542	2	2,267	47	2,970	31	3,624	22	1,566	4,034	158
Protection activities (Secret Service)	311	354	14	433	22	473	9	529	12	316	554	75
Other enforcement	486	487	0	514	6	603	17	734	22	443	766	73
Total	4,167	4,341	4	5,675	31	6,631	17	7,127	7	4,305	7,869	83

Federal litigative and judicial activities

Civil and criminal prosecution and representation	819	913	11	1,311	44	2,147	64	2,722	27	821	2,888	252
Federal judicial activities	1,072	1,181	10	1,584	34	2,143	35	2,959	38	1,052	3,191	203
Representation of indigents in civil cases	519	411	-21	402	-2	358	-11	396	11	466	438	-6
Total	2,411	2,505	4	3,296	32	4,657	41	6,090	31	2,339	6,530	179
Federal correctional activities	656	656	0	1,022	56	2,223	117	2,593	17	700	2,987	327
Criminal justice assistance	1,240	250	-80	423	69	788	86	1,634	107	1,487	2,704	82
Total	8,451	7,734	-8	10,417	35	14,300	37	17,443	22	8,812	20,090	128

Source: *Sourcebook of Criminal Justice Statistics*, annual volumes, 1978–94.
a. Includes estimates for 1995–97.

defeat the antiterrorism bill and to push for investigations into the practices of federal law enforcement agencies, suggests that uneasiness about the reach of government authority can find a home in both parties.[67] Calls for a victims' rights amendment to the Constitution and for revisions to the Federal Sentencing Commission's mandatory minimum sentences for drug possession promise to keep these debates alive, as do policy decisions to require drug rehabilitation in prisons and to supervise probationers and parolees more closely.

It is important to realize that such a debate, though it could easily start with crime issues, would not necessarily be restricted to this area of social policy. Popular social policy options in this period rely increasingly on interventionist approaches. Take, for example, suggestions that the government should reward welfare recipients for finding work or penalize them for having children out of wedlock; provide incentive programs for businesses to provide jobs in the inner city, treat their workers well, or protect the environment; pay children to stay in school or to read books; or assess higher medicare premiums upon people with unhealthy habits. Although people of different political persuasions offer different kinds of interventions, such proposals all involve efforts to enforce various types of personal behavior.[68] In discussions of "values" that now find a home in both parties, as in one strand of the American historical tradition, such proposals seem sensible, even righteous. But their flip side is a level of surveillance and implicit coercion, which equally strong American traditions have condemned.

If approaches to social policy do indeed fall out over the level and permissibility of intervention, the ensuing debate should cause as much turmoil within the parties as between them. As the overarching claims made by proponents and opponents about the level of permissible government intervention into private behavior expand, the political gain from packaging them into a coherent public philosophy—a set of principles about the reach and role of government—expands as well. But precisely because beliefs about the level of intervention are both strong and inconsistent across issues and issue frames, the principles one wing of a party chooses may not be the same principles that a different wing of the same party would advocate. Both political parties, and the shape and direction of activist social policy, would be reinvented by such a debate.

In comparison with this possibility, federal involvement in crime policy could take a much more modest direction that would come not from reconfiguring the debate but from reshaping the practices of policymaking to involve states and localities more actively. This would encompass federal efforts to claim a place in state and local law enforcement decisionmaking by bringing something to the table: the possibility of federal money but also the promise of federal networking and coordination. With these to offer, the federal government can attach conditions, and thus exercise influence, in ways that constitutional limitations and jurisdictional distance would otherwise preclude. But the promise is something more than just static cooperation: the possibility of creating a more truly unified and efficient system of criminal justice beckons.

A previous attempt by the federal government to become more active in crime fighting offers some important lessons. In 1968, a Democratic president, Lyndon Johnson, and a Democratic Congress passed the Safe Streets Act. Among its provisions was the establishment of the Law Enforcement Assistance Administration (LEAA), which provided law enforcement block grants to states. In its twelve years, the LEAA provided $7.5 billion in grants. But when it expired, its death was applauded by Republicans and Democrats alike. Not only had violent crime increased in all but one of the years of LEAA's tenure, the block grant process was widely viewed as a pork barrel for states. A study written at the demise of LEAA in 1980 concluded, "These days it is fashionable to talk about the *limits* of government. But the limits of government are a pallid excuse for the political exploitation of the crime issue, the mismanagement of LEAA, and the ineffective national leadership that characterized so much of the war on crime."[69]

But the LEAA was not merely a symbol of failure. Its projects included a sophisticated data-gathering operation, which, in its current incarnation as the Bureau of Justice Statistics, has now grown to be the country's most reliable source of information on crime, prevention, and law enforcement. Nor did all states mismanage the LEAA; some states, such as Illinois, New York, Texas, and Michigan, were able to use the LEAA state planning process to rethink their entire criminal justice budget.[70] This small example suggests that federal aid for crime control need not be massive to be successful. But it must provide services that complement rather than duplicate existing efforts and that encourage states to rethink rather than simply re-fund their law enforcement efforts.

Today, the possibilities created by information technology almost beg for a coordinating body to make them useful. Until recently, apart from professional conferences and FBI workshops, there was no obvious way for jurisdictions to share information about various innovations or get advice on solving particular problems. But the Department of Justice has now helped to develop an information search and retrieval system known as PAVNET (Partnerships Against Violence Network), which includes information on crime-fighting innovations, funding sources, and technical assistance.[71] Similarly, in the United States today, there is no way to track a convicted criminal's past criminal history, except by calls to individual states where the convict may (or may not) have been active. The federal government is the most obvious site of coordination for a national database.

But of course, possibilities for coordination are not limited to information sharing. As indicated, the development of professional networks spanning federal, state, and local law enforcement, and the ability of the federal government to cajole private and nonprofit groups to cooperate with states and localities on law enforcement projects, can be just as important. In all of these areas, the federal government plays an indispensable role, given its resources, its prestige, and its ability to keep track of trends that occur across jurisdictional boundaries. To the extent that the federal government can channel its efforts into these directions, a nationally directed but community-led reinvention of crime policy can occur.

A focus upon this type of coordination, however, requires its own political context. Since any effort to coordinate across jurisdictional boundaries involves not only several different law enforcement agencies but also several different political boundaries, mediating among partisan priorities, credit claiming, and the ability to sustain commitment over several years is crucial. In other areas of social policy, the failure to do this has been disabling: notice the difficulties in settling, or even starting, enterprise zone projects, as described by John Mollenkopf in his chapter for this volume. As crime policy begins to involve more organizations than the police, similar intergovernmental and interorganizational conflicts are bound to occur, and it is not clear that researchers, politicians, or practitioners have the systematic knowledge that would make solving them easier. As devolution takes hold, the need for this kind of knowledge becomes even greater.

Crime policy burst onto the national scene in 1993 with the momentum of public fear and political advantage propelling it. By taking advantage of this momentum as dramatically as he did, President Clinton remade the partisan identification of crime as a Republican issue, changing a rhetorical frame that had been fixed since the 1960s. That political achievement made it possible for latent factions within both parties to jockey with the issue for power; for interest groups to bargain with the parties for policies that would advance their cause; and for states and cities to make a claim on federal assistance for a set of distinctly local concerns. It also sowed the seeds for a new crop of crime debates: a perennial one over the reach of government into the regulation of private behavior and a nascent one over the political challenges of devolution. Viewed from this angle, President Clinton's impact upon the content and the uses of crime as an American political issue is truly significant. But whether that legacy will ultimately help to reconfigure the political parties, to build more stable interest group partners, or to truly extend the crime-fighting capacity of states and localities, remains to be seen.

Notes

1. Leslie McAneny and David W. Moore, "Republicans Now Seen as Better Able to Handle 'Most Important' National Problem," *Gallup Poll Monthly* (August 1994), p. 17.

2. Leslie McAneny, "The Gallup Poll on Crime," *Gallup Poll Monthly* (December 1993), p. 18.

3. Princeton Survey Research Associates for the Pew Research Center, "People and the Press Media Consumption Survey," Question 66; survey administered April 19–April 25, 1996; source document released May 13, 1996.

4. Marianne W. Zawitz and others, "Highlights from 20 Years of Surveying Crime Victims," *Bureau of Justice Statistics Reports* (Department of Justice, NCJ-144525, October 1993), pp. 6, 21.

5. Leslie McAneny, "Americans Discouraged by Government's Ineffective War on Crime," *Gallup Poll Monthly* (December 1993), p. 29.

6. David W. Moore and Frank Newport, "Public Strongly Favors Stricter Gun Control Laws," *Gallup Poll Monthly* (January 1994), p. 18.

7. Leslie McAneny, "Racial Overtones Evident in Americans' Attitudes about Crime," *Gallup Poll Monthly* (December 1993), p. 37.

8. William J. Clinton, July 16, 1992, speech accepting the Democratic presidential nomination, reprinted in *1992 Congressional Quarterly Almanac*, p. 55-A.

9. Confidential interview with House staff, July 14, 1995.

10. "Senate OK's Omnibus Anti-Crime Bill," *1993 Congressional Quarterly Almanac*, p. 293.

11. Interview with Bruce Reed, deputy assistant to the president for domestic policy, July 10, 1995.

12. David Cole, "Strict Scrutiny: Destruction of the Habeas Safety Net," *Legal Times*, June 19, 1995, p. 33.

13. The quote is from Craig Shirley, a public relations specialist retained by the NRA to lead its anticrime bill effort. The quote itself and general information about the NRA's campaign comes from Dan Balz and Ronald Brownstein, *Storming the Gates: Protest Politics and the Republican Revival* (Little, Brown, 1996), pp. 189–97.

14. Editorial, "Soft on Crime, Heavy on Fat," *Wall Street Journal*, August 3, 1994, p. A10.

15. For instance, the Local Partnership Act, a community development block grant sponsored by Conyers, resurfaced in the crime bill; it had originally been part of the president's blocked economic stimulus package. Community schools, a program that had the support of Senate Republicans like John Danforth of Missouri as well as Democrats like Edward Kennedy of Massachusetts, was further expanded by the House. Other measures, such as the youth employment services program and model intensive grants, were also targeted at localities, offering the prospect of geographical benefits for legislators to take home.

16. Interview with Paul McNulty, majority counsel, House Subcommittee on Crime, August 3, 1995.

17. Representative Dick Armey, speech delivered at the signing of the "Contract with America," September 27, 1994, Republican National Committee.

18. Balz and Brownstein, *Storming the Gates*, p. 198.

19. James G. Gimpel, *Fulfilling the Contract: The First 100 Days* (Allyn and Bacon, 1996), pp. 60–61.

20. Letter quoted in Legi-Slate, "Overview and Outlook: S. 735 by Sen. Robert Dole, Comprehensive Terrorism Prevention Act of 1995; Victims of Terrorism Act of 1995."

21. Holly Idelson, "House Strips New Powers from Terrorism Bill," *Congressional Quarterly Weekly Report*, March 16, 1996, p. 705.

22. Holly Idelson, "Crime Provisions in Anti-Terrorism Bill," *Congressional Quarterly Weekly Report*, March 16, 1996, p. 703.

23. Questions 16-18, *Los Angeles Times* poll, released April 28, 1995.

24. Question 28, *Los Angeles Times* poll, released April 28, 1995; and Richard L. Berke, "Dole Sends Message of Inclusion to Abortion-Rights Republicans; He Shrugs Off NRA in His Move to the Center," *New York Times*, July 22, 1996, p. A1.

25. Osha Gray Davidson, *Under Fire: The NRA and the Battle for Gun Control* (Henry Holt, 1993), p. 129.

26. "Remarks by the President in State of the Union Address," *Weekly Compilation of Presidential Documents*, January 30, 1995.

27. Balz and Brownstein, *Storming the Gates*, p. 191.

28. Alan Greenblatt, "Repeal of Assault Weapons Ban Unlikely to Go Beyond House," *Congressional Quarterly Weekly Report*, March 23, 1996, p. 803.

29. National Rifle Association, "The Politics of Crime: Winning Strategies for Your Campaign," internal videotape prepared for 1994 congressional candidates.

30. Interview with Elizabeth Swasey, senior counsel for policy, Crimestrike, NRA, July 13, 1995.

31. Ibid.

32. Greenblatt, "Repeal of Assault Weapons Ban Unlikely to Go Beyond House," p. 803.

33. During the battle to pass McClure-Volkmer, its sponsors had claimed the support of police organizations when in fact those organizations had withdrawn their support; the NRA sent out letters to its membership citing support from the National Sheriffs' Association when in fact that group had come out publicly against the bill. See Richard Corrigan, "NRA, Using Members, Ads and Money, Hits Police Line in Lobbying Drive," *National Journal*, January 4, 1986, p. 8.

34. Jay Mathews, "Police, Prosecutors Meet with Reagan on Bork; Campaign Launched for Senate Confirmation," *Washington Post*, August 29, 1987, p. A3.

35. Philip J. Garcia, "Law Enforcement Groups Criticize Bush," United Press International, August 4, 1988.

36. Rumors suggested that the FOP president had engineered the endorsement in order to be appointed to a government post; NAPO's president openly accused Justice Department officials of lobbying members, a violation of the Hatch Act. See Daniel Klaidman, "Charges Fly Over DOJ Bid to Lobby Police," *Legal Times*, October 19, 1992, p. 11.

37. "Paralyzed Police Officer Supports Dole," *New York Times*, August 15, 1996, p. A21.

38. Senator Joseph Biden Jr., quoted in Daniel Klaidman, "Cop Vote Is Clinton's to Lose," *New Jersey Law Journal*, July 24, 1995, p. 14.

39. Interview with Daniel Rosenblatt, executive director, International Association of Chiefs of Police, July 17, 1995.

40. According to a Gallup Poll taken in December 1993, 87 percent of whites and 88 percent of blacks see crime on the rise. See Leslie McAneny, "Most Americans Again See Crime on the Rise," *Gallup Poll Monthly* (December 1993), p. 18.

41. Holly Idelson, "An Era Comes to a Close: Costly Victory on Crime Bill Exposes Democratic Weakness, Foreshadows GOP Takeover," *Congressional Quarterly Weekly Report*, December 23, 1995, p. 3872.

42. Letter to the Hon. Kweisi Mfume, from the U.S. Conference of Mayors, July 14, 1994.

43. Confidential interview, Senate staff, July 14, 1995.

44. See Jo Freeman, "Whom You Know versus Whom You Represent: Feminist Influence in the Democratic and Republican Parties," in Mary Katzenstein and Carol Mueller, eds., *The Women's Movements of the United States and Western Europe* (Temple University Press, 1987), pp. 216–41.

45. Confidential interview, Senate staff, July 14, 1995.

46. See David S. Broder, "Reagan Runs into Resistance on Transferring Programs to the States," *Washington Post*, March 2, 1981, p. A11; Paul E. Peterson, Barry G. Rabe, and Kenneth K. Wong, *When Federalism Works* (Brookings, 1986); and Paul E. Peterson, *The Price of Federalism* (Brookings, 1995).

47. Thomas E. Cronin, Tania Z. Cronin, and Michael E. Milakovich, *U.S. v. Crime in the Streets* (Indiana University Press, 1981), chap. 7.

48. Interview, Jon Felde, senior committee director and general counsel, National Conference of State Legislatures, July 11, 1995.

49. Letter from Robert Connor, President, National Conference of State Legislatures, to Victor Ashe, President, U.S. Conference of Mayors, August 11, 1994.

50. Confidential interview, interest group representative, July 19, 1995.

51. Reed interview.

52. McNulty interview.

53. Confidential interview, interest group representative, July 10, 1995.

54. Felde interview.

55. Allen Beck and Lawrence Greenfield, "Violent Offenders in State Prison: Sentences and Time Served," *Bureau of Justice Statistics: Selected Findings* (Department of Justice, NCJ-154632, July 1995).

56. Jon Felde, remarks at Brookings Institution, October 18, 1994, p. 5.

57. Rosenblatt interview.

58. Peterson, Rabe, and Wong, *When Federalism Works*.

59. Catherine Conly and Daniel McGillis, "The Federal Role in Revitalizing Communities and Preventing and Controlling Crime and Violence," *National Institute of Justice Journal* (August 1996), pp. 24–30.

60. "Presidential Debate in Hartford," *Weekly Compilation of Presidential Documents*, October 14, 1996, p. 1978.

61. Clifford Krauss, "New York City's Gift to Clinton: A Lower National Crime Rate," *New York Times*, September 1, 1996, p. E5.

62. Fox Butterfield, "'Three Strikes' Rarely Invoked in Courtrooms," *New York Times*, September 10, 1996, p. A1.

63. Chain gangs, adopted in Alabama in 1995, were halted in 1996 after the numerous safety hazards involved in chaining inmates together surfaced. California's law was also moderated in 1996 when the California State Supreme Court decided that judges needed more discretion over disregarding prior convictions. See Associated Press, "Chain Gangs Are Halted in Alabama," *New York Times*, June 21, 1996, p. A8; and Carey Goldberg, "California Judges Ease 3-Strike Law," *New York Times*, June 21, 1996, p. A1.

64. Nolan Jones, "A Balanced Approach to Fighting Crime," *University of Dayton Law Review*, vol. 20 (Winter 1995), pp. 795–802.

65. United States Conference of Mayors, "A National Action Plan to Combat Violent Crime: Recommendations of Mayors and Police Chiefs to the President of the United States," December 9, 1993, p. 5.

66. The decision in *Lopez* was further reinforced in *Seminole Tribe* v. *Florida* (1996), where the same 5–4 majority decided that under the Eleventh Amendment, the Seminole tribe had no right to sue Florida for the state's failure to follow a federal law specifying procedures for setting up a casino on federal land. This "right of private enforcement" has long been considered a key tool to keep states accountable to federal law, because it allows anyone harmed by a state's noncompliance to seek redress. The new ruling stated that states can be held accountable for violating federal rules only if the federal government sues the state itself or regulates states using nonjudicial measures. The justices did, however, make an explicit exception for private enforcement in Fourteenth Amendment cases, which involve due process, equal protection, or voting rights; the majority opinion stated that the Fourteenth Amendment was in fact intended to reallocate power from the states to the federal government in these particular areas. See Linda Greenhouse, "Justices Curb Federal Power to Subject States to Lawsuits," *New York Times*, March 28, 1996, p. A1; and Nina Bernstein, "An Accountability Issue: As States Gain Political Power, a Ruling Seems to Free Them of Some Legal Reins," *New York Times*, April 1, 1996, p. A1.

67. "NRA, ACLU, Others Unite in Asking for Federal Civil Liberties Reforms," NRA-ILA Crimestrike Press Release, October 24, 1995.

68. See Lawrence M. Mead, ed., *The New Paternalism: Supervisory Approaches to Poverty* (Brookings, 1997).

69. Cronin, Cronin, and Milakovich, *U.S. v. Crime in the Streets*, p. 182. Most of my discussion of the LEAA is based on this work.

70. Ibid., pp. 153–55.

71. Laurie Robinson, "Linking Community-Based Initiatives and Community Justice: The Office of Justice Programs," in *National Institute of Justice Journal* (August 1996), pp. 4–7.

PART THREE

Recasting Policies for the Disadvantaged

Chapter 9

Ending Welfare as We Know It

R. Kent Weaver

MOST of the chapters in this volume report a pattern of relatively modest legislative change or complete stalemate in federal legislation in the first Clinton administration, while substantial "subterranean" change was being produced by state governments and private sector actors. There was a different pattern of change in policies toward low-income families. Although there was considerable change in the states, there were also two major legislative changes at the national level. In the first year of his presidency, Bill Clinton won a huge expansion in the earned income tax credit (EITC). In 1996, near the end of his first term, he signed a welfare reform bill largely on Republican terms that replaced the aid to families with dependent children (AFDC) program with a block grant to the states and made major cuts in the food stamp program and assistance to legal immigrants.

These two legislative bookends to the first Clinton term are in fact linked: both reflect the impact of President Clinton's strategic vision for reorienting Democratic social policy and the party's image with the electorate. The former reflects an early success of that vision. The latter reflects two unforeseen consequences of the same vision: Clinton's welfare policy initiatives helped to push Republicans to shift their own welfare reform stance to the right in order to avoid losing the welfare issue to Clinton, and the president's leverage to resist a Republican-oriented bill was severely weakened once he lost control over the welfare reform agenda in 1994.

The author would like to thank Martha Derthick, Lawrence Mead, Theda Skocpol, Gilbert Steiner, and Joseph White for comments on earlier versions of this chapter.

The Clinton administration and the new Republican congressional majority in the 104th Congress both came into office with ambitious policy agendas for low-income families. The content of those policy agendas was quite different, however. Bill Clinton promised in his 1992 presidential campaign to "make work pay" by dramatically expanding the earned income tax credit and increasing and indexing the minimum wage. He also pledged to "end welfare as we know it" through a package of reforms to the AFDC program that stressed work requirements, training, and supportive services and improved child support enforcement. Of these three planks, only the EITC expansion was enacted before the Republicans won control of Congress in 1994.

The new Republican majority in the House of Representatives came into office with a family policy agenda that was even more ambitious and far less favorable to low-income families. The House Republicans' Contract with America proposed a welfare reform plan very different from the administration's proposal: it would have capped and reduced AFDC funding to the states, ended individual entitlement to AFDC benefits, restricted benefits for women who have children outside marriage, and placed time limits on receipt of AFDC benefits. The contract also proposed a family tax credit that, because it was nonrefundable, gave most of its benefits to middle- and upper-income Americans. And after the Republicans gained control of Congress and began to deal seriously with the costs of their pledges to lower taxes and balance the budget, they proposed substantial cutbacks in the EITC to help pay for those promises. The new Republican agenda initially encountered serious obstacles. The Republican welfare initiative, the family tax credit, and EITC cutbacks were all rolled into the December 1995 budget reconciliation package that Clinton vetoed, and he vetoed the welfare reform bill again in January 1996. But in the summer of 1996, when congressional Republicans passed a welfare reform bill that met some of the president's objections and omitted unpopular medicaid cuts, he agreed to sign it. The family tax credit was passed in 1997, but major EITC cuts were not revived.

Dramatic change was occurring on a piecemeal basis at the state level throughout this period, as the Clinton administration let it be known that it would approve almost any request made by the states for a waiver in AFDC rules. States used waivers granted by the federal Department of Health and Human Services to experiment with a variety of approaches, including family caps (denial of additional benefits for children born or conceived while a mother received AFDC), work requirements, and time limits on receipt of benefits. The pace of change at the state level accelerated even more after passage of welfare reform legislation in 1996.

Developments in policies toward low-income families during the first Clinton administration show some clear patterns: a contested and rapidly changing family policy agenda, initial failure but eventual passage of comprehensive welfare reform legislation at the federal level, substantial innovation at the state level, and expansion but increasing controversy over the EITC. To explain these developments, this chapter argues that Clinton's effort to reposition the Democratic party on the racially charged issue of welfare both widened the range of alternatives on the agenda for low-income families and opened the door to changes far more radical than those he initially envisioned.

Party polarization and competition, intense public antipathy to welfare in its current form, and budgetary constraints lowered political barriers to welfare reform and altered reform options. Reflecting the primacy of partisan competition in policymaking, welfare reform became the object of strategic games in which most of the major participants' positions rested not just on their views of the policy merits but also on their relation to the positions of other participants. In trying to prove himself a "New Democrat," Clinton tried to position himself between congressional Republicans and congressional Democrats. But many moderate and conservative congressional Democrats pursued a second relational strategy: they were desperately seeking political cover from the charge that they were "soft on welfare" by avoiding positions to the left of the president. Thus every time President Clinton accepted Republican positions, he dragged a number of congressional Democrats to the right with him. Congressional Republicans were torn between a desire to reach a legislative deal for which they could claim credit and a third relational strategy of "strategic disagreement," that is, maintaining policy distance from Clinton and the Democrats so that they could continue to claim that they were the ones who were interested in "real" welfare reform while Clinton was really trying to obstruct it. Knowing that neither the president nor Democratic legislators wanted to be in the position of appearing to defend the status quo in the leadup to the 1996 election, congressional Republicans were in a very strong position to enact legislation on their own terms when they switched from a strategy of strategic disagreement to one of passing legislation in the summer of 1996, reversing a sixty-year federal commitment to assist poor single-parent families regardless of their work status.

Low-Income Families as a Policy and Political Challenge

In the early 1990s, the federal government channeled federal aid to low-income families through a number of programs. Some of these programs (notably AFDC, the EITC, and school-based nutrition and child nutrition programs) are targeted especially toward low-income families. Other programs, such as food stamps, medicaid, and supplemental security income, serve other low-income individuals as well as families. Still other programs, such as the child tax exemption in the Internal Revenue Code, benefit families at a variety of income levels. Figure 9-1 shows expenditure trends for major means-tested income transfer, nutrition, and health programs with a substantial clientele of low-income families. Real expenditures on low-income families channeled through these programs have grown substantially over the past twenty years, especially since the late 1980s, but there is a tremendous variation across programs. Most expenditure growth is accounted for by tremendous expenditure increases in the EITC and medicaid, while spending for AFDC has been relatively stable. Despite these programs, poverty among children is higher in the United States than in most other advanced industrial countries, having risen from 15.7 percent in 1978 to 21.1 percent in 1992.[1]

The most politically controversial program for low-income families was AFDC, a federal-state program that gave the states enormous leeway over both eligibility and benefits. AFDC provided cash benefits and automatic access to medicaid. Originally intended for widows, AFDC increasingly served families where the father was absent from the home as a result of divorce or separation or never had a marital tie to the mother.[2] Moreover, more than 90 percent of AFDC mothers in the early 1990s were not in the paid labor force—a growing political problem when a majority of non-AFDC mothers were working. Black families were heavily overrepresented among AFDC recipients relative to their share of the population, as they are among poor families generally.[3] The racial skewing of the AFDC caseload gave the program a racial cast that contributed to its extreme unpopularity with the public.[4] Partially as a result of this unpopularity, the real value of state-set AFDC benefits fell substantially after the early 1970s.

FIGURE 9-1. *Combined Federal and State Spending on Major Programs for Low-Income Families with Children, 1977–95*

Constant 1996 dollars

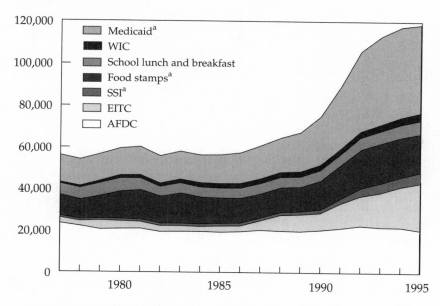

Sources: *1996 Green Book: Background Material and Data on Programs within the Jurisdiction of the Committee on Ways and Means,* Committee Print, 104 Cong. 2 sess. (Government Printing Office, 1996), pp. 458, 809, 896, 906, 925, 926, 928; *Budget of the United States Government, Historical Tables, Fiscal Year 1998,* table 11-3; *Social Security Bulletin, Annual Statistical Supplement,* 1996, tables 7B1, 8E2; *Health Care Financing Review,* vol. 6 (Winter 1984), p. 103; and U.S. Department of Agriculture, Food and Nutrition Services, National Data Bank, "Food Stamp Program Information for FY 1980 through 1995," April 1996.
    a. Expenditures shown are only those for low-income families.

Despite the unpopularity of AFDC, efforts at comprehensive reform of the program had generally failed.[5] Three obstacles have been particularly critical in limiting the prospects for successful welfare reform initiatives. First and most important is the dual clientele of any programs to aid low-income families. Most welfare reform proposals raise concerns either about rewarding parents of questionable "deservingness" and creating long-term dependence on the one hand, or harming innocent children on the other. Guaranteed income proposals like Nixon's family assistance plan are particularly likely to give rise to the former concerns; work requirements and time limits approaches, the latter. Financing problems have been a second critical factor in the failure of welfare reform initiatives. Most of the welfare reform proposals on the agenda before the 1990s would have cost more money in the short run than the status quo, and the combination of budget deficits and unpopularity of the AFDC program made spending more money on welfare recipients a tough sell politically. Finally, the multiple veto points in the U.S. legislative process create a strong bias toward the status quo, especially when there are deep divisions among political elites.

The earned income tax credit supplements the wages of low-income families with at least one worker in the labor force by giving them a refundable tax credit. The EITC enjoyed three major expansions, in 1986, 1990, and 1993, the last as part of the Clinton administration's budget package.[6] As figure 9-1 shows, by 1995 the federal government was spending more on EITC benefits than the federal and state governments together spent on AFDC benefits. The success of the EITC in a period when AFDC and other means-tested social programs were being challenged has several roots. First, the fact that EITC parents were by definition working meant that both parents and children were more likely to be perceived as more "deserving" than mostly nonworking AFDC families. Moreover, because the EITC uses carrots rather than sticks to secure desired parental behavior, EITC policymaking has not gotten bogged down in fights over how to avoid harming children. Second, although the EITC contains numerous perverse incentives, they have generally been overwhelmed by the message that the EITC "makes work pay." A third critical advantage that the EITC enjoyed over welfare reform is procedural: EITC expansions, including the one in 1993, were generally considered as part of big tax or reconciliation packages where significant new revenue was generated by other provisions. This became particularly important after restrictions on new spending were tightened by the Budget Enforcement Act of 1990.

The supplemental security income (SSI) program provides cash assistance to low-income persons who are aged, blind, or disabled. Although it is federally funded, many states supplement SSI benefits. The SSI program is targeted at adults but is also available to children with a "medically determinable physical or medical impairment of comparable severity" to that of adults.[7] After a 1990 Supreme Court decision substantially increased the access of children to the SSI program, the child SSI population tripled in the early 1990s, leading to increasing concerns that children with behavioral disorders and those coached by parents to "act crazy" were driving up the SSI rolls.[8]

In addition to cash assistance programs, substantial assistance to low-income families is transferred through a variety of nutrition programs; indeed, there is substantial overlap in recipiency of such programs.[9] The largest of these programs, food stamps, provides federally financed vouchers to all types of low-income households and individuals. About 60 percent of such households in recent years have included children.[10] The school lunch and school breakfast programs subsidize free or re-duced-price school meals to low-income children. And the special supple-mental feeding program for women, infants and children (WIC) provides nutritious foods (or more commonly, vouchers to purchase those foods) to pregnant and postpartum women, infants, and young children. Nu-trition programs for children have generally been more politically resil-ient than AFDC or food stamps in recent years, reflecting strong public sympathy for the idea that poor children should not go hungry.

Conflicting Approaches to Reform

Five distinctive approaches to policy toward low-income families un-derlie the shifting agenda in the early 1990s, posing different diagnoses of the nature of the problems posed by low-income families and distinc-tive solutions flowing out of those diagnoses.

Liberals, diagnosing the problem as low wages, inadequate services, and insufficient opportunity, tend to support incentives and prevention or rehabilitation approaches to family poverty. The first approach con-centrates on removing disincentives to work and maintain two-parent families, while trying to "make work pay" and weaken "poverty traps" that make it difficult to leave welfare. Making affordable health care available to low-income working families so that they do not have to rely on medicaid is perhaps the most prominent example of incentive-oriented approaches to welfare reform. Subsidizing low-income work through the EITC, increasing the minimum wage, and disregarding some of the earned income of welfare recipients to ease their transition into the work force are also consistent with this approach. Incentives for family breakup can be reduced by making both single-parent and two-parent families eligible for programs such as AFDC and public housing.

The prevention or rehabilitation approach focuses on overcoming human capital deficiencies in low-income families and removing structural barriers to labor market entry through the provision of services such as basic education, job training, family planning, and child care.

A third approach, "new paternalism," is associated with conservative writers like Lawrence Mead, but has increasingly been voiced by New Democrats like Bill Clinton as well.[11] It begins with the argument that current policies demand too little of recipients; public policies must demand responsible behavior and sanction irresponsible behavior. The centerpiece of new paternalist approaches is work requirements, with sanctions for noncompliance. Sanctions can also be applied to younger parents, for example, by lowering welfare benefits for recipients who do not stay in school or do not get their children immunized.

A fourth approach, deterrence, has increasingly been suggested by social conservatives. As the label suggests, this approach argues that it is not enough to provide obligations for people in low-income families; it is also necessary to prevent undesirable behaviors (notably out-of-wedlock births and long-term dependency on AFDC) from occurring in the first place. The former can be addressed by prohibiting payments to mothers for children conceived while the mother was receiving AFDC (family caps) and banning cash payments to teenage mothers (teen mother exclusions). Long-term receipt of benefits can be addressed by hard time limits, a set period after which recipients will be eligible neither for cash benefits nor a government-provided or -subsidized job.

Finally, a fifth approach, devolution, has been embraced in part by both New Democrats and Republicans. It suggests that uniform federal policies are unlikely to lead to adequate solutions to the problems of teenage pregnancy, family breakup, and nonparticipation in the labor force. A better mechanism is to devolve most responsibility for such families to the state level, allowing a number of experiments to produce new knowledge about which policies to pursue.

Each of these approaches has its own set of advantages and disadvantages, some of them obvious and some more subtle. Most of the incentive, prevention or rehabilitation, and work-oriented new paternalist approaches, for example, require spending more money in the short term. Moreover, many conservatives are philosophically opposed to increasing government's role in income distribution and increasing the number of persons dependent on government transfers. Deterrence approaches run into the most fundamental source of public ambivalence toward assistance toward low-income families with children: while people want to be tough on adult recipients whose deservingness they suspect, they do not want to punish innocent children.[12]

Devolution is perhaps the most complex in its effects. While devolution of responsibility for income support to the states offers an opportunity to test new programs to deal with dependence and welfare-to-work transitions, it may also radically transform the nature of the debate away from concerns about protecting children and toward concerns with meddling by Washington. If critics charge that Washington is abandoning poor children, defenders of block grants could ask in response why critics think that state governors would be any less willing to defend children than politicians in far-off Washington.

Some specific proposals are consistent with several approaches, and most welfare reform packages—including those of the Clinton administration in 1994 and congressional Republicans in 1995—draw upon several approaches. But while there was some overlap in specific proposals, the range of options under consideration grew, making a consensus on policy direction less likely.

A Polarized Political Environment

The broadened set of alternative approaches to reforming policy for low-income families on the agenda in the early 1990s confronted the same multiple veto points that had long stymied major social policy initiatives. But major changes in the political environment were also occurring, as outlined in Margaret Weir's introductory chapter to this volume. In the case of low-income families, the interaction of these changes in the political environment not only opened windows for major change in policy but also shaped the direction of that change. Elite polarization introduced new approaches—deterrence and devolution—that dramatically shifted the nature of the debate on how to respond to the welfare problem. Partisan competition and public discontent with welfare created incentives for Bill Clinton to make a bold promise to "end welfare as we know it" in order to capture the vast middle ground that polls showed supported work-based solutions to welfare reform. But his pledge also raised expectations about how much change was possible, further undercut public support for an already very unpopular program, and gave Republicans an incentive to criticize the president's proposals and attempt to "outbid" him, dramatically shifting the welfare reform agenda.[13] The growth of social conservative groups allied with the Republican party upset the old pattern of welfare policymaking dominated by Washington-based intergovernmental groups and advocates for the poor, adding political clout to the conservative push for deterrence approaches. And new budget pressures and procedures pushed the policy debate toward both spending retrenchment and the use of procedures, such as budget reconciliation, that risked a complete legislative meltdown.

Divided Elites

In the late 1980s there was a brief moment of widespread elite agreement on an approach to welfare that stressed increased work requirements, transitional services (such as health care and child care), and child support enforcement to move welfare families into financial independence. One of the most prominent proponents of a work-based approach to welfare reform was Harvard economist David Ellwood, who argued that families that were working very hard to keep themselves out of poverty should be rewarded through mechanisms to supplement their incomes and make work pay, notably an expansion of the EITC and an increase in the minimum wage. Families that needed temporary assistance (as a result of family breakup, for example) could draw on cash assistance. Those who needed longer-term support would be required to work at minimum wage jobs—half time for single-parent families, full time for one parent in two-parent families—in exchange for assistance. And all Americans would be guaranteed access to medical care (although Ellwood was not very clear about the mechanism for providing it) in order to avoid the perverse incentives of welfare recipients having access to care while other low-income families did not. Ellwood did not include detailed cost estimates, but allowed that his proposals "may cost well over $20 or even $30 billion to do everything right."[14]

Coming at the end of eight years of Reagan administration criticism of AFDC and in the middle of the debate over what was to become the Family Support Act of 1988, Ellwood's agenda was perceived as a bold alternative to retrenchment, informed by the latest research on "what works" in lessening welfare dependence. Less clear at the time was another effect: it legitimized among mainstream welfare scholars the idea of putting time limits on cash welfare benefits, albeit with a job guarantee at the end.

But the prospect for an enduring elite consensus on a work-based approach to welfare evaporated in the wake of alarming social trends, discouraging social science research results, and the interpretations put on those results by conservative scholars and activists. Trends in out-of-wedlock births were particularly worrisome to conservatives. In 1993, 69 percent of all births to black mothers were out of wedlock.[15] In that same year, white illegitimacy rates approached 24 percent, close to the level that had led Daniel Patrick Moynihan to argue in the 1960s that the black family was near collapse. Conservative writers like Charles Murray charged that "illegitimacy is the single most important social problem of our time—more important than crime, drugs, poverty, illiteracy or homelessness because it drives everything else."[16] Conservative critics of the current system also charged that welfare benefits acted as a lure to illegitimacy and dependence and as a serious deterrent for work among welfare recipients. These arguments were disputed by advocates for the poor and by many mainstream economists, but they gained widespread acceptance by the public.[17]

Social science research produced a steady stream of unsettling results on other aspects of welfare but failed to promote an elite consensus on how to respond. Research on the dynamics of entry to and exit from welfare rolls, for example, suggested that many recipients stay on the rolls for a decade or more, and that those who do not leave the rolls within two years are particularly slow to exit thereafter, further increasing concern over long-term dependency.[18] Research suggesting that children raised in single-parent families tended to fare worse scholastically and become less self-sufficient than those raised in two-parent families (even after controlling for known educational and class characteristics of their parents) further increased concern over issues of family structure and illegitimacy.[19] Perhaps most important, later evaluations of welfare-to-work experiments conducted by the states suggested that those programs had limited capacity to raise large numbers of people out of poverty, undercutting consensus on the work-training-services approach taken in the Family Support Act of 1988.[20]

Concern over programs for low-income families was further exacerbated by a more encompassing definition of welfare pressed by congressional Republicans and their allies in the conservative policy and advocacy communities. Traditionally "welfare" was identified with AFDC, and defenders of programs targeted at the poor were able to argue that AFDC constituted a tiny (never more than 2 percent) part of the federal budget. But in 1994, Robert Rector of the Heritage Foundation began arguing that the entire spectrum of federal means-tested programs—seventy-five or more, including the gigantic medicaid program, which gave most of its benefits to the elderly rather than families with children—should be counted as welfare. Taken together, he argued that these programs had spent more than $5.4 trillion (in 1993 dollars) over the past thirty years—and they represented an incredibly costly failure of the Great Society.[21] Leading Republican legislators quickly picked up this figure as stunning evidence of a welfare state monster that had spun out of control.

Social science research and the intellectual and political debates that surrounded that research were eroding the fragile consensus on work and training-based policies to assist low-income families. Moreover, political competition between President Clinton and the Republicans to appear tough on welfare and public hatred of the policy status quo helped to legitimize new approaches despite a paucity of evidence suggesting that they would work any better. Many conservatives, in particular, shifted away from work-based policies to deterrence approaches, expanding the policy agenda to include new, generally untested, policy initiatives. Murray, for example, proposed that single mothers be made ineligible for AFDC, food stamps, and public housing in order to weaken incentives for, and strengthen social stigma (and parental pressure) against, out-of-wedlock childbirth.[22] Murray's severe proposals won few adherents among moderate or liberal policymakers and policy experts, and most social conservatives focused on a combination of illegitimacy deterrents (such as family caps), hard time limits, and stiff work requirements. There is little question, however, that conservatives were intellectually on the offensive—and on the move toward more deterrence-oriented approaches—in the 1990s. This shift both moved the overall welfare debate to the right and widened the policy distance that needed to be crossed in any revision of policy toward low-income families.

Angry Voters

The public, too, was, expressing growing anxiety about the welfare system, although with some uncertainty about what to do about it. The rise in AFDC caseloads from 10.9 million children and parents in 1988 to 14.4 million persons in early 1994 after a period of substantial stability in the 1980s further undercut confidence that policymakers had a firm grip on the "welfare problem."[23] Public opinion on some issues was quite clear and consistent. There was widespread belief, for example, that the current welfare system fostered dependence on the part of recipients and needed a fundamental overhaul. There was also a growing consensus, consistent with the "new paternalism" paradigm, that recipients, even the mothers of very young children, should work in exchange for cash benefits. On other issues, responses frequently varied widely depending on whether the wording of questions elicited primarily sympathy for children or anger at the behavior of welfare parents.[24]

Overall, the evidence suggests four conclusions about the structure and impact of American public opinion in the most recent round of welfare reform. First, most Americans did not completely abandon their concern for poor children or complex views of the roots of poverty; these continued to exist (albeit uncomfortably) alongside their dislike for welfare programs and their perception that the behavior of many adult welfare recipients was irresponsible and unacceptable. But when conflicting beliefs coexist, which ones dominate depends heavily on whether or not they are "primed" by opinion leaders and the media.[25] Republican initiatives were aided substantially by the fact that powerful opinion leaders, Democratic as well as Republican, repeatedly primed concerns about welfare dependence. New conservative arguments that the welfare system actually hurt children more than it helped also stimulated broad public approval for Republican welfare initiatives.

Second, the eventual success of the Republican welfare initiative cannot be traced to a public consensus that Republicans in Congress would provide superior leadership to President Clinton on welfare. Indeed, public views on this question were quite volatile (figure 9-2). Clinton came into office with a huge lead over congressional Republicans in trust on the issue of welfare, but this lead evaporated during his first eighteen months in office. Similarly, the new Republican majority in the 104th Congress enjoyed a substantial advantage over the president in public trust when they took over, but this advantage had largely evaporated by the end of their first year in control. Poll data suggest the public has high hopes and demands for reform but is also quick to lose faith when politicians fail to deliver on welfare reform or propose a program that they believe has serious flaws.

Third, although there was a trend toward more conservative positions on several approaches toward welfare policymaking, there was by no

FIGURE 9-2. *Public Opinion about Whether President Clinton or Republicans in Congress Will Do a Better Job of Reforming Welfare*

Percent

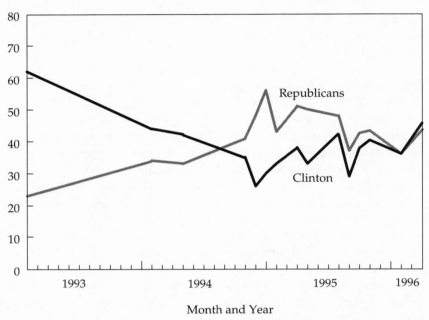

Month and Year

Sources: Data are derived from multiple polls using slightly different wordings, all variations on the question of whether the respondents thought President Clinton or the Republicans in Congress were doing a better job of dealing with reforming the welfare system. Where multiple polls were available for a single month, results of the polls were averaged. The polls are as follows: January 1993, Greenberg/Lake; January 1994, Blum and Weprin for NBC; April 1994, October 1994, and September 1995, *Los Angeles Times*; November 1994, January 1995, August 1995, September 1995, October 1995, and January 1996, Hart/Teeter for the *Wall Street Journal* and NBC; December 1994, two CBS/New York Times polls and a third poll by Princeton Survey Research Associates for *Newsweek*; January 1995, April 1995, and October 1995, CBS/*New York Times*; March 1995, July 1995, and September 1995, ABC/*Washington Post*; October 1995 *Washington Post*; September 1995, Princeton Survey Research Associates/Times Mirror; and March 1996, Gallup poll for the Cable News Network and *USA Today*. Details and exact wording of poll questions available from Roper Center.

means a public consensus on a specific package of changes. Indeed, the proposal by the Clinton administration was probably closer to that of the mythical "median voter" than the welfare provisions of the Contract with America. But that would prove be of little aid to Clinton and the

TABLE 9-1. *Public Support for Various Welfare Reform Packages*
Percent

Response	Replace welfare with tax credits and enhanced child support enforcement[a]	Clinton 1994 welfare package[b]	Swap federal support of medicaid for state control of welfare[c]	April 1995 House-passed welfare provisions[d]	Final welfare reform legislation[e]
Approve or favor	67	91	58	57	82
Disapprove or oppose	21	7	24	34	14
No difference (volunteered)	1				
Don't know, unsure, or refused	11	2	18	9	4

a. Tarrance Group and Mellman, Lazarus, and Lake poll for *U.S. News and World Report*, November 30, 1993.

b. The package was not identified as the Clinton administration's welfare reform package. It was described as requiring "all able-bodied welfare recipients, including women with preschool children, to go to school for two years to learn a skill while receiving benefits. After that, they would be required to either get a job or take a job the government would give them and their welfare benefits would be discontinued." *Los Angeles Times* poll, April 16–19, 1994.

c. Harvard/Kaiser poll, December 27–29, 1994.

d. The provisions were described as "reforming welfare to provide block grants to states that would end cash benefits after five years and stop cash benefits for all unmarried parents under age 18." Princeton Survey Research Associates poll for Times-Mirror, April 6–9, 1995.

e. The legislation was identified as a bill that had just passed and President Clinton had said he would sign. The description stated that the legislation "requires that welfare recipients work within two years of applying for benfits, it eliminates eligibility for most benefits for most legal immigrants until they become citizens, it requires able-bodied adults with no children to work 20 hours per week in order to be eligible for food stamps, and it imposes a five-year lifetime cap on welfare benefits whether or not a person can find a job." *Los Angeles Times* poll, August 3–6, 1995.

Democrats after they failed to move a welfare bill before the 1994 election. Public opinion polls throughout the Clinton-Gingrich round of welfare reform also showed that the public preferred almost *any* possible package of reforms over the status quo (table 9-1).

Finally, the extreme antipathy of the public toward the current AFDC program meant that agenda control would be a critical element of the welfare debate. Because the public demanded policy change, whoever could control the agenda in Congress would have an important advantage in getting reform enacted on their terms, since public pressure on the president to accept whatever Congress passed would be intense. In short, public opinion ultimately worked to the acceptance of the Republican welfare reform package in 1996 less because of public identification with Republican positions or deference to Republican leadership than because congressional Republicans' control of the agenda meant that Clinton would have to choose between approving a bill written largely on Republican terms or appearing to prefer the universally despised status quo.

A More Complex Interest Group Environment

An additional challenge to the status quo in policy toward low-income families was a change in the interest group environment for those policies. With the exception of a brief period in the late 1960s when the National Welfare Rights Organization was active, the major constituencies in welfare politics had long been Washington-based intergovernmental lobbies, notably the National Governors' Association, American Public Welfare Association, and National Conference of State Legislatures.[26] In the 1980s, intergovernmental groups had been joined by groups such as the Center on Budget and Policy Priorities, Center on Law and Social Policy, and Children's Defense Fund, which combined (in varying combinations) research and advocacy functions on behalf of the poor.[27] These groups relied primarily on their policy expertise and their ability to get favorable attention in the media to gain entree into the policymaking process, and they depended on foundations for their funding support. None of these groups had a mass political base, but they did have close links to many Democratic clienteles and legislators, making them difficult for politicians, especially Democratic ones, to ignore.

In the 1990s, a third set of groups—conservative "pro-family" organizations such as the Christian Coalition, Family Research Council, Eagle Forum, and Traditional Values Coalition—became engaged in the welfare issue.[28] These groups, several of which had links to leaders in the evangelical Christian community, were attracted to the welfare policy arena both because of their concern about the breakdown of two-parent families and because they wanted to develop appeals beyond traditional social conservative issues such as abortion and school prayer. Some of these organizations do have a mass political base and engage in such techniques of modern mass politics as the issuance of voter guides. The pro-family groups also benefited from the very effective leadership of Robert Rector, a policy analyst at the Heritage Foundation, who aided in building coalitions between groups, provided a steady stream of critiques of the current welfare system, and built links to junior Republican legislators who pressed for deterrence-oriented welfare reform within the Republican congressional caucuses.[29]

The social conservative groups had a very different diagnosis of the nature of the welfare problem than the liberal advocacy groups. They also had a different set of proposed solutions centered around reducing out-of-wedlock births and deterring long-term dependence.[30] In their effort to solidify support among these groups, Republicans in Congress would be pulled to the right by the new social conservative groups, just as liberal advocacy groups were pulling Democratic politicians to the left. Thus the prospects for finding a consensus solution to welfare reform were almost nonexistent; any move to find a middle ground would offend important constituencies.

Budgetary Stress

Pressures to reduce budget deficits, along with budget procedures adopted to meet that objective, shaped debates about policy toward low-income families in several critical ways in the 1990s.

First, political pressures and new statutory mechanisms to reduce budget deficits limited the resources available for any reform package (notably those employing the prevention or rehabilitation and new paternalism approaches) that was likely to cost more in the short term. New budget pressures and procedures also increased existing incentives to roll costly initiatives into huge multiprogram packages (most commonly, the budget reconciliation bill). Reconciliation could make change easier by weakening the multiple veto points in the federal legislative process and obfuscating direct trade-offs between individual spending and tax policies required by the Budget Enforcement Act. But because it increased the risk of overloading a single budget bill, reconciliation also made it more likely that the entire legislative program could collapse under the weight of the most unpopular parts of a package. Finally, reconciliation biased the potential for policy innovation toward initiatives (such as an expansion of the existing EITC) that could most plausibly be rolled into big budget reconciliation bills with limited debate, and away from initiatives (such as comprehensive AFDC overhaul) where legislators were likely to demand a separate debate.

The Clinton Administration and Family Policy

Policy for low-income families was an important political priority for the Clinton campaign and the new presidential administration. The administration's proposals combined elements from the incentives, prevention or rehabilitation, new paternalist, and devolution approaches. Borrowing from David Ellwood, the Clinton campaign endorsed a combination of EITC expansion, training, time limits on cash benefits, and jobs at the end of a specified period. Under the catchy slogans of "ending welfare as we know it" and "making work pay," welfare reform and EITC expansion became central planks of the presidential campaign.[31]

Family Policy and the New Democrats

This approach to the problems of low-income families offered some potentially important political advantages. A public philosophy that emphasized work and individual responsibility offered the opportunity to seize the moral high ground in the welfare debate, inoculate Democrats against charges that they coddle the (disproportionately minority) nonworking poor, and take away one of the race-tinged "wedge" issues that had long alienated blue- and white-collar constituencies from the Democratic party.[32] Moreover, pressing the ideals of "making work pay" and ensuring that people who "work hard and play by the rules should not be poor" resonated well with constituencies that had suffered declining or stagnant real income in recent years.

This approach fit well with other planks and themes of the Clinton platform. The need to implement universal health care as a way to address families' fear of losing health care if they moved from welfare to the low-wage labor market obviously reinforced the administration's call for health care reform. The notion of converting welfare offices from bureaucracy-laden payment and enforcement centers to entrepreneurially oriented employment and training centers fit well with the Clinton theme that government needed to be reinvented.

The Clinton administration's efforts to construct a new approach to poor families—and in particular, its campaign pledge to "end welfare as we know it"—also posed important risks, however. First and most important, it implicitly reinforced conservative critiques of AFDC—and the notion that nothing could be worse for poor children than the status quo. This ultimately would place the administration at a severe bargaining disadvantage with a Republican-controlled Congress. Having wholeheartedly condemned the status quo, Clinton would be in a very awkward position if he vetoed Republican-inspired welfare reform legislation. This was not a concern at the time that the pledge was made: candidate Clinton was at that time understandably concentrating on the grand strategic game of realigning the image of the Democratic party on welfare issues rather than legislative bargaining games to follow. Nor could he anticipate the Republican takeover in Congress that would take away his control of the welfare reform agenda and force him into a defensive posture on welfare issues.

A second risk was that the administration might not be able to keep its promises: transforming AFDC without simply cutting off recipients is a complex and very expensive process. But given its commitment to end the existing welfare system, the administration risked being politically hammered by the Republicans if it did not come up with a proposal that could plausibly be portrayed as doing so. Indeed, postelection research by the new administration's pollsters showed that welfare reform ranked third on the list of the administration's most important promises.[33]

Third, the administration's acceptance of time limits with a work requirement pushed Republicans in the direction of deterrence strategies (notably time limits with no work guarantee) in order to differentiate themselves from the Democrats as tougher on welfare. All of these processes threatened to push the welfare debate further to the right.

The new administration's policies toward low-income families also posed potential strains toward traditional Democratic constituencies, especially organized labor. Labor applauded the proposals to expand EITC and increase the minimum wage. But the proposal to dramatically increase the scope of public service "workfare" programs risked alienating public service employee unions, an important Democratic constituency that feared that their members would be replaced by workfare recipients.[34]

The prospect for using family policy to revitalize Democratic coalitions in Congress was also highly problematic. The potentially punitive aspects of the Clinton administration's welfare proposals were anathema to liberal Democrats in Congress and to the Congressional Black Caucus. But if congressional liberals did not support the administration's welfare initiatives, Clinton would have to rely on at least some Republican votes, and their asking price would likely be high. In short, welfare reform risked shattering rather than strengthening the Democratic coalition in Congress and in the electorate.[35]

Making Work Pay

The twin planks of expanding the EITC and increasing the minimum wage both aimed to fulfill the administration's campaign platform pledge to move families with one full-time worker out of poverty. But, faced with strong business opposition, the administration quickly dropped the minimum wage proposal (see chapter 7 by Margaret Weir in this volume).

The campaign pledge to raise the value of the EITC was more successful and became the administration's greatest achievement in antipoverty policy. In addition to the campaign commitment, EITC expansion was also needed to offset for low-income families the impact of increases in energy taxes that the administration included in the 1993 budget. And it enjoyed powerful allies in the liberal advocacy community.[36] The cost of an EITC expansion sufficient to move most families of four with a full-time minimum wage worker out of poverty was high: the administration's proposal to Congress was budgeted at $28.3 billion over five years. Passing such an expenditure increase independently would have been almost impossible: meeting the provisions of the Budget Enforcement Act would have required too many explicit cutbacks in other programs or increases in taxes. What made the Clinton administration's EITC initiative possible was its inclusion in the administration's big budget package, which involved huge offsetting revenue increases (especially on upper-income taxpayers). But because the package did contain so many unpopular measures, the relatively uncontroversial EITC measure was almost dragged down with the rest of the package. Ultimately, Congress raised EITC expenditures by $20.8 billion over five years, $7.5 billion less than the president had asked for. The credit was also phased in gradually over time, with full phase-in occurring in the presidential election year of 1996.

The Clinton Welfare Reform Initiative

The decision by the Clinton campaign to adopt a work-oriented welfare reform proposal forced a number of difficult and internally divisive choices on the new administration.[37] Conservatives and New Democrats within the Clinton administration pushed for time limits, both on cash benefits without a work requirement ("soft time limits") and on subsidized job slots ("hard time limits"). Liberals in Congress, upon whom the administration would depend to pass its welfare package, opposed both kinds of time limits, especially leaving recipients without either cash benefits or a job guarantee. Inability to reach a consensus on these issues contributed to the delay in unveiling of the administration's welfare reform package until mid-1994.[38] The Clinton administration ultimately rejected including hard time limits in its welfare reform proposal.

The debate over proposals to decrease out-of-wedlock births through teen mother exclusions and family caps was also highly contentious. Most liberals opposed both, but family caps were fairly popular with the public, and several states had applied for authority to implement family caps under waiver authority from the Department of Health and Human Services. The Clinton administration ultimately decided in its welfare reform plan to allow family caps as a state option (no longer requiring a waiver from the federal government).

The administration also confronted serious concerns that its proposal might lure more people onto the welfare rolls by offering training and child care assistance to recipients.[39] Early drafts of the Clinton plan proposed substantial spending on child care for the working poor to lessen AFDC's attractions for this group. Ultimately, the child care provisions of the bill had to be reduced to meet the limited financing available.

Interaction between the administration's health care and welfare initiatives complicated planning, budgeting, and scheduling for the latter. The administration hoped that health care reform would extend health insurance to the working poor, thus easing the way for AFDC recipients to leave welfare for low-paying jobs. This meant that the projected costs and caseload estimates for welfare reform would be lower (and thus easier to sell politically and to get through the budget scorekeeping process) after comprehensive health care reform passed Congress than before it passed. But the administration could reap these advantages only by delaying welfare reform until after health care reform passed—which it never did.[40] Moreover, delaying welfare reform risked antagonizing

Senator Daniel Patrick Moynihan, the new chair of the Senate Finance Committee, who had been the chief author of Nixon's family assistance plan and the chief architect of the 1988 Family Support Act. Early in 1994, for example, he argued that "We don't have a health crisis in this country. We do have a welfare crisis. And we can do both." Moynihan accused the administration of using welfare as "boob bait for Bubbas" and threatened obliquely to hold up health care reform if a welfare reform proposal was not forthcoming, but it was less clear what Moynihan wanted the bill to include.[41] Despite Moynihan's complaints, welfare was repeatedly put on the back burner to avoid interfering with the health reform initiative.

Probably the most critical obstacle to the administration's welfare proposal was finding financing for new spending on jobs, training, and child care, especially given the deficit-neutrality provisions of the Budget Enforcement Act. The administration was reluctant to propose tax increases, and congressional Republicans and conservative Democrats were vehemently opposed to them. No constituencies volunteered to have their taxes increased or benefits cut.[42] Thus cuts in other entitlement programs became the most likely source of funds for welfare reform. But which programs to cut? Social security? Programs for disabled veterans? Medicare? It did not take a lot of imagination for the Clinton administration's welfare policymakers to figure out the headlines—and the uproar from affected groups—if they appeared to be taking resources from one of these constituencies to give to welfare mothers. The central budgetary challenge, then, was to come up with entitlement programs to cut that were less popular than AFDC—and very few fit that description. Ultimately, the administration relied heavily on benefit cuts to unpopular and weak clienteles—immigrants and persons deemed disabled as a result of drug and alcohol abuse—to finance much of its welfare reform proposal.

The image the Clinton administration sought to convey to the public in its June 1994 reform proposal was that of an income transfer program being transformed into a work program. The reality of the Clinton administration's proposal was quite different, however. Many welfare mothers were not expected to work, either because they were caring for infants or because they were seriously disabled or caring for disabled children. An even bigger hurdle was money. Providing jobs, even low-skilled jobs, takes lots of it, for administration, transportation, and child care. Providing jobs to all AFDC parents could cost over $20 billion a year. Thus the Clinton plan called for a slow phase-in (beginning with younger mothers) and many exemptions. By 2000, parents in less than 10 percent of AFDC cases were projected to be at work in government-provided or -subsidized jobs.[43] Such a phase-in was both fiscally necessary and administratively prudent, but it did not constitute "ending welfare as we know it"—at least not in the short term. Republicans immediately denounced the plan as "weak on work."

President Clinton's welfare reform package also sparked enormous controversy among Democrats. Liberal Democrats and members of the Congressional Black Caucus opposed provisions they feared would deprive many families of cash benefits. Conservative Democrats did not like its slow phase-in of work requirements. The Hispanic Caucus objected to the cutbacks to immigrant benefits. Public sector unions worried that a large public jobs program would displace their workers, while conservatives feared that it could turn into another big public service employment program.

The administration's repeated delays in getting a package to Congress, and unclear signals about how quickly it wanted action once the package was released (caused in part by a desire to keep the decks clear for health care reform), meant that there were only a few months left between the June 1994 unveiling of the package and the November election. Nor was there a "must pass" legislative vehicle to which welfare reform could be attached to push it through Congress quickly.

By the late summer of 1994, congressional Republicans were anticipating substantial gains in the fall election, so they had no incentive to facilitate quick passage of welfare reform: delaying consideration of welfare until the next Congress would increase the prospects of getting a welfare reform package closer to the median preferences of Republican legislators. It would also deny the president a legislative victory and the political credit that would therefore accrue to him and would allow Republican candidates to continue to use the welfare issue that was working very well for them in the election campaign.[44] Welfare reform in the 103d Congress thus died not with a bang, but with a whimper: while the House Ways and Means Committee held hearings on the Clinton proposal in the summer of 1994, it never proceeded to mark up the bill, let alone report it to the full chamber.

Some critics have portrayed the Clinton administration's failure to move more swiftly to develop and pass a welfare reform package early in its first term as "the fundamental strategic mistake of the Clinton presidency. . . . If President Clinton had pushed for welfare reform rather than health care reform in 1994, we would now be talking about a great Democratic realignment, rather than a great Republican realignment."[45] But it seems clear in retrospect that the window of opportunity for welfare reform in the 103d Congress was extremely narrow, if it existed at all. It is doubtful that welfare reform could have gone before health care reform in 1993–94 because the Clinton administration needed comprehensive health care reform to keep the costs of welfare reform down to politically plausible levels. Moreover, a prolonged congressional debate in the 103d Congress would probably have fractured the Democratic party publicly, as it did less publicly in the formulation stage of the administration's proposal. Indeed, it is far from clear that the administration could have passed a welfare reform plan even if it had made doing so a top priority, just as it failed to pass a top-priority health care plan. If the administration had moved toward Republican positions on welfare reform, it is likely that Republicans would have pursued a policy of strategic disagreement, raising the policy ante high enough that the president would have alienated much of his core Democratic base in Congress, while the Republicans would have refused to accept anything that the president proposed.

Republicans and Low-Income Families

The Republican takeover of both houses of Congress in the 1994 election redefined the agenda for low-income families, the coalition of support that had to be built to enact a package, and the barriers to policy change. Republicans envisioned welfare reform that drew primarily on the new paternalist, deterrence, and devolution approaches rather than incentives and prevention or rehabilitation. Only by saving money on programs serving the poor, such as welfare and the EITC, would they be able to enact their ambitious plans for a balanced budget and a family tax credit primarily benefiting middle-income families.

Family Policy and the Contract with America

The Contract with America, the House Republicans' electoral manifesto in 1994 and their blueprint for action in the 104th Congress, sought to articulate both an overarching philosophy and a coherent and politically attractive set of programs consistent with that philosophy. Several themes were particularly important to policy toward low-income families: a smaller role for Washington, devolution of program authority to the states, a balanced budget, and an emphasis on strengthening traditional two-parent families. The contract's welfare provisions were intended to reduce spending levels in the short term and to ensure lower spending in the long term by putting a firm cap on spending for AFDC and a number of other means-tested programs rather than preserving them as an open-ended entitlement. In so doing, they contributed to the contract's extremely ambitious goals of simultaneously reducing taxes and balancing the budget.

The contract's welfare provisions also reflected an ideological commitment to shrink the welfare state and return power to states from Washington, which many Republican leaders saw as dominated by a coterie of liberal interest groups, bureaucrats, and legislators that sustained the welfare state.[46] The Republicans' effort to articulate an attractive and coherent public philosophy was not without tensions and contradictions, however. Perhaps the greatest conflict among Republicans involved the amount of flexibility to be given to states in reforming welfare. Some conservatives argued that getting Washington out of the welfare business and ending individual entitlement to benefits was the key reform. But many activists, notably Robert Rector of the Heritage Foundation, argued that it was irresponsible to give states money without mandating deterrence approaches—such as family caps, a ban on benefits to teenage mothers, and time limits—that states might not adopt on their own.[47]

Deterrence-oriented approaches to welfare reform offered a real opportunity for Republicans to solidify links with conservative pro-family groups, but also posed the risk that those groups could sink reform by blocking compromise. Moreover, because some deterrence measures (notably family caps and teen mother exclusions) were likely to encourage an increase in abortions, the Republican agenda risked splitting the "pro-life" constituency that was an increasingly important part of the party's political base.

While deterrence-oriented approaches to welfare reform energized a core group of Republican members of the House and Senate, especially among the newer and more conservative members, they also increased the probability of friction in the Senate—where Republicans had not signed on to the contract and the moderate wing of the Republican party was stronger—and with Republican governors. Devolution of policy-making authority offered an opportunity to gain support from governors for otherwise unpopular cutbacks in federal funds. But governors were likely to endorse such a trade-off only if it served their interests. Cutting back on AFDC and other grants to the states also raised the specter of formula fights over how to allocate the pain of cutbacks. Because these issues tend to divide congressional delegations on the basis of state population, wealth, and growth rates (all of which may enter into grant allocation formulas) rather than ideology, they posed special dangers for keeping the Republican coalition together.

Finally, the commitments made in the Contract with America to cut taxes through a family tax credit and to balance the budget complicated the process of building a financing package and finding an appropriate legislative vehicle for policy change. Indeed, these commitments would drive the Republicans to make cuts not just in AFDC but also in popular programs—like the EITC, medicare, and medicaid—that were not targeted for cuts in the Contract with America. This in turn led toward reliance on the budget package as a way to push through unpopular measures, which in turn increased the risk that the Republicans' entire legislative program could be dragged down by its least popular elements.

Republicans and Welfare Reform

Despite nearly universal support among Republicans for welfare reform, it took more than eighteen months to resolve internal substantive and strategic disputes within the party and maneuver President Clinton into signing a bill.

INITIAL BIDS. The initial Republican welfare reform initiatives of 1995 were contained in the proposed "Personal Responsibility Act," one of the ten pieces of legislation included in the Contract with America. The bill proposed capping the growth in AFDC and allowing states to convert their AFDC grants from the federal government into block grants with which they could design their own programs to serve low-income families with children.[48] In addition, the bill converted a number of nutrition programs, including food stamps, into a block grant that would no longer have entitlement status.

The proposed legislation would also have imposed new deterrence-oriented mandates on the states, however. In particular, it required states to exclude permanently from AFDC eligibility almost all children for whom paternity had not been established; all children born to mothers under age 18, unless the mother married someone who assumed legal responsibility for the child (states had the option of increasing this to mothers under age 21 at the time of birth); and children born to mothers who received AFDC at any time during that pregnancy.[49] The bill also set a five-year lifetime limit for all AFDC aid and allowed states to terminate aid for anyone who had received aid for as little as twenty-four months if that aid included at least twelve months under the work program. Abortion counseling was also forbidden. In addition, the bill required parents in single-parent AFDC families to work for at least thirty-five hours a week if they had been receiving assistance under the program for at least two years, and it limited nonwork assistance to a total of two years. States were required to meet an escalating set of work participation rates for their family assistance caseloads. Work requirements were likely to be particularly costly to the states because they entailed providing transportation, child care, and supervision; the bill committed the federal government to provide almost $10 billion in new funding to help finance the work program. Overall, the bill (excluding nutrition components) was estimated to produce net savings to the federal government of about $30 billion over five years, with more than half of those savings coming from denial of means-tested benefits to noncitizens who are legal residents of the United States.

If the Personal Responsibility Act's expenditure reductions reflected a desire to lessen Washington's role and produce savings for tax cuts and deficit reduction, the bill's efforts to reduce out-of-wedlock births reflected the growing importance among congressional Republicans and the Republican electoral coalition of conservative groups such as the Christian Coalition. In putting together the welfare provisions in the contract, the House Republican leadership generally sided with the social conservative groups, in part to compensate them for the omission from the Contract with America of high-priority issues—notably abortion and school prayer—that party leaders had decided were too divisive among Republican legislators and candidates.[50]

These conservative mandates pitted social conservatives against Republican governors, who favored block grants with as few strings attached as possible. As Republican Governor John Engler of Michigan put it, "Conservative micromanagement is just as bad as liberal micro-management."[51] Although the contract's welfare provisions eliminated many existing strings, in other ways it was close to the states' worst nightmare: it reduced and capped their AFDC funding, reduced state discretion with a number of new mandates including very tough (and costly) work requirements, and had the potential to transfer obligations to support legal immigrants from the federal government to the states.

Shortly after the 1994 election, the House Republican leadership and Republican governors began negotiations that resulted in a replacement welfare bill with more flexible work requirements, in exchange for which the governors agreed to a basic family assistance block grant with no increases in nominal funding levels—and thus a decline in real fund-ing—for five years. But congressional Democrats and the Clinton White House attacked efforts to reduce state work participation requirements and the absence of requirements that states maintain their own funding effort as evidence that the Republicans were "weak on work" and "tough on kids." Work requirements were stiffened again as the legislation moved through the House. The revised Personal Responsibility Act passed the House of Representatives on a largely party-line vote, re-flecting both extraordinarily effective Republican leadership and strong individual and collective incentives for House Republicans to hang together.

The most obvious collective incentive for Republican legislators in the House was the desire to show Republican unity, and in particular to demonstrate that the Republicans could govern effectively and end gridlock. In addition, there was a desire to avoid losing the welfare issue back to the Democrats. Clinton had used the issue of welfare re-form effectively in the 1992 election, but the House Republicans, with their very aggressive stance, had regained the initiative, and public confidence, in 1994.[52] And while there were deep substantive divisions among House Republicans on some elements of the Personal Respon-sibility Act, almost none of them wanted a stalemate, which would probably preserve the policy status quo. The timing of House consid-eration of welfare reform was also a help: because it came at the end of the first one hundred days of the 104th Congress, there was enormous pressure on exhausted Republican members to vote for the bill to "com-plete the Contract." Finally, the Republican leadership benefited from the fact that most Republican members—with a few exceptions, such as Cuban American representatives from Florida, whose constituents would be disproportionately affected by the immigrant provisions—did not have a strong constituency interest in resisting the cutbacks to means-tested programs.

House Republicans did not succeed in winning many Democrats over to their bill, however. Democrats were sharply divided, and the more liberal of two Democratic substitute bills that the Rules Committee allowed to come to a vote was overwhelmingly defeated. But Democrats united around a conservative Democratic alternative (sponsored by a soon-to-be Republican, Nathan Deal of Georgia) and stayed united in opposing final passage of the Republican bill.[53] Thus the House debate contained both good news and bad news for Republicans. The critical good news was that Clinton had backed the Deal bill although it contained hard time limits, something the administration had ultimately backed away from in its own welfare package the previous June. Thus the president had been nudged an important step to the right, giving the Republicans additional leverage to insist on hard time limits in a final welfare reform package. But on the negative side, the unity of the Democrats in the House suggested that it would probably be hard to gain Democratic support for a Republican bill in the Senate where, given the narrow margin of Republican control and the opportunities that the chamber's nonmajoritarian procedures provided for obstruction, help from some members of the minority party would be needed.

STOP AND GO IN THE SENATE. Indeed, the Republican welfare reform initiative did come close to collapsing in the Senate. In 1995, the institutional characteristics of the Senate that tend to enhance minority veto power were complicated further by presidential politics. Senate Majority Leader Robert Dole, the leading Republican contender, faced conflicting pressures. As the only presidential contender in a congressional leadership position, Dole needed to show that he was an effective leader in getting legislation passed—never an easy task in the fractious and individualistic Senate. To do so, Dole needed to solidify support among moderate Republicans and gain support from Republican governors. Dole's personal policy preferences also suggested attempting a bipartisan approach to welfare: in January, he criticized the evolving House Republican bill on welfare reform—and in particular its ban on cash benefits to young mothers—as overly radical.[54] But Dole faced competition in the Republican primaries from competitors placing themselves to his right—notably Senator Phil Gramm—and he was under pressure to move in that direction to appeal to conservative activists, who tend to vote disproportionately in Republican primaries.[55]

Senate floor consideration of welfare reform was delayed several times by disputes over illegitimacy reduction issues and a funding formula fight. But Dole eventually succeeded in smoking out the center of policy gravity in a series of votes, built a majority for a bill including work requirements and hard time limits, and co-opted the White House into the process of reform on largely Republican terms. When Clinton endorsed the Senate bill in principle in September 1995, most Senate Democrats jumped on the bandwagon. Dole then offered a package of amendments intended to solidify the support of a broad coalition of moderate Republicans and Democrats for his bill, including more money for child care and for states facing economic downturns. Conservative Republicans were outvoted, mustering only eleven votes in opposition to the package. They were joined by only one Democrat: Senator Moynihan, who, having decided that the bill would lead to a major increase in poverty and homelessness for children, refused to back amendments that would increase its prospects for passage. In the subsequent vote on final Senate passage of the revised Dole bill, it was liberal Democrats who were isolated on the losing end of an 87–12 vote.[56]

The passage of the Senate welfare reform bill with a quasi-endorsement from the president and the support of an overwhelming majority of Democratic senators is perhaps the most important single event in the history of the legislation; it fundamentally altered the nature of later bargaining over welfare reform. Having already endorsed the Senate bill, Clinton could not later refuse to back a bill with similar provisions without being vulnerable to Republican charges that he was not really interested in reforming welfare. The majority of Senate Democrats who had voted for the legislation (and who did not in any case want to take a position to the left of the president) were in the same boat: they would also have problems backing away from the Senate legislation.

Republicans gained critically on both individual components of welfare reform and in more general bargaining leverage. Since the president and most Democratic senators had already conceded an end to individual entitlement and the imposition of hard time limits in signing on to the Senate welfare reform bill, there was no reason for Republicans to make concessions on those issues in future negotiations. Passage of the Senate bill allowed Republicans to try to push welfare reform further to the right while setting a default position to which Republicans could return at any time if negotiations with the administration broke down. Thus from September 1995 on, the critical questions in welfare reform negotiations would not be whether an agreement on legislation was possible, but rather how much further the administration could be pushed to the right, whether Republicans could reach an agreement among themselves on a welfare reform package near or somewhat to the right of the Senate bill, and whether Republicans would put a higher priority on passing legislation (while sharing some of the credit with the president) or on having an election issue—Clinton's unwillingness to agree on welfare reform legislation—with which they could bash the president.

ENDGAMES. Moving from Senate passage of welfare reform legislation to a presidential signature took almost a full year and several additional rounds of negotiations between Congress, the president, and governors. Just reconciling the House and Senate versions of the welfare reform bill took more than three months, with much of the delay concerning not AFDC but rather a dispute about whether the school lunch program should be turned over to the states in a block grant. The conference agreement was sent to President Clinton in December for his signature as part of a congressionally passed reconciliation bill that included unpopular cuts in the medicare and medicaid programs, and the president vetoed it.[57] Congress then sent a separate welfare package to the president without the health care cuts. But the bill still contained controversial cuts and structural changes in the food stamp and school lunch programs and immigrant benefits, and the president focused on those provisions in vetoing welfare reform again, arguing that the welfare bill "was designed to meet an arbitrary budget target rather than to achieve serious reform."[58]

As a result of these vetoes and the failure of budget negotiations between the president and Republican congressional leaders, the Republican deficit reduction and devolution agendas both appeared to be in shambles in the first half of 1996. A package of reforms assembled by the National Governors' Association combining devolution, flexibility, and increased funding helped to jump-start interest in welfare reform but failed to unite the disparate interests at stake.[59] Particularly problematic was Republican governors' insistence on linking welfare reform with medicaid reforms—a much bigger item in state budgets, where they hoped for substantial savings and flexibility. The White House repeatedly insisted that Republican medicaid cuts were unacceptable, and the president dared Republicans to send him a separate welfare bill stripped of medicaid provisions.

The stalemate presented Republicans in the Dole presidential campaign and on Capitol Hill with the classic strategic question of whether it was better to have a bill or an issue.[60] Some Republicans, such as Ways and Means subcommittee chair Clay Shaw of Florida, wanted to get a welfare reform bill through that would make it into law. Others wanted to keep sending the president welfare bills that he was likely to veto in order to be able to paint him as hypocritical in his pledge to reform welfare. Still others wanted to do nothing, arguing that two vetoes were enough to run against the president and fearing that if the Republican Congress sent him a bill that was even partially acceptable, he would sign it and get most of the public credit for "ending welfare as we know it."[61] But doing nothing also had problems so long as Dole remained in the Senate (he resigned in mid-May), for the president could blame Dole for not moving a welfare bill.

Congressional Democrats also faced a political dilemma that revolved around avoiding blame. Liberal Democrats were certain to oppose any bill the Republicans might bring forward, and some conservatives were almost equally certain to support such a bill. Many moderate Democrats were on the fence, however: they had deep reservations about elements in the Republican bill, but they did not want to end up on the wrong side of a popular legislative initiative. The NGA's bipartisan endorsement of a welfare reform package made resistance to welfare reform even more difficult.

From Democratic legislators' perspective, the worst-case scenario would be to vote against a Republican welfare bill that passed anyway and was then signed by the president: to do so would play right into the hands of Republican accusations that they were too liberal in the upcoming elections.[62] In deciding how hard to resist Republican welfare reform initiatives, they were constantly looking over their shoulders for assurances that the president would provide them with political protection. What they saw was not very reassuring. The president's chief political advisor, Dick Morris, was pushing a "triangulation" strategy in which the president positioned himself ideologically between congressional Republicans and Democrats: he confronted the Republican majority on issues where the Democratic position had broad popular support (such as opposition to cuts in medicare and medicaid) and worked with the Republicans on issues where their positions were more popular (like balancing the budget).[63] The unpopularity of AFDC made it a poor candidate for presidential confrontation. And the president was likely to veto a congressional welfare reform bill only if it had encountered solid Democratic opposition in Congress, which his own unclear signals were making much less likely.[64] Indeed, Clinton put himself further into a strategic box during this period with repeated requests that the Republicans send him a "clean" (that is, without medicaid provisions) bill. These requests were intended to reinforce the president's credentials as a welfare reformer and also lower the chance that the Republicans (who feared Clinton's ability to claim credit for welfare reform) would actually send forward a bill. But these presidential pleas also undercut his leverage to veto such a bill if he got one.

As Republicans blasted presidential obstructionism on welfare, President Clinton used several strategies to inoculate himself against those charges. He signed executive orders forcing states to implement tougher rules on keeping teenage mothers in school and requiring AFDC mothers' cooperation in locating their children's fathers.[65] He also trumpeted his record in granting state waivers and promising to "end welfare one state at a time" through waivers if the Republicans failed to pass acceptable legislation.[66]

House and Senate Republicans introduced their revised welfare proposals in May 1996 as Republican bills including medicaid cuts, rather than bipartisan bills.[67] The prospects for welfare reform remained uncertain as the Republicans moved their bills through committees on largely party-line votes, because the Republicans could drop the contentious medicaid provisions at any time if they decided that they wanted to have a statute rather than an issue. Republicans also had bargaining leverage if they decided to move a separate welfare bill quickly: by designating the welfare reform bill as a deficit-reducing reconciliation bill, they reduced the prospects that it could be subject to procedural delays, multiple amendments, and even filibuster in the Senate.

As long as welfare reform and medicaid reform were linked, however, the stalemate between the Republican Congress and President Clinton was unlikely to be broken. But a changing mood among Republican members in the House eroded their commitment to this linkage. Polls in the early summer of 1996 showed that the Republicans might lose control of Congress in the upcoming election.[68] These polls served as a dual wake-up call to House Republicans. First, if members hoped to get reelected, they should enact welfare reform so that they would not be vulnerable to Democratic charges that their revolutionary fervor had resulted in little legislation.[69] Enacting welfare reform would show that they had accomplished something in the 104th Congress, even if it meant sharing the credit with Clinton. Second, if they might lose control of Congress in the fall, they should act quickly to reform welfare on Republican terms.[70]

On July 11, Republican leaders in Congress announced that they were de-linking medicaid and welfare reform. Sending the president a separate welfare reform bill, Republicans hoped, would force him either to veto it, dividing the Democratic party on the eve of his renominating convention, or reveal his promise to "end welfare as we know it" as hypocrisy.[71] The president tried to improve his bargaining position by demanding additional changes in the bill, but administration officials also undercut their ability to get more changes by avoiding direct veto threats and sending signals that he would sign whatever the Republicans sent.[72] Despite White House urging that House Democrats vote against the bill to give them additional leverage in conference negotiations, the bill passed the House with almost solid Republican support and thirty Democrats defecting to back the bill.[73] Five days after House action, the Senate approved a slightly softer bill with nearly solid Republican support and half the Democratic senators voting in favor. While the White House called for additional concessions in conference committee, it did not say that it would veto if they were not made.[74]

Conferees moved quickly, seeking to head off pressure from liberal advocacy groups and to force the president to declare before the Democratic convention whether he would sign a final welfare bill. In their accord, conferees moved toward Senate positions on a number of provisions but did not go as far as the president had requested. Congressional Democrats sought a strong signal from the president about his intentions. In the words of Representative Robert Matsui, Democrat of California, "Most members would like to know what he is going to do. If the President supports it, they will support it. . . . A lot of members just don't want to be to be to the left of the President on welfare."[75] The morning of the scheduled House vote, the president held a long meeting with his top policy and political advisors, in which most of his policy advisors urged a veto and Vice President Al Gore urged that he sign it.[76] The president then simultaneously announced that he would sign the bill and work for revisions (mostly in non-AFDC provisions) in the next Congress. Both chambers quickly passed the welfare bill by large margins, with Democrats strongly split.[77]

A NEW WELFARE LAW. The legislation signed by the president, the Personal Responsibility and Work Opportunity Reconciliation Act (PRWORA) of 1996, was expected to save about $54 billion overall through fiscal year 2002.[78] The family assistance and child care provisions taken together did not save money over current law in that period. In fact, the Congressional Budget Office estimated that they would result in a net increase in outlays of about $3.8 billion over the period from 1997 through 2002, largely because of increased funding for child care. The big savings were in reduction of benefits to legal immigrants and other changes in the food stamp and SSI programs, including stricter definitions of disability for children receiving SSI benefits.

The changes to family assistance programs were nonetheless dramatic.[79] The AFDC program was abolished, replaced by a block grant to the states called temporary assistance to needy families (TANF). Individual entitlement to family assistance benefits was ended. TANF funds are an essentially fixed sum in nominal terms, based on the total amount currently spent by the federal government on AFDC, the job opportunities and basic skills (JOBS) program, and AFDC administration. Thus TANF funds will decline in real terms over time; in the near term, however, many states receive more funds from TANF than they would have under the old AFDC program, because AFDC caseloads are currently falling. Individual states' shares of the block grant are based on their historical allocations of AFDC funds. There are limited contingency funds for periods of recession. States are required to maintain 80 percent of their own current spending to draw down their full share of block grant funds (states that meet work requirements need maintain only 75 percent).

Proponents of deterrence approaches enjoyed mixed success, winning on hard time limits but doing less well on illegitimacy mandates. The statute puts a five-year time limit on adults' receipt of cash assistance using TANF funds (states can set lower limits if they chose). Nor can TANF funds be used for vouchers for those who have exhausted the time limit. States can, however, exempt up to 20 percent of their caseload from time limits. Teenage parents were required to live with parents or in an adult-supervised setting, a provision that the Clinton administration had also endorsed. No requirement for family cap or teenage mother exclusions was included, but states can impose those restrictions themselves if they so choose. To placate social conservatives for the loss of illegitimacy mandates, the bill provides competitive bonuses of up to $20 million a year for as many as five states if they are successful in reducing illegitimacy.

Competition between congressional Republicans and the Clinton administration to appear "tough on work" led to strict, escalating work requirements for recipients, with rising penalties for states that do not meet the requirements but significant discretion for the federal Department of Health and Human Services on whether to impose those penalties. By 2002, states will be required to have 50 percent of their caseloads in work activities. The act provides additional funding for child care but no entitlement to that care. Families with children under age 6 are protected from a benefit cutoff if they cannot find child care.

REPRISE. The months after passage of PRWORA saw further maneuvering and posturing on welfare reform. In the 1996 presidential election, Clinton tried for the political equivalent of having his cake and eating it, too: he simultaneously appealed to conservative and moderate voters by claiming credit for "ending welfare as we know it" while arguing to liberals that if reelected, he would "fix" a flawed welfare law. The president's priorities focused more on immigrant and food stamp provisions of PRWORA than on the new TANF program, however, and they explicitly did *not* include trying to restore individual entitlement to AFDC, now recognized by all sides as a lost cause. Republican leaders in Congress, meanwhile, vowed to block substantial changes in the new law until it had been given a chance to work.[80] Congressional Democrats, still fearing the appearance of being to the left of the president on welfare issues and well aware that the prospects for a rollback of the statutory transformation of AFDC were a political nonstarter, were content to let the president take the lead on welfare. Republican governors pressed for easing of PRWORA's immigrant provisions, which they feared would leave them to pick up the tab in caring for those groups. But, under pressure from Republican leaders in Congress who feared erosion of PRWORA budget savings and the creation of an opening for Democratic pressure to reverse many PRWORA statutory changes, Republican governors also insisted that they did not want a major reopening of debate on the TANF provisions of welfare reform.[81]

The prospects that Clinton would be able to make major changes in the TANF provisions of the 1996 welfare reform law were further limited when Republicans retained control of both chambers of Congress in the 1996 election. In this situation, the president's only vehicle to force the Republican Congress to act on welfare legislation was the balanced budget bill under negotiation between the White House and congressional leaders through the first seven months of 1997. These negotiations naturally focused on spending provisions rather than the statutory changes (loss of entitlement, time limits, work requirements) that were at the heart of PRWORA's provisions affecting low-income families. Short-term pressures for changing PRWORA were also minimized by the slow phase-in of PRWORA's work requirements and hard time limits and by the relatively flush financial condition of the states (caused by a combination of falling TANF caseloads, a fixed TANF block grant that provided most states with more funds than they would have under the old caseload-sensitive AFDC law, and added child care funding).

The Balanced Budget Act of 1997 made a number of changes in the 1996 welfare reform statute. It provided substantial additional funding for immigrant benefits and a bit more for food stamps. The provisions regarding low-income families changed only modestly. The states received additional federal funds ($3 billion over two years) for welfare-to-work activities, but the new grants would "sunset" at that time. At the urging of the Clinton administration, a temporary tax credit was provided to employers who hired long-term welfare recipients, despite evidence that similar programs in the past had proven ineffective in increasing employment among those recipients.[82] The balanced budget act also reaffirmed earlier Department of Labor regulations requiring states to meet federal minimum wage law requirements in workfare assignments—a requirement that had been strongly advocated by public sector unions and vehemently opposed by many governors and congressional Republicans.[83] At the same time, however, the act stipulated that workfare "earnings" would not count for receiving the EITC, making private sector earnings relatively more attractive to welfare recipients as an income source than workfare. The new act also lessened HHS's discretion to exempt states from penalties for failing to have a required share of their caseload in work activities.

The Family Tax Credit and the EITC

Besides welfare reform, the second major component of the Contract with America affecting low-income families concerned transfers through the tax code. By 1995, the bipartisan consensus in favor of the EITC had weakened. Congressional Republicans proposed significant cutbacks in the EITC as part of their 1995 budget package, including elimination of the credit for families without children and freezing of the phaseout points and maximum credit.

The political vulnerability of the EITC was in some ways the direct result of the program's prior political success. As a result of the 1993 expansion, the EITC became much bigger and a much more visible target. EITC expenditures (including the outlay equivalent of forgone revenue) totaled more than $24.8 billion in fiscal year 1996, almost double what the federal government would spend on AFDC benefits—and the gap would grow wider over the next four years.[84]

The coming of a Republican congressional majority in 1995 changed EITC policymaking in several additional ways. Probably the most important were several promises contained in the House Republicans' Contract with America: pledges to balance the budget, reduce taxes, and enact a $500 per child nonrefundable tax credit for families earning less than $200,000. The first of these pledges meant that there would be intense pressures for expenditure reductions to meet the balanced budget target. The latter two added to those pressures by further reducing government revenues; the family tax credit alone would cost an estimated $105 billion over five years.[85] And the EITC was, due to the liberalizations of 1986, 1990 and 1993 (especially the latter) the fastest growing of the welfare cash programs, making it a particularly visible target for conservative critics.

Rapid expenditure growth alone might not have been sufficient to call into question support for the EITC had it not been accompanied by credible critiques of the deservingness of some program clientele and of perverse incentives in the program.[86] The 1993 expansion exacerbated a number of problems already latent in the program, notably weak targeting on the poor (by increasing the maximum income at which benefits were received) and work disincentives (by increasing the phaseout rate from a maximum of 13.14 percent in 1992 to more than 20 percent in 1996). There was a cascade of criticism on many (and often inconsistent) grounds, especially after the 1993 expansion. The Internal Revenue Service and General Accounting Office both issued studies noting widespread claiming of the EITC by ineligible families, and the IRS uncovered a number of organized EITC fraud rings.[87] Republicans also questioned the 1993 provision extending the EITC to childless families. Congressional Republicans gave prominent play to an economist's estimate that high marginal tax rates in the phaseout range of the EITC meant that the EITC probably lowered not only work effort but total disposable income for workers in that range.[88] At the same time, however, many Republicans criticized the fact that large numbers of people well above the poverty line were eligible for the credit—a policy that could be changed only by lowering the amount of the credit or by increasing marginal tax rates in the phaseout range even further. President Clinton gave strong support to the EITC, however, suggesting that he might veto any bill that contained cutbacks.[89]

Of course, Republican proposals also faced issues of targeting, notably on the family tax credit proposal for a nonrefundable tax credit of $500 per dependent child. The family tax credit was strongly backed by the Christian Coalition and other social conservative groups viewed by congressional Republicans as key elements of their coalition.[90] Democrats criticized the family tax credit for giving benefits to the wealthy while excluding "10 million working American families with nearly 24 million children."[91] Cognizant of the deficit-increasing potential of the family tax credit, and wanting, in the words of Representative Henry Hyde, Republican of Illinois, "something that defangs Democrats' charges that we are the party of the rich," 102 House Republicans signed a letter to the Rules Committee as it was considering the GOP tax package in March 1995, asking the committee to permit a vote on an amendment limiting the tax credit to families earning less than $95,000 a year.[92] However, other House Republicans and social conservative groups adamantly opposed the amendment, and the Rules Committee refused to allow consideration of it.[93]

The family tax credit faced more opposition in the Senate, where more Republicans put a higher priority on deficit reduction than tax cuts. But under pressure from House Republicans and presidential aspirant Phil Gramm, the Senate Finance Committee agreed in October to a tax cut package including the family tax credit, although with lower phaseout levels than in the House bill.[94] The conference agreement generally followed the Senate bill. It added a special political twist, however. The timing of the credit was moved up to allow a partial credit for 1995, with the IRS directed to notify taxpayers in a special mailing that Congress had enacted a new credit. The IRS was also directed to calculate the 1995 refund separately from 1996 returns and mail out the checks less than a month before the 1996 election—a clear symbol of the dividend to middle-class families provided by a Republican Congress.[95] Once again, however, procedural factors proved to be critical: Republican efforts to cut the EITC and enact a broad nonrefundable family tax credit fell victim to their inclusion in the overburdened budget reconciliation bill vetoed by President Clinton in December 1995. When congressional Republicans decided not to proceed with a massive tax cut bill in 1996, the family tax credit and EITC cuts died as well.

Republicans gained another opportunity to make changes in tax provisions for families in 1997 budget negotiations. A substantial nonrefundable family tax credit was one of the primary objectives of congressional Republicans in the negotiations, reflecting strong pressure from social conservative groups. President Clinton, while agreeing to a family tax credit, sought to lower the income level at which the credit would begin to phase out. He also wanted to provide benefits to some families whose income was too low to qualify for a nonrefundable credit.

The budget agreement-in-principle reached between the White House and congressional leaders on May 2 set an overall tax cut target of $135 billion over five years (to be partially offset by closing of loopholes). This agreement in turn helped to prevent a bidding war over the child tax credit; instead negotiations over tax cuts turned into a fixed-sum game among proponents of the child tax credit, tax cuts for educational purposes, business interests, and lower estate taxes, each of which sought to increase their share of the tax cut. Child tax credit provisions were one of the last elements of the final budget package to be resolved. In the end, both sides got much of what they wanted: Republicans won a permanent child tax credit with high income phaseouts ($110,00 for a two-parent family) that was estimated to cost $85.3 billion between 1997 and 2002, while the president won partial refundability for large low-income families.[96] The EITC once more emerged almost unscathed from budget-cutters' scalpels, reflecting the Clinton administration's refusal to accept substantial cuts in that program.[97]

Implementing Welfare Reform in the States

While policy toward low-income families was being debated and eventually radically altered at the federal level, a parallel process was occurring in many states.[98] Changes at the state level were being driven by many of the same forces influencing policy change in Washington, including rising caseloads, budgetary pressures, increasing public hostility, and partisan competition. But the national and state-level processes were not just parallel: they were also deeply intertwined with each other.

The federal Family Support Act of 1988 made it easier for state governments to obtain waivers to requirements of the AFDC program; the Bush and Clinton administrations both encouraged state experimentation through the waiver process; and the political dynamics of the 104th Congress encouraged states to seek maximum discretion and weakened the Clinton administration's ability to veto state initiatives.

Early state experiments in welfare reform did not follow a single approach. Indeed, many of them were explicitly designed as packages that combined elements of several approaches in order to attract a broader range of political support. The 1992 New Jersey legislation, for example, combined earnings disregards and transitional medicaid assistance for those who left welfare for work (the incentives approach) with family caps (deterrence) and increased funding for training programs (rehabilitation).[99] Wisconsin's many welfare waiver requests included earnings disregards, medicaid extensions for families leaving the rolls, sanctions for teenage parents who do not stay in school, and a two-county demonstration of hard time limits.

Once the welfare reform bandwagon began to roll, many other states jumped on. But the process was not one of state emulation of successful innovations, as long described by political scientists.[100] Instead, it was a politically driven process in which states often adopted innovations before their efficacy had been carefully evaluated. Politicians quickly absorbed lessons about the politics of welfare reform without formal evaluations. As one astute observer put it, "No state wants to be left behind in the welfare reform sweepstakes. No governor wants to be perceived as doing nothing. Neither political party wants to be perceived as soft on welfare."[101]

The future direction of state initiatives in welfare reform is decidedly murky now that the 1996 welfare reform law has given states substantially more leeway in designing some aspects of their family assistance programs while also mandating some major constraints on state choice, notably hard limits and stiffened work requirements. Most states moved quickly to maximize their dollars received by switching to block grants rather than wait until July 1997 to move over from the existing AFDC system, even though this meant triggering individual recipients' time limits for work requirements and hard time limits earlier than would otherwise have been the case. Given the confusion over policy and administrative requirements, maximizing the inflow of federal dollars was a simple decision rule to follow in both budgetary and political terms.[102]

There are major differences across states in the resources available to move poor families from welfare to work, resulting both from basing the TANF funding allocation on historical funding levels and from differences across states in the recent falloff in welfare caseloads. Texas and Mississippi, for example, received less than $2,500 per TANF family in federal TANF funds for fiscal 1997, while Michigan and Connecticut got about twice as much per family.[103] States with higher funding levels will have far more capacity to provide expensive services like child care than poor states and thus may be less tempted to simply cut recipients off.[104] Slower welfare caseload declines in inner cities have also led to major differences in resources available across counties *within* states; Milwaukee County, for example, has only about one-half of the statewide average funding per recipient in its Wisconsin Works program.[105] And in some states, legislatures have given increased responsibility (backed by incentives and penalties) to county governments to design their own programs—a move that detractors fear will intensify a "race to the bottom" as county governments try to make their programs less attractive than those of their neighbors.[106]

In the short term, no states have chosen radical paths of reform (such as doing away with cash benefits entirely). However, several states have chosen to impose stricter hard time limits than the federal maximum of five years, and California immediately announced its intention to cut benefit levels—a step that the Clinton administration had not previously allowed it to take.[107] Most state welfare offices appear to be sending clearer messages to adult recipients that they are expected to begin work immediately rather than undergoing additional training or basic education first. And many states have become more flexible in what they are willing to pay for—for example, car repairs and work clothes to allow recipients to work and even assistance to allow recipients to move from job-poor rural areas to places where jobs are more plentiful.[108]

Other aspects of state policy are still in flux. PRWORA provisions enabling states to pay new migrants the benefit level in their prior state of residence for up to a year have been challenged in the courts, and it will be some time before these cases are fully resolved.[109] Also unclear is the extent to which states will take advantage of ambiguities and loopholes in the law to soften some features of PRWORA—for example, allowing a greater share of their caseloads to avoid the five-year time limit for benefit cutoffs or lessening the probability that states will incur sanctions for failing to meet work requirements.[110]

Politically, the first year of PRWORA was a great success. The availability of TANF caseload data and the desire of federal and state politicians to use caseload declines as an indicator of the effectiveness of their policies have made caseloads the dominant focus of recent evaluations of welfare reform implementation. And there is no question that welfare rolls are down dramatically. AFDC rolls peaked at 14,225,591 in 1994; by July 1997 they had fallen to 10,258,000, a decline of more than one quarter and below the number of recipients before AFDC recipiency began its rapid rise in 1989.[111]

While federal and state politicians rushed to claim credit for the decreases in caseloads, experts have been far more cautious in interpreting those declines. Clearly economic expansion and low unemployment rates have been very helpful.[112] Work requirements have reduced welfare rolls both by accelerating exits and reducing takeup: they have "smoked out" some recipients who were already working but not reporting their income, while in other cases recipients who would otherwise have gone onto welfare rolls have been "diverted" into the regular work force without going onto welfare.[113] Most experts believe, however, that the caseload declines have disproportionately drawn off the relatively "easy" cases in which parents have higher skills and fewer drug, alcohol, or psychological problems that make it difficult for them to get and keep jobs. There is no consensus yet as to what percentage of those remaining on the welfare rolls are unlikely to become self-sufficient. Nor is there clear evidence on the extent to which former welfare recipients have simply displaced other workers, often at a significantly lower wage rate.[114] Also lacking is information on people who have left the welfare rolls ; indeed, most states do not have the capacity to effectively trace such families, even to find out if they have remained employed.[115]

The choices made by individuals in this new environment, and their long-term effects on child welfare and dependency, are unlikely to become clear for some time. Even in an optimistic scenario, however, it is difficult to imagine that the prospects for most poor children will be significantly improved. The low level of education and skills of most low-income mothers (and fathers) suggests that even if welfare dependency is significantly reduced, economic insecurity and poverty among low-income families are likely to grow.[116]

What will happen when the nation's economy enters a downturn remains the most critical unknown about welfare reform. At present, low unemployment and a growing economy make the states' task easier in a self-reinforcing "virtuous cycle": jobs for low-skilled workers are relatively plentiful; caseload declines combined with fixed TANF federal funding make it easier for states to spend more per recipient on transportation, child care, employment subsidies, training, and the intensive and directive case management needed to move welfare recipients into work and keep them there through the repeated crises in transportation, health, and child care that characterize their lives; and overall economic growth lessens fiscal pressure on states to reduce spending on the poor. When a recession hits, however, all elements of the cycle turn vicious, posing tougher choices for government and recipients. Problems of placing and maintaining low-skilled employees in jobs will grow. States will also be fiscally stressed and reluctant to spend money on poor families, especially since increased state effort will no longer attract matching funds from the federal government. Washington could bail the states out when this situation arises: indeed, at the time that welfare reform was being debated, proponents of reform argued that if more money was required later, Washington would likely supply it. But this was before passage of the 1997 balanced budget law, which firmly committed the Clinton administration as well as congressional Republicans to reaching and maintaining a balanced budget. It seems questionable at best that substantial new funding would be forthcoming from the federal government in this new fiscal environment.[117]

The other major unknown is whether adequate information to evaluate the implementation of welfare reform will be available in the future. The recent history of state-level welfare reform initiatives suggests that what is likely to be most important for state politicians is not whether a welfare reform initiative is well designed and well implemented, but whether government appears to be doing something about "the welfare mess."[118] They will have few incentives to conduct careful evaluations that might show their innovations failed. In this political environment, the most likely outcome is less likely to be an immediate and highly visible "race to the bottom" than a steady but much less visible erosion of programs, with programs being revised to fit budgetary targets and observers lacking sufficient information to evaluate carefully either the magnitude of the changes or their effects on poor children and their parents.[119]

Notes

1. Child poverty rates for households with a male parent present in 1992 were 10.4 and 19.4 percent for whites and blacks, respectively, while white and black female-headed households had poverty rates of 45.3 and 67.1 percent. *Overview*

of Entitlement Programs: Background Material and Data on Programs within the Jurisdiction of the Committee on Ways and Means, Committee Print, 103 Cong. 2 sess. (Government Printing Office, 1994), p. 1150. (Hereafter *1994 Green Book.*)

2. In 1983, parents of 44.3 percent of children receiving AFDC had no marriage tie. By 1994, this had grown to 55.7 percent. *Overview of Entitlement Programs: Background Material and Data on Programs within the Jurisdiction of the Committee on Ways and Means,* Committee Print, 104 Cong. 2 sess. (GPO, 1996), pp. 473–74. (Hereafter *1996 Green Book.*)

3. In 1992, 37.2 percent of AFDC parents were African Americans, about three times their share of the overall population. *1994 Green Book,* p. 402.

4. For a recent review, see Martin Gilens, "'Race Coding' and White Opposition to Welfare," *American Political Science Review,* vol. 90 (September 1996), pp. 593–604; and Gilens, "Racial Attitudes and Opposition to Welfare," *Journal of Politics,* vol. 57 (November 1995), pp. 994–1014. See also Paul M. Sniderman and Thomas Piazza, *The Scar of Race* (Harvard University Press, 1993). On the role of race in antipoverty programs generally, see Jill Quadagno, *The Color of Welfare: How Racism Undermined the War on Poverty* (Oxford University Press, 1994).

5. On the fate of President Nixon's reforms, see Henry J. Aaron, *Why Is Welfare So Hard to Reform?* (Brookings, 1973); and Daniel Patrick Moynihan, *The Politics of a Guaranteed Income: The Nixon Administration and the Family Assistance Plan* (Vintage Books, 1973). On the Carter initiative, see Laurence E. Lynn Jr. and David F. Whitman, *The President as Policymaker: Jimmy Carter and Welfare Reform* (Temple University Press, 1981). On Reagan's reforms, see Edward D. Berkowitz, "Changing the Meaning of Welfare Reform," in John C. Weicher, ed., *Maintaining the Safety Net: Income Redistribution Programs in the Reagan Administration* (Washington: American Enterprise Institute, 1984), pp. 23–42. The Family Support Act of 1988 made a strong rhetorical commitment to improving education, training, transitions to work, and child support enforcement and required the states to meet work participation requirements, but it provided very little in the way of new funding. See Lawrence Mead, *The New Politics of Poverty: The Nonworking Poor in America* (Basic Books, 1992), pp. 198–209; as well as Erica B. Baum, "When the Witch Doctors Agree: The Family Support Act and Social Science Research," and Ron Haskins, "Congress Writes a Law: Research and Welfare Reform," *Journal of Policy Analysis and Management,* vol. 10 (Fall 1991), pp. 603–15, 616–32.

6. See Christopher Howard, "Happy Returns: How the Working Poor Got Tax Relief," *American Prospect,* no. 17 (Spring 1994), pp. 46–53.

7. On the origins of SSI, see Martha Derthick, *Agency under Stress: The Social Security Administration in American Government* (Brookings, 1990); and Bob Woodward and Benjamin Weiser, "Costs Soar for Children's Disability Program," *Washington Post,* February 4, 1994, p. A1.

8. *Sullivan* v. *Zebley,* 493 U.S. 521. See also Woodward and Weiser, "Costs Soar

for Children's Disability Program"; and General Accounting Office, *Social Security: Rapid Rise in Children on SSI Disability Rolls Follows New Regulations*, HEHS-94-225 (September 1994).

9. In 1995, 87.2 percent of AFDC households received food stamps, 24.7 percent received benefits under the special supplemental nutrition program for women, infants, and children (WIC), and 63.1 percent received free or reduced-price school lunches. *1996 Green Book*, p. 856.

10. About half of food stamp households are female-headed and include children. Ibid., p. 880.

11. See Mead, *New Politics of Poverty*; and Mead, ed., *The New Paternalism: Supervisory Approaches to Poverty* (Brookings, 1997).

12. On this "dual clientele trap" in welfare, see R. Kent Weaver, "The Politics of Welfare Reform," in Weaver and William T. Dickens, eds., *Looking Before We Leap: Social Science and Welfare Reform* (Brookings, 1995), pp. 91–108; and David T. Ellwood, *Poor Support: Poverty in the American Family* (Basic Books, 1988), chap. 2.

13. On strategic disagreement and bidding wars, see the excellent analysis by John B. Gilmour, *Strategic Disagreement: Stalemate in American Politics* (University of Pittsburgh Press, 1995).

14. Ellwood, *Poor Support*, pp. 110–16, 241. Ellwood's reform package also included a uniform child support assurance system that would guarantee a minimum benefit to every child, even if the noncustodial parent could or would not pay that amount.

15. Stephanie Ventura and others, "Advance Report of Final Natality Statistics, 1993," *Monthly Vital Statistics Report*, vol. 44, no. 3, Supplement (September 21, 1995), pp. 1–2.

16. Charles Murray, "The Coming White Underclass," *Wall Street Journal*, October 29, 1993, p. A14; and Murray, *Losing Ground, American Social Policy, 1950–1980* (Basic Books, 1984).

17. For a review of evidence on the incentive effects of welfare, see Robert Moffitt, "Incentive Effects of the U.S. Welfare System: A Review," *Journal of Economic Literature*, vol. 30 (March 1992), pp. 1–61; and Gregory Acs, "Do Welfare Benefits Promote Out-of Wedlock Childbearing," in Isabel V. Sawhill, ed., *Welfare Reform: An Analysis of the Issues* (Washington: Urban Institute Press, 1995), pp. 51–54. For a liberal critique of the Murray analysis, see Sharon Parrott and Robert Greenstein, *Welfare, Out-of-Wedlock Childbearing, and Poverty: What Is the Connection?* (Washington: Center on Budget and Policy Priorities, January 1995).

18. See especially Mary Jo Bane and David T. Ellwood, *Welfare Realities: From Rhetoric to Reform* (Harvard University Press, 1994).

19. See Sara McLanahan and Gary Sandefur, *Growing Up with a Single Parent: What Hurts, What Helps* (Harvard University Press, 1994).

20. See Gary Burtless, "When Work Doesn't Work: Employment Programs for Welfare Recipients," *Brookings Review*, vol. 10 (Spring 1992), pp. 26–29; and Daniel

Friedlander and Gary Burtless, *Five Years After: The Long-Term Effects of Welfare-to-Work Programs* (New York: Russell Sage, 1995).

21. See, for example, Robert Rector and W.F. Lauber, *America's Failed $5.4 Trillion War on Poverty* (Washington: Heritage Foundation, 1995). The programs are listed in *1996 Green Book*, pp. 1321–24. For a critique, see Sharon Parrott, *What Do We Spend on Welfare?* (Washington: Center on Budget and Policy Priorities, February 13, 1995).

22. Murray, "The Coming White Underclass." On the growing importance of the illegitimacy issue for conservatives, see Dan Balz and Ronald Brownstein, *Storming the Gates: Protest Politics and the Republican Revival* (Little, Brown, 1996).

23. *1994 Green Book*, p. 325; and *Budget of the United States Government, Fiscal Year 1997: Supplement*, p. 71. The caseload increase can be attributed in part to economic recession and to changes in AFDC policy included in the 1988 Family Support Act. See the discussion by William T. Dickens in Weaver and Dickens, eds., *Looking before We Leap*, pp. 42–47.

24. A majority of the public was willing to help welfare recipients try to make a transition to independence with money for training, education, child care, and transitional assistance. Deterrence approaches remained the most controversial. By 1993 a majority of the public supported the notion of family caps but continued to oppose teen mother exclusions in most polls. Support was substantially higher for time limits where recipients could continue to receive benefits in exchange for work than for an absolute cutoff of benefits. See R. Kent Weaver, Robert Y. Shapiro, and Lawrence R. Jacobs, "Public Opinion on Welfare Reform: A Mandate for What?" in Weaver and Dickens, eds., *Looking Before We Leap*, pp. 109–28; Steve Farkas and others, *The Values We Live By: What Americans Want for Welfare Reform* (New York: Public Agenda Foundation, 1996); and Henry J. Kaiser Family Foundation, Kaiser-Harvard Program on the Public and Health-Social Policy, *Survey on Welfare Reform: Basic Values and Beliefs; Support for Policy Approaches; Knowledge about Key Programs* (January 1995).

25. See, for example, Shanto Iyengar, "Television News and Citizens' Explanations of National Affairs," *American Political Science Review*, vol. 81 (September 1987), pp. 815–31.

26. On intergovernmental groups, see Beverly A. Cigler, "Not Just Another Special Interest: Intergovernmental Representation," in Allan J. Cigler and Burdett A. Loomis, eds., *Interest Group Politics*, 4th ed. (Washington: Congressional Quarterly Press, 1995), pp. 131–53; and Anne Marie Cammisa, *Governments as Interest Groups: Intergovernmental Lobbying and the Federal System* (Westport, Conn.: Praeger, 1995).

27. On liberal advocacy groups, see Douglas Rowley Imig, "Resource Mobilization and Survival Tactics of Poverty Advocacy Groups," *Western Political Quarterly*, vol. 45 (June 1992), pp. 501–20; Imig, *Poverty and Power: The Political Representation of Poor Americans* (University of Nebraska Press, 1996); Jeff Shear,

"Tightfisted Liberals," *National Journal*, September 3, 1994, pp. 2021–25; and Marilyn Werber Serafini, "Not a Game for Kids," *National Journal*, September 21, 1996, pp. 2011–14. On increasingly blurred boundaries between research and advocacy groups, see R. Kent Weaver, "The Changing World of Think Tanks," *PS: Political Science and Politics*, vol. 22 (September 1989), pp. 563–78.

28. On conservative groups and welfare policymaking, see, for example, Peter H. Stone, "All in the Family," *National Journal*, October 28, 1995, pp. 2641–45; and Gregg Zoroya, "Flying Right," *Los Angeles Times*, October 1, 1995, p. E1.

29. Hilary Stout, "GOP's Welfare Stance Owes a Lot to Prodding from Robert Rector," *Wall Street Journal*, January 23, 1995, pp. A1, A10.

30. Moreover, many of these groups argued for an increased role for private charities in provision of social services to the poor, because only private charities can offer the individually tailored programs and the moral regeneration that are needed for truly changing the lives of the spiritually as well as economically impoverished. See Marvin Olasky, *The Tragedy of American Compassion* (Washington: Regnery, 1995); and Robert Rector, "Welfare Reforms on the Sidelines," *Washington Times*, May 31, 1996, p. A16.

31. Bill Clinton and Al Gore, *Putting People First: How We Can All Change America* (Times Books, 1992), pp. 164–68.

32. See Stanley B. Greenberg, *Middle Class Dreams: The Politics and Power of the New American Majority*, rev. ed. (Yale University Press, 1996), especially pp. 206–07; Thomas Byrne Edsall with Mary D. Edsall, *Chain Reaction: The Impact of Race, Rights and Taxes on American Politics* (Norton, 1992); and Will Marshall and Elaine Ciulla Kamarck, "Replacing Welfare with Work," in Will Marshall and Martin Schram, eds., *Mandate for Change* (Berkley Books, 1993), pp. 217–36.

33. Bob Woodward, *The Agenda: Inside the Clinton White House* (Simon and Schuster, 1994), p. 109. The first two promises were providing more jobs and reforming health care.

34. See David T. Ellwood, "Welfare Reform as I Knew It," *American Prospect*, no. 26 (May–June 1996), p. 24.

35. See David S. Broder, "A Party Split," *Washington Post*, August 7, 1996, p. A19.

36. See Timothy Noah and Laurie McGinley, "Advocate for the Poor, Respected on All Sides, Secures a Pivotal Role in Expanding Tax Credit," *Wall Street Journal*, July 26, 1993, p. A12.

37. See Jason DeParle, "The Clinton Welfare Bill Begins Trek in Congress," *New York Times*, July 15, 1994, p. A1; Jeff Shear, "Pulling in Harness," *National Journal*, June 4, 1994, pp. 1286–90; and David Whitman and Matthew Cooper, "The End of Welfare—Sort of," *U.S. News and World Report*, June 20, 1994, pp. 28–37.

38. Jason DeParle, "Proposal for Welfare Cutoff Is Dividing Clinton Officials," *New York Times*, May 22, 1994, sec. 1, p. 20; Eric Pianin, "Tenet of Clinton Welfare Plan Faces Test," *Washington Post*, May 20, 1994, p. A6; DeParle, "Clinton Plan-

ners Facing a Quiet Fight on Welfare," *New York Times*, March 18, 1994, p. A18; and DeParle, "Clinton Welfare Bill Begins Trek in Congress."

39. See Mickey Kaus, "Tough Enough," *New Republic*, April 25, 1994, pp. 22–25.

40. See Jason DeParle, "Clinton Puzzle: How to Delay Welfare Reform Yet Seem to Pursue It," *New York Times*, January 5, 1994, p. A13.

41. William Claiborne, "Moynihan Presses Welfare Reform; White House Warned Not to Defer Issue Because of Health Care Debate," *Washington Post*, January 10, 1994, p. A6.

42. On one short-lived administration revenue-raising initiative, see Jason DeParle, "Casinos Become Big Players in the Overhaul of Welfare," *New York Times*, May 9, 1994, p. A1. See also DeParle, "Democrats Face Hard Choices in Welfare Overhaul," *New York Times*, February 22, 1994, p. A16; and DeParle, "A New Strategy for Welfare Overhaul," *New York Times*, April 21, 1994, p. D24.

43. Department of Health and Human Services, *Work and Responsibility Act: Detailed Summary*, June 1994.

44. Jeffrey L. Katz, "Welfare Issue Finds Home on the Campaign Trail," *Congressional Quarterly Weekly Report*, October 15, 1994, pp. 2956–58.

45. Mickey Kaus, "They Blew It," *New Republic*, December 5, 1994, p. 14.

46. See, for example, Elizabeth Drew, *Showdown: The Struggle between the Gingrich Congress and the Clinton White House* (Simon and Schuster, 1996), pp. 26, 84.

47. Robert Carleson, "Can Welfare Reform Survive Friendly Fire," *Washington Times*, February 29, 1996, p. A21; and Robert Rector, "Stringing Along," *National Review*, April 17, 1995, pp. 50–53.

48. To prevent migration in search of higher welfare benefits, states were to be allowed to use the eligibility and benefit standards that would have been used in the new migrant's former state of residence for up to twelve months after the migration.

49. States were to be given grants equal to the amount that federal expenditures were reduced by exclusion of those families.

50. Representative Richard Armey, who was responsible for managing development of the contract as chair of the House Republican Conference (he became majority leader in the 104th Congress), argued that those omissions "made the welfare provisions tougher and more imperative because we had a very, very important, significant part of our base already disappointed." Balz and Brownstein, *Storming the Gates*, p. 39.

51. See Lori Montgomery, "In Welfare Debate, Engler Is Both a Model and a Maverick," *Detroit Free Press*, January 20, 1995, p. 1A.

52. For data on public confidence in President Clinton and congressional Republicans to handle the welfare reform issue, see Weaver, Shapiro and Jacobs, "Public Opinion on Welfare Reform."

53. Five Republicans voted against H.R. 4 on final passage, while nine Democrats voted for it. Two of the five Republicans voting against it were Cuban

Americans, and one opposed it because of concerns that it would increase abortion. See Robert Pear, "House Backs Bill Undoing Decades of Welfare Policy," *New York Times*, March 25, 1995, p. 1.

54. Bill McAllister, "Dole Criticizes House Plan; Teen Mothers' Welfare Cutoff Called Unlikely," *Washington Post*, January 23, 1995, p. A4.

55. See Ronald Brownstein, "Dole Walks Fine Political Line in Bid for Presidency," *Los Angeles Times*, April 4, 1995, p. A1; Hilary Stout, "After Early Success, GOP's Effort to Overhaul Welfare System May Be Derailed in the Senate," *Wall Street Journal*, July 6, 1995, p. A10; and Richard L. Berke, "Dole and Gramm Clash on Revising Laws on Welfare," *New York Times*, July 16, 1995, sec. 1, p. 1.

56. One Republican, Lauch Faircloth, voted against the bill on final passage.

57. The conference agreement would have turned AFDC into a block grant that would remain essentially fixed in nominal terms—and thus decline in real dollar value—for five years (minor adjustments were allowed for states growing rapidly in population and for those undergoing recession). Thus it would largely freeze in place the existing interstate distribution of funds that advantages wealthier states. The conference agreement would also have imposed some new specific policy mandates on the states, generally splitting the difference between the House and Senate bills.

58. "Message to the House of Representatives Returning without Approval the Personal Responsibility and Work Opportunity Act of 1995," January 9, 1996, *Weekly Compilation of Presidential Documents*, January 15, 1996, pp. 30–32.

59. The NGA proposal included an additional $4 billion in entitlement funds for child care and an additional $1 billion in contingency funds. State flexibility was increased by higher allowable caseload exemptions to the five-year time limit, making family caps a state option rather than a mandate with state opt-out, and easing work participation rate requirements. See National Governors' Association, "Welfare Reform," February 6, 1996. NGA modified its February proposal in early March to require a state match for additional child care funds and a maintenance of effort requirement to receive recession-related contingency funds. For a discussion of why the NGA was able to reach an agreement, see R. Kent Weaver, "Deficits and Devolution in the 104th Congress," *Publius: The Journal of Federalism*, vol. 26 (Summer 1996), pp. 45–85. Overall, the Congressional Budget Office estimated that the governors' proposal would reduce seven-year nonmedicaid savings from about $60.4 billion over seven years in the conference agreement to about $43 billion. Memorandum from Paul Cullinan, Budget Analysis Division, Congressional Budget Office, February 16, 1995.

60. See Gilmour, *Strategic Disagreement*, chap. 2.

61. See Patrice Hill, "GOP Has New Strategy for Getting Welfare-Medicaid Bill to Clinton," *Washington Times*, March 7, 1996, p. A4; and Jeffrey L. Katz and David S. Cloud, "Welfare Overhaul Leaves Dole with Campaign Dilemma," *Congressional Quarterly Weekly Report*, April 20, 1996, pp. 1023–26.

62. See Jeffrey L. Katz, "Voter Call for Revamped Welfare Poses Problem for Democrats," *Congressional Quarterly Weekly Report*, April 20, 1996, pp. 1027–29.

63. See, for example, Michael K. Frisby and John Harwood, "Clinton Steals Republicans' Thunder by Moving to the Right on Some Controversial Social Issues," *Wall Street Journal*, May 7, 1996, p. A24.

64. See Jeffrey L. Katz, "GOP's New Welfare Strategy Has Democrats Reassessing," *Congressional Quarterly Weekly Report*, July 13, 1996, pp. 1969–70.

65. See Barbara Vobejda, "President Limits Teens on Welfare," *Washington Post*, May 5, 1996, p. A1; and John F. Harris and Judith Havemann, "Clinton Vows Tougher Rules on Finding Welfare Fathers," *Washington Post*, June 19, 1996, p. A2.

66. Clinton also publicly praised a dramatic welfare plan submitted for federal approval by Wisconsin's Republican governor, Tommy Thompson, and then more quietly backed away from his endorsement. Republicans responded by introducing legislation to give automatic approval to the Wisconsin waiver request. See Judith Havemann, "Clinton Backs Proposal to Scrap Welfare," *Washington Post*, May 19, 1996, p. A1; John E. Yang and Judith Havemann, "House, Bypassing Clinton, Votes to Grant Wisconsin Welfare Waiver," *Washington Post*, June 7, 1996, p. A8; and Robert Pear, "Clinton Wavers after Backing Welfare Plan," *New York Times*, June 15, 1996, p. A1.

67. While the bills contained many of the NGA proposals, they contained others that were closer to the Republican congressional bill of 1995. Moreover, the bills proposed cutting $10 billion more than the NGA proposal and linked welfare and medicaid reform. Democratic governors and the administration pronounced several of the provisions unacceptable. See Jeffrey L. Katz, "Ignoring Veto Threat, GOP Links Welfare Medicaid," *Congressional Quarterly Weekly Report*, May 25, 1996, pp. 1465–67; Robert Pear, "G.O.P. Submits New Bill to Revamp Welfare and Medicaid," *New York Times*, May 23, 1996, p. B9; Cheryl Wetzstein, "GOP Takes Offensive on Welfare," *Washington Times*, May 23, 1996, p. A4; and Judith Havemann and John F. Harris, "Governors' Welfare, Medicaid Deal Blows Up amid Charges of Partisanship," *Washington Post*, May 30, 1996, p. A7.

68. Richard L. Berke, "Poll Indicates Stable Ratings for President," *New York Times*, June 5, 1996, p. A1; and Richard Morin and Mario Brossard, "Key Voters Are Fleeing House GOP," *Washington Post*, June 17, 1996, p. A1.

69. See Janet Hook, "GOP Pares Legislative Wish List in Run-Up to Elections," *Los Angeles Times*, July 7, 1996, p. A6.

70. See Jeffrey L. Katz, "GOP May Move to Split Medicaid, Welfare," *Congressional Quarterly Weekly Report*, June 22, 1996, pp. 1761–62; and Laurie Kellman, "GOP Lawmakers Urge Welfare Split from Bill," *Washington Times*, June 28, 1996, p. A10.

71. House Majority Leader Richard Armey said that Republicans wanted to

force the president to have to decide whether "to sign this bill and satisfy the American people while he alienates his left-wing political base, or if he's going to veto the bill in order to satisfy the left wing of the Democrat Party, and thereby alienate the American people." E. J. Dionne Jr., "Clinton's Choice," *Washington Post*, July 23, 1996, p. A17.

72. See Robert Pear, "White House Is Optimistic about Chances of Welfare Bill with New G.O.P. Moves," *New York Times*, July 13, 1996, p. 10; Dan Balz, "Clinton Prods Congress on Welfare Overhaul Bill," *Washington Post*, July 17, 1996, p. A6; Elizabeth Shogren, "House Takes Up Welfare Reform Bill," *Los Angeles Times*, July 18, 1996, p. A5; and Robert Pear, "House Approves Shift on Welfare," *New York Times*, July 19, 1996, p. A1.

73. See Jeffrey L. Katz, "Conferees May Determine Fate of Overhaul Bill," *Congressional Quarterly Weekly Report*, July 20, 1996, pp. 2048–51.

74. See Barbara Vobejda, "White House Hoping for More 'Progress' as Welfare Bills Head to Conference," *Washington Post*, July 25, 1996, p. A4.

75. Elizabeth Shogren, "House and Senate Conferees Approve Welfare Overhaul," *Los Angeles Times*, July 31, 1996, p. A1.

76. See John Broder, "Decision on Welfare Reform Was Difficult for Clinton, Tough on Dole," *Los Angeles Times*, August 1, 1996, p. A16; and Todd Purdum, "Clinton Recalls His Promise, Weighs History, and Decides," *New York Times*, August 1, 1996, p. A1.

77. The House passed the bill by a margin of 328–101, with Democrats split 98–98. The Senate passed the bill 78–21, with Democrats split 25–21 in favor of passage. Only one of seven Democratic senators up for reelection, Paul Wellstone of Minnesota, voted against the conference report.

78. Congressional Budget Office, *Federal Budgetary Implications of H.R. 3734, The Personal Responsibility and Work Opportunity Reconciliation Act of 1996*, August 9, 1996, p. 1.

79. For a summary of provisions of the new law, see *1996 Green Book*, pp. 1325–1415.

80. See Jeffrey L. Katz, "Changes in New Law Hinge on Budget Deal," *Congressional Quarterly Weekly Report*, November 23, 1996, pp. 3310–11; and Robert Pear, "Clinton Considers Move to Soften Cuts in Welfare," *New York Times*, November 27, 1996, p. A1. On divisions within Republican ranks, see Sandy Hume, "Welfare Plan Splits Republicans," *The Hill*, December 4, 1996, p. 1.

81. See, for example, Judith Havemann, "GOP Governors Reject Reopening of Welfare Bill But May Seek Some Aid," *Washington Post*, February 2, 1997, p. A7; Dan Balz and Barbara Vobejda, "Under GOP Pressure, Governors Soften Welfare Stance," *Washington Post*, February 3, 1997, p. A4; Robert Pear, "Governors Limit Revisions Sought in Welfare Law," *New York Times*, February 3, 1997, p A1; and Janet Hook, "Wilson Joins Call to Help Immigrants Facing Cuts," *Los Angeles Times*, February 3, 1997, p. B1.

82. See Robert Pear, "Clinton Will Seek Tax Break to Ease Path off Welfare," *New York Times*, January 28, 1997, p. A1; and Rochelle Sharpe, "A Tax Credit Designed to Spur Hiring Seems Promising—At First," *Wall Street Journal*, August 21, 1997, p. A1.

83. For a detailed summary and explanation of these provisions, see Mark Greenberg, *Welfare to Work Grants and Other TANF-Related Provisions in the Balanced Budget Act of 1997* (Washington: Center for Law and Social Policy, August 1997). Opponents of the application of minimum wage laws argued that doing so would limit state capacity to put more recipients into work activities and, in low-benefit states, make it difficult to comply with PRWORA requirements that a specified percentage of their caseload activities be engaged in work activities twenty or more hours per week (thirty hours beginning in 2000) for single-parent families unless those states increased benefit levels. See Steve Savner, *The Implications of Applying Federal Minimum Wage Standards to TANF Work Activities* (Washington: Center for Law and Social Policy, April 1997); Marilyn Werber Serafini, "Wimping Out," *National Journal*, October 18, 1997, pp. 2072–75; and Barbara Vobejda, "GOP Backs Off in Fight against Workforce Protections," *Washington Post*, October 10, 1997, p. A17.

84. *Budget of the United States Government, Fiscal Year 1998: Analytical Perspectives*, pp. 83–84.

85. See Michael Wines, "Republican Dissidents Want Narrower Family Tax Credit," *New York Times*, March 22, 1995, p. A1.

86. On rapid growth of program expenditures as a contraindicator of the deservingness of program clientele, see R. Kent Weaver, "Controlling Entitlements," in John E. Chubb and Paul E. Peterson, eds., *The New Direction in American Politics* (Brookings, 1985), pp. 307–41.

87. See General Accounting Office, *Earned Income Tax Credit: Design and Administration Could Be Improved*, GGD-93-145 (September 1993). For early press reports on EITC fraud, see James Bovard, "Clinton's Biggest Welfare Fraud," *Wall Street Journal*, May 10, 1994, p. A18; Lucinda Harper, "U.S. Is to Combat Abuse of Tax Credit on Income Earned by Poor Workers," *Wall Street Journal*, October 27, 1994, p. A8; and Steven Pearlstein and Edward Walsh, "Tax Credit for Poor Comes under Attack," *Washington Post*, July 30, 1995, pp. A1, A8.

88. See Edgar K. Browning, "Effects of the Earned Income Tax Credit on Income and Welfare," *National Tax Journal*, vol. 48 (March 1995), pp. 23–43. For an earlier and more positive evaluation of the EITC, see Saul D. Hoffman and Laurence S. Seidman, *The Earned Income Tax Credit: Antipoverty Effectiveness and Labor Market Effects* (Kalamazoo, Mich.: W.E. Upjohn Institute for Employment Research, 1990).

89. See Todd S. Purdum, "Clinton Defends Income Tax Credit against G.O.P. Cut," *New York Times*, September 19, 1995, p. A1.

90. See Major Garrett, "GOP Lawmakers Split over Child Tax Credit," *Wash-*

ington Times, March 20, 1995, p. A1; and Jonathan Peterson, "Christian Group Adds Budget Items to Agenda," *Los Angeles Times*, October 30, 1995. p. A1.

91. Jim McDermott, "'Bait-and-Switch' on the Family Credit," *Washington Post*, April 5, 1995, p. A19.

92. Alissa J. Rubin, "Unity Frays within House GOP over Family Tax Credit," *Congressional Quarterly Weekly Report*, March 25, 1995, p. 857. See also Wines, "Republican Dissidents Want Narrower Family Tax Credit."

93. See the letter of John T. Doolittle of California and thirty-four other House Republicans to Speaker Gingrich, of March 22, 1995, which argued that "family tax relief should not be means-tested," and that allowing families "to keep more of what they earn, and to reward families for doing the vital job of raising their own children . . . is not, and must not become, an argument of class warfare."

94. See Clay Chandler, "GOP Senators Agree on $245 Billion Tax Cut," *Washington Post*, October 14, 1995, p. A1.

95. For details of the conference agreement, see *Balanced Budget Act of 1995*, H. Rept. 104-350, 104 Cong. 1 sess. (GPO, 1995), pp. 1292–94. See also Jackie Calmes, "Republican Leaders Seek Ways to Make Child Tax Credit Effective This Year," *Wall Street Journal*, November 9, 1995, p. A2.

96. The child tax provisions are described in *Taxpayer Relief Act of 1997*, H. Rept. 105-220, 105 Cong. 1 sess. (GPO, 1997), pp. 330–35, 776.

97. Provisions in the Taxpayer Relief Act of 1997 did clarify that workfare payments were not to be counted as wages for purposes of qualifying for the EITC.

98. See especially Donald F. Norris and Lyke Thompson, eds., *The Politics of Welfare Reform* (Thousand Oaks, Calif.: Sage Publications, 1995).

99. See Ted George Goertzel and John Hart, "New Jersey's $64 Question: Legislative Entrepreneurship and the Family Cap," in ibid., pp. 109–45.

100. The classic study is Jack Walker, "The Diffusion of Innovations among the American States," *American Political Science Review*, vol. 63 (September 1969), pp. 880–99.

101. Thomas J. Corbett, "Welfare Reform in Wisconsin: The Rhetoric and the Reality," in Norris and Thompson, eds., *Politics of Welfare Reform*, p. 42.

102. Dave Lesher, "Welfare Payment Reductions a Step Nearer," *Los Angeles Times*, October 10, 1995, p. A3.

103. These figures are based on September 1997 Health and Human Services estimates of the fiscal year 1997 TANF grants and June 1997 TANF family caseloads. See U.S. Department of Health and Human Services, Administration for Children and Families, "Estimated FY 1997 State Family Assistance Grants under P.L. 104-93," September 1997; and "TANF 2-Parent Families as Percentage of Total Families on Welfare by State," September 1997.

104. Judith Havemann, "Some States Are Hobbled in Race to Welfare Reform," *Washington Post*, October 22, 1996, p. A4.

105. Joel Dresang and Crocker Stephenson, "W-2 Resources Vary Widely by County," *Milwaukee Journal Sentinel*, October 13, 1997, p. 1.

106. Judith Havemann, "Welfare Reform Still on a Roll as States Bounce It Down to Counties," *Washington Post*, August 29, 1997, p. A19.

107. Robert Pear, "So Far, States Aren't Rewriting the Book on Welfare Plans," *New York Times*, October 15, 1996, p. A21.

108. Jane Gross, "Poor without Cars Find Trek to Work Can Be a Job," *New York Times*, November 18, 1997, p. A1; and Eric Lipton, "Fairfax Offers Welfare Recipients Rides to Work," *Washington Post*, November 25, 1997, p. B8.

109. Robert Pear, "Judge Rules States Can't Cut Welfare for New Residents," *New York Times*, October 14, 1997, p. A1.

110. See Steve Savner and Mark Greenberg, *The New Framework: Alternative State Funding Choices under TANF* (Washington.: Center for Law and Social Policy, March 1997). See also Dana Milbank, "Lawyer Helps States See the Loopholes in Welfare Law," *Wall Street Journal*, March 14, 1997, p. A18.

111. U.S. Department of Health and Human Services, Administration for Children and Families, "Aid to Families with Dependent Children (AFDC), Temporary Assistance for Needy Families (TANF), 1960-1997," November 1997.

112. A May 1997 Council of Economic Advisers report attributed 44 percent of the caseload decline through 1996 to improvement in the economy, with another 31 percent due to the effects of state welfare reform experiments under federal waivers and the rest due to other factors, such as enrichment of the EITC and improved child support enforcement. See Council of Economic Advisers, "Explaining the Decline in Welfare Receipt, 1993-1996," May 9, 1997; and "Technical Report: Explaining the Decline in Welfare Receipt, 1993-1996," May 9, 1997. For a critical evaluation, see Alberto Martini and Michael Wiseman, "Explaining the Recent Decline in Welfare Caseloads: Is the Council of Economic Advisors Right?" *Challenge*, vol. 40 (November–December 1997), pp. 6–20. Republicans have stressed both the role of activist governors from their own party and recipients' anticipation of, and later experience with, the 1996 PRWORA law. See Barbara Vobejda, "Welfare Drop Attributed to Economic Rise," *Washington Post*, May 10, 1997, p. A9.

113. See, for example, Barbara Vobejda and Judith Havemann, "Welfare Clients Already Work, Off the Books," *Washington Post*, November 3, 1997, p. A1.

114. See Crocker Stephenson and Joel Dresang, "W-2: Cases Become Fewer, and Tougher," *Milwaukee Journal-Sentinel*, September 28, 1997, p. 1; and Michael H. Hodges, "'Deep Needers' Require Extraordinary Intervention to Succeed," *Detroit News*, September 23, 1997, p. A1. Several states have taken steps to prevent or limit displacement. See, for example, Louis Uchitelle, "Welfare Recipients Taking Jobs Often Held by the Working Poor," *New York Times*, April 1, 1997, p. A1; and Uchitelle, "Maryland Order Limits Hiring of People in Welfare Programs," *New York Times*, July 1, 1997, p. A15.

115. See, for example, Wendy Wendland, "Welfare Rolls Slashed, Many People Find Jobs," *Detroit Free Press*, August 12, 1997. See also General Accounting Office, *Welfare Reform: States' Early Experiences with Benefit Termination*, HEHS-97-74 (May 1997).

116. A recent Urban Institute study of women with very low basic skills (attributes shared by about one-third of the 1991 AFDC caseload) found that only about one-sixth were able to move rapidly into steady employment and less than half were able to move into steady employment by their late twenties. Even among extremely low-skilled women with no children, only 61.5 percent were working steadily by ages 26–27. LaDonna Pavetti, *Against the Odds: Steady Employment among Low-Skilled Women* (Washington: Urban Institute, July 1997). See also Pavetti, *How Much More Can They Work? Setting Realistic Expectations for Welfare Mothers* (Washington: Urban Institute, July 1997).

117. See Avrum D. Lank, "What Happens to W-2 When Economy Stumbles?" *Milwaukee Journal-Sentinel*, October 26, 1997, p. 1.

118. Corbett, "Welfare Reform in Wisconsin."

119. Mark Carl Rom, "Sinking Swiftly and Silently: Welfare Policy at the Millennium," *Georgetown Public Policy Review*, vol. 1 (Spring 1996), pp. 107–21.

Chapter 10

Race and the Politics of Social Policy

Linda Faye Williams

A RGUABLY, race has been the most endemic cleavage in
American politics and social policy. The stability of the
New Deal coalition rested in good part on preserving racial inequality
in the distribution of program benefits and refusing to enfranchise southern blacks. It was not until dramatic political changes were wrought in
the 1960s that African Americans, other people of color, and women were
finally included in America's welfare state. As black insurgency, violent
confrontations with students, and urban strife became the order of the
day, the meaning and object of American social policy was refocused.
The fusion of race, poverty, and crime in particular became the tacitly
accepted starting point among liberals and conservatives alike for debates about social policy reform. In turn, a new and cryptic vernacular
for racial politics developed. As Thomas and Mary Edsall put it in 1991,
"When the official subject is presidential politics, taxes, welfare, crime,
rights, or values . . . the real subject is RACE."[1]

The link between race and social policy in the American mind set up a
political dilemma for both President Clinton and the congressional Republicans as they approached the issue of reform. Clinton wanted to
reduce the political salience of race as a central cleavage but at the same
time retain strong black and Latino political support. His question was
how to avoid a key challenge that other Democrats have faced: how to
signal whites (especially white males) that the party was not a captive of
so-called special interests (increasingly perceived by many whites as
"minorities" and allied groups) and yet claim to be a party inclusive
enough to discourage a popular black candidate from opposing him, to
maintain black and Latino leadership support, and to inspire people of
color to turn out to vote in large numbers.

Clinton's political learning from the efforts of Michael Dukakis in 1988 showed that it was not enough to pose as a pragmatic centrist. Thus he decided to carefully stake out his claim to represent a new kind of Democrat. His attempted solution relied on three interrelated strategies.

The first strategy was to seek to control racial symbols. For instance. crime had been Dukakis's weakest point. Thus as a candidate in 1992 Clinton attempted to distance himself from his party's image of being soft on criminals by promising to get tough on crime while posing for photographers with a formation of mostly black convicts providing the backdrop. His pose was extra insurance since Clinton had already arranged to mark his position on criminals when he was governor of Arkansas by allowing the execution of Rickey Ray Rector, a severely brain-damaged African American who had killed a police officer.[2]

The second strategy was to emphasize responsibility over rights. Thus Clinton's 1992 campaign manifesto, *Putting People First* (coauthored with vice-presidential nominee Al Gore), was "thin on civil rights." "Race rated less space in a Civil Rights chapter than sexual preference or physical disability and did not make the thirty-one 'crucial issues' listed and addressed in alphabetical order from Agriculture to Women."[3] By contrast, Clinton was much less reticent in his calls for personal responsibility. Often addressed at exclusively black audiences, the message of personal responsibility allowed the president to play off many whites' highly negative perceptions of minorities as "irresponsible," "lazy," and "violence prone."[4]

Clinton's third strategy for managing the politics of race was to emphasize universal social policies instead of race-specific ones. Thus he pledged to create a universal health care system, to provide increased opportunities for college students, and to raise the minimum wage. This was clearly a retreat from Lyndon B. Johnson's understanding that there were legacies to two centuries of slavery and a third one of Jim Crow that required compensatory actions to level the playing field.[5]

The Republicans, long the beneficiaries of the political salience of race, faced an entirely different set of questions. With the sole exception of 1976, the party had won the White House with less than 15 percent of the black vote in every election since 1968.[6] The party's stock in trade was a politics permeated by race, which played on whites' anxieties. Thus the Republicans, with an obviously more racially homogeneous base, could play the race card in a way Democrats could not. Their challenge, however, was to escape vulnerability to charges of racism.

To deflect charges of racism, Republicans pursued three main strategies. First, they sought to convince a growing public that blacks and their families were the main "victims" of misguided welfare policies and antidiscrimination measures, which had sapped their potential. The result, Republicans asserted, is a black "underclass" of enormous proportions and a black middle-class insecure of its footing. Slicing benefits and eliminating "racial preferences," Republicans concluded, would not only stimulate the economy and create jobs but would also force poor people and black people into an independence that, in the long run, would make them happier and better off.

Second, Republicans claimed that civil rights leaders exaggerate the degree of racism in the United States to keep their cause alive and that the intensity and institutional embodiment of racism had lessened significantly, if not disappeared.[7] The racism that did exist was blacks' own fault. Typical refrains of party spokespersons, especially black ones, went something like this: There would be no racism if it weren't for black crime; we've created racism that maybe wasn't there before affirmative action; racism exists because whites are sick of paying higher taxes to take care of "them." What is needed, the party spokesmen claimed, were genuinely color-blind policies.[8]

Third, Republicans sought to exile civil rights organizations and Democratic black elected officials to the margins of public importance. Hence, these leaders were portrayed as just "another group of special pleaders who just want to line their pockets." In addition, the party sought to manufacture overnight a new black conservative leadership as a political counterweight.[9]

This chapter examines how each of these strategies—Clinton's and the Republicans'—developed regarding key racially targeted and racially charged social policy issues in Clinton's first term.

Social Policy and the Significance of Race

The development of social policy in the United States has been complicated by and inextricably linked to the politics of race since its inception. Race played a crucial role in shaping a three-legged American welfare structure composed of social insurance, employer-provided benefits, and programs targeted toward the poor and especially minorities. Race became mapped to social policies in a way that reproduced a racial social order even as it undercut the potential for a comprehensive welfare state.

Partisan Polarization, Race, and Social Policy

The burst of policy innovation during the New Deal that created social insurance did nothing to address severe racial economic inequalities, nor did it address the denial of basic civil rights to black Americans. Social security and welfare were both designed and implemented in ways that sharply disadvantaged blacks. Civil rights too were submerged in order to maintain greater party unity.[10] The political economy of the southern cotton plantation areas, southern dominance of the committee system in Congress, the coalition needs of President Franklin D. Roosevelt and the Democratic party, and the concomitant politics of race dictated that American social policy would not undermine the control of black labor by the dominant planter class in the South. Blacks were also disadvantaged in the system of employer-provided benefits that emerged after World War II. Since these benefits were disproportionately provided to unionized or professional workers, much of the low-wage working population was excluded. People of color and women concentrated in such jobs were particularly disadvantaged.

Thus both the first and second legs of the New Deal system hardly tinkered with the system of unequal outcomes for African Americans. The failure to include blacks in the first two legs stymied the development of blacks, organized labor, and indeed, the American welfare state. The bonds that might have united workers across race lines were never forged; instead, by the late 1940s it appeared that a coalition composed both of southern whites and northern blacks and liberals could endure only so long as the issue of race was submerged. Roosevelt had succeeded in doing this during his lifetime, but Democratic party and congressional leaders found it an increasingly difficult issue to manage during the late 1940s and 1950s.

Throughout the 1950s Republicans and Democrats appeared almost equally identified with the cause of civil rights. As a result, according to Democratic pollster Stanley Greenberg, polls before 1963 showed that American public opinion was sharply divided on the question of which party was good for civil rights.[11] Even as late as 1960 a substantial minority of blacks continued to vote for the Republican party. In the contest between Richard M. Nixon and John F. Kennedy, 32 percent of black voters cast their ballots for the Republican nominee.

Only four years later the partisan politics of race had shifted decisively. When Lyndon B. Johnson signed the Civil Rights Act of 1964 and Republican nominee Barry Goldwater ran a campaign highlighting his opposition to the act, a healthy black majority for the Democrats became a nearly unanimous bloc. Democrats emerged from the 1960s with the image of being not only the liberal party but the party for civil rights. Conversely, Republicans emerged from the 1960s with the image of being not only the conservative party but the party against civil rights. In 1964, race, party, and state became intimately linked much more than class, party, and state, a development with major consequences for the coalition-building potential of the two major parties. It is scarcely exaggerating to conclude that the national party order of the last thirty years was shaped by the enactment of the Civil Rights Act of 1964 and the Voting Rights Act of 1965. As Edward G. Carmines and James A. Stimson conclude, in 1964 Republicans turned their back on one hundred years of racial leadership, while the historic party of slavery became the home for blacks.[12] Just as surely, the Democratic party's tenuous ties first with the white voters of the South and increasingly with many white voters of the North were broken.

Yet it was not just civil rights that divided the two parties. While the New Deal failed to address the status of African Americans in any fundamental way, the programs of the Great Society targeted African Americans for inclusion. The Economic Opportunity Act of 1964 created programs like VISTA, Head Start, and the Job Corps, which provided blacks with greater educational and job training opportunities. Housing assistance grew substantially, and the federal government began to support economic development aimed at the cities. Blacks benefited considerably from many of these programs, since they were disproportionately represented among the ranks of the ill-housed, the poorly educated, the un- and underemployed, and the recipients of inferior health care. In particular, conditions greatly improved for a growing segment of blacks (the middle class) who manned the new public sector jobs created by the programs, and income maintenance for poor blacks grew significantly.[13]

Some black leaders of the day tried to push change farther. As early as 1957, civil rights activist Bayard Rustin urged Martin Luther King Jr. not only to issue a call for action but also to stress the need to expand the civil rights struggle on all fronts. Beyond the right to vote, Rustin believed the civil rights movement must focus on economic uplift: "A part of this is the realization that men are truly brothers, that the Negro cannot be free so long as there are poor and underprivileged white people."[14] In the leadership of his last campaign, the Poor People's March, King heeded Rustin's call. But to address poverty in these terms would have required something the nation never had—a tradition of social rights— and policymakers in Washington turned a deaf ear to such urgings. Instead, officials refused to substantially increase the state's redistributive capacities or to directly confront class-based inequalities.

Locked in by the segmentation that characterized the first two legs of American welfare, policymakers in the 1960s simply tried to build a third leg that included people of color and women in their own particularistic programs. In this way, race was mapped to the policies of the 1960s, politically isolating relatively powerless groups and leaving programs that benefited them vulnerable to attack.[15] To be sure, each leg of the welfare state included some members of all classes and races, but segmentation remained tangible. The white nonpoor (especially white males) continued to be advantaged by the two legs of the welfare state (social insurance and unionized welfare) created before the 1960s, while blacks, other people of color, and middle-class and poor white women were the primary beneficiaries of the new services and income maintenance programs of the Kennedy, Johnson, and Nixon years.

As the funds for a much larger war on poverty dried up in the late 1960s, assistance for the poor and minorities took two different tracks. The first was the expansion and liberalization of aid to families with dependent children (AFDC) as more eligible families claimed benefits. The second was the emergence of affirmative action, for which Kennedy and Johnson had laid some groundwork, but which took an explicitly race-conscious form under Nixon.[16] This framework of segmented social policy plus affirmative action proved particularly vulnerable to attack from the right, especially once the economic growth of the 1960s stalled. The question for conservatives (especially Republicans) was how to launch the attack and regain control of the national government. Given the utter failure of Goldwater's campaign in 1964, Republicans fashioned a new politics of race in which unvarnished race appeals were replaced with racial symbols and code words.[17] There were four aspects to this effort.

The first built upon Nixon's "law and order" theme. Thus Reagan and Bush sought to win votes by linking crime to blacks and blacks to Democrats through a campaign of at best thinly veiled racial symbolism. This effort reached its nadir during the campaign of 1988, when Bush became irrevocably known as the Willie Horton candidate.[18] The second message fanned white fears of affirmative action. To make the argument, Republicans began with the claim that racial injustice no longer existed and any past injustices were not at issue. What was now needed were color-blind policies where rewards were allocated on the basis of merit. The color-blind argument marked not only the escalation of the attack upon affirmative action but the increasing sophistication of the way the Republicans played the race card. For millions of white families, merit was their only connection to the American dream. What the Republicans understood was that many white people resented both the old special preferences for the white rich and what they perceived were the new ones for blacks. In essence, the color-blind argument transformed white people's class concerns into racial ones.

The third message flowed directly from the second, for it was necessary to explain why, if racial injustice no longer existed, blacks ranked at the bottom of every socioeconomic indicator. The answer, according to Reagan and Bush, was that it was African Americans' own behavior and self-destructive culture and values. Thus they invoked the image of a new and menacing black underclass as a political issue. "The concept of the *underclass* captured the mixture of alarm and hostility that tinged the emotional response of more affluent Americans to the poverty of blacks increasingly clustered and isolated in postindustrial cities."[19] By grounding the sources of poverty in the deficiencies of individuals and redefining unemployment and underemployment as instances of social pathology and Great Society policies (not of structural, cyclical, or general crises of the market), Republican administrations sought to create an ideological cover for the mushrooming poverty and deepening schism between the rich and poor that occurred in the 1980s.

The final message aimed to undermine black leadership. It generally began with the claim that black leadership was "out of step" with the black masses and no longer spoke for them. Next, black leaders were portrayed as little more than "pimps" or "shakedown artists" who urge their followers to settle for excuses and handouts, thus encouraging the view that hard work and perseverance will not pay off since the deck is stacked against them.[20] Such self-pity generated a denial of personal responsibility. To promote divisiveness among people of color, blacks were compared unfavorably with other minority groups, usually Asian

Americans.[21] Finally, to demonstrate the irrelevance of traditional black civil rights leaders, Bush and Reagan refused to meet with them.[22]

In sum, just as the submergence of race had been required to enact and secure the New Deal, the constant invocation of racial code words and symbols during the Reagan-Bush administrations undercut and weakened support for the nation's welfare state. The policies and programs that suffered most during the Reagan-Bush years were those created in the 1960s, which had a disproportionately high black and Latino clientele in particular and benefited the working poor in general.[23]

It is hardly surprising in this context that, despite thirty years of racial change, black and white Americans share such different outlooks toward race and social policy that analysis of one recent poll concluded that blacks and whites no longer appear to be living in "two societies," but rather on "two different planets."[24] According to the poll, conducted in August and September 1995, the white image of people of color is so distorted that whites believe they compose only half the population of the United States rather than the roughly three-fourths they actually do. By contrast, blacks, who actually compose 12 percent of the population, were thought by most whites to compose almost 25 percent. Those with the most exaggerated ideas about the size of the black population revealed a persistent note of fear and animosity toward African Americans. And despite the fact that blacks do far worse than whites on almost every socioeconomic indicator imaginable, a majority of whites said blacks fared as well as or better than whites in the job market and in education, while more than two out of five said the same for housing and income.

How whites saw black circumstances was closely tied to social policy preferences. "Two-thirds of whites . . . who saw little difference between the social and economic conditions of blacks and whites also opposed additional federal spending to help low-income minorities. That compared with just 32 percent of those who knew that blacks on average still fared . . . worse than whites on most measures of economic well-being."[25] Moreover, the more whites were misinformed about the conditions of blacks, the more they favored such actions as cutting food stamps and aid to the cities and limiting affirmative action.

Whites minimized the importance of discrimination and traced the source of black problems to blacks themselves, "with 58 percent of whites citing the breakup of the black family as a major cause of problems in the black community." Although whites and blacks shared a fear of the economic future, the poll suggested that whites have become more hostile to people of color, fearful that more minorities would further erode their diminishing quality of life, and far less sympathetic to attempts by the federal government to address problems that poor people of color face. By contrast, the survey found that for blacks the dimming of the American dream suggested the need for more government intervention, not less.[26]

This 1995 poll demonstrated the continuation of a long-term trend. John R. Petrocik's analysis of the decline of the New Deal coalition indicated that defections from the Democratic party among union members, Polish and Irish Catholics, and lower-status white southerners in the 1970s were connected to attitudes on racial and welfare issues and the perceived position of the Democratic party on these issues. While blacks became overwhelmingly liberal on such issues and thus more strongly Democratic over the 1970s, white ethnics became less liberal and less Democratic.[27] In sum, there was a sharpening bifurcation within the Democratic party between the New Deal and unionized welfare constituencies on one side and the Great Society constituencies on the other that paralleled their structural relationship to the American welfare state.

Possibilities for Transforming Racial Politics in the 1990s

These political and social policy legacies set the stage for debates over race and social policy in the 1990s. Republicans had mastered a politics permeated by race-coded messages that played on anxieties of white Americans, intensifying their fears that their identities, interests, and standards of living were under serious attack. Democrats, however, included two sharply divided groups with dramatically different views about the social policy agenda and the role of race in politics.

Liberals and progressives (traditional Democrats) argued that Republicans had won most presidential contests since 1968 by consciously and aggressively spreading the politics of divisiveness. What the Democrats needed to do was not to desert social policies that worked and a strong defense of civil rights, but to also speak more forcefully to the pocketbook issues that had once guaranteed the party success. Moderates and conservatives (New Democrats) countered that just such "liberal fundamentalism" was itself the real problem. In this lament, progressive agendas lost credibility, and Democrats lost the White House, because they had become identified with "special interests," thereby alienating the Democratic party's white working- and middle-class constituencies, which carried the fiscal burden for social programs. In this view, race was at the center of the party's dilemma.[28] The party's identification with blacks had destroyed the Democrats' coalition, putting the party at risk of becoming a permanent minority in presidential elections. To rebuild, new Democrats counseled, the party should deemphasize issues of racism, poverty, civil rights, and affirmative action and instead focus on the concerns of the middle class in terms of lower taxes, opposition to quotas, and a tough approach to welfare and crime.[29]

As Democrats debated the role race played in the problems of their party, new opportunities for exploiting racial politics became apparent as a result of the increasing diversity of the minority population, the potential for class cleavages within each minority group, and the obsolescence of many civil rights organizations.

In some places, conflicts among minority groups surfaced over policies designed to promote equal access and equity for different groups.[30] According to several studies, for instance, while Latinos strongly supported bilingual education, blacks tended to fear that this policy would shift resources from the effort toward desegregation and thus did not support it. Other policy issues of concern to Latinos that were not perceived as being supported by blacks included the English-only movement, employer sanctions, immigration, and the extension of coverage to Latinos in amendments to the Voting Rights Act. Blacks and Latinos also collided over the fruits of majority-minority redistricting and affirmative action, with Latinos questioning whether blacks have fairly shared the benefits of these policies (primarily new districts and public sector jobs).[31] Also, it is often claimed that Asian Americans harbor resentments against affirmative action in education, which some studies conclude decreases their representation in colleges and universities.[32] Finally, some survey data suggest that hostility and distrust are growing among blacks, Latinos, and Asians, often confined to the same urban space, as they compete for political offices, jobs, housing, and other scarce resources.[33] These differences not only make the politics of race more complex but open up the potential to drive wedges among people of color.

In addition, three developments in black politics in particular suggested new possibilities for reframing racial issues. The first is the increasing significance of class. Since the 1960s the economic schism among African Americans has deepened, producing a stable and prospering middle class (some represented at the higher echelons of the occupational world, in the professions and in corporate management, but especially in the public sector) and a far larger group of working-class and poor blacks (locked in poverty and the secondary labor market, characterized by high rates of unemployment and low pay).[34]

Recent analyses of survey data demonstrate that the objective class differences among blacks have begun to produce subjective differences in political opinions. Middle- and working-class blacks are not in lockstep on all political issues. Michael C. Dawson, for example, found that blacks with higher incomes are much more likely than blacks with low incomes to blame poor blacks for their own plight and to favor cutting welfare spending.[35] Middle-class blacks are, however, equally or more likely than less affluent blacks to hold liberal positions on civil rights. In general, class differences in the political opinions of blacks remain small compared with class differences in the political opinions of whites. Race still remains more salient than class in understanding black political behavior. However, the more the subject is not civil rights, the better the opportunity for politicians to exploit the class differences among blacks.

The declining strength of major civil rights organizations that traditionally have provided black politics a sense of unity also opens up new possibilities for exploiting divisions among blacks. Of the "big five" organizations of the 1960s civil rights era (the NAACP, the Urban League, the Southern Christian Leadership Conference, the Congress of Racial Equality, and the Student Nonviolent Coordinating Committee), only the NAACP and Urban League remain relatively prominent in national politics.[36] Until recently, at least, these two organizations, too, have been plagued by several interrelated problems: poor fiscal conditions, leadership succession struggles, poor public relations apparatuses, technological backwardness in their communications and fundraising processes, disharmony among the rank and file, failure to update visions, strategies, and organizational structures, and, in the case of the NAACP, declining membership.[37] The National Rainbow Coalition (which grew out of the Chicago-based Operation PUSH, itself an outgrowth of SCLC) has failed, thus far, to make the transition from Jesse Jackson campaign organization to policy arm.[38]

It is also important to note that there is not one strong national political action committee in black America. Practically every well-known black organization is a nonprofit, with the attendant limits on political activity legally defined. Nor is there a think tank resolutely committed to black interest activity.[39] Thus black politics is bereft of the institutional capacity to bring "penetrating analysis and knowledge into alliance with political purpose," in the way, for example, the Heritage Foundation does for conservatives.[40] Black churches, still the institutions in the black community with the most autonomy and important financial holdings, continue to play an important political role (for example, in motivating and registering blacks to vote and in fundraising for candidates such as Jesse Jackson as well as local, state, and congressional candidates).[41] But the black church has not become a force at the national level in terms of lobbying for a clearly defined policy agenda as white evangelical groups such as the Christian Coalition have done. Finally, black interest groups increasingly have only a meager attachment to the grass roots. Almost all black interest groups suffer from low rates of membership and high turnover rates.[42] In sum, the civil rights lobby has nearly lost the capacity to act, a weakness leaving blacks organizationally unprepared to meet challenges to their interests.

This weakness has provided the open space for the Nation of Islam's controversial leader, Louis Farrakhan. Perhaps more than any other development, Farrakhan's appeal reflects the failure of the black political elite to connect to the black poor. His rise also demonstrates the negative views many members of the black middle class have of the black poor. The predominantly middle-class "million" black men who marched behind Farrakhan apparently were not turned off by a message concentrating on the "irresponsibility" of black men (read, *poor* black men), validating the right's explanation of poverty and inequality.[43] An opportunity to call for direct civic action was replaced by a call for self-help.

Moreover, Farrakhan's bootstrap economic nationalism (which has never worked) taps nascent hopes of blacks for their own successful businesses, if only blacks would "buy black." His brand of black nationalism is far more the hope for the conservative black middle class than the downtrodden black poor whom he has massively failed to organize. In general, black nationalist sentiments appear to be growing dramatically, and the increase in support comes primarily from a shift among middle-class blacks, the group whose class, but not race, problem has been solved.[44]

Finally, black politics is changing as a result of the creation of a cadre of extremely conservative black spokespersons intent on challenging the traditional civil rights leadership. Some gained prominent positions in Republican administrations. Others have become highly visible spokespersons against affirmative action, welfare, and "black crime." Their views, which sometimes provide cover for even the most bizarre discussions of race, are heavily reported in the press as evidence of a significant black divide—giving them exposure far disproportionate to the numbers of blacks whose views they actually represent. Financed by wealthy white contributors, black conservative Republicans now have some of the best organized entities in the black community.

The Clinton Balancing Act

"Where I come from we know about race-baiting," Bill Clinton said in his presidential campaign announcement at the Old State House in Little Rock, Arkansas. He promised not to let "them" get away with a campaign predicated upon "the politics of division." Instead, he pledged, if elected, he would not only turn the nation around economically but also end a dozen years of racial and social strife.[45] Once in the White House, Clinton pursued a balancing act on matters of race. On the conservative side, he embraced the New Democrat message that personal responsibility held priority over social rights. While establishing his conservative credentials on racially charged issues, Clinton came across as nearly a Great Society liberal on others (particularly health care).

Managing Racial Conflict in Crime and Welfare Reform

Clinton's decision to stress responsibility over rights in racially charged policies, such as welfare and crime, generated conflict between the administration and its minority allies. But the president also showed that he could manage such conflict because of the underlying divisions among black leaders, the difficulties that black organizations had in mobilizing grass-roots support, and the class divisions among blacks.

In his omnibus crime bill, the president proposed capital punishment for an ever-expanding list of federal violations, more than sixty in all. More than any other factor, it was the federalizing of death penalty cases that produced an explicit battle over rights. Suspected racism in the application of capital punishment made the attempt to broaden its use problematic. Responding to the perceived threat, several black interest groups formed a coalition that included the NAACP, NAACP-Legal Defense

Fund, National Conference of Black Lawyers, and National Black Police Association. Staffers of the Congressional Black Caucus (CBC) and representatives of civil libertarian groups (especially the American Civil Liberties Union and the Sentencing Project) met with the coalition dozens of times for nearly a year. One proposal to grow out of the coalition was the Racial Justice Act of 1994 (RJA). Supported by the CBC, the Congressional Hispanic Caucus, and the Progressive Caucus, the RJA proposed that death penalty defendants would be allowed to use statistical evidence to demonstrate whether race was a significant factor in the decision to invoke capital punishment.

The CBC, realizing that it did not have the votes to get its own bill passed, decided to concentrate on winning inclusion of the RJA in Clinton's bill. To do so, they chose a White House strategy rather than a grass-roots one, negotiating with the Clinton administration rather than mobilizing mass support. The CBC's goal was to get the Clinton administration to lobby senators to support the RJA. The decision to negotiate caused a split between the CBC and black interest groups, who up to this point had been central in drafting and promoting the RJA. By the late spring of 1994, the coalition had fallen apart.

Meanwhile, the White House had its own strategy. It was preparing to outflank the CBC on every front. For months, the president refused to meet with the CBC, obscuring his own inclinations. When he finally met with the caucus in late June 1994, the CBC, which had to accept all the bill's new death penalties in order to vote for it, thought it had a deal with the administration.[46] The president would say publicly that the RJA was a desirable part of a balanced crime bill and would lobby for it. But as late as mid-July, not a sound came from the administration to advance or defend the racial justice provision.

In fact, the administration was courting black interest groups and local elected officials for its version of the bill, which did not include the RJA. The White House turned to two main sources. First it successfully lobbied the United States Conference of Black Mayors, which included the then ten big-city black mayors, to support its version of crime reform. It appealed to this group on the basis of the prevention programs included in the bill (such as community development corporations, drug treatment programs, midnight sports leagues, antigang grants, and programs aimed at ending violence against women and seniors).[47] The mayors in turn sent CBC chair Kweisi Mfume a letter urging the CBC "not to oppose a crime bill which includes so many vital provisions for the people of our cities because it may not include the Racial Justice Act." With the exception of Baltimore's Kurt Schmoke and Washington's Sharon Pratt Kelly, every big-city black mayor signed the letter. The CBC never formally responded to the mayors' letter, but as Representative Robert C. Scott, Democrat of Virginia, noted in a fax to Mfume, the July 14, 1994, date of the mayors' letter indicated that the "White House was busy getting signatures" while the CBC thought that "everything was still on the table for negotiation."[48]

Second, the president lobbied black ministers to pressure the CBC to drop its opposition to his version of the bill. Speaking at a black church in Washington, he portrayed passage of the crime bill as a "morally right thing to do" and "the will of God."[49] Later, he invited twenty-five black clergy to the White House and urged them to pressure CBC members to vote for the bill. These tactics led the CBC to accuse the White House of failing to negotiate in good faith and circumventing them in order to pass the bill.

By then the White House was totally in charge of the actual ground rules for negotiation with the CBC. Ignoring the RJA, the White House began to incorporate many of the prevention programs supported by black interest groups into its omnibus proposal. Black interest groups and CBC members continued to argue, however, that the prevention provisions did not offset the harm that would come from other provisions in the bill. Thus the CBC threatened to launch a protest vote against the procedural rule that would bring the conference version of the bill to the House floor, an action that is usually extremely partisan. In response, Clinton called a July 25 meeting at the White House, finally admonishing the CBC that he could and would get the bill passed even if all the black voting House Democrats stood in the way—an unlikely scenario in any case.[50]

Not surprisingly, the White House never intended to let the CBC as a whole vote against its bill. Even as the CBC began to raise the volume of its objection to the removal of the RJA, the administration was picking off CBC members one by one. Within days of the White House meeting, at least four members were prepared to vote for the procedural rule as well as for the bill.[51] In the end, despite the deletion of the racial justice provision in the House-Senate conference, the Clinton crime bill not only passed the House 235 to 195, but the vast majority of CBC members, twenty-four of the thirty-nine members in the House, voted for the bill; twelve voted against it, and three did not vote.[52] Theoretically, CBC unity could have made the difference. Only twenty votes separated passage and failure on the crime bill. Had the CBC's twenty-four members who voted for the bill joined the twelve who voted against it, the vote would have been 211–219 to defeat the bill. The influence of CBC unity would have been decisive. Clinton's strategy had clearly worked: he had divided and conquered with ease.

The crime bill proved not only how easily the CBC could be had, but made apparent for all to see the disintegration of its ties to the grass roots. Neither the CBC nor black interest groups mobilized their constituents in opposition to the crime bill. No mass phone calling or letter writing was organized; no public education campaign was planned or implemented. Not even one single press release was issued by the CBC outlining its position. Interest groups produced no research arguing their case. The testimony of black interest groups and floor speeches of black members of Congress received little or no coverage in the black press. Few op-ed articles appeared in the majority press. In the end not only were CBC members left to split off willy-nilly in support of the bill, white members of Congress received almost no pressure from blacks at all. Thus the broad public education and developed networks that would have enabled the black community to live to fight another day failed to materialize. Instead, the 1994 National Election Study found that an overwhelming majority of blacks (83 percent) reported favoring the Clinton crime bill, more than the 73 percent of whites who also favored the bill.[53] By the time the Republicans gained control of Congress in 1994, there was not even enough of a residue of organization among African Americans to begin to fight for preserving the prevention funding.

The racial politics of welfare played out somewhat differently. Among the many problems raised about the president's welfare reform proposal, African American interest groups concentrated most on its failure to seriously address job creation for those whose time limits on welfare receipt had expired as well as for poor fathers who were expected to meet child support requirements. What is more interesting about welfare was the absolute weakness of blacks' response to the Republicans' extreme bill in the 104th Congress. In a very real sense, black, Latino, and women leaders never prioritized welfare reform. To be sure, the CBC held one press conference decrying the bill's potential effects on poor children and many of its members made eloquent, haunting speeches on the floor of the House, but it fell to the Progressive Caucus to seek to organize an opposition. Nor did blacks organize a coalition to write an alternative bill, as had happened with the crime bill. As discussed below, welfare reform did not inspire the kind of high-visibility mobilization that occurred over affirmative action, an issue that has a disproportionately middle-class clientele.

The politics of crime and welfare showed how the president could retain black support even as he used the divisions within the black community to enact policies that deemphasized rights and social benefits. The struggle over the crime bill cast in bold relief the divisions between civil rights leaders and local black leaders confronted with crime and deteriorating communities.[54] Both the welfare bill and the crime bill revealed the lack of grass-roots mobilizing capacities of established black and Latino interest organizations. The lack of mobilization around welfare suggested a role for class divisions as well. Both pieces of legislation revealed the dilemma that confronted minority leaders and voters; despite their differences with Clinton, their opposition to Republican proposals was still greater.

Appealing to Minority Interest Groups and the Antidiscrimination Agenda

Throughout his first term, Clinton stayed away from Congress on matters of race.[55] Instead of new policy proposals to appeal to minority constituencies, Clinton chose to make numerous appointments and to delegate most civil rights responsibilities to the Justice Department's civil rights division, with the Departments of Housing and Urban Development (HUD) and Labor playing subsidiary roles. As much as possible, a wall of silence would surround the work of these departments' civil rights actions.

In fact Clinton looked like a traditional Democrat when making appointments. He promised and largely delivered a race- and gender-balanced cabinet that would "look like America." His first cabinet included five African Americans, two Latinos, and four women. Clinton also was true to his campaign pledge to appoint judges of more diverse backgrounds to fill the slew of vacancies he found waiting for him as the first Democratic president in twelve years. One of his two choices for the Supreme Court—"the first High Court appointments by a Democratic President in twenty-six years—was a woman, Ruth Bader Ginsburg"; and by the end of his first term, "more than half of . . . Clinton's 196 appointments [were] women or . . . minorities or both" (30 percent women, 20 percent blacks, and 7 percent Latinos), almost twice the proportion among those chosen by Bush.[56] Yet, as Gerald Horne noted, "the administration's rainbow of hues [was] not . . . matched by a rainbow of views." All of the minority cabinet members were considered to be political moderates.[57]

Beyond appointments, the other benefit accruing to minorities was stepped-up enforcement of civil rights laws. The Civil Rights Division under the leadership of Assistant Attorney General Deval Patrick was the site of most action. For example, Justice reached a $54 million settlement with Denny's restaurant chain, which had been accused of racially discriminatory practices. Similarly, it reached an agreement with a subsidiary of the Fleet Financial Group, resulting in the payment of $4 million in damages to African Americans and Latinos who were charged higher prices for home mortgage loans than comparably qualified whites.[58] As a result of this success, Justice broadened its coverage to include the huge portion of the lending industry that is unregulated, including finance companies, direct mortgage lenders, and others often used by poor and low-income people. Just as the Denny's settlement had ripple effects throughout the restaurant industry, so too did the Fleet settlement begin to alter mortgage-lending bias in the industry. As a result, a record volume of lending to minority borrowers occurred during Clinton's first term.[59]

The administration also submitted amicus curiae briefs on the side of expanding civil rights in a number of cases, including a case to make the Civil Rights Act of 1991 apply to suits that were pending when the law was passed; a Piscataway, New Jersey, reverse discrimination case involving two equally qualified teachers, one minority and one white, in an otherwise all-white department; and a North Carolina case involving majority-minority redistricting.[60]

Other actions that could favorably affect people of color included HUD and Agriculture's implementation of empowerment zones and enterprise communities in more than one hundred cities and rural communities. HUD also tackled the task of desegregating public housing projects, most visibly in Vidor, Texas, a small town known for its racism. Finally, at the Department of Labor, the Office of Federal Contract Compliance Programs stepped up compliance reviews and complaint investigations. Financial settlements for victims of discrimination, debarments, and back pay awards soared compared with the record during the Reagan-Bush years.[61]

How much the White House was behind the renewed enforcement efforts, however, is unclear. Most not only appeared to be department initiatives, but in some instances seemed to depend on the initiative of individual staff rather than the department as a whole. For example, just how aggressively the federal government should enforce affirmative action was the subject of a simmering debate among Justice officials. Patrick (who left at the end of Clinton's first term) was a tough, staunch defender of affirmative action. When Patrick took on the reverse discrimination case in Piscataway and conservatives furiously criticized him (calling him a "quota lover" and mispronouncing his first name Deval as "devil"), both Clinton and Attorney General Janet Reno publicly gave him a lukewarm endorsement. Behind the scenes, however, Reno is reported to have been unhappy that Patrick chose to take a stand on the New Jersey case.[62]

The administration's balancing act was not an unqualified success. The attempt to conduct civil rights policy in an atmosphere of near secrecy meant that the administration also got little or no credit for its positive actions. But the biggest problems surfaced in the appointments strategy, where missteps engendered as much anger as goodwill. The most spectacular case angering civil rights groups was the jettisoning of the nomination of Lani Guinier for assistant attorney general for civil rights.[63]

Other criticisms from minority groups arose over the administration's tortoise-like pace in filling civil rights positions. For more than a year after Clinton was elected, important vacancies at Justice, Labor, and the Equal Employment Opportunity Commission (EEOC) left on hold a variety of issues affecting women, people of color, and the disabled.[64] For instance it was not until February 1, 1994, almost fourteen months after the president took office, that the civil rights position at Justice was finally filled. It was nearly two years after his election before the Senate confirmed Gilbert F. Casellas, a Latino attorney, as head of the EEOC, the last major unfilled civil rights position in the administration. Five weeks later the Republicans won control of both houses of Congress.

In 1994 it looked as if the rising crescendo of minority groups and liberal Democrats unhappy with Clinton's handling of racially charged social policies on one side, and the increasingly rancorous complaints of New Democrats unhappy with the president's appointment politics and friends of the court briefs on the other, would become a real problem for the administration. But then along came the results of the 1994 midterm elections to scare both kinds of Democrats back in place. In the atmosphere of despair for all Democrats after the Republicans took control of Congress, New Democrat William A. Galston glumly noted: "If we don't all stick together, we'll all hang separately." From the opposite end of the party, when asked why the CBC did not step up its criticisms of Clinton for doing so little for blacks, Representative Charles Rangel of New York angrily retorted: "Clinton is all we've got!."[65]

Republicans, Democrats, and the Politics of Affirmative Action

Republicans swept into the 104th Congress with a clear legislative plan, the Contract with America. Almost everything in the contract threatened to be injurious to African Americans. Proposed spending cuts in education, training, employment, housing, and antipoverty programs would disproportionately harm blacks, while few would benefit from proposed tax cuts. The contract's welfare reform proposal targeted particularly those groups that were heavily black: teenage mothers, long-term recipients, and children whose paternity had not been established. The block grant proposals would result in substantial reduction of a host of other antipoverty programs, from public housing to medicaid to food and nutrition.

The revival of racial symbolism and code words was central to the Republican strategy. Gingrich's often repeated refrain evoked racially linked images to attack all of social policy: "No civilization can survive for long with twelve-year-olds having babies, fifteen-year-olds killing one another, seventeen-year-olds dying of AIDS, and eighteen-year-olds getting diplomas they can't read. Yet every night on the local news, you and I watch the welfare state undermining our society."[66] The Speaker, who fancied himself not only a historian but a futurist, pointed out that in some other time, some other civilization, these people may have been tolerated, but no more. The racial subtext in the message was so thinly veiled that people of color, blacks especially, could hardly not know they were under attack. Thus it was hardly surprising that blacks were far more likely than whites to disapprove of House Republican proposals. When asked whether they agreed or disagreed with most of what the Republicans in Congress were proposing, 80 percent of African Americans, compared with 39 percent of whites, disagreed.[67]

The ten planks of the contract, however, proved to be only the tip of the iceberg. It soon became clear that although the contract had not mentioned it, eliminating affirmative action was its eleventh plank. Even before the new Congress convened, Senator Orrin G. Hatch of Utah, chair of the Judiciary Committee, talked about his intention to review every civil rights law since *Brown* v. *Board of Education* in 1954. In January 1995, the House Economic and Educational Opportunities Committee held hearings on the Clinton administration's civil rights agenda. The oversight hearings attempted to demonstrate that the Clinton administration's civil rights policies far exceeded the original intent of Congress. Those hearings, according to the committee's chair, Representative William F. Goodling of Pennsylvania, might lead to amending or writing new civil rights laws. On February 5, 1995, appearing on NBC's "Meet the Press," Senate Majority Leader Bob Dole queried: "Has it [affirmative action] had an adverse or reverse reaction? . . . Slavery was wrong. But should future generations have to pay for that?" Dole, once a firm supporter of affirmative action, now requested a review. Concomitantly Representative John Boehner of Ohio, chairman of the Republican Conference, announced in early February 1995 that both the House and Senate would review affirmative action laws.[68] By February 21, 1995, the first product of retrenchment was realized. The House voted to abolish a set of tax breaks given to communication corporations that sold their companies to minority group members.[69]

To be sure, the storm clouds that surrounded affirmative action in the 104th Congress had been gathering for decades. As long as the Democrats controlled Congress, however, Republican presidents could not completely wipe out the policy, and in any event, many congressional Republicans supported aspects of affirmative action. Indeed, affirmative action protections were expanded in several instances during the Reagan-Bush era. For example, the Civil Rights Act of 1991 overturned a raft of Supreme Court decisions that had made it harder for women and people of color to sue for job discrimination and for the first time allowed punitive damages in sex discrimination cases.[70] Other civil rights bills, for example, the Americans with Disabilities Act, were passed during the Reagan-Bush years.

Moreover, during the Reagan-Bush administrations, despite the Court's making affirmative action more difficult to pursue (especially in *Richmond* v. *J. A. Croson*, where the "strict scrutiny" standard was required in state and local government minority contracting), it did not overwhelmingly rule out affirmative action. For example, *Johnson* v. *Transportation Agency* and *United States* v. *Paradise* upheld affirmative action in narrowly tailored circumstances.[71] The Reagan-Bush effort to erode civil right protections in schools, hiring, and firing proved harmful to further progress by women and people of color. It accomplished this mainly by deliberate nonenforcement, by withholding operating funds, and by installing anti–civil rights judges and other appointees. Still, Reagan-Bush represented substantially less than fundamental change. The change in rhetoric was considerably larger than the change in drastic programmatic alternatives. The situation in the 104th Congress, however, bore more ominous portents. The opponents of affirmative action now dominated.

The Republicans understood that they had to keep the focus on "preferences" and "quotas," for polls showed that the more people of all races thought of affirmative action in these terms, the more likely they were to oppose it.[72] By comparison, when affirmative action was asked about in a straightforward manner or when a justification was given for the policy, support for the policy increased among whites as well as blacks. In March 1995 polls, for example, a focus on preferences reduced support for affirmative action among whites by more than thirty percentage points— thus the importance of the Republicans' constant invocation of "preferences," "special rights," and "quotas" in their framing of the debate. Polls also showed that when asked about affirmative action for women as opposed to minorities, white support for affirmative action tended to rise by more than ten percentage points.[73] Thus it was also clear that the Republican effort to eliminate affirmative action would benefit most if they kept the focus on blacks.

In the Senate, Dole opened the attack on affirmative action. Releasing a report he had requested the Congressional Research Service (CRS) to prepare, he claimed to have found 160 federal preference programs, and he promised to introduce legislation to eliminate every one of them.[74] In fact, only 42 of the programs listed made any reference to giving "preference" as a means of outreach to minorities and women. Since quotas are illegal, none included quotas, a fact that reportedly surprised politically naive freshman Republican members of Congress.[75] Even goals and timetables were rare, with fewer than one out of every four programs on Dole's list either specifying or directing agencies to establish them. Nonetheless, Dole's claim to have found 160 preference programs became the object of pack journalism, repeated over and over as if it were an accurate portrayal of the CRS list.

In the House, Representative Charles Canady, Republican of Florida and chair of the Judiciary Committee's Constitution Subcommittee, promised to move parallel legislation to Dole's through the subcommittee. He began a series of hearings that took place throughout 1995. Because he exercised tight control over witness lists, the African Americans and Hispanics who were called to testify read like a who's who of the party's minority conservatives. Meanwhile, a large number of requests from groups that supported affirmative action were turned down.[76]

During the same period, the Supreme Court was reviewing a bumper crop of cases that had the potential to alter substantially the future course of affirmative action, on topics including awarding federal contracts, providing federal oversight for school desegregation, and creating majority-minority districts. Other cases percolating their way up to the Court included affirmative action cases involving minority scholarships at universities and the pursuit of faculty diversity.[77]

Clinton's Affirmative Action Review

The Republican challenge and the actions of the courts threatened the delicate balance on racial issues that was central to Clinton's political strategy. Republican use of affirmative action as a wedge issue could be fatal to Clinton, and the legal climate suggested that the ground was shifting away from affirmative action. The president responded by ordering an "intense, urgent review" of affirmative action, telling the Democratic caucus, "Let's see what we can defend and what we can't."[78]

Civil rights activists greeted Clinton's review with skepticism, especially when the president declared at a conference in Ottawa on February 24, 1995, "What we need to guarantee is genuine equality of opportunity. We shouldn't be defending things we can't defend."[79] He expressed doubts about whether some of the programs were needed and whether criteria other than race, for instance, class, ought to be used. Speaking to college newspaper editors, for example, the president asked: "So the question is: How do we now go forward? And let me tell you the questions I've asked my folks to answer. I've said, first of all, how do these programs work, and do they have a positive effect? . . . . Secondly, even if they work, are they sometimes, at least, unfair to others? Could you argue that in some cases there is reverse discrimination, and if so, how? Thirdly, are there now others in need who are not covered by affirmative action programs?"[80]

Presidential aide George Stephanopoulos, generally regarded as a liberal in the White House, oversaw the review and recruited Christopher Edley Jr., a Harvard Law professor who had just left the Office of Management and Budget, to coordinate the operation. The questions about possible changes to affirmative action were wide-ranging. Most significant were considerations about whether criteria other than race could be used to assist the disadvantaged, for example, class or place. But other questions about how broad affirmative action should be were also considered, including whether women and Latinos should be covered.[81]

Administration officials were sharply divided over which side the president should take: whether he should defend affirmative action, modify it in some way, or abandon it altogether. According to Elizabeth Drew, White House officials coming out of the Democratic Leadership Council "urged a phasing out of set-asides—the reserving of certain contracts for minorities [and women]—and their replacement with programs encouraging economic empowerment."[82] Chief of Staff Leon Panetta, whom Richard Nixon fired as director of the Office of Civil Rights at the Department of Health, Education and Welfare for being too aggressive on busing, reportedly wanted the president to disavow affirmative action so thoroughly that he should back Proposition 209 (the California ballot initiative banning affirmative action programs in the state and its local governments).[83]

On the other side of the debate, HUD Secretary Henry Cisneros, HHS Secretary Donna Shalala, Attorney General Janet Reno, Labor Secretary Robert B. Reich, Commerce Secretary Ronald Brown, Energy Secretary Hazel O'Leary, and White House Public Liaison Alexis Herman argued for supporting affirmative action. Key elements of the Democratic base, including women and minorities, benefited from affirmative action; without their enthusiastic support, Democrats would be doomed in the next election.[84]

Reno's and Reich's departments played critical roles in affirmative action's defense. At Justice, both Reno and Patrick made calls on the CBC and other progressive members of Congress, encouraging them to help Justice make the fight to maintain affirmative action. Reich's Labor Department supplied new research findings to arm its defenders. For instance, although a major report of Labor's Glass Ceiling Commission had been in the works for months, the commission issued a preliminary version of the report, which detailed how white women and people of color were still excluded from the nation's top posts.[85] The substantial media coverage that followed the report repeated time and again that although white men compose only 37 percent of the nation's adult population, they occupy 95–97 percent of the top positions in Fortune 1500 companies. Stories also emphasized the continuing stark differences in wages and wealth between white men and everyone else. The clear indication was that affirmative action had produced the limited progress that had occurred since 1970 and was still desperately needed. A few weeks later, Labor issued a second report that would play a marked role in the debate. The report pointed out that of the 90,000 complaints of employment discrimination based on race or gender the federal government received in 1990–94, fewer than 3 percent were for reverse discrimination and that a "high proportion" of the claims brought by white men were "without merit."[86]

Minority and women's groups and their congressional allies used these reports in their counteroffensive to those opposing affirmative action. For instance, on the same day the Glass Ceiling Commission issued its preliminary report, women's organizations and minority organizations headed by women, such as the Lawyers' Committee on Civil Rights and the NAACP-Legal Defense Fund, held a press conference declaring their opposition to cutting back affirmative action, followed by a march to the White House and a meeting with White House officials. For the Leadership Conference on Civil Rights, Ralph Neas arranged for the views of prominent businessmen who favored affirmative action to be heard at the White House. Civil rights groups organized a briefing for Democrats on the House Judiciary Committee that incorporated their views in a position paper issued by Representative Richard Gephardt, Democrat of Missouri. The CBC organized an affirmative action task force that held a press conference each week throughout May, June, and July.

The National Rainbow Coalition also held a series of press conferences in which Jesse Jackson suggested that his decision on whether to launch a race for the presidency hung on the president's decision on affirmative action. According to Jackson, "There is no question about it. My position on it was quite public, and I stated it to him. I had no inclination to run. My choice was, rather, to support him. But if he had taken away that program for equal opportunity, he would have crossed the line."[87]

When the *New York Times* published a story about a leaked draft of the anticipated White House review indicating that the president was going to sharply stiffen the rules governing minority set-asides, a firestorm broke out among black groups.[88] While vowing to battle GOP attempts to gut affirmative action policies, the chair of the CBC task force, Representative Mfume, also warned on June 5 that White House efforts to date had left black members of Congress concerned and that "the president runs the risk of permanently losing large segments of his base." He said he told the White House and Clinton adviser George Stephanopoulos that CBC members "believe that we need bold presidential leadership. And bold presidential leadership is not a polite tap on the shoulder."[89] He promised there would be protests in the form of economic boycotts and street demonstrations if the president's review curtailed affirmative action.

A group of the nation's top one hundred black businessmen, responding to the threat to eliminate or seriously alter minority set-asides, organized a political action committee (MOPAC). In early June, leaders of MOPAC met with Clinton to press their demands, but the *New York Times* also reported that one Clinton official said there might be a political benefit to black businessmen criticizing the president's eventual proposal. "We want black businessmen to scream enough to let angry white males understand that we've done something for them," said the unnamed official.[90]

Throughout the five-month review period, Clinton acted much as he did in the fight over the racial justice provision. For example, despite the CBC's persistent requests for dialogue, the White House did not consult or meet with the group. It was late June 1995 before the president dispatched Stephanopoulos and Edley to meet with the caucus. Both White House aides listened to the CBC's concerns but provided few insights into the president's position. Meanwhile, Clinton had Panetta making the rounds on Capitol Hill to see what fellow Democrats would do if the administration signaled its support for California's Proposition 209.[91]

The Supreme Court weighed in on June 12, 1995, ruling in *Adarand* that federal affirmative action programs are subject to the most rigorous level of court review, known as strict scrutiny. The decision appeared to cast doubt on many federal programs, although the justices did not actually strike down any programs and a majority said that affirmative action may indeed be appropriate in some circumstances. As it turned out, however, Clinton and the Democrats were able to capitalize on the court decision. Even before the president issued his review, House Democrats cited *Adarand* as a basis for their unwillingness to consider new legislation in 1995. As Representative James E. Clyburn, a member of the Democratic task force on the programs, put it in late June 1995: "We have a court decision, and that ought to guide us."[92]

In fact, as Steven A. Holmes concluded, the decision carried a silver lining for the administration. "In effect the Justices had said, mend it, don't end it." Thus "the decision allowed the administration to modify affirmative action programs in ways that preempted the criticisms raised by Republicans while fending off" blacks, Latinos, women, and other liberals by saying the changes he made were mandated by the Supreme Court.[93] It also gave the president a way to sound principled by not having to openly break with his well-known, long-held views supporting antidiscrimination and equal opportunity.

On July 19, 1995, Clinton delivered his long-awaited speech on affirmative action. He asserted that the record of the past thirty years shows— "indeed, screams"—that "the job of ending discrimination in this country is not over." "When affirmative action is done right, it is flexible, it is fair, and it works. . . . . Let me be clear: affirmative action has been good for America." "Mend it, don't end it," the president said. He also acknowledged that "some people are honestly concerned about the times affirmative action doesn't work, when it's done in the wrong way." He vowed that when the administration found such cases, it would fight them in court, by filing reverse discrimination suits if necessary. But pointing to data in research by Alfred W. Blumrosen and the Glass Ceiling Commission report, Clinton's central argument was that there is little evidence to back up Republican assertions that whites are being broadly discriminated against and minorities unfairly rewarded in government employment and the awarding of contracts and other benefits. Clinton concluded that "most of these [discrimination] suits . . . affect women and minorities for a simple reason—because the vast majority of discrimination in America is still discrimination against them." Hence most of the current backlash, Clinton said, comes not from cases of reverse discrimination, but from "sweeping historic changes" taking place in the global economy that have left many lower- and middle-income whites struggling to keep pace. "Affirmative action did not cause the great economic problems of the American middle class," Clinton said. "If we're really going to change things, we have to be united."[94]

But there were things in the review directly devoted to reassuring his centrist supporters. In the case of set-asides per se, the review focused on how these programs could be reformed to eliminate abuse.[95] It suggested that recent audits of the section 8(a) contracts showed some recipients were disguising their net worth and that the law setting up the program needed to be changed to require fuller reporting. Overall, the review said, an interagency group should come up with ways to tighten the test of who is economically disadvantaged, develop new standards for when any individual firm no longer needs special help in receiving government work, establish more stringent safeguards against front firms, and establish measures to reduce concentrating set-asides in certain business fields. It also called on Vice President Al Gore to find a way to expand government set-aside programs to firms located in economically disadvantaged areas, regardless of the race or gender of their owners. In short, in the review, the new standard being promoted for set-asides was place-, not race-, based affirmative action.[96] In the end, it was the classic Clinton balancing act. His "mend it, don't end it," gave comfort to both camps of his party. As Drew noted, "He managed to please a large segment of the party's base without driving away its center."[97]

The overall response to Clinton's address was better than either politicians or pundits predicted when the review began. Polls taken after the president's address showed that a majority of the public agreed with Clinton.[98]

The Republican Response

Outflanked by Clinton, the immediate response of Republicans, particularly those on the presidential campaign trail, was to condemn the president's message and promise to continue to move full steam ahead on comprehensively eliminating affirmative action. Dole promised he would still introduce his bill, but the scramble for the nomination complicated his aims. Trying to beat Dole to the punch and claim the mantle as the one who had eliminated affirmative action, Texas Senator Phil Gramm, another Republican presidential nomination contender, offered an amendment in July 1995 to an appropriations bill that would prohibit the government from giving preference to female- or minority-owned companies for contracts awarded from funds in the bill. Not to be beaten, Dole engineered the defeat of Gramm's measure, encouraging the Senate to wait for his bill.

In the House, Representative Gary A. Franks (then one of only two black Republicans in Congress), was blocked in late July from bringing an amendment similar to Gramm's to the floor. On July 27, 1995, shortly before Dole resigned from the Senate to pursue the presidential race full time, he and Representative Canady introduced their legislation. Emphasizing the code words that produce opposition to affirmative action, Dole claimed his bill would end any "preferential treatment" on federal contracts or employment for minorities and women. He said that such programs, designed as temporary remedies, had wrongly become permanent and amounted to a ridiculous pretense of quota tokenism.[99]

But by then, it was clear that there would be no action on affirmative action in either chamber until late fall of 1996 or after the presidential election. What had brought about this remarkable shift? From the start of the 104th Congress, it was clear that eliminating affirmative action could not be placed on the fast track in the Senate, given that body's rules, greater Democratic unity, and more moderate Republicans, but the House had proven, by passing nine of the ten planks of the Contract with America in its first one hundred days, that it could act swiftly. Why was it unable to do so on affirmative action?

The answer is to be found not only in Clinton actions, helped along by the Supreme Court, but in splits within the Republican party on affirmative action. Conservatives found it hard to agree on how best to eliminate affirmative action. Concerned about their image as the rich white men's party, some Republicans wanted to try a balancing act of their own.[100] Gingrich and the Civil Rights Working Group ("a collection of conservative legal advocates and several Republican congressmen and their staff, . . . headed up by Clint Bolick, vice president . . . for the Institute of Justice") favored not eliminating affirmative action, but rather rewriting affirmative action laws so they favored the poor instead of certain racial and ethnic groups.[101] As Gingrich put it in April 1995: "I'd rather talk about how do we replace group affirmative action with effective help for individuals, rather than just talk about wiping out affirmative action by itself."[102] But these ideas were not universally shared. Other Republicans sharply opposed any idea of class-based preferences, viewing them as even worse than race and gender quotas.[103] This group wanted simply to eliminate affirmative action. There were yet others, Republican moderates—including many prominent governors—who opposed quotas but supported retaining "goals and timetables" as part of affirmative action.[104]

Dole's presidential campaign camp reflected these divisions. When the Dole-Canady bill was submitted, an advisor commented that "no one was going to get to the right of Dole on this subject." But according to veteran journalist Bob Woodward, New York Senator Alfonse D'Amato, a key Dole advisor, lectured other Dole advisors that opposing affirmative action would hurt Dole politically.[105] Unable to agree on a positive program that would replace affirmative action, many Republicans felt they would be vulnerable to charges of racism if they eliminated affirmative action.

Also, as Dole's selection of Jack Kemp to be his running mate showed, Republicans for the first time since 1960 had some intention of going after some of the black vote. Representative J. C. Watts (a black Republican from Oklahoma) and Representative James M. Talent, Republican of Missouri, had been working to produce a package of legislation designed to help the inner cities, including enterprise zones and school choice. According to one Republican aide, "They were afraid that the publicity raised by an assault on [affirmative action] would interfere with their efforts."[106] Indeed, the split between the two black Republicans in Congress (Watts and Franks) and their public sparring over affirmative action on the floor of the House perhaps best symbolized the ambiguity and divisions in the party over the policy.

Republican governors were also divided. While many were opposed to affirmative action, most of the best known were in favor of the policy. This latter group told the press they had no plans to become recruits in the war, clarifying that they objected both substantively and politically to the attack on affirmative action. Ohio's Governor George V. Voinovich's comments were typical: "A lot of us believe [affirmative action] is good for America. . . . Making this an issue is not good for the country—or the Republican party." Or as Massachusetts's William F. Weld put it, "in a country 'where black unemployment is twice that of white unemployment' and 95 percent of the top corporate jobs in America are held by white men, affirmative action is still needed."[107] Many of the businesses that were heavy contributors to the Republicans were also in favor of affirmative action. An impressive number of CEOs issued statements saying they valued and remained fully committed to affirmative action.[108]

Finally, Republican attempts to eliminate affirmative action were frustrated in part because of the nature of the issue. In many ways affirmative action is an issue like reproductive choice. Those who feel strongly about it are deeply committed and tightly knit into opposing camps. But the issue had little salience in 1996. Unlike welfare reform, which ranked among the top three or four "most important" issues in most polls, few named affirmative action as an important issue. An October 1996 poll conducted for *U.S. News and World Report* found only "one half of 1 percent of respondents chose ending the policy as the top political priority. On the list of major issues, it ties for 30th, after reforming the tax code and abolishing the IRS."[109]

To be sure, references to "quotas" or "preferences" tap into economic worry and racial resentment and sway white opinion to the negative, but the more economic worries subside, the less interest whites show in affirmative action. In 1996, the economy appeared healthy, with low inflation and unemployment declining. It was not the context for Republicans to make affirmative action the ultimate wedge issue. The policy's detractors among the public proved to be diffuse; its supporters vocal and united. In this context, "mend, not end" proved to be the silver bullet, enabling Clinton to put the Republicans on the defensive. Though Dole introduced his bill, neither he nor any other Republican pressed it, and the 104th Congress ended without having enacted any broad-based ban on affirmative action.

The Future of Race as a Political and Policy Issue

Although the Republicans failed to pass legislation eliminating affirmative action, it has been trimmed significantly. The Clinton administration has not ended the policy, but it has been doing a great deal of "mending." For example, although in July 1995 Clinton said he had found evidence of the "very real, ongoing impact of discrimination," three months later the Defense Department suspended a major contracting rule (the "rule of two," "which since 1987 has been applied to all the department's contracting business").[110] This suspension was especially important since the Pentagon was by far the biggest federal player in the realm of affirmative action contracting.

Then in May 1996 the administration announced new federal procurement rules toughening participation standards in all federal contracting.[111] Changes included using race-neutral alternatives as frequently as possible, ending exclusive set-aside programs for two years, and tightening eligibility requirements for minority firms.

Under the new rules, members of specified protected groups must identify the particular group membership that entitles them to be judged as socially and economically disadvantaged, ending the automatic presumption that all minorities are disadvantaged and moving closer to the requirement for individualized inquiry into the economic disadvantage of participants. Agencies are allowed to use sole source contracting and sheltered competition or bidding credits of up to 10 percent of the fair market price to reach minority contracting or subcontracting benchmarks. Benchmarks may also be used for minority hiring and promotion in each agency. Only 6 percent of federal contracts were performed by minority and women firms in 1995, and the number had already declined as a result of *Adarand*, according to the OMB. The new rules are expected to speed up the decline.

These public sector effects represent only the tip of the iceberg. Although the *Adarand* decision applied directly only to federal affirmative action programs, new standards of fairness are being examined in the private sector as well. As a result, the development of new programs has slowed or stopped. Some managers contend they are concerned with changes in the law. Others were already ambivalent about affirmative action, and current law allows them to act on their ambivalence. Cautious reaction has had the effect of reducing even race-conscious outreach and recruiting efforts.

Meanwhile, a raft of challenges is mounting in the states. In 1997 the Supreme Court refused to reconsider California's Proposition 209, which outlaws affirmative action in the state and local governments. Buoyed by their victories, Proposition 209's supporters have sought to keep up the momentum they gained with its passage. Ward Connerly, the best known black supporter of the initiative, has launched a national organization to promote similar challenges in other states. Their success is by no means guaranteed. The 1997 vote approving affirmative action in Houston demonstrated the importance of framing the issue. When affirmative action is posed as preferences, as in California, it is on much weaker ground than when it is framed as a matter of opportunity.[112]

Nonetheless, the future of affirmative action remains cloudy. Already affirmative action as it has been practiced by colleges and universities has been cut back dramatically. Race-based affirmative action was eliminated in the California state higher education system even before enough signatures had been gathered to place Proposition 209 on the ballot. On the mid-Atlantic coast, after the Supreme Court refused to hear *Podberesky* v. *Kirwan*, the University of Maryland was forced to eliminate its race-based Banneker scholarship program. In the following year, the number of merit-based scholarships going to blacks at the University of Maryland dropped by half.[113] A federal appeals court decision in 1996, *Hopwood* v. *Texas*, which ruled against affirmative action for purposes of diversity, sent ripples throughout higher education, as one institution after another began reviewing its affirmative action program.[114] The University of Michigan became the next target. A pending case there "is emerging as the next pivotal battle in the growing campaign that conservative groups are waging against affirmative action on the nation's campuses. The dispute could decide whether universities can keep the practices that many have relied on for a generation to create racially diverse enrollments."[115]

Increasingly majority-minority redistricting also has been portrayed as an affirmative action issue. Here, too, the Supreme Court, predisposed to dismiss race as a factor, has been critical in reversing gains made during the civil rights era. While in 1996 the Court stopped short of absolutely ruling out race as a factor in redistricting, its use was sharply curtailed. Before the 1996 elections, in Georgia, Florida, Louisiana, and Texas alone, seven majority-minority districts (six majority black and one majority Hispanic) were held to be unconstitutional and required to be redrawn.

Far more damaging to the future of poor people of color than the plight of affirmative action, however, is the so-called devolution revolution. Since at least the end of Reconstruction in the late nineteenth century, the way governments "closest to the people" handled matters of civil rights and social policy has been highly suspect. It was states' rights that returned blacks to a condition of servitude and established Jim Crow laws. The different historic experience of blacks and whites with state governments was one of the reasons a 1996 poll showed that nearly twice as many blacks placed more confidence in the federal government than in state governments while more than twice as many whites held the opposite view.[116] Although in the late 1990s most of the nation's state legislatures include some minorities, posing the possibility that the experience with state governments could be different this time around, the problem is that state performance has already proven to be inadequate in delivering social welfare in many places.[117]

Part of the problem is that different states have vastly different taxable resources and poverty-related needs. Blacks especially tend to live in the least wealthy and most poverty-stricken states with the least ability to impose new taxes even if they wanted to do so. In wealthier states, they are often concentrated in cities, which have little control over state spending and are themselves fiscally strained.[118] Clearly, real choices about levels of taxes, services, and amenities are open only to wealthy states with modest poverty needs. Poor states, however, have choices only in theory and "are simply forced into the 'provide-less, cut-more, and tax-more' vicious circle" that makes them less and less attractive to families and businesses wealthy enough to be able to move away. This migration toward the more affluent states inevitably further erodes the tax bases of poor states, requiring some combination of higher rates to collect the same revenues and further cutbacks in services, thus providing even stronger incentive for middle-class flight. The demand for assistance to help the poor is greatest in precisely the states that have weak economies and tax bases and the longest histories and current realities of racial segregation.[119] Turning over programs to those "closest to the people" in this setting can only mean further policy failure and deepening poverty for the minority poor.

Economic and demographic trends strengthen the probability of this result. Already the segment of the labor market most accessible to former welfare recipients is characterized by low and falling wages and high and rising unemployment.[120] These problems are heightened for poor minorities ghettoized in the nation's largest central cities, where occupational shifts in place for over a decade have contributed to precipitous net declines in slots filled by unskilled and poorly educated persons and rapid increases in slots filled by those with at least some college training.[121] In short, availability of low-skilled and semiskilled jobs is at a historic low precisely in the places where most poor minority welfare recipients live.

Forcing welfare mothers, the majority of whom are unskilled and non–college educated, into the labor market is likely to further lower wages and increase unemployment in big cities.[122] As a result, the numbers of working poor will multiply. Even the provision of tax incentives to employers who hire welfare recipients may have little or no impact on job creation. For instance, in a "similar plan during the Carter administration, . . . 'at least nine times out of ten, the subsidy went to a job that the business would have filled anyway.'" Nor did the Carter tax credit create many additional opportunities. "'Studies showed that more than half of subsidized workers would have gotten the same jobs without the [tax] break. And unscrupulous employers could 'churn' the credit by replacing workers when credits ran out.'" This time around, business leaders, including black ones such as Earl Graves of *Black Enterprise* magazine, are warning Clinton that tax credits will be even less successful. Big companies in the 1990s simply have fewer unskilled jobs suitable for people on welfare than they had in the 1970s.[123]

It would be comforting to conclude that minority political organizations will play a role in meeting the new challenges poor people of color face, but it would also be indulging in an illusion. In the post–civil rights era, most black political organizations have demonstrated little interest or ability in assisting the black poor. From time to time, leaders of both the NAACP and the Urban League, for example, have themselves decried their lack of outreach to the black poor.[124] However, little about the caliber of these organizations' current leaders demonstrates they have the broad social vision and concrete political agenda needed to lead a struggle on behalf of the poor. Instead, they have provided a ringing endorsement for "self-help," with its subtly self-serving undercurrents.[125]

Indeed, there has been a disturbing turn in black politics in the post–civil rights era. The increasing trend is to define the concrete goals of black politics in terms of a form of racial trickle-down, a narrow class agenda in which gains for upper-status, comparatively well-off black people—bankers, architects, beverage distributors, advertising executives, or high appointive government officials—are held to be exactly the same as benefits for all.

Significantly, the dominant defense of affirmative action focuses on how that policy is necessary to help women and people of color achieve elite status, "break the glass ceiling." Thus, in the case of affirmative action, class interests and public values tend to go hand in hand for those who provide the policy's visible defense, indicating that increasingly civil rights leaders fight hard and extensively only for those rights they perceive as both just and serving their class interests.

In this regard, poor minorities are especially disadvantaged. Social science documents the myriad ways in which economic inequalities get translated into political inequalities. The poor are less likely to participate in politics than other Americans.[126] Indeed, poverty remains a greater handicap than gender or race in the political process. Middle- or upper-class women, blacks, Asians, and Latinos occasionally win seats in the House and Senate, but people on welfare lack the wherewithal even to run for local political offices. The poor are particularly disadvantaged with respect to their capacity to make large political donations to friendly candidates. No one could confuse MOPAC (the black business lobby) with the Chamber of Commerce, but pro-minority set-aside political actors contribute far more to political campaigns than welfare recipients. As a result, they have greater influence on elections than welfare rights organizations interested in securing basic necessities for all. Although Martin Luther King Jr.'s last campaign was a march for poor people, no well-known leader has chosen to seriously take up his mantle. This is unlikely to happen as long as organizations on the "left" refuse to face up to clear class problems.

Conclusion

In 1992 Clinton promised to turn back a dozen years of the politics of racial division. By linking together a get-tough approach to the racially charged issues of welfare, crime, immigration, and quotas, the president reduced his vulnerability to accusations of liberal fundamentalism that had plagued his party for decades. At the same time, he retained the lion's share of political support from people of color—both leaders and led.[127]

To some it may have seemed ironic that people of color would give such strong support to a president who restrained the growth of spending on social programs; ended the federal guarantee of a modicum of income security for the nonworking poor; placed new restrictions on both immigration and minority set-aside contracting; supported international trade agreements as unpopular among people of color as they were among organized labor; and engaged in other actions that signaled a shift toward a more conservative, business-oriented philosophy within the Democratic party. However, to assume that such considerations should have kept blacks and Latinos at arm's length from Clinton presumes a set of choices that did not exist in 1996. To which other political party might they have given their support? The Republican party remained not only patently unwilling to make any fundamental racial commitments that might have changed black voting patterns, but stepped up its campaign against immigrants, vigorously pushing to strip legal immigrants of a host of benefits in the new welfare reform law and making legal entry into the country more difficult. Thus, in light of the available options and the Republican presidencies that had gone before, the black and Latino embrace of Bill Clinton stood not in contravention of the best interests of their groups, but as a realistic response to the political circumstances of the times. It may have been tragic that it took so little to win the votes of people of color in the last presidential election of the twentieth century, but in fact they had nowhere else to turn.

Meanwhile, Clinton's policies left many of the problems affecting people of color—especially poor ones—untouched and may have exacerbated them. It was this potential that provided the context for a spate of news stories and poll findings revealing deepening racial polarization in the 1990s.[128] It also undergirded Clinton's decision to announce, early in his second term, a new initiative on race.[129] Even as the initiative (defined as a year-long "great and unprecedented conversation about race") began, there were copious signs that the retreat by the Democratic party from progressive social policies and an interventionist government was likely to continue. Many Democrats believe that the electoral victories of Clinton verify that to win in national elections, the party must continue its rightward drift. Determined not to turn off white constituents, the party will not take a step forward on race without plotting a step back, and so the balancing act is likely to continue. Whether this strategy will work as well for another Democratic president, especially if the economy sours, is an unstable proposition. Already the racial policies of New Democratic politics, joined to the programmatic bankruptcy of current black politics and the failure of the established civil rights leadership to build a force capable of mobilizing its base, threaten to alienate blacks from mainstream politics, spurring them toward the evasive leadership of Louis Farrakhan. Analogously, Latinos, a group increasingly critical to the Democratic party's fortunes, may be temporarily mollified by the modest restorations of benefits to current legal immigrants and alterations in the new immigration law. But concern surrounding these issues is likely to reemerge as the prospects for future immigrants remain uncertain.

Perhaps losing the center of political gravity is the real problem: from now through the first part of the twenty-first century, conservatives in both parties will be setting the parameters of social policy debate—and the parameters are moving farther and farther right. As the ugly politics of race grows more divisive, people of color and progressives in general may find themselves at the limit of what can be accomplished through the two-party system.[130] If this happens, the necessity of political mobilization directed toward transforming the nation's social policy will become manifest, and the nation will turn to a new, more powerful rhetoric of still another insurgent movement that seeks to replace both the Republican and New Democratic ascendancy.

Notes

1. Thomas Byrne Edsall with Mary D. Edsall, "When the Official Subject Is Presidential Politics, Taxes, Welfare, Crime, Rights, or Values . . . the Real Subject Is RACE," *Atlantic Monthly* (May 1991), pp. 52–86.

2. Kenneth O'Reilly, *Nixon's Piano: Presidents and Racial Politics from Washington to Clinton* (Free Press, 1995), p. 411.

3. Ibid., p. 410. The candidates pledged to "actively work to protect the civil rights of all Americans," but they also vowed to "oppose racial quotas." See Bill Clinton and Al Gore, *Putting People First: How We Can Change America* (Times Books, 1992), pp. 32, 63–66.

4. For example, in a December 1990 National Opinion Research Center (NORC) poll, more than half of the white respondents (57 percent) rated blacks and almost half (46 percent) rated Latinos as preferring to live off welfare. Almost half of whites (47 percent) rated blacks and 37 percent rated Latinos as lazy. A majority of whites (54 percent) thought blacks were violence prone, and 42 percent thought Latinos were violence prone. Asian Americans were rated more unfavorably than whites on these traits, but significantly more favorably than blacks and Latinos. Tom W. Smith, "Ethnic Images," NORC, GSS Topical Report 19 (December 1990).

5. See, for example, "Remarks of the President at Howard University, June 4, 1965," in Lee Rainwater and William L. Yancey, *The Moynihan Report and the Politics of Controversy* (MIT Press, 1967), p. 125.

6. David Bositis, "Blacks in the 1996 Republican National Convention," Joint Center for Political and Economic Studies, Washington, 1996, p. 16; and Marjorie Connelly, "Portrait of the Electorate," *New York Times*, November 10, 1996, p. 28.

7. For an example of Ronald Reagan's views on this point, see Transcript, "The Reagans," *Sixty Minutes*, CBS News (January 15, 1989), p. 4.

8. For examples of these arguments, see Robert Woodson, "We Need to Examine the Side Effects of the Civil Rights Movement," *Issues and Views* (Fall 1991), pp. 4–8, 10; and Paul A. Gigot, "Potomac Watch: The Real Reason the Black Caucus Opposes Thomas," *Wall Street Journal*, July 19, 1991, p. A10.

9. "The Reagans"; and Fred Barnes, "Inventanegro, Inc.," *New Republic*, April 15, 1985, pp. 9–10.

10. Jill Quadagno, "From Old-Age Assistance to Supplemental Security Income: The Political Economy of Relief in the South, 1935–1972," in Margaret Weir, Ann Shola Orloff, and Theda Skocpol, eds., *The Politics of Social Policy in the United States* (Princeton University Press, 1988), pp. 244–45.

11. Stanley B. Greenberg, *Middle Class Dreams: The Politics and Power of the New American Majority* (Times Books, 1995), p. 103.

12. Edward G. Carmines and James A. Stimson, *Issue Evolution: Race and the Transformation of American Politics* (Princeton University Press, 1989), pp. 45–47.

13. See Michael K. Brown and Steven P. Erie, "Blacks and the Legacy of the Great Society: The Economic and Political Impact of Federal Social Policy," *Public Policy*, vol. 29 (Summer 1981), pp. 299–330.

14. Quoted in David J. Garrow, *Bearing the Cross: Martin Luther King, Jr., and the Southern Christian Leadership Conference* (Vintage Books, 1988), p 93. For a

detailed discussion of efforts of civil rights leaders to promote a fuller social policy agenda, see Dona Cooper Hamilton and Charles V. Hamilton, *Dual Agenda: Race and Social Welfare Policies of Civil Rights Organizations* (Columbia University Press, 1997), pp. 122–45.

15. For discussion and data on Great Society programs and the racial composition of their beneficiaries, see Michael K. Brown, "The Segmented Welfare System: Distributive Conflict and Retrenchment in the United States, 1968–1984," in Brown, ed, *Remaking the Welfare State: Retrenchment and Social Policy in America and Europe* (Temple University Press, 1988), pp. 192–96.

16. See Frances Fox Piven and Richard A Cloward, *Regulating the Poor: The Functions of Public Welfare* (Pantheon, 1971); and John David Skrentny, *The Ironies of Affirmative Action: Politics, Culture, and Justice in America* (University of Chicago Press, 1996), pp. 177–221.

17. Analyzing survey data, Martin Gilens has shown that welfare policies are now widely viewed as "coded" issues that activate white Americans' negative views of blacks without explicitly raising the "race card." He shows that the single most important influence on whites' views of welfare is their views of blacks. Those who stereotype all blacks as "lazy" are the most likely to hold negative views toward welfare and to oppose increased spending on it. As he notes, the role of the "unspoken agenda" of racial imagery "has troubling implications for electoral politics. . . . Such 'race-coded' issues are attractive to some politicians precisely because they can exploit the power of racial . . . animosity while insulating themselves from charges of [racism]." Moreover, since race is rarely explicitly discussed, racial (indeed racist) claims are difficult to challenge and rebut. See Martin Gilens, "'Race Coding' and White Opposition to Welfare," *American Political Science Review*, vol. 90 (September 1996), pp. 593–604.

18. For discussion of the Bush campaign's use of William Horton Jr., see Andrew Hacker, *Two Nations: Black and White, Separate, Hostile, Unequal* (Ballantine Books, 1995), pp. 226–27.

19. Michael B. Katz, *The Undeserving Poor: From the War on Poverty to the War on Welfare* (Pantheon, 1989), p. 185.

20. Black conservatives most typically promoted this message. See, for example, Glenn C. Loury, "Thomas's Black Foes Fear His Leadership," *Newsday*, August 1, 1991, p. 99; Walter E. Williams, "Race, Scholarship, and Affirmative Action," *National Review*, May 5, 1989, pp. 36–38; and Shelby Steele, "I'm Black, You're White, Who's Innocent? Race and Power in an Era of Blame," *Harper's Magazine* (June 1988), p. 51. For a more recent recitation, see J. C. Watts's response to President Clinton's State of the Union Address on February 4, 1997, in "Our Problems Can't Be Solved by Legislation," *Washington Post*, February 5, 1997, p. A17. Watts was the only black Republican member of the 105th Congress.

21. For a book written by a conservative developing these themes, see Jared Taylor, *Paved with Good Intentions: The Failure of Race Relations in Contemporary America* (New York: Carroll and Graf, 1992).

22. Reagan, for example, went eight years without meeting with a single traditional civil rights leader, and Bush's single meeting with these leaders as a group was after the Los Angeles riots in the summer of 1992. Carl T. Rowan, *The Coming Race War in America: A Wake-Up Call* (Little, Brown, 1996), p. 55.

23. For trend data and analysis of program expenditures in the 1980s, see *Overview of Entitlement Programs: 1993 Green Book: Background Material and Data on Programs within the Jurisdiction of the Committee on Ways and Means*, Committee Print, 103 Cong. 1 sess. (Government Printing Office, 1993), p. 1368ff.

24. *Report of the National Advisory Commission on Civil Disorders* (GPO, 1968), p. 1; Richard Morin, "A Distorted Image of Minorities: Poll Suggests That What Whites Think They See May Affect Beliefs," *Washington Post*, October 8, 1995, pp. A1, A27; and Malcolm Gladwell, "Personal Experience, the Primary Gauge," *Washington Post*, October 8, 1995, p. A26.

25. Morin, "Distorted Image of Minorities."

26. See Jennifer L. Hochschild, *Facing Up to the American Dream: Race, Class, and the Soul of the Nation* (Princeton University Press, 1995).

27. John R. Petrocik, *Party Coalitions: Realignment and the Decline of the New Deal Party System* (University of Chicago Press, 1981), pp. 77–97.

28. Stanley B. Greenberg, *Report on Democratic Defection* (Washington: The Analysis Group, 1985), pp. 13–18, 28.

29. Thomas Byrne Edsall with Mary Edsall, *Chain Reaction: The Impact of Race, Rights and Taxes on American Politics* (Norton, 1992).

30. Paula D. McClain and Joseph Stewart Jr., *"Can We All Get Along?" Racial and Ethnic Minorities in American Politics* (Boulder: Westview Press, 1995), p. 129.

31. Angelo Falcón, "Black and Latino Politics in New York City: Race and Ethnicity in a Changing Urban Context," in F. Chris Garcia, ed., *Latinos and the Political System* (University of Notre Dame Press, 1988), pp. 178–79; and National Council of La Raza, "Background Paper for Black-Latino Dialogue," Washington, 1990.

32. For discussion of Asian American views of affirmative action, see Kenneth Lee, "Angry Yellow Men," *New Republic*, September 9, 1996, p. 11. For discussion of the impact of affirmative action on college admissions of diverse racial and ethnic groups, see Theodore Cross, "Suppose There Was No Affirmative Action at the Most Prestigious Colleges and Graduate Schools," *Journal of Blacks in Higher Education*, no. 3 (Spring 1994), pp. 50–51.

33. James H. Johnson Jr. and Melvin L. Oliver, "Interethnic Minority Conflict in Urban America: The Effects of Economic and Social Dislocations," *Urban Geography*, vol. 10 (September 1989), pp. 449–63.

34. William Julius Wilson, *The Declining Significance of Race: Blacks and Changing American Institutions*, 2d ed. (University of Chicago Press, 1980).

35. Michael C. Dawson, *Behind the Mule: Race and Class in African-American Politics* (Princeton University Press, 1994).

36. Robert C. Smith, *We Have No Leaders: African Americans in the Post–Civil Rights Era* (State University of New York Press, 1996), pp. 88–98.

37. The Urban League is not a membership organization.

38. In 1996 Jackson merged Operation PUSH and the National Rainbow Coalition and moved the new organization's national headquarters to Chicago. One key goal of Rainbow-PUSH is to build grass-roots connections among a wide variety of civil rights constituencies including blacks but also other people of color, women, religious organizations, and gays.

39. By the early 1980s, the Joint Center for Political and Economic Studies (a Washington-based research organization often referred to in the press as a "black think tank") announced that it would become a "national research organization in the tradition of Brookings and the American Enterprise Institute," rather than simply a "technical and institutional support resource for black elected officials." See Juan Williams, *The Joint Center: Portrait of a Black Think Tank* (Washington: Joint Center for Political and Economic Studies, 1995), pp. 23–26, 32. The Congressional Black Caucus Foundation sought to establish a think tank in 1993 but suspended the effort in 1995 after a series of leadership conflicts.

40. In the early 1970s, political scientist Matthew Holden Jr. recommended the creation of such a think tank. See Matthew Holden Jr., *The Politics of the Black "Nation"* (New York: Chandler, 1973), p. 180.

41. Fredrick C. Harris, "Something Within: Religion as a Mobilizer of African-American Political Activism," *Journal of Politics*, vol. 56 (February 1994), pp. 42–68; and Ronald E. Brown and Monica L. Wolford, "Religious Resources and African-American Political Action," *National Political Science Review*, vol. 4 (1994), pp. 30–48.

42. Katherine Tate, *From Protest to Politics: The New Black Voters in American Elections* (Harvard University Press and Russell Sage, 1993), pp. 92–95, 105–07. The decline in group membership is especially precipitous among poor blacks. See Cathy J. Cohen and Michael C. Dawson, "Neighborhood Poverty and African American Politics," *American Political Science Review*, vol. 87 (June 1993), pp. 286–302.

43. For data on class composition of the marchers, see Mario A. Brossard and Richard Morin, "Leader Popular among Marchers," *Washington Post*, October 17, 1995, pp. A1, A23; and Lorenzo Morris and others, "Million Man March: Preliminary Report on the Survey," Howard University, Department of Political Science, 1995.

44. Michael C. Dawson, "Structure and Ideology: The Shaping of Black Public Opinion," paper prepared for 1995 annual meeting of the Midwest Political Science Association, p. 29, n. 23.

45. O'Reilly, *Nixon's Piano*, p. 407.

46. Interview with Representative Craig Washington, June 21, 1994.

47. Clarence Lusane, "Interaction and Collaboration between Black Interest

Groups and Black Congressmembers in the 103rd Congress: A Study in Race-Conscious Policy Innovation," Ph.D. dissertation, Howard University, 1997, pp. 326–52.

48. Letter from the United States Conference of Mayors to the Honorable Kweisi Mfume, July 14, 1994; and fax to Rep. Kweisi Mfume from Rep. Bobby Scott, July 15, 1994.

49. "It's Still a Crime (Bill)," National Rainbow Coalition, *JaxFax,* August 18, 1994; and Lusane, "Interaction and Collaboration," p. 341.

50. "Hill Briefs," *Congress Daily,* July 26, 1994, p. 4; and Lusane, "Interaction and Collaboration," pp. 357–61.

51. Mary Jacoby, "Black Caucus Acts to Kill Crime Rule," *Roll Call,* July 18, 1994, p. 20.

52. Roll Call 416, *Congressional Record,* daily ed., August 21, 1994, p. H9005.

53. National Election Studies and Inter-University Consortium for Political and Social Research, Institute for Social Research, "American National Election Studies, 1948–1994," CD-ROM (May 1995).

54. See the discussion in J. Phillip Thompson, "Urban Poverty and Race," in Julia Vitullo-Martin, ed., *Breaking Away: The Future of Cities* (New York: Twentieth Century Fund Press, 1996), pp. 13–32.

55. The only piece of legislation signed by the president that minority interest groups lobbied heavily for was the National Voter Registration Act of 1993. Seen as a benefit to minorities and the poor because it allowed citizens to register to vote while they were renewing driver licenses, applying for welfare, or joining the military, the "motor voter" bill was proposed long before Clinton was elected. Still it was one genuine gain that flowed to people of color from having a Democratic administration, because both Reagan and Bush had opposed it.

56. Neil Lewis, "In Selecting Federal Judges, Clinton Has Not Tried to Reverse Republicans," *New York Times,* August 1, 1996, p. 20.

57. Horne called this "a superficial multiculturalism." Gerald Horne, "Race: Ensuring a True Multiculturalism," in Richard Caplan and John Feffer, eds., *State of the Union 1994: The Clinton Administration and the Nation in Profile* (Boulder, Colo.: Westview Press, 1994), p. 186.

58. James S. Hirsch, "Fleet Agrees to Pay $4 Million to Settle Complaints of Bias," *Wall Street Journal,* May 8, 1996, p. A4.

59. Interview with Susan Patterson, Federal Bank Examiner, Charlotte, North Carolina, October 27, 1996. See also Janet Reno, Transcript of Justice Department Briefing, November 14, 1996.

60. See W. John Moore, "Collision Course," *National Journal,* December 3, 1994, pp. 2830–34.

61. Linda Newborn, "OFCCP: Back in Business," *Black Collegian,* vol. 25 (February 1995), pp. 107–11; Gary Glaser and Edmund Cooke Jr., "The Scrutiny Intensifies," *HR Focus,* vol. 73 (April 1996), p. 5; and "OFCCP 1994 Enforcement Data," *Labor Law Journal,* vol. 46 (January 1995), p. 64.

62. Lincoln Caplan, "A Civil Rights Tug of War," *Newsweek*, February 13, 1995, p. 34. The administration subsequently pulled back its support. In 1997 the case was settled before the Supreme Court could rule on it. A coalition of civil rights groups, believing the case was weak, raised funds to settle the case out of court. Joan Kiskupic, "Rights Groups Pay to Settle Bias Case," *Washington Post*, November 22, 1997, p. A1.

63. For discussion, see O'Reilly, *Nixon's Piano*, pp. 417–20.

64. Stephen Labaton, "Administration Leaves Top Civil Rights Jobs Vacant," *New York Times*, October 31, 1993, p. 18.

65. Interviews with William A. Galston, November 21, 1994, and Representative Charles Rangel, February 4, 1995.

66. Newt Gingrich, *To Renew America* (Harper Collins, 1995), pp. 8-9.

67. Hart-Teeter proprietary poll on Republican proposals, April 3–5, 1995.

68. Transcript of "Meet the Press," NBC News, February 5, 1995, p. 12; and "Affirmative Action Will Be Examined in Senate, Dole Says," *New York Times*, February 6, 1995, p. A15.

69. Paul Farhi and Kevin Merida, "House Rejects Tax Break: Viacom Sale to Minority Group Spurred Vote," *Washington Post*, February 22, 1995, p. A1.

70. Richard E. Cohen, "Rights Act Deal Cuts Cannery Workers," *National Journal*, November 16, 1991, p. 2817.

71. *Richmond* v. *J. A. Croson Co.*, 488 U.S. 469 (1989); *Johnson* v. *Transportation Agency, Santa Clara County, California*, 480 U.S. 616 (1987); and *United States* v. *Paradise*, 480 U.S. 149 (1987).

72. See the discussion and polls reported in Lawrence Bobo and Ryan A. Smith, "Antipoverty Policy, Affirmative Action, and Racial Attitudes," in Sheldon Danziger, Gary D. Sandefur and Daniel H. Weinberg, eds., *Confronting Poverty: Prescriptions for Change* (New York: Russell Sage Foundation, 1994), pp. 378–79; and Charlotte Steeh and Maria Krysan, "The Polls: Trends, Affirmative Action and the Public, 1970–1995," *Public Opinion Quarterly*, vol. 60 (Spring 1996), pp. 128–58.

73. Hart-Teeter and Princeton Survey Research Associates proprietary polls, March 1995.

74. David Maraniss, "Campaign '96—With Roots in the Middle, Dole Shifted Uneasily on a Racial Issue," *Washington Post*, October 31, 1996, p. A1.

75. Interview with Vin Weber, codirector of Empower America, May 14, 1995.

76. Interview with Sherille Ismail, House Judiciary Committee staff assistant to Representative John Conyers, Democrat of Michigan, April 7, 1995.

77. *Adarand Constructors, Inc.* v. *Pena*, 515 U.S. 200 (1995), involving a white subcontractor whose low bid was rejected in a Denver highway construction grant; *Missouri* v. *Jenkins*, 515 U.S. 70 (1995), involving the scope and duration of federal oversight of the Kansas City Metropolitan School District's desegregation efforts; *U.S.* v. *Hays*, 94-558 (1995), involving the constitutionality of drawing a second majority-black district to provide Louisiana's poorest section of

460   Linda Faye Williams

blacks the opportunity to elect the representative of their choice; *Podberesky* v. *Kirwan*, 38 F.3d 147 (4th Cir., 1994), cert. denied, 115 S. Ct. 2001 (1995); and *Piscataway Township Board of Education* v. *Taxman*, cert. granted June 27, 1997, 117 S. Ct. 763 (1997) (case later settled out of court).

78. Quoted in Elizabeth Drew, *Showdown: The Struggle between the Gingrich Congress and the Clinton White House* (Simon and Schuster, 1996), p. 290. For accounts of the review, see Drew, *Showdown*, pp. 289–96; and Steven A. Holmes, "On Civil Rights, Clinton Steers Bumpy Course between Left and Right," *New York Times*, October 20, 1996, p. 16; see also the analytic account in Christopher Edley Jr., *Not All Black and White: Affirmative Action, Race, and American Values* (New York: Hill and Wang, 1996).

79. Quoted in Drew, *Showdown*, p. 290.

80. "Remarks to a Question-and-Answer Session with the College Press Forum," *Weekly Compilation of Presidential Documents*, March 27, 1995, p. 460.

81. See Drew, *Showdown*, p. 291.

82. Ibid., p. 292.

83. This was Panetta's position, according to Representative Maxine Waters, Democrat of California. According to Waters, while Edley did not support Proposition 209, he did support placing stiff new restrictions on minority set-asides. In response, Waters said she had stopped returning phone calls from Edley and Panetta. Interview with Maxine Waters, May 10, 1995.

84. See Drew, *Showdown*, p. 293.

85. Federal Glass Ceiling Commission, *Good for Business: Making Full Use of the Nation's Human Capital* (GPO, March 1995).

86. Alfred W. Blumrosen, "Draft Report on Reverse Discrimination Commissioned by Labor Department," no. 56 (Washington: Bureau of National Affairs, 1995), p. E1.

87. Holmes, "On Civil Rights, Clinton Steers Bumpy Course."

88. Robert Pear, "Report to Clinton Has a Mixed View on Minority Plans," *New York Times*, May 31, 1995, pp. A1, B6.

89. Remarks of Kweisi Mfume, Co-Chair of Congressional Black Caucus (CBC) Task Force on Affirmative Action, CBC Press Conference, Washington, June 5, 1995.

90. Pear, "Report to Clinton Has a Mixed View," p. B6.

91. Various members of the CBC (Representatives Bennie Thompson of Mississippi, Carrie Meek of Florida, and Maxine Waters of California) discussed Panetta's meetings with members of Congress regarding Proposition 209 at a June 1995 CBC meeting. Author's notes from CBC meeting, June 28, 1995. See also Steven V. Roberts and others, "Affirmative Action on the Edge," *U. S. News and World Report*, February 13, 1995, p. 32.

92. Interview with Representative James E. Clyburn, Democrat of South Carolina, June 30, 1995.

93. Holmes, "On Civil Rights, Clinton Steers Bumpy Course."

94. President William Jefferson Clinton, "Remarks by the President on Affirmative Action," Office of the Press Secretary, The White House, July 19, 1995.

95. George Stephanopoulos and Christopher Edley Jr., *Affirmative Action Review: Report to the President* (GPO, 1995), p. 74.

96. See the later discussion of place-based affirmative action in Paul M. Barrett and Michael K. Frisby, "Politics and Policy: 'Place, Not Race,' Could Be Next Catch Phrase in Government's Affirmative-Action Programs," *Wall Street Journal*, October 19, 1995, p. B16.

97. Drew, *Showdown*, p. 296.

98. For instance, a late July–early August *Wall Street Journal*/NBC News poll found that by a margin of 57 percent to 26 percent, respondents reported that federal programs giving preference to women and minorities "should continue with reforms." Also by a 47 percent to 41 percent margin, respondents thought the current national debate over affirmative action was "a divisive and negative development." Ronald G. Shafer, "Washington Wire: The Wall Street Journal/NBC News Poll; A Special Weekly Report from the Wall Street Journal's Washington Bureau," *Wall Street Journal*, August 4, 1995, p. A1.

99. Bob Dole and J. C. Watts Jr., "A New Civil Rights Agenda," *Wall Street Journal*, July 27, 1995, p. A10; and Steven A. Holmes, "G.O.P. Lawmakers Offer a Ban on Federal Affirmative Action," *New York Times*, July 28, 1995, p. A17.

100. See "Republicans Retreat on Key Issues: Education, Environment, Quotas," *Human Events*, vol. 51 (July 7, 1995).

101. This group talked about creating "a socio-economic 'index,' based on a myriad of factors including family income, quality of education, and general childhood background. Using this index, the government would enforce preferences for the 'economically disadvantaged' throughout society, in college admission, the awarding of government contracts and even private hiring." Quoted in "Republicans Retreat on Key Issues."

102. Quoted in Will Marshall, "From Preferences to Empowerment: A New Bargain on Affirmative Action, Executive Summary," Progressive Policy Institute, Washington, August 3, 1995, p. 2.

103. See the comments of Roger Pilon of the Cato Institute and Linda Chavez, president of the Center for Equal Opportunity, in "Republicans Retreat on Key Issues."

104. See Steven A. Holmes, "Preferences Are Splitting Republicans," *New York Times*, July 29, 1995, p. 6; and Michael A. Fletcher, "Losing Its Preference: Affirmative Action Fades as Issue," *Washington Post*, September 18, 1996, p. A12.

105. "Republicans Retreat on Key Issues"; and Bob Woodward, *The Choice* (Simon and Schuster, 1996), p. 226.

106. Quoted in "Republicans Retreat on Key Issues."

107. David S. Broder and Robert A. Barnes, "Few Governors Join Attack on Racial Policies," *Washington Post*, August 2, 1995, pp. A1, A21.

108. Alan Farnham, "Holding Firm on Affirmative Action," *Fortune*, March

13, 1989, pp. 87–88; and James P. Pinkerton, "Why Affirmative Action Won't Die," *Fortune*, November 13, 1995, pp. 191–98. See also Federal Glass Ceiling Commission, *Good for Business*.

109. Lincoln Caplan, "The Hopwood Effect Kicks in on Campus," *U.S. News and World Report*, December 23, 1996, p. 26.

110. See Ann Devroy, "Rule Aiding Minority Firms to End: Defense Dept. Move Follows Review of Affirmative Action," *Washington Post*, October 22, 1995, pp. A1, A8.

111. Paul M. Barrett, "Affirmative Action for U.S. Contracts Is Limited in Rules Using 'Benchmarks,'" *Wall Street Journal*, May 23, 1996, p. A4; and Steven A. Holmes, "In New Guide, U.S. Retreats on Contracts for Minorities," *New York Times*, May 23,1996, p. A26.

112. Sam Howe Verhovek, "Houston Vote Underlined Complexity of Rights Issue," *New York Times*, November 6, 1997, pp. A1, A26.

113. The number of blacks receiving merit-based scholarships at the university fell from thirty-eight in 1994 to nineteen in 1995. Roland King, Office of University Relations, University of Maryland, College Park, citing data from the university's Office of Institutional Statistics.

114. *Hopwood* v. *Texas*, cert. denied July 1, 1996, 861 F. Supp. 551, 78 F. 3d 932.

115. Rene Sanchez, "Applicant's Challenge Emerges as Pivotal Affirmative Action Case," *Washington Post*, December 5, 1997, pp. A1, A35–A36.

116. Joint Center for Political and Economic Studies National Opinion poll, January 1996.

117. Analyses of the job opportunities and basic skills (JOBS) training program, for example, demonstrated most states' inability to dedicate enough resources to move AFDC recipients out of poverty. See, for example, General Accounting Office, "Welfare to Work: States Move Unevenly to Serve Teen Parents in JOBS," HRD-93-74 (July 1993). See also Demetrios Caraley, "Dismantling the Federal Safety Net: Fictions versus Realities," *Political Science Quarterly*, vol. 111 (Summer 1996), pp. 225–58; and Center on Budget and Policy Priorities, "The Kassebaum Federalism Proposal: Is It a Good Idea?" Washington, December 1994, p. 4.

118. For this argument, see Caraley, "Dismantling the Federal Safety Net." For states' percentages of black residents and per capita income, see Courtenay M. Slater and George Hall, *1996 County and City Extra: Annual Metro, City and County Data Book* (Lanham, Md.: Bernan Press, 1996), pp. lxxxi, 8.

119. Caraley, "Dismantling the Federal Safety Net," p. 235.

120. Jared Bernstein and Lawrence Mishel, "Trends in the Low-Wage Labor Market and Welfare Reform: The Constraints on Making Work Pay," Economic Policy Institute, Washington, February 22, 1994.

121. John D. Kasarda, "City Jobs and Residents on a Collision Course: The Urban Underclass Dilemma," *Economic Development Quarterly*, vol. 4 (November 1990), pp. 313–19.

122. Elaine McCrate, "Welfare and Women's Earnings," *Politics and Society*, vol. 25 (December 1997), pp. 417–42; and Bernstein and Mishel, "Trends in the Low-Wage Labor Market," p. 4.

123. Ruth Conniff, "Girding for Disaster: Local Officials and Private Charities Brace Themselves for Welfare Reform," *The Progressive*, vol. 61 (March 1997), pp. 22–24; and John F. Harris, "Clinton Welfare Outreach Nets an Earful: In Harlem, President Hears Grievances on Law from Executive, Recipient," *Washington Post*, February 19, 1997, p. A4.

124. Both Hugh Price, president of the Urban League, and Earl Shinhoster, then acting executive director of the NAACP, have argued that the two associations have paid too little interest to the problems of poor blacks and should refocus their efforts.

125. At the annual meeting of the NAACP in February 1997, NAACP head Kweisi Mfume declared, "We must depend more on self-help." Hugh Price of the Urban League was already on record attributing black Americans' difficulties to a race-neutral "global economic shift" that lies beyond Americans' intervention. This requires, he claims, that "self-help" efforts take priority over fighting for racial equality.

126. Raymond E. Wolfinger and Steven Rosenstone, *Who Votes* (Yale University Press, 1980), pp. 13–36; Sidney Verba, Kay Lehman Schlozman, and Henry E. Brady, *Voice and Equality: Civic Voluntarism in American Politics* (Harvard University Press, 1995), pp. 186–227; and Mark A. Graber, "The Clintonification of American Law: Abortion, Welfare, and Liberal Constitutional Theory," *Ohio State Law Journal*, vol. 58, no. 3 (1997), pp. 731–818.

127. Eighty-four percent of black voters supported Clinton in 1996 (a figure indistinguishable from his black support in 1992), and his share of the Latino vote rose substantially (from 61 percent in 1992 to 72 percent in 1996). Although a majority of Asian Americans continued to vote for the Republicans, Clinton's vote among Asians also rose (from 31 percent in 1992 to 43 percent in 1996). Voter News Service exit poll, 1996, and Voter Research and Surveys exit poll, 1992. See Connelly, "Portrait of the Electorate."

128. For an example of poll findings demonstrating perceptions among blacks and whites of continuing and increasing racial polarization, see "The Gallup Poll Social Audit: Black/White Relations in the United States," Gallup Organization, Princeton, N.J., June 10, 1997.

129. William J. Clinton, "Remarks by the President at University of California at San Diego Commencement," White House Press Office, June 14, 1997.

130. According to Diane Colasanto of Princeton Survey Research Associates, 1995–96 polls show that 57–68 percent of Americans favor creation of a third party. Telephone interview, February 12, 1997.

Chapter 11

Urban Policy at the Crossroads

John Mollenkopf

U RBAN POLICY exemplifies the challenges facing
President Clinton as he attempted to pilot the Democratic
party away from traditional programmatic liberalism while simultaneously fending off Republican attacks on those programs.[1] Clinton had
good reason to distance his administration from the urban programs
enacted during the New Deal and the Great Society. Many voters associated them with unpopular constituencies and thought they did not work.
The nation's political center had also shifted away from big central cities
toward the suburbs. At the same time, big cities still contained the core
of the Democratic vote and provided Clinton's margin of victory. By
1992 many had experienced worsening long-term problems with economic decline, poverty, crime, and fiscal distress as well as the short-
term effects of the 1989–92 recession. Therefore, despite the constraints
he faced, Clinton could not ignore the problems of the cities.

Urban policy was an inherently difficult policy area in which to develop a political strategy that would unite the interests and fates of the
poor and the middle class. By the 1990s, the place-targeted spending

The author is grateful to Kirk Vandersall and Victoria Allen for research assistance, to Harold Wolman for sharing prepublication versions of his work, and
to Demetrios J. Caraley, Peter Dreier, Bennett Harrison, Brian Holland, Michael
Rich, and Phillip Thompson for comments on previous versions of this paper.
Deep thanks are due to the many participants in the urban policy process who
shared their scarce time and insights with me. As usual, the remaining errors,
misunderstandings, and misinterpretations are my fault, not theirs.

programs that characterized traditional liberalism had lost broad public support, and deficit politics made it unlikely that they would be revived. Newer proposals to link the fate of the urban poor and the suburban middle class through metropolitan approaches to urban problems would surely provoke considerable suburban opposition since they meant confronting the racial divisions that characterize most metropolitan areas. As a consequence, some Democrats, primarily in the White House, argued for turning policy away from traditional urban programs. They proposed instead to build on the off-budget and regulatory urban policies launched in the 1980s to promote community economic development. They focused on delivering on the president's campaign promises, which included creating empowerment zones and community credit financial institutions and strengthening the Community Reinvestment Act. Others—who were more likely to be found in the agencies, on Capitol Hill, and among the local beneficiaries—favored putting more resources into modestly revised versions of traditional programs. Although these groups failed to win passage of the 1993 stimulus package that would have substantially boosted urban spending, they did secure modest spending increases for such urban programs as community development block grants. A small minority sought, rather unsuccessfully, to promote metropolitan policies aimed at reducing the isolation of the urban poor.

The administration's difficulty in resolving these internal conflicts put it at a disadvantage after Republicans assumed control of Congress in 1994. While Democrats might not agree on *how* the federal government should address urban problems, they believed it should do so. The Republicans saw urban programs as fundamentally flawed and wished to repeal or sharply reduce them. Devolution, deregulation, and reduced spending were the hallmarks of urban policy for congressional Republicans. The modest accomplishments of the Clinton administration's first two years thus gave way to a more profound reconsideration of federal urban policy. Urban programs proved an easy target for Republican spending cuts, but equally significant was the effect of the 1994 elections on the Department of Housing and Urban Development itself. Faced with Republican threats to dismantle his agency, HUD Secretary Henry Cisneros proposed dramatic new administrative changes that would greatly reduce the regulations governing all urban programs and especially loosen federal control over local housing authorities. Although none of these programs was enacted, their positive reception in Congress suggested the likely direction of future policy.

Cities in National Politics

For laymen and experts alike, most federal urban programs had become identified with minority poor people, socially disorganized neighborhoods, and high-taxing, patronage-ridden, union-dominated city governments. These programs had come under increasing criticism not only from a new breed of Republican mayors, like Brett Schundler of Jersey City, but also from New Democrats. Few experts, whether on the left, right, or center, would argue that federal urban expenditures had improved the quality of urban life. To the contrary, many criticized programs like public housing and section 8 for deepening racial and class segregation within metropolitan areas. Prominent writers argued that community development programs, from urban renewal to model cities to urban development action grants, had not only failed to revitalize poor urban neighborhoods but had made matters worse.[2] Such views found a fertile ground in public opinion, which had become increasingly disenchanted with the federal government in general and antipoverty programs in particular, especially welfare.[3]

The voting power of large, old, central cities had also diminished over time. One study of twelve such cities found that while they cast 21.8 percent of the national vote in 1948, they contributed only 13.3 percent in 1968 and 6.5 percent in 1992. National exit polls found that residents of cities with populations over 500,000 cast 11 percent of the total vote in 1992 and 10 percent in 1996.[4] Between the early 1970s and the early 1990s, the number of central-city congressional districts fell from 103 to 84, a decline of 18 percent, while suburban districts rose from 131 to 214, a 63 percent gain. Excluding the relatively conservative central cities of the South and West, urban House districts fell even more sharply, from 57 to 37.[5]

By contrast, the suburban vote grew steadily. One observer hailed 1992 as the first year it made up a majority of the electorate. Suburbanites surged to 55 percent of the total, according to the 1994 exit polls, then subsided to 49 percent in 1996.[6] In the 1980s, suburbanites gave Republican candidates between 55 and 61 percent of their votes. It was hardly surprising, therefore, that Clinton and his strategists identified northern, white, ethnic, suburban "Democratic defectors" as pivotal to their project of realigning national politics. Clinton's 1992 campaign pollster, Stanley Greenberg, spent the 1980s studying this population and argued that the Democratic party's focus on urban blacks had "crowded out" the "forgotten middle class" of white suburbanites. He found that these descendants of New Deal supporters had decided that the urban poor lacked basic values and got an unwarranted share of federal aid. By playing on these themes during the 1980s, Republicans had generated many "Reagan Democrats." Along with the gradual and perhaps more permanent loss of southern whites to the Republicans, Greenberg argued suburban defection was a key ingredient of Republican national presidential majorities.[7] Winning them back would therefore be the central task of the 1992 Clinton campaign.

Nonetheless, President Clinton could not ignore urban problems. The 1992 Los Angeles riot and urban unrest in New York and Miami had captured national attention and led many to call for renewed federal attention to urban problems.[8] Although the population and real median household income of large cities like New York and Los Angeles grew during the 1980s, reversing trends of the 1960s and 1970s, they declined in many other cities, like Detroit and St. Louis. Poverty became increasingly concentrated in central cities, leading to sharp increases in urban inequality and sharp declines in the quality of life in poor neighborhoods. These trends fed, and were fed by, increases in crime, drug abuse, family breakup, joblessness, and social disorganization; they also carried a fiscal penalty for central cities, which on balance lost further ground to their suburbs in terms of median income and fiscal capacity.[9] When combined with the especially negative impact of the 1989–92 recession on large, old central cities, these trends led many to call for a federal response on the scale of programs launched in similar circumstances by earlier Democratic presidents.

The continuing importance of central-city voters within the Democratic electorate reinforced this case. In many key 1992 primary states, central-city voters gave Clinton the edge over his competitors. In the general election, the constituencies that were most likely to favor Clinton—blacks, Hispanics, Jews, white liberals, union households, and senior citizens—were all concentrated in central cities.[10] As a southern Democrat who was elected governor by a biracial coalition, Clinton knew he needed black votes and was comfortable campaigning in black venues. Although grass-roots organization has become less important as political advertising has become more potent in national campaigns, big-city party organizations and public employee unions staffed the Clinton campaign's field operations. Were he to offend this base, Clinton might well face a primary challenge from Jesse Jackson in 1996. The president was thus obliged to appoint people from big-city and minority backgrounds to high office, to advocate funding for programs they favored, and to create new programs to address their unmet needs.

Republicans, of course, faced the reciprocal challenge. Except for Gerald Ford's loss to Jimmy Carter in 1976, Republican presidential candidates used the "subtractive" politics of metropolitan cleavage to win every presidential election between 1964 and 1992. Republican presidential and congressional candidates did best in rural constituencies and white, predominantly Protestant suburbs. To extend their presidential victories into control of Congress, House Republicans would have to improve their position in suburban districts, especially Catholic districts. During the 1980s, the antiurban urban policies of Republican presidents had not enabled Republicans to defeat suburban House Democrats. (Not every Republican espoused these policies, of course. For example, Jack Kemp, a former member of the House from Buffalo and secretary of HUD, felt that a radically new market-oriented approach to urban policy could win urban and minority votes for the Republicans and undercut the Democrats.)

To broaden their suburban support, a new generation of Republican congressional leaders sought to capitalize on suburban resentment over paying taxes for programs that benefited urban constituencies. In so doing, they were not hampered by the cleavages that divided central-city and suburban Democrats. White, Catholic suburbs were socially closer to the white, Protestant, rural and small-town base of the Republicans than they were to central cities. Republicans could seek the moral high ground by asserting that the welfare state fostered urban dependency. Republican conservatives could argue for terminating failing programs and getting the government out of the taxpayers' wallets, while Republican progressives could stress using targeted tax credits and deregulation to encourage private investment in central cities in order to expand the Republicans' urban base.

The State of Federal Urban Policy

The national debate over the proper direction for urban policy was opportune because, after decades of oscillation between Democratic attempts to expand these programs and Republican efforts to reform and contract them, the edifice of urban programs had begun to experience serious structural faults. These programs stretched across several cabinet agencies, notably HUD, Health and Human Services, and Transportation, and addressed a plethora of objectives, including promoting investment in central cities, aiding poor urban families, and coordinating urban programs across cabinet agencies and across functions at the local level to operate more effectively. Between 1965 and 1978, these programs had grown in scope and, as block grants were enacted, had gradually become less targeted at poor, inner-city neighborhoods. Subsequently, however, the urban aid programs came under increasingly severe pressure and were clearly in trouble.[11]

Table 11-1 describes trends in real federal outlays on the various components of urban policy between 1978, the year that federal aid to localities peaked, and 1994, reflecting the final budget proposed by the Bush administration. Spending on programs that provided infrastructural investment, fiscal assistance, and social services in cities contracted sharply in real and relative terms, while spending on poor individuals in cities grew enormously.[12] The Reagan administration was particularly effective in reducing federal domestic discretionary programs that benefited urban constituencies.[13] As a result, federal aid became a much less important factor in city budgets, which exposed them to greater fiscal strain. In the twenty-four largest central cities, the federal share of local government expenditures fell from 11.9 percent in 1980 to 3.4 percent in 1990, and its real value declined by 38 percent. At the same time, the suburban share of federal aid to local governments increased.[14]

Congressional Democrats sought to compensate by finding points of bipartisan agreement and off-budget methods of encouraging urban investment. They succeeded in enacting the low-income housing tax credit (LIHTC) in 1986, adopting President Bush's HOME housing block grant in 1990, and making federal transportation funds more flexible and requiring metropolitan transportation planning through the Intermodal Surface Transportation Efficiency Act in 1991. At the same time, community groups pursued the avenues opened up by the Community Reinvestment Act of 1977 (CRA) and the Home Mortgage Disclosure Act of 1975. None of these measures was self-executing, and the usefulness of each new tool depended on whether local communities were well enough organized and had sufficient technical expertise to take advantage of it.

Urban policy was further harmed by the deep administrative troubles of the Department of Housing and Urban Development, the main agency designated to carry out federal urban policy. Federal housing and urban

TABLE 11-1. *Federal Urban Program Outlays, Fiscal Years 1978–94*
Thousands of 1994 dollars

Program category	1978	1994	Real change, 1978–94 (percent)
To or through city governments and local agencies			
Infrastructure			
Community development block grants	6,204	3,684	-40.6
Urban Mass Transit Administration	4,502	3,267	−27.4
Local public works	6,596	0	−100.0
Public housing authorities	1,467	2,584	76.1
Highways[a]	12,325	18,139	47.2
Airports	1,193	1,620	35.8
Water and sewer	6,764	1,962	−71.0
Subtotal	39,051	31,256	−20.0
Subtotal minus highways	26,726	13,117	-50.9
Fiscal assistance			
Antirecessionary fiscal assistance	2,821	0	−100.0
General revenue sharing	14,481	0	−100.0
Subtotal	17,802	0	−100.0
Social service			
Community Service Administration	1,140	0	−100.0
Legal Services	333	375	12.5
Education title I	5,658	6,819	20.5
Special education	480	2,748	472.9
Vocational education	1,467	1,292	−11.9
Social services block grant	5,962	2,728	−54.3
HHS children and family services	2,375	3,998	68.3
HHS foster care	0	3,030	
HHS substance abuse and mental health	1,284	2,132	66.0
DOL training and employment	9,022	3,310	−63.3
Comprehensive Employment and Training Act	10,122	0	−100.0
Subtotal	37,842	26,412	−30.2
To individuals concentrated in cities			
Medicaid	22,667	82,034	261.9
Supplemental security disability	11,206	23,700	111.5
Aid to families with dependent children	13,562	16,508	21.7
Food stamps	11,671	25,441	118.0
Child nutrition	5,656	7,044	24.5
Women, infants and children	787	3,249	312.6
Housing assistance (Section 8)	6,369	19,861	186.4
Earned income tax credit	1,870	10,950	485.6
Subtotal	73,789	188,787	155.8

Source: *Budget of the United States Government, Fiscal Year 1996, Historical Tables*, tables 10.1, 11.3, 12.2.
a. Most highway aid is not spent within city boundaries.

development programs had multiplied rapidly during the 1960s from the initial base of public housing, the Federal Housing Administration, and urban renewal. Despite the Nixon and Ford administrations' efforts at consolidating these programs into block grants, HUD continued to manage a huge number of discrete categorical programs for various facets of housing and urban development. Some were criticized, deservedly so, for being poorly targeted to the urban needy, while others were criticized for fostering the spatial concentration of the urban poor.[15]

HUD had also suffered several major scandals. In the 1970s, lax HUD administration abetted unscrupulous developers and lenders in abusing the section 235 home ownership program, while the section 236 subsidized rental housing program experienced severe financial difficulty. In the 1980s, top staff to HUD Secretary Samuel Pierce and close associates of Senator Alfonse D'Amato, then the ranking minority member of the Senate Banking, Housing, and Urban Affairs Committee, were implicated in schemes to distribute housing contracts in return for political favors.[16] Despite appointing Jack Kemp as HUD secretary, the Bush administration continued to cut HUD's programs and vetoed Kemp's favorite initiative, federal urban enterprise zones.[17]

In addition, HUD presented a looming financial crisis. The number of households receiving federal housing assistance actually grew by 49 percent between 1980 and 1988 as federal housing policy shifted away from production of housing and toward vouchers. During this period, a bulge of housing production authorized in the late 1970s continued to reach completion, while the number of section 8 vouchers and certificates grew slowly. By 1989 a total of 1,650,000 households were in project-based programs and 1,060,000 had section 8 certificates and vouchers. By contrast, only 1,360,000 households lived in public housing.[18] Sustaining the existing project-based subsidized housing while continuing to expand the number of tenant-based certificates and vouchers meant that HUD was overseeing a large and rapidly growing share of federal outlays, approaching $30 billion, including $20 billion for section 8 alone. Because funds for the out-year costs of housing programs were appropriated at the time the initial commitments were made, HUD had also accumulated the largest amount of unexpended budget authority ($233 billion) of any agency. To minimize the apparent size of this problem, in the early 1980s Congress shortened the length of section 8 contracts from twenty years to five years, thereby cutting their apparent cost by three-quarters without reducing the government's actual obligation.[19] To continue to fund these commitments, HUD outlays would have to continue to rise. Given the desire of the White House and Congress to balance the budget while holding social security harmless, HUD would inevitably become a major target.

HUD owned a great deal of housing for which book value exceeded market value or rents were higher than those in comparable private housing. It had to find a way to demolish, write down, or otherwise provide new subsidies for these units. The FHA had already foreclosed on 48,000 units that would cost $2 billion to improve or write off. In 1992 the National Commission on Severely Distressed Public Housing found that 6 percent of all public housing, or 86,000 units, was in bad shape and should be torn down or fixed up, which would cost $7.5 billion.[20] While Secretary Kemp wished to sell off public housing to its tenants, he was not able to secure legislative authorization for this goal. Finally, many units built in the 1970s under section 236 and similar programs would come to the end of their twenty-year mortgages in the 1990s; the cost of preserving them as part of the subsidized housing stock was projected to rise from $750 million in 1993 to $4 billion in 1997. If all this were not enough, HUD studies of "worst case" housing needs showed that an additional 5.1 million households needed assistance.[21]

The location of public housing projects and section 8 new construction had fostered the very concentration of the urban poor that had come to be seen as the major urban problem.[22] As HUD Secretary Cisneros later observed, "Too often, [public housing] concentrates dependent families, reinforces their social isolation, provides its youth with few working adult role models, exposes people to crime, and is physically decayed."[23] Well-meaning efforts by liberals to target federal aid to the neediest populations had the effect of reinforcing the spatial concentration of poverty.

Finally, decisions about federal low-income housing programs in the 1980s also narrowed their base of support from the interest groups that had traditionally supported them. Peter Dreier and John Atlas observed that "real estate industry groups—the homebuilders, bankers, realtors—pay little attention to federal housing policy for the poor," that "unions are no longer a major voice for federal housing policy," and "mainstream business groups . . . sit on the sidelines when it comes to HUD and housing policy." The remaining direct beneficiaries of federal subsidized housing programs, such as big-city mayors, private landlords with section 8 tenants, and community development corporations, were "politically weak, fragmented, and generally viewed unfavorably."[24] As federal aid had become a steadily smaller share of their budgets, they experienced less incentive to focus on Washington as a source of revenues. Indeed, the "urban lobby" was surprisingly quiet as the Republicans cut federal aid during the 1980s.

These trends placed candidate Clinton, and later President Clinton, in a substantive as well as a political bind. Clinton could not simply throw more money at traditional urban programs, as the U.S. Conference of Mayors urged him to do. But neither could he follow his Republican predecessors by ignoring urban problems and cutting troubled urban programs. His campaign manifesto, *Putting People First,* sidestepped the increasing spatial concentration of poverty in central cities and the problems of existing federal programs. Eschewing "federal handouts," it emphasized the primary importance of national economic expansion. Its explicitly urban component recommended a modest program of infrastructure investments, community development banks, CRA enforcement, and urban enterprise zones, an idea borrowed from Jack Kemp and the Heritage Foundation. The document placed greater emphasis on improved job training, expanding the earned income tax credit, welfare reform, crime initiatives, and health care reform, all of which, it argued, would benefit cities.[25] This tension between addressing urban problems and avoiding costly new urban programs continued after Clinton was sworn in. As the president observed to the U.S. Conference of Mayors six months after the inauguration:

> I want to move beyond the politics of both parties in Washington, beyond the politics of abandonment, of the politics of entitlement. . . . We can't do everything for the cities or the people of America, but we can't turn our backs on you either. And, frankly, that's what you've had for the last 12 years. I want a new spirit of empowerment that offers you a hand up, not a hand out. . . . I want to offer more opportunity and demand more responsibility.[26]

If it was clear that the president would not be giving handouts, however, it was far less obvious what he actually meant by a "new spirit of empowerment."

One source of ideas was the Democratic Leadership Council (DLC), which Clinton cofounded and chaired in the mid-1980s to create "an ideas-based movement focused on shaping a specific mainstream alternative identity for the [Democratic] party."[27] On urban issues, the DLC

followed the lead of a new generation of white mayors elected to succeed black mayors in New York, Los Angeles, Chicago, and Philadelphia. These mayors stressed controlling expenditures, reducing taxes and
regulations, reining in social programs, increasing law enforcement, and
promoting business. They opposed group quotas and sought to appeal
to minority populations, particularly Latinos and Asians, with an entrepreneurial approach to group advancement, not the rights-based approach associated with blacks. Many of these mayors were openly
skeptical of federal aid.[28]

Drawing on the experiences of these mayors, prominent DLC think-
ers like Bruce Reed, William Galston, and Elaine Kamarck conceptual-
ized the nation's urban problem in terms of strengthening the social fabric
of communities, not providing city governments with federal money.
Thus they were skeptical of the whole idea of an urban policy. The DLC
manifesto for the new administration, *Mandate for Change*, did not mention urban policy or housing policy and made only passing reference to
cities when addressing education, family policy, crime, and welfare reform. It discussed HUD only as a case study of how not to deliver federal assistance. Instead, the DLC, like the Clinton campaign document,
advocated charter schools, national service, community policing, and
welfare reform.[29]

But New Democrats were not the only source of ideas for the Clinton
administration's urban policy. Big-city mayors and their allies had been
busy developing new rationales for federal aid. They downplayed the
need for social welfare and instead emphasized how central cities drove
regional economic growth and competitiveness but badly required a new
round of federal investment in infrastructure, schools, and fiscal assistance.[30] Unlike the mayors on whom the DLC drew for inspiration, most
big-city mayors clearly wanted Clinton to reverse the pattern of declining
federal aid, though they agreed that it should arrive with fewer strings.

The emerging national network of community development corporations (CDCs) provided yet another perspective. Supported by funding
cobbled together from foundations, community development block grant
(CDBG) funds, development fees from constructing subsidized housing, the low income housing tax credit, and the CRA, CDCs argued for a
place-based approach to the regeneration of urban neighborhoods in
which they, not city government, would play the central role.[31] National
intermediaries like the Local Initiatives Support Corporation and the
Enterprise Foundation, created to funnel private investment in low-

income housing tax credits into CDCs, provided technical expertise, national visibility, and their own advocacy for this viewpoint. These efforts meshed well with new scholarly attention to "social capital" and the need to strengthen neighborhood social networks.[32] National foundations had also initiated collaborative efforts at community building in cities across the country, the most prominent of which was the Atlanta Project, spearheaded by former President Jimmy Carter.[33] Like the DLC policy entrepreneurs, these initiatives offered a model for national programs and provided candidates for key appointments.

A fourth, quite divergent perspective emerged from the scholars and policy analysts who had concluded that the ghetto could not be gilded and that federal policy should instead promote mobility for the urban poor.[34] Since housing discrimination was a primary barrier to mobility and a major force in concentrating poverty in cities, fair housing and lending enforcement would have to be at the heart of mobility strategies.[35] A mobility approach would also use reverse commuting schemes to connect inner-city residents with suburban labor markets and make federal housing subsidies portable across city lines, following the model of the Gautreaux program in Chicago. This perspective coincided with a "new regionalism" that stressed the interdependence between cities and suburbs and espoused metropolitan solutions to urban problems. According to proponents like former Albuquerque Mayor David Rusk, metropolitan fragmentation and the polarization between older central cities and their suburbs was the main urban problem to be overcome.[36]

Profoundly conflicting political and ideological forces thus pushed the Clinton administration simultaneously toward and away from urban policy. Given the president's strong support from cities, proposing a new federal urban strategy was politically compelling yet also politically dangerous because he needed to win over suburbanites who disliked urban blacks and costly urban programs that they thought rewarded bad behavior. The adverse trends in crime, homelessness, and social disorganization that flowed from concentrated urban poverty deserved federal attention, yet the array of policy entrepreneurs and advocates spoke with many voices about how to solve these problems.

Forging a Clinton Urban Policy in the 103d Congress

All these perspectives found places within the administration, complicating the task of developing a coherent urban policy. Prominent New

Democrats like Bruce Reed, William Galston, and Elaine Kamarck joined the presidential and vice presidential staffs, where they would have a strong hand in shaping the administration's domestic policies. But Clinton also appointed many traditional urban advocates to cabinet departments. Secretarial appointments included Henry Cisneros, former mayor of San Antonio, to HUD; Federico Pena, former mayor of Denver, to Transportation; Donna Shalala, former assistant secretary of HUD, president of Hunter College in New York, and board member of the New York City Municipal Assistance Corporation, to Health and Human Services; Ron Brown, who had grown up in Harlem politics, to Commerce; and Robert Rubin, a New York investment banker who had advised his city and state's Democratic mayor and governor on urban policy, to head the National Economic Council and later the Treasury Department.

These cabinet officers appointed deputy and assistant secretaries with strong professional credentials in urban policy analysis and advocacy. For example, Cisneros recruited a former staff director for the House Banking, Housing, and Urban Affairs Committee; a former mayor of St. Paul; a former big-city public housing authority director; a former city council member from San Francisco; the son of New York's former Democratic governor and a leading developer of housing for the homeless; and a city planning professor and foremost analyst of urban housing markets. This clearly set the stage for internal differences over what the Clinton administration's urban policy should be and even whether it should have one.[37]

This divergent and sometimes conflicting cast produced a diverse set of policy initiatives. The White House focused on delivering on the president's campaign promises. In practice, this meant winning enactment for urban enterprise zones and community development banks, strengthening CRA regulations, creating new housing for the homeless, and establishing a national service program.[38] These relatively low-profile, low-budget initiatives occupied a far less central place in the administration's legislative agenda than the stimulus package, the expanded EITC, deficit reduction, NAFTA, the crime bill, health care reform, and welfare reform. As one subcabinet officer observed, "However narrowed down compared to past urban agendas, the table was set."[39]

Figure 11-1 summarizes the Clinton administration's urban initiatives. They include programs to increase the flow of financial resources into central cities and urban neighborhoods, changes to entitlement programs that would have a disproportionate impact on central cities, and efforts

FIGURE 11-1. *Clinton Administration Urban Policy Initiatives*

Aid to or through city governments
Fiscal assistance to city governments
    Stimulus package (failed)
Programs to promote public and private investment in central cities
    Empowerment zone (HUD/Agriculture/Treasury)
    Community development financial institutions (independent
    agency)
    Revised CRA regulations (Treasury)
    HUD reinvention: block-granting community development
    programs
    HUD reinvention: block-granting housing produciton programs
Programs to provide and promote access to affordable housing
    Increasing housing production, public housing modernization,
    section 8 (HUD)
    Increased support for housing for the homeless (HUD)
    Fair housing and fair lending enforcement (HUD, Justice)
    Moving to opportunity (HUD)
    Addressing expiring section 236, section 8 contracts (HUD)
    HUD reinvention: deregulating public housing authorities
    Preservation of LIHTC (Treasury)
Programs to deliver social services to the urban poor
    Empowerment zone program social spending (HUD)
    Crime bill "prevention" programs (Justice)
Programs to shape urban labor markets
    School to work transition (Education/Labor)
    Summer youth employment (Labor)
    Employment and training (Labor)
Programs to shape neighborhood organization
    AmeriCorps (National Service Corporation)
    Empowerment zone program planning and administration process
    (HUD)
Programs to assist individuals concentrated in cities
    EITC expansion (Treasury)
    Health care reform (HHS) (failed)
    Welfare reform (HHS)
    HUD reinvention: block-granting housing assistance in voucher
    program (legislation pending)
Efforts to define urban policy across agencies
    National Urban Policy Report
    Community Empowerment Board
    Interagency proposal to reward progress toward metropolitan
    performance targets

to coordinate federal urban policy across agencies. Despite the fact that, in the words of one senior White House domestic policy advisor, "the administration had no confidence that a 'Marshall Plan for the cities' was either politically possible or the right way to proceed," its first initiative involved a traditional attempt to pump money into cities.[40] In early 1993 the White House offered a $16.3 billion stimulus package that would fund urban infrastructure development, summer youth employment, and Head Start expansion and increase CDBG by $2.5 billion. Senate Republicans filibustered the bill, successfully attacking it as urban "pork." In defeat, the administration debated whether the battle had been worth fighting and resolved to make the deficit its controlling priority.[41]

The focus of the Clinton administration's urban strategy subsequently shifted to the adoption of modest but symbolically important measures designed to increase the flow of capital into urban neighborhoods, such as the community development financial institutions initiative, the empowerment zone legislation, and revised CRA regulations. Since these programs had far less political or budgetary salience than health care reform, NAFTA, or even the crime bill, they were largely able to avoid being caught in partisan and ideological conflict in Congress.

In addition to these White House objectives, cabinet secretaries had their own agendas. HUD Secretary Cisneros sought to reinvigorate HUD's ability to deliver its programs and "reinvent" the way it went about its mission. He had little use for debating "people" versus "place" approaches to urban problems and felt both were needed. He wanted to improve ongoing programs, such as the Bush administration's HOME block grant program, and expand the number of section 8 vouchers and certificates. He also embraced new initiatives, such as implementing the empowerment zone legislation. But he was also keen to tackle more difficult issues, such as demolishing distressed public housing and vigorously enforcing fair housing legislation, which were likely to arouse opposition. He wished to curb the practice of concentrating subsidized housing in poor neighborhoods and to use section 8 vouchers to expand the geographic mobility of the inner-city poor. In early 1993 he described these initiatives as promoting five values: respecting and strengthening community, supporting families, providing economic lift, balancing rights and responsibilities, and attacking the systemic barriers that create spatial separation by race and income.[42] By the time the president's National Urban Policy Report was released two years later in August 1995, these had been trimmed to "linking families to work," "leveraging private investment," "promot[ing] solutions that are locally crafted and implemented by entrepreneurial public entities, private actors, and the growing network of community-based corporations and organizations," and "affirm[ing] traditional values." Attacking racial discrimination had been muted into "encourag[ing] coalitions of common interest that cut through barriers of race, income, and artificial jurisdictional boundaries."[43]

Promoting Investment in Cities and Neighborhoods

The Clinton administration's most visible urban policy success was the $3.5 billion, ten-year empowerment zone and enterprise community program. Many factors conspired to make this legislation possible. The basic notion of enterprise zones had been around since the beginning of the Reagan administration, when conservative policy thinker Stuart Butler imported the idea from the Thatcher government. Republican Jack Kemp had championed waiving federal taxes and regulations in urban industrial zones as a Republican approach to urban policy. Although Congress did not adopt his idea during the 1980s, forty states, including Arkansas, implemented some 2,000 enterprise zones on their own. As governor, Clinton used these zones as an economic development tool and included a federal enterprise zone program in his 1992 campaign platform. Equally important, in the wake of the Los Angeles riot in 1992, the House and Senate finally agreed upon enterprise zone legislation that included federal spending as well as tax expenditures. Bush vetoed the bill the day after he lost the election, arguing that it had become a legislative Christmas tree, but it was clear that a revised bill could provide the Clinton administration with an early victory.[44]

The Clinton proposal was part of the Omnibus Budget Reconciliation Act of 1993 narrowly adopted by Congress and signed into law on August 10. It authorized the secretaries of HUD and Agriculture to designate six urban and three rural empowerment zones and sixty-five urban and thirty-five rural enterprise communities that met certain population and poverty criteria and that, through a local planning process to devise innovative approaches to urban problems, had written the best proposals. Communities designated as empowerment zones would benefit in two ways: city governments would receive $1 billion over ten years in direct spending previously appropriated for HHS social ser-

480   John Mollenkopf

vices block grants, or $100 million per empowerment zone, while employers would receive up to $2.5 billion in tax credits valued at $3,000 (20 percent on the first $15,000 of wages) for each resident employed in the zone. Employers could also expense an additional $20,000 in property or equipment purchases per company, while local authorities in empowerment zone cities could issue additional industrial development authority bonds over previously established caps. The more numerous enterprise communities were essentially consolation prizes compared with the empowerment zones; they would each receive only $3 million in social services block grants.[45] Either status also brought priority consideration for any federal grant that might aid the implementation of the city's strategic plan; some federal agencies set aside funding pools for this purpose, while others awarded bonus points to applicants for these two programs.

This initiative departed from the original conservative version proposed by Jack Kemp in three ways: it added social service spending on top of the tax incentives provided to private businesses, it called for a "bottom up" planning process to generate a comprehensive, holistic plan to address community needs, and it established a Community Empowerment Board (CEB) of cabinet secretaries to give these zones and communities top priority for waivers and grants from other existing programs. In the words of the president, the program was supposed to "cut out a lot of the federal rules and regulations, letting you consolidate the funds that you're getting from these different government agencies, and getting you the chance to develop . . . a coordinated strategy at the grass-roots level." It would give cities "a single point of contact so that the federal government contributes to rather than stifles the rebirth of your communities."[46] By using specifically defined distressed urban areas as a laboratory for coordinating federal programs in a new way, the proposal resembles the model cities program (1966–72) at least as much as the "free market" approach advocated by the initial proponents of enterprise zones, a fact that they bitterly criticized.[47]

To many cities, the empowerment zone and enterprise community program seemed like the only urban policy game in town, though many feared the designations would be politically "wired." After a six-month planning process leading to a June 1994 deadline, HUD received 74 applications for urban empowerment zone designations and 219 for urban enterprise community designations, with many cities submitting more than one. An interagency team led by HUD Assistant Secretary Andrew

Cuomo reviewed the proposals for their substance as well as for evidence that community participation played an important role. When the administration announced the winning cities in December 1994, however, empowerment zone status was granted as expected to New York, whose representative, Charles Rangel, had been pivotal both to the enactment of the legislation and the submission of the application, as well as to Atlanta, Baltimore, Chicago, Detroit, and Philadelphia/Camden. To deal with disappointments in jurisdictions that were politically important, the administration granted "supplemental empowerment zones" of $125 million in HUD grants (but no tax incentives) to Los Angeles and $90 million to Cleveland, as well as four "enhanced enterprise communities" ($25 million each in HUD and social services block grant funds) for Boston, Houston, Kansas City, and Oakland. While less than half the thirty-four empowerment zone applicant cities had Democratic mayors, all the awardees did except for New York, which was represented by the key author of the measure; a similar tilt could be observed among the enterprise community designations.[48]

The enterprise zone program is inherently difficult to evaluate, and its results, like those of state enterprise zones, are likely to be mixed at best.[49] In its start-up phase, the program seems to have fallen prey to the problems experienced by the model cities program, such as conflict over who at the local level will decide how to spend the money, a lack of coordination across functional policy areas, and disagreement between federal and state monitors over how localities spend the money. Although the cities that received designation are mostly Democratic, the state governments that monitor them are often governed by Republicans. Marilyn Gittell and her team of researchers found that the planning period had indeed actively involved community-based organizations and challenged them to rethink their community's problems in most of the six successful cities, but that mayors and governors had moved to assert control in the process of formalizing memorandums of agreement with HUD. This has disappointed community activists and led to political contention.[50] For example, in New York, Governor George Pataki held up the implementation of the empowerment zone in order to assert his priorities and control the process. Assistant Secretary Cuomo had to threaten to withdraw federal funds in order to get all the parties to reach an agreement.

The Community Empowerment Board, chaired by Vice President Gore, which was supposed to coordinate all federal departments, did not meet in the first half of 1995 and has subsequently had a small staff and low profile, working mainly to expedite grants from various federal agencies to applicants located in or serving empowerment zones and enterprise communities. It took HUD until early 1996, more than a year after the designations, to conclude memorandums of agreement with the empowerment zone cities because of local wrangling and the time it took local jurisdictions to generate the information HUD requested for setting benchmarks by which to measure subsequent progress. The administration did succeed, however, in promptly disbursing the appropriated funds to the localities so that they could not be subjected to rescission by the 104th Congress. Only in late 1996, more than two years after cities had submitted their applications, were local empowerment zone organizations making their first funding commitments.

The Clinton administration also undertook two other initiatives that deeply interested the community development industry, if not always big-city mayors: the community development financial institutions (CDFI) program and the overhaul of Community Reinvestment Act regulations. The CDFI legislation, signed into law in September 1994, created a $382 million fund administered by the Treasury Department to provide financial and technical assistance to community development–oriented banking operations, including start-ups of freestanding institutions modeled on the South Shore Bank in Chicago and the establishment or expansion of community lending divisions in existing credit unions and other insured depository institutions. Its proponents hoped the CDFI would leverage $4.8 billion in additional private funds; by 1994, 310 existing community development finance organizations in forty-five states had managed $1 billion in capital and had made $3 billion in loans.[51] Advocates of these organizations successfully argued that the legislation should grant assistance only to banks, credit unions, and loan funds solely devoted to community lending, not to the community development lending arms of established banks.

Since it embodied a market-oriented approach to increasing investment in poor areas, the measure received considerable Republican support; it passed the Senate unanimously and the House by 410 to 12.[52] The first administrator of the fund had worked with Equitable Life Insurance to develop alternative vehicles for institutional investors to lend to affordable housing and other community-related real estate projects. In signing the legislation, President Clinton commented that "I've long admired the way [South Shore Bank] steered private investments into previously underprivileged neighborhoods, to previously undercapitalized and underutilized Americans, proving that a bank can be a remarkable source of hope and still make money" and noted that he had called on South Shore officials to help him establish a similar bank for rural Arkansas.[53]

An even more significant effort to increase the flow of capital into urban neighborhoods was the reform of the CRA's regulations, administered by the Controller of the Currency, one of the four federal bank regulatory agencies housed within the Treasury Department. Initially passed in 1977, the CRA established that federal bank regulators should consider a bank's record in making loans to residents of low-income neighborhoods in deciding whether to approve that bank's request to open new branches or undertake a merger or acquisition. The related Home Mortgage Disclosure Act of 1975, as amended in 1990, required banks to make available data on loan applicants and lending decisions. Community advocates could use these data to scrutinize bank lending practices and build a case against a bank's CRA record. By filing a complaint, or threatening to, these community advocates could bargain with banks to take more proactive measures to lend in underserved communities.[54] Banks responded to this pressure by making more loans to residents of poor and minority neighborhoods and by setting up community development lending windows to provide construction financing, bridge loans, and mortgages for government-subsidized housing developments sponsored by community development corporations. Some banks discovered that the latter activity was not only good politics, but could also be good business compared with the commercial real estate loans they made in the 1980s. By one estimate, the CRA led federally chartered banks to make $4 billion to $6 billion in additional credit available each year to low-income areas.[55] The existing CRA regulations did not, however, provide a clear measure for evaluating banks' CRA performance. The regulations also had little force with smaller banks that were not expanding and none with state-chartered lending institutions, mortgage lenders, or insurance companies.[56]

President Clinton charged the Controller of the Currency with carrying out his campaign promise to thoroughly overhaul the regulations. The original idea was to set targets for low-income neighborhood lending so federal bank examiners could move away from consulting community groups toward more objective performance measurements. Proponents felt this would make administration of the CRA less cumbersome and more effective. The controller and community groups also wanted to extend CRA standards to small business loans and to apply the rules to small banks, which, because they were less likely to undertake mergers and acquisitions, had not previously been affected by CRA regulations. These proposals encountered strong resistance from the banking industry, however, and the regulators themselves could not agree on how to measure community-based housing lending or document and track minority small businesses loan requests. The Office of Legal Counsel at the Department of Justice also ruled that regulators could not impose fines or issue cease and desist orders to banks held to be systematically ignoring poor areas. By the spring of 1995, the regulations had been revised to accommodate these criticisms, but they still provided stronger and clearer performance criteria than had previously been the case. The final rules published in May 1995 established lending, investment, and service tests for banks with assets over $250 million and a "streamlined" examination for smaller banks, but dropped a requirement that banks report small business lending by race, gender, and census tract.[57]

In the same vein, HUD undertook a number of innovative steps to increase the amount of private financing for housing in low-income urban areas. It pushed the two government secondary market institutions, the Federal National Mortgage Association and the Federal Home Loan Mortgage Corporation (colloquially known as Fannie Mae and Freddie Mac), to increase the percentage of mortgages they were insuring in underserved areas to 18 percent of their total in 1995 and 21 percent in 1996. It used $100 million of section 8 funds to match union pension fund investments for the development of approximately 10,000 units. HUD also contributed $20 million to an $88 million National Community Development Initiative Fund that the Local Initiatives Support Corporation and the Enterprise Foundation would use to make loans to 2,000 community development corporations in twenty-three cities. The Rockefeller Foundation matched HUD's money with $15 million, as did J. P. Morgan with $12 million.[58] In these ways, the administration took small but real steps to increase the supply of financing for housing and small business development in underserved urban areas.

Given the well-documented, unmet need for affordable housing, together with the litany of criticism of HUD's difficulties in providing it, Secretary Cisneros set a high priority on expanding and improving HUD's subsidized housing programs and fair housing enforcement. More than any other cabinet member, Cisneros identified racial discrimination,

housing segregation, and the concentration of the poor in urban neighborhoods (often in public or publicly assisted housing) as targets of federal government action. In the first two years of the administration, HUD
sought to increase the number of new section 8 certificates, to address
the financial problems besetting its subsidy programs (for example, the
oversubsidy of rents in many project-based section 8 units), and to encourage public housing authorities to demolish dilapidated units.

Among Cisneros's more courageous and controversial stands was to
confront housing segregation and the spatial concentration of the poor.
Audit studies by HUD and others had revealed continued racial discrimination in the real estate industry. With other housing market regulators, HUD undertook more vigorous enforcement of the fair housing
and fair lending laws.[59] The secretary received wide and positive notice
for seizing control of public housing in Vidor, Texas, in order to enable
black families to move in. Other efforts, however, encountered more difficulty. Assistant Secretary Roberta Achtenberg, in charge of HUD's enforcement activities, received negative press comment in the summer of
1994 when she considered investigating citizen protests against housing
for recovering addicts and the mentally disabled in Berkeley, California,
and the Gramercy Park area of New York City. Nonetheless, the administration continued to win notable victories in this area. HUD settled a
number of lawsuits alleging that the location of public housing com-
pounded racial segregation. The housing section of the Civil Rights Division of the Justice Department also actively—indeed, in the minds of
some, too actively—pressed lenders to make more loans in underserved
areas. A Justice Department complaint led the Chevy Chase Federal Savings Bank to agree in the summer of 1994 to open new branches in Prince
Georges County, Maryland, an area of growing black suburbanization.[60]

More controversial were Secretary Cisneros's efforts to promote mobility for the urban poor. To do so, he sought to expand Chicago's
Gautreaux housing program to four other cities with an initiative called
"moving to opportunity." In 1976, in the wake of a suit against the Chicago Housing Authority, *Gautreaux* v. *Kemp*, the plaintiffs, the housing
authority, and HUD had agreed to set up a regional program that would
enable 4,100 public housing families to use section 8 certificates to move
to 114 suburban jurisdictions. Evaluations of the experiment showed that
it had a modest but positive impact on the lives of these families, particularly in removing them from violent environments. Extensive counseling of the families and their wide dispersion successfully averted

protest from the receiving communities, and few families reported hostile treatment.[61]

To build on this experience, Secretary Cisneros developed a $235 million demonstration project to use 3,000 section 8 certificates each year for two years to enable public housing families in Boston, New York, Los Angeles, and Baltimore to move to the suburbs. HUD hoped that the success of these demonstrations would allow it to extend similar practices to the entire base of section 8 vouchers and certificates.[62] Unfortunately, the initiative encountered quick resistance. A *Wall Street Journal* columnist attacked it as "sowing chaos in suburban neighborhoods, rewarding those who are dependent on the state, and alienating middle class Americans who end up paying for apartments that they themselves could not afford." Worse, residents of Essex and Dundalk, white, blue-collar towns east of Baltimore, protested against what they feared would be the arrival of 18,000 black public housing tenants from the central city. Maryland Senator Barbara Mikulski, ranking Democratic member of the Senate Banking, Housing, and Urban Affairs Committee, expressed strong reservations about the program, and Congress cut off its funding for future years.[63]

For the most part, however, in its first two years, the Clinton administration forestalled political controversy over urban policy by promoting small regulatory initiatives. After the failure of the stimulus package, the administration avoided further proposals for significant spending increases and quickly backed off from the racially charged mobility initiatives. But most of the programs that the president had promised in the 1992 campaign had been delivered. The modesty of these achievements reflected the initial orientation of the administration, which, in the view of one participant, "compartmentalized urban issues to one small set of programs."[64] Within the cabinet agencies, particularly HUD, the new management teams grappled with long-term problems and sought, with some degree of prompting and support from the White House and the Office of Management and Budget, to develop new approaches to them. As they began to understand the depth of these problems, they gradually moved toward more unorthodox and eclectic responses.

Defining and Coordinating Urban Policy across Agencies

Many observers think that the federal government does not have an urban policy decisionmaking process. One study found that the urban policy arena was not characterized by an "iron triangle" of congressional committee members and staff, agency bureaucrats, and local beneficiaries nor even by a "policy subsystem," but only by "an incomplete issue network . . . with very loose ties to . . . policy making" about which we lack "a systematic body of knowledge."[65] Though Congress mandated in 1977 that the president issue a biennial National Urban Policy Report, the resulting documents did not articulate coherent federal approaches to urban problems, much less give the White House a mechanism to force cabinet agencies to hammer out their differences and coordinate their actions.[66] To the contrary, HUD went through a protracted and contentious discussion with the White House over the administration's first National Urban Policy Report and did not issue it until August 1995, a year after the nominal deadline. One participant found "putting the report together was an extraordinarily difficult experience because everyone had a veto but no one had the power to say yes," while another commented that "it was an undirected process that gave everyone the chance to fingerpaint."[67]

The 1995 National Urban Policy Report clearly reflected the Republican victory in the 1994 congressional election and anticipated the president's 1996 reelection campaign. It gave more space to justifying the administration's positions than to analyzing the source of urban problems or proposing new urban initiatives. For example, one section extolled the virtues of the president's budget-balancing plan, middle-class tax relief, and the positive impact of NAFTA and GATT on world trade, while the introduction stressed the administration's commitment to promoting "traditional values," including "hard work, family, and self-reliance."[68]

The report referred briefly to an intriguing idea circulating within the administration on the eve of the 1994 elections. It said that the Clinton administration would develop "performance partnerships" as a "third way" between overly detailed categorical grants and insufficiently accountable block grants. The federal government would collaborate with localities to establish performance criteria for how localities would progress toward national goals. These pacts would leave the means for achieving these goals up to the localities but specify ways to measure outcomes. In return, the federal government would consolidate federal grants into a flexible pool of funds localities would use to carry out their plans. The federal government would also set aside some funds to reward the localities that made the most progress, thus creating "strong incentives for good performance."[69] Federal urban policy would thus shift from managing programs to articulating national goals, establishing specific performance criteria, collaborating with local planning processes, and monitoring outcomes.

Consideration had been given to proposing that this process be organized on a metropolitan basis. A memorandum prepared for an interdepartmental working group on urban policy, entitled "The Next Phase of the Clinton Urban Policy: Metropolitan Empowerment Zones," strongly advocated such an approach. It called for senior administration officials to engage leaders from metropolitan areas in a collaborative discussion about how to overcome the fragmentation of federal programs and the barriers to metropolitan cooperation. These discussions would lead to the establishment of measurable goals each metropolitan area would seek to achieve by using an unfettered pool of federal assistance. The federal government would reward the metropolitan areas that made the most progress with additional funds. The draft memorandum drew explicitly on Anthony Downs's call for forging new "bonds of community and social solidarity" between central cities and suburbs.[70] Although the administration shelved this proposal after the 1994 elections, it was undoubtedly the administration's boldest vision for urban policy.

If framed in ways that did not exacerbate tensions between central cities and suburbs, such an approach to urban policy might well have spoken to the Democrats' need to bolster suburban support. However, given the experience with the "moving to opportunity" program, it was feared that any effort to put the weight of federal expenditures behind promoting racial and class integration on a metropolitan scale would provoke great opposition. Although the National Urban Policy Report did not mention metropolitan enterprise zones, HUD's subsequent budget requests continued to request the establishment of performance bonus pools to reward local jurisdictions that successfully addressed such issues as promoting mobility.

The 104th Congress, Budget Cuts, and the Fate of National Urban Policy

The November 1994 congressional elections and advent of Republican majorities in the Senate and House dramatically altered the political environment for federal urban policy. The Contract with America, the Republican stance on fiscal year 1995 rescissions and the 1996 budget, and emerging Republican initiatives on urban policy posed a grave threat not only to the Clinton administration's fledgling initiatives, but to the basic framework of existing urban programs, including the continued existence of HUD. As drastic as this situation was for groups and individuals benefiting from these programs, it freed the administration from its reliance on the Democratic majority in Congress, which many White House and vice presidential staff members saw as an albatross around the necks of those who would forge a New Democratic policy framework.

Since the new Republican majority wished to move quickly to reduce the federal budget deficit while simultaneously cutting taxes and maintaining spending on defense and social security, they had to make deep cuts in domestic discretionary spending and more rapidly slow the growth of entitlements, especially medicare and medicaid. As a first installment on this campaign, the new Congress extracted $16.5 billion in rescissions from the previously adopted fiscal year 1995 budget, with $6.3 billion coming from HUD alone, largely from public housing and section 8. This represented a 24.9 percent decrease in the department's budget. After initially vetoing the bill in order to win some concessions from the Republicans and save his pet initiatives, such as CDFI and the national service program, President Clinton signed the bill in July 1995. This proved a warmup for the protracted fight over the fiscal 1996 budget, which began with administration budget requests in early 1995 and concluded, after a series of presidential vetoes, in April 1996, seven months into the fiscal year.

Anticipating the need for budget cuts in order to move along his own path to deficit reduction, the president's 1996 HUD budget request proposed a reduction from the previous base budget of $64 billion over five years, including an $800 million cut realized by reducing HUD staff from 11,900 to 7,500, shortening section 8 contracts to two years, and restructuring the financing of FHA-insured properties. Cisneros had already trimmed 1,500 of HUD's staff members, reduced the number of field offices from eighty-one to sixty, and decreased the HUD budget by $800 million in fiscal 1994.[71] But the 1996 budget negotiations, like the 1995 rescissions, hit HUD and other urban programs especially hard.

According to a senior White House domestic policy advisor, the House Republican leadership targeted "every single program with the Clinton imprimatur, despite conservative support for many of them."[72] During the 1996 budget process, the appropriations subcommittees concerned with various urban policy made the rescissions permanent, defunded the CDFI and the president's cherished national service initiative, AmeriCorps, and attached language undoing many of the steps taken to strengthen the CRA. The House appropriations housing subcommittee cut HUD's budget request by $5.6 billion, or 23 percent, from the 1995 level, leaving a budget authority of $19.1 billion. Like the rescissions, this reduction came primarily from section 8 and public housing, while maintaining CDBG and HOME, the programs local officials favored most, at previous levels.[73] It also adopted language preventing HUD from taking Fair Housing Act enforcement actions against the insurance industry. In other actions that would affect cities, other House appropriations subcommittees cut mass transit operating assistance by $310 million (44 percent) and education Title I funding by $1.1 billion (17 percent) and reduced or eliminated new funding for Head Start, summer youth employment, education and training, substance abuse treatment, energy assistance, the EITC, and the LIHTC. They also proposed cuts for medicare and medicaid that would have an enormous effect on urban hospitals.[74]

In the late fall of 1995 and winter of 1996, the president and the Republican Congress battled over these appropriations bills. After a series of vetoes and government shutdowns, agreement was finally reached in April 1996. In the process, the president was able to save a few of the programs dearest to him, such as CDFI, CRA, AmeriCorps, the LIHTC, and HUD's right to enforce fair housing laws, while also softening the medicare and medicaid cuts. But the fiscal 1996 omnibus budget reconciliation act eliminated all new section 8 vouchers and made deep cuts in section 8, public housing, and other programs for the urban poor. As one participant in the process commented, "It basically seemed like the White House was willing to jettison all the major programs in order to save its own initiatives." Robert Reischauer, former director of the Congressional Budget Office, called the act "historically unprecedented" in its disproportionate negative impact on city governments, city economies, and the urban poor.[75]

Remarkably, the Department of Housing and Urban Development managed to survive this onslaught. Since the Contract with America promised to abolish one or more cabinet departments, HUD appeared to be a prime candidate for termination in late 1994 and early 1995. Even White House staff considered eliminating HUD as one way to respond to the Republicans' momentum. To forestall this outcome, Cisneros devised a bold plan immediately after the 1994 election entitled "Reinvention Blueprint."[76] It proposed to consolidate HUD's sixty programs into a Community Opportunity Fund similar to the CDBG program but with a new emphasis on job creation and cleaning up contaminated "brownfield" sites, an Affordable Housing Fund based on the HOME block grant, which would consolidate all assisted housing production programs, and a Housing Certificate Fund, which would combine all voucher and project-connected rental housing subsidies.

The Reinvention Blueprint also called for deregulating public housing authorities and spinning off FHA as an independent, government-owned corporation that would work out the problems with FHA-insured HUD projects. Over time, HUD would wean local public housing authorities from operating subsidies and force them to compete with private landlords for tenants with housing vouchers. Noting that "the current public housing system is plagued by a series of deeply rooted and systemic problems," HUD called for an "orderly and prudent" but nonetheless "dramatic transformation of public housing." Regulations for other programs would also be radically reduced. States and localities would be required to develop plans with specific performance targets in order to receive the money allocated to them. The nascent proposal for "performance partnerships" would be pursued by setting aside 10 percent of the block grant totals to provide bonuses to jurisdictions that did best in meeting national objectives.[77]

The boldness of this plan, combined with effective advocacy from the secretary, deterred the White House and Congress from abolishing HUD, but it created a wave of concern from the beneficiaries of HUD's existing programs. In essence, HUD was aiming to get out of the business of producing and managing subsidized housing, shifting toward an income support or voucher strategy, marking down its untenable real estate, and becoming a much smaller agency that would write checks to recipients and monitor, evaluate, and reward performance by other players in the housing market. Advocacy groups like the Low Income Housing Information Service, the National Housing Law Project, and the Council of Large Public Housing Authorities criticized the proposal on many counts. They argued that the plan did not commit enough resources to achieve its objectives and that HUD lacked the credibility to enforce performance standards on localities. They were skeptical that HUD would really reduce onerous regulations and concerned that the proposal was insensitive to the tenants and projects that would be left stranded in the policy shift.

Many of the Reinvention Blueprint proposals received a friendly hearing in the 104th Congress. Although ultimately none were enacted in authorizing legislation, many were embodied in appropriations bills. According to one HUD budget negotiator, "a quiet revolution took place in who ran housing policy on the Hill" as the appropriations committees allowed HUD to pursue its reforms in compensation for its budget being cut.[78] Sooner or later, these changes will pass into authorizing legislation. For example, both chambers passed measures to revamp public housing, but, as the 1996 election loomed, they did not make it to conference.

The House Banking Committee's Subcommittee on Housing and Community Opportunity, chaired by Republican Rick Lazio of New York, proposed the most thoroughgoing revision. His bill, H.R. 2406, repealed the Housing Act of 1937, the Brooke amendment (which required tenants to pay no more than 30 percent of their income in rent), and the requirement to replace demolished public housing units on a one-for-one basis. It deregulated public housing authorities, allowed them to use modernization funds to demolish dilapidated units, and consolidated the section 8 certificate and voucher programs.[79] The bill was reported out of committee and passed the House, with 91 Democrats joining 224 Republicans against 107 of their colleagues. Although most northern urban Democrats opposed the bill because they feared public housing tenants might be displaced or have to pay higher rents, Charles Schumer, Democrat of New York, a coauthor of the LIHTC in 1986, endorsed the bill in the subcommittee and on the floor.[80] Lazio observed that "the old housing policies ensure that no one is well-served by the gigantic hulks of despair all too often associated with public housing," and that his measure "makes a commitment to families struggling to make ends meet."[81] While this bill did not become law, something like it stands a good chance of enactment.

HUD has also pursued the goals of the Reinvention Blueprint by reforming its administrative regulations. For example, it established a consolidated plan that combined the planning, application, and peformance paperwork for four large programs (CDBG, HOME, Emergency Sheltergrants, and Housing Opportunities for Persons with AIDS) into one document. The administration budget request and the fiscal 1997 HUD appropriations bill adopted new program categories moving toward those suggested in the Reinvention Blueprint. The final appropriations bill, H.R. 3666, signed on September 26, 1996, retained the president's favored programs, the Corporation for National and Community Service (AmeriCorps) and the CDFI fund and slightly increased

HUD's overall budget authority, allowing HUD to renew all expiring section 8 contracts. As in the previous year, it provided no new section 8 vouchers and did not appropriate the "bonus funds" requested by Secretary Cisneros. Representative Lazio rejected performance bonuses on the grounds that they might be handed out to political allies.[82]

Congressional Republicans had challenged the entire structure of urban policy. They had sought not only to reduce spending on traditional housing programs and eliminate Clinton's initiatives, they had also attempted to undo the incentives and regulations enacted in the 1980s, such as the LIHTC and the CRA, that undergirded the activities of local community development groups. Their success was only partial; spending on urban and housing programs had been significantly reduced, but the traditional urban programs and the regulatory measures enacted in the 1980s and extended by Clinton were still standing by the 1996 election. Nonetheless, the Republicans had succeeded in shifting the ground for urban policymaking. The initiatives of Secretary Cisneros suggested that a new era of deregulation and devolution was not far off.

The Future of Federal Urban Policy

How can the Clinton administration's urban initiatives best be judged? From the point of view of city budgets and the dependent poor, the record bordered on disastrous. The Clinton administration did not reverse the downward trend in urban program spending; rather, it accepted the need to cut these programs further in order to reduce the deficit and move toward a balanced budget over seven years. The urban lobby prevailed on the president and Congress to maintain the most popular programs, particularly community development block grants and the HOME block grant. But many other federal grant programs important to local governments, such as mass transit, were trimmed.

More important, Congress disproportionately cut entitlement programs supporting the urban poor and the health care and social service institutions that address their needs, particularly AFDC, medicaid, and medicare. Ending the eligibility of legal immigrants for AFDC, food stamps, and supplemental security income will particularly undercut the fiscal position of the cities where they are concentrated and reduce income to these communities. Such measures will also undoubtedly have a long-term effect on the city governments, which are ultimately obliged to provide some level of assistance to these populations. Philadelphia Mayor Ed Rendell observed,

> County and city governments are the last of the food chain; and if my state won't pick up that [additional shelter-care cost that will come from cuts in AFDC]—and I doubt they will—what happens? We've just eliminated a billion-dollar-plus deficit. We produced the first cut in our wage tax in fifty years. But this one thing . . . could eradicate our tax cut, maybe force us to raise taxes. If we raise taxes, all we do is drive people out in the long run and worsen the city's problems.[83]

If taking money out of systems that serve the urban poor does not, as Republicans predict, reduce urban poverty, then city budgets will suffer considerably, even if these governments cut service levels. The few places where the Clinton administration managed to increase funds flowing to city governments, such as the empowerment zone program or housing for the homeless, do not compensate for these cuts, especially as localities have been slow to spend this money.

These budget trends will also reduce the production of subsidized housing in poor urban neighborhoods, no matter how much housing developers make creative use of tax expenditure programs like the LIHTC. Nonprofit community development corporations typically account for most housing construction in poor neighborhoods. To build it, they splice together funding from many sources, public and private, national and local.[84] Such projects require at least some tenants who have section 8 vouchers because they provide a long-term rent that makes the overall project bankable.[85] Without new section 8 vouchers and certificates, the whole intricate nonprofit housing production system is at risk. If the number of section 8 vouchers is actually cut in the future, as seems likely, this crisis will become even more severe. As one senior local government housing official observed, "This is a sophisticated delivery system. Talented people are drawn to these organizations. It could deliver far more product, but the organizations are thinly capitalized and strangled by their dependence on project fees. We are at the beginning of a real shake-out. Lots of people are in denial."[86]

If the issue is no longer whether urban aid can be increased or even maintained, but "how to use Washington's newfound determination to control spending as an opportunity to effect changes in federal policies and programs that will benefit cities," then what have cities gained in procedural flexibility?[87] The administration and the Republican congressional leadership have both stressed the need to reduce federal regulations and mandates, increase the flexibility of federal funds, and focus on results over procedure. Apart from the waivers HHS granted for welfare, little seems to have happened at the ground level. One senior local administrator who had extensive dealings with HUD commented,

> The tone of business was a lot better. We had more access and a lot of the new people in the agency wanted to make the kind of changes needed. But they ran into a stone wall in DC. There was no improvement in the bureaucracy, changing the rules, being open to local initiative, getting paper processed. Absolutely no improvement.[88]

Certainly, the vision for radically reorganizing HUD held by Cisneros has yet to be realized, though Secretary Cuomo continues to push in this direction.

The empowerment zone program and the Community Empowerment Board offer cases in point. Touted as a laboratory for demonstrating the administration's urban policy that would devolve power and resources to a local decisionmaking process, the empowerment zone program instead got bogged down in the local political marshes. The Community Empowerment Board has not enabled the vice president and the relevant cabinet secretaries to coordinate federal responses to localities and dramatically reshape intergovernmental relations. Although the CEB's small staff, drawn from the White House and relevant agencies, expedited grants for empowerment zone cities, they did not change interagency relations. As one staff member involved with the CEB said, "Never will you get agencies to cooperate. They run programs, not solve problems." A senior HHS administrator added, "Once in a while we take time out to talk about the problems of cities, but the crush of business pushes it aside."[89]

When judged by the narrow standard of candidate Clinton's campaign promises, President Clinton delivered almost every urban program set forth in *Putting People First*. During his first two years, he won enactment for the community development financial institutions initiative, urban enterprise zones, national service, and the urban crime package. He strengthened the Community Reinvestment Act, liberalized the EITC, and expanded job training, summer youth employment, the HUD budget, homeless housing, Head Start, and Chapter I school funding. The only salient urban planks in his platform that did not materialize were increased infrastructure investment and health care reform. The Clinton administration also took some steps away from rigid, centralized, "one size fits all" federal programs toward more flexible approaches. But it did not succeed in its more ambitious schemes to fold urban programs into flexible grant pools that could be used to cement new forms of political cooperation between Washington, the central cities, and the suburbs.

More consequential for the future of cities than these modest achievements, however, was the agreement between New Democrats and Republicans on an agenda of budget restraint, deregulation, and devolution. These decisions may well reverberate through the framework of federalism to produce long-run changes in the balance of political interests within the Democratic party and the nation. Those who favor devolution argue that states and localities understand urban problems better, are more responsive to local needs, and can design more innovative programs. They note that states made important changes in various domestic programs as the federal government reduced its level of commitment in the Reagan administration.[90] Others counter, however, that the states stepped in to support programs with broad constituencies and offered the least help with programs aiding the urban poor. Moreover, block grants have other characteristics that might work against cities. Typically, they have not required states to continue their contributions. Historically, the federal government has not sustained their real funding levels compared with categorical programs. Block grants broaden the range of potential beneficiaries and therefore weaken their ability to organize to lobby in favor of the program. They also shift the scene of decisionmaking from one focal point, Washington, to fifty state legislatures, where cities have been at an increasing disadvantage.[91]

From the point of view of economic theory, states, like cities, are less able than the national government to engage in redistributive activities without promoting the flight of asset holders. Thus, as redistributive responsibilities are pushed lower in the federal system, they face more structural obstacles. As Mayor Rendell observed, the result is a Hobson's choice: maintain spending, increase taxes, and suffer further flight of business and the middle class, or cut programs, ignore the need, and attempt to export the poor. As devolution proceeds, it may well further undercut the base of support for urban liberalism, foster the election of more conservative mayors, and place greater stress on city budgets. This could result in mayoral efforts to get the poor to leave the cities or otherwise insulate city budgets from the costs of poverty.

How meaningful were these successes in the larger sweep of federal

urban policy? Do they materially address the issues scholars have identified as central to the problems facing our cities? While it may be too soon to
answer these questions, the Clinton administration's urban policy initiatives appear to be symbolic gestures more than substantive achievements.

If broad fiscal and political constraints prevent any sizable increase in
federal spending on cities, if entitlement spending on poor individuals
concentrated in cities is also likely to decline, and if interagency policy
coordination remains an ephemeral goal, what hope is there for urban
policy in the future? What steps might address the substantive problems without spending more money? And how might they affect the
balance of political alignments?

The Clinton administration has considered important, if halting, steps
toward using federal incentives to promote cooperation within metropolitan areas and to unwind the intrametropolitan political fragmentation and competition that, by many accounts, severely exacerbate urban
problems. Vigorously pursuing such a policy direction need not have a
major impact on the federal budget. Current funding could, as suggested
by HUD's Reinvention Blueprint and its plans for bonus pools for meeting performance targets, be conditioned on planning solutions and
achieving performance goals on a metropolitan basis. Such incentives
could provide a backdoor to promoting residential mobility and choice
for the concentrated urban poor, which proved so controversial in HUD's
"move to opportunity" program. Congress could also abate the fiscal
competition between suburbs and central cities by outlawing the use of
tax incentives or tax-free bonding to lure investment from one jurisdiction to another, encouraging metropolitan tax sharing schemes like that
of Minneapolis–St. Paul, and favoring areas with strong regional planning in the award of various federal grants.

If the responsibility to solve urban problems is being thrust back on
states, metropolitan regions, and cities, they must develop a stronger
institutional capacity to address them. Otherwise, the prevailing jurisdictional competition within metropolitan areas and declining city influence in state legislatures will only compound the underlying problems
of the spatial isolation of the central-city poor. If, as Harold Wolman and
his colleagues have concluded, disparities between the central cities and
the suburbs lie at the heart of urban problems, there is also "an ominous
lack of consensus [about] how to create a viable political strategy to persuade the majority of Americans who are not poor and do not reside in
cities to respond to the needs of these areas."[92] The Clinton administra-

tion's search for a "third way" between traditional urban liberal Democrats and conservative, rural and small-town Republicans will succeed only if it can find a geopolitical path that forges a metropolitan majority that will address problems that are at once urban, suburban, and national in scope. The ultimate test of the Clinton administration's urban policy is the extent to which it moves us toward this end.

Notes

1. Urban policy is defined to include federal programs or regulations designed to affect urban jurisdictions and White House or intercabinet efforts to coordinate such programs across agencies. Because other chapters analyze the major federal programs affecting inner-city residents, they will be discussed here only in passing. "Non-urban urban policies," that is, federal programs or regulations that do not have an explicit urban focus but strongly affect the spatial distribution of economic activity, such as the defense budget, are not examined here.

2. See, for example, Nicholas Lemann, "The Myth of Community Development," *New York Times Magazine,* January 9, 1994, pp. 27–60.

3. Times Mirror Center for the People and the Press, *The New Political Landscape* (Washington, October 1994), pp. 22–24, 29–32; and Karlyn Bowman and Everett Carll Ladd, "Opinion Pulse: Gauging the 1994 Vote," *American Enterprise,* vol. 6 (January–February 1995), pp. 101–11.

4. Richard Sauerzopf and Todd Swanstrom. "The Urban Electorate in Presidential Elections, 1920–1992: Challenging the Conventional Wisdom," paper prepared for 1993 annual meeting of the Urban Affairs Association, fig. 2; Gerald M. Pomper, "The Presidential Election," in Pomper, ed., *The Election of 1992* (Chatham, N.J.: Chatham House, 1993), p. 139; and "Portrait of the Electorate," *New York Times,* November 10, 1996, p. 28.

5. Harold Wolman and Lisa Marckini, "Changes in Central City Representation and Influence in Congress," paper prepared for 1997 annual meeting of the Urban Affairs Association, tables 4, 6.

6. William Schneider, "The Suburban Century Begins," *Atlantic Monthly,* July 1992, pp. 33–44; Pomper, "Presidential Election," p. 139; and CNN and others, Presidential Election Poll Results, Allpolitics web site (http://cgi.pathfinder.com/cgi-bin/report-o-matic).

7. Stanley B. Greenberg, *Middle Class Dreams: The Politics and Power of the New American Majority* (Times Books, 1995), pp. 278–83.

8. Michael J. Rich, "Riot and Reason: Crafting an Urban Policy Response," *Publius,* vol. 23 (Summer 1993), pp. 115–34.

9. George C. Galster and Ronald B. Mincy, "Understanding the Changing Fortunes of Metropolitan Neighborhoods, 1980 to 1990," and John Kasarda, "Inner-City Concentrated Poverty and Neighborhood Distress: 1970 to 1990," *Housing Policy Debate*, no. 3, vol. 4 (1993), pp. 1–53, 253–302; George C. Galster and Edward W. Hill, eds., *The Metropolis in Black and White: Place, Power, and Polarization* (New Brunswick, N.J.: Rutgers Center for Urban Policy Research 1992); Kathryn P. Nelson and John C. Edwards, "Intra-Urban Mobility and Location Choice in the 1980s," in G. Thomas Kingsley and Margery Austin Turner, eds., *Housing Markets and Residential Mobility* (Washington: Urban Institute Press, 1993); and Robert J. Sampson, "Unemployment and Imbalanced Sex Ratios: Race-Specific Consequences for Family Structure and Crime," in M. Belinda Tucker and Claudia Mitchell-Kernan, eds., *The Decline in Marriage among African Americans* (New York: Russell Sage Foundation, 1995), chap. 8.

10. Pomper, "Presidential Election," pp. 138–39.

11. For good accounts of the evolution of federal urban programs, see Harold L. Wolman and Elizabeth J. Agius, eds., *National Urban Policy: Problems and Prospects* (Wayne State University Press, 1996); Benjamin Kleinberg, *Urban America in Transformation: Perspectives on Urban Policy and Development* (Thousand Oaks, Calif.: Sage Publications, 1995); and George Galster, ed., *Reality and Research: Social Science and U.S. Urban Policy since 1960* (Washington: Urban Institute Press, 1996).

12. See also Kenneth Bickers, "Federal Domestic Outlays: Trends and Issues for State and Local Governments," *La Follette Policy Report*, vol. 5 (Fall 1992), pp. 6–10; and Demetrios Caraley, "Washington Abandons the Cities," *Political Science Quarterly*, vol. 107 (Spring 1992), pp. 1–30.

13. Harold Wolman, "The Reagan Urban Policy and Its Impacts," *Urban Affairs Quarterly*, vol. 21 (March 1986), pp. 311–35.

14. Howard Chernick and Andrew Reschovsky, "Urban Fiscal Problems: Coordinating Actions among Governments," *La Follette Issues* (University of Wisconsin, LaFollette Institute, 1995), p. 17; and R. Andrew Parker, "Patterns of Federal Urban Spending: Cities and Their Suburbs, 1983–1992," *Urban Affairs Review*, vol. 31 (November 1995), p. 195.

15. Michael J. Rich, *Federal Policymaking and the Poor* (Princeton University Press, 1993), pp. 320–21; and Rich, "UDAG, Economic Development, and the Death and Life of American Cities," *Economic Development Quarterly*, vol. 6 (May 1992), p. 169.

16. Steven Waldman, "The HUD Ripoff," *Newsweek*, August 7, 1989, pp. 16–22.

17. Wolman, "Reagan Urban Policy and Its Impacts"; William R. Barnes, "Urban Policies and Urban Impacts after Reagan," *Urban Affairs Quarterly*, vol. 25 (June 1990), pp. 562–73; and Caraley, "Washington Abandons the Cities."

18. Connie H. Casey, *Characteristics of HUD-Assisted Renters and their Units in 1989* (U.S. Department of Housing and Urban Development, Office of Policy

Development and Research, Housing and Demographic Analysis Division, March 1992), p. 2; and William Green, "Washington and the Cities: Housing," speech to conference on "Washington Abandons the Cities," Cooper Union, New York City, October 12, 1995.

19. Stephen Kohashi, "Housing Budgetary Analysis," Senate Committee on Banking, Housing, and Urban Affairs, November 29, 1994, pp. 1–3.

20. National Commission on Severely Distressed Public Housing, *The Final Report: A Report to Congress and the Secretary of Housing and Urban Development* (Government Printing Office, 1992), p. 15.

21. Jason DeParle, "Big Bills Coming Due at HUD, Crimping Expansion," *New York Times,* April 8, 1993, p. A1; and U.S. Department of Housing and Urban Development, *Worst Case Needs for Housing Assistance in the United States in 1990 and 1991* (Office of Policy Development and Research, Division of Policy Development, 1994).

22. Michael H. Schill and Susan M. Wachter, "The Spatial Bias of Federal Housing Law and Policy: Concentrated Poverty in Urban America," *University of Pennsylvania Law Review,* vol. 143 (May 1995), pp. 1285–1342; and Harold Pollack, "Don't They Want to Go? Section 8 and Efforts to Relocate Residents of Poor Neighborhoods," paper prepared for conference on "Social Networks and Urban Poverty," Russell Sage Foundation, New York City, March 1–2, 1996.

23. U.S. Department of Housing and Urban Development, "Reinvention Blueprint," December 19, 1994, pp. 1, 3.

24. Peter Dreier and John Atlas, "U.S. Housing Policy at the Crossroads: A Progressive Agenda to Rebuild the Housing Constituency," Occidental College, International and Public Affairs Center, January 1996, pp. 15–16.

25. Bill Clinton, "Bill Clinton on Rebuilding America's Cities" (Little Rock: Clinton Presidential Campaign, August 1992); and Bill Clinton and Al Gore, *Putting People First* (Times Books, 1992).

26. Bill Clinton, "Remarks by the President in Satellite Feed to the Conference of Mayors," *Weekly Compilation of Presidential Documents,* June 28, 1993, p. 1151.

27. Jon F. Hale, "The Making of the New Democrats," *Political Science Quarterly,* vol. 110 (Summer 1995), p. 219.

28. Jim Sleeper, "The End of the Rainbow," *New Republic,* November 1, 1993, pp. 20–25; and Fred Siegel, "Rudy in Disguise: Giuliani Talks Like a New Democrat. Can He Walk Like One?" *New Democrat,* vol. 6 (April–May 1994), pp. 9–14.

29. Will Marshall and Martin Schram, eds., *Mandate for Change* (Berkley Books, 1993).

30. Ronald Berkman and others, eds., *In the National Interest: The 1990 Urban Summit* (New York: Twentieth Century Fund Press, 1992); Joseph Persky, Elliot Sclar, and Wim Wiewel, *Does America Need Cities? An Urban Investment Strategy for National Prosperity* (Washington: Economic Policy Institute, 1991); and American Federation of State, County, and Municipal Employees, *The AFSCME Agenda*

for Urban America: The Report of the AFSCME Urban Affairs Advisory Committee (Washington, 1992), pp. 4, 5.

31. National Congress for Community Economic Development, *Tying It All Together: The Comprehensive Achievements of Community-Based Development Organizations* (Washington, 1992); and Avis Vidal, *Rebuilding Communities: A National Study of Urban Community Development Corporations* (New York: New School for Social Research, Community Development Research Center, 1992).

32. Robert D. Putnam, "The Prosperous Community: Social Capital and Public Life," *American Prospect*, no. 13 (Spring 1993), pp. 35–42.

33. Michael J. Rich, "Empower the People: An Assessment of Community-Based, Collaborative, Persistent Poverty Initiatives," paper prepared for 1995 annual meeting of the Midwest Political Science Association.

34. President's Commission for a National Agenda for the Eighties, *A National Agenda for the Eighties* (Government Printing Office, 1980); James E. Rosenbaum and Susan J. Popkin, "The Gautreaux Program: An Experiment in Racial and Economic Integration" (Northwestern University, Center for Urban Affairs and Policy Research, 1991); Mark Alan Hughes, "Antipoverty Strategy Where the Rubber Meets the Road: Transporting Workers to Jobs," in Kingsley and Turner, eds., *Housing Markets and Residential Mobility*; and John M. Quigley, "New Directions for Urban Policy," *Housing Policy Debate*, no. 1, vol. 5 (1994), pp. 97–106.

35. Douglas Massey and Nancy Denton, *American Apartheid* (Harvard University Press, 1993).

36. Anthony Downs, *New Visions for Metropolitan America* (Brookings, 1994); Hughes, "Antipoverty Strategy Where the Rubber Meets the Road"; Larry C. Ledebur and William Barnes, *"All in It Together": Cities, Suburbs, and Local Economic Regions* (Washington: National League of Cities, February 1993); Neal Peirce with Curtis Johnson and John Stuart Hall, *Citistates: How Urban America Can Prosper in a Competitive World* (Washington: Seven Locks Press. 1993); and David Rusk, *Cities without Suburbs* (Washington: Woodrow Wilson Center Press, 1993).

37. One White House Domestic Policy staff member commented to me early in the administration that "we do not like to talk about an urban policy. It is not something we believe in. We prefer to talk about a community empowerment policy." Such comments caused one urban lobbyist to remark that "there is some sort of urban policy development process going on over there, but it is being put together by a bunch of under-30 white males who are very brilliant, but who have never run a city and have no interest in talking to anyone who has." Jonathan Walters, "Not a Local Hero Anymore," *Governing*, vol. 6 (September 1993), p. 33.

38. Clinton, "Bill Clinton on Rebuilding America's Cities."

39. Author's interview, February 25, 1997.

40. Author's interview, August 10, 1995.

41. Rich, "Riot and Reason," p. 128; and Bob Woodward, *The Agenda: Inside the Clinton White House* (Simon and Schuster, 1994).

42. Henry Cisneros, "Remarks to the HUD-SSRC Round Table on Family Self-Sufficiency and Community Economic Development," Washington, July 13, 1993, author's notes.

43. U.S. Department of Housing and Urban Development, *Empowerment: A New Covenant with America's Communities, President Clinton's National Urban Policy Report* (Washington, August 3, 1995), pp. 4–5.

44. Richard Cowden, "Enterprise Zones: A Case Study in American Urban Policy" (Washington: American Association of Enterprise Zones, 1993), pp. 8–35.

45. Ibid., p. 27; and Sarah F. Liebschutz, "Empowerment Zones and Enterprise Communities: Reinventing Federalism for Distressed Communities," *Publius*, vol. 25 (Summer 1995), pp. 117–32.

46. Bill Clinton, "Remarks in a Teleconference on Empowerment Zones and an Exchange with Reporters," *Weekly Compilation of Presidential Documents*, May 10, 1993, pp. 744–45.

47. See Stuart Butler's position, cited in Cowden, "Enterprise Zones," p. 52; see also Mitchell Moss, "Where's the Power in the Empowerment Zone?" *City Journal*, vol. 5 (Spring 1995), pp. 76–81.

48. Liebschutz, "Empowerment Zones and Enterprise Communities," pp. 130–31.

49. Ibid.; and Franklin James, "The Evaluation of Enterprise Zone Programs," in Roy E. Green, ed., *Enterprise Zones: New Directions in Economic Development* (Newbury Park, Calif.: Sage Publications, 1991).

50. Marilyn Gittell, "Growing Pains, Politics Beset Empowerment Zones," *Forum for Applied Research and Public Policy*, vol. 10 (Winter 1995), pp. 107–11.

51. Kathryn Tholing, *Community Development Financial Institutions: Investing in People and Places* (Chicago: Woodstock Institute, 1994)

52. Mark A. Pinsky, "Coalition of Lenders and Investors Help Create the Community Development Financial Institution Act of 1994," *Shelterforce*, no. 79 (January–February 1995).

53. Bill Clinton, "Remarks on Signing the Riegle Community Development and Regulatory Improvement Act of 1994," *Weekly Compilation of Presidential Documents*, September 26, 1994, p. 1827.

54. Gregory D. Squires, ed., *From Redlining to Reinvestment: Community Responses to Urban Disinvestment* (Temple University Press, 1992), pp. 9–17.

55. Federal Reserve Board Governor Lawrence Lindsey, quoted in John Taylor, "CRA Transcends Political Party Boundaries," *The Fair Housing Report* (Fair Housing Council of Greater Washington, Fall 1995), p. 15.

56. Squires, *From Redlining to Reinvestment*, p. 252.

57. National Community Reinvestment Coalition, "Final CRA Regulation Released, But Congressional Action Threatens Two Years of Work," *NCRC Reinvestment Compendium*, vol. 2 (June–August 1995), pp. 1, 3.

58. U.S. Department of Housing and Urban Development, Office of Community Planning and Development, *Government's Working: 1996 Annual Report* (Washington, 1997), chap. 7.

59. George Galster, "Minority Poverty: The Place-Race Nexus and the Clinton Administration's Civil Rights Policy," in Citizens' Commission on Civil Rights, *New Challenges: The Civil Rights Record of the Clinton Administration Mid-Term* (Washington, 1995), pp. 47–49.

60. Saul Hansell, "Stretching the Borders," *New York Times,* August 25, 1994, p. D1.

61. Rosenbaum and Popkin, "Gautreaux Program"; Mary Davis, "The Gautreaux Assisted Housing Program," in Kingsley and Turner, eds., *Housing Markets and Residential Mobility;* and "The Promise of Housing Mobility Programs," *Urban Institute Policy and Research Report,* vol. 25 (Winter 1995–96), pp. 4–6.

62. U.S. Department of Housing and Urban Development, Office of Policy Development and Research, "Residential Mobility Programs," *Housing and Development Brief,* no. 1 (September 1994), pp. 5–6. In December 1994, HUD also settled a lawsuit against the Pittsburgh Housing Authority, *Sanders* v. *HUD,* by providing $58 million in section 8 and community development funds so public housing tenants could disperse through Allegheny County. Thomas J. Henderson and Stacy E. Seicshnaydre, "*Sanders v. HUD:* A Multi-Faceted Remedy for Housing Segregation," *Poverty and Race,* vol. 4 (July–August 1995), pp. 9–10, 14.

63. James Bovard, "Clinton's Wrecking Ball for Suburbs," *Wall Street Journal,* August 4, 1994, p. A12; and Karen DeWitt, "Housing Voucher Test in Maryland Is Scuttled by a Political Firestorm," *New York Times,* March 28, 1995, p. B1.

64. Author's interview with HHS staff, August 15, 1995.

65. Harold Wolman, "Urban Policy Processes at the National Level: The Hidden World of Urban Politics," paper prepared for 1993 annual meeting of the American Political Science Association, pp. 9–15.

66. Wolman and Agius, eds., *National Urban Policy,* p. 48.

67. Author's interviews with HUD staff, September 7, 1994, and February 20, 1995.

68. HUD, *Empowerment,* chap. 3, p. 4.

69. Ibid., p. 66.

70. Christopher Edley, "The Next Phase of the Clinton Urban Policy: Metropolitan Empowerment Zones," draft memorandum, Office of Management and Budget, October 1, 1994, p. 1; and Downs, *New Visions.*

71. Guy Gugliotta, "HUD Plan Savings Put at $64 Billion," *Washington Post,* January 20, 1995, p. A19.

72. Author's interview, August 14, 1995.

73. U.S. House of Representatives, VA-HUD Appropriations Subcommittee, "FY 1996 Budget Overview," July 10, 1995; see also Cameron Whitman, "HUD Appropriations Down 23 Percent," *Nation's Cities Weekly,* vol. 18 (July 17, 1995),

p. 12. The bill also provided for a minimum $50 per month rent in public housing, increased section 8 rents to 32 percent of adjusted gross income, and lifted the Brooke amendment cap on public housing rents.

74. U.S. Department of Housing and Urban Development, Office of Policy Development and Research, "Impact of the FY 1996 House Appropriations Bills and the Congressional Budget Resolution on American's Metropolitan Communities," August 8, 1995.

75. Author's interview with HUD staff, February 27, 1997; and Robert Reischauer, speech to conference on "Washington Abandons the Cities? Trends, Consequences, and Solutions," Cooper Union, New York City, October 12, 1995. See also Demetrios Caraley, "Dismantling the Federal Safety Net: Fictions versus Realities," *Political Science Quarterly*, vol. 111 (Summer 1996), pp. 225–58.

76. U.S. Department of Housing and Urban Development, "Reinvention Blueprint," December 1994.

77. U.S. Department of Housing and Urban Development, "HUD's Reinvention: From Blueprint to Action," March 20, 1995, p. 15.

78. Author's interview, February 27, 1997.

79. *United States Housing Act of 1996*, H. Rept. 104-461, 104 Cong. 2 sess. (GPO, 1996). "Lazio and Cisneros share a similar vision of what HUD could become," according to Rochelle L. Stanfield, "Gimme Shelter," *National Journal*, February 10, 1996, p. 335.

80. Guy Gugliotta, "House Votes for Overhaul in Housing," *Washington Post*, May 10, 1996, p. 1; and "Votes in Congress," *New York Times*, May 12, 1996, p. 32.

81. "House Passes Lazio's Bill Overhauling U.S. Housing Laws," press release, House Committee on Banking and Financial Services, May 8, 1996.

82. Susan Vanhorenbeck, "Appropriations for FY1997: VA, HUD, and Independent Agencies," *CRS Report for Congress* (Congressional Research Service, October 4, 1996), pp. 8–17.

83. Mayor Edward Rendell, remarks to a conference on "The 'Contract with America'? What Does It Mean for Our Nation's Cities," Taub Urban Research Center, New York University, June 1, 1995 (author's notes).

84. Langley C. Keyes and others, "Networks and Nonprofits: Opportunities and Challenges in an Era of Federal Devolution," *Housing Policy Debate*, no. 2, vol. 7 (1996), p. 205; Kenneth Rosen and Ted Dienstfry, "The Economics of Housing Services in Low-Income Neighborhoods," paper prepared for conference on "Community Development: What We Know, What We Need to Know," Brookings, November 15–16, 1996; Christopher Walker, "Nonprofit Housing Development: Status, Trends, and Prospects," *Housing Policy Debate*, no. 3, vol. 4 (1994), pp. 369–414; and James E. Wallace, "Financing Affordable Housing in the United States," *Housing Policy Debate*, no. 4, vol. 6 (1995), pp. 785–814.

85. For the New York experience, see Alan S. Oser, "Housing Programs Strained as Cutbacks Take Hold," *New York Times*, March 24, 1996, p. 7; and Alex F. Schwartz

and Avis C. Vidal, "Between a Rock and a Hard Place: The Impact of Federal and State Policy Changes on Housing in New York City," paper prepared for a conference on "Housing and Community Development in the New Fiscal Environment: New Directions for New York City" (New York University School of Law, Center for Real Estate and Urban Policy, March 28, 1996), pp. 16–25.

86. Author's interview, March 25, 1996.

87. Hugh O'Neill and Megan Sheehan, "The Impact of New Federal Budget Priorities on America's Cities," New York University, Taub Urban Research Center, September 1995, p. 11.

88. Author's interview, March 25, 1996.

89. Author's interviews, April 20, 1996, and August 15, 1995.

90. For some of these arguments, see the symposium on "The Devolution Revolution," *Rockefeller Institute Bulletin* (Albany, N.Y.: Rockefeller Institute, 1996).

91. See Margaret Weir, "Big Cities Confront the New Federalism," paper prepared for the project on "Big Cities Confront the New Politics of Child and Family Policy," Columbia School of Social Work, April 12, 1996; Weir, "Central Cities' Loss of Power in State Politics," *Cityscape*, vol. 2 (May 1996), pp. 23–40; Steven D. Gold, "The Potential Impacts of Devolution on State Government Programs and Finances," testimony to the House Budget Committee, March 5, 1996; and U.S. General Accounting Office, "Block Grants: Characteristics, Experience, and Lessons Learned," HEHS-95-74 (February 1995).

92. Wolman and Agius, *National Urban Policy*, p. 26.

Chapter 12

American Politics and the Future of Social Policy

Margaret Weir

T HE CONFLICTS that divided Clinton and congressional Republicans are not unique to the United States: as economic and social shifts have sharpened inequality and strained existing social programs, struggles about the future of social policy have emerged across the industrialized West. What is distinctive about the United States in comparative perspective is the relatively limited public response to these shifts—especially in levels of spending.[1] As a candidate, Bill Clinton's New Democratic approach promised a blend of economic populism and market-oriented reform that would reinvigorate the public role. As I argued in the introduction to this volume, this deliberately ambiguous formula contained two political possibilities: the first would remake the Democratic coalition by uniting middle- and lower-income people around common interests in a stronger public sector; the second would move the party to the center of the existing political spectrum by reducing the federal government's social role and appealing primarily to the middle class. In fact, neither of these political scenarios occurred. Instead, Clinton moved to the center of a political spectrum that had itself been pushed sharply to the right by the congressional Republicans. As the president moved right, he pulled a substantial bloc of congressional Democrats with him on most major issues.

These political shifts have affected social policymaking in three major ways. First, the centrality of the balanced budget has blocked new spending and increased the emphasis on taxes as a tool of activist social policy.

I would like to thank E. J. Dionne Jr., Jennifer Hochschild, Thomas Mann, Mark A. Peterson, Ted Perlmutter, and R. Kent Weaver for helpful comments and suggestions.

Second, major responsibility for the poor—especially the nonworking poor—has shifted away from the federal government toward the states. Third, broad-based entitlement programs are threatened by new measures designed to peel off the most healthy and wealthy beneficiaries by offering them attractive publicly subsidized private options. Together these changes point social policy in a direction that promises to widen the social divide between the well-off and the less prosperous. Although the brunt of the shift falls most immediately on the poor, the erosion of public programs offering opportunity and security through insurance also threatens growing numbers of working families.[2]

Despite the comparative quiet after the 1996 election, debates about what role the government should play in ensuring social and economic well-being are far from settled. Much about those debates will depend on the political context in which they take place. As the contributors to this book have argued, the partisan battle for dominance is a central fact of the new political environment, as is a new style of politics that connects most people to politics only through advertising. In the first Clinton administration, the advertising style of politics encouraged politicians to frame their goals in the most sweeping and provocative of terms and lent a new shrill tone to public debate. The intense activism of Washington-based interest groups contrasted with the loose political engagement of most Americans. Together they created a hyperactive but thinned-out world of policymaking in which interests were narrowly construed and defense became the most successful strategy. Moreover, each party had to contend with the limitations and new rhythms of policymaking imposed by budget politics. The constraints of budgetary politics naturally hurt Democrats most, but also confronted Republicans with politically unattractive choices.

In such a charged but narrowly cast partisan atmosphere, the strategic concerns of the parties dominate policymaking. Thus the challenge of understanding political and policy outcomes must go beyond simply documenting the operation of Madisonian constraints; it must make sense of the strategic decisions that this political environment sets up for politicians and how politicians navigate them. For most of Clinton's first term, as this book has emphasized, Democrats and Republicans took turns proposing major policy shifts that they hoped would transform politics. Even once-routine compromises became difficult as policymaking degenerated into "pitched battles over issue ownership" and issue definition.[3] These episodes showcased the barriers that American political institutions pose to policy activists, but the shifts in the policy agenda indicate that such obstacles do not prevent change: the sweeping character of the proposals, such as Clinton's health reform, often altered policy in decisive ways even when they failed. Moreover, these features of politics did not inevitably lead to legislative stalemate: as the compromises on welfare, the minimum wage, and the balanced budget indicate, parties at times judged it to their advantage to compromise.[4]

These two strategic struggles—battles over issue definition and ownership and assessments about the value of "strategic disagreement" versus enacting legislation—are the key political dynamics that will shape future debates about social policy.[5] The increased homogeneity of parties and the enhanced ability of congressional leaders to enforce party discipline mean that partisan divisions will dominate these dynamics. But differences within parties will also remain significant. Such internal divisions will affect the way issues are framed and what issues parties prefer to have on the agenda.

In this conclusion I return to the social policy challenges outlined in the introduction—policies toward the poor and disadvantaged, policies that address the needs of working families, and the broad entitlement programs—to assess how strategic politics changed the terms of debate in each and consider how they set the agenda for the future. As I do so, I also consider what kinds of politics and policies are needed to build a new consensus that addresses the conflicting concerns of Americans about social policy. I highlight the threads of a new social populism that offers a forthright defense of social as opposed to budgetary goals, couches policy in terms of deeply felt and broadly held moral concerns, and emphasizes a politics of social mobilization and broad coalition building rather than advertising.

Race, Poverty, and the Politics of Wedge Issues

One of Clinton's chief priorities was to reposition the Democratic party so that it was no longer vulnerable to the wedge issues of race, poverty, and "values." In the thirty years after the Great Society and the civil rights movement, Republicans had used public antipathy to welfare, opposition to racial "quotas," and concern about crime against Democrats. When these issues came to the fore, Democrats paid a price.[6] Democratic politicians traditionally sought to address this disadvantage by steering debate toward economic fairness, which invoked a more favorable set of issues for Democrats. Clinton, however, addressed wedge issues directly, stressing that rights should be balanced by responsibilities.

In fact, during his administration, policy toward the poor and disadvantaged shifted in ways that ultimately placed considerably more emphasis on responsibility than rights. The new welfare act exposed women and children in particular to new insecurities by removing the federal guarantee of assistance to families without work. Although Clinton ultimately called for "mending" rather than ending affirmative action, the federal government did little to respond to a spate of judicial rulings that now jeopardize minority opportunity in such critical domains as education. And even as the federal government took steps away from the poor and disadvantaged, it stepped up its support in criminal justice, an area where its impact on local practices was minimal. The major exception to this pattern of withdrawal was the substantial increase in the earned income tax credit (EITC), which significantly boosted the income of low-wage workers.

A comparison of welfare, affirmative action, and the EITC reveals how these outcomes emerged from partisan competition as it interacted with the distinctive politics surrounding each policy and with pervasive budgetary constraints. The broad and intense negative public opinion regarding welfare, its role as a lightning rod for a whole set of highly charged issues concerning race, sex, and urban poverty, and its status as a historic marker between the two parties since the 1960s helped open up a range of possible reform options that sharply departed from existing policy. Welfare was also unusual because there were so few interest groups to weigh in: the beneficiaries were weak and unorganized, and the usual intergovernmental pressure from governors had been neutralized by Republican governors supporting devolution. As R. Kent Weaver's chapter shows, Clinton's promise to "end welfare as we know it" gave Republicans an opening, intensely negative public opinion allowed them to push debate to the right, and weak interest group support provided little effective resistance to the rightward shift. Affirmative action, by contrast, was strongly supported by the black Democratic leadership, who, as Linda Faye Williams's chapter shows, wielded the threat of a primary challenge if Clinton backed away from affirmative action. Moreover, affirmative action had a more complex public opinion profile, making Republicans cautious about launching an aggressive attack on it. And, in any case, both parties knew that the main action on affirmative action was taking place in the courts. A range of judicial rulings eliminating or greatly restricting affirmative action allowed the president to pledge his support at a much reduced political cost even as they handed Republicans a substantive victory that spared them the political risks of a major assault on affirmative action.

The success of the EITC highlights the greater ease of enacting programs that rely on tax expenditures rather than spending, as Clinton's own plan for welfare reform would have done. And in contrast to welfare, the EITC had comparatively low visibility; its link with a working, and therefore deserving, clientele allowed it to avoid the negative public image that surrounded welfare. The EITC was not a promising target for controversy and politicization, although congressional Republicans tried with little success to make it one. Moreover, its status as a tax expenditure offered the EITC procedural protection: proposed reductions had to be included in the huge budget bill that failed in the wake of the congressional-presidential stand-off in 1995.

What are the political and substantive implications of these changes in policy toward the poor and disadvantaged? Some evidence suggests that Clinton's attempts to reposition the Democratic party succeeded. Public opinion polls after the 1996 election showed that Republicans now enjoyed only a small advantage on such matters as crime, drugs, and welfare, issues on which they had long fared far better than Democrats.[7] But Clinton's political success in neutralizing wedge issues must be measured against initial aspirations—however ambivalent—to alter the existing political and policy spectrum in ways that would build Democratic strength in the future. By this measure, his success is more questionable. Clinton did not alter the political spectrum; rather he inoculated himself on these issues by moving to the center of a political spectrum that was itself shifting right. This strategy at least temporarily removed welfare and divisive racial issues as pivotal concerns in national electoral politics, but it did not address the underlying problems and the political tensions they create.

One of the greatest dangers in our new system of assisting the poor is the prospect of creating a new large category of "undeserving poor"— largely children—for whom the federal government bears no responsibility and for whom state action is optional. Before 1996, only able-bodied working-age people who were not working and did not have children could fall into this category; this group did not qualify for federal assistance other than food stamps. Some states provided low levels of aid through general assistance programs, although these programs have been substantially reduced in recent years, and the 1996 welfare law greatly limits their access to food stamps. The 1996 welfare law has the potential to expand greatly this pool of "undeserving poor" that is guaranteed assistance by no level of government. As able-bodied welfare recipients with children reach their two-year time limit for receiving assistance (or their five-year lifetime limit) and cannot find work or will not work, they—and their children—are in danger of becoming part of this much enlarged category.

Devolution to the states is quickly becoming the dominant way of assisting the poor.[8] Defenders of this role point to the increased capacities of the states and their ability to tailor programs to local needs. But many of the same political dynamics that now limit assistance to the poor at the national level also operate in the states. When their budgets are flush, states are more likely to provide generous assistance to the poor even in the context of unfavorable political factors. This has largely been the case since the 1996 welfare legislation, when most states not only have had strong economies but also enjoyed a short-term financial windfall of federal funds due to the terms of the law. When these extra funds dry up—as they are scheduled to do—or when their economies turn sour, states are less likely to resist the political logic of the "race to the bottom" in which competitive bidding among the states reduces benefits to the poor in favor of activities that promote economic development. These dynamics may not immediately result in reduced benefits to the poor, but they create pressure to divert resources away from the poor that may be difficult to resist in the future.

The pressing question for the future is whether these changes in policy can provide a backdoor for alternative approaches to enhancing the opportunity and security of the poor, which were largely missing from New Deal–era social policies. Three possibilities stand out. The first is to build a politics and promote policies to support the working poor. Until now the emphasis on the moral and behavioral problems of the poor has directed public attention away from the problems of the low-wage labor market. A focus on work and wages makes it easier to defend assistance to the poor, as the debate over the EITC in 1995 revealed.[9] Similarly, the fight over the minimum wage in 1996 revealed strong public support for rewarding people who work. Such views have been a long-standing feature of American political culture; Robert B. Reich has gone so far as to call them "the moral core of American capitalism."[10]

Welfare reform has created new possibilities both for expanding the ranks of the working poor and for directing attention to their needs, which were all but ignored because of the political focus on welfare. The conflicts over providing a minimum wage and the basic protections of the Fair Labor Standards Act to people on workfare, which erupted soon after the passage of the 1996 law, suggest the new possibilities for altering the politics of poverty.[11] Other initiatives along these lines would reform unemployment insurance to make it possible for part-time and contingent workers to receive benefits. Two other sets of issues, which I discuss below, are of broad concern but are especially relevant to low-wage workers and welfare recipients: the availability and adequacy of job-related benefits, such as health care and pensions, and the difficulties of combining work and family responsibilities. These issues are especially compelling to the poor because inadequate health care and child care can become significant barriers to regular employment, and our system of social support now provides no place for the able-bodied nonelderly poor who do not work.

A second, more controversial approach would attack state and local barriers to opportunity. The efforts of suburbs to protect themselves from urban ills have created barriers that prevent the urban poor from taking advantage of the economic growth and job opportunities there. They have contributed to the concentration of poverty and strained resource base that characterize many cities. As John Mollenkopf's chapter indicates, the Department of Housing and Urban Development considered, although it did not succeed in enacting, various ideas to promote metropolitanization, including resource sharing, administrative cooperation between cities and suburbs, and promoting access to suburban housing for the urban poor. Breaking down the barriers to opportunity for urban residents is essential to long-term efforts to address poverty. The federal government has long stayed aloof from these issues because they infringe on local autonomy and raise the prospect of racial conflict.[12] It has instead focused diminishing resources on community development, as in the empowerment zones. But, as the Kerner commission pointed out thirty years ago, community development and "opening up the suburbs" are both essential strategies.[13] The decline of inner suburbs in many metropolitan areas and concerns about the environmental consequences of suburban sprawl have altered the political balance in ways that now create new possibilities for metropolitan initiatives.[14] The federal government can do much to advance this agenda through the way it structures block grants and creates incentives to open opportunities to the poor throughout a metropolitan area.

Even if work opportunities and benefits and wages for the working poor (including people on workfare) improved, the issue of jobs for those unable to find work would remain. This problem would be most severe during periods of recession, but it would be persistent in some geographical areas. Some proportion of welfare recipients are likely to remain unattractive to private employers and will not be able to make ends meet after they reach their limits for assistance. These problems point to the need for public jobs as a last resort or other arrangements that combine responsibility with benefits, such as compensation for structured volunteering.[15] This approach places the well-being of the family at the center of policy while acknowledging the broader public desire that benefits be combined with work.

Finally, the question of affirmative action must be confronted. Although Clinton called for "mending, not ending" affirmative action, he stayed aloof from controversies over state-level efforts, such as California's Proposition 209, to end affirmative action programs. The president has often highlighted racial disadvantage as a key American problem, but his initiatives—such as his national commission on race—propose talk, rather than action. The rollback of affirmative action at the state level is not inevitable, as the vote to retain affirmative action in Houston in November 1997 revealed. The public's ambivalence on the issue, depending on how it is posed, leaves much room for leadership to build support for some types of affirmative action.[16] But action is also needed in instances where the courts have ruled affirmative action illegal, especially regarding access to higher education. Much of this may occur in the states, but the federal government also needs to be engaged in formulating new opportunity programs that open access to higher education.

These initiatives—improving pay and benefits for the working poor, opening opportunity throughout metropolitan areas, providing work as a last resort—all aim to bring the welfare poor into the mainstream of social and economic opportunity and put the problems of the working poor on the national agenda. Defending affirmative action and the reenergizing of our national commitment to opportunity are essential to avoid widening the social divide and reinforcing its racial character. Building support for this agenda requires more than removing wedge issues; it requires positive arguments and initiatives that appeal to norms of fairness and opportunity that have been missing from the more narrowly focused welfare debates.

Social Policy for Working Families

Growing wage inequality, the problems of two-wage-earner families (adequate child care, time to spend with children) and single-parent households, and the decline in job-related social benefits compose a cluster of issues related to the needs of working families that existing social policy does little to address. Clinton's campaign policies devoted considerable attention to these issues. Key among them were health care reform, which would address an important feature of inequality across jobs and a major source of insecurity for working families; the promise of a significant investment program, which included but was not restricted to human capital; expansion of the EITC and an increased minimum wage for the working poor; a new emphasis on job training and educational assistance; and passage of the Family and Medical Leave Act (FMLA). Underlying these initiatives was the conviction that the federal government, through its spending and regulatory powers, could assist working families with the challenges thrown up by the economic and social changes of the past two decades.

Although some of these measures were enacted, most of them were not, either because, like health reform, they were defeated, or because, like the investment program, the administration abandoned them in order to pursue deficit reduction. Many of the initiatives that did pass, like family leave, were significantly watered down. The greatest successes were the EITC and the increased minimum wage. The enactment of a higher education assistance plan in 1997 was a political triumph, but its effect on educational opportunity is more doubtful. On balance, the Clinton administration did not succeed in significantly redeploying public power and resources to improve the opportunities and security of working families.

In some respects, the Republican vision was more successful but it, too, failed to capture this broad realm of policy in any decisive way. Despite important differences among social and economic conservatives, both camps shared a fundamental vision that tied the well-being of families to reduced government spending and lower taxes. Both also emphasized individual morality and discipline as key to addressing the problems that families faced. Their greatest success was on budget issues, most clearly evident in the president's acceptance of the Republican goal of balancing the federal budget in seven years. The inability of Republicans to win support for tax cuts in 1996 when they were pitted against entitlements was the most spectacular Republican failure, indicating that the low-tax antigovernment formula had its limits.

Why was there so little policy change in an area of such broad salience? The most important reason was the limited range for movement available to either party, which stemmed from policies they inherited but also from the political choices they made. One route to preserving good jobs—protectionism—was ruled out by elite consensus on free trade, which helped create a somewhat tenuous bipartisan agreement. The president hoped to combine free trade with investment in people and infrastructure as a way of joining economic and social goals, but he quickly dropped the investment route in favor of deficit reduction. On this issue, Clinton was playing on a terrain that was far more favorable to Republicans. As Paul Pierson's chapter argues, Democrats themselves had participated in making the deficit a central policy goal by elevating attacks on the deficit to a prominent position in their political message during the 1980s. By committing to reduce the deficit, the administration gravely restricted what it could propose in the way of spending to improve the opportunity and security of working families. Its greatest successes, the EITC and the increased minimum wage, relied on tax expenditures and regulation, not spending.

Mandates on business provided another possible route for improving the security of working families. Business mandates were a natural way to assist working families, not only because possibilities for federal spending were limited but also, as Cathie Jo Martin's chapter points out, because a significant proportion of working families had traditionally received social benefits from their jobs. But, given their close ties to business constituencies, Republicans not surprisingly opposed most such mandates. And Democrats found that the dominance of health reform on the domestic agenda during the first two years of Clinton's presidency left little room to press for other business mandates that would assist working families or to make a broader case for a business role in promoting family security. Internal divisions among Democrats also checked any push for mandates. New Democrats associated with the Democratic Leadership Council tended to be more probusiness and less willing to support mandates on business (preferring the EITC to the minimum wage, for example), than traditional Democrats, who were generally more game to take positions that business opposed. In any case, because it needed business support for its health plan, the administration avoided other policy proposals that it feared would antagonize business. Thus Clinton would not argue that business practices were a central reason for the problems middle-class people confronted, nor would he propose new mandates on business, apart from the FMLA, which had already won congressional approval twice.

In this context, policymaking toward working families became a blend of conflicts over issue definition and tactical maneuvering around symbols. In health reform the conflict over issue definition took center stage, with Clinton claiming that such reform was essential to middle-class security and congressional Republicans arguing that the plan threatened middle-class security because it empowered "big government." After the 1994 elections, Clinton largely retreated into manipulating symbols. In contrast to the way he handled his health care plan, which aimed to redefine policy in order to cement new Democratic majorities, the president now played a purely tactical game aimed at winning short-term advantage. In the course of these political maneuvers, Clinton periodically acknowledged that working families needed help in negotiating the new economy and asserted that government could assist them. Congressional Democrats made this a key point of partisan contention, as in the fight for the minimum wage and the Kennedy-Kassebaum health reform. But in critical ways, the president blunted this partisan difference in his battle for tactical advantage. Not only in his much-quoted renunciation of "big government," but more so in his decision to embrace the Republican proposal to balance the budget in seven years, the president accepted Republican terms of policymaking. This strategy successfully deprived Republicans of a campaign issue but drastically reduced the future possibilities for using government to assist working families.

What are the consequences of blurring these issues and making tactical maneuvers so central to policy and rhetoric? One danger is that the economic problems of working families will be ignored in favor of values issues narrowly defined, as in the V-chip and school uniforms, which were key themes in the 1996 presidential campaign. The return of widespread optimism with the rebounding economy seemed to confirm the administration's decision to relegate the issue of economic security to the back burner.[17] Yet concerns about values and economics are intertwined for working people as they strive to find time for their families and ensure their well-being.[18] In the era of the two-wage-earner family and single parents, social supports—including child care, after-school care, and leave to care for children with minor illnesses—are essential both to economic security and to family stability.

A second danger is that Congress and the president will respond to family concerns in ways that benefit only higher-income workers, effectively exacerbating inequalities. The FMLA and the Kennedy-Kassebaum health insurance portability measures are examples of regulations that are far more useful to higher-wage rather than lower-wage workers. The FMLA provides only unpaid leave, and the health portability measure does nothing to control the costs of health insurance, much less help workers who have no insurance. Even the child tax credit, which was expanded to cover more of the poor after its scope became a sticking point in the 1997 budget negotiations, does not benefit a significant portion of the poor.[19] Politicians have substantial incentives to continue addressing economic insecurity with measures that mainly assist middle- and upper-income workers. Not only are such initiatives likely to be less costly, they also appeal to the sector of the population most likely to vote.

A final danger is that political compromises will produce results that appear balanced—and that both parties have an incentive to claim are balanced—but that actually lock in structural advantages for the rich over the long term. The 1997 budget act created several new programs for the poor and the middle class in addition to the sizable tax benefits it offered the rich. Over time, however, the act will exacerbate inequality because the advantages to upper-income taxpayers will grow while spending on the poor is likely to erode or the assistance is slated to end altogether.[20] Given the squeeze on discretionary expenditures due to budget rules, it is most likely that any compromise combining tax benefits for the well-off with discretionary expenditures for the poor will exacerbate inequality over time.

What are more desirable directions for future policy and politics concerning working families? Foremost is the need to acknowledge the intertwining of economics and values in family policy. This means a renewed focus on the atrophy of job-related social benefits, such as medical care and pensions, as well as attention to the new needs of families as they relate to the workplace. These issues are more pressing, as Martin's chapter points out, because the limits on job-based social benefits that have long affected lower-income workers are now also spreading to many middle-income workers. This is a major shift in the American welfare state, in which job-related benefits have provided an essential piece of social protection for working-age adults. It is critical that public policy acknowledge the erosion of this key element of social protection and respond with measures that do not simply exacerbate the widening in-equality in the private sector.

Second is a greatly increased federal attention to education. Students of comparative social policy have long pointed to the early and exten-sive role of public schooling in the United States, calling it the American equivalent of the more generous social programs in European nations.[21] Clinton emphasized education and training as a means to help workers prosper in the new economy and sought to make support for education a key issue distinguishing him from Republicans. But given the small role the federal government has traditionally played in financing public education, it is a field rife with symbolic politics. Especially after the 1994 elections, Clinton's efforts to use education as a political issue pro-duced initiatives that were neither equitable or effective. Policies that are driven solely by the need to appeal politically to the middle class are prone to fall short on both counts. One of Clinton's education initiatives reveals the dangers. It was first packaged as a "Middle Class Bill of Rights" immediately after the 1994 election and included tax credits for college tuitions and vouchers for training. The higher education initia-tive was rightly widely criticized for providing a boon to universities, which would simply increase their tuition in response to the increased ability of students to pay. It was also initially biased against lower-in-come students until congressional critics succeeded in adding more funds for Pell grants in the final legislation.[22] But such grants are more easily cut in the future than are tax expenditures. In the face of such problems, it is important to ask whether this approach or others like it are the most effective ways to spend new educational funds. Even as the president was insisting on his higher education initiatives, he agreed to eliminate funds for the repair of deteriorating public elementary and high schools. Yet the problems in elementary and high school education deserve far more attention and assistance from the federal government. Poor edu-cation in K-12 may be the ultimate barrier to getting access to many forms of advanced training and higher education.[23]

In the domain of job training, the federal government needs to play a stronger role in promoting local and regional capacities to connect work-ers with jobs and to promote the use of training and high-skill workers among employers. Simply handing workers vouchers for training is not enough: workers need to be able to connect to a system of training and placement. There is no guarantee that states on their own will create such systems, and there is a substantial danger that states will use federal money to undercut competing states to lure corporations. Such beggar-thy-neighbor actions have been so prevalent that some states are urging Washington to enact legislation to prevent states from using federal money, including job training funds, to attract out-of-state corporations.[24] These problems suggest that the federal government still has an important role to play as system builder, setting the fundamental rules of the game and providing support for regional institutional building that connects workers, training, and firms.

Underlying many of the problems that workers now confront is the globalization of the economy and the type of corporate behavior and practices it has helped to spawn. The trade issue cuts too many ways for purely protectionist arguments to have much broad appeal, nor is it clear how successful protectionism would actually be in sustaining the supply of good jobs. Yet our politics has done a poor job in promoting a frank consideration of the costs and benefits of trade. The elite consensus around free trade has distorted debate as proponents of free trade tout the long-run macroeconomic benefits, seriously underplaying the real costs to significant sectors of the population and the general rise in insecurity experienced by much of the work force.[25] We need a much less ideological national discussion about the costs of trade and what kinds of public action are needed to address them, including much more significant investments in human resources, stronger provisions regarding labor and environmental goals in trade agreements, and an activist stance in international trade forums.

Many of the policy directions outlined here are sure to provoke vigorous business opposition. Clinton sought to avoid this type of conflict, searching instead for consensual solutions. By contrast, Republicans, who routinely chastise Democrats for practicing a politics of "class warfare," established a close partnership with business, especially the formidable organizations of small business. Clinton's combination of a top-down technocratic approach to policy and tactical maneuvering must be replaced with a much more explicit social strategy that relies on appeals to lower- and middle-income voters and mobilizes these forces to counter business organizations.[26] Such a class strategy must differ in significant ways from the past: most important, it must mobilize women, who are most attracted to this agenda, and particularly working women, who bear the brunt of balancing family needs with work life. The recent efforts of organized labor to regain its former political and economic strength are critical for such a strategy to succeed. The appeal of the increased minimum wage in 1996 suggests that concern for the working poor and for economic security may be much more politically potent if there are active efforts to mobilize these sentiments. But if labor is to be successful in providing a strong political counterweight to business, it will have to maintain a broader perspective and devote more attention to the concerns of families than it has in the past. This requires more than political advertising; it entails a more far-reaching process of mobilization and organizational revival.

The Future of Entitlements

Entitlements that serve Americans regardless of income—social security and medicare—constitute the bulk of social welfare spending by the federal government. Medicaid, too has de facto become a broad social welfare entitlement as it has taken over much of the burden for long-term care. Policymakers have long resolved issues related to the financial stability of these entitlements in bipartisan agreements, either in commissions designed to keep them out of the limelight (as in the 1983 commission on social security) or by highly technical administrative reforms, such the medicare reforms in the 1980s designed to keep costs down.[27]

But throughout the 1980s, mounting conservative arguments about the affordability of these programs grew into attacks on their ultimate desirability. Concern about future financing became the occasion to launch arguments about fundamental changes in policy. In this context, it became difficult to agree on reform. In 1994, Clinton's bipartisan Entitlement Commission disbanded in disagreement between those who advocated major structural changes in the programs and those who supported only incremental shifts designed to preserve the universal and mildly redistributive character of entitlement programs. The following year, widespread opposition caused congressional Republicans to withdraw their proposals to cut medicare. Now the action centers on policy innovations, such as medical savings accounts and IRAs, that bore into entitlement programs, creating new inequalities by offering attractive alternatives that are far more likely to be used by those who are better off.

The unraveling of the elite consensus that once supported these social benefits means that the battle over entitlements will dominate future social policymaking. Underlying these new rifts are fundamentally different views about what the role of the government should be in helping individuals achieve economic security. The collective vision underlying social security and medicare charges government with creating broad pools of beneficiaries across which risk is spread. This approach is animated by the idea that all workers face common risks regardless of their income level. Some redistribution from the well-off to the poorer is inherent in these arrangements, but in the peculiarly American version of a collective vision, the framers of social security linked participation to past contributions and pegged benefits to wages. This older perspective is now challenged by a market-oriented vision, which breaks up these publicly defined pools to offer individuals more opportunities to seek out arrangements that they judge will best meet their needs. Rather than setting the terms for policy in ways that spread risk and promote some redistribution, the government plays a much more residual role of providing last-resort assistance to the most needy.[28]

But views about entitlements are not only matters of broad vision. Material interests are also at stake. Because public and private arrangements for social protection are intertwined, changes in major social insurance programs not only threaten groups and interests benefiting from existing arrangements; they also offer tremendous new opportunities for profit making. The growth of defined contribution pensions in the private sector and the booming mutual fund industry in the 1980s laid the groundwork for new arguments about privatizing social security. Not surprisingly, the mutual fund industry has played an important behind-the-scenes role in arguing for privatization.[29] Similarly, changes to medicare greatly shift costs and benefits among the complex of private interests involved in medical care. As Mark Peterson's chapter shows, the move to managed care after the failure of Clinton's comprehensive health reform, for example, proved a boon to private insurance companies and costly to hospitals. The spread of medical savings accounts would likewise benefit insurance companies by segmenting off an attractive pool of claimants.

In addition to their effects on private groups, shifts in entitlement programs have important distributional consequences, with implications for partisan politics. By breaking up the larger pools that link the fates (and resources) of the wealthy with those of the less well-off (and the sick with the healthy in medicare), market-oriented reforms of social insurance programs offer the well-off a better deal even as they impose more risk on the poor. But for those in the middle, the effects are murkier. In contrast to the past fifty years, when a rapidly growing economy and a smaller beneficiary pool meant that all social security beneficiaries received more than they paid into the system, the high costs of the programs today mean that some middle-income people, may in fact, be better off under alternative arrangements. But because the exact lines defining who will benefit and who will be hurt depend on how reforms are designed as well as on unforeseen circumstances in individual lives, there is much room for political maneuver around these issues. The partisan fight is for each party to win over the ill-defined middle class to its future vision for entitlement programs.

The course of that battle will depend in part on how the issues are framed. The spread of the term *entitlements* connotes a rights orientation and maintains a focus on individuals. This way of framing the issue provides proponents of market-oriented reforms with two potent arguments. They can attack the notion of unearned rights inherent in the concept of entitlements, an appealing argument as rights rhetoric has become a focus of political controversy over the past twenty years.[30] But the entitlements framework also assists market-oriented reforms by keeping the focus on individuals. Individualistic rhetoric provides a good fit with proposed reforms, which allow individuals to seek out the arrangements that best fit their needs. By contrast, an alternative framework— using the term *social insurance* rather than *entitlements* and family strategies for managing risk rather than individual benefit—offers more support for the government-organized collective pools that now exist. Such defenses of social security and medicare have not been much in evidence in recent years, reflecting the bureaucratization of these programs and the heavy reliance on legal rights in much of American policy rhetoric.[31] However, major efforts to revamp social security and medicare may alter the debate. When congressional Republicans proposed substantial cuts in medicare and medicaid in 1995–96, they provoked a reconsideration of family strategies and social insurance as supporters of the existing programs reminded middle-class families that parents and grandparents would depend more on their children for support without these federal programs.[32]

Even more important is how the debate about entitlements becomes intertwined with the politics of the budget. In 1995–96, congressional

Republicans found that the balanced budget—especially when combined with tax cuts—did not trump support for medicare. Polls showed that congressional Republicans did have some success in convincing the public that reforms would be needed to stave off the impending bankruptcy of medicare.[33] The trust fund mechanisms for funding medicare and social security, originally designed to instill faith in the programs, now threaten them. Bankruptcy—the function of an accounting device—became the pretext for dramatic change.[34]

Democrats have been reluctant to take on the balanced budget issue, but they will not be able to avoid it if they are to defend social insurance programs. It is even more pressing if they hope to alter the social policy agenda to address the problems of work and family and economic inequality. Because Republican efforts to balance the budget have been combined with proposals to cut taxes, they offer Democrats an advantageous starting point for counterposing the agendas of the two parties. But Democrats will also have to confront directly the popularity of the balanced budget. The projected increases in future spending on social insurance mean that this issue will not go away.

The projected decline in the deficit during the first Clinton administration offered an opportunity to question how low a deficit was needed for a healthy economy and whether other policies should take priority. But in 1996, Clinton, faced with a Republican Congress and anxious to remove the budget as a political issue, instead announced his support for a balanced budget. The elimination of the deficit is unlikely to usher in a new era in spending. For one thing, the price of the bill was significant tax cuts for the wealthy. Democrats must understand that the spiral of tax cuts, deficits, and deficit reduction has no fixed endpoint and that this cycle is fatal to spending programs. Moreover, the rules that govern policymaking are still dominated by budgetary concerns: social policy remains fiscalized. Democrats who support social insurance and also want to launch new initiatives will have to be prepared to defend those social projects as more important than tax cuts or a balanced budget. This may entail building broad support for such alternative ideas as public investments and for accounting devices such as capital budgets. As Clinton discovered when his investment program collapsed, this is a long-term project. It is also one that must engage the broad public since the weight of expert advice is against such initiatives.

The course and outcome of the entitlements battle will also depend on who the participants are and how they are organized. Although programs for the elderly, and social security in particular, have been dubbed the "third rail of American politics," they are in fact much more vulnerable than the name implies.[35] In the past decade, the imbalance in social assistance provided to the elderly compared with children has sparked a new debate about intergenerational equity, in which the elderly have been cast as receiving more than their fair share. And with a 1996 poverty rate of 11.7 percent, the elderly are indeed better off as a group than children, who have a poverty rate of 21.8 percent.[36] Functionally organized interest group politics in which groups representing the elderly, such as the American Association of Retired Persons, are the main defenders of social security and medicare (although medicare also engages a range of health care providers as well) reinforces these arguments about generational inequity. Such concerns—especially if joined with new questions about whether the upper middle class benefits from current social insurance programs—can provide powerful opposition to existing programs.

If they are to confront these generational arguments, defenders of social insurance must build a broader coalition, including groups lobbying for children as well as the elderly. In a constrained budgetary environment, with groups that have little history of working together, this is not a simple task. It requires uniting groups whose interests do not coincide on every issue around a broader policy vision from which all should benefit in the long run. Such coalitions have become more common in Washington. Republicans showed that it was possible to unite diverse groups with the disparate "leave us alone" coalition that joined forces in support of the congressional Republican agenda to limit federal spending.[37] But Republicans also found how difficult it is to sustain such a coalition once their broader agenda collapsed.

But perhaps the most important question is how broad the debate about entitlements is. Inside-the-beltway elites dominated the discussion when both parties had an incentive to keep the issues quiet as they negotiated bipartisan agreements. The breakdown of consensus about the future of these programs, however, makes it imperative that the debate be broadened. Proposals to reform both social security and medicare involve many technical issues that may be difficult for nonspecialists to understand. But they also raise fundamental questions of deep concern to all Americans about what role government should play in promoting economic security. Broad public debate about the government role is all the more urgent because the ongoing erosion of employer-provided benefits and changes in the economy pose new insecurities for growing numbers of families.

Politics and Social Policy

The cumulation of dissatisfactions, doubts, and gaps in the current public-private system of social provision has brought us to a turning point. As the chapters of this book have documented, it is one that our political system is ill equipped to manage in a way that brings both expertise and broad political engagement to bear on decisionmaking. The shrill partisan debate that characterized social policymaking in the first Clinton administration and the mobilization of Washington-based interests to defend their turf only reinforced public disengagement from government. This kind of politics will make it very difficult to reform social policies in ways that promote security and opportunity for people across the income spectrum. Instead, this political process is likely to exacerbate already widening inequalities and place heavier burdens on those striving to manage family and work lives under new social and economic conditions.

I have argued here that stemming the erosion of social benefits and curbing growing inequality will require a new social populism that challenges existing assumptions about politics as well as policy. It is essential to reassert broader social aims in order to challenge the primacy of narrowly defined budget and economic goals. The argument that government can advance deeply held American values about fairness and opportunity in changed economic circumstances must stand as a counterweight to the perspective that places budgets above all else. Advocates of a strong federal social role cannot win on a terrain defined by budget goals. This is especially so because, when linked to tax cuts, the balanced budget can simply become a cover for shrinking government in ways that have far-reaching distributional consequences.

Likewise, those who support a strong public social role cannot win when their opponents hold a monopoly on moral argument; the technocratic approach characteristic of American social policymakers since the Great Society and replicated in Clinton's health policy proposals must be subordinated to appeals that connect with deeply held moral concerns.[38] This does not mean simply embracing the views of the right: widely shared sensibilities about fairness and opportunity provide the basic elements for making policy arguments for a strong government social role that also resonates with core values.

Finally, an alternative politics of social populism needs to challenge the limited terms and narrow scope of public engagement in politics. The top-down approach of Clinton's first two years in office sought to overcome political obstacles primarily through policy design. But because this strategy required big policy proposals with many intricately connected parts, it proved no match for the narrow and agile style of interest group politics that dominates Washington policymaking. Only a bottom-up coalition-building strategy, too long absent from Democratic politics, can temper such interests.[39]

This approach contrasts with the effort to blur differences and search for the center of a narrowly defined political universe with which most people have only loose connections. On the contrary, what is required is a more robust partisanship in which the public is brought into the discussion. The differences that underlie partisan divisions are real, and it is important that they be debated nationally. But parties and interest groups must engage in more grass-roots organizing so that people learn about choices and form their preferences in a context other than advertising. Likewise, the resources and power that narrow Washington-based interests now command must be balanced by a more broadly organized politics. These political tasks are all the more pressing because of the marked bias in political participation: in the past thirty years, participation has increasingly become an activity monopolized by citizens with higher incomes and education.[40] But the decisions about what the government should do to promote economic security will particularly affect the lives of the less well-educated and less well-off. Linking a more inclusive politics to policymaking is an essential precondition for redesigning social policy in ways that promote broad opportunity and security in an altered economic and social world.

Notes

1. For a comparative perspective, see the essays in Katherine McFate, Roger Lawson, and William Julius Wilson, eds., *Poverty, Inequality, and the Future of Social Policy: Western States in the New World Order* (New York: Russell Sage Foundation, 1995); and Gosta Esping-Andersen, ed., *Welfare States in Transition: National Adaptations in Global Economies* (London: Sage, 1996).

2. Theodore R. Marmor, Jerry L. Mashaw, and Philip L. Harvey argue that opportunity and insurance are the fundamental motivations for most American social policy. See Marmor, Mashaw, and Harvey, *America's Misunderstood Welfare State: Persistent Myths, Enduring Realities* (Basic Books, 1990), pp. 22–52.

3. Stephen Skowronek, "President Clinton and the Risks of 'Third-Way' Politics," *Extensions: A Journal of the Carl Albert Congressional Research and Studies Center* (Spring 1996), p. 12.

4. See David W. Rohde, "Parties, Institutional Control, and Political Incentives: A Perspective on Governing in the Clinton Presidency," paper prepared for colloquium on "The Clinton Years in Perspective," Université de Montréal, October 6–8, 1996, p. 10; and John Aldrich, "Rational Choice Theory and the Study of American Politics," in Lawrence C. Dodd and Calvin Jillson, eds., *The Dynamics of American Politics: Approaches and Interpretations* (Boulder, Colo.: Westview Press, 1994), pp. 208–33.

5. John B. Gilmour, *Strategic Disagreement: Stalemate in American Politics* (University of Pittsburgh Press, 1995).

6. Edward G. Carmines and James A. Stimson, *Issue Evolution: Race and the Transformation of American Politics* (Princeton University Press, 1989); and Thomas Byrne Edsall with Mary D. Edsall, *Chain Reaction: The Impact of Race, Rights, and Taxes on American Politics* (Norton, 1991).

7. For example, a Yankelovich Partners survey on May 7–8, 1997, found that 48 percent of respondents trusted Clinton more than Republicans on the issue of crime, and only 31 percent trusted the congressional Republicans more. A Gallup/CNN/*USA Today* poll conducted on February 24–26, 1997, found that 51 percent of respondents approved and 38 percent disapproved of the way Clinton was handling welfare policy, and 45 percent approved and 43 percent disapproved of the way he was handling crime policy. In general, Republicans fared better in questions that pitted the Republican party against the Democratic party rather than the president against the congressional Republicans. Even so, in a January 17–19, 1997, poll by Wirthlin Worldwide, 43 percent of respondents thought Republicans could best handle "changing welfare for the better" and 40 percent believed that Democrats could; on "reducing crime and drugs," however, 42 percent preferred Republicans and 34 percent preferred Democrats.

8. Most of the new initiatives designed to assist the poor in the 1997 budget agreement were block grants to the states. See Robert Greenstein, "Looking at the Details of the New Budget Legislation: Social Program Initiatives Decline over Time While Upper-Income Tax Cuts Grow," Center on Budget and Policy Priorities, Washington, August 12, 1997.

9. See the testimony in *Earned Income Tax Credit*, Hearing before the Subcommittee on Oversight and Subcommittee on Human Resources of the House Committee on Ways and Means, 104 Cong. 1 sess. (Government Printing Office, 1996).

10. See Robert B. Reich, "Up from Bipartisanship," *American Prospect*, no. 32 (May–June 1997), p. 30.

11. This protection was extended in the 1997 budget agreement. See Mark Greenberg, "Welfare-to-Work Grants and Other TANF-Related Provisions in the Balanced Budget Act of 1997," Center on Law and Social Policy, Washington, August 1997.

12. See the discussion in Michael N. Danielson, *The Politics of Exclusion* (Columbia University Press, 1976), pp. 199–242.

13. *Report of the National Advisory Commission on Civil Disorders* (New York Times, 1968); and Anthony Downs, *Opening Up the Suburbs: An Urban Strategy for America* (Yale University Press, 1973).

14. On the new political possibilities, see Myron Orfield, *Metropolitics: A Regional Agenda for Community and Stability* (Brookings and Lincoln Institute of Land Policy, 1997); for an analysis of metropolitan solutions to urban problems, see Anthony Downs, *New Visions for Metropolitan America* (Brookings and Lincoln Institute of Land Policy, 1994).

15. See William Julius Wilson, *When Work Disappears: The World of the New Urban Poor* (Knopf, 1996).

16. See Sam Howe Verhovek, "Houston Voters Maintain Affirmative Action Policy," *New York Times*, November 6, 1997, p. A1. On the complexity of public views more generally, see Lawrence Bobo and Ryan A. Smith, "Antipoverty Policy, Affirmative Action, and Racial Attitudes," in Sheldon H. Danziger, Gary D. Sandefur, and Daniel H. Weinberg, eds., *Confronting Poverty: Prescriptions for Change* (Harvard University Press, 1994), pp. 365–95.

17. With the improving economy, the administration focused on the good news, highlighting the number of new jobs created since Clinton had taken office and claiming that most of these were "good jobs." Council of Economic Advisers, "Job Creation and Employment Opportunities: The United States Labor Market, 1993-1996," April 23, 1996.

18. See Ruy Teixeira, "Living Standards as a Values Issue: A New Synthesis for a New Majority," paper prepared for New Majority Project Workshop, January 10–12, 1997), pp. 31–32; and E. J. Dionne Jr., *They Only Look Dead: Why Progressives Will Dominate the Next Political Era* (Simon and Schuster, 1996), p. 289.

19. Greenstein, "Looking at the Details of the New Budget Legislation."

20. Ibid.

21. See Ira Katznelson and Margaret Weir, *Schooling for All: Class, Race, and the Decline of the Democratic Ideal* (Basic Books, 1985).

22. See Rochelle L. Stanfield, "The Old College Try," *National Journal*, December 14, 1996, pp. 2700–03. See also William G. Gale, "Tax Reform Is Dead, Long Live Tax Reform," Brookings Institution Policy Brief 12 (February 1997).

23. The dismal record of schools that serve poor minority children becomes all the more salient as public universities dismantle their affirmative action pro-

grams. See Charles Krauthammer, "Race and Classrooms," *Washington Post*, May 23, 1997, p. A29.

24. See Charles Mahtesian, "Saving the States from Each Other: Can Congress Dictate an End to the Great Smokestack Chase?" *Governing*, vol. 10 (November 1996), p. 15.

25. See Dani Rodrik, *Has Globalization Gone Too Far?* (Washington: Institute for International Economics, 1997). As Rodrik notes, this elite consensus is now jeopardized by opponents from the left and the right, in part because it does not recognize the increased insecurity that workers now confront. The ability of congressional Democrats to defeat fast track authority in November 1997 underscored the political vulnerability of free trade agreements.

26. The 1996 election did evidence this pattern. See Teixeira, "Living Standards as a Values Issue."

27. On the 1983 social security reform, see Paul Light, *Artful Work: The Politics of Social Security Reform* (Random House, 1985); on medicare reform, see David G. Smith, *Paying for Medicare: The Politics of Reform* (New York: Aldine de Gruyter, 1992).

28. See Theodore R. Marmor and Jerry L. Mashaw, "The Case for Social Insurance," in Stanley B. Greenberg and Theda Skocpol, eds., *The New Majority: Toward a Popular Progressive Politics* (Yale University Press, 1997), pp. 78–103; and Julie Kosterlitz, "Do It Yourself," *National Journal*, November 23, 1996, pp. 2532–36.

29. See Brett D. Fromson, "Wall St.'s Quiet Message: Privatize Social Security," *Washington Post*, September 20, 1996, p. F1.

30. See Mary Ann Glendon, *Rights Talk: The Impoverishment of Political Discourse* (Free Press, 1991).

31. On the centrality of legal tools in American policymaking, see Robert A. Kagan, "Adversarial Legalism and American Government," *Journal of Policy Analysis and Management*, vol. 10 (Summer 1991), pp. 369–406; and Robert A. Kagan and Lee Axelrad, "Adversarial Legalism: An International Perspective," in Pietro S. Nivola, ed., *Comparative Disadvantages? Social Regulations and the Global Economy* (Brookings, 1997), pp. 146–202. The best case for social insurance is in Marmor, Mashaw, and Harvey, *America's Misunderstood Welfare State*.

32. These issues became particularly salient when congressional Republicans proposed a "family responsibility" clause to medicaid that would have allowed states to recover part of the costs for long-term care from families able to pay. The proposal was dropped. See the discussion in Judith Havemann, "Medicaid Cost May Hit Home; GOP Plan Could Make Families Pay," *Washington Post*, December 18, 1995, p. A1.

33. See the *Washington Post*, Harvard University, and Kaiser Family Foundation poll, March 1997, as discussed in Eric Pianin and Mario Brossard, "Americans Oppose Cutting Entitlements to Fix Budget: Poll Finds Pessimism on Medicare, Social Security," *Washington Post*, March 29, 1997, p. A4.

34. Jill Quadagno, "Social Security and the Myth of the Entitlement 'Crisis,'" *Gerontologist*, vol. 36 (June 1996), pp. 391–99.

35. Henry J. Aaron, "The Myths of the Social Security Crisis: Behind the Privatization Push," *Washington Post*, July 21, 1996, p. C1.

36. *1996 Green Book: Background Material and Data on Programs within the Jurisdiction of the Committee on Ways and Means*, Committee Print, 104 Cong. 2 sess. (GPO, 1996), p. 1223, table H-1.

37. Dan Balz and Ronald Brownstein, *Storming the Gates: Protest Politics and the Republican Revival* (Little, Brown, 1996), pp. 159–202.

38. See Hugh Heclo, "The Social Question," in McFate and others, eds., *Poverty, Inequality, and the Future of Social Policy*, pp. 665–91.

39. See Margaret Weir and Marshall Ganz, "Reconnecting People and Politics," in Greenberg and Skocpol, eds., *New Majority*, pp. 149-71.

40. See Sidney Verba, Kay Lehman Schlozman, and Henry E. Brady, *Voice and Equality: Civic Voluntarism in American Politics* (Harvard University Press, 1995).

Contributors

John Ferejohn
*Stanford University and
New York University*

Lawrence R. Jacobs
University of Minnesota

Ann Chih Lin
University of Michigan

Cathie Jo Martin
Boston University

John Mollenkopf
City University of New York

Mark A. Peterson
University of Pittsburgh

Paul Pierson
Harvard University

Robert Y. Shapiro
Columbia University

R. Kent Weaver
Brookings Institution

Margaret Weir
*Brookings Institution and
University of California, Berkeley*

Linda Faye Williams
University of Maryland

Index

Defense, U.S. Department of, 447–48
Defense spending, 14, 131, 133, 145, 159
Deficit: fluctuations, 134–35, 168; sources, 129–34; as symbol of government failure, 135–37, 142. *See also* Deficit reduction
Deficit hawks, 140–41, 143, 149, 151, 200
Deficit reduction: business support, 256; Clinton priority, 16, 79, 127–29, 135, 139–44, 171; discretionary spending, 15, 133, 517; impact on social policymaking, 14–16, 377–78, 506–07, 514–15; limiting effect on Democratic agenda, 30, 31, 36, 146, 507, 523; as political strategy, 136–37; public opinion, 109–10, 115, 127, 135, 152, 159, 163. *See also* Budget policy; Republican policy agenda
Delaware, 342
DeLay, Tom, 76, 102
Democratic Congressional Campaign Committee, 258
Democratic Leadership Council (DLC), 28, 440, 473–74, 515
Democratic party: African American voters, 317, 333–34, 418, 420–21, 425, 452–53; budget factions, 140, 148–51; change in grass-roots structure, 12; changes in voter patterns, 88–90; civil liberties image, 315; Clinton coalition-building problems, 29, 51, 55–56, 363; constituency changes, 10, 50, 71, 425, 466–67; crime policy factions, 319–21, 325, 326–27, 330–31; crime policy image, 314-15; defectors, 466–68; deficit reduction as political strategy, 136–37, 143, 156, 523; electoral impact of Clinton policies, 56–59, 67, 152, 201, 322–23; identification with race, 317, 378, 421, 425–26, 453, 466–67, 508; impact of regulation

as social policy, 78, 274–75; labor and employment factions, 278, 286, 515–16; labor unions, 86, 273–74, 295–96, 379; medicare public opinion strategy, 107–08; minimum wage increase, 64; New Deal coalition, 11, 86; new-old Democrat differences, 9, 27–28, 59-61, 464–65, 488–89, 496, 515–16; repositioning strategy, 50, 59–61, 77–78, 242, 378, 452–53, 506, 508–09, 510; role of business, 230–32; welfare factions, 379–80, 381, 383, 392. *See also* Clinton, Bill; Democrats, House; Democrats, Senate; New Democrats
Democrats, House: affirmative action, 442–43; budget factions, 161–62; cohesion, 50–51, 70, 76–77, 201; crime policy factions, 55, 319–21, 431–32; effect of procedural changes, 68–69, 71; effect of realignment of the South, 10, 71; family leave, 247; health care reform, 196; housing assistance, 492; labor factions, 286, 292; welfare reform factions, 389, 394. *See also* Clinton, Bill; Democratic party; Democrats, Senate
Democrats, Senate, 70, 201; crime control legislation, 318–19; family leave, 247; job training and welfare link, 293; welfare reform, 390, 394. *See also* Clinton, Bill; Democratic party; Democrats, House
Demographics, and entitlements, 25, 26
Denny's restaurant chain, 434
Denver, Colorado, 476
Deportation of criminal aliens, 324. *See also* Antiterrorism legislation
Detached middle, in electorate, 10, 12, 35, 85, 182, 188, 193, 507
Detroit, Michigan, 467, 481

benefits, 7, 143; medicare, 207; minority programs, 418, 421, 422; public opinion research, use of, 95–96

Johnson v. *Transportation Agency*, 438

Jones, Bryan D., 6

Judiciary Committee, U.S. House of Representatives, 325, 439, 441

Justice, U.S. Department of: affirmative action, 440; civil rights enforcement, 433, 434, 435, 484; fair housing enforcement, 485; law enforcement coordination, 342–43, 343–44, 351–52

Juvenile violence, 314, 343

Kamarck, Elaine, 474, 476

Kansas, 342

Kansas City, 481

Kasich, John R., 76, 105, 151, 156–57, 162, 200

Kassebaum, Nancy Landon, 215, 293

Kelly, Sharon Pratt, 431

Kemp, Jack, 446, 468, 471, 472, 473, 479, 480

Kennedy, Edward (Ted), 215, 216–17, 293

Kennedy, John F., 95, 421, 422

Kennedy-Kassebaum bill. *See* Health Insurance Portability and Accountability Act

Kernell, Samuel, 71

Kerner commission, 512

Kerrey, Bob, 136, 149

King, Martin Luther, Jr., 421–22, 451–52

Kingdon, John, 6

Klein, Ethel, 243

Koresh, David, 326

Kristol, William, 193, 252

Labor, U.S. Department of: affirmative action, 440–41; Clinton appointments, 277–78, 435; compliance reviews, 433, 434; Employment Service, 285–86;

minimum wage and workfare, 397; policy factions, 284, 296–97; skill grant proposal, 291–92; Women's Bureau, 287; workplace innovation, 281, 282, 287, 296; youth wage subsidies, 287. *See also* Reich, Robert

Labor and Human Resources Committee, U.S. Senate, 189, 215, 293

Labor law reform, 275, 276, 281–82

Labor unions: and changes in economy, 22–23, 271; decline in political impact, 22, 86–87, 88, 273–74, 276–77, 279, 298; health care reform, 30, 184; housing assistance programs, 472; importance to Democratic coalition, 11–12, 273–74, 327; job training priority, 276, 284, 287, 301–02; labor law priorities, 281–82; "living wage" campaigns, 303; opposition to Reemployment Act, 285–86, 299–300; post–Clinton election agenda, 275–76; welfare reform, 379, 383, 397. *See also* AFL-CIO

Lamp, Virginia B., 244

Latinos, 417, 426, 432, 451, 453, 474

Law and order theme, 315, 317, 333, 422–23. *See also* Crime control; Racial issues in politics

Law Enforcement Assistance Administration (LEAA), 351

Law enforcement networks, 343, 350–52. *See also* Crime control

Law Enforcement Steering Committee (LESC), 331–32

Lawyers' Committee on Civil Rights, 441

Lazio, Rick, 492, 493, 494–95

Leadership Conference on Civil Rights, 441

Least-common-denominator politics, by big business, 238–39, 241, 250

The Brookings Institution

The Brookings Institution is a private nonprofit organization devoted to nonpartisan research, education, and publication in economics, government, foreign policy, and the social sciences generally. Its principal purposes are to aid in the development of sound public policies and to promote public understanding of issues of national importance. The Institution was founded on December 8, 1927, to merge the activities of the Institute for Government Research, founded in 1916, the Institute of Economics, founded in 1922, and the Robert Brookings Graduate School of Economics and Government, founded in 1924.

The Institution maintains a position of neutrality on issues of public policy to safeguard the intellectual freedom of the staff. Interpretations or conclusions in Brookings publications should be understood to be solely those of the authors.

The Russell Sage Foundation

The Russell Sage Foundation, one of the oldest of America's general purpose foundations, was established in 1907 by Mrs. Margaret Olivia Sage for "the improvement of social and living conditions in the United States." The Foundation seeks to fulfill this mandate by fostering the development and dissemination of knowledge about the country's political, social, and economic problems. While the Foundation endeavors to assure the accuracy and objectivity of each book it publishes, the conclusions and interpretations in Russell Sage Foundation publications are those of the authors and not of the Foundation, its Trustees, or its staff. Publication by Russell Sage, therefore, does not imply Foundation endorsement.